COPING WITH DEFEAT

Coping with Defeat

SUNNI ISLAM, ROMAN CATHOLICISM, AND THE MODERN STATE

JONATHAN LAURENCE

PRINCETON UNIVERSITY PRESS

PRINCETON & OXFORD

Published by Princeton University Press
41 William Street, Princeton, New Jersey 08540
6 Oxford Street, Woodstock, Oxfordshire OX20 1TR

press.princeton.edu

All Rights Reserved

Library of Congress Cataloging-in-Publication Data

Names: Laurence, Jonathan, author.
Title: Coping with defeat : Sunni Islam, Roman Catholicism, and the modern state / Jonathan Laurence.
Description: Princeton : Princeton University Press, [2021] | Includes bibliographical references and index.
Identifiers: LCCN 2020040053 (print) | LCCN 2020040054 (ebook) |
    ISBN 9780691172125 | ISBN 9780691220543 (hardback) | ISBN 9780691219783 (ebook)
Subjects: LCSH: Religion and state. | Islam and state. | Church and state.
Classification: LCC BL65.S8 L38 2021 (print) | LCC BL65.S8 (ebook) |
    DDC 261.7—dc23
LC record available at https://lccn.loc.gov/2020040053
LC ebook record available at https://lccn.loc.gov/2020040054

British Library Cataloging-in-Publication Data is available

Editorial: Fred Appel, Jenny Tan, and James Collier
Production Editorial: Mark Bellis
Jacket Design: Layla Mac Rory
Production: Brigid Ackerman
Publicity: Kate Hensley and Kathryn Stevens
Copyeditor: Cynthia Buck

Jacket Credit: Abandoned locomotive once belonging to T. E. Lawrence (Lawrence of Arabia) and Prince Emir Faisal, manufactured by the North British Locomotive Company, Glasgow. Image courtesy of Paul Stallan.

This book has been composed in Arno

Printed on acid-free paper. ∞

Printed in the United States of America

10 9 8 7 6 5 4 3 2 1

For Patricia and Stuart

C'était le moment le plus heureux de ma vie, je ne le savais pas. Aurais-je pu préserver ce bonheur, les choses auraient-elles évolué autrement si je l'avais su?

—ORHAN PAMUK, *MUSÉE DE L'INNOCENCE*
(TRANSLATED BY VALÉRIE GAY-AKSOY, GALLIMARD, 2011)

CONTENTS

List of Illustrations   xi
List of Tables   xix
Abbreviations   xxi
Acknowledgments   xxiii

INTRODUCTION: COPING WITH DEFEAT	1
1 Sunni Islam, Roman Catholicism, and the Modern State	3
THE FIRST DEFEAT: THE END OF EMPIRE	45
2 The Fall and Rise of Roman Catholicism	47
3 The Plot against the Caliphate	77
4 The Rise and Fall of Pan-Islam	118
THE SECOND DEFEAT: THE NATION-STATE ERA	159
5 Nation-State Catholicism	161
6 Nation-State Islam	196
THE THIRD DEFEAT: THE ERA OF BELIEVERS WITHOUT BORDERS	237
7 Catholicism in the United States	239
8 Islam in Europe	284
9 Nation-State Islam versus the Islamic State	328

CONCLUSION: EMBRACING SPIRITUAL POWER   391

10   Out of Office: Rejoining Civil Society   393

Regime Timelines: 1500–Present   439
Glossary   445
Interviews   449
Notes   457
Bibliography   519
Illustration Credits   555
Index   567

ILLUSTRATIONS

1.1.1 and Figure 1.1.2. Twenty-First century: Pope Francis at the European Parliament (2014); Abu Bakr al Baghdadi in Mosul (2014)   4

1.2.1 and Figure 1.2.2. Nineteenth century: Sultan Abdülmecid with British royals; Pope Pius IX at Vatican Council I   6

1.3. The First Defeat: The Ottoman Empire and the Roman Catholic Church   20

1.4. The Relationship between Loss of Territory and the Ottoman Religious Affairs Budget, 1864–1924   25

1.5. Catholic and Muslim-Origin Populations in the United States and Europe, 1850–1930 and 1950–2030   31

1.6. Regional Breakdown of the Cardinal College: Italy and the Americas, 1903–2013   37

1.7. Islamic Affairs Spending in Turkey, Morocco, Algeria, and Tunisia, per Person, 2000–2015   42

2.1. The decline of Roman Catholicism, eleventh century to seventeenth century   48

2.2. The desert north of Cologne (Planisfero Anonimo, 1530)   48

2.3. "Bringing Down a Station of the Cross" (Germany, sixteenth century)   52

2.4. The Destroyed Cathedral of St. Andrews, Scotland (1559–1561)   54

2.5. Apartment of Ignatius of Loyola, Rome   59

2.6. The Council of Trent (1545–1563)   60

2.7. Catechism of the Council of Trent   61

2.8. Roman Catholic Dioceses before, during, and after the Reformation, per Country   63

2.9. Confessional map of the German Empire   64

2.10. Religious Education in Rome and Europe, 1348–1702   66

2.11.1 and Figure 2.11.2. Letter from Ignatius of Loyola regarding the
    German College, Rome (1552)   67

2.12. The Collegio Germanico, Rome (1580)   69

2.13. Palace of the Holy Congregation of Propaganda Fide,
    Rome (1626)   71

2.14. Typesets of the world (Holy Congregation of Propaganda Fide)   72

2.15. The Size of the College of Cardinals before and after the
    Protestant Reformation, 1050–1600   75

3.1.1, Figure 3.1.2, and Figure 3.1.3. The decline of the Ottoman Empire,
    seventeenth century to twentieth century   78

3.2. The Global Muslim Population, 1907   79

3.3. "England Bent on Ousting Turkey from Mecca"
    (*New York Times*, March 5, 1911)   87

3.4. "So, do you have any recurring dreams?"
    (*Iznogoud* comic by René Goscinny and Jean Tabary)   90

3.5. Maréchal Lyautey dines with Sultan Yusuf in Fez,
    Morocco (c. 1925)   94

3.6. The Dutch consul in Jedda authorizes pilgrims from the
    East Indies to visit Mecca   97

3.7. "Disputed Lands of Near East That Hold World Attention
    Today" (*Literary Digest Atlas*, 1922)   102

3.8. Vahdettin leaves Yıldız Palace for the last time (1922)   107

4.1. The Longest-Lasting Islamic Caliphates and Sultanates   122

4.2. Proposed Kandilli-Rumelihisarı Bridge, Istanbul (1900)   124

4.3. Hamidiye Mosque and Minaret in Yıldız, Istanbul (1890)   124

4.4. Friday Selamlık procession on Yıldız Palace grounds,
    Istanbul (1890)   125

4.5. "Prevailing Religions: Muslims, British Indian Empire (1909)"   127

4.6. Portrait of Sultan Abdülhamid II (1890)   129

4.7. The Ka'bah, Mecca (1900)   131

4.8. Hejaz Railroad, Jordan (1902)   131

4.9. Bab el Fetvahane, Istanbul (1904)   136

4.10. Ottoman Populations Lost and Muslim Refugees Gained,
    1805–1920   137

4.11. The Unintended Islamization of the Ottoman Empire, 1836–1923 138

4.12. Mosquée du Pacha, Algeria (nineteenth century)   139

4.13. The First Defeat and the Ottoman Response: Religious Affairs Budgets, 1840–1926   140

4.14. A fallen locomotive that once pulled pilgrims on the Hejaz Railroad, built by the Ottoman Empire   155

4.15. "Four Flags That Rule Arabia" (1900)   156

5.1. Inauguration of the statue of Giordano Bruno, Rome (1888)   162

5.2.1 and Figure 5.2.2. The Church's Encounter with the Nation-State, 1780–2000   164

5.3. "Abbé Francois Nicolas under the Gun" (1793)   168

5.4. Bishops from Austria, France, and Poland, 1431–1922   170

5.5. "The Separation: 'Let's separate—I'll keep your property'" (1905)   172

5.6. Republican female fighters besiege a monastery in Madrid (1936)   175

5.7. Monument to the Siccardi Law abolishing the Ecclesiastic Courts, Turin (1853)   178

5.8. Pope Pius IX blesses papal Zouaves in St. Peter's Square, Rome (1870)   183

5.9. Roman Catholic Establishments of Higher Education in Nineteenth-Century Europe   186

5.10. Roman Catholic Churches and Clergy in England and Wales, 1840–1910   188

5.11. Via della Conciliazione, Rome (1929)   192

6.1.1 and figure 6.1.2. Post-Ottoman Administration of Religious Affairs (Twentieth century)   197

6.2. Islamic Encounters with the Nation-State, 1780–2000   199

6.3. Turkey: Official Mosques and State-Employed Religious Personnel (Diyanet), 1924–2000   208

6.4. Turkey: Post-Coup Hiring Spurts by the Diyanet, 1950–2000   209

6.5. Turkey: Directorate of Religious Affairs (Diyanet) Budget Allocations (1924–2000)   212

6.6. Turkey: İmam Hatip Schools and Students (1950–2000)   213

6.7. Morocco: Sultan Mohammed V, with son Hassan II (1950)   216

6.8. Morocco: The Rise in Religious Affairs, 1970–1990   219

6.9. Algeria: The Mosque in La Place du Gouvernement,
Algiers (1955)   222

6.10. Tunisia: The Ministry of Religious Affairs, Tunis (1992)   233

7.1. Annual Catholic Migration to the United States, 1820–1940   240

7.2. The National Shrine of the Assumption (Baltimore Basilica)
(1806)   244

7.3 [triptych of 7.3.1, 7.3.2, and 7.3.3]. St. Patrick's Cathedral
(New York City), St. Nicolas Kirche (New York City),
and Cathedral of the Holy Cross (Boston)   247

7.4. Illustration from *Saint Joseph Baltimore Catechism: The Truths
of Our Catholic Faith Clearly Explained and Illustrated: With
Bible Readings, Study Helps, and Mass Prayers* (Baltimore, MD:
Catholic Book Publishing, 1964)   250

7.5. A contingent of North American papal Zouaves, New York (1868) 251

7.6. "At it again! Through the Ballot-box to the Constitution"
(*Puck*, 1885)   254

7.7. Dynamite attack in the French Chamber of Deputies,
Paris (1893)   255

7.8. Bombing of the Liceu Theater, Barcelona (1893)   256

7.9. Editorial offices of *La Questione Sociale* in Paterson, New Jersey
(1900)   259

7.10. Gaetano Bresci assassinates King Umberto in Monza,
Italy (1900)   261

7.11. Leon Czolgosz assassinates President William McKinley in
Buffalo, New York (1901)   262

7.12. Paterson, New Jersey: "Anarchists Live Here" (1900)   263

7.13. President Theodore Roosevelt and Cardinal James Gibbons
in a friendly exchange (date unknown)   267

7.14. Clerical Visas to the United States Granted and Enrollment
in the North American College in Rome, 1856–1910   267

7.15. Catholic Churches and Clergy in the United States,
1820–1940   269

7.16. Catholic Clergy in the United States, 1835–1925   271

7.17. Catholic Schools in the United States, 1815–1930   272

7.18. Catholic Schools and Students in the United States, 1830–1940 273

7.19. North American College in Rome   275

7.20. St. Mary's Seminary in Baltimore (1851)   275

7.21. Roman Catholic Dioceses and Cardinals in the United States, 1830–1940   278

7.22 [triptych of 7.22.1, 7.22.2, and 7.22.3]. [7.22.1]: John Carroll, SJ, first US-born bishop (1789); [7.22.2]: John McCloskey, first US cardinal (1875); [7.22.3]: James Gibbons, First US-born cardinal (1886)   280

7.23. St. Mary's Seminary, Class of 1919   282

7.24. Catholic elementary school class, United States (1930)   282

8.1. The Growth of the Muslim Population of Europe, 1950–2030   285

8.2. The unofficial French "Foreign Legion" in Syria (Facebook, 2016)   290

8.3. "The New Editors" (*Daily Mail*, 2015)   291

8.4. "A Breeding Ground for Terrorists" (Molenbeek, Belgium, 2015)   292

8.5. Turkish Islamic Infrastructure in Western Europe, 1973–2018   296

8.6. Islamic theology students from Germany at the University of Marmara, Istanbul (2009)   297

8.7. Turkish President Recep Tayyip Erdoğan meets in Ankara with Turkish association leaders from Strasbourg, France (2015)   299

8.8. The Growth of Moroccan-, Algerian-, Tunisian-, and Turkish-Origin Populations in Western Europe, 1973–2015   300

8.9. French foreign affairs minister Laurent Fabius and Moroccan Islamic affairs minister Ahmed Toufiq signing an imam exchange agreement in front of King Mohammed VI and President François Hollande (2015)   305

8.10. French Imams studying at the Mohammed VI Institute meet with French senators in Rabat, Morocco (2016)   306

8.11. Dalil Boubakeur, recteur of the Grande Mosquée de Paris, with French president Jacques Chirac, Paris (2004)   309

8.12. Dalil Boubakeur with Mohammed Aïssa, Algerian Minister of Religious Affairs, Paris (2015)   311

8.13. The Al-Ghazali Institute recruitment stand at the annual Bourget conference for French Muslims (2018)   313

8.14. Cover of guide for imams abroad, Algiers (2012)   314

8.15. Ayman Mazyek, chairman of the Central Council of Muslims in Germany, with Chancellor Angela Merkel and President Joachim Gauck (2015)   316

8.16 [triptych of 8.16.1, 8.16.2, and 8.16.3]. The grand mosques of Rome (1974), Strasbourg (2009) and Cologne (2014)   325

9.1. The twenty-first-century "Caliphate" of the Islamic State (2015)   329

9.2. Islamic Affairs Spending per Capita, 2000–2018   332

9.3. Trajectory of Spending on Nation-State Islam in Turkey and North Africa as a Percentage of GDP, 1998–2015   335

9.4. Cross-National Mosque Comparison, 2017   335

9.5. Spending on Nation-State Islam in Turkey and North Africa, 2016   336

9.6. Turkey: Religious Affairs Spending per Capita, 2000–2016   339

9.7. Turkey: Mosque Construction and Religious Affairs Hiring, 2000–2014   340

9.8. Turkey: Mosques and Imams per 10,000 Citizens, 2000–2015   340

9.9. Turkey: Religious Education Enrollment in İmam Hatip and Qur'an Courses, 2000–2016   342

9.10. Morocco: Spending on Habous, Mosques and Imams, 2001–2015   353

9.11. Algeria: Twenty-First-Century Institutionalization of Religious Affairs, 2005–2016   364

9.12 [diptych of 9.12.1 and 9.12.2]. Ministry for Religious Affairs and grand mosque projects, Algiers (2016–2020)   365

9.13. A Mosque under construction in Oran, Algeria (2014)   366

9.14. Religious affairs officials with tablet and brush at the Abu Bakr Issadek Mosque in Oran, Algeria (2014)   369

9.15. Tunisia: The Minister of Religious Affairs and the Mufti of the Republic inaugurate a new mosque, Tunis (2016)   378

9.16. Mosque construction in postrevolutionary Tunisia (2010 versus 2016)   380

9.17. The new Tunisian Ministry of Religious Affairs, Tunis (2016)   383

10.1. Foreign fighters in Syria and Iraq (Soufan Group, 2016)   400

10.2. Great Mosque of Tirana in Albania under construction (2017)   404

10.3. Turkish president Recep Tayyip Erdoğan receiving Palestinian president Mahmoud Abbas, Ankara (2015)   405

10.4. German chancellor Angela Merkel with Turkish president Recep Tayyip Erdoğan at Yıldız Palace, Istanbul (2015)   411

10.5. A stylized geography of Sunni Islamic jurisprudence   412

10.6. King Mohammed VI kisses the Qur'an with Malian leaders (2014)   413

10.7. Worldwide Growth of Catholic Dioceses, 1431–2017   417

10.8. The Size of the College of Cardinals, 1050–2010   419

10.9. Diplomatic Recognition of the Vatican, 1860–2015   421

10.10. The Demography of Global Religions in the Twenty-First Century   425

10.11. The Demography of Global Islam, 1950–2010   426

10.12. North America: Dioceses versus Apostolic Delegates, 1493–1940   431

10.13. Second Vatican Council (1963)   433

TABLES

1.1. Standardizing Religion   15

1.2. The First Defeat: The End of Empire   24

1.3. The Second Defeat: The Rise of the Nation-State   29

1.4. The Third Defeat: Minorities of Mass Migration   35

1.5. Civilian Rule of the Military (Huntington, 1966)   40

2.1. The Creation of Roman Colleges, 1551–1735   70

2.2. Instructions for Catholics Abroad, Seventeenth Century   74

3.1. European Challenges to the Religious Authority of the
Ottoman Caliphate, 1774–1907   80

3.2. The British Empire in the Majority-Muslim World, 1800–1984   85

3.3. The French Empire in the Majority-Muslim World, 1830–1977   91

3.4. Caliph Candidates, 1924–1932   113

3.5. Caliphate Conferences, 1924–1931   114

4.1. The Institutions of Ottoman Islam   137

4.2. Education: Ottoman Empire, 1839–1915   139

4.3. The Pan-Islam Caliphs, 1808–1918   145

4.4. Hierarchy: Abdülhamid II's Cabinet of Sheikhs   147

5.1. Nineteenth-Century State Offices for Church Oversight   165

5.2. Ecclesiastic Officials in National Parliaments
(*Annuaire Pontificale*), 1907   181

6.1. Islam in Twentieth-Century Arab Political Development
(Dessouki, 1987)   201

7.1. International Terrorism Tied to Catholic Perpetrators, 1874–1933   242

7.2. European Organizations Supporting Catholics in the
United States in the Nineteenth Century   245

7.3. Milestones in US Catholic Church History, 1784–1893   268

8.1. International Terrorism with Ties to Muslim Countries,
2004–2016   287

9.1. Objective Civilian Control in the State-Religion Relationship   334

10.1. The Missing Caliphate: Twenty-First-Century Global
Contenders   396

10.2. The Turkish Republic's Gestures toward Jerusalem, 2004–2016   408

10.3. Overlapping Influences in Funding and Expertise for Mosque
Construction, Imam Training, and Religious Studies   416

ABBREVIATIONS

AKP Justice and Development Party (Turkey)
AQMI Al Qaeda in the Islamic Maghreb
CCME Consultative Council for Moroccans Residing Abroad
CCMTF Coordinating Committee of Muslim Turks in France
CFCM Council of the Muslim Faith (France)
CHP Republican People's Party (Turkey)
COEM Council of Moroccan Ulema in Europe
DIB Directorate of Religious Affairs (Diyanet)
DİTİB Turkish-Islamic Union for Religious Affairs
EUTD European Turkish Democrats
FEERI Spanish Federation of Islamic Religious Entities
FIS Islamic Salvation Front (Algeria)
FLN Front for National Liberation (Algeria)
FNMF National Federation of French Muslims
GCC Gulf Cooperation Council
GDP Gross domestic product
GIA Armed Islamic Group of Algeria
GICM Moroccan Islamic Combat Group
GMP Grande Mosquée de Paris
GSPC Salafist Group for Preaching and Combat
HCI Supreme Islamic Council (Algeria)
HDP People's Democratic Party (Turkey)
IHL İmam Hatip Lise (school)
IRI International Republican Institute (United States)
IGGÖ Independent Islamic Community of Austria

ISIS   Islamic State of Iraq and al Sham (the Levant)

MARE   Ministry of Religious Affairs (Algeria)

MHP   Nationalist Movement Party (Turkey)

MRA   Ministry of Religious Affairs (Tunisia)

MRE   Moroccans residing abroad

MSP   National Salvation Party (Turkey)

NATO   North Atlantic Treaty Organization

NGO   non-governmental organization

OIC   Organization of Islamic Cooperation

PJD   Justice and Development Party (Morocco)

PKK   Kurdistan Workers' Party

RMF   Rally of Muslims of France

TESEV   Turkish Economic and Social Studies Foundation

TIKA   Turkish Cooperation and Coordination Agency

UGTT   Tunisian General Labor Union

YEE   Yunus Emre Institute (Turkey)

ZMD   Central Council of Muslims in Germany

ACKNOWLEDGMENTS

THIS BOOK was made possible by research support and writing residencies from the Norway Research Council and the Fafo Research Foundation, the American Academy in Berlin, the Jenesis Foundation and the Brookings Institution, LUISS Guido Carli University in Rome, Wissenschaftszentrum Berlin, and the Centre d'études et de recherches internationales at Sciences Po-Paris. Boston College sustained this project with a sabbatical year and provided funding for fieldwork and research assistance from the Office of the Dean of the Morrissey College of Arts and Sciences, the Office of the Provost, and the Clough Center on Constitutional Democracy. The Burns, Bapst, and O'Neill Libraries of the university provided crucial documentary assistance.

I am grateful to readers of early drafts for their thoughtful responses, especially Sid Tarrow, Ines Michalowski, Noah Dauber, Will Phelan, Wayne te Brake, Rahsaan Maxwell, and Nora Fisher Onar. I was extremely fortunate to receive critical feedback on the manuscript from two anonymous readers. A number of scholars helped refine my ideas, including Ruud Koopmans, Ahmet Kuru, Justin Vaïsse, Karen Barkey, Mark Lilla, Osman Balkan, Jytte Klaussen, Jean-Marc Dreyfus, Lisa Anderson, Sheri Berman, Jose Casanova, Mohammed Hashas, Jesse Ausubel, and H. A. Hellyer. The team at Fafo—Lillevik Ragna, Sindre Bangstad, Olav Elgvin, Marcel Maussen, Oddbjørn Leirvik and Jon Rogstad—were ideal colleagues to have at a formative moment in the book's trajectory.

I was fortunate to try out the book's material in recent years at seminars, debates, and conferences with audiences hosted by the American Academy in Berlin; Wissenschaftszentrum Berlin; Mercator Stiftung; German Marshall Fund; the US embassies in Algiers, Brussels, and Rome; the Assemblée nationale in Paris; the Ministry of Habous and Islamic Affairs in Rabat; the Directorate for Turks Abroad in Ankara; the École nationale supérieure des sciences politiques in Algiers; the King Abdelaziz Foundation in Casablanca; Beit el Hikma in Carthage; the US Senate's Aspen Congressional Program; the Ditchley Foundation; Harvard's Center for European Studies; the North American Association of Islamic and Muslim Studies; Princeton University; the College of William and Mary; the annual meetings of the Council for European

Studies; Oakland University; Forum Saint Laurent; the University of North Carolina; Bilgi University, Sabanci University, and Fatih University in Istanbul; LUISS Guido Carli University in Rome; the École normale supérieur and the Institut français des relations internationales in Paris; the Université libre de Bruxelles; the Catholic University of Leuven; the Junge Islam Konferenz in Berlin; and the European Council of Moroccan Ulema. I am grateful to my hosts and fellow participants at all of these events.

At Boston College, I benefited from a faculty study group on religion and the modern state and from the insights gleaned during conversations with knowledgeable colleagues, including Jim O'Toole, James Keenan, Alan Rogers, Erik Owens, Joseph Appleyard, Gregory Kalscheur, David Dipasquale, Ali Banuazizi, Kathy Bailey, Tim Crawford, Nasser Behnegar, Peter Skerry, Natana Delong-Bas, Sean McGraw, Charles Gallagher, and Oliver Rafferty. Dana Sajdi's feedback was insightful, as was that of an audience at the Jesuit Institute. I am grateful for reading suggestions from colleagues Kay Schlozman, Susan Shell, James Cronin, and Juliet Schor.

My undergraduate research fellows and graduate assistants at Boston College were indispensable to the organization and presentation of vast amounts of empirical information. The exceptional team formed by Emily Murphy, Alexander Hayden, Sarya Baladi, and Perin Gokçe worked tirelessly to draft figures and track down sources in multiple languages. Valuable research and editorial assistance was also provided by Sofia Yepes, Alexander Schroeder, Austin Kim, Daniel Fu, Anthony Kim, Amelie Trieu, Deniz Demirci, Narintohn Luangroth, Katerina Katsouris, Ellen Boettcher, Austin Bodetti, Christopher Splaine, Emily Vassiliou, Jeff Lambart, Lior Sapir, Katie Tsante, William Provost, and Elizabeth Wollan.

In addition to benefiting from the knowledge of hundreds of interview respondents, scores of others helped introduce me to scholarly material, primary sources, religious institutions, and government bureaucracies around the Mediterranean. My fieldwork in Algeria was facilitated by Mohamed Yazid Bouzid and Mohamed Lamine Nait Youcef as well as the extraordinary Abderrezak Sebgag, with the support of the Presidency of the Republic. Karim Ouaras and Robert Parks were gracious interlocutors, Azzouz Mustapha Nazim provided expert research assistance, and Jesse Lichtenstein, Michael Driessen, and Anne Giudicelli generously shared their knowledge and experience of Algeria. In Berlin, I happily relied upon advice from Thorsten Benner, Züli Aladag, Veysel Özcan, Andrea Dernbach, Pia Castro, Sena Löper, Judd Ernster, Hans-Michael Giesen, Frank Zimmer, Gökçe Yurdakul, Günilla Finke, Ines Kappert, Adelheid Müller, Semjon H. N. Semjon, Dodi Reifenberg, Gary Smith, Rauf Ceylan, Cem Özdemir, Thomas Kleine-Brockhoff, Mohammad Shoeb Irshad, Alexander Schwenkenberg, Sergey Lagodinsky,

Cemal Aydin, and members of JUMA. Peter Constantine taught me a great deal about the late Ottoman Empire and generously shared family photos, documents, and introductions. In Turkey, I especially valued my interactions with Istar Gözaydin, Murat Borovali, Ahmet Yukleyen, Dilek Kurban, Murat Somer, Nuri Tinaz, and Talip Kücükcan. For help with Ottoman archives, I am grateful to Tahsin Özcan of Marmara University and Önur Öner of Bahcesehir University. I savored the opportunity to interview the historians Serif Mardin and Ilber Ortayli. The director of the 29. Mayis Library kindly received me and oriented me in the collections. Serhan Göngür guided me through the tombs, mosques, and palaces of Ottoman Istanbul.

My fieldwork in Morocco was facilitated by the advice of Michel Zerr, Mounir Azzaoui, Hakim el Ghissassi, and the hospitality and friendship of Tarek Elariss and Nada Amchaar. In Tunis, I am grateful to Valérie Gaist, Laurence M'Rad, Nadia Marzouki, Stephen Kochuba, Mohammed Haddad, and Daniel Rubenstein. In France, I benefited from the insights of Riva Kastoryano, Denis Lacorne, Bayram Balci, Elise Massicard, Bernard Godard, Roland Dubertrand, Didier Leschi, and Romain Sèze. The time I shared with Alessandra Fanari, Altinaï Petrovitch-Njegosh, Hubert Sauper, Elie Barrau, Jessica Boyd, Fabrice Ferrier, Elie Barrau, Isabelle Arrighi, Justin Vaïsse, Jean-Pierre Guardiola, and Nathalie Serfaty was always a pleasure and never enough. In Italy, I thank Alessandro Orsini, Cecilia Rinaldini, Federica Caciagli, Sebastiano Cardi, Peter Brownfeld, Chiara Galbersanini, Enrico Biale, Sofia de Benedictis, Simone Disegni, Federica Zoja, Marco Lucidi, Alessandro Lanni, Letizia Durante, Volker Kaul, Mohammed Hashas, Raffaello Matarazzo, Yahya Pallavicini, Leland de la Durantaye, Flavia Giacobbe, Khalid Chaouki, Zouhir Louassini, Fabio Benincasa, and Francesco Rosetti for their friendship and expertise. For assistance with access to Roman archives, I thank Father James Grummer of the Jesuit Curia and Cristina Berna of the Archivio Storico at the Pontificia Università Gregoriana. I consider myself lucky to have met Nina zu Fürstenberg and Giancarlo Bosetti, cofounders of Reset Dialogues on Civilizations, which has enriched intellectual life across the Mediterranean and the Atlantic.

In Washington, DC, I was fortunate to have colleagues like Kemal Kirisci, Andrew Moffatt, Spencer Boyer, Phil Gordon, Jeremy Shapiro, Martin Indyk, and Fiona Hill with whom to discuss these issues while at Brookings, in addition to regular interactions with a host of talented officials and diplomats at the US State Department. In Boston, I would like to thank Kristen Fabbe, Janine Hanrahan, Rotem Bar-Or, Omür Buduk, Helmut Landes, Jesse Sage, and Cigdem Benem Tunc for their conversations and advice, and Shabillah Nunsebuga for her friendship. Juliana Mishkin was a source of inspiration in the final stretch.

At Princeton University Press, my sincere thanks to Fred Appel for his stewardship of this volume. Other colleagues at the press, including Jenny Tan, Dimitri Karetnikov, and Mark Bellis, were a tremendous help during the production process. I would also like to express my gratitude to Cynthia Buck for her careful copyediting. I am grateful to Hannah Townsend and Andrew Wylie of the Wylie Agency for their advice and support.

Finally, I thank my family and friends for their company while this book came to life: Salomé, Limor, Solal, and my ex-wife Rachel, to whom this book is dedicated, and Ilana, Jeremiah, Peter, Kevin, Leland, Devin, Noah, Ines, Ruud, Rahsaan, Marion, Allegra, Naomi, Jamie, Jacob, Wei, Roger, Emma, Lew, Shilpa, and little Alex. In token of my affection, this book is inscribed to my parents.

INTRODUCTION
Coping with Defeat

1

Sunni Islam, Roman Catholicism, and the Modern State

TWENTY-FIVE YEARS have passed since the opening frenzy of Islamist attacks targeting the symbols and civilians of Western democracies, and it has been nearly sixty years since the Second Vatican Council aligned Church doctrine with modern society in those same countries. The riveting scenes that unfolded around the Mediterranean Sea in the twenty-first century might therefore appear predestined, or at least unsurprising. In Syria, a rogue Islamic Caliph exhorted Muslims to revolt against nation-states and the international order. He executed infidels in his desert redoubt and dispatched masked assassins to silence apostates across the globe in editorial offices and nightclubs, from Paris to Istanbul.[1] Midway across the Mediterranean, meanwhile, the Roman Catholic pope fielded invitations to address the European Union Parliament and United States Congress, prayed alongside a rabbi and an imam in the Vatican gardens, and urged secular legislators to "keep democracy alive" (see figure 1.1).[2]

This striking divergence in religious attitudes toward the state is unexpected. Just 150 years ago, the interested observer would have predicted opposite trajectories for Roman Catholicism and Sunni Islam. In the 1860s, Pope Pius IX barricaded himself behind Vatican walls, angrily asserting personal infallibility and his prerogative to depose princes and potentates. His encyclicals condemned religious pluralism, banned books, and forbade Catholics from voting in democratic elections. Pius enlisted 18,000 irregular fighters from Europe and North America to fend off "the accursed infidels in red shirts"—the Italian patriots unifying the country—leading several countries to bar the international travel of young men seeking martyrdom in defense of the Holy Father's earthly rule.

While the pope "recoiled from the appeal of the times," the *New York Times* reported in 1859, the Ottoman caliph in Istanbul "appears as the champion and nearly as the martyr of Progress."[3] The figurehead of Sunni Islam exhibited

FIGURE 1.1 Twenty-First Century: Pope Francis at the European Parliament (2014);
Abu Bakr al Baghdadi in Mosul (2014)

FIGURE 1.1 (*continued*)

worldliness and toleration while fulfilling the guardianship of the holy cities of Mecca and Medina (see figure 1.2). He inaugurated legislative sessions, toured European capitals, and expanded religious tolerance across a multi-confessional empire.[4] Sultan Abdülmecid (1823–1861) sent the American republic a tribute of friendship etched in marble for inclusion in the Washington Monument, and he received Persian dignitaries for shared Sunni-Shi'a prayer in the Hagia Sofia Mosque.[5] As caliph, Abdülmecid and his six successors projected a layer of religious uniformity over the Sunni Muslim world, embodying the ideal of political independence, self-determination, and glory to God at a time when more than 80 percent of Muslims worldwide lived under European rule in the British, Dutch, French, Russian, and Austro-Hungarian empires.

The last half-dozen sultan-caliphs sat atop a growing international network of clerics, seminaries, and religious schools, providing spiritual leadership and hundreds of daily fatwas from Istanbul to most of the world's Sunni Muslims—from Sarajevo, Cairo, Damascus, and Tunis to Java and Hyderabad. But Muslims under siege by European empires had no illusions that the Islamic cavalry was on its way. The Ottomans compensated for political loss with spiritual gains, transforming a regional sultanate into a global caliphate. Well into the twentieth century, by contrast, many Roman Catholics, holding out hope that

FIGURE 1.2 Nineteenth Century: Sultan Abdülmecid with British Royals;
Pope Pius IX at Vatican Council I

the Prince of Rome would be restored to his rightful place in temporal power, defied democratization and secular efforts to build up new nation-states.

By the twenty-first century, however, the international Catholic and Muslim religious institutions had abandoned their earlier approaches to executive power and switched roles. The Roman Catholic Church abruptly relinquished its 1,000-year claim to political rule and focused instead on advocacy, global spiritual influence, and its evangelizing mission. Catholic positions on social and political issues became increasingly progressive while the worldview of Islamic jurists regressed in the direction of Rome's antimodern *Syllabus of Errors* (1864).[6] The controversial and inconsistent acceptance by Islamic authorities of the modern nation-state—and thus their renunciation of political office-holding—opened up an enduring fracture in Muslim communities worldwide. The epicenter of the fragmentation is the Mediterranean core of the old Ottoman Empire, rippling outwards from Turkey, North Africa, and the Arabian Peninsula. The unresolved political-religious divide is at the heart of today's "Islamic Question."[7]

This book makes two arguments to decipher religious politics in countries with significant Catholic and Muslim populations. First, today's theological disunity within Sunni Islam can be traced to Europeans' decisions to undermine the caliphate in lands they briefly ruled across the Middle East, North Africa, and South and Southeast Asia. That set the conditions for two fateful events: Turkish nationalists' abolition of the caliphate and the Saudi Wahhabi takeover of Mecca and Medina, Islam's two holiest cities. Ironically, the British, Dutch, French, and Russian empires, while occupying powers over two centuries, did everything short of kidnapping or assassinating the caliph to ensure this outcome instead of the alternative—the caliphate's survival as a spiritual figurehead. As a result, it is bearers of Islamic extremism who travel the Pan-Islamic path furrowed by Ottoman religious diplomacy.

The second argument concerns the contrast between Rome's and Istanbul's respective experiences with turn-of-the-century European governments. While European nations strong-armed, expropriated, violated, and humiliated the Catholic hierarchy, they never disbanded it. When Italian nationalists invaded the Papal States and made Rome their new political capital, the Red Shirts halted at the Vatican's bronze gates. European powers in the early 1900s considered relocating the pope abroad but ultimately spared the Roman Catholic Church the destabilizing experience of having either no pope—an empty see (*sede vacante*)—or an illegitimate one. Within national borders, the Church came under the administrative control of European states, which usurped clerical appointments and religious education. But the Vatican had the time and space to build up organizational resources and compete for religious authority. The defeats and shocks of modernity guided Church actors and activities away from the unrealistic goal of political office-holding and toward advocacy, missionary work, and ritual uniformity.

Two sets of related consequences are crucial to the state-religion divide today. First, the Vatican returned from exile a changed organization. The diplomatic isolation of the Church's desert-crossing—also known as the "Roman Question"—lasted nearly seventy years (1861–1929) before the Lateran Accords with Italy resurrected independent statehood for the Vatican. It entered the new world order as a sovereign state, with its global community united under pontifical guidance—albeit on a strictly symbolic basis. The pope has hundreds of millions of followers and admirers, but he governs over fewer than 1,000 citizens. Resolving the Roman Question granted the Church a spiritual afterlife in the nation-state era. Governments along the northern and western shores of the Mediterranean restored organizational independence to Catholic officialdom on their soil. In one country after another, the Church won back autonomy over its internal affairs—from clerical training to bishop nominations—even in places that had banned the hierarchy for centuries. The soft restoration of Roman Catholicism reverted control over religious matters from state oversight to independently appointed community leaders, despite their foreign ties to the Vatican. A city-state under Roman Catholic rule was a face-saving solution that provided a model Catholic polity where God's shadow on earth could rule in sovereignty. This outcome, at once triumphant and circumscribed, mitigated the kind of politicization of religion that took root in the Muslim world.

No such bridge to the past was projected on the Mediterranean's southern and eastern banks. Since the Turkish republic exiled the last caliph and abolished the institution in 1924, the question of which Muslim ruler would receive the pledge of loyalty (*bai'a*) and the *umma*'s daily benediction has remained wide open. The other consequence is that the leadership once exercised by Istanbul—in the Balkans, down the Arabian Peninsula, and across North Africa—is now siloed within national Islamic affairs ministries. More than half of the world's Muslims reside in countries where Islam is partly or fully established, as is the case for around half of the fifty or so Muslim-majority nation-states globally. But it is true for virtually all who live in former Ottoman territories across North Africa and the Middle East, where religion has become a third rail of national politics. Each of these ministries' religious legitimacy is actively contested by nongovernmental movements, from the elections-oriented Muslim Brotherhood as well as from violent rivals like al Qaeda and and the Islamic State.

The caliph's empty seat set off a century-long supernova of pretenders and Islamists spanning the Islamic Crescent, intensifying in the decades leading up to the abolition's centenary (2024). The popularity of Islamist parties

whose leaders question the state's basic legitimacy attests to the ongoing politicization of religion in North Africa and Turkey. Yet even when the circle of
eligible candidates and officeholders was expanded to include Islamists in
Turkey (2002), Tunisia (2011), and Egypt (2011), the state did not revert
autonomy to traditional religious authorities. Despite minimal gestures toward
soft restoration—such as delegating civil powers of marriage to clerics or
allowing the local election of state *muftis*—none has seriously considered spinning off religious affairs to nonstate actors. Instead, it is governments that
license and train imams, oversee mosques, and remain the arbiters of acceptable religious expression.

The tension between nonstate transnational Islamic actors and official
Nation-State Islam feeds political instability around the globe. The Islamist
dissidents, for whom Islam stands above all (including the nation), resemble
the fervent romantics of interwar Europe. For Islamists, the Treaties of Sèvres
and Lausanne (1920–1923) formalized the evisceration of the last Muslim empire. As with the Treaty of Versailles for German nationalists, a century-long
narrative has built up that internal foes in alliance with external enemies have
delivered the proverbial stab in the back. In a similar way to the idealized vision of German empire superseding all other subnational political units
("Deutschland über alles"), the missing ingredient that could rescue political
systems for Islam was a greater God ("Allahu Akbar").

The existential challenge to regimes in the Muslim-majority world has been
mirrored in the disrupted religious lives of millions of immigrant-origin communities residing across the sea in western Europe. The missing caliphate
trapped Muslim communities in a purgatory populated by colorful transnational pretenders like the Egyptian doctor Yusuf al-Qaradawi, the Yemeni
sheikh Osama bin Laden, and the Iraqi theologian Abu Bakr al Baghdadi, on
the one hand, and the state-appointed *ulema* and national ministers of Islamic
affairs in Muslim-majority nation-states, on the other. Absent the rudder of a
robust sense of affiliation, some in the diaspora drifted away from the distant
winds of their ancestral religious references—and toward the gales of dissident
and politicized Islam, which emanated, ironically, from the outer frontiers of
the former European empires. Afghanistan and Somalia, Syria, Iraq, and Libya,
were staked out as "authentic" Islamic enclaves in defiance of the rule of law
and the international state system.

Essential Differences?

After a long and winding road, international Catholic and Muslim religious
institutions effectively traded political positions vis-à-vis the state. How have
these once omnipotent religions contended with displacement by the state in

their customary realms of prestige and power? Even if there is no precise formula for the transition of religious authorities to the rule of law, it is urgent to identify the factors that promote the mutual acceptance of religious communities and the modern state. How should the evolution of religious authorities' attitudes toward the modern state be understood? How should those attitudes be placed in the context of today's configuration of state-Islam relations? Under which conditions do the less zealous win out? What fosters the paradoxical result wherein religious leaders endure state subjugation yet retain their dignity?

Many fail to see the puzzle. They point to the underlying unity of faith and politics in Islam (religion and state, *din wa dawla*), on the one hand, while insisting that Christianity was always destined to comply with contemporary norms separating church and state. For Sunni Muslims to catch up with Saint Augustine's vision of two cities—one earthly and the other heavenly—the argument goes, contemporary governments would need to start by giving up their current religious monopoly. Much of the scholarship on Islam and politics today either implicitly or explicitly argues that Islam needs to undergo a Protestant Reformation style of political theology or asserts that such a development is intrinsically impossible. Yet the initial shift of fourth-century Christians from preaching to governing was also unexpected. The maxim to "render unto Caesar that which is Caesar's" pertained only for as long as Christian believers were in the minority. "Once Caesar is Christian," Harvard divinity scholar Shai Cohen writes, "things lined up differently."[8] A closer look at history in this book reveals a host of contingencies for why the papacy survived intact into the twenty-first century while the caliphate succumbed. Moreover, Protestant and Catholic churches and their associated political regimes resisted religious pluralism and liberalism for centuries yet still ended up as proponents of democracy.

This is not a study of essential differences or of historical destiny. The key ingredients are to be found in neither the scripture nor the stars. There are so many strains of religious interpretation and historical cases from which to choose that defining state-religion *compatibility* can be selective and ad hoc. The direct comparison of Sunni Islam and Roman Catholicism—notwithstanding geographic divergences and differences in doctrine and prayer—can be justified by shared traits like creeds, codes of conduct, and notions of a global confessional community.[9] Both faiths have proselytized across many cultures, and at different historical moments both have allowed for degrees of separation between divine and secular rule. In theory, Western Christendom was a monolithic spiritual realm governed by the pope, whose authority transcended all boundaries. In practice, national Catholic churches reflected the political map of Europe in the nation-state era, and secular rulers required their clergy to be loyal subjects. In the words of one scholar, Catholicism rested upon "a reasoned legal framework that links God and humankind" with ideas and norms that implicated the state, political systems, and public policy.[10] Catholicism, etymologically traceable to mean "all-concerning," was unlikely to embrace religious pluralism and democracy. The Roman Catholic Church's renunciation of political office-holding and its embrace of democracy seemed remote as recently as the 1950s.

Then the unimaginable started happening. The Church underwent a series of modernizations at the Second Vatican Council (1962–1965). To the surprise of observers like Samuel Huntington, a towering scholar of twentieth-century state-society dynamics, the pope became a leading global human rights actor and an engine of democratization. "Cultures evolve, and historically are dynamic, not passive," Huntington concluded. To argue otherwise, he said, was no "more viable than the thesis that Confucianism prevents economic development" against the evidence of China's bustling global marketplace. Quite unpredictably, then, rigid cultural communities can suddenly acknowledge defeat and "reinterpret their traditions so as to make them compatible with the democratic political practices—Catholicism made that adjustment."[11]

How and why did that take place? The Second Vatican Council forged the final link in a chain of interlocking defeats stretching back centuries. By gathering data from eight national states and two transnational empires over several centuries, this book weaves a tapestry of religious authorities' path to political disempowerment and transformation. The evidence suggests that similar dynamics are under way within Sunni Islam, which in all of its global diversity may yet follow the path of Catholicism. A historical-institutional portrait of Roman Catholic and Sunni Muslim religious authorities emerges over time, as they have coped with defeat in geographic, political, and demographic terms.

The Argument: Modernity's Three Defeats

It may baffle the reader to evoke religion's defeat amid a global spiritual renaissance. Around the world, believers wage godly battles both figurative and literal. Many seek to insert their faith into electoral politics and constitutions. In dozens of countries, terrorists inflict violence on nonbelievers. But violent idealists have spilled over borders to threaten public safety *because* they have been defeated and forced out of somewhere else. They are not the triumphant envoys expanding a successful revolution. In the domestic sphere of the nation, Islam and Catholicism have been roundly subdued by modern states. On a daily level, the state took on roles previously held by religious authorities, from education to legal codes and the regulation of diet, birth, burial, marriage, and divorce.[12] Since around 1800, Western political leaders have displaced the authority of religious leaders and devalued traditional institutions through a process often described as functional differentiation. The French sociologist Émile Durkheim was the first to recognize that the modern state would take over religion's role in structuring social cohesion.[13] The German theorist Max Weber assumed that science would eventually obviate the need for religion. Historical accounts of secularization single out the roles played by capitalism, nationalism, the scientific revolution, and the Reformation.[14] Indeed, modernization theory presumed that separation of religion and state would be one of its natural outcomes. The reality, however, was not a unilinear, teleological story of religious decline and privatization.[15] It is a difficult and long journey from religious preeminence over the state to the soft restoration of legal subjecthood, going from a position of omnipotence to the realms of civil society and family law.

This book's central argument is that three shocks, or defeats, eroded the political ties between the last major Christian and Muslim political-religious empires—the Papal States and the Ottoman Empire—and their believers. The shocks differed in timing for Catholics and Sunnis but have had the same revolutionary effect of gradually binding religious authorities to the rule of law. Three parts of the book are organized around these critical junctures: Part 1, "The End of Empire," part 2, "The Nation-State Era," and part 3, "The Era of Believers without Borders." Each historical shock moved religious authorities further along the spectrum of state-religion relations—from a position of supremacy to the semi-autonomy of the contemporary state-religion bargain.

Each defeat erected new legal borders between the religious leadership and the faithful and ground their political sovereignty down to a nub. Surrender to state supremacy (civilian rule) was the cost paid by religious authorities to preserve uniformity of rite in territory they did not physically control. They strengthened three aspects of their organization: infrastructure, educational institutions, and hierarchy. The expansion of Catholic dioceses, colleges, and seminaries took place to *counteract* the efforts of religious rivals and modernizing nation-states. The Ottoman development of formal religious training and standardized religious content—occasionally customized for local constituencies—also took place in reaction to European efforts to replace it. The result was that priests, prelates, imams, and ulema went from being an uneven bunch—some educated, some ignorant, some mendicant, some noble—to a professional corps. These institutions had always existed in some shape, but infrastructure, clerical training, and religious education were highly informal, irregularly distributed, and subject to little quality control. Some of the best-known features of the caliphate and the papacy—and their most intense periods of internationalization—were relatively recent developments.

Engaging this argument requires a willingness to reinterpret state-religion relations since the sixteenth-century Counter-Reformation and the advent of nineteenth-century Pan-Islam. Although the first centuries of the spread of Islam and Christianity were characterized by aggressive expansion and subjugation to Christian or Muslim religious-political authority, the institutions forged in the modern era were *defensive* and depended on the recognition of other states for their existence and operations. A good place to start reinterpreting is by questioning the assumptions underlying this unusual comparison. The evidence arrayed suggests significantly more overlap than might be expected. The initial evangelizing mission central to both Christianity and Islam drove each to spread over the same southern and southeastern shores of the Mediterranean basin, just a few centuries apart. That was the period during which the geographical heartlands of Western Christendom and the Islamic Crescent took their familiar shapes.

The book traces the path of these two "political" religions toward peaceful cohabitation with the modern state. It is the history of Roman Catholicism and Sunni Islam in the long descent from their most recent apex of political and spiritual power. Popes and caliphs have served as chief apostles and defenders of their respective faiths. The pontiff is Guardian of the Two Swords of Saint Peter and Bishop of Rome, while the caliphs have been Holy Warriors (*ghazi*), Custodians of Mecca and Medina, and Guardians of the Holy Relics.[16] For the latter half of their existence, the Papal States (Stato Pontificio, 752–1870) and the Ottoman Caliphate (Osmanlı Devleti, 1299–1924) were the preeminent religious authorities and the longest-reigning dynasties of the world's two largest religious denominations. Yet each had only four centuries of spiritual and political hegemony: Western Christendom between the Great Schism (1054) and the Protestant Reformation (1517), and Sunni Islam from the taking of Baghdad (1517) to the exile of the last caliph (1924).

Wasn't Catholicism always centralized? And isn't authority within Islam diffused and not concentrated in any single institution? On the one hand, compared to Roman Catholicism's firm organizational chart, Ottoman Islam had a lower grade of centralized institutionalization. The sultan-caliphs left room for local religious authority, maintaining looser control in southeastern Europe, North Africa, and Arabia. Nonetheless, Sunni Islam was more centralized than is generally acknowledged, and Roman Catholicism's hierarchical monopoly was less airtight than its reputation. The Ottomans were one of a small handful of Islamic regimes in history with custodianship of Islam's holiest sites in Mecca, Medina, and Jerusalem. As measured by the extent of land and people under the rule of a unified religious-political hierarchy, the Reformation marked the precipitous decline of the Papal States, and the rise of the British and French empires spelled the end of the caliphate. At their moment of political extinction, the pope (1870) and the caliph (1922) ruled over territorial states with relatively small populations: 2.5 million Papal States citizens and 14 million Ottoman citizens. As supreme religious leader, however, each man had a *spiritual* influence over believers whose numbers greatly exceeded these population figures.

The sultan-caliphs inspired hundreds of millions of Muslims living under British, Dutch, French, and Russian rule. Although their political influence had peaked in the seventeenth century, in the first quarter of the twentieth century the sultan-caliph became the spiritual leader for around 80 percent of the world's 350 million Muslims.[17] The last time the Roman Catholic pope could claim similar projection power as a religious beacon within Christianity was before the Reformation. But he cultivated influence over a similar number of Catholics in Europe and the Americas. More than half of the 500 million Christians worldwide in 1925 were Roman Catholic. Beginning in the late nineteenth century, there was a dramatic increase in the global share of Muslims who included the Sunni caliph in their prayers or lived in states at least nominally aligned with his authority. If the religious necessity of a caliphate is hotly debated, its historical persistence is unavoidable. The attempt of modern nation-states to fulfill the role makes its absence that much more felt.

A close examination of modern Muslim-majority states, moreover, shows that the widespread understanding of Islam as a radically decentralized religion without a clergy is fundamentally inaccurate. The widespread notion among many Muslims and non-Muslims that there is "no Islamic hierarchy to fix doctrine, combat heresy or compete for power" is belied by the reality of Sunni ulema and religious authorities who vie with or accommodate political rulers.[18] The American scholar Jonathan Brown compares state ulema to a priestlike class of scriptural guardians who, despite the lack of an international ordination procedure, maintain an "interpretive monopoly" over law and dogma within Sunni Islam.[19]

In the course of my extensive interviews in each country under examination—Algeria, Morocco, Tunisia, and Turkey—religious affairs officials, from the minister down to the neighborhood imam, volunteered the view that state control prevented a situation of *fitna* (intracommunal strife)—shorthand for dividing the community with competing mosques and imams. One Turkish observer referred to the danger of being "pulverized by the destructive millstone" of sectarianism.

The national religious affairs ministries and agencies of the Ottoman and post-Ottoman world are not exact equivalents to the Catholic hierarchy, but they have played a comparable role as the exclusive administrators of spiritual affairs and religious education and the arbiters of scriptural interpretation. It turns out that the process of professionalization played a critical role. Formal-

TABLE 1.1. Standardizing Religion

Roman Catholicism	Sunni Islam
Infrastructure	
Churches and Priests	Mosques and Imams
Roman Catholic Europe: 1550–1648	Ottoman Empire: 1826–1924
Protestant states and New World: 1650–1830	Ottoman successor states: 1950–2000
Americas: 1830–1940	Western Europe: 1980–2015
Education	
Catholic Universities, Seminaries, Colleges, and Parochial Schools	Islamic Theology Faculties, Seminaries, and Schools
Europe: 1555–1700	Ottoman Empire: 1900–1924
Europe: 1820–1960	Ottoman successor states: 1970s–
Americas: 1820–1980	Europe: 1980–
Hierarchy	
Apostolic Delegates, Bishops, and Cardinals	Ambassadors, Ulema, and Ministries of Islamic Affairs
Europe: 1650–1850	Ottoman successor states: 2000–
Europe: 1850–1960	Europe: 2000–
Americas: 1800–1960	

ized training drastically changed the clerical corps from a motley assortment of clerics to a professional body with uniform training and a standardized liturgy. The religious-administrative revolution marks the shift from providing small, decentralized services to training a large standing religious bureaucracy. The resulting Catholic and Sunni institutional infrastructure—schools, seminaries, and *madrassas*—survives in every formerly Ottoman or Catholic state today (see table 1.1).

Nation-State Islam, for Now

The relationship between Islamic authorities and the modern state in the twenty-first century appears to be stuck in a phase where national governments guard a close monopoly on religious expression. The liberal demand to do away with Islamic affairs ministries and official muftis in the twenty-first-century Muslim world—to disestablish official Islam—is more likely to harm, not help, democratization. Even proponents of secular liberalism acknowledge that the state cannot retreat entirely and will always have "to regulate the role of religion in order to maintain its own religious neutrality."[20] State oversight of religious affairs comes in many forms, but it arguably represents the most plausible attempt to reconcile Islamic organizations with the national rule of law in the absence of consensual religious leadership. Instead of seeing bureaucratization as a fatal weakness, it should be seen as part of a sequence of professionalization that is indispensable to any religion's coexistence with the nation-state. Establishment can be found almost everywhere in the Muslim-majority world, where *waqf* departments, Islamic affairs ministries, state theology faculties, and government-appointed ulema form a barrier to movements or political parties aspiring to enter the religious marketplace or to link up with a transnational umma.

Nation-State Islam should not be rushed offstage before progress is made in repairing the breach of political and religious legitimacy of Islamic authorities across the former Ottoman Empire. To dissolve the public bureaucracy and dismiss the corps of imams and religious officials would be the spiritual equivalent of disbanding the army and devolving national security to unregulated militias. The desire to erase the symbols of a preceding order is understandable, but the political abuse of public religious institutions by some actors should not be permitted to discredit the whole enterprise. Denial and repression tend to leave vacuums filled by shadowy alternatives. Just as democratic nation-states struggled to find the right balance of power in civil-military relations, an apolitical framework for civil-religious relations is required for democracy to thrive. Paradoxically, establishment—despite its discrimination against religious minorities—may be more compatible with democratization than disestablishment.

Measuring Defeat

The experience of the Roman Catholic Church as a civil society actor in the twentieth and twenty-first centuries demonstrates that religion and secularism are not fixed categories.[21] It also shows that there is no clear relation between adapting to church-state relations, on the one hand, and accepting the liberal precepts of most of the states where it operated, on the other.[22] The distinction between this world and the next one is not always clear-cut.[23] Augustine, the first to coin the term *saeculorum*, had in mind a temporal imperative toward such collective action. The real-world policy of providing for the poor, for example, may be based on religious convictions. The political scientist Anna Grzymala-Busse has shown that, in the absence of establishment, the Church has been able to transcend its circumscribed roles and achieve a "specifically political form of moral authority" in several contemporary European countries. Her recent study asks how churches influence policy if they have no formal legislative role.[24] Whereas Grzymala-Busse and others look at politicization, this book, by contrast, is interested in *depoliticization* and the dethronement process itself. Why did religious authorities lose their legislative role, and how did political exile shape their current organizational stances? Churches did not reemerge intact in the contemporary nation-state and pick up where they left off. The defeats described herein—the decline of empire, the spread of nationalism, unruly diasporas—are a subset of larger problems that religions face in their encounter with a modernizing world. Who dispenses grace?[25] Who can conduct or has access to modern-day sacraments? The three phases of defeat all conspired to shape the operations and aims of religious organizations in the era of nation-state sovereignty.

When considering such apparently dissimilar cases, this book will engage in systematic paired comparison to argue that they share a common progression of the state-religion relationship. This adopts what the political sociologist Sidney Tarrow defines as an analytical strategy "to work through complex empirical and historical materials,"[26] distinct from large-N analyses and single-case studies.[27] The strategy is to identify nearly identical processes in a broad range of cases.[28] Only by "going inside the process to specify its connective mechanisms," Tarrow writes, "can we understand how the chain of causation operates."[29] What are the mechanisms and processes that translate defeat into depoliticization—what Tarrow calls the "sources of intra-systemic behaviors"?[30] This approach embraces the proper names of case studies and its intimacy and attention to empirical detail depart from regression analysis and methodology-driven political science.

This book pairs comparative-historical cases and process-tracing with the experiences of officials charged with managing contemporary politics and religion. There is abundant evidence of a connection between political defeat and institutional expansion, as demonstrated in charts and tables compiled from my unique database containing archival research on Roman Catholic institutions (in western Europe and the Americas) and two centuries of institutionalized Islam in the Muslim-majority world formerly under the sway of the Ottoman Empire. Parts 1 and 2, on the end of empire and the rise of the nation-state, present original research from Vatican and Ottoman archives aggregating records of institutional growth and budgetary lines for religious affairs. Parts 2 and 3 focus on the experiences of Algeria, Morocco, Tunisia, and Turkey in comparison with those of Italy, France, Germany, and Spain. Part 3 draws on interviews and conversations that I conducted in North Africa, Turkey, and western Europe from 2011 to 2019. I interviewed more than 100 officials responsible for Islamic affairs or public religious education in Algiers, Ankara, Casablanca, Istanbul, Oran, Rabat, and Tunis and another fifty with interior ministry and foreign ministry officials in Berlin, Brussels, The Hague, Madrid, Paris, and Rome who were responsible for relations with Islamic affairs representatives.

Despite its aim for completeness, the book does not tackle the development of Nation-State Islam in Libya and Egypt or of Nation-State Catholicism
in Ireland and Poland. There are reasons for this: Libya stands apart for its relative underdevelopment of formal religious institutions, and Egyptian Islam's
multiple internal layers of authority proved too unwieldy to fit neatly into this
comparative work.[31] I also shied away from fieldwork in Egypt or Libya during
the turbulent decade of the 2010s. The consolation for these missing cases is
that they are less relevant to the argument than the featured countries. Religious affairs and scholarly life in both Libya and Egypt were far less Ottomanized than in other corners of the empire.[32] Similarly, although Poland and
Ireland were both majority-Catholic states, they were governed by non-
Catholic regimes (in Moscow, Vienna, and London) during the period under
examination. The book does contain references to both the Cairo-based Al-
Azhar and Muslim Brotherhood, however, in addition to Libyan and Egyptian
leaders whose influence on twentieth-century Islam is impossible to escape.
And the arrival of immigrants on US shores pulls key figures from Ireland and
Poland into the book's narrative.

The central focus here is on religious professionalization and institution-
building as the concrete expression of political defeat. These processes—the
construction of houses of worship and the hiring of clerics, the establishment
of educational organizations, and the creation of religious hierarchies—took
place over centuries. Several years of field research allowed for their enumera-
tion here, and an exhaustive review of contemporary histories permits this
book's correlation of their growth with other political developments.[33] My
implicit premise is in harmony with the comparative historical notion that
institutions structure politics by influencing actors' calculations, shaping their
identities and preferences.[34] The book's illustrations contain charts to provide
a clear and relatively objective measure of the connections between state development and the formalization of organized religion. At its extreme, such an
exercise can become a rigid, structuralist model of explanation that is dismis-
sive of purposive action. The empirical sections of this book therefore strive
to describe these processes with rich detail and address why similar situations
do not always lead to the same outcomes. The comparison shows where things
stand and also how they might realistically develop, beyond the political uses
of religion by national governments.

The most important parallel that the two religions share—with a time lag—
is visible in their institutional responses to the three great shocks. At the same
time that Rome's and Istanbul's religious legal authority became null and void
in their former territories—and ultimately even in their immediate
surroundings—they fashioned ways to bring their spiritual influence across
borders in a clerical and hierarchical capacity. The only way for Rome and

Istanbul to resist without force of arms was to rationalize and improve their houses of worship, preachers, and teachers. The methodical expansion of infrastructure, education, and hierarchy was undertaken by the Roman Catholic Church after the sixteenth-century Council of Trent and by the Ottoman Empire beginning in the mid-nineteenth century.

Roughly a century of Counter-Reformation (starting around 1540) and Pan-Islam (starting in 1826) would leave a strong institutional legacy and mark the first stage of the modern professionalization of Catholicism and Islam. The shock of the Reformation and the tribulations it imposed made the papacy and the Church what they are today. Both periods provoked a transformation and renewal of religious institutions to battle heretical movements encroaching on their remaining territory—and to protect their believers trapped under infidel rule. The political displacement of the Prince of the Papal States and the Sultan of the Ottoman Empire had the effect of *spiritually* reinforcing them as divine or prophetic emissaries. Being weakened politically reinforced their cross-border ethereality as truly the Shadows of God on Earth.

Part 1: The First Defeat—and the Counterpunch

Part 1, comprising chapters 2, 3, and 4, picks up the history of Roman Catholicism and Sunni Islam when their dominant political systems featured spiritual-temporal fusion: the religious and political authorities were rolled into one, the pope guarding the Two Swords of Saint Peter while the caliph served as guardian of the Sword and Flag of the Prophet. Their first shock in the modern era—the Protestant Reformation and the dismemberment of the Ottoman Empire—inflicted territorial losses and introduced sectarian competition. In the space of one generation, the Protestant Reformation and European colonial expansion deprived Rome and Istanbul, respectively, of access to vast reservoirs of land, people, and religious authority. Lutheranism and other Protestant movements in the mid-sixteenth century spread wildly across northern and western Europe—from Germany to England, Denmark, Norway, Sweden, and a large chunk of the Low Countries, Switzerland, and France.[35] In the words of one nineteenth-century historian, the revolt "thrust its sickle into the Pope's harvest."[36] Within fifty years, schismatic churches had swallowed up one-third of Europe's Catholic population and half the landmass under Rome's dominion. This crisis, the worst for the Church in half a millennium, reduced it from a realm of 64 million followers spread over 4.2 million square kilometers to 45 million people on half that much land (see figure 1.3).[37] The movement that traversed northern Europe stranded Catholic minorities in Protestant countries, which banned or severely restricted the presence of the Church and its hierarchy on their national territory.

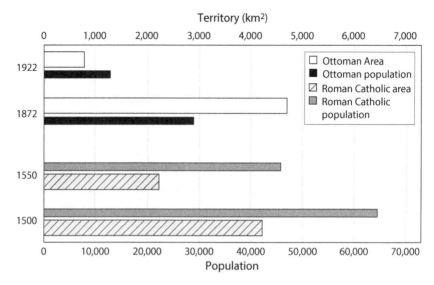

FIGURE 1.3. The First Defeat: The Ottoman Empire and the Roman Catholic Church

At the summit of Ottoman might, the sultans boasted of ruling over 40 million subjects "in seven climates." Starting in the late eighteenth century, the Ottomans' European nemeses clawed back influence and direct rule around the Adriatic, Mediterranean, and Black Seas. European military might reduced them to one-quarter of the population—the biggest losses came in 1868—in one weather zone. In the early twentieth century, nearly 90 percent of the world's Muslims lived under colonial rule. France, Britain, Italy, Russia, Austria, and the Netherlands had a combined Muslim population of 230 million. The Ottomans' spiritual authority was disputed in Central Asia, the Balkans, the Middle East, and North Africa through warfare and diplomatic pressure from the French, British, Austro-Hungarian, and Russian empires. Just as the new Lutheran and Protestant governments rejected the notion of a princely pope—and made life miserable for loyalist holdouts—the new rulers in the former Ottoman realm also went to great lengths to undermine the caliphs' claim to the mantle of the Prophet. Occupiers cultivated alternative religious leadership to replace the caliph: France and Britain in Africa and Arabia, and Russia and Austro-Hungary in Europe.[38] The Ottoman caliph's realm diminished from 30 million souls on 4.5 million square kilometers in the year 1862 to 13 million on 780,000 square kilometers in 1922 (see figure 1.3).[39]

None of the territories flipped from Christianity to Islam during these contractions, or vice versa. Instead, each religious community was separated from its traditional center of authority—the pope or the caliph—in new institutional arrangements. The results ranged from sectarianism to schism. In a sectarian out-come, the new authorities offered an alternative national path to the same God and heaven—for example, the Anglican and Swedish churches, or Bosnian and Bulgarian Islam. Catholic and Muslim communities' spiritual parting of ways from Rome and Istanbul appeared to be political disputes cloaked as a latter-day crisis of investiture. By contrast, schismatic cases, such as the Lutheran, Wahhabi, and other Reformist movements, were based on substantive differences over re-ligious ritual and meaning. In such cases, two sets of beliefs were exclusive and contradictory, and conflict could rise to the level of mutually assured damnation. The serial declarations of religious supremacy by new national actors raised new barriers between Rome, Istanbul, and tens of millions of followers.

The barriers were raised by rivals who stood to inherit a lot. Reformation and occupation sparked Henry VIII–style reasoning, and there was no short-age of would-be local sovereigns. Every Henry, Frederick, John, and Philip spotted the chance to be pope in his own court. In the Middle East, the Sauds, Hashemites, and Alaouites saw an opportunity to cooperate with a European invader for the ultimate power grab. Other challengers who stood to gain were Mahdists in the Sudan, Sanussiyas in Libya and Wahhabis in Arabia. Why settle for *sharif* when you could run your own emirate? The European empires were entertaining applications for leadership of the umma and the custodianship of Islam's holy cities.

The history of Rome's decline as the capital of Western Christendom and that of Istanbul's demise as the center of global Islam are shrouded in self-serving legends and contradictory lore. In the narrative that emphasizes the power of leadership and ideas, men like Martin Luther and T. E. Lawrence advanced the causes of individual and collective self-determination in a vic-tory over the forces of corruption and despotism. Lutheranism and its ilk spread wildly across northern and western Europe as national churches swal-lowed up one-third of Europe's population and half the landmass of Rome's former dominion.[40] Luther and Lawrence and others pushing for spiritual secession from Rome or Istanbul peddled persuasive arguments, but they were taking battering rams to crumbling walls.

The dysfunction and abuses imputed to the Ottomans were not cooked up. The Ottoman ulema, like the clergy of late medieval Europe, were so patronage-laden that they formed an aristocracy. They became a patrimonially encrusted, opulent, and tax-exempt class apart.[41] In Europe, priests and bishops were exempt from lay jurisdiction.[42] Against the original intentions of their found-ing fathers, church leaders and ulema had become a self-reproducing elite. Family connections and nepotism determined the religious careers of Otto-man officialdom.[43] Certain families came to dominate the senior mollah posi-tions in Istanbul and cardinals' seats in Rome.[44]

Despite the universalist rhetoric and dogma, neither religious capital was very good about integrating its own communal periphery. Unequal representation within the religious hierarchies left many unsatisfied customers open to new management. With 15 million inhabitants, Germany was the largest land—nearly one-quarter of Western Christendom—yet going into the 1500s it had virtually no representation in the College of Cardinals and thus virtually no influence in Rome. Similar complaints accumulated in the Arab provinces about the Ottomans, whose hereditary dynasty had always named a Turk to the position of Sheikh-ul-Islam. In the 400 years preceding Martin Luther, 90 percent of the popes were Italian—there were also six French and Spanish popes. In Germany, the Lutheran Reformation overlapped with the pursuit of sovereign statehood.[45] In North Africa, similarly, the European conquests emboldened Islamic Reformists, some of whom cooperated with the occupiers to pursue a social and intellectual agenda independent from the declining caliphate.[46]

In the late nineteenth century, the French and British empires replaced their makeshift, regional Islamic authorities with more serious efforts to enduringly capture global Sunni religious authority. It was a fight to the spiritual death, and Europeans reached deep, all the way into the key seminaries, mosques, and holy cities that formed the heart (and rump) of the Ottoman Empire. Possible solutions ranged from the establishment of a "Mahometan Vatican" to the convening of major international conferences to designate a successor caliph. The tug-of-war over the caliphate was a critical precursor to state-Islam relations in the post-colonial Middle East and North Africa. European efforts to weaken the sultan-caliph and to build up their own alternatives had an enduring impact on the geopolitics of Sunni (and Shi'a) Islam well into the twenty-first century. For the first time in centuries, widespread confusion reigned over the spiritual direction of the Muslim caliphate. This created a chaotic transition from Ottoman to British and French rule that implicated the religious lives of hundreds of millions.

In contemplation of the sultan-caliphs' formal disappearance, western European capitals intensely debated who should follow in Ottoman footsteps. Part 2 of the book unearths this incredible saga of colonialist chutzpah. Newly released documents from diplomatic archives chronicle the interference by London and Paris—and by Rome, Vienna, and Moscow—in the spiritual affairs of the global umma. They denigrated the Ottomans and promoted substitutes. Vienna appointed its preferred grand mufti (*rais ul ulema*) in Bosnia and Herzegovina; the British invented a mufti of Jerusalem and inflated the sharif of Mecca; and the French considered installing the Moroccan sovereign atop a Western caliphate.

More than a half-dozen prominent individuals and regimes—from Syria, Jordan, Libya, Egypt, and Saudi Arabia to India—expressed interest in filling the position. Major international caliphate conferences were held in Cairo and Jerusalem, producing much intrigue but no consensus to achieve something like the Vatican city-state to replace the defunct Islamic dynasty.[47] The fall of the last Sunni bastions that were still free of European rule spelled the end of the Muslim state as a unified spiritual and political entity, in the same way that the fading of the Papal States prefigured the death of political Catholicism as an executive power. But whereas the caliphate expired, the papacy got a new lease on life.

The Church Responds to Defeat

When considering which leader was most influential for the Church's relationship with the modern state, one might first think of Constantine, who made Christianity the religion of state, or Charlemagne for his unification of European empire through mass conversions, or perhaps John XXIII for convening the Second Vatican Council. But it was Pope Paul III who set in motion an institutional revolution that expanded and standardized the way the Church was run—that is, with catechism, dioceses, seminaries, priests, and bishops. Paul commissioned the Jesuits to undertake a major educational expansion, and he convened a monumental gathering of church leadership at the Council of Trent. The council's July 15, 1563, session marked the beginning of the professionalization of clergy and educational institutions, notably with the law that coined the word "seminary," incorporating the metaphor of a seedbed, and instituted a requirement that every diocese be equipped with one to provide formal clerical education.

Despite losing a quarter of its population and nearly half its territory, the Holy See nearly doubled the number of episcopal sees (dioceses) worldwide, from 206 in 1500 to 378 in 1600. The creation of a system of national colleges in Rome—such as the Collegio Romano, Collegio Germanico, English College, and French College—professionalized the cadre of priests destined to serve in countries where Catholicism had come under political and spiritual attack (see table 1.2). The colleges introduced highly organized religious instruction and codified oral catechism in writing.[48] The most emblematic office was the Propaganda Fide (1622), the Vatican congregation devoted to minority Catholic populations and missions to oversee the propagation of the faith. Missionaries and church officials chartered Catholic universities and theology departments at home and abroad. For example, my analysis of Vatican records revealed that the share of German bishops increased from 8 percent of all bishops worldwide in 1431 to 18 percent in 1788—a reflection of the importance that Rome assigned to manning the front line against Lutheranism. Church officials also significantly increased the number of cardinals coming

TABLE 1.2. The First Defeat: The End of Empire

	Protestant Reformations	European Imperial Expansion
Who	Rome-based curia and papacy	Istanbul-based ulema and caliphate
What	Counter-Reformation: Churches, priests, dioceses, bishops, seminaries, and schools	Pan-Islam: Mosques, imams, muftis, qadis, ulema, and schools
Where	Western Europe and Central Europe (Americas, Asia)	Balkans, North Africa, and Arab countries (South Asia)
When	sixteenth century to eighteenth century	nineteenth century to twentieth century

from *outside* Italy and enlarged the body to seventy papal electors—modeled after the Sages of Zion—from a pre-Reformation average of twenty-five. These national dynamics are illuminated in country shares of dioceses and seats in the episcopate and the College of Cardinals, signaling the rise and fall of national influences over its most important policymaking bodies. Over time, the centralized organisms became more responsive to the new periphery and integrated their concerns into the decision-making center.

The Ottoman Response to Defeat

With each territorial loss in North Africa, the Balkans, and the Middle East—from Algeria (1830) to Bosnia (1882) to the Hejaz (1916) and Jerusalem (1918)—"the sovereign writ of the Sultan" became an "unexecuted right" (*nudum jus*).[49] Abdülaziz and his successors did not have the military capacity to reclaim the legal authority and political jurisdiction undermined by "hectoring [from] Europe," L. Carl Brown observes, so they aimed to exercise *spiritual* leadership over Muslims "wherever they [may] be."[50] As the Ottoman Empire shrank, the caliphs made Islamic lemonade from European lemons. From their perspective, their failure at the head of a *political-military* project did not preclude their continued viability as *spiritual* stewards of the global umma. The House of Osman hoped to emulate the nineteenth-century papacy, whose last grains of earthly power were also slipping into the lower bulb of the hourglass.

The caliphs incorporated stranded followers in North Africa and the Balkans into a larger spiritual umma that spanned the Sunni Muslim world. The most significant caliphs for the contemporary state-Islam relationship were the pair who ruled for seven decades of Islamic *grandeur*, Abdülmecid (1839–1861) and Abdülhamid II (1876–1909), who professionalized the ulema, established a religious education system, and chartered an Islamic hierarchy of

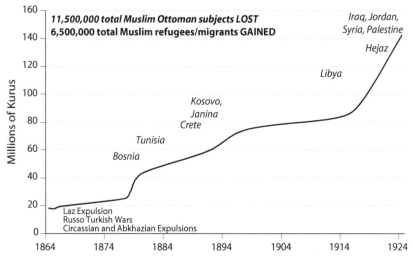

FIGURE 1.4. The Relationship between Loss of Territory and
the Ottoman Religious Affairs Budget, 1864–1924

qadis, naïbs, and muftis. They brought courts and schools under bureaucratic oversight.[51] This included Counter-Reformation-style activities as the Ottomans "competed for the souls, minds and bodies of [their] subjects" by constructing mosques and assigning teachers of religion in the rural countryside.[52] William Ochsenwald says that they "transformed the system of state patronage of religious activities and informal religious acceptance of the state authority into a state-dominated version of Islam [with] high standards and credentials for teachers, judges and interpreters of the faith."[53]

As more Muslims lived outside the empire, Istanbul exponentially increased spending on imams, muftis, and qadis—in response, it said, to requests from those under assault by Christian and Wahhabi missionaries (see figure 1.4). They founded schools and mosques and hired ulema to shore up legitimacy at home and in restive Arab territories like Syria and the Transjordan. In the late nineteenth century, refugees increased the Muslim population of the Ottoman Empire from 2.5 million to 6.3 million. Spending on the religious apparatus followed the arrival of refugees and the stranding of former Ottoman subjects outside imperial borders. By the turn of the century, the effort had borne fruit: scholars document 188,000 imams, *muezzins*, and *hafizler*, 1,700 Qur'an schools, and 12,000 madrassa students across the empire.[54]

My compilation of original data from Ottoman archive sources shows that the shrinking empire increased religious spending from 1 percent to over 4 percent of total budgetary expenditures (see figure 1.4). The eminent centers of Islamic learning in Fez, Cairo, Tunis, and elsewhere continued to be respected, but since those were under European occupation, Istanbul increasingly sought to replace them. In the tradition of the Counter-Reformation, the sultan not only built theological seminaries and mosques and maintained holy sites but also devised a system of local rais-ul-Islam (Islamic chieftains) and other preachers and sheikhs to serve in missionary territories as diverse as the Balkans, Cape Town, and the United Kingdom, as well as in Muslim-majority Indonesia, North Africa, and the Levant. These endeavors began as a defensive maneuver against frontal assault but ended up provoking significant institutionalization.

For both Rome and Istanbul, the projection of religious influence aimed to strengthen what remained of empire, and above all to project spiritual hegemony abroad. The pope, like the caliph, maintained pretensions of deposing sovereigns and aimed to exercise more than merely symbolic executive powers. Ambition should not be mistaken for self-delusion: the concept of defunct *legal* jurisdiction was already familiar to both dynasties. The insertion of weekly prayers honoring the caliph or the pope's spiritual leadership—recited by citizens with standing political allegiance to their national rulers—shifted believers' religious loyalty toward the metaphorical and metaphysical. The success of modern popes and caliphs at enhancing their role in believers' rituals of faith, however, underscored their political irrelevance at home and abroad.

The denouement of the relationship between the Great Powers' colonial empires and the Ottoman caliph unspooled from the 1880s to the 1920s. In almost exactly the same period, another religious head of state would not go quietly as the papal drama and the Roman Question played out.

The Church and Islamic institutions were hostile to the nation-state as a political unit, and both declared holy war on the nationalist armies closing in on them. By the time Pope Pius IX (in 1860) and Ottoman Sultan Mehmed V (in 1914) called for holy war on Western democracies in a last-ditch attempt to save their two empires, their appeals fell on largely deaf ears. The thousands of volunteers the pope mobilized were only a small fraction of 1 percent of military-age Catholic men in Europe. The irregular fighters nonetheless played a critical role at the margins by buying time at a crucial juncture. The papacy itself survived thanks in part to the paramilitary mobilization of Zouaves, who held off assault on Rome. For Ottomans, the Indian Khilafa movement was less militarily accomplished, but it diplomatically persuaded the British and French not to invade the caliph's palaces. The failure of both Rome and Istanbul to rally their usual allies or more foreign fighters is rightly seen as proof of political impotence, and it reinforced the shift in their role from political to spiritual leaders. Pius IX's encyclical advising against Catholic participation in Italian elections illustrated the growing preeminence of citizenship over religious affiliation. But it was as ineffective as the later Ottoman fatwa declaring nationalist Turks to be infidels.[55] Turkish nationalists terminated and scattered the religious power of the Ottoman caliphate in 1924, but Amsterdam, Vienna, London, Paris, and Rome had already undermined and emptied it of meaning for the preceding half-century.

Part 2: The Second Defeat: The Rise of the Nation-State

After the nationalists' military victory, the founding fathers of the Italian and Turkish nation-states—home to the religious capitals of Rome and Istanbul, respectively—terminated the remnants of their religious rivals' *temporal* power and pondered the cost of keeping them intact. Eventually, the religious hierarchies were evicted from all independent roles in public life.[56] This is consistent with Michael Walzer's 2017 book about the "disturbing pattern in the history of national liberation": the militancy of the liberationists.[57] Governments disowned most of their religious heritage but coveted religious holdings on their territory. It is estimated that as much as half of Rome and three-quarters of Istanbul, including holy sites, were seized and nationalized. The new nation-states swept away centuries-old religious establishments in a matter of decades, taking actions such as closing universities and high schools, eliminating theology chairs, and prohibiting teaching religion to children. Finally, they imposed a top-down subservience of the hierarchies to fashion Nation-State Catholicism and Nation-State Islam, with official control over their internal organization. The insecurities of early nationalists led them to engage in retributive behavior.

As detailed in chapters 5 and 6, the Church experienced almost a century and a half of political subordination (1790–1929) in Spain, France, and Italy, while authorities in the Republic of Turkey (1923–) and the North African states (1950s–) established state control of Islam that remains open-ended to this day. The behavior of independent governments in postcolonial North Africa and Turkey (1925–2000) was strikingly similar to actions taken by their Catholic predecessors. They consolidated their nation-states by enforcing a secular monopoly over general education and eliminating the remaining clerical or ulema privileges from the premodern era. Unlike during the first defeat, these changes did not represent a schismatic challenge. Sometimes known as Caesaro-Papism, Josephism, or Nasserism, the state simply substituted itself at the traditional apex of the hierarchy and demanded loyalty from the clergy. These were not sectarian rivals: the majority-Catholic and Muslim-majority populations brought their own religion to heel. The role played by the ministries of Islamic affairs upon national independence was strikingly similar to that of national governments in the nineteenth-century Catholic world. One commentator in 1896 wrote wistfully, "In such cases where church and state occupy but a single sphere, the lion and the lamb lie down together it is true, but the lamb is inside the lion."[58]

For example, European capitals forced Rome to submit names to the government for approval, and all bishops and clerics were required to take an oath of loyalty to nation, law, and constitution.[59] In 1866, the Italian king nationalized all Church property and decreed the end of all religious corporations; his royal consent, frequently withheld, was required before any bishop or archbishop could assume office.[60] In Prussia, the crown monopolized the appointment of all priests and bishops. The Spanish court also cut Rome out of the process of bishop nomination. France renamed the months of the year, slashed the number of bishoprics by 40 percent, and turned parish priests and bishops into elected positions.[61] Catholic states were vicious in suborning the Church because they considered the papacy virulently antimodern. In Catholic states, the Church was not necessarily treated worse than it was in Protestant lands—like Britain and Scandinavia—that banned the Catholic hierarchy and outlawed the religious sacraments.

The religions could not be banned outright—although Robespierre, Atatürk, and Bourguiba arguably tried—because many citizens remained faithful, and many still revered the ancestral birth, marriage, and death rituals. The fear of revanchists who espoused ultramontanism or Islamism, respectively, led nation-states—first across western Europe, and later in the Arab world and North Africa—to demote and humiliate religious authorities on what was left of their home turf. The religions' preservation by the state was accompanied by severe restrictions on their activities. Church bells and muezzins' calls were silenced, and heretics were enshrined in place of saints. The new national governments in North Africa and Turkey banned Muslim religious orders, seized their property, nationalized the ulema and fatwa councils, centralized education and the justice system, and tightly restricted the activities of Muslim theologians and clergy (see table 1.3). Each postcolonial head of state arrogated to himself the role of guardian of the national religion and appointed a civilian leader atop the religious hierarchy. There is a direct parallel between nineteenth-century constitutional bishops in the large Catholic countries and the twentieth-century muftis of the republic in North Africa. The state religion survived under a new regime, but under strict control. Bureaucracies of the era have persisted and thrived, in the central religion offices in the European ministries of the interior or justice and, of course, in the ministries of Islamic affairs.

The repression in these periods was marginally more civilized than during antiquity or the Middle Ages. In lieu of bonfires and the gallows, there were

TABLE 1.3. The Second Defeat: The Rise of the Nation-State

	Nation-State Catholicism	Nation-State Islam
Who	France, Italy, Germany, Spain, etc.	Turkey, Morocco, Algeria, Tunisia, etc.
What	Central religion offices in ministries of the interior versus ultramontanes	Ministries of Islamic affairs versus Islamism
Where	Former Catholic heartland	Former Ottoman heartland
When	Nineteenth century	Twentieth century

restrictions on political participation and religious brotherhoods were suppressed. For a period of time after the French Revolution, priests were forced to marry. The early Republic of Turkey opened farms to raise halal pork. But for the most part, in the succinct formulation of the religion scholar Ani Sarkassian, "rather than throwing Christians to wild animals in the arena," modern states made laws to keep them out of political power.[62] At the extremes, however, the governments harassed religious officials with anticlerical legislation and made religious exercise more cumbersome and sometimes impossible.

Notwithstanding the eventual occupation and annexation of the Papal States and Rome, the Vatican itself was preserved in its native location and the pope's person left alone. Nineteenth-century Italian nationalists decided to ignore the pope, stopping short at his palace gates and granting the Church a final clerical exemption. That allowed for a critical and difficult adjustment by the pope and the curia. The Vatican experienced a full decade of complete political impotence before Italians conquered Rome in 1870, and it enjoyed another sixty years of institutional reorganization before independent statehood. During that time, Rome remained a beacon of religious reference. The popes held the First Vatican Council, signed the Lateran Accords, and in other ways laid the groundwork for coexistence with democracy and with other religions to come in Vatican Council II. With the pontiff denied a state to govern, however, there were no longer any Catholic states. As one observer wrote in 1915, "Catholicism has become an individual attitude, and ceased to be a corporate fact."[63] The only European governments professing Catholicism as an official religion were statelets like Andorra, Lichtenstein, Malta, and Monaco. The Roman Question was resolved when the pope was given full political and legal sovereignty on his own piece of land. The sovereign Roman Catholic Church is now encompassed on 140 hectares of Vatican City, around the size of New York's Central Park.

After the fall of the Ottoman Empire, there would be no such thing as a Sunni Muslim state anymore either. The key difference between current-day Sunni Islam and Roman Catholicism, ironically, is that the caliph received no such reprieve. There was no equivalent to the Vatican's happy-enough ending, with sovereignty restored to the Holy See and a Via della Conciliazione paved outwards from St. Peter's Square. The twentieth-century Turkish republic and successor states to the Ottoman Empire did to Islam what the nineteenth-century French, Italian, and Spanish republics had done to Catholicism—but they never walked it back. In Turkey, the imperial palaces were seized and the Ottoman dynasty was banished. The National Assembly abolished the caliphate, leaving the Prophet without a Shadow on Earth. This marked the first time in Islamic history that Muslims had no Islamic epicenter or Defender of the Faith, disputed or otherwise, around which to rally, and hundreds of millions were left in the lurch. The world's Muslim populations were pressed into the outlines of the Westphalian state system, itself an outcome of a centuries-old Christian internecine war, and compelled to live according to the colonialists' norms of interstate rules and borders. The Roman Question and the issue of the missing caliphate dogged Catholic- and Muslim-majority nation-states for generations. The caliphate's embers also ignited a slow-burning conflagration in the former colonial periphery, which gradually spread *inwards* to the European capitals through labor migration—compounding one irony upon another—at the turn of the twenty-first century.

Part 3: The Third Defeat: Believers without Borders

Chapters 7 and 8 discuss the great westward migration of Catholics to the United States (1850–1930) and of Muslims to western Europe roughly one century later that led to the massive, unplanned, and voluntary settlement of minority diaspora communities outside the religious heartland. Their movement coincided with a range of threats that were felt both at home and abroad. For the Muslim countries of origin with an operational monopoly over religion, just as for the Roman Catholic hierarchies, the development of such large minorities in diaspora presented a new missionary front full of dangers and opportunities. For centuries, the United States did not figure in the Catholic Church's strategic growth plan, and Europe was considered an unlikely locus of expansion of Sunni Muslim communities. Suddenly, millions of Catholic and Muslim nationals lived permanently beyond "enemy lines," vulnerable to secularization, proselytism, and doctrinal dilution within oases of free expression. Religious adaptations and dispensations existed for Catholics and Muslims who found themselves living outside of their communities, but only for believers who were forced to stay under infidel regimes against their will. The voluntary, self-initiated nature of Mus-

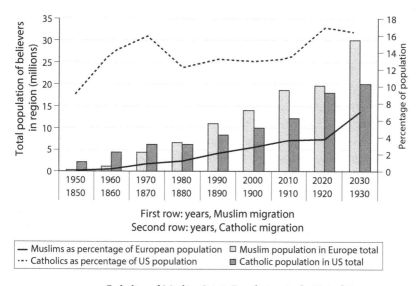

FIGURE 1.5. Catholic and Muslim-Origin Populations in the United States
and Europe, 1850–1930 and 1950–2030

lims' minority status in the United States and western Europe was uncharted territory.

The influxes reflected the relative positions of the Global South and the Global North. American gross domestic product (GDP) per capita in the year 1900 was far ahead of European economies. Twentieth-century western European countries in postwar economic expansion, similarly, had an average GDP valued at multiples of those of Turkey and North Africa. Emigrants were invited by entrepreneurs who were searching for cheap labor and who stimulated emigration via steamships and charter planes.[64] The United States absorbed a transatlantic population transfer of 35 million immigrants, including 15 million (43 percent) from majority-Catholic countries, as rural Europe emptied out and its birth rates plunged between 1820 and 1920. Catholics went from being virtual nonexistent among the US population in 1800 to 17 percent in 1900. Despite immigration restrictions, moreover, the Catholic population continued to grow for another century: between 1820 and 2020, their absolute numbers rose from 100,000 (1 percent) to 75 million, or 23 percent of Americans. The immigrant-origin Muslim population in twenty-first-century western Europe is only fifty years into its permanent settlement (see figure 1.5). Nevertheless, the sudden growth of Muslim immigrant communities surprised their host societies. The population of Muslim Europeans similarly rose from several hundred thousand (0.4 percent) to 20 million between 1965 and 2015, or around 5 to 10 percent in Europe circa 2020.[65]

Two types of emigrants were most significant for the purpose of religious planners: labor migrants and their families, and political refugees who adhered to a dissident political, social, or religious ideology (for example, anarchists or Islamists). The first century of Catholics' experience in the United States transpired at a moment of ideological turmoil and halting democratization in western Europe. Emigration was spurred by a combination of "crisis, revolutions, famines and financial panics."[66] In the second half of the nineteenth century, the region was throwing off empires and old caste systems, slowly entering the modern economy and the era of democratic citizenship. In the mid to late twentieth century, Turkey, North Africa, and the Arab world were shaking off the colonial and secularist yoke. European Muslims' fifty-year experience as a new religious minority also coincided with chaos and instability that have yet to be resolved. Religious-political control over territory and scriptural interpretation in the Middle East and North Africa remain highly politicized and contested.

The governments of the United States and western Europe did not lament the end of the formal political powers of both the Roman Catholic papacy and the Ottoman caliphate, and in fact many hastened it. But they would pay a price for the demise of these powers by reaping political instability in affected diaspora populations one generation later. The groups repressed in the predominantly Muslim late twentieth-century Middle East and North Africa—and those in the predominantly Catholic late nineteenth-century western Europe cropped up in immigrant settlements. The spread of the modern "-isms"—nationalism, anarchism, socialism, fascism, Islamism, Wahhabism—was aided by a sociopolitical landscape that had been cleared of religious brush. Southern Europe was a reliable wellspring of anarchists, and North Africa later provided a disproportionate share of Islamists.

The effect that migration would have on religious authority was not immediately apparent. Religious capitals did not initially adapt their institutions to the new demographic situation. Rome put off accepting the permanence of the American minority, keeping the United States in the "missionary" category and without direct representation in the church hierarchy, all while it sanctioned the spread of schools and seminaries. Similarly, the Turkish, Algerian, Moroccan, and Tunisian governments did not at first pay much attention to migrants in western Europe. Islamic scholars debated their juridical status and the temporary or permanent nature of their presence in Europe. The delay fostered an infrastructural deficit in the diaspora. The dearth of prayer spaces, clergy, and sites of religious education was leaving citizens open to other influences. Compared to a homeland rate of one cleric for every 1,000 of the faithful, sending governments mustered only modest contingents to face down ideological threats in the diaspora. In 1900, there were only 250 Italian priests for 1.2 million Italian Catholics in New York City; in France one century later, there were even fewer Moroccan imams for 1.8 million Moroccans residing abroad.[67] In fact, there were more Italian priests who converted to Protestantism preaching in churches and missions abroad than in Italian-American Catholic churches in 1913.[68] In western Europe in the year 2000, similarly, it was surmised that the Saudi monarch had more Moroccan imams under his indirect employ than the Moroccan king did. Activist political refugees alongside the labor migrants took advantage of the license to publish, gather openly, and engage in political activism against the old regimes they had fled. As Gerald Shaughnessy wrote of early twentieth-century United States, the Catholic capitals of Europe had reason to fear that the faithful would "fall away to apathy, atheism— or worse."[69]

Immigration and Political Violence

In both cases, the movements' diaspora extremists were caught up in a cycle of violent conflict in the old world. Anarchists in southern Europe and Islamists in North Africa traded assassinations and attacks on officials with imprisonment, torture, and executions. Late nineteenth-century exile, mass imprisonment, and massacres in Paris, Sicily, and Milan were echoed 100 years later by similar consequences for Islamists in North Africa. Turn-of-the-century Europeans were scandalized and incredulous that American authorities permitted such hornet's nests to flourish without intervening. Likewise, Moroccan, Tunisian, and Turkish governments in the early 2000s could not fathom why European countries allowed groups with names like the Caliphate State or the Great Eastern Islamic Raiders Front to hold meetings on their territory and circulate propaganda.

Between the 1880s and 1910s, ideology and activists spawned in immigrant America inspired or committed assassination attempts on multiple heads of state around the world. Many hit their target with newly patented American revolvers, which were easily concealed and whose multiple chambers required no time-consuming reloading. In the early 2000s, similarly, immigrant-origin (and Christian-origin) Islamists used European passports and satellite phones to facilitate lethal attacks on their societies of origin—in Djerba, Casablanca, and Istanbul.[70] A century apart, industrial urban areas like Molenbeek and Paterson were hotbeds of radical thought, but were relatively unnoticed by local authorities. When that became too difficult, the second generation turned to softer targets right at home. In 1901, an immigrant-origin anarchist from Detroit assassinated the president of the United States. In 2015, a Molenbeek-based cell sowed terror with machine guns and suicide bombs in central Paris. Despite the contradiction of murder and mayhem with Christian and Islamic teachings, a vast majority of anarchists were born Catholic, just as Islamists came from a Muslim background.

The social disadvantages of having a certain background accumulated: migrant-origin Catholics and Muslims were overrepresented within the prison population, and their young men were willing to assassinate leading figures and to bomb crowds. Both the nineteenth-century United States and twenty-first century Europe faced a foreign fighter crisis as young men flowed out to wage holy war abroad. The refusal of US dioceses to hold memorials for assassinated heads of state and immigrant newspapers' glorification of assassins—including Italian migrant workers who had lived in Paterson, New Jersey—was equivalent to mosques declining to mobilize their congregants for the "Je Suis Charlie" movement honoring the *Charlie Hebdo* satirists slain in 2015 in Paris.[71]

In the early 1900s, the immigrant-origin terrorists in the United States prompted the first formalization of national borders, passports, and immigration policy. Similar reforms of nationality and citizenship policies have been elicited, and religious liberties tightened, in twenty-first-century western Europe. There were over 10,000 arrests and nearly 1,000 deportations during the anti-anarchist fight in the United States, just as thousands of arrests and deportations accompanied the two-decade wave of Islamist terrorism at the turn of the twenty-first century.[72]

The third shock prompted the professionalization of informal networks and political patronage in the religious minority Sunni Muslim and Roman Catholic communities. First came infrastructure: the places of worship and clergy to guide the first generation (see table 1.4). When elements within these diasporas turned on their host societies, the cultural preservation agenda of the centers of religious authority aligned with the nation-states' agenda to preserve public order. The underlying source of political violence was self-evident to the countries of origin. The number of churches and mosques expanded faster than prayer leaders and sermonizers could arrive or be trained. The vacuum of religious infrastructure in the nineteenth-century United States and twenty-first-century Europe left open trajectories for Catholic boys to grow up to be assassins, or Maliki youth to turn themselves into human bombs. Next came religious schools to socialize the second generation and train local clerics. Finally, the hierarchy was dispatched as the third generation signaled the minority's institutional maturity. Part 3 of the book explores the road to native-born personnel and a degree of organizational autonomy, such as the right for each religion to choose its own textbooks and to propose its own hierarchy of locally born imams, bishops, muftis, cardinals, and ulema.

In the early 1900s, the United States was home to 14 million Catholics, who represented 17 percent of the population.[73] They were still part of the Propa-

TABLE 1.4. The Third Defeat: Minorities of Mass Migration

	The Catholic Diaspora	The Muslim Diaspora
Who	Rome and sending countries (Ireland, Germany, Italy, and Poland)	Riyadh, Doha, and sending countries (Algeria, Morocco, Tunisia, Turkey, etc.)
What	Local dispensations; churches; priests; schools; local bishops and cardinals	Local dispensations; mosques; imams; schools; local imams and ulema
Where	United States	Western Europe
When	Nineteenth century to twentieth century	Twentieth century to twenty-first century

ganda Fide Congregation overseeing missionary countries: the Vatican considered them to be under infidel rule, so to speak. This required a constant rotation of foreign personnel parachuting in from the organizational center. It was not until 1908 that the United States was removed from the jurisdiction of the missionary Holy Congregation of Propaganda Fide and integrated as its own national Church hierarchy. Within a generation, the number of US-born priests, bishops, and cardinals increased dramatically: the ratio of priests to congregants improved to one for every 630 Catholics by 1940, one of the best ratios worldwide.[74] Within two generations, American Catholics found themselves with a large inventory surplus.

This is not unlike the succession of statuses enjoyed by Muslims in twenty-first-century Europe vis-à-vis their own ancestral countries, who first considered them to be only temporarily abroad and did not sufficiently provision their religious institutions. As with Catholics in the United States, the religious affairs hierarchies in the Islamic world eventually acknowledged that the diaspora was no longer part of a missionary community in hostile territory (*dar al harb*). It is counterintuitive for any universalist religious community to acknowledge its own permanent *minority* status. In the case of Sunni Muslim jurisprudence (*fiqh*), this makes the difference between considering western Europe a House of War (Dar al Harb) or a House of Islam (Dar al Islam) or Contract, as well as the difference between centrally appointed and locally cultivated leadership. It has concrete implications for the rules governing the recruiting, training, hiring, and firing of religious officials—from prayer leaders (imams) to interpreters of religious texts (ulema). The ratios of imams and mosques have also been improving for Muslims living in Europe, standing at one for every 2,000 believers, which is roughly half the rate in their countries of origin.[75]

In the Church's view, you remain a Catholic for life after baptism. From the Moroccan kingdom's perspective, you remain a Maliki Muslim and Moroccan through the generations, no matter where you are born, ad infinitum. For such communities, "letting go" requires adjusting that mentality in religious affairs bureaucracies to the actual lack of political jurisdiction. Living as a permanent minority implied operational autonomy as a fully licensed branch. In this way, the third shock reinforced the shift from temporal to spiritual oversight. For the tens of millions living as a religious minority in Western countries, Roman Catholicism and Sunni Islam became an appendage to their "nationality," a sentimental pendant on the golden chain of citizenship.

An unintended result of political control over Catholic hierarchy in the traditional heartland was to give a bigger role to leadership *outside* of the European nation-states, especially in liberal democracies whose economies had attracted millions of labor migrants. The Vatican did this by increasing the number of dioceses worldwide by one-third at the height of Nation-State Catholicism in the nineteenth century—from 610 dioceses to 815, including 126 dioceses established by Pius IX (1846–1878) alone. The crackdown of nationalist governments in Europe led to an increasingly diverse College of Cardinals with arrivals from other continents. A wave of appointments was made to foreign dioceses in order to preclude Italian interference in the hierarchy's internal discussions.[76] The First Vatican Council (1870), which enshrined immaculate conception and papal infallibility, was convened when nearly two-thirds of cardinals came from Italy.

American Catholic adjustment unfolded in several stages. The first milestone came when the US diaspora was no longer governed as a missionary division. After 1908, American Catholics enjoyed greater autonomy in appointments of bishops and gained a louder voice in Rome's policymaking bodies—the episcopate, the curia, and the College of Cardinals. Second, the Vatican city-state resolved the issue of temporal sovereignty for the pope. And third was the holy grail of social integration: the formal reconciliation of Catholic values and doctrine with democracy and pluralism. That took another generation, until the 1960s, by which point the proportion of cardinals of Italian origin was halved to one-third. Vatican Council II introduced milestone rulings on religious tolerance, the use of vernacular, and the role of laity (see figure 1.6). The theologian and historian Mark Massa observes that the council heralded the end of the "hermetically sealed brand of counter-Reformation belief and practice" that had defined the Church for centuries.[77]

It is still early going, but something analogous has begun taking place thanks to the internationalization of the twenty-first-century centers of Sunni Islam, many of which have ties with immigrant-origin Muslim minorities in western Europe. Ulema councils in the national capitals increasingly take the minority experience into account in hiring new personnel and issuing new rulings that affect all self-identified believers in the community. The surprise emergence of

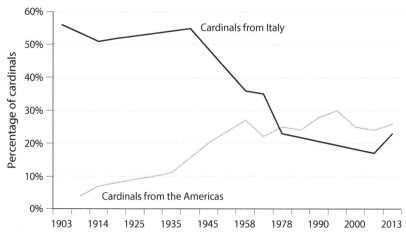

FIGURE 1.6. Regional Breakdown of the College of Cardinals:
Italy and the Americas, 1903–2013

a diaspora has introduced new feedback mechanisms and animated Islamic affairs ministries with new life and purpose. The process of maintaining ties and
training imams and ulema in minority contexts has produced a range of compromise positions on previously immovable themes, from usury to prayer to
gender and minority rights. These compromises are also moving Islamic authorities toward soft restoration, with professional autonomy and self-government of
internal affairs, and mitigating the apparent success of an expanding presence of
Catholics in the United States and Muslims in Europe. Chapters 9 and 10 consider how the most recent historical defeat has forced religious hierarchies to
adapt to a landscape designed by modern states if they intend to survive the
twenty-first century.

Why Religions Are Like the Military

Critical insight into the Catholic and Islamic paths to civil-religious relations
can be found in an unlikely source: Samuel Huntington's book *The Soldier and
the State* (1957). It was written four decades before his *Clash of Civilizations*, at
a time when generals, not mullahs, were the chief impediment to electoral
democracy amid military coups and coup attempts in South America, the
Middle East, and Southeast Asia. Huntington was interested in the question
of how to resolve the tensions between civilian government and the military,
which he describes as a "complex equilibrium" of the "authority, influence and
ideology" of both military and nonmilitary groups in society.[78] Democratic
nations need armed forces willing to submit to alternating political majorities

and electoral outcomes. Huntington argues that the armed forces of modern states professionalized as a counteraction to an episode of defeat. It was the humiliation "of loss or threatened loss" that provided the impetus for Prussia, Great Britain, and France to standardize the training of their officer corps. He notes that "immediately after the Napoleonic Wars, most nations established institutions of military education," and that by 1875, "all nations of Europe had acquired the basic elements of professionalism."[79] Only then "did officers begin to acquire a specialized technique to distinguish themselves from laymen."[80] This built on an earlier centralization of military command, the early modern "shift from small, decentralized knight service to large standing armies."[81]

The relationship between defeat, professionalization, and civilian rule is relevant to the institutionalization processes undergone by religious hierarchies within Roman Catholicism and Sunni Islam. "Like the lawyer and physician," Huntington writes, the officer "is concerned with only one segment of the activities of his client"—in this case, military defense.[82] But unlike medicine or the law, the military and the church represent peculiar challenges unlike those posed by other civil society associations. From the perspective of the modern state, military and religious leadership share a mix of organizational traits: they are both hierarchical, honor-bound, and paternalistic, and both operate as an all-encompassing fraternity. Moreover, like violence, religion is a concept whose exercise is extremely hard to limit—anyone can do it—and thus can carry out the dissuasive, deterrent legitimacy of a recognized authority. This book presents evidence of a depoliticizing process—an institutional defanging—that takes place when the professional parameters of the military and the church are overseen by civilian leadership. The causal mechanism being examined is the process that facilitates this transition.

It is surprising to learn how relatively recent are the roots of standardized and professionalized education of the clergy, the catechism, and the diocesan seminary. They are artifacts of operating under the modern rule of law. Just as it helps to produce a centralized military with carefully circumscribed activities and a civilian appointed as chief administrator (for example, the minister or secretary of defense), the religious authority's powers are reduced to some amount of sovereignty over ecclesiastical affairs, overseen by a state agency responsible for religious affairs. In state-church terms, it is a refracted image of what Thomas Hobbes (1588–1679) proposes in *Leviathan*: "The state ought to control religion by providing the authoritative interpretation of scripture and banning interpretations that encourage sedition of secular state authority."[83]

Huntington argues that the modern state thus resolved a question that had dogged rulers for centuries: how can military leaders, who have their own coercive resources, be kept loyal to political rule? Military force and corporal punishment are brought under state oversight as part of what Huntington calls "managed violence."[84] Huntington says that "the military function was socialized: national control replaced private control," and he identifies the professionalization of an independent officer corps "free of partisan or class allegiance" as the key to what became the widespread model of *civilian rule* of the military.[85] Professionalization meant standardizing training to replace a variety of decentralized and informal practices. A civilian-led bureaucracy developed to plan "quantitative issues of size and recruitment" and determine the "proportion of state resources" to dedicate to the military.[86] The explicit bargain here for the military, in exchange for civilian oversight, is "an independent military sphere . . . organized in accordance with interests and principles of its own," with reasonable internal autonomy for the military hierarchy within its domain. The military belongs unquestionably to the executive branch of government, but it maintains a special status within it, of which the court-martial system is the readiest example. The establishment of a "mutually recognized independent officer corps," he says, is the surest guarantee against the military control of civilian life.[87]

It took time for states to get a handle on the use of force. According to Charles Tilly, states did not monopolize violence for centuries. Instead, territories were overrun with "urban militias, private armies, fiscal agents, armies of regional lords, police forces, and state armies." Asserting the state's monopoly of "physical force" required "a long-lasting process of political expropriation" in which all of these "other communities [were] deprived of the means of coercion."[88] This was the passage from "dispersed, overlapping and decentralized" activity to centralization, monopoly, and made hierarchy.[89] This did not require the establishment of a new order so much as the official defense of order. Overcoming the resistance of existing social groups through a series of bargains—such as those made with the old aristocracy—were stops along the way to exercising authority.[90] This meant restoring a degree of sovereignty to the military, entrusting it to conduct its own affairs. Simultaneously, the depoliticization of the military was furthered by laws making legislative office incompatible with military office. Huntington argued that civilian control can be politically neutral in only one of its many guises: when it is "objective."[91] He dreamed of making the military "politically sterile and neutral."[92] The revolution in civilian oversight follows the same pattern for religious communities as for military affairs: a shift from small, decentralized services to a large, standing bureaucracy organized in accordance with the logic of the state.

Surrounded by examples of coups d'état during the post–World War II international state system, Huntington ruled out any domestic political role for the military because that would necessarily favor one political faction over another and *subordinate* the military establishment rather than granting it a degree of autonomy. Governments "who use the military to shore up their

TABLE 1.5. Civilian Rule of the Military (Huntington, 1966)

Balance	Equilibrium of "the authority, influence and ideology" of military and nonmilitary groups
Professionalism	"The principal focus is the relation of the [officer] corps to the state" "Professionalization renders them politically sterile and neutral"
Nationalization	"The shift from small, decentralized knight services to large standing armies" "National control replace[s] private control"

own power abuse this relationship." Civilian oversight does not eliminate civil-religious tensions but instead provides forums for addressing them (see table 1.5). The building up and adaptation of infrastructure, education, and hierarchy were triggered by overlapping waves of political and legal defeat. The moments at which a given nation-state seizes the upper hand in regulating public religious behavior is just as critical for national cohesion and civil peace as when the nation-state achieves civilian control of the military. Why have other scholars—including Huntington himself—missed this analogy? Several social scientists have in fact elided the subject by examining the formalization of priesthoods as processes of professionalization.

The sociologist Max Weber first observed the link between bureaucratization and professionalization. These are complementary processes—"the priest, and the soldier are, in the Occident, examples of bureaucratic-professionals."[93] Weber cited the rise of the professional priesthood as the most important transition away from the medieval church and toward the development of Western rationality. The priesthood appears in the occupational and organizational sociology literatures as one of the "people-processing devices" that defined Western rationalization and modern state-building. The priest and the soldier, then, are ideal-typical professionals whose legitimacy originates in the rational, institutional nature of their training—"specialized knowledge, fixed doctrine and vocational qualifications."[94] That and their existence within a compulsory organization (the priesthood or the officer corps) place them at the far end of the spectrum away from the brute force of the mercenary or the charismatic authority of the magician. Weber also singles out bureaucratic structure as the precondition for "professional standing armies."[95]

In terms of the French intellectual Michel Foucault's understanding of disciplinary power, the seminary-trained clergy were produced by the same methods that summoned "the organized powers of armies and other distinctive institutions" of modern states. For most of recorded history, Foucault writes, institutions were "amorphous gatherings of idle and inactive men."[96]

Each new training apparatus of the modernizing state, however, "appeared somehow greater than the sum of its parts." The professionalizing process also laid the bases for claims to organizational autonomy within the modern state.[97] The exclusivity of training and the institutional monopolization of knowledge helped carve out a sphere of autonomous activity.[98]

Preachers and soldiers share another professional characteristic of relevance to the privileged role they seek. Their ritual practices do not need to produce any material outcome outside the practices themselves. Catholic sacrament and military pomp can be their own ends. This differs from the actions of other professionals—say, the lawyer's advocacy or the doctor's interventions—which instrumentally pursue specific legal or medical *outcomes*. Many professional rituals of religious leaders and soldiers, instead, have intrinsic significance—maintaining appearances and validating the organization—but no concrete effects.[99] The resulting "aura of mystery," the sociologist Andrew Abbot argues, "haloes professional tasks" and guards the profession's monopoly.[100]

On the other hand, the professional titles and educational accreditation of military officers and religious leaders have legal meaning thanks only to the permissions granted by state licensing.[101] Modern nation-states will never restore the complete jurisdiction that these leaders once had under a different regime. But they may hope for advisory jurisdiction in the new one.[102] In an influential treatise on organizational sociology, the MIT scholars John Van Maanen and Edgar H. Schein described organizational culture as a lengthy apprenticeship formed by a series of conflicts and challenges. Formal institutions are developed to "cope with and make sense of a given problematic environment," they write, and are designed to outlast their founders' lifetime.[103] Scholars have not, as yet, framed the evolution of religious professions as a direct response to political and legal defeat, which is one focus of this book.[104]

Civilian Rule

In majority-Muslim countries, the national religious affairs bureaucracies exercise a monopoly over the licensing of mosques and imams, the religious education of schoolchildren and theologians, and the appointment of ulema and muftis.[105] Oversight rests in the hands of the elected or appointed official in charge who can enforce state omnipotence—for example, by replacing the religious leadership or revoking the tax-exempt status of a religious nonprofit association. The lay authorities exercise powers previously reserved for divine monarchs, rule on what is permissible, and sit de facto at the summit of the organizational pyramid. Under the modern state, the ministry or agency overseeing charitable foundations is the ultimate head of every religious hierarchy,

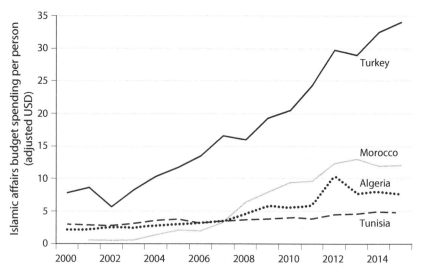

FIGURE 1.7. Islamic Affairs Spending in Turkey, Morocco, Algeria, and Tunisia, 2000–2015

just as the defense minister overrules the military hierarchy. The head of a modern state is the chief arbiter of legal status and its final court of appeal.

Across the southern Mediterranean, bureaucracies dedicated to religious affairs expanded so much that they came to rival each country's largest ministries; with spending increasing in the last fifteen years, they now account for over 1 percent of their national budgets on average (see figure 1.7). Nation-State Islam thrived under all shades of government, and its growth outpaced any other bureaucracy, extending institutional religious coverage over the entire national territory and frequently beyond it. In the twenty-first century, per capita spending by religious affairs ministries in Turkey and the Maghreb has grown by at least 60 percent. The mean level of state support for religion in Muslim-majority countries, Jonathan Fox has found, is nearly twice the global average.[106] Regardless of whether a state has officially aligned with Islam or Catholicism, however, having an established religion reduces its overall freedom ranking by an astounding 20 percent.

Given the extent of religiously inspired revolutionary ideologies, establishment appears to have been in the rational state interest. The ministries of Islamic affairs across North Africa have provided a buffer in defense of national identity and against the influence of brotherhoods, missionaries, and political groups considered seditious. Officials warn their subjects against foreign fatwas, which arrive as well-funded Wahhabi and Islamist messages beamed from the Arabian Peninsula and the Levant via satellite and internet into homes everywhere. The advent of this modern Islamic establishment—the tens of thousands of imams and preachers licensed by national states across the Muslim world—has followed a similar path to the professionalization of the officer corps.

Governments in Turkey and across North Africa increased the resources they devoted to Nation-State Islam in the first decades of the twenty-first century, both before and after the Arab Spring. The ostensible policy aim, as articulated by each Islamic affairs minister I interviewed, was to achieve *depoliticization* of Islam and avoid communal discord (fitna). But the professionalized Islamic corps is not independently operated, and the state has itself been accused of politicizing religion. Nathan Brown quotes an imam who "observed wryly . . . 'If I endorse the constitution, that is not political. But if I oppose it, that is political.'"[107] Indeed, many scholars share the view that more resources for Nation-State Islam simply makes more flunkies available to spout more of the same propaganda.

Scholars do not generally entertain the possibility of a state role without political abuse and the weakening of religion. When seeking to explain the majority-Muslim world's "noncompetitiveness" and "illegitimacy," the unity of political and religious spheres is cast as a major obstacle to democratization. Many treatises on "what went wrong" in the modern history of the region specifically concern state-religion relations and the dynamic between rulers and Islamic jurists. Scholars from Bernard Lewis to Abdul Filaly-Ansary have argued that Islam had no natural experience with the state-religion differentiation.[108] The influential mid-twentieth-century Islamist Sayyid Qutb referred to state ulema as "religious mercenaries."[109] This was also the viewpoint of Salafis, who have long fingered the establishment ulema as the source of Muslims' divisions and weakness in the world. An impressive recent tome by the political scientist Ahmet Kuru singles out the ulema-state alliance as the death knell for intellectual creativity and economic competition.[110]

Overregulation has been blamed for low prayer attendance, and many argue that the Islamic affairs ministries inevitably violate the equal rights of non-Sunni Muslims—and of all non-Muslims.[111] Everywhere, the logic of the nation-state prevails, but it is as yet incomplete. Absent the conditions for soft restoration and the achievement of *objective* civilian control, the faithful are left thirsting on their national islands. There is Islam, Islam everywhere, but not a drop to drink. Given the creative twentieth-century political solutions to the Roman challenge and the Jewish Question, it is incongruous that the world's other major monotheism was left to such an uncertain international fate. There is no model Islamic society—a caliphate for the nation-state era was the colonial path *not* taken.

The blind spot of critics of Nation-State Islam is to persistently conflate the state control of religion with top-down Islamization. They tend not to consider the infrastructural deficit resulting from decades of strict secularism: the shuttered mosques, religious schools, and theological faculties all amounted to unilateral spiritual disarmament in a religious war that others were still waging. Islamic affairs is frequently the only agency or ministry to be physically housed in the prime minister's or president's office. Contemporary Muslim states and their constitutions make a public display of piety, with constitutional articles claiming *shari'ah* as a source of law. But none of the successor states of the Ottoman Empire has a religious head of state: the religious authorities are constrained and serve at the pleasure of the government. There is therefore a practical reason for maintaining established religion in the hotspots of the Islamic world today. Civilian-led government ministries of religious affairs, like civilian-led ministries of defense, guarantee stability through the management and oversight of services in realms where the state's omnipotence is of existential proportions. The shaping of religious education has been a critical element in postcolonial state-building, as the historian Sarah Feuer demonstrated in a recent study.[112] It is impractical to simply disband these bureaucratic corps.

Because of religion's imbrication with national identity, precipitous disestablishment would be rash. Thomas Hobbes was a firsthand observer of the religious strife tearing apart Western Christendom at the peak of the Reformation and the Counter-Reformation. Hobbes argued that the state ought to control religion by providing the authoritative interpretation of scripture and banning interpretations that encouraged sedition of (secular) state authority. The only possibility for compatibility, in other words, is the state endorsing and promoting a version of religion that is not hostile to the nation-state.

The following section on the end of empire lays out how the territorial retrenchment and sectarian assault on Rome and Istanbul prepared religious authorities for their ultimate defeat and surrender to state rule. Defeat inspired the institutional reinvention and transformation of Sunni Islam and Roman Catholicism into their contemporary institutional forms.

The End of Empire

2

The Fall and Rise of Roman Catholicism

TALLYING THE DESTRUCTION wrought by the secessionist churches upon his diminished empire—the loss of chapels, cathedrals, cloisters, and countless souls over generations—it was said that Pope Paul III might weep by the Tiber.[1] Rome had weathered serious uprisings and schism before, but the Reformation presented the greatest existential threat to date. After the Orthodox split to the east and the Islamic border to the south, the Protestant Reformation added a northern front bifurcating the Christian world (see figure 2.1).[2] Martin Luther's religious views spread even more rapidly than Muhammad's prophecy in the Arabian Peninsula eight centuries earlier. Within months of the appearance of his publications, Luther won tens of thousands of adherents in Berlin, Copenhagen, Rotterdam, Geneva, and Zurich.[3] The city of Amsterdam was home to 105,000 supporters within the space of two years.[4] One Catholic historian compared the Reformation's astonishing speed to the third day of Creation, when "Protestant lands separated from Catholic, like land and water."[5] A defiant set of national churches arose in England, Norway, Sweden, Denmark, and Scotland. Large Reformist pockets opened in mostly Catholic Austria, Hungary, and the Netherlands.[6] Half of Switzerland and Germany adopted a Reformed Church, which by the late sixteenth century extended northeast to Estonia, Latvia, and the Baltic coast.[7] Entire regions of France—which prided itself as Rome's "eldest daughter"—stood on the verge of conversion. Only Italy and Spain reemerged (almost) wholly Catholic (see figure 2.1).[8]

The Reformation did not come as a shock out of nowhere: it was the culmination of centuries of conflict with the papacy, Europe's largest feudal overlord. The peasant revolts and the religious wars that followed were part of a historical shift in state structures away from feudalism and toward the emergence of market-ordered societies.[9] But certain changes occurred quickly. Thousands of bishops and priests were imprisoned, exiled, and lynched. The

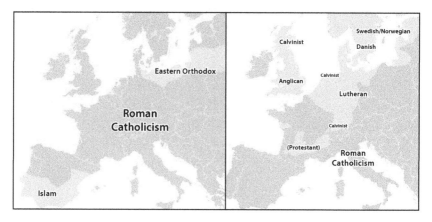

FIGURE 2.1. The Decline of Roman Catholicism, Eleventh Century to Seventeenth Century

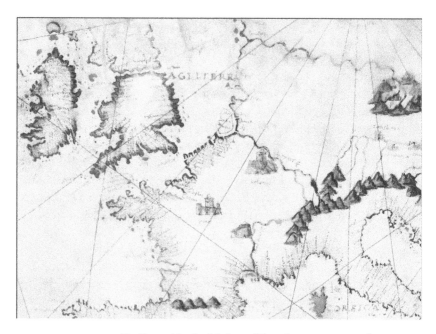

FIGURE 2.2. The Desert North of Cologne (Planisfero Anonimo, 1530)

pope was a helpless spectator to the fate of the Spanish Armada.[10] All points north of Cologne became a vast and inhospitable *terra incognita* (uncharted territory) for Roman Catholicism, populated not with mythical dragons but flesh-and-blood Lutherans: *hic sunt heretici* (here be Protestants) (see figure 2.2). Small Catholic minorities survived there clandestinely, under another rule of law. The political and military defeat in northern Europe prefigured the Church's eventual fate in the modern nation-state era. The experience transformed the Roman Catholic political-executive entity—embodied by the Papal State—into a spiritual and non-governmental organization.

That is not how historians usually characterize the Counter-Reformation, an imperfect term that denotes the collective political, diplomatic, and military retaliation (and offensives) against Protestant churches and governments from around 1540 to 1780.[11] The Holy See did not stand by idly after the ships burned to the waterline and the northern cathedrals were seized. The bloodshed of the wars of religion and the infamous corporal punishments of the Inquisitions courses through this period of European history. The instances of belligerence and repression, however, obscure another more enduring legacy. The tribulations shaped the papacy and its supporting institutions into the global network that it oversees up to the present day. The initial papal response to the Reformation was delayed and incoherent, but the sixteenth century marks a clear turning point toward professionalization of the global Church.

The several dozen popes who managed the Church's *political* demise also oversaw its largest-ever *institutional* expansion through the creation of hundreds of dioceses, bishops, seminaries, and congregations. From a defensive crouch, Church officials coped with defeat by expanding their *spiritual* perimeter, converting temporal power into a spiritual beacon. That required separating the religious from the political, despite the intermingling of the spiritual and the temporal in its core activities, for example, the Church's monopoly over the seven Holy Sacraments regulating believers' civil status and personal life.[12] This was an impressive ability: Machiavelli himself expressed admiration for how the clergy held sway over "states they do not defend and subjects they do not govern."[13] Tradition on the Italian peninsula held that a militarily weak papacy built more churches where it could not build barracks. Similarly, Church officials knew that they could not execute their way out of a spreading Reformation. At a time before treaties establishing religious toleration, Catholic believers who were stranded abroad needed instructions for how to observe Church teachings without landing afoul of the local law. The Lutheran rout coincided with Spanish and Portuguese expeditions in the New World, opening a second front in furtherance and in contestation of Roman Catholicism's hegemonic ambitions. On large sections of the globe, Church influence could only pass through the modern world's new borders by way of spiritual institutions operating under new rules of non-Catholic governance.

This process was neither crisp nor sudden. However, two post-Lutheran developments in particular helped improve the quality and quantity of Catholic institutions, services, and personnel. Pope Paul III gave his blessing to the institutions that enabled the Church to survive the millennium: the international

Jesuit order (1540), and the massive undertaking of the Council of Trent (1545–1563).[14] Many items on the agenda at Trent were being addressed by the fifteenth-century Conciliar Movement and were not simply a reaction to the Reformation.[15] The adaptations amount to an acknowledgment of the decadence that preceded the fall, and a reassessment of the corrupt or hollow institutions that had allowed the Lutheran overthrows to take place.[16] Slowly but surely, new Catholic institutions with global clerical detachments materialized to support the loftiest of ambitions: the reconquest of lands that had fallen into the hands of Anglicans, Lutherans, and Calvinists.[17] Where total re-Catholicization was unrealistic, authorities rallied to preserve Catholic minorities abroad and in their own borderlands, such as southwest Germany (Bavaria) and southwest France (Toulouse), where Protestant sects evangelized aggressively. As Catholic missionaries pushed into the far corners of colonial America, Asia, and Africa, their operational map came to include those parts under English or Dutch Protestant rule.[18]

The period from 1600 to 1650 witnessed a supernova of monasteries, seminaries, colleges, and universities, the inauguration of nunciatures around Europe, and the appointment of apostolic vicars across the rest of the world. Global operations were centralized in the Holy Congregation of Propaganda Fide (1622), which divided the world into Catholic countries and missionary lands—in other words, not-yet-Catholic countries. Internally and externally, Church officials standardized religious education and training, and they chartered common manuals to guide priests in the Holy Sacraments they administered. One historian summarized the Propaganda Fide Congregation's aims as the reconquest, "by spiritual arms, by prayers and good works, by preaching and catechizing," of the countries that had been lost in the "*débâcle* of the sixteenth century."[19] The Catholic landscape shifted, glacially but unmistakably, from small, decentralized providers to a large standing religious bureaucracy.

The medieval church may have functioned as the first multinational corporation, but the post-Reformation Roman Church became the first global enterprise. The Reformist movements delivered the exogenous shock that built the modern Catholic Church. Wherever possible, supporters extended infrastructure, educational institutions, and representatives of the Roman hierarchy. Church governing boards carefully balanced the nationalities of leadership positions, from bishops to the rectors of the Roman congregations.[20] The result was better-prepared clergy and envoys from the Church hierarchy who were parachuted in from Catholic Europe to defend the faith. At first these institutions were aimed at persecuted minority Catholics, but they later expanded to also provide tailored local solutions for Catholics who lived as a majority. The creation of a national hierarchy and self-standing religious education system in the target missionary country was the final step before removal from the Propaganda Fide Congregation and full national representation in the curia, the high administration of the Church. Rome created new cardinals' seats where it judged there to be greater chances of shoring up its base, and it withdrew cardinal seats from nation-states that it had no chance of winning back into the Church fold.[21] These appointment practices led, over time, to the reverse importation of personnel and influence from periphery to center, reflected in the global distribution of bishops and the national makeup of the College of Cardinals, who elect the pope.

Germany: The Lutheran Assault

What determined whether a country got caught up in the Protestant winds? The revolts are typically portrayed as the result of pent-up anger over taxation, incompetence, and corruption. A lack of professionalism placed Church defenses at a low ebb. The Reformation was not a one-man show, but Luther was the super-catalyst in a mixture of motives that included sincere religious belief and genuine anger with clerical institutions.[22] Because clerical appointments in early modern Europe required no formal training, episcopal sees were frequently filled with well-connected but religiously incompetent noblemen. German sensitivities to corruption were rising at the turn of the sixteenth century.[23] One Bavarian prince served as archbishop of Cologne and four other sees despite never having been ordained as a priest.[24] Certain cities teemed with men of the cloth lacking religious knowledge. The clergy in Worms accounted for fully 10 percent of the population, Cologne's 40,000 residents included 6,000 clerics, and Hamburg's 12,000 inhabitants included 450 parish priests. The popes had come to resemble any other Renaissance princes, driven foremost by financial and diplomatic considerations.[25] In the view of modern sociologists, the path to heaven offered by the premodern Church resembled a monopolistic toll road with different rates depending on personal wealth.[26] Setting too high a price for indulgences, church offices and bishoprics invited the entry into the religious marketplace of rival churches offering a better deal.[27] Local elites sought to hold on to more of what they were sending in tribute to Rome.[28]

On Halloween of 1517, Martin Luther, an obscure monk living at the center of a German-speaking realm, proposed nearly 100 theses for debate at the University of Leipzig. Most provocatively, Luther denied the divinity of the pope's appointment and contested Church authority. In his letter to the "Christian nobility of the German nation," Luther offered local aristocrats political and economic emancipation on a platter.[29] Armed revolt was necessary to set themselves free from the *Roman robber*.[30] At a time when one-quarter of real

FIGURE 2.3. "Bringing Down a Station of the Cross" (Germany, Sixteenth Century)

estate was under Church control, heads of state and local lords across northern Europe stood to inherit an enormous portfolio.[31] Parliaments, urban magistrates, territorial princes, and peasant referendums enacted national Protestant reformations to reclaim it.[32] Bringing this to fruition, Luther argued, would require "washing our hands in their blood."[33] The Leipzig debate was never held, but the theses were reprinted in Wittenberg and four more cities within months of Luther's posting, and he quickly achieved notoriety in the heart of Catholic Europe.[34]

Not all of Luther's broadsides were novel, but his means of communications took advantage of the latest technology. Previous reform movements in the Church did not have Luther's multiplying effect of typeset printing. Publishers in Wittenberg released vernacular books for export—for example, English and Lettish Bibles, among others—foreshadowing the imminent ruptures in England and Latvia.[35] Luther was miraculously prolific: his collected writings stretch to 60,000 pages.[36] Rome excommunicated him in 1521.[37] It was in a German parish in 1523 that a Reformist service in the vernacular language replaced the Latin-rite Mass for the first time.

The practice radiated outwards from Wittenberg and southern Germany, often followed by attacks on Church icons and artwork. Fundamentalist mobs upholding the Old Testament injunction against graven images or divine likenesses smashed statuaries, destroyed stained-glass windows, and tore down crucifixes (see figure 2.3).[38] Between 1523 and 1546, rulers across the German-speaking lands, including Switzerland and Austria, appropriated Church property and severed the local Church hierarchy from Rome, creating territorial churches.[39] Chronologiclly, local rulers tended to convert *after* their subjects had already done so themselves.[40] States confiscated Church property in hundreds of small polities and replaced Catholic bishops with committees of theologians and electoral officials.[41] In 1527, the first Protestant university in Germany opened in Marburg, initiating the standardized production of Protestant preachers and launching a formal war of clerics in German-speaking pulpits. In Wittenberg, enrollment in theology studies rose from 162 students in 1516 to 552 in 1520.[42] After Rome's condemnation of Luther, tougher restrictions were imposed on students from Catholic areas, and enrollment dipped before rising again to 800 in 1550. A total of 16,000 students matriculated from 1520 to 1560, with most coming from southern Germany and Austria-Hungary.[43]

England and Sweden: From Sectarianism to Schism

The early sixteenth-century kings of England recognized the Roman pontiff as their spiritual ruler and feudal overlord.[44] The cardinal assigned there from Rome effectively cogoverned with the House of Tudor. Immediately after the dissemination of the ninety-five theses, Henry VIII (1491–1547) wrote a polemical essay against Martin Luther—for which the pope awarded him the title Defender of the Faith.[45] After the pope refused Henry a divorce when he requested one, however, a dynamic of separation from Rome set in.[46] Parliament recognized Henry as Supreme Head of the English Church and its clergy.[47] The 1534 Act of Supremacy gave him complete control over all Church institutions and the hierarchy in his territory, starting with the country's bishops and senior cleric, the archbishop of Canterbury.[48] Henry thought of himself as charting a middle way between Wittenberg and Rome, and he maintained a blend of Catholic, Lutheran, and Calvinist practices.[49] He kept the parish clergy in place, but criminalized communion, priestly celibacy, and the Catholic Mass.[50] To demonstrate his equanimity on one occasion in 1540, he executed three papal loyalists and burned three Evangelicals in a single act of royal justice.[51] His son Edward VI (1547–1553) sealed the schism with Rome by introducing a new Anglican catechism and *Book of Common Prayer*.[52] A second wave of Reformation passed over Scotland after a Calvinist network from Geneva spread anti-Catholic fervor leading to the destruction of numerous churches, including the Cathedral of St. Andrews in 1559 (see figure 2.4).

In Scandinavia, too, theological differences coincided with worldly interests. As King Gustav of Sweden put it, "The church's wealth belonged to the nation."[53] Gustav took over nominations of bishops and seized hundreds of monasteries and cloisters as well as dozens of reliquaries and valuable property.[54] Soon thereafter, Christian III of Denmark abolished Catholicism,

The Cathedral at St. *Andrews.*

FIGURE 2.4. The Destroyed Cathedral of St. Andrews, Scotland (1559–1561)

looted Church holdings, exiled the clergy, and arrested all nine bishops in the country. Like Gustav, he placed his own Reform bishops in the former Roman dioceses and imposed the Lutheran style of worship, removing all images and relics. Bishops and clergy who resisted were exiled or prosecuted; the Bishop Aresen von Holum, a Roman loyalist, was executed in Iceland in 1550.[55] As a bulwark against missionaries, all foreigners were required to endorse the Foreign Articles. By 1555, less than twenty years after Denmark embraced Lutheranism, the kingdom had only a tiny stranded minority of Catholic residents.[56]

In the Netherlands, where groups of Calvinist preachers arrived from Geneva to advocate religious freedom, Erasmus's translations were wildly popular, and the Anabaptist movement thrived in the mid-1530s, amid the flowering of subversive Evangelical activity.[57] The city of Münster was a hub of Dutch Protestant activism just over the border, playing the same role that Geneva had done for France. The first Calvinist church appeared in Antwerp in 1555 and then in the southern Walloon regions. Despite the arrival of Spanish troops in 1559 to enforce repressive edicts, hundreds of Dutch-language Evangelical books were printed in the 1560s. During the *Bildersturm* in 1566, churches in Antwerp and Ghent were sacked and their artwork was destroyed. Open-air Evangelical services were held outside major cities. While they were sovereign rulers of the Netherlands, the Spanish crown executed several thousand heretics (mostly Anabaptists).[58] In 1581, the Northern Provinces—joined by the ruling nobility, who went along with Calvinist revolutionaries— declared independence from Spain.[59] The Netherlands ended up resembling Scandinavia when William of Orange banned Catholicism and made the Kingdom of the Netherlands officially Calvinist.[60]

France: A Close Call

As the Protestant movement's center of gravity and the hub for propaganda for Francophone populations in Europe, Strasbourg earned the nickname of "New Jerusalem."[61] It was the first refuge of Jean Calvin, a lawyer from Picardie who preached that salvation could only come as "an act of free grace from God," not from Rome.[62] From the perspective of the Catholic Church, Calvin added a Latinate threat—French speakers—to the existing threat posed by German-speaking Luther. Despite the risk of arrest for possessing heretical literature and a royal prohibition against French-language Bibles, over 100,000 copies of the vernacular New Testament circulated within two years of its publication.[63] As Reformist influence spread, provocative demonstrations indicated that a Protestant underground was at work around the country. In 1528, an icon of the Virgin Mary was smashed on a prominent Paris street corner. In 1534, Evangelicals hung posters attacking the Catholic Mass in prominent places throughout the kingdom—including the king's bedroom in his Loire Valley chateau.[64]

Authorities judged the movement to have significant growth potential, and a royal arrest warrant pushed Calvin to flee in 1534, when he discovered the charms of Switzerland, then still a poor country with under a million people. Geneva was strategically situated for convening Protestants from across Europe, and it was right next door to the ripe target of France.[65] In his model polity of Geneva (1536), Calvin trained Protestant leaders and missionaries to return to preach in their majority-Catholic homelands.[66] He cultivated a printing industry aimed at a French readership, consolidating followers scattered across Francophone Europe into an imagined community.[67]

The Evangelical movement also spread through locally organized, independent religious education.[68] Thirty Calvinist religious colleges were established in French cities between 1530 and 1560.[69] Protestants concentrated in the south of France, where their numbers grew to around 2 million adherents active in more than 1,000 congregations.[70] Protestant militias even temporarily seized power in the cities of Lyon, Orléans, Le Mans, Rouen, Caen, and Toulouse.[71] As Genevan influence spread throughout the French "hexagon," the movement drew the attention and adherence of aristocrats who saw a chance to improve their own sort and standing.[72] In the subsequent decade, it has been estimated that around 10 percent of the general public and as much as 40 percent of French nobility embraced Calvinism.[73] Calvinists had enough gall to hold a general synod in 1559 in Paris, where they made a formal profession of faith. During the decades of civil war that followed, hundreds of cathedrals and abbeys and thousands of churches were burned to the ground, and thousands of priests and members of religious orders were assassinated.[74] At the end of the century, King Henri IV (1553–1610) decided that "Paris vaut bien une messe" ("Paris is well worth a mass"), preserving France's Catholic monarchy for two more centuries.[75]

The Age of the Auto-da-fé

Sovereigns across Europe, Protestant and Catholic alike, issued severe policies to suppress religious opposition.[76] Dissenting views were tantamount to sedition or heresy. Attending a forbidden service and distributing banned literature were treated as acts of defiance against both civil and church authorities. Religious violence and capital punishment were therefore viewed as a political necessity on all sides of the 1530s fault lines. The Spanish Inquisition executed only a dozen or so suspected Protestants, but authorities in England, France, Italy, and Switzerland spilled more blood on behalf of the Church.[77] It is estimated that at least 1,300 Protestants—perhaps as many as 6,000—were put to death between 1523 and 1566.[78] In October 1534 alone, 30 Protestants were burned alive (*autos-da-fé*) in Paris's Place Maubert.[79] Under Calvinist rule, Geneva hosted frequent trials for "Witchcraft and Magic, or erroneous teaching on the Son of God."[80] On average, Genevans burned one Catholic at the stake every month over the period from 1542 to 1546.

In Rome, a sense of existential menace grew as pockets of heretics cropped up closer and closer to home. Italy's lengthy sea borders and active commerce exposed residents to Reformist ideas through contact with foreign Calvinists trading in Lyons and Geneva. Some Evangelicals circulated in disguise as merchants or, more deviously, in the garb of Catholic priests.[81] Their preaching helped stir up Reformist uprisings in cities like Lucca (in Tuscany), proving that the Protestant phenomenon was not restricted to northern European agglomerations. The pope appointed an inquisitor to Lucca and wherever else Protestants—or religious innovation—surfaced in the small republics surrounding the Papal States. In Venice, another well-known haven for heresy, religious trials were held on a monthly basis.[82] Inhabitants were prosecuted for offenses ranging from iconoclasm to consorting with heretics and accepting false religious doctrines. The Roman Inquisition carried out executions in the cities of Faenza, Amandola, Bologna, Genoa, and Palermo. During the five-year period from 1567 to 1572, one auto-da-fé was held every three to four months on average in Rome's Piazza della Minerva, just behind the Pantheon. Belated repentance could save the heretic's soul but not necessarily spare his or her life. Out of 2,000 people who stood trial in the Roman Inquisition, 220 individuals (11 percent) died in flames, tied to a stake (*il rogo*). Another 720 people received the lesser sentence of being burned in effigy.[83]

The Inquisition grew into a sizable juridical bureaucracy that strengthened the pope elsewhere on the Italian peninsula. Its warrants and indictments were enforceable by law only in the Papal States, so its prosecutors relied on the goodwill of other governments.[84] Friendly Catholic regimes were sometimes willing to hand over offenders for judgment in the court of the Roman Inquisition, but extradition requests frequently met resistance.[85] If anything, the crisis strengthened the hand of Catholic monarchs vis-à-vis Rome. The Inquisition helped suppress the Reformation in Italy, however, perhaps sparing the country a bloodier religious war or a ruinous campaign against sacred images.[86] The Church also began to rely on old-fashioned miracles to shore up its base. After a fire devastated the town center of Faenza, a Lutheran bastion, Church officials announced that an image of the Madonna had miraculously emerged unscathed and invited Catholic pilgrims to bear witness.[87] At around the same time, in 1588, Rome established the first miracles commission. The verification of such events had been previously reserved for processes of beatification. The Protestant challenge increased the urgency of absorbing local religious activity and grassroots fervor.[88] The Roman Church did not vest its future, however, in either the supernatural or the stake. New institutional remedies were devised that were inaccessible to both the Inquisition and the hand of God.[89]

Compagnia di Gesù: "To Combat Lutherans and Confirm Wavering Catholics"

A Spanish student and religious pilgrim, Ignatius of Loyola, arrived in Paris shortly before Calvin fled France. Entering a spiritual awakening after a battle injury, he began a seven-year residency on the city's Left Bank.[90] In August 1534, he gathered his closest companions to burrow in high above the city in the crypt of a chapel in Montmartre. Just across the river from where dozens of Protestants were burned alive in the Place Maubert, Ignatius founded a movement that aimed to achieve a different kind of incendiary effect. To buttress the Church against the embers of Reformation and raise it out of its doldrums, "Jesuits" reclaimed the initiative and prepared "to set the world aflame."[91]

Within five years, Pope Paul III formally recognized the new Compagnia di Gesù, or Society of Jesus—*compagnia* also means "companions"—and exempted Jesuits from the usual jurisdiction of bishops. Rome's stovepiping strategy—outsourcing to a new clerical corps independent of the traditional hierarchy—indicated an awareness that the old hierarchy was rotten in some places. It afforded the pope direct powers over the order, instead of having to pass through the chain of command down to the local see. Unlike the Franciscans or the Dominicans, Benedictines, or Sulpicians, the Jesuits served under the watch of not just any patron saint, but of Jesus himself. Organized under their own superior general, they swore an additional pledge of personal loyalty to the pope alongside their vows and came to be known as "the shock troops of the Counter-Reformation."[92] At the time, many Jesuits embraced an Ultramontane outlook stressing papal authority over that of princes and other monarchs, which sometimes put them on the wrong side of the law. The Jesuits were repeatedly expelled from numerous countries, and a coalition of the French, Spanish, and Portuguese rulers even pressured Rome to suppress the order temporarily (1773–1814).

For the first two centuries following the Reformation, the Papacy granted the Society carte blanche as in-house education experts. The preaching, schools, and missionary activity of this new clerical corps formed a major component of the Church's overall professionalization. The pope entrusted the Jesuits with the French and German translations of the new catechism.[93] When asked by his Dutch companion Peter Canisius how the Jesuits could help save Germany, Ignatius is said to have replied: "Colleges." Ignatius and Canisius consulted local rulers and the Church hierarchy to plan Jesuit schools and seminaries. Global operations were based in simple chambers within the baroque headquarters of Chiesa del Gesù (Jesus Church) in the heart of Rome (see figure 2.5). The Jesuits heralded the formalization of Roman Catholic education, a system that would make an imprint upon hundreds of millions worldwide over the next five centuries. As the historian John O'Malley writes, they were the first order "to undertake, systematically, the operation of full-fledged schools for any students."[94] In short order, the Society established colleges in key Catholic hubs across the continent: Paris, Louvain, Cologne, Padua, Alcalà, Valencia, and Coimbra. By the end of the 1540s, there were nearly 60 endowed Jesuit colleges.[95] In the 1550s, they opened four or five schools per year.[96] Local authorities across Catholic Europe sought to attract the deluxe school facilities to their region as the order became known as the "educators of the governors."[97]

Jesuits paid special attention to sensitive areas in France, northern Italy, Germany, and Switzerland where Lutherans and Calvinists had made inroads. Bishops sent clerics to study in Jesuit schools, eleven of which were opened in Germany in the course of the 1560s.[98] Another bastion of the Counter-Reformation was Bavaria, where local dukes engaged Jesuits to conduct parish-to-parish combat against Lutherans by teaching theology in local com-

FIGURE 2.5. Apartment of Ignatius of Loyola, Rome

munities.[99] John O'Malley writes that Peter Canisius personally dispatched handfuls of preachers "to combat Lutherans and confirm wavering Catholics."[100] The Society is also credited with quelling nascent rebellion by the Duke of Mantua in northern Italy. The Jesuit-trained archbishop of Milan led the Counter-Reformation effort in Switzerland, sending young men to study in the relative safety of seminaries in northern Italy until a college could be established; the first one in Lucerne (1577) was followed by another in Fribourg, where Peter Canisius served as director (1580).[101] After Protestants mounted armed seizures of French cities and lay siege to Toulouse, the Jesuits counterattacked in 1563 and fostered networks of anti-Protestant brotherhoods.[102]

Twenty-five years after papal recognition of the Society, there were 3,000 Jesuit priests and 150 colleges on three continents—120 of which were outside the Italian peninsula—with tens of thousands of students enrolled. Born in the age of Copernicus and Galileo, the founding generation of Jesuits was not weighed down by the medieval baggage of other orders that also ran educational operations. Their Collegio Romano (1551), for example, was the first church school to incorporate the new physical sciences into its curriculum.

Not all Jesuit efforts in schismatic lands and global missions succeeded. The Society achieved less impressive results in the Nordic countries, where only

FIGURE 2.6. The Council of Trent (1545–1563)

tiny communities of Catholics remained after the Reformation.[103] Similarly, their missionary mandate in China and Japan (1585) yielded limited demographic gains. Over the next two centuries of the Counter-Reformation, however, they implemented their newly codified pedagogy (*Ratio Studiorum*, 1599) in 700 schools across Europe and 100 schools in the rest of the world.[104]

The Council of Trent (1545–1563)

The Jesuits were particularly useful to the Church during a period when the papacy was distracted by distant conflicts with the Ottoman sultan and French king. After settling those disputes with treaties (1544), the pope turned his focus back to his near enemies: Martin Luther and Jean Calvin. Paul III convened a rare gathering of hierarchs—an ecumenical Church Council—that had taken place only a handful of times before and has seldom been convened since (see figure 2.6).[105] The Council of Trent met in twenty-three sessions over eighteen years "to oppose the errors of the swarm of Protestant sects" and to set a strategy to combat the rejection of Church authority.[106] The final session (1563)

FIGURE 2.7. Catechism of the Council of Trent

was the most influential. The six cardinals, three patriarchs, 25 archbishops, 168 bishops, and seven heads of clerical orders collectively voted to formalize priestly ordination and approved a new law recommending the establishment of a seminary in every diocese.[107]

With this step, Rome began to rationalize, standardize, centralize, and consolidate its spiritual jurisdiction—and to police its brand.[108] A professionalized clerical caste slowly replaced the motley assortment of medieval clergy, many of them untrained and unprepared.[109] Local accountability would also rid the Catholic landscape of mendicant friars who operated without any oversight and "preached and taught what they pleased."[110] Church planners focused on achieving optimal ratios of priests to congregants and enforced the requirement of priestly ordination to celebrate Mass.[111]

The internal war on ignorance and superstition moved the Church to generate printed religious materials.[112] Standardized handbooks were printed for priests worldwide to use as a common set of instructions for performing Mass, teaching catechism, and interacting with parishioners about sensitive issues (see figure 2.7).[113] In the late 1560s, new editions were released of the *Revised*

Breviary, the *Roman Martyrology*, the *Septuagint*, the *Vulgate*, the *Missal*, the *Ceremonial*, and the *Pontifical*. Tridentine-inspired practices followed later with a wave of dioceses and seminaries and the introduction of uniform ordination titles (1700).[114]

The professionalizing trend upended the patronage practices that had bequeathed a sclerotic episcopal network. Bishops were increasingly learned and not just politically connected. The Council of Trent empowered bishops to act as papal delegates while introducing measures to centralize and standardize their quality control.[115] They were henceforth required to reside within their diocese and needed to submit a personal loyalty oath to the pope within two months of appointment before receiving definitive confirmation (1564).[116] Central control was further tightened in 1596: an additional consecration from two current bishops would be required of new bishops within three months of appointment in order to assume the office's full powers.[117]

Infrastructure

My archival research illustrates how the Church overhauled its institutions. Maintaining the equilibrium of competing national interests within the pool of existing dioceses, bishoprics, and cardinals was vital to the Counter-Reformation's success. Regional balancing of constituencies had always been necessary, throughout Church history, to avoid infiltration and power grabs by ambitious monarchs. The decades after Trent saw the dramatic increase of dioceses, in absolute and relative terms, and the adjustment of their geographical distribution.[118] The bishops occupying each diocese helped set Church policy and doctrine and helped steer the distribution of resources— from cathedrals and hospitals to schools and universities—toward their constituents.

In the year 1500, there were three dioceses per 1 million Western Christians worldwide. By the late sixteenth century, that number had risen to seven dioceses per 1 million Catholics. Despite the loss of millions of believers to Lutheranism in Germany—half of the population—the number of German dioceses *increased*, from thirty-nine to sixty-one during the sixteenth century (see figure 2.8).[119] The Church also nearly doubled the number of dioceses in Austria-Hungary, from seventeen to thirty-one. Accordingly, there were substantial changes in the ratio of bishop to congregants between 1500 and 1600.[120] Territorial coverage was enhanced through the creation of new dioceses to replace those lost to Protestantism. Rome doubled diocesinal coverage in France, Italy, Spain, and Austria-Hungary and tripled the number of

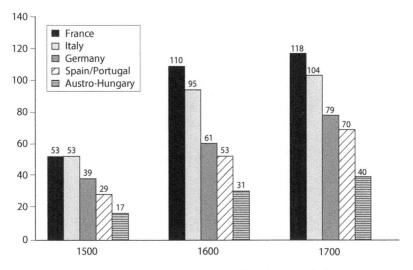

FIGURE 2.8. Roman Catholic Dioceses before, during, and after the
Reformation, per Country

bishops per Catholic faithful. In 1500, there were three bishops for every 1,000
French citizens; one century later, there were twice as many—six bishops per
1,000.[121] Italy went from five dioceses to nine per 1,000 citizens, Spain from
three to five, and Austria-Hungary from one to two. Germany, a clear priority
on the front lines against Lutheranism, went from four bishops per 1,000 to
twelve bishops per 1,000 in the year 1600.[122]

The growth in dioceses elsewhere diluted the proportion of local *Italian*
inhabitants within the curia. Italy's share of total dioceses shrank from
38 percent of all dioceses worldwide in 1431 to 23 percent in 1591—at the height
of American exploration. Italy was not a colonial power in the New World, and
the Reformation lands lay beyond its reach. By contrast, France's share of all
bishops rose from 18 percent in 1431 to 27 percent in 1591, and Spain and Portugal improved their share by half (from 8 percent to 13 percent).[123] Germany
improved its standing by two-thirds (from 9 percent to 15 percent), and
Austria-Hungary quadrupled its representation (from 2 percent to 8 percent).
Paris was elevated to an archdiocese in 1622, followed by Vienna in 1722, keeping up in rank, if not in substance, with the new rising stars of the Catholic
reform.[124] By the end of the 1600s, Catholics numbered 60 million
worldwide—including 5 to 10 million in the American colonies—double the
number three centuries earlier. With 19 million (in 1700), France accounted
for almost one-third of all Catholics. Germany had a similar overall population

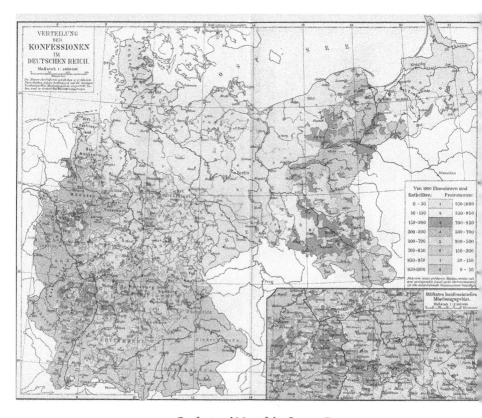

FIGURE 2.9. Confessional Map of the German Empire

to France, but half of the Germans were Protestant; only 8 to 10 million were Catholic, around the same as Italy (see figure 2.9).[125]

Education

The Church struggled to supply priests with the new training required to perform Mass. The average level of formal education increased slowly, but weaknesses persisted for nearly 100 years after Trent.[126] The Reformation's forces took an immediate toll at universities. The German state of Würzburg graduated 115 new priests in 1521, but only five in 1530. Only two newly ordained priests joined Viennese parishes between 1534 and 1554.[127] Thousands of pulpits were up for grabs in a parish-by-parish combat of words. Sermons confronted heresy and the struggle for doctrinal purity at a time when oral culture still prevailed.[128] While Latin remained the language of instruction, Catholic seminaries began training students to preach in the vernacular to stay competitive with Protestant rivals.[129]

Universities

Geographical proximity to a university theology faculty was critical in the struggle between the Roman Church and its detractors. Cities exposed to Evangelical activism through student mobilization were more likely to institute Reform, which was more easily avoided when loyal Catholics were supported by their own loyal local student activists.[130] In 1517, there were a total of seventeen universities in the Holy Roman Empire.[131] The Church had established seven theological faculties between the mid-fourteenth century and the late fifteenth, notably in Louvain, Belgium, and in the greater German-speaking sphere (for example, Wittenberg in 1502).[132] The University of Cologne was a bulwark of Roman orthodoxy that prepared agents to defend the Church around Europe. The Cologne Cathedral's spires reached fifty-six meters into the heavens, and the religious fervor of the city's inhabitants against the eruption of Lutheranism earned it new monikers: Holy Cologne, the German Rome, and the True Daughter of the Church.[133] The city played the role of a Teutonic Esau to wavering France's Jacob, aiming to counterbalance Protestant strongholds in Wittenberg as well as the budding New Jerusalem in nearby Strasbourg.

Faculties became battlegrounds in the wars and rivalry between Roman Catholicism and Lutheranism. Reinforcements were sent in and resources were reallocated. Pope Julius III (1550–1555) promoted the German theology faculties in Heidelberg, Ingolstadt, Würzburg, and Dillingen from college to university status. The number of Catholic universities Europe-wide doubled to thirty-four by 1600. The universities became ideological hubs to vaccinate whole regions against Evangelical movements. Of course, not all religious education was centrally administered by Rome. Numerous nonstate actors also worked alongside—and sometimes preceded—the Holy See. Brotherhoods and clerical orders founded their own seminaries in Protestant lands and in the New World. The Jesuits and the Sulpicians were among the most influential, but older orders, like Dominicans and Benedictines, also played a key role. Their involvement in religious education stoked the centralized reaction coming from Rome and led to the expansion of pontifical centers of learning (see figure 2.10). Julius III endowed the University of Rome, funded the Biblioteca Apostolica, and oversaw the growth of numerous *athenaeums* and faculties. These new departments were modeled on the thirteenth-century University of Paris: they were overseen by Rome and *not* run by a missionary order. The consolidation effort culminated with Pope Sixtus V's establishment of a new

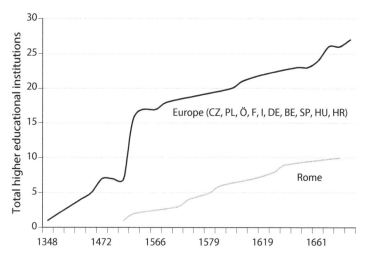

FIGURE 2.10. Religious Education in Rome and Europe, 1348–1702

Sacred Congregation (1588) to supervise Catholic universities across the globe, with an eye to doctrinal purity, reconquest, and re-Catholicization.[134]

Colleges

Catholic clergy in missionary countries operated under oppressive and secretive conditions. It was either impractical or impossible to train clergy for pastoral service in places like England, Scotland, and most of Germany, which was divided into dozens of statelets, dukedoms, and principalities.[135] Julius III entrusted Jesuits to combat Reformist ideas and influence from the safety of the Papal States, shielded from political interference and protected from Protestant plotting. An influential new category of seminaries and colleges came of age during this period. The Collegio Romano (1551) was the first international site for training young men from "regions infected with heresy"— in other words, northern Europe.[136] The period of the Augsburg Treaty, which established the legal separation of Catholic and Lutheran lands (1555–1648), was an era of "national conformity and international diversity," as one Church historian put it.[137] Priests sent to serve Catholic minorities risked arrest in transit or upon arrival. Next to come was the Collegio Germanico, for which Ignatius began to solicit students from Cologne and Vienna in 1552. In handwritten correspondence I discovered in the Jesuit archives—one of 7,000 letters Ignatius drafted in his chambers above the Chiesa del Gesù—the future saint wrote to a powerful cardinal of the Counter-Reformation to request his assistance (see figure 2.11). In the letter, Ignatius asked for the cardinal's aid "in the holy work" of bringing the new Germanic college to the

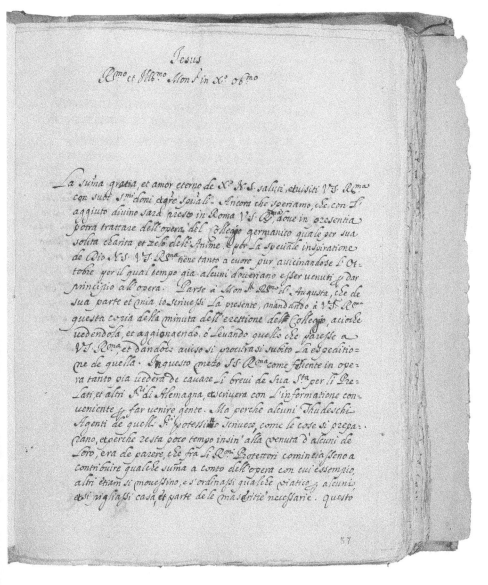

FIGURE 2.11.1 AND FIGURE 2.11.2. Letter from Ignatius of
Loyola regarding the German College, Rome (1552)

attention of the priesthood and others in German-speaking lands to "get
people to come."[138]

The Germanico opened its doors in 1555 and immediately took on a key role
in the attempts to restore Catholicism in German towns and cities, turning
Rome into a center for clerical training (see figure 2.12).[139] One motive was

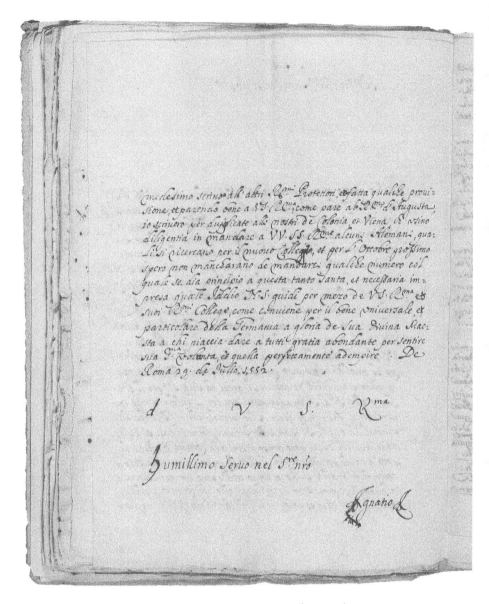

FIGURE 2.11.1 AND FIGURE 2.11.2. (*continued*)

that the clergy-in-training "contracted manifold ties and habits which made them *Romtreu* (loyal to Rome)" and engendered their "steadfast loyalty to the Catholic and the papal cause."[140]

The promulgation of *Adolescentium Aetas* on July 15, 1563, during the twenty-third session of the Council of Trent called for the creation of semi-

FIGURE 2.12. The Collegio Germanico, Rome (1580)

naries in all dioceses in order to standardize and formalize religious training under the direct jurisdiction of the local bishop.[141] The effect was immediate: forty-three new colleges and seminaries were founded in the mid-1560s, many of them in Rome and surrounding areas (see table 2.1).[142] The Seminario Romano (1565) was placed under Jesuit oversight. The Jesuit-inflected Collegio Germanico served as a model for seminaries established in Germany by Pope Gregory XIII (1572–1585), who was an enthusiast of education and the sciences. He is the namesake of the Gregorian University and the monthly calendar still in use worldwide. Rome founded more than twenty colleges for the education of Catholic youth under British rule, including, in 1600, the English College and the Scottish College, followed by the Irish College (1628). Pope Urban VIII (1623–1644) also oversaw a wave of colleges created *outside* Rome to train clergy to do missionary work in their home countries. Together with smaller satellite institutions like the English colleges in Valladolid (Spain), Lisbon (Portugal), and Douai (France), the Irish college in Paris, and the Maronite college in Ravenna (Italy), these seminaries quietly dispatched a steady flow of priests to serve minority communities abroad.[143]

The impact of professionalization and standardization upon quality control and quantity was palpable. Hundreds of students passed through the Collegio Romano and the Collegio Germanico in the 1560s and early 1570s.[144] Between 1565 and 1765, the Church established 800 colleges and seminaries in southern Europe and in European colonial possessions.[145] The result was an increasingly

TABLE 2.1. The Creation of Roman Colleges, 1551–1735

Year	College
1551	Seminario Romano (and Gregorian University)
1575	Collegio Germanico–Ungarico
1577	Collegio Greco di Sant'Atanasio
1579	Collegio Inglese di San Tommaso di Canterbury
1580	Angelicum–College of St. Thomas
1600	Scottish College in Rome
1627	Collegio Urbano di Propaganda
1628	Irish College in Rome
1687	Sant'Anselmo all'Aventino (Benedictine)
1715	Collegio o Seminario Greco di Palermo
1735	Collegio dei Cinesi di Napoli
1735	Collegio o Seminario Greco di San Benedetto in Ullano

well-educated hierarchy. Whereas only one of every six Spanish bishops under King Charles V (1519–1556) was trained in theology at university, half of those in office under his successor, Philip II (1556–1581), attended one of the new *colegios mayores*, and more than two-thirds obtained a university degree.[146] By the early seventeenth century, 84 percent of French bishops held a degree, and the rate kept increasing.[147] Only the growing German episcopate formed an exception to this trend. The spike in demand for German-speaking bishops led to such a rapid rise in their ranks that some still lacked a degree or ordination, although many had attended the Collegio Germanico for some amount of time.[148] From the 1560s onwards, nearly one in five of all German bishops and one in three of all Austrian bishops passed through the Collegio Germanico in Rome.[149] The Collegio Romano also remained an elite training ground for future Church leaders. Prominent alumni included Pope Gregory XV, who later beatified Ignatius and commissioned a grand Roman church in honor of the founder of the Jesuits (Chiesa di Sant'Ignazio di Loyola, 1622).

Holy Congregation of Propaganda Fide

Spanish missions spread across the entirety of New Spain (1511–1851), from Las Californias to Las Floridas (as the territories were then known) and to the island of Puerto Rico, across Mexico and through Central America, down the western coast of South America, across the Pacific, and into the Philippines. For their part, the Portuguese reached Goa and also created missions along the coast of Brazil, around the western coast of Africa, into the Persian Gulf, and across the East Indies.[150] By 1610, there were five archbishoprics, twenty-seven bishoprics, and 400 residences of Catholic religious orders in South

FIGURE 2.13. Palace of the Holy Congregation of Propaganda Fide, Rome (1626)

America.[151] Fifty years later, there were seven dioceses and two apostolic delegates in North America. By the seventeenth century's end, a handful of bishops and archbishops had even taken up residence in Japan and China.

The sudden and significant increase in missionary activity led to the creation of a special department for it in Rome.[152] Gregory XV centralized command over missions under the Sacred Congregation of the Propagation of the Faith (Holy Congregation of Propaganda Fide, 1622) (see figure 2.13).[153] Its official aim was "to regain the faithful in all those parts of the world where Protestantism had been established, and to bring the light of the true faith to the heathen lands."[154] But as J. Fréri wrote in 1903, "The ambition of the Propaganda is immense, which is to convert the whole world."[155] It was the last of nine major congregations of the Roman Curia to be established, but it rapidly became the most powerful arm of the Church bureaucracy. From the perspective of Church governance, it was considered a minor luxury to fall under the Propaganda Fide's jurisdiction. The congregation's offices abroad were a stovepipe from the periphery directly to the Vatican, reducing the bureaucratic process when requesting personnel or resources. Like the empowerment of the Jesuit order, this was an act that consolidated papal power.

Beyond institutional presence or density, Lutheranism also challenged the Catholic Church to match the immediacy and accessibility of the Reformation's God and the liveliness of its vernacular. To succeed in its mission, the

FIGURE 2.14. Typesets of the World (Holy Congregation of Propaganda Fide)

Church embraced the tools of its nemesis: in addition to better sermonizing, another Holy Congregation was created to run the Vatican's first printing press.[156] It began printing in the late 1580s, in every local vernacular. In 1626, an in-house publishing operation—the Tipografia Poliglotta di Propaganda—was up and running. By 1759, Rome's polyglot typographers were printing in twenty-seven languages, including some with multiple alphabetic variations (see figure 2.14).[157] An eighteenth-century defense of absolutism, *Politics Drawn from the Very Words of Holy Scripture*, even invited the Catholic reader "to consider the biblical data for himself, as a protestant would, rather than to rely on clergy and bishops."[158]

Modern-Day Apostles

With global responsibilities for operating in missionary lands that had no national Catholic hierarchy, the Propaganda Fide at first prioritized European reconquest in, for example, Great Britain, the German states, Norway, Sweden, Denmark, Holland, Luxembourg, Switzerland, Greece, Crete, and the Balkans.[159] Its most active centers were in German-speaking and Anglophone Europe, where it established apostolic prefectures—the first step in the territory's enrollment in the Holy Congregation of Propaganda Fide. Based on written reports from these delegates, officials in Rome decided where to send missionaries or clerics and where to facilitate the construction of churches.[160] In 1647, the Propaganda Fide created the title of Vicariat Apostolic so as to exercise closer supervision of missionary activities in Protestant Europe and in the French, Portuguese, and Spanish colonies in the Americas.[161] It determined in each case whether to establish a prefecture or a vicariat or to propose a new diocese, although the permission of sometimes hostile rulers was required.[162] Apostolic vicars were denied entry to Scandinavian territories but allowed into Württemberg and Prussia—where they were forbidden, however, from performing any episcopal functions.

Determining what was licit and what was illicit for the unprecedented minority experience—demographically or juridically—required redefining the duties, habits, expectations, and rules for being a good Catholic. I encountered a seventeenth-century document in a Jesuit archive in Rome with forty pages of handwritten instructions for those living in Calvinist or Lutheran lands.[163] Such a situation was presumed to be temporary and considered acceptable only for unspecified "grave and justified reasons to reside for some time" outside of Catholic rule. Two guiding imperatives were articulated. First, remain "resolutely celibate within the true faith and satisfy the obligations of a good Catholic." And second, "behave in public commerce or conversation on daily and political topics such that the Calvinists cannot discern that you are Catholic from your deeds or your words" (see table 2.2). Catholic converts living in England received a dispensation from attending Mass on holidays and to forgo fasting days so as to hide their true faith. Another memorandum (1702) from two cardinals revisited a centuries-old obligation to avoid contact with heretics, which was impracticable for those living as a minority in a heretical country.[164]

Representatives were sent from Rome to interpret and reconcile the nuanced advice for daily life as a minority.[165] Apostolic vicariates served as stand-ins for episcopal sees and, later, cardinalates once a country exited the Propaganda Fide, shed its missionary status, and restored its own national hierarchy. Catholics in Great Britain formed a tiny minority, around 1 percent of the English population and 2 percent of the Scottish population. Ireland was home to the world's only majority-Catholic population (60 percent) under non-Catholic rule.[166] The situation in England improved after the Glorious Revolution, when Rome sent four apostolic vicars (1688) and one to Scotland (1694) to oversee the religious life of 100,000 or so Catholics.[167] Rome succeeded in restoring a national hierarchy in Ireland in the early eighteenth century, although it took until 1851 to do so in the rest of Great Britain. Despite the virtual absence of Catholic inhabitants in Scandinavia, the Swedish, Norwegian, and

TABLE 2.2. Instructions for Catholics Abroad, Seventeenth Century

---

In certain circumstances Catholics in Germany may attend heretical sermons and religious services that declare many impertinences, insults, and calumny against the Catholic religion.

Catholics have no obligation to rise and fight back to uphold the honor of the offended religion.

The best advice (if not to say obligation) is to have as a general rule to never go to hear Protestant preaching.

You may have your marriage contact approved by the civil magistrate but *not by the Calvinist minister or pastor.*

A Catholic living *incognito* must abstain from anything that includes the personal declaration of Calvinist faith. This includes singing in their churches together with them before and after the sermon.

In no case may you negate your Catholicism in telling the perverse lie of affirming being Calvinist and denying being Catholic.

If asked in private conversation if you are Catholic, you can avoid answering, change the subject, or declare that you do not want to report your conscience to others. Protestants and especially Calvinists, in Germany and particularly in Holland, do not usually press for an answer.

Danish monarchies refused the arrival of a single apostolic vicar appointed from Rome until the last third of the nineteenth century.[168]

Hierarchy

The sixteenth-century northern European defections to Protestant faiths provoked a new sensitivity in Rome to geographic diversity in the Church's governing bodies. In a bid to galvanize papal authority, Rome placed Princes of the Church in the new European periphery and across the New World.[169] As discussed earlier with regard to the post-Reformation redistribution of dioceses and bishops, popes reinforced wavering countries by giving them more electoral weight in the College of Cardinals. The College, which elects the pope, was enlarged to accommodate a more diverse and besieged Church. It grew from a pre-Reformation average membership of twenty-five cardinals to seventy in 1565 (see figure 2.15). My archival research shows that Germany was the biggest beneficiary. Eleven German bishops were promoted to become cardinals between 1520 and 1650, compared to a grand total of just five before then. The number of cardinals in Italy also improved during the Lutheran scare, going from seven for every 1,000 citizens in 1500 to ten per 1,000 in 1600.[170]

Conversely, the relative position of other countries decreased after crackdowns by national authorities persuaded Rome that cardinals there would not be able to be politically independent. England was treated as a lost cause, receiv-

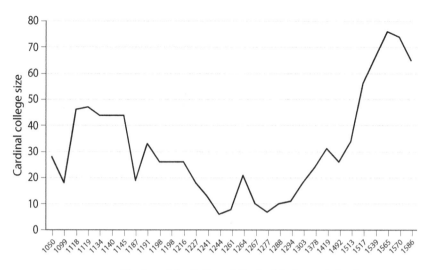

FIGURE 2.15. The Size of the College of Cardinals before and after the
Protestant Reformation, 1050–1600

ing no new appointments to the College of Cardinals for almost three centuries
after Henry VIII. Eighteenth-century France's representation in the college declined from two cardinals per 1,000 citizens to just one per 1,000. Spain's ratio
decreased from three per 1,000 citizens to one per 1,000. These diminished numbers were not the result of a demographic shift in France or Spain. The Church
did not alter its supply of priests and churches in these two countries. Instead,
the national imbalances can be explained by the papacy's efforts to resist the
pressure from Catholic rulers, especially the Spanish and French, to approve
their candidates for church offices, a type of appointee known as a crown cardinal. When the papacy rejected the names proposed by monarchs, those leaders
sometimes threatened to cut off the military aid required to defend against heretics and Ottoman armies. In turn, Rome sought to use its hierarchical appointments to exploit national divisions and competition among emperors and kings
in the hope of preserving its own operational independence.[171]

Rome after Ignatius

The chain reaction that began with Martin Luther's theses and schismatic national churches across northern Europe heralded the Catholic Church's historical destiny: the transition from temporal to spiritual power. Rome's decline
as a temporal power coincided happily with the reality of a less militaristic
Europe. The continent went from being in a state of war, on average, more than
two-thirds of the time between 1550 and 1650 to half of the time from 1650 to
1750, and eventually to less than one-quarter of the time from 1850 to 1900.[172]

The papacy, a central target of Luther's wrath, emerged strengthened in the lives of the Catholic faithful.[173] In response to those who questioned the pope's representative legitimacy, the Church commissioned monumental paintings showing Jesus personally handing the keys of the Church to Peter, the first in the line of 266 popes.[174] Papal authority, in other words, came directly from the Lord in the flesh.[175] Church artists and architects were instructed to avoid Lutheran iconoclasm and instead create ever more glorious sacred images as "a bible for the poor" and illiterate and "to bring them closer to Salvation."[176] The aesthetic language of the Counter-Reformation was the baroque, and Rome was its epicenter.[177] One fresco in Rome's Chiesa di Sant'Ignazio depicts the apostles being dispersed throughout the world, including Africa and Asia. It was a grand artistic justification of centralized executive oversight, through apostolic prefectures and the Holy Congregation of Propaganda Fide. Religious authority was visually reinforced with the credibility of Saint Peter and Jesus's own disciples.

This is the period when the great Papal Basilica of St. Peter was completed, and when Pope Paul V commissioned the piazza and colonnade abutting the Vatican, as well as the dual domes of Santa Maria del Popolo. The building style of a preferred papal architect of the moment, Francesco Borromini (1599–1667), spread north to Austria-Hungary and Germany. The turn of the seventeenth century also marked Rome's rise as the modern capital of Western Christianity. The attention earlier lavished by Ignatius of Loyola and his companions on the city helped turn the Holy See from a relative backwater—it had been sacked as recently as 1527—back into the preeminent center it had once been.

Church leaders used the nonmilitary arms at their disposal—miracles, saints, bishops, and cardinals—to bring those on the periphery into the system. In the end, the Church conserved the outer edges of the German realms, from the large Bavarian dukedom to Münster and Cologne, in addition to numerous Catholic islands in a sea of Protestant regimes in Germany and Switzerland (see figure 2.8).[178] Northern Italy and southwest France also remained in the Catholic firmament. At the end of the nineteenth century, majority-Catholic countries had on average one church and a priest or clergyman for every 400 to 600 residents. The work of the Propaganda Fide, in countries where Catholics were a minority, kept the ratio at around one cleric for every 900 to 1,800, or half to one-third as much coverage. The trained clergy and bishops, the ample houses of worship, and the institutions of religious education were the product of defensive gestures and adaptation to potentially extinguishing challenges.

3

The Plot against the Caliphate

THREE CENTURIES AFTER the Reformation, the Ottoman caliphate faced a situation analogous to that endured by the papacy at the hands of Lutheran rulers. The sultan-caliphs found themselves cut off from tens of millions of Muslim believers by European states at the turn of the twentieth century, a development that paradoxically led to the caliphate's rise in stature and institutional profile between 1800 and 1920. Europeans' imperial expansion reached from London, Paris, and The Hague all the way to Hyderabad, Tunis, Cairo, Java, and Bukhara. More and more Muslim subjects—in North Africa, the Balkans, Palestine, Transjordan, Syria, and Arabia—found themselves outside Ottoman borders (see figure 3.1). By the early 1900s, the world's preeminent Muslim powers were Great Britain (which had 75 million Muslim subjects), the Netherlands (30 million), France (25 million), and Russia (17 million)—all of which already outnumbered the shrinking Ottoman population (see figure 3.2). The spiritual orientation of Islam's holy cities had implications for daily individual prayer directed toward Mecca. European capitals considered Islamic religious affairs to be too entwined with their own legitimacy as colonial rulers and too sensitive to be left to others, especially to a geopolitical rival.[1]

The caliph was the most common symbol of Friday's collective prayer, customarily a moment featuring an appearance by the political ruler, to whom the presiding imam would express loyalty (*bai'a*). The annual pilgrimage (*hajj*) made by scores of thousands of Muslims under European rule, for example, depended on Ottoman control. As a religious duty for all who could afford it, the pilgrimage presented an annual opportunity for Ottomans to ply their religious leadership in person. The European empires also coveted Ottoman ports and straits—specifically, access to the Red Sea's Gulfs of Aden, Aqaba, and Suez—and open passage was too valuable to be left to the fickle humors of a rival divine ruler.

Like the Reformation, whose ripples took decades to reach the farthest shores, the dismantling of the caliphate took place in two stages: first in the

77

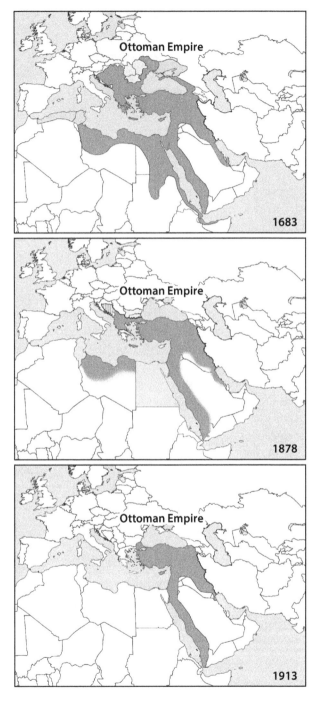

FIGURE 3.1.1, FIGURE 3.1.2, AND FIGURE 3.1.3. The Decline of the Ottoman Empire, Seventeenth Century to Twentieth Century

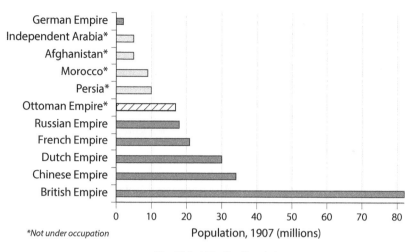

FIGURE 3.2. The Global Muslim Population, 1907

Ottoman provinces of North Africa and the Balkans in the late nineteenth century, and then in its heartland of Arabia and the Levant in the early twentieth. At first, each European empire coming into possession of large Muslim populations had formally cordial terms with the Ottoman caliph, sometimes exercising control jointly to allow local Muslims to pay respects to the caliphate's spiritual hegemony. Religious personnel changed their insignia and nominally paid respect to the supreme caliph—in Friday prayer or by requesting approval of appointments made by local rulers. For the former Ottoman subjects, there was no change in religious rite except the prayer for the ruler, which was divided in two, including one for the caliph in Istanbul as a spiritual sovereign. It resembled the early years of the Anglican Church—when the hierarchy still paid symbolic homage to the pope. But with each new treaty and every defeat across the Balkans, North Africa, and the Middle East, Yahya Birt writes, "the sovereign writ of the Sultan" became "an unexecuted right (*nudum jus*)."[2]

The rupture with the caliph became as meaningful as the rupture of national Churches with Rome. The nineteenth-century colonial leaders sought to impose a spiritual blockade to avoid all traces of Ottoman Islam in their possessions.[3] Reluctant to extend their own evolving models of separation of church and state, European rulers used other elements—tribe, nation, local religious identity—to cut off their Muslim subjects from Istanbul, and from one another.[4] Their assault on the caliphate deployed the scorched-earth tactics of the Lutheran and Calvinist Churches vis-à-vis the papacy in Rome.[5] In one territory after another, the regimes ended the circular flow of institutions and personnel between the Ottomans and the Muslim populations in the Balkans and North Africa and throughout the Middle East (see table 3.1). They

TABLE 3.1. European Challenges to the Religious Authority of the Ottoman Caliphate, 1774–1907

Year	Challenger	Challenge to Religious Authority
1774	Russia	Crimea: Treaty of Küçuk Kainardja, which recognized the Ottoman sultan as the Supreme Caliph with no political or civil authority over the Tatar people
1782	Russia	Orenburg Muhammadan Ecclesiastical Assembly: State body made up of mufti and three law judges; clerics appointed by local mosques
1798	France	Egypt: New Mahdi declared
1810	Russia	Administration of Religious Affairs: All appointments made by the state after exam by Orenburg assembly and local governor's approval
1830	Egypt	Egypt: Mehmet Ali claimed West Anatolia
1842	France	Algeria: Directorate of Arab Affairs established
1861	France and Great Britain	Tunisia: New constitution enacted
1870	Russia	Bulgaria: Bulgarian government named twelve muftis and twenty-five deputy muftis elected by the community
1870	France	Algeria: Commission for the Administration and Supervision of the Muslim Religion established
1872	Great Britain	Egypt: Dar al 'Ulum, a teacher training school, established
1875	France	Algeria: Mosque employees enrolled in civil service
1877	Great Britain	India: Anglo-Mohammedan College at Aligarh founded
1877	Great Britain	Egypt: Khedive Abbas Hilmi encouraged to lay claim to the caliphate
1877	Russia	Romanian government: Took over all rights and attributions with regard to preachers, imams, and mosque officials, who were paid by the state (1880)
1880	Great Britain	Saudi Arabia: Emir of Mecca assassinated while visiting the British consul in Jeddah, by a man dressed as a Dervish
1881	Great Britain	Sudan: Mahdi movement occupied the Ottoman vice-regency
1882	Great Britain	Egypt: British occupation ended Ottoman control over Egyptian Islam
1882	France	Tunisia: French authorized Friday prayer for the Ottoman sultan, but revoked Ottoman suzerainty
1882	Austria-Hungary	Bosnia: Government chose the Rais-ul-Ulema from Bosnian ulema; six regional muftis named by local governments
1884	Greece	Greece: Government appointed four muftis and a commission composed of Greek citizens
1887	France	Algeria: French citizenship granted to former Ottoman parliamentarian/publisher
1892	Great Britain	Turkey and Saudi Arabia: Campaigned to transfer the caliphate from Istanbul to Mecca
1902	Great Britain	Sudan: British reorganized shari'ah courts and established a board of ulema
1904	Great Britain	Yemen: Sheikh Hamid Eddin marched on Ottoman garrisons
1904	Great Britain	Yemen: Imam Muhammad al Mansur and Imam Yahya revolted against Ottomans
1905	France	Algeria: The three regions (départements) of Algeria considered part of France exempted from law separating church and state
1907	France	Algeria: Law for recruitment and payment of official Muslim clergy passed

appointed new Islamic muftis and judges to oversee a large network of state-paid clerics, mosques, and regional councils.[6] Echoes of the Reformation can also be found in the spread of written propaganda targeting the caliph's sway in their colonies, and in the way they quarantined their Muslim subjects from his spiritual, political, and cultural influence.[7] There was already a complex internal dynamic under way among Muslim reformers, ambitious Islamic monarchs, and modern fundamentalists, as well as tribal and ethnic rivalries.[8] European powers weighed in on that debate by identifying and supporting a range of intellectuals and institutions that could cast doubt on the Ottoman caliph's legitimacy and necessity.

In addition to the generous stipends, European empires gave local elites the prospect of religious dominance within their new international borders.[9] Colonial officials wrested the laurels off of the Ottoman caliphate and foisted them upon locally available leaders, reenacting one modern-day Act of Supremacy after another.[10] The transfer of religious sovereignty had concrete implications for the funding, operation, and leadership of Islamic institutions that had long been under Ottoman oversight.[11] Between 1914 and 1923, the British declared a protectorate in Egypt and marched into Jerusalem, while their ally in Mecca, Hussein bin Ali (1853–1931), launched a military takeover of the Hejaz. The French took Damascus and Beirut, and thousands of Italian troops joined British and French armies in Istanbul in the final years of the Ottoman Empire.[12]

European empires never dared to physically terminate the caliphate—not even when they had the chance to do so during the allied occupation of Istanbul after World War I.[13] Their constant abuse of the caliph guaranteed his spiritual demise, however, which they achieved via allied control of Mecca, Medina, and Jerusalem. The occupiers uprooted and repurposed centuries-old religious endowments and encouraged the emergence of Islamic leadership that was independent from Istanbul. Like the bearers of Reformation in northern Europe, European empires offered Muslim populations in their colonies a range of services—including military protection—on more favorable terms than the distant hegemon in Istanbul could offer. The French convinced the sultan of Morocco to take on the title of king in an effort to shore him up as Caliph of the West in their quadrant of occupied Africa. The British invented the offices of Grand Mufti of Jerusalem and Imam of the Two Holy Cities. The Dutch employed a Javanese sheikh in their imperial service, while Italy, Austria-Hungary, and Russia promoted a set of autocephalous Islamic communities in their areas of influence.[14] In the Balkans, Bulgaria, Greece, Serbia, and Romania all opted for religious administrations with a national mufti at the summit.[15] Hundreds of millions of Muslims in British India and the Dutch East Indies were made to rededicate Friday prayers away from the sultan-caliph in Istanbul and toward whomever the British, French, and Dutch states decided. This fragmentation was a definitive rebuke to Ottoman religious authority.

The First Balkanization

Two decades before Napoleon (1769–1821) invaded Egypt and long before the French navy landed in the port of Algiers, Russia was the first European empire to recognize the Ottoman sultan's extraterritorial religious authority. After a Russian military victory, an important treaty signed at Küçük Kainardja (a village on the Bulgarian-Romanian border) enshrined him as the Supreme Caliph of the Muhammadan Faith for Muslims residing in conquered territory—but *without* political or civil authority. This resembled European empires' own ambitions to protect Christian minorities and holy sites under Ottoman control, and it also mirrored the contemporary Pan-Slavic ambitions of the Russian czar.[16] With the Congress of Berlin (1878), the Balkans were the first European region to be severed from Istanbul in a century.[17] The experiences that followed owed much to the eighteenth-century treaty with Russia.[18]

The Austro-Hungarian occupation of Bosnia-Herzegovina (1878–1914) shaped the new national awareness of a specifically Bosnian Islam.[19] The new rulers inherited oversight of nearly 1,000 religious schools, including sixty for higher religious education and training. Austro-Hungarian authorities broke with Istanbul by creating a Bosnian *rais al ulema* (Grand Mufti, 1882), who presided over six regional muftis and a committee of religious overseers (*mejdlis*).[20] Formal approval (*manshur*) of his appointment was requested from Istanbul—but only after Vienna had already chosen from among three candidates presented by a special meeting of Bosnian ulema.[21] Ottomans negotiated the inclusion of a Friday prayer for the caliph in the Bosnian rite, recognizing the sultan as head of the Bosnian Muslim community and its "theoretical" sovereign. Bosnian Muslims thus "remained part of the global Muslim community presided by the Caliph," but under Habsburg administration.[22] The rift with Istanbul deepened with the establishment of a Bosnian institution for scholars of shari'ah (1887) and the declaration of theological independence from the caliphate (1892).[23] With the caliphate successfully severed, Vienna removed itself from the administration of Bosnian Islam: the Austro-Hungarian Empire ratified this with its 1912 recognition of the iGGÖ (Independent Islamic Community of Austria), in which "the Bosniaks administered their religious, waqf and educational affairs autonomously."[24]

The Ottoman agreement with Serbia stated that "no obstacle may be made to the relations of communities or individual Muslims with their spiritual leaders who will depend upon the Sheikh ul Islam in Constantinople." An article of the Ottoman-Serbian treaty guaranteed that "the name of His Imperial Majesty the Sultan as Calif will continue to be pronounced in the public prayers of Muslims."[25] At the Belgrade mosque, built during the rule of Suleyman II (1642–1691), the Ottoman flag was flown every Friday.[26] The mosque's imam and muezzin were appointed by the Serbian government, however, and the Serbian government created its own seminary to train muftis for national service.[27] In reality, Muslim Serbian voters elected their own leaders; formal approval was sought from Istanbul only after the king of Serbia named his choice of chief mufti.[28]

Bulgaria won independence with the aid of the Russian army during the Russian-Turkish War of 1877–1878. The Principality of Bulgaria formally remained within the Ottoman Empire as an "autonomous province of Eastern Rumelia" for several decades, during which the Bulgarian government insisted that Muslim communities elect their own muftis, whose names were submitted to the Ottomans to formally grant approval after the fact.[29] Under the agreement of "suzerainty" with Bulgaria, Istanbul continued to appoint and pay religious teachers and to pay the mufti of Philopoppoli. In Croatia and Slovenia, Muslims were permitted to practice their religion freely and allowed to maintain ties with the Ottoman caliphate, but shari'ah law was banned. Muftis submitted appointments of local qadis to Istanbul for Ottoman approval. Muslims in Montenegro nominated a mufti together with Turkey, choosing a leader of Pomak ethnicity as the national mufti in the capital of Podgorica.[30] During the country's first period of national sovereignty (1879–1918), Montenegrin Muslims wishing to pursue Islamic studies traveled to Istanbul, Izmir, and Salonica for postprimary religious training.[31]

Romania and Greece, finally, made a clear-cut rupture with Istanbul. With its 1880 law organizing Islam in the Principality of Romania, the state assumed the costs for employing personnel and maintaining mosques in nine cities. To replace the Ottoman seminary, a new Muslim seminary was established in the city of Babadagh to train mosque personnel and offer religious education to Romanian Muslims. Greece achieved its independence from Istanbul in 1832 but did not address the issue of Islam until 1884, when the government appointed muftis in four cities with large Muslim populations and named a commission to oversee mosques; the position of Grand Mufti of Greece was created but never filled.[32]

The British Eastern Caliphate

British rule is sometimes portrayed as more respectful of local power structures than other nineteenth-century empires, but examples like Britain's Northern Nigeria Protectorate, where religious leaders and institutions enjoyed full autonomy, were exceptions and not the rule.[33] For a period of time in the mid-nineteenth century, Her Majesty's Government still found uses for the Ottoman caliphate—for example, during the Crimean War (1853–1856) against Russia. The Sepoy Uprising of 1857 exposed a British vulnerability to unruly Muslim subjects, and officials requested a letter from Istanbul addressed to Indian Muslims, imploring them not to join the revolt.[34] The British used the "influence of the Caliphate," the *New York Times* wrote in 1887, "to check the spread of the mutiny, to rally to the English standards the Mussulman races of India."[35] The relationship got more complicated once Britain took full control of India. Because India was home to a sizable share of the world's Muslim population, England considered itself "more deeply interested than any other country in obtaining the satisfactory settlement of the Eastern Question."[36] The British government became more suspicious and less deferential toward Ottoman attempts to influence India's Muslims. This was especially true after the British deposed the last Mughal ruler, who died in a British prison (1862), and millions of British subjects began to embrace the caliph more overtly. London framed the "Eastern Question" as a matter of self-defense against conquering Muslim armies. One diplomatic petition portrayed religious ties between the Ottoman caliph and Indian Muslims as "political conspiracies organized under the cloak of religion."[37]

The British assault on the caliphate began slowly in the 1860s and built to a frenzy over a fifty-year period. At first, they sponsored reform movements by encouraging a sympathetic network of schools, mosques, and clergy outside the caliphate's spiritual chain of command. The Deoband Madrassa (1867) was the first of several thousand to be opened under British rule.[38] Colonial authorities also helped establish a *dar al ifta*—a fatwa council—to field religious inquiries from Muslims across India. In 1877, Sayid Ahmad Khan (1817–1898) founded the Anglo-Mohammedan College in the city of Aligarh to promote Neo-Islam and "make the Mahometans of India worthy and useful subjects of the British Crown."[39] British officials were cognizant of the uphill battle they faced: the college's first uniform included the Turkish *fez* as "an expression of Pan-Islamic sympathies."[40] The college promoted substituting vernacular languages for the holy Arabic and encouraged interpreting and adapting Islam to contemporary circumstances.[41]

The British arrival in Cairo in 1882 set them on a collision course with the caliphate. At first, they asked the Ottoman caliph to bless their rule in Egypt—which was an Ottoman vice-regency at the time—but London grew uncomfortable that the large Muslim population directed their loyalties every week toward Istanbul. They preferred religious leadership amenable to guaranteeing British access to Mecca—the hajj was a destination of millions of British subjects—and to avoid any possibility that holy war might be directed against them. Moreover,

TABLE 3.2. The British Empire in the Majority-Muslim World, 1800–1984

Year	Place	Region
1800–1960	Sierra Leone Protectorate	Africa
1858–1947	British Raj (now India/Pakistan/Bangladesh)	India
1869–1963	Aden Protectorate (now Yemen)	Gulf
1873–1971	Persian Gulf Residency	Gulf
1880–1971	State of Bahrain	Gulf
1882–1971	Sultanate of Oman	Gulf
1884–1947	British Somaliland	Africa
1887–1965	Maldives	Indian Ocean
1888–1946	British North Borneo	Southeast Asia
1888–1984	Brunei	Gulf
1892–1971	Trucial States (Now United Arab Emirates)	Gulf
1895–1946	Federated Malay States	Southeast Asia
1896–1963	Zanzibar	Indian Ocean
1899–1961	State of Kuwait	Gulf
1899–1956	Anglo-Egyptian Sudan	Africa
1900–1914	Northern Nigeria	Africa
1909–1946	Unfederated Malay States	Southeast Asia
1914–1960	Colony/Protectorate of Nigeria	Africa
1916–1971	State of Qatar	Gulf
1920/1921–1932	Kingdom of Iraq	Middle East
1920–1948	Mandatory Palestine	Middle East
1921–1946	Emirate of Transjordan	Levant/Middle East
1922–1953	Khedivate of Egypt	Africa
1948–1957	Federation of Malaya	Southeast Asia

access to the Red Sea would halve the sea voyage to British India. William Gladstone (1809–1898), the prime minister who dominated British politics during the last third of the nineteenth century, took a hard-line position based upon these imperatives of empire. He exerted pressure to bring Islamic movements in the empire under civilian (British) oversight.[42] The British government became the most fervent advocate of "returning" the caliphate to its Arab allies and putting an end to Ottoman domination: "The one thing required to convince the Egyptian that ... his connection with the Turk is severed for ever will be the disappearance of his former sovereign from the Golden Horn."[43] From the outside, Great Britain appeared to be "weaving a vast web of intrigue against the spiritual oversight of the Sultan Caliph." Rumors flew of "England's aim to transfer the Great Caliphate from Istanbul to Jedda in Arabia or to a place in Egypt" or Baghdad, governed by an "Englishman appointed for life."[44]

British officials encouraged the Egyptian viceroy (*Khedive*) to personally lay claim to the caliphate.[45] The Ottomans gradually lost control over Egyptian

Islam as the British severed Islamic institutions from Istanbul.[46] Al-Azhar University was expanded and diversified to be of service to the overseas British Empire and its Muslim subjects. The British granted administrative autonomy to the Ministry of Justice to manage the shari'ah, the personal courts subdivision, and the waqf department, which ran the religious schools (*kuttabs*) and Al-Azhar.[47] The British also supported a handful of rival Islamic leaders while overtly and covertly undermining the Ottoman caliph's spiritual legitimacy and sowing doubt about his authority within their vast empire of Muslim subjects. They excoriated the sultan for violating minority rights in the empire, especially those of Orthodox Christians, and described his Islamic leadership as faulty and "unprincipled."[48] Cairo became a den of "anti-Hamidian fervor" (a reference to Sultan Abdülhamid II) under British rule, Walter Bullock writes, harboring editors and publishers in exile from the Ottoman Empire. Cairo printers published criticism of "Islam's decay" under Turkish watch and called for a return to an Arab caliphate.[49]

British rule lifted the curtain on the competing tendencies roiling beneath the surface. In Anglo-Egyptian Sudan, another Ottoman vice-regency, an imam declared himself the Mahdi and Allah's messenger, saying, "I am the expected guide."[50] He announced plans to overtake the Ottoman Empire, "severing its provinces one by one," and to "impose his caliphate on the entire Islamic world."[51] The Ottomans deployed troops and worried about his impact in Arabia, but the movement ended with the Mahdi's death in 1885.

Several years later, in British-ruled Punjab, Mirza Ghulam Ahmad (1835–1908) founded a new Islamic tendency independent of the Ottoman Empire. He too declared himself the Mahdi and initiated a remarkably tolerant and easygoing line of Ahmadiyya Muslim caliphs. Ahmadiyya are seen with conspiratorial suspicion by some in the Arab world who say that their sect was "created to express loyalty to the British colonial power and continues to be used as a tool against Islam and Muslim countries."[52] In 1895, the mufti of Egypt was installed in the new bureaucracy responsible for issuing fatwas (dar al ifta). An Egyptian nationalist wrote that "Great Britain's ambition is to realize the dream of Napoleon—taking over the Caliphate and the moral domination of all Muslims—but Khedive will never consent to be their tool."[53] Under British rule, however, the Egyptian Khedive did allow the British to help set up specialized "colleges" for European empires to train their own imams at Al-Azhar, far from the sultan's influence.

At around the same time, the British propagandist W. S. Blunt (1840–1922) launched a media campaign to gather support for "transferring the caliphate from Istanbul to Makkah under an Arabic speaking Quraishi."[54] Legal arguments were put forth in the British parliament claiming "the illegitimacy of

FIGURE 3.3. "England Bent on Ousting Turkey from Mecca" (*New York Times*, 1911)

the Ottoman Caliphate" because the Ottomans were not of Arab descent: "the Quraish qualification is wanting to one and all of the Turkish Sultans."[55] Like the French, they projected their experience of political rupture with Rome upon the periphery of the Ottoman caliphate.[56] Blunt thought that the Islamic world "needed freeing of its thought ... by a 'religious reformation.'" By promoting reformers like Muhammed Abduh (1849–1905), Britain could "encourage the better elements of Eastern thought." British regard for the caliph's spiritual influence was minimal: "the sole trace of recognition" was that he was "prayed for in the mosque."[57]

When the sultan's fundraising campaign for the Hejaz Railroad received voluntary contributions from the Muslims of Central Asia, India, and Afghanistan, British authorities saw the makings of a potential "uprising of Muslims."[58] In an article titled "England Bent on Ousting Turkey from Mecca," a journalist described King George V as "the greatest Moslem ruler of the universe" because half of the world's 200 million Muslims "are subject to his way and are content with his rule" (see figure 3.3). The journalist outlined the king's aim to "restore the complete independence of Arabia" and have "the holy cities of Mecca and of Medina in the possession of friends rather than of foes."[59] The Foreign Office confirmed this view in a "Memorandum on Future Control of the Middle East region," in which the Hejaz was described as "a country in which His Majesty's Government, as the greatest Mohammedan power in the world, cannot fail to be deeply interested."[60] They would not lose interest until they evicted the Ottomans from three cities holy to Muslims worldwide: Jerusalem, Mecca, and Medina.

Hussein versus Husseyni

The most prominent British candidate for the caliphate was Hussein bin Ali (1852–1931), the sharif of Mecca, of the Hashemite clan.[61] Hussein checked several boxes for London: He had Qureyshi ancestry and the potential to rule over the holy cities, since the family had generations of leadership experience as local governors of the Hejaz under the Ottomans. He also portrayed himself as "moderate, modern and compatible with European global interests."[62] Like other sharifs, he spent an extended period of time residing at the Ottoman court in Istanbul. Moreover, his two adult sons—Feisal (1883–1933) and Abdullah (1882–1951)—represented Mecca and Jedda in the Ottoman parliament and were available to help govern other areas liberated from the Ottomans. In 1915, the British replaced Hussein's Ottoman stipend with their own funding. Hussein bin Ali sent a memorandum to the British high commissioner in Cairo asking him to "acknowledge the territorial independence of Arab countries and the proclamation of an Arab Caliphate within thirty days."[63] In reply, High Commissioner Henry McMahon wrote a letter in which he "promised British assistance" for an Arab state and caliphate.[64] Foreshadowing the British deal made with Zionist leaders two years later, the McMahon Letter was a Muslim variant of the Balfour document that promised a Jewish state on the Ottoman lands they conquered.[65] Arab armies attacked the Ottoman garrison in Mecca in the summer of 1916, overrunning the "tiny Turkish force in Mecca and, with the help of a British naval bombardment, the all-important port of Jeddah."[66]

The British recognized Hussein as king of the Hejaz and thus sovereign over Mecca and the Medina, and he and his sons were set to rule all Arabia. Hussein took the title of Imam al Harameyn (Imam of the Two Holy Cities) and declared the expiration of the Ottoman caliphate, although without announcing his own to replace it.[67] Eager to seal the transfer, Abdullah told London that his father, Hussein, should be declared "King of the Arabs in order to show they are not under any power." With regard to Abdülaziz al Saud (1875–1953) and other contenders, Abdullah argued that there had never been a perfectly unified umma. "Let everyone rule his part, it does not make any difference," he said, adding, "It is not important whether those people would agree or not."[68] Meanwhile, the British continued to rely on Arab rebels to engage Turkish soldiers so as to cover their invasion of Palestine.[69] British forces occupied Jerusalem by the end of 1917, followed by Damascus in 1918.[70] They installed Hussein's son Feisal as king of Syria and Palestine and placed Abdullah several hundred kilometers away, on the throne of Transjordan.

The high watermark of British fulfillment of promises made in the McMahon Letter came between 1918 and 1920. They ordered that Hussein's name be substituted for that of Sultan Mehmed V (1844–1918) in Friday prayers throughout all the mosques in their empire, including Palestine and Syria. For McMahon's promises to remain on track, however, Hussein needed more overt assistance to obtain the title of caliph.[71] An impatient Feisal wrote to Whitehall urging London to announce "the reward of the Arabs, who were the principal instrument in ruining the Turkish Mohammedan Empire."[72] He recalled the existence of "certain understandings and obligations between us" and noted that "every Mohammedan believes that his Holy Places should be under the protection of a Caliph or an independent ruler." The British hesitated to commit to Hussein bin Ali as caliph, however.[73] Moreover, the Ottoman caliph's popularity persisted outside Arabia, as British and French prime ministers recognized in private discussions though they publicly denied it.[74] In the absence of consensus in favor of Hussein in the role of caliph, they reneged on McMahon's promises and signaled the position's availability to several rivals, including the Aga Khan, an Afghan amir, and Abdulaziz al Saud.

The British also invented a new position, the Grand Mufti of Jerusalem, and they named Kamil al Husseyni (1867–1921) to it. He was to supervise all waqfs and shari'ah courts and to "exercise the functions formerly vested in the Sheikh-ul-Islam."[75] Like the Hashemites of Mecca, the Husseyni family of Jerusalem had generations of leadership experience under the Ottomans. The British high commissioner declared that henceforth "Palestine is cut off from the Government of Constantinople and the Turkish authority in these matters, the Sheikh-ul-Islam." However, no effort was made to subsume the new Grand Mufti of Jerusalem under the authority of Sharif Hussein bin Ali, Imam of the Two Holy Cities. Hussein went unmentioned in the agreement. Instead, Muslims in Palestine were meant to have the feeling that "they have management of their own religious affairs," as one memorandum put it.[76] Soon thereafter, Kamil al Husseyni was singled out as the only *religious* leader worldwide to be granted royal honors for service to the empire as Mufti of Jerusalem. Under his direction, the Supreme Muslim Council emerged as the most independent of all Muslim religious authorities in the British Empire.[77] A new shari'ah court in Jerusalem replaced the Ottoman Ministry of Justice in 1918.[78]

Supporting Husseyni allowed Great Britain to hedge its extensive bets on the Hashemite sharif of Mecca and his two sons.[79] In furtherance of the McMahon Letter's principles, however, the British violated the terms of *another* secret document, from 1916—the Sykes-Picot Accord signed with France. Taken together, the new court and council, and control over Haram al-Sharif (the Dome Mosque) all endowed the Grand Mufti of Jerusalem with international credibility and a serious "leadership role vis-a-vis the Muslim community"—whose spiritual and political borders were profoundly in flux.[80] This aroused French suspicions, enough to spur them to add more of their own

FIGURE 3.4. "So, do you have any recurring dreams?"
(*Iznogoud* comic by René Goscinny and Jean Tabary)

candidates to the mix to balance the pro-British leadership in Islam's three holiest cities.

The French Western Caliphate

Decades of French experience in North Africa had given Paris a head start on British efforts with regard to the colonial administration of Islam. France's interference with the caliphate—and its support of Arab-ruled Islam to replace it—began with Napoleon's invasion of Ottoman Egypt in 1798. The French historian Henri Laurens writes that the French occupation exposed the Ottoman sultan-caliph as "unable to protect his Egyptian subjects or al Azhar," the university at the core of the empire. In Cairo, Laurens writes, Napoleon "presented himself as the friend and even the Mahdi of the Muslims," and he also enforced shari'ah law in Islamic courts, attended a public celebration of the Prophet's birthday, and had his proclamations "translated into Qur'anic Arabic" to give his rule the veneer of religious legitimacy.[81] French Egypt was short-lived, however, so it was not until the occupation of Algeria (1830)—another Ottoman regency like Egypt—that Islam policy "found expression in the French imperial management of North African religious affairs."[82] The French expression "to want to be caliph in place of the caliph" is idiomatic for using calculating means to unseat someone important (see figure 3.4).

The stakes rose with the growing French presence in North Africa and western Africa—sometimes referred to as Algeria's "annexes" (see table 3.3).[83]

TABLE 3.3. The French Empire in the Majority-Muslim World, 1830–1977

Years	Place	Region
1830–1962	French Algeria	North Africa
1841–1975	Comoros	Indian Ocean
1848–1960	Four Communes (now Senegal)	Africa
1880–1960	French Sudan (now Mali)	Africa
1881–1956	French Protectorate of Tunisia	North Africa
1882–1891	Southern Rivers (now Guinea)	West Africa
1889–1960	Ivory Coast/Côte d'Ivoire*	Africa
1894–1958	French Guinea	West Africa
1896–1967	French Somaliland	Africa
1900–1960	Territory of Chad	Africa
1902–1904	Senegambia and Niger	Africa
1903–1958	Ubangi-Shari (now Central African Republic)*	Africa
1903–1960	Colony of Mauritania	Africa
1904–1922	Upper Senegal and Niger	Africa
1912–1956	French Protectorate of Morocco	North Africa
1918–1960	French Cameroon*	Africa
1919–1932	Upper Volta (now Burkina Faso)	Africa
1922–1960	Colony of Niger	Africa
1958–1960	Central African Republic*	Africa
1967–1977	Afars and the Issas (now Djibouti, replaced French Somaliland)	Africa

* (Muslim minority)

France openly aspired to be an Islamic power (*puissance musulmane*), and colonial thought-leaders engaged the "peculiar characteristics of each region" at international conferences like the Congress of Orientalists in Algeria, the Congress of North Africa in Paris, and the Colonial Congress in Marseille.[84] In a context of ongoing concern about Ottoman influence and plots to aid dissidents in North Africa, French administrators, the historian George Trumbull writes, "perceived any organized form of Islamic piety as a menace." They began to sever institutional and religious ties with the sultan-caliph and to ensure that any international Islamic mobilization on French territory took place under French oversight.[85] According to Victor Bérard, France "maintained agents in all of the theological centers, from al Azhar to the mosque of Fez and the mosques of India."[86] They spread rumors undermining Istanbul's religious legitimacy, making reference to the "So-called Caliph, since this title which Abdülhamid shamelessly appropriated does not belong to him," and they accused him of having "usurped it."[87] France granted citizenship to a former Ottoman MP and Abdülhamid critic who used his newspaper (*al Basir*) to praise their colonial policies and highlight their concern for their Muslim subjects.[88]

Algeria

In Algeria, France created a director of Arab affairs with authority over the country's qaʾids, sheikhs, qadis, and muftis. To undermine any Ottoman sympathizers, the French employed at least 625 imams, muftis, and other official "religious agents."[89] France required loyalty from these agents, who in turn requested freedom from state involvement.[90] Given the French fear of an Islamic uprising directed from Istanbul, disestablishing the religious authorities entirely would leave the Maghreb open to Ottoman influence. A consequence of French nationalization of the waqfs was to cut funding for traditional religious seminaries that depended on nonprofits for their operating revenue.[91] In their place, the state offered free "traditional Islamic education" at three madrassas and religious centers in Algiers, Tlemcen, and Mostaganem. All mosque officiants, judiciary clerks, and those in other administrative roles were thereafter recruited solely from among graduates of these three schools.[92] An 1851 decree "bureaucratized the Muslim clergy and created "a caste of [state-paid] mosque officiants" with a monopoly on all mosques and preaching.[93] Any independent ulema—that is, those who were not trained at a state madrassa—were removed from circulation.[94] After the Algerian revolts in the 1860s, the French deported or expelled *thousands* of "Muslim leaders and religious dignitaries" and later did so "on a smaller scale" in Morocco and Tunisia.[95] These religious officials dominated urban Islam and did their best to compete with the brotherhoods and *zawiyyas* in the countryside. Napoleon III (1852–1870) portrayed himself as "Emperor of the Arabs," and from the 1870s onwards, qadis trained in the French madrassas enforced the shariʿah-based Indigenous Code. The hands-on approach to Islam ignored an emerging French tradition of *laïcité*. Colonial rulers were inconsistent in applying the 1905 law separating religion and state across North Africa.[96] Algeria received its own separate decree in 1907 granting the French state control of Islam in the public and national interest. The contravention of the 1905 law was rooted in authorities' fear of Algerian religious fanaticism.[97]

Tunisia

France took a slightly different tack in Tunisia. Officials there maintained the facade of the Ottoman *bey*'s religious legitimacy, including public oaths of allegiance by leading ulema, all "to give an appearance of co-governance."[98] Authorities decided "that the imams could mention the Ottoman Sultan—the nominal suzerain of the *Beylik* of Tunis—in the Friday sermon," as had been done for hundreds of years.[99] This was the nineteenth-century French version of Russia's 1774 concession to recognize the caliph's religious supremacy in the Treaty of Küçuk Kainardja. While political ties to Istanbul were cut, France acknowledged the caliph's preeminent position with gestures of respect. The local Husaynid dynasty (unrelated to Kamil al Husseyni or Hussein bin Ali) was given symbolic sovereignty over religious matters. On the other hand, the rupture of religious ties with the Ottoman Empire had really begun when France and Great Britain imposed the country's first constitution upon the Tunisian bey (1861).[100] In a context of persistent Ottoman influence in Algeria, it has been argued that French motives for seizing Tunisia as a "protectorate" included countering Pan-Islam.

The French helped King El Amine Bey establish independence from Istanbul, seizing control of both the Islamic law faculty (fiqh) and the financial output of the waqfs. The Zeitouna, the highly esteemed university, and the mosque-university of al-Kairouane were influential across Africa, drawing students from Mali, Senegal, and Morocco. The bey transferred these prestigious religious establishments and significant infrastructure (hundreds of mosques, madrassas, and religious courts) away from Ottoman influence and control.[101] Under French rule, traditional Islamic representatives of the Ottoman caliphate were constrained to accept French-imposed educational reforms. The Resident-General also reportedly "meddled in the succession of Husaynid religious leadership," leading to "frayed cooperation with the ʿulema."[102] He empowered the brotherhoods by "transferring enormous subsidies to the Tekkés and Zawiyas of the Regency," reorganized the Zeitouna's mosque and university, and, as in Algeria, opened a new establishment to educate Muslim administrators (Sadiqi College).[103] Finally, they reformed the Islamic educational system by combining religious studies with a modern curriculum. Decrees issued in 1875 and 1912 outlined the "subjects studied and books used at the Zeitouna."[104]

Morocco

When France came into control of Morocco in 1912, its colonial leadership already anticipated that their British rivals would support Hussein bin Ali's move to take Mecca. The French groomed a counterweight and prepared to install the Moroccan sultan Moulay Yusuf as the Caliph of the West, for Muslims in French colonies, in anticipation of the moment when the British would recognize Hussein as King of the Hejaz and Imam of the Holy Cities. The French resident general thought Moulay Yusuf to be the legitimate claimant to "spiritual suzerainty in Northwest Africa" and believed that he already enjoyed the following of Algerians.[105] The Sykes-Picot Accord of 1916 quieted this talk by settling spheres of influence, but the British-backed installation of Hussein bin Ali's son Feisal in Damascus less than two years later had repercussions. Officials of the French Protectorate of Morocco also made use of the Islamic networks they found on site. The Treaty of Fez (1912) "preserved or restored the religious authority of the Sharifian Alaouite dynasty" in which the Moroccan sultan-king was the recognized Commander of all the Faithful—and

FIGURE 3.5. Maréchal Lyautey dines with Sultan Yusuf in Fez, Morocco (c. 1925)

the spiritual leader of the Maliki tradition within Sunni Islam.[106] The French representative in Morocco wrote at the time that he had "carefully removed all European promiscuities—automobiles and champagne dinners—and surrounded him with old Moroccan rituals. His honest character and nature as a good Muslim did the rest. . . . I believe Moulay Yusuf is my greatest success" (see figure 3.5).[107] While under French protection, theological studies at al-Kairouane University in Fez were formalized for the first time in "number, content, purpose and location." The protectorate also restricted the subjects and texts that could be taught in mosques; unauthorized activities were punishable by law. French officials encouraged al-Kairouane graduates to "circulate around learned religious circles" in the Ottoman Empire's former sphere of influence across North Africa.[108] The western caliphate had a figurehead ready to counter the British power grab for Islamic hegemony through its allies in Arabia.

Syria

As early as the 1850s, France had expressed interest in detaching Syria from the sovereignty of the Ottoman sultan.[109] The French obtained control over Syria following the Sykes-Picot agreement "in return for giving Britain a free hand in the rest of the Arab world and its plans for an Arab Caliphate"—but the honeymoon was brief.[110] When the French took over Damascus from Feisal bin Hussein bin Ali in 1920, they reminded the British of their disapproval of his father, Sharif Hussein bin Ali, as a potential caliph. The French were ambivalent about the utility of a supranational Islamic religious authority and wary of British activity. Pro-French Arab notables were associated with campaigns to discredit Sharif Hussein, and there were signs among local subjects of persistent loyalties to Istanbul's siren call. Periodic "khutba scares" occurred in Palestine, Jordan, Syria, and Iraq when defiant ulema or imams restored the Ottoman caliph's name to their Friday sermon.

The immediate effect of moving Feisal bin Hussein bin Ali from Syria to the throne of Iraq in February 1920 was the revival of the Ottoman caliph's Pan-Islamic role: the Friday prayer reverted to the sultan in Istanbul. From one week to the next, imams in British Jerusalem and French Damascus were intoning the Ottoman caliph's name in their Friday *khutba*, in defiance of British orders to pray exclusively for the health of their man in Mecca. The Khutba Revolt spread to Baghdad, despite the British invasion there and their installation of Feisal as king of Mesopotamia, and Friday sermons continued to be dedicated to the Ottoman sultan.[111] In Jerusalem, the "first time local Khatibs [preachers] dedicated Friday sermons to the Ottoman Caliph," the British district governor ignored it, "since blessings offered to the Sultan were preferable to expressions of support for the nationalist forces of Mustafa Kemal."[112] The Grand Mufti of Jerusalem also played it down. But British intelligence officers viewed the dedication as "politicization" and "a dangerous innovation," and they suspected the French were behind it. Diplomatic cables show that the Civil Secretary's Office ordered reports on "the effect of the introduction of the Caliph's name on the population" and "any information they had about individuals/groups behind this development."[113] Louis Massignon identified the khutba controversy as "the key to the balance: if the Friday prayer continues to be said in Baghdad and Damascus for Hussein then the Ottoman Caliphate is at risk of disappearing." The division into rival camps and the disappearance of the caliphate predicted by Massignon took place, but not because of Hussein's popularity.[114]

Gallican Islam

France also interfered with the Ottoman sultanate by serving as safe harbor for Ottoman exiles in Paris, including the "Young Turk" military officers who deposed Abdülhamid II (1842–1918) in 1909. It was rumored, Kemal Karpat writes, that French intellectuals and spies in Paris "educated them in the antireligious positivism that came to be known as secularism."[115] As Henri Laurens observes, "Following the Young Turk revolution [of 1909], France could not resist." It wanted to prove that "it was the friend of Muslims . . . to be a *'puissance musulmane'* [Muslim power]."[116] France created its first administrative body to coordinate its complex *politique musulmane*, the Commission interministerielle des affaires musulmanes. Describing how politicians in Paris envisioned Islamic education "as the instrument of a *Concordat* with Islam," Jean-Pierre Luizard captures the bottom line: they believed, he writes, that "France should try to create a Gallican Islam as it had done with the Roman Catholic Church."[117]

To prevent any single Islamic authority from dominating internationally, the French sponsored overlapping networks. Despite their support for the Moroccan king as Commander of all the Faithful (Emir al-Mu'minin), the French also promoted Sufism in Morocco's backyard by financing mosque construction and Arabic language training for Islamic schools in Senegal. Jean-Louis Triaud found that they "portrayed so-called 'Arab Islam' as alien to African culture and sought closer cooperation with Sufi clerics who did not challenge French rule."[118] They sent Senegalese officials to "attend major Sufi ceremonies" and subsidized Sufi religious leaders' pilgrimages to Mecca.[119] French concern about Ottoman influence extended to the city of Wadai, the center of African Pan-Islamism, which they seized in 1910. One contemporary observer wrote that thanks to the French, local Muslims "did not listen to the call to the jihad by the caliph in Constantinople [in 1914 . . .] but they now listen when the call goes forth from their own *Mahdi*."[120] Given the extent of their involvement, the French prime minister seemed disingenuous when he publicly insisted, shortly before World War I, that France "had no Muslim policy."[121] In reality, France's tens of millions of Muslim subjects were a force to be reckoned with in the Muslim world. The French government laid further claim to its hybrid imperial identity as a *puissance musulmane* when it built the monumental Grande Mosquée de Paris (1922–1926) in the heart of its capital city, out of gratitude to Muslim subjects' sacrifices during World War I.

Sayyid ʿUthman, Dutch Lion

Tens of millions of Dutch subjects were another exposed flank of the Ottoman-led umma. Javanese Muslims first pledged allegiance to the Ottoman caliph in the sixteenth century and remained attached to Istanbul for most of Dutch rule in the East Indies (1800–1949). Its actual impact was doubtful for much of that time. Machteld Allan describes the Dutch colonial mentality: "The Ottoman Sultan had no real power over Muslims in the areas he lost to the European Empires, let alone over the Muslims in Southeast Asia."[122] Nonetheless, technological advances in travel and communication presented new challenges to Dutch authorities. The Ottomans sponsored Javanese students to pursue higher Islamic studies in Istanbul. The sultan was known to embrace new technologies, from the telegraph to the telephone. Periodic rumors that the caliph had called upon Muslims to prepare for jihad "frayed Dutch nerves" and led them to take new "precautions."[123] From The

FIGURE 3.6. The Dutch consul in Jedda authorizes pilgrims from the
East Indies to visit Mecca

Hague's point of view, Ottoman Pan-Islam created "needless confusion for the thirty-five millions of Mohammedans whom history placed under [Dutch] guardianship."[124]

The new railway and steam-powered travel by sea linking early twentieth-century pilgrims to the Hejaz increased the share of Malaysian and Indonesian pilgrims going on the hajj. Despite being "the Muslim majority located furthest away from Mecca on the planet," they provided one-quarter of all pilgrims worldwide at the turn of the century (see figure 3.6).[125] Dutch officials worried that during hajj, "each European power's own pilgrims disappeared from sight—nationalities fall away and Muslims form an international under the green flag."[126] Since consular officials, as non-Muslims, were barred from entering Mecca, they feared that pilgrims "could easily fall into the clutches of Turkish agents of Pan-Islam."[127]

The Dutch sought to counter that influence by cultivating a loyal religious leader, the Islamic scholar Sayyid 'Uthman bin Yahya (1822–1914). Born in the large Yemeni community of Dutch Batavia, 'Uthman claimed Qureyshi descent lineally from the Prophet Muhammad. He advised Dutch colonial officers and served as the liaison for all Islamic issues in Nederlands-Indië as Grand Mufti of Batavia. A map in a Dutch imperial collection traces 'Uthman's travels and religious pilgrimages back and forth across the Indian Ocean—to Egypt, the Balkans, western Europe—all while conspicuously avoiding Istanbul, which was unusual for the time.[128]

When Dutch forces encountered ferocious resistance in Sumatra during the Aceh War (1873–1910), they noticed that local nobility were emboldened by "pan-Islamic ideas broadcast from Istanbul" and were being egged on by local pro-Ottoman ulema who were largely of Arab origin.[129] Nonetheless, linguistic barriers with Istanbul and the failure of local leaders to enlist Ottoman military support during Aceh's war of independence limited the relationship's actual threat to their interests. The Dutch were still moved to lodge regular diplomatic complaints against the Ottoman consul's zealous Pan-Islamist propaganda.[130] 'Uthman also duly issued a fatwa supporting the colonial army's campaigns, and upon request, he authored a ruling banning the use of Edison's recordable wax cylinders for fatwas. The Dutch rewarded the community with support for mosques and religious schools. When Queen Wilhelmina (1880–1962) took power at the height of the colonial onslaught against Abdülhamid in the Balkans and North Africa, Sayyid 'Uthman composed a prayer for her coronation in anticipation of her replacing the caliph in Dutch Muslims' prayers. In it, he praised the Dutch government for "bringing stability and for allowing Muslims to practice their religion without interference," as well as for the maintenance of mosques and remuneration of Islamic judges. The prayer ended with a supplication that God bless Wilhelmina and give her a long and healthy life. Like his Jerusalem counterpart, Sayyid 'Uthman, he helped European occupiers keep colonial Muslim subjects out of Istanbul's reach, and the Dutch Queen Wilhelmina rewarded him with the Order of the Dutch Lion.

Italy

When the Italian kingdom conquered Eritrea and Libya, the 1912 treaty between Italy and Turkey formed a compromise similar to the one arrived at in French Tunisia. The treaty specified that Istanbul could "appoint a high official to look after the *waqfs* and other local Islamic interests, while Italy shall recognize the spiritual prerogatives of the Sultan-Caliph." Italians "guaranteed complete respect for all Muslim practices, respect for *waqfs* and no interference between the people and the ulema. On the one hand, the Caliph chose a former Minister of Evkaf as his representative in Libya," but like the qadi in British Egypt, "his salary was paid by the Italians." As in the Balkans, this was largely a face-saving measure for Istanbul: Italians were sending Libyan and Eritrean imams for training at a special college in Al-Azhar University in Cairo, out of Ottoman reach. The Italian kingdom also created advisory committees comprising Libyan Muslim notables "appointed by the minister of colonies at the governor's suggestion."[131] Another decree that year "reserved the [waqf] revenues for . . . financial subsidies to the Tripolitania students at al-Azhar" as well as at the Zeitouna in Tunis—both seminaries in the British and French empires, outside the Ottoman influence of Istanbul's reach. The Italian government established a college and hostel there for 150 students "to train students to teach the coming generation in Tripoli the Islamic doctrine, the Arabic tongue, and love of Italy."[132]

A Muslim Vatican?

The aftermath of World War I and the impending collapse of the Ottoman Empire broke the "Caliphate Question" wide open. In religious terms, the British and French conquest into the heart of the Middle East was unlike earlier colonial ventures. Elsewhere, the propping up of new Islamic chieftains to rival Istanbul were limited to bounded Islamic communities—for example, in the Balkans and North Africa, as in India and the East Indies. Recently declassified American, British, and French correspondence captures the diplomatic reasoning behind the final assault on the caliphate.[133] After the French and British victory in World War I, the Allies faced the decision as to whether and how to punish Turkey—in Asia and/or in Europe.[134] Discussions took place after the Paris Peace Conference in 1919, in preparation for the Treaty of Sèvres. The last Ottoman sultan, Mehmed VI (also known as Vahdettin, 1861–1926), had precious little political power during his rule (1918–1922): the Turkish nationalists were about to abolish the sultanate. The British, French, and Italian zones prepared the former empire for further dismemberment.

Having arrived at the citadel gates, the interallied forces faced the question of what to do with the supreme religious leader. It was a situation analogous to one faced by the Italian nationalists occupying Catholic Rome since 1870. Their negotiations paralleled the discussion of the Roman Question, which was also still open. The occupying powers considered contradictory appeals to do away with or preserve the caliphate. They were aware that Istanbul (referred to in discussions by its former name, Constantinople) was a cosmopolitan city composed of Greeks, Jews, Armenians, and hundreds of thousands of non-Turkish Muslims, but they were uncertain of the repercussions that might follow the caliphate's abolition. To explore the possibilities for leveraging the caliphate in their favor, the British held conversations with the French (1919–1920) and later with the sultan (1921–1922) in alliance against the Kemalist nationalists. Both powers had confronted issues related to Islamic rule before, but never at such close range to its source of authority.

Diplomatic archives reveal that the French and British government ministers worried that leaving the caliph in place would leave the mistaken impression that Turks had been on the winning side of World War I. French and British credibility was at stake because they had threatened the sultan-caliph on at least three occasions that expulsion from Europe would be "the price of defeat." According to the French, "if the Sultan was left at Constantinople there would be a danger of the Mahometans saying that the Turks had never been beaten, and that the Allies had not dared to remove him." The British representative chimed in: "and to prove it they would point to the fact that he was still in possession of Constantinople and Adrianople, from which places he continued to exercise his full powers as Khalif."[135]

They hesitated to keep the caliph in place in Istanbul, but there was no consensus on where to move him—the city of Bursa and the island of Malta were among the options being mooted. To settle the Eastern Question, four senior officials representing Paris and London—Prime Minister George Clemenceau of France (1917–1920) and Prime Minister Lloyd George of Great Britain (1916–1922), with their deputies, George Curzon and Pierre Berthelot—debated the finer points of Islamic religious legitimacy. For example, one British diplomat cabled the deputy foreign secretary to ask "whether the Caliphate might not be vested in a purely spiritual personage surrounded by representatives from Islamic countries and maintaining touch with them through representatives of an ostensibly ecclesiastic character in those countries?"[136] And, he added, did this need to be in Istanbul? Lord Curzon argued that:

> The Khalif is Khalif wherever he resides. When he was in Asia Minor centuries ago his residence was "Roum" [Rumelia] to the Eastern world. When he migrated to Europe Byzantium became Roum. If he goes back to Asia, Brusa [Bursa] or Konia [Konya] will become Roum. Constantinople has never had, and has not now, any associations of peculiar sanctity or prestige to the Indian Mohammedan.

Curzon continued:

> Perhaps the Sultan should be established in a sort of Vatican at Constantinople. He should be given Yıldız Kiosk. We might say to him: "Brusa [Bursa] is your capital, but you can have Yıldız Kiosk as a residence and as the religious centre of Islam." He would be allowed to have a small Turkish guard, just as the Pope had his guard in the Vatican. But the Allies would be in occupation of all the surrounding country and of the Golden Horn.

The closest they came to adopting this was when Berthelot presented a lower-grade option "to give Vahdettin a palace at Constantinople, just as the Pope was allowed to live in the Vatican without his being specified as spiritual head of the Roman Catholic religion." The British representative confirmed that the "advantage to us of the Vatican proposal is that it would help us with the Mahometans."

If the religious necessity of staying was uncertain, by contrast, the dangers of leaving the sultan in place were obvious to the French and British leadership when they gathered in late 1919 and early 1920. There were those who saw "great risk . . . in leaving them there to brood over their former greatness."[137] They predicted consequences for the Muslim-majority territories in the colonies: "All the memories and prestige of the past" would be "inevitably trouble [for] the French in Tunis and Algeria [and Italians] at Tripoli no less than on the British in Egypt and India." They also predicted that the caliph "would attempt to divide the Powers" with "constant intrigues, etc."[138] Prime Minister Clemenceau also opposed the plan: It was already "quite bad enough to have one Pope in the West."[139] There was no need to establish a holy place in Constantinople, since "the Mahometans already had Mecca"[140] and besides, in the French estimation, "Constantinople is in [no] way whatsoever a Holy City of Islam."[141]

This led the British to muse: "What is to prevent France from assuming the role of champion of the *new* Islam, and organizing the Moslems of the Western World from Morocco to Syria against the Moslems of the East, i.e., Mesopotamia, Arabia, Persia, Afghanistan, and India?"[142] Regarding the open question of Islamic religious authority, moreover, allowing the sultan-caliph to remain in a "Mahometan Vatican" might set off a spiritual arms race—temporarily averted by the Sykes-Picot Accord—and France would return to grooming the Moroccan sultan as a counterweight. Prime Minister Lloyd George articulated the bottom line: if the British did not actively protect their own interests, another power would assert itself instead. The British worried about Berlin's tightening relationship with Istanbul and assumed that the Germans coveted the city's strategic location on the Bosphorus linking the Black Sea and the Mediterranean. From the British perspective, "complete control of the Straits would not be assured unless Constantinople was in the hands of an inter-allied force." This view was shared by its US ally: the Americans encouraged London to "expel the Turk from Europe once and for all" (see figure 3.7). It was thought that only open-ended Allied occupation would prevent Istanbul from being used by Germany as a gateway to the Middle East.

Nonetheless, the British hesitated to act. The imperial "left brain" in Cairo was swept up with the need to remove the Ottomans and install an Arab caliph. But the "right brain" in imperial India, which was familiar with a larger cross-section of global Islam, was outright hostile to Britain's main Arab options: Hussein bin Ali and Abdulaziz ibn Saud. The British did not pull the trigger on the Ottoman caliphate when they had the chance. German consular assessments from Cairo observed astutely that while "British policies . . . aimed at detaching the Caliphate from the Sultan," if the caliphate were to disappear, the reality of "Indian Muslims' respect for the Sultan as spiritual

FIGURE 3.7. "Disputed Lands of Near East That Hold World Attention Today"
(*Literary Digest Atlas*, 1922)

leader" would put British interests "in great jeopardy," not only in India but in
Egypt and Arabia as well.[143]

The Muslim identity of His Majesty's Empire helped set British priorities
in the region, even as London assessed its realistic options for withdrawal. One
British official pleaded the view to Lloyd George that, for centuries, "Sunni
Muslims had been praying daily for the health of the Caliph in Constantinople: if their spiritual leader was turned out . . . the Muslims of India would be
estranged, probably permanently, from British rule."[144] Finally, in the spring
of 1920, the Western alliance "decided to allow the Turk to remain in Europe,
and at Constantinople to continue the functions of his political and religious
administration."[145]

Prime Minister Lloyd George acknowledged that "since the Mahometans
did, in fact, recognize the Sultan as their spiritual head, he would actually continue to be so whether designated or not." In a moment of comparable lucidity,
British political officer Gertrude L. Bell wrote a cable from Baghdad arguing
against "the early creation even in name of an Arab Administration."[146] She
advised that "a Turkish Administration would have less difficulty asserting
itself in the [Syrian and Mesopotamian] provinces than an Arab government;

the tradition of the past 200 years and the [memory] of the Sultanate and Caliphate are still strong." In Bell's assessment, "the atmosphere of resentment" was "favorable to the spread of Turkish pan-Islamic doctrines." Making clear her lack of confidence in Hussein bin Ali, she added, "We have no effective antidote" to the "spread of Turkish pan-Islamic doctrines."[147] When the opportunity presented itself to issue the coup de grâce to Istanbul as a holy city, His Majesty's Government proved circumspect. Despite brazenly undermining the caliph's religious legitimacy wherever they ruled, France and England balked when they finally had the chance to do something about it. The net effect, unintentionally, was to enhance the Ottoman caliph's spiritual appeal worldwide, even while weakening its political power.

The Pan-Islamic Central Khilafat Committee and International Reaction

How could the British miss the opportunity, in Lord Curzon's words, to settle once and for all the "source of distraction, intrigue, and corruption in European politics" for nearly five centuries?[148] A German periodical wagered that "what is preventing British government from driving Turks out of Europe, and finally replacing the Sultan, is that they discovered that the Caliph has too great political meaning for the entire Mahometan world, 300 million people from Morocco to India," and that the British were intimidated by the Khilafat Committee's transnational activism.[149] The British may have been on their way out of the Middle East, but they had no intention of leaving India, home to 90 million Muslim subjects. Despite their claims of the caliphate's illegitimacy and weakness, they could not destroy it because it was too popular and strong. The Ottoman jihad may have been ineffective, but decades of global Pan-Islamic public diplomacy before that had paid dividends.

Opinion remained broadly favorable to the Ottoman caliph in British India, the legacy of Ottoman envoys' efforts "to convince Indian Muslims that the Caliphate would remain intact" during and after World War I. Great Britain and France had important colonial holdings in India and North Africa—two of the regions where Abdülhamid focused his Pan-Islamic activities.[150] His public diplomacy campaign reaped rewards ten years after he was deposed, in the form of the Khilafa movement.[151] British diplomats did not have to look far to determine "the importance in the Moslem mind of the retention of Constantinople."[152] The Muslim minds came to them because of the caliph's standing.[153]

The height of Indian Muslim mobilization on behalf of the caliphate took place between the Balkan Wars in 1911 and the abolition of the caliphate in 1924. The caliphate's greatest defender and direct heir, the Khilafa movement,

had offices in India and England. It successfully pressured the British government not to expel the caliph from Istanbul. A delegation to London, led by the
Aga Khan in 1912, lobbied on behalf of Ottoman territories under assault by
European armies. The delegation of Indian Muslims traveled to Paris in 1919
to "appear before the Council of Four [at Versailles] to urge that the Sultan
should be left in Constantinople." British officials acknowledged that, "owing
to propaganda or otherwise, the question bulks large in India," where Muslims
were not impressed by British demonstrations that Constantinople has "not
always been the seat of the Caliphate." Moreover, the official continued, it "is
a factor of some weight in Egypt where there is an important Turkish element
among the notables."[154]

Mawlana Hasan was one prominent leader of the khilafa movement. The
author of anti-British fatwas, Hasan held the title Shaykh of India, sided with
Gandhi's Indian nationalist movement, and became a major pro-Ottoman
troublemaker in Indian Islam. "The enemies of Islam . . . strike against and
harm its honor and prestige," Hasan claimed. "Iraq, Palestine and Syria that
were won over by the Prophet's companions and his followers," after great
sacrifice, "[are] again targets of greed of the enemy." After the British sought
his arrest, Hasan traveled to Mecca to request the protection of the Imam of
the Holy Cities. Sharif Hussein bin Ali did not endear himself to Indian Muslims when he "handed over his guest" by arresting and extraditing Hasan. The
British imprisoned Hasan for three years in Malta. The episode worsened Hussein's standing in the eyes of global opinion.[155]

Muslims in the Dutch East Indies also had no reflexive solidarity with Hus-
sein. It appeared that the vast majority of the world's Muslims considered an
independent caliphate to have been part of Muslim heritage at least since the
Abbasid caliphate in Baghdad. During Abdülhamid's reign, Indian Muslims
grew from 40 million to 100 million. They were the overriding reason that the
British could never pull the trigger on the caliphate. The role of the Central
Khilafat Committee (1919) was "to protect temporal and spiritual power of the
Turkish Caliphs."[156] The Hijra/Khilafa movement (1920) originated in the
Northwest Frontier province of India to protest the postwar dismemberment
of the Ottoman Empire. They acted upon a perceived religious duty to leave
dar al harb (a situation of war) and migrate to the dar al Islam (Muslim-ruled
territory). Approximately 18,000 Muslims moved to Afghanistan; thousands
of others left for Anatolia or the Soviet Union.[157] The Central Khilafat Committee supported the Ottoman state and pressured the British to guarantee the
security of the caliph and the holy cities.[158] The scholar Melissa Hafez discovered that Indian Muslims in London published a volume called *The Future of
the Muslim Empire: Turkey* in English and in Ottoman Turkish. The work took
up President Woodrow Wilson's fourteen-point program for world peace, one

of which was that self-determination required no outside involvement, in order to defend the caliphate. For the majority of Indian Muslims who rejected the British foisting Sharif Hussein bin Ali upon them as spiritual leader, the Khilafa movement proved to be the "most powerful expression of the pan-Islamic dimension . . . part of Indo-Muslim identity."[159] They provided Red Crescent medical services to tend to Ottoman troops, while another committee was dedicated to preserving Islam's holy sites in southern Anatolia.[160]

In Turkey, the Committee on Union and Progress set up a new Pan-Islamic association, which the British called "nationalists' [attempt] to enlist support and coordinate efforts of all anti-foreign and disaffected elements in Islamic countries."[161] At around the same time, the Jemiet-ul-Islam announced that a Pan-Islamic Congress would be convened to discuss a potential "League of Moslem Nations, in opposition to the European League of Nations."[162] Martin Kramer describes how the Soviet Union facilitated a meeting between Turkish nationalists and Islamic organizations that sought to reclaim territory from the British and French empires "to promote Islam and thereby weaken the British."[163] The first congress was convened in Moscow in 1921 and was financed by Russia.[164] The transnational aspirations of the committee were out in the open: one Turkish Islamic leader claimed to represent "a union of revolutionary organizations of Morocco, Algeria, Tunisia, Tripoli, Egypt, Arabia and India."[165]

The Fog of Interregnum (1920–1922)

Coming in the midst of English-French-Italian pressures and zones of influence, the nationalist movement of the future Turkish statesman Mustafa Kemal (1881–1938) to evict the foreign occupation gathered steam. The British had grown wary of nationalists' intentions toward northern Syria, Mesopotamia, and Greece, and shortly after the Grand National Assembly was seated, the British occupied Istanbul (March 1920). Kemal's use of a Turkish caliphate and his government's pursuit of Pan-Islamic policies further alarmed the British. An admiral in Constantinople reported to Lord Curzon that "the Pan-Islamic policy . . . actively revived by Mustafa Kemal is said to be to secure the liberation of all Moslem countries from European domination, and to make the Caliphate the basis of a temporal and spiritual union among them." He proceeded to describe a loose alliance among coreligionaries, a kind of Holy Ankaran Empire:

> Each nation will . . . be completely independent, but will be bound to other Moslem countries by offensive and defensive alliances. The ultimate object . . . is to make the Caliphate the recognized guarantor of the independence of

every Moslem country, with the final result of Turkish hegemony over the whole Islamic world.

This was the Vatican-style solution feared by Curzon and Berthelot: one that would provoke "constant intrigues &c.," but one that they had declined to avert. This was expected to pose a fearsome challenge, leaving Europeans helpless to defend their spheres of influence.

> If European Governments complained against interference by Turkey in the affairs of other Moslem nations, the reply could be made that, . . . the Turkish Government . . . had no desire for territorial acquisition of any kind, it was only natural for Moslem countries to aspire towards unity under their Caliph.[166]

Despairing of his future, Vahdettin (Mehmed VI) initiated a rapprochement with the British occupying forces in Istanbul against Kemal and the nationalists in the French zone of central Turkey. Vahdettin communicated with the English representative in increasingly urgent private audiences in 1921 and 1922, signaling that he might request asylum in England. The caliph's strategy against the nationalists was simple: he refused the permanence of the new situation and maintained that the spiritual and political roles of the office were inseparable. "The Sultanate and Caliphate are two complementary parts of a single whole," he explained, "not like the Papacy"—which had been denied its temporal powers and was still under occupation, languishing under the Italian Law of Guarantee.[167] The British ambassador reported the sultan-caliph's suspicions of what nationalists would do next: Ankara's "leaders might set up a Caliph of their own" and force the ulema to perform "a semblance of [the bai'a]; . . . or might [appoint] some junior member of his house . . . or transfer it . . . to some Prince or Sherif or such like." He sensed that the government's impulses were not antireligious per se, but instrumental: it sought official oversight of Islam with diminished operational autonomy to favor the state's goals. The diplomatic cable concluded that, "if the Caliphate were taken Eastward . . . under control [of Ankara], it would become an instrument in the hands of [nationalists] wolves who loved the air of a fog."[168]

Sultan Vahdettin was correct that something was afoot. The Allies inadvertently precipitated the final confrontation between the old empire and the new regime when they sent two invitations for the Lausanne Conference in October 1922. One was expedited to Atatürk in Ankara and the other to Vahdettin in Istanbul. This annoyed Kemal, who scheduled a legislative session to consider abolishing the caliph's remaining *temporal* powers on October 30, 1922.[169] Kemal announced that he would block Vahdettin from attending Lausanne, in the interest of a "totally new Turkey." He also argued

FIGURE 3.8. Vahdettin leaves Yıldız Palace for the last time (1922)

for separating the sultanate from the caliphate and handed the task to a legislative commission. They "will discuss the issue of abolition," he said, and
"maybe some heads will be cut down." Within a week, the sultanate was
abolished, on November 4, 1922. The decapitation rhetoric made Vahdettin
nervous: he was aware that four years earlier the Russian czar, Nicholas II,
had been executed along with the empress, their children, and their servants.
Some lynchings of Ottoman officials—including the future British leader
Boris Johnson's Turkish grandfather—brought this closer to home. Vahdettin applied for British protection, sending a message to Charles Harrington
with a request for help. He fled Yıldız Palace and boarded a British navy
vessel, the *HMS Malaya*, two weeks after the sultanate was abolished (see
figure 3.8). His destination was Mecca, now under Hashemite control, where
he personally submitted his application for asylum as "Vahdettin, Caliph of
the Muslims."[170]

Pan-Islamic Kemalism (1922–1924)

Even after Vahdettin boarded the *HMS Malaya*, Mustafa Kemal gave a lengthy
speech at the Grand National Assembly in which he vigorously justified preserving a symbolic spiritual role for the caliphate. There had been Arab caliphs
in Islamic history without political power, he noted, arguing that the religious
function could be separated from the sultan's temporal rule: "The institution

of the Caliphate will be exalted as the central link of the spirit, the conscience and the faith of the Islamic world."[171]

One observer argued that this was actually "a concession to conservative Moslem opinion in Turkey as well as to the opinion of the Western chancelleries, who pointed out that the caliphate must, in all circumstances, be preserved on account of their sensitive Moslem subjects." The British, in turn, saw the separation of temporal powers as a ruse for nationalists to make a neo-imperial power grab. "It seems probable that Angora [Ankara], in abolishing the Sultanate, hoped to strengthen the religious appeal made to other Moslem countries in the name of the Caliphate" because it was less threatening to their "hard-won independence." After dispatching Vahdettin and abolishing the sultanate, Mustafa Kemal supported an "evolutionary constitution on the model of England, with the Sultan-Caliph as the constitutional head of state." But he gave it a revolutionary flair: the Turkish Grand National Assembly was charged with electing a member of the Ottoman dynasty "who was worthy and fitting in learning and character."[172] The caliphate remained in the House of Osman, but the state chose which member of the house ruled, similar to the Second Constitutional Period, which began in 1909. It was argued that the novel electoral procedure would actually endow the caliph with de facto temporal powers: "The election of such a dignitary by a laic and self-appointed Assembly was an innovation."[173]

The Grand National Assembly elected a new Caliph of the Republic by a wide margin: 114 to 14 in favor of Abdülmecid II Effendi (1868–1944), the oldest imperial prince in line by the Ottoman law of succession. In a perfect illustration of the modern nation-state's fastidiousness, he was elevated to caliph in two steps, like a nineteenth-century bridegroom. First came the *civil* ceremony at Topkapı Palace, followed by a *religious* service at the Fatih Mosque several kilometers away. The Prophet's beard and Caliph Omar's sword and battle standard were handed over in an investiture otherwise "devoid of regal splendor" and with no other members of the *ancien régime* present. A simple red fez betrayed his prerevolutionary origins: he was not permitted to wear the robes and turban of the office.[174] The small group proceeded by automobile—not in the customary horse-drawn carriage—to the ceremony at Fatih Mosque, where the new caliph mounted the imperial throne in civilian clothes to receive prayers glorifying him and "invoking the blessings of Allah upon the Caliph and the Turkish people" as the thirty-eighth successor to Mohammed in the House of Osman. For the first time in history, these prayers were said in Turkish, not Arabic. The nationalists had successfully installed a quiescent caliph who compliantly accepted the loss of temporal power, just as Vahdettin had predicted in his audience with the British ambassador. From November 1922 until March 1924, Caliph Abdülmecid II retained his spiritual powers but forfeited temporal rule to the new Turkish government.

In January 1923, an increasingly desperate Hussein bin Ali hoped to convince the newly elected Abdülmecid to "reverse voluntarily the forced seizure of the Caliphate by Sultan Selim I in 1517 from the last Arab Caliph."[175] Hussein requested British help in "securing the treasures of the Medinan haram"—the Prophet's regalia—which he thought would help "increase his importance in the Muslim world, particularly after the Caliph had been stripped of his temporal authority."[176] Ankara refused, because Abdülmecid II was still making use of them in his capacity as a religious leader.[177] But the request forced a debate about the importance of executing political power as the leader of Islam. Even though Abdülmecid II was next in line, formalizing his succession through the Grand National Assembly was distasteful to hard-liners—or at least served as a good excuse. The French worried what the Muslims of "India, Afghanistan, Egypt, Morocco, Tunis and Algeria will think of a Commander of the Faithful chosen by parliamentary sub-committee." The *Journal des débats* asked: "Will the Grand Sharif of Mecca, the King of Egypt, the Sultan of Morocco and the Amir of Afghanistan recognize the authority of a man who is the simple instrument of his electors? He will be only the shadow of a Caliph"—far short of the Shadow of God. "What would the Catholics of the world think of the election of a Pope by Italian Deputies?" The French held that other Muslim countries should be given a vote because Turkey "is only a little island of 12 million in a sea of 300 million Muslims."[178] King Abdullah of Transjordan declared that Abdülmecid II could not logically be caliph because the government deprived him of "the power to safeguard the interests of the faith of Islam." The caliph needed to have temporal powers to be able to protect Islam.

In Ankara, meanwhile, the young nationalist government was transforming the caliphate into an international instrument of Turkish interests—but now completely free of territorial claims. Atatürk formally replaced the caliph as head of state, becoming president in October 1923, and he proposed a republic to replace the empire. Mustafa Kemal declared that he was depoliticizing Islam once and for all: "The Moslem religion . . . must be freed from its role as a political instrument." According to a British diplomatic cable, Atatürk had long aimed

> to secure the liberation of all Moslem countries from European domination, and to make the Caliphate the basis of a temporal and spiritual union among them. Each nation will, it is suggested, be completely independent, but will be bound to other Moslem countries by alliances. . . . [I]f European Governments complained against interference by Turkey . . . the reply could be made that the Turkish Government . . . had no desire for territorial

acquisition of any kind, it was only natural for Moslem countries to aspire towards unity under their Caliph.[179]

Being aware of the legitimacy problem stemming from Abdülmecid's election by parliament, Mustafa Kemal had the government convene a caliphate congress in Istanbul. One by one, delegations of Afghanis, Syrians, Palestinians, Egyptians, and Indians confirmed their agreement to a future "Istanbul Caliphate." An Ottoman Islamist theorist provided the "religious rationale for a radical secularist" agenda: "Because the issue of Caliphate, rather than being a religious matter, is a worldly issue; the noble Messenger—may God bless him—left it to the [umma], as well as he left—after his death—to the members of the community to choose and define the Caliphate, without any prescription."[180] Atatürk planned for a Muslim congress under his supervision to elect a new caliph and to force Abdülmecid's abdication.

Out of One Caliph, Many

A major opportunity for European intervention arose in the period of limbo between the elimination of the sultanate and the abolition of the caliphate (1922–1924). The Muslim population of the British, French, and Dutch empires had grown to 185 million, while those under the sultan-caliph in Istanbul numbered only 13 million, with no Arab lands remaining in its sway. There was international criticism of the "Kemalists' cavalier treatment of the caliphate" from Cairo.[181] Letters began to arrive in Turkey from the Aga Khan claiming to be the leader of the Sunni sect in India. Messages also came in from the Amir Amanulla of Afghanistan "warning the new Turkey against its apostasy in robbing the Caliphate of its temporal prerogatives." In July 1923, one correspondent wrote that the Aga Khan, a proud British subject, was "honored by King George and recognized by the whole Moslem World as the direct descendant and heir of Muhammad and who may become Caliph."[182]

Hussein bin Ali was drumming up support for his candidacy with a tour of the Transjordan when the Republic of Turkey suddenly abolished the caliphate on March 3, 1924.[183] King Hussein falsely claimed that the Turkish government would back him as the next caliph, and on March 5, 1924, he formally declared a caliphate. Hussein's son Abdullah announced that "the Khalifate has come back to Arabia," and that by doing away with the Ottoman dynasty the Turks had "rendered the greatest possible service to the Arabs." He said that he felt like "sending a telegram thanking Mustafa Kemal." The following day in Damascus, the first Friday prayers were hastily dedicated to King Hussein of Arabia, and at a rally of 15,000 on March 10 the succession was publicly presented for popular approval.

Early reports hinted at discord: "Despite the optimism of British observers," one journalist wrote, "not all of Islam is well disposed toward King Hussein and his two sons, rulers of Mesopotamia and Transjordania" (modern-day Iraq and Jordan).[184] Within two days, an American diplomat cabled to Washington that "some of the leading Moslems" in Damascus still held that the Ottoman heir, Abdülmecid II, was the legitimate caliph. He described "mingled feelings of sorrow and rejoicing." On the one hand, it was "a humiliation of Islam" that entailed "ignominious treatment of the representative of the Prophet" (the caliph in Istanbul). On the other hand, "the precious gift was returned to the Arabs": the British had brought "the Caliphate back to Arabia from where it was stolen by the Turks over four hundred years ago." Thanks to the British, there was finally an Arab descendant of the Prophet with "an independent country and an army."[185]

The tables turned: Ankara warned Turks against pilgrimages to Mecca and Medina. Diplomatic records reveal that only the British thought Hussein bin Ali to be potentially "formidable as the leader of the Arabian nationalist movement."[186] The French, unsurprisingly, "regretted the choice" of Hussein to declare a caliphate because they considered him to be under British influence. An American diplomat wrote that "it is held by many that Abdülmecid is influenced by the French . . . in their efforts to transfer the caliphate to French territory and to counter British influence in Arabia."[187] On March 13, 1924, "the pro-French government in Damascus issued confidential instructions to all mosque preachers to refrain from mentioning King Hussein in their prayers, directing instead that the prayers be dedicated to the *Emir-el-Mu'minin* (i.e. the generic 'commander of the faithful') instead of to King Hussein." The machinations upset enough locals that an armed mob materialized to pressure the preachers of the mosques. Nonetheless, when "preachers said their prayers in the name of King Hussein," the assembled militia "departed, without disorder, to their homes."[188] And like that, Abdülmecid II was no longer caliph in the Levant.

While Britain's Cairo office had supported Hussein, its Indian imperial office was not impressed with the Hashemite (also known as Sharifian) dynasty. Hussein was tepidly received by the vast majority of Britain's Muslim subjects. Officials fished deep for signs of support: British intelligence reported "discussions in Islamic circles" in Switzerland—including "among Turks, many of whom were supporting Hussein [bin Ali] for the Caliphate." Some preferred the status quo, while others took exception to the British "treatment of the Caliph's throne as a prize to bestow" and could not help but notice the non-Muslim hand guiding his victory in the Hejaz. In other words, Hussein failed the elementary test of military independence.[189] The British began to feel much the same after Hussein's conquest of Mecca was "met with resounding silence" and he appeared unable to inspire "a broader Arab uprising." More-over, according to diplomatic cables, Caliph-King Hussein was "anxious to increase the strength of the Arab national movement" by getting rid of the British "mandates in Mesopotamia, Palestine and Syria and [imposing] the complete domination by an Arab Moslem state."[190] This contributed to British fatigue with Hussein and helped shift their preferences to the ruler of Nejd in eastern Arabia, Abdulaziz al Saud. Deaf to protests from Indian Muslims, they allied with Abdulaziz, a military figure whom they had harbored in Kuwait in the early 1900s.[191]

In sum, one British colonial official wrote, "it would be a good thing if Ab-dulaziz did establish himself at Mecca."[192] The British never again openly sup-ported Sharif Hussein after he laid claim to the caliphate, nor did they defend Feisal in Damascus. (He was transferred 1,100 kilometers east to Baghdad.) In fact, they never wholly committed to any of the alternatives to Istanbul's spiri-tual hegemony, for two related reasons. First, the sharif had detractors in Brit-ain's India and Baghdad offices. The Sauds were allied with the fundamentalist Wahhabis who in 1800 destroyed the black stone of the Ka'bah. From a mod-ernization perspective, they unfavorably contrasted with Hussein who had in-stalled the first telephone in Mecca.[193] But diplomats and analysts were uncon-vinced that either Hussein or his sons had the wherewithal to substitute the Ottoman caliph anywhere but the bai'a. Gertrude L. Bell issued a forceful, prescient warning to Whitehall from Baghdad in 1919: "If we raise members of the Sharifian family [Hussein, Faisal, Abdullah] to pre-eminence . . . we shall have before long to support them by force of arms against a formidable group" of several dissidents, of whom she named Abdulaziz first. She added that she doubted whether "the Sharifian family can reckon on popular or democratic support."[194]

After two centuries of unsuccessful Wahhabi revolts, the British expulsion of the Ottomans provided the ultimate opportunity. The India office's "whis-per campaign" against Hussein attempted to belittle him by promoting Abdu-laziz in internal documents. Abdulaziz described Hussein as "trivial and un-stable" and denied that he ever supported Hussein's religious leadership. Scott Anderson writes that Abdulaziz became "British India's man in Arabia, with a close relationship going back to before the war."[195]

At the same time, London was reminded of the Ottoman caliph's loyal fol-lowing in India through the Central Khilafat Committee; it was unwilling to be associated with the institution's actual extinction. They had little desire to rile up a restive minority at the exact moment of Mohandas Gandhi's anticolonial mobilization—or to incur the eternal resentment of future generations of Brit-ish Indian Muslims.[196] Their worries were not confined to India: "In Arabia, Afghanistan, Mesopotamia, Syria and Azerbaijan," a British member of the

TABLE 3.4. Caliph Candidates, 1924–1932

Candidates	Origins/Credentials	Supporters
Hajj Amin al Hussayni	Grand Mufti of Jerusalem	Great Britain, Indian Muslims
Abdülmecid II	Thirty-eighth Ottoman caliph	France, Indian Muslims
Selim I	Eldest son of Abdülhamid II	France
King Idris I	Libya	Self-nominated
Aga Khan	Prophetic descendance	Great Britain, Indian Muslims
King Fuad	Circassian/Albanian	Self-nominated
Sheikh Kattani	Morocco	Senusiyas of Libya

General Staff wrote that "the Caliphate question will always be used as a political weapon when required by their leaders and spokesmen."[197]

British diplomat T. E. Lawrence argued that Medina should not be taken, because "despite posing as Islamic reformists with all the narrow-minded bigotry of the puritan, Abdulaziz and his Wahhabis were hardly representative of Islam." According to Anderson, Lawrence judged that "if it prevailed, we would have in place of the tolerant, rather comfortable Islam of Mecca and Damascus, the fanaticism of Nejd."[198] The fictional portrayal of T. E. Lawrence by actor Peter O'Toole distills the British approach. In one scene of the film, he plays with matches and extinguishes the flame with his fingertips: "The trick, my dear, is to not mind that it hurts." Their real-life pain threshold was lower. Neither Lawrence's nor Gertrude Bell's warning against replacing the House of Osman with the Hashemite dynasty was heeded, nor were her misgivings about Abdulaziz and his austere brand of religion from eastern Arabia. Within months, Hussein was overrun by Abdulaziz and lost his throne. Great Britain sat out the war between its two allies, and the Sauds successfully occupied the Hejaz within a year.

Despite its abject failure, Hussein's assertiveness gave the French an unexpected idea. Two months after the abolition of the caliphate, they were discussing plans to resurrect it. In May 1924, it was reported in a confidential diplomatic note that "the French administration suggested to Syrian Moslem Notables the designation of Selim, the eldest son of Abdülhamid II as Amir (Prince) of Syria," after which "his designation as Caliph would be acceptable," with the enlisted support of Muslims in Tunis and Algeria.[199] Meanwhile, King Fuad (1868–1936) in Cairo thought that "Egypt was better suited to the caliphate than a desert nomad like Hussein . . . because [the Egyptian state] took the lead in religious education and had a vast number of highly educated and intelligent Muslims." Abdulaziz, who seized the two holy cities from Hussein, was one of the few leaders who never put forward a claim to the caliphate; the

TABLE 3.5. Caliphate Conferences, 1924–1931

Year	Location	Conference
1924	Mecca	Pilgrimage Conference: Thwarted ambitions of Sharif Hussein of Mecca
1926	Cairo	General Islamic Congress for the caliphate to unite all of Islam
1926	Mecca	Simultaneous preparation of a rival Muslim congress in Mecca: At odds with the caliphate of India (Ali)
1927	London	Western Islamic Association: Amir Khalid Sheldrake
1931	Jerusalem	General Islamic Conference: 145 participants from Muslim countries, including a representative from the caliphate of India; Turkey and Saudi Arabia did not send delegates

family lacked Qureyshi roots. The leaders of Al-Azhar and the ulema stepped up out of a desire to "end the disarray in to which the Turkish decision [to abolish the caliphate] had cast the Muslim world."[200]

A competition between Cairo and Jerusalem ensued. The Egyptians did not want there to be a theological faculty in Jerusalem to rival Al-Azhar.[201] Jerusalem was used as a showcase to compete with growing Zionist interest in the land. High-profile Pan-Islamic figures, including Muhammad Ali and King Hussein, were buried in Jerusalem in the Haram al-Sharif.[202] It was argued, however, that the Egyptian King Fuad could not be elected caliph because Cairo was under British influence—which impaired "the prime function of the Caliphate: the conduct of a policy of union of all Moslems throughout the world because that would be against British interests."[203]

The French sociologist Louis Massignon, chair of Muslim Sociology at the Collège de France, joined calls for an international caliphate convention to "split the difference" between Arabs and Turks, thus returning the institution to the "consultative principle of its origins."[204] International representatives failed in Jerusalem, Mecca, and once more in Cairo. In the run-up to each instance, rumors flew about the reestablishment of the caliphate and the possible election of the ex-Ottoman caliph Abdülmecid. One meeting was initiated by the Grand Mufti of Jerusalem, who had cultivated a following among Indian Muslims and was thought to be planning to restore Abdülmecid as the Ottoman caliph in Jerusalem.[205] One journalist wondered whether the British would "acquiesce in the establishment of an Islamic headquarters in Jerusalem."[206] There was also "a movement afoot in France to give Caliph Abdülmecid asylum in Tunis, with the prospect of making him commander of the faithful," a move that would have to be "harmonized with the views of the Sultan of Morocco."[207] It coincided with the French effort to raise the king of Morocco as Caliph of the West during the Jerusalem conference (see table 3.5).[208]

The potential candidacy of Abdülmecid maddened the Turkish government, which denounced the congress as reactionary. The last Ottoman Sheikh-ul-Islam issued a fatwa from exile in Cairo to "save the Caliphate from the enemies of Islam."[209] But mobilizing international consensus for a successor was a Sisyphean task. Yearning persisted for an independent caliphate, free of European fingerprints.

Conclusion

The race to destroy Istanbul's religious infrastructure and networks has had untold unintended consequences. After the European conquests there would not again be a consensual Islamic "center" around which to rally. British policies pried their imperial subjects from the Ottoman sphere, diverting Indian and Arab affection for the sultan. But they never successfully reassigned those ties, thus leaving huge numbers of believers who were open to other influences—especially the political Islam movement growing in the 1920s in British-occupied India and Egypt. In the view of those who considered the Hashemites and al-Sauds to be illegitimate or inappropriate successors to the caliphate, Islam's holy cities lost their historic sovereignty when the British helped install those two dynasties in Jerusalem and Mecca and Medina, respectively. This moment was the culmination of a decades-long military and propaganda war to undermine the religious authority of the Ottoman caliph, an effort that the Russian, Austro-Hungarian, and Dutch empires also pursued.

The French and British treatment of the caliphate in the interwar period was characterized by vindictive, short-term thinking familiar from diplomatic negotiations under way in post–World War I Paris, which had been visited by an Indian delegation of pro-caliph Muslims. The Allies' punitive measures in the Treaty of Versailles that ended World War I inadvertently abetted a nationalist fury in western Europe that expanded outwards, swallowing all in its path. The treaties signed by the Ottoman Empire at Sèvres and Lausanne completed an unraveling of a different kind. Those treaties and the League of Nations dismantled the Ottoman Empire, redrew Turkish borders, and legalized the Allied occupation from Amman and Baghdad to Jerusalem, Damascus, and Mecca. As for the legacy of European intervention and imperialism, the Ottoman scholar Bruce Masters concludes that "the caliphate was, with historical hindsight, an exaggerated issue for European imperial planners," who had either a shared "paranoia of a mass Muslim uprising" or an unrealistic optimism that an "alternative Arab claimant would stymie the Ottoman Empire."[210]

Regarding the caliphate, Louis Massignon wrote, "The less the European states intervene in this intra-Muslim *querelle*, the better it will be for everyone."

He reminded Prime Minister Clemenceau that "France was the first to recognize Israel's *droit de cité*"—Jewish temporal, political sovereignty following the Balfour Declaration—"and owes it to itself to take the same initiative for Islam."[211] As one colonial report put it, before the integration of the Balfour Declaration into the Treaty of Sèvres, "the Moslem looks upon Turkey as the embodiment of the temporal power of Islam and does not desire to see Islam reduced to the position of Israel, a religion without temporal status."[212] For the caliph to be properly caliph, he would need to have some sovereign territory— in other words, temporal and spiritual power. In fact, in a manner analogous to the Balfour Declaration recognizing a Jewish homeland in Palestine, Her Majesty's Government had already promised "the independence of Arabia and Caliphate" to the Hashemite dynasty.[213] Despite High Commissioner Henry McMahon's letter to Sharif Hussein bin Ali committing Her Majesty's Government, events overtook McMahon's promises.[214] After Hussein bin Ali proved unviable, the historian David Motadel writes, "Whitehall ignored the protests of its own Muslim subjects about Wahhabi doctrine in order to establish an alliance with the new guardians of the Ka'bah": the Sauds.[215]

A century of European conquest and military interventions enacted a policy of subdividing Islam according to the colonially redrawn map. This process amounted to religious schism-by-international-law. The new sovereign rulers refused the caliph's customary right to independently appoint regional muftis and a local rais-ul-Islam (grand mufti). The decade from World War I to the abolition of the caliphate marked the passage from a relatively coherent global Islamic community under one caliph (1517–1924) to an umma with as many de facto caliphates and muftis as there were Muslim nation-states. Ottoman religious legitimacy was like a centuries-old cistern of refined oil—a repository, reprocessor, and redistributor of inputs from Istanbul, Arabia, India, and Islamic populations around the world. The Europeans burst the cistern, earning the British preeminence on the Sinai Peninsula and Red Sea coast of Arabia for several decades and solidifying their commercial domination of the Gulf, while the French occupied North Africa. They provoked an oil-letting that saturated the regional fabric and left a Muslim world in search of unity and self-government.[216]

European empires forced an international debate about the temporal relevance of Islam itself and proffered self-serving and contradictory answers. Similar to what was taking place in the Ottoman Empire, the new civil and criminal courts imposed by Europeans limited the jurisdiction of shari'ah to matters of "family law, personal status, and religious endowments."[217] But in other respects, European empires stalled processes differentiating Islam and the state. For example, it was the French Republic of Egypt that organized the rule of Al-Azhar sheikhs.[218] And it was the French resident general, not the

Moroccan king, who banned the consumption of alcohol in Morocco, barred non-Muslims from entering mosques, and put in place fines for violating the Ramadan fast. The geopolitical contest, by contrast, raised the question of whether the caliph had to have political sovereignty over Mecca and Medina—or, indeed, whether a caliph was even necessary—and the need for the shari'ah to be incorporated into Westphalian-style national rule of law.[219] The failure to resolve these questions left the caliphate's embers glowing—igniting a slow-burning conflagration in the former colonial periphery.[220] It was in that context that the Muslim Brotherhood (Ikhwan) and Jamaat-i-Tabligh first emerged (in British Egypt and British India), the same time as the Khilafa movement's proposed re-creation of a caliphate, whether in Istanbul, Damascus, or somewhere else.[221] After decolonization, the open conflict gradually spread *inwards* to the European capitals, through labor migration—compounding one irony upon another—in the late twentieth century.

4

The Rise and Fall of Pan-Islam

LATE OTTOMAN RULERS struck a ginger balance between Islamic duty and
the new imperatives of modern statecraft. The sultan-caliph's diplomatic tour
of western Europe in 1867 confronted religious scholars and trip planners with
a logistical paradox. Ottoman law held that the sultan-caliph was sovereign
wherever his feet tread, and foreign military conquest was the only justification to leave the empire. The ulema agonized before reaching a compromise:
bring a supply of soil from Istanbul to London, Paris, Berlin, and Vienna and
periodically apply a layer of dust to the sultan's shoes so that he would never
step off land under his control. Presented with a tangle of religious-political
contradictions, religious scholars found pragmatic ways to slice the knot. Following the European incursions into its former territories, the Ottoman Empire itself was home to an ever-smaller share of global Islam—far less than the
rival empires of Great Britain, China, the Netherlands, and France.[1] Istanbul
experienced an unprecedented level of religious contestation when millions
of former subjects were stranded outside their borders, under the jurisdiction
of European-appointed muftis. Each loss of land tested the caliphs' ability to
withstand jurisdictional separation from a growing share of believers. It fell to
the late nineteenth-century caliphs to apply a layer of Ottoman essence to the
souls of Muslims worldwide, so that they too would always remain symbolically within the Ottoman caliphate.

Between 1830 and 1920, the European empires invaded Ottoman North
Africa, the Balkans, and the Middle East, where they commandeered the economic, political, and religious lives of more than 100 million Muslims, eradicated the old order, and installed their own preferred Islamic hierarchies.[2]
Despite the *political* concessions made in one treaty after another, Istanbul did
not abandon believers abroad. The institutional renaissance of Ottoman Islam
was comparable to the Vatican's sixteenth-century efforts to contain the damage of the Reformation. The initial impulse of Ottoman Pan-Islam was to
stymy the new sectarian authorities in their backyard and to shore up the wavering in its remaining strongholds.[3] Like the Vatican, the Ottoman caliphate

survived its own declining political fortunes thanks to savvy global engagement in the face of defeat.

Ever since Ottoman military preeminence started to decline in the eighteenth century, the sultans in Istanbul had bent their spears into pruning hooks and put in place an international spiritual leadership. Like the pope, another religious-political leader with increasing numbers of stranded flocks, every new border where the caliph acknowledged the loss of political sovereignty eroded the universal nature of his claims. It pushed him closer to the realm of symbolism, and further from temporal rule. The subsequent professionalization and adaptation of religious infrastructure to support cross-border operations were the first steps toward the civilian control of Islam in the modern era.

One step consisted in signing treaties with Russia, Great Britain, Austria, and Italy to officially guarantee Istanbul's postwar role in Muslim spiritual life in these countries, at least on paper. Ottoman advisers successfully negotiated the inclusion of a Friday prayer for the caliph in Turkestan, India, Tunisia, parts of the Balkans, and North Africa and worked to the end of the empire to get this provision codified in international law. They inserted claims into international agreements that affirmed that the empire's chief religious official (Sheikh-ul-Islam) would retain religious authority over Muslim subjects and ensured that the Turkish sultan would continue to be referred to as "Caliph." Nonetheless, as the scholar Jacob Landau writes, a prayer for the caliph was not to be confused with "any desire to be political subjects of the Ottoman government."[4] One and the same person, as "Sultan," recognized military defeat, thereby allowing himself to live and rule another day as "Caliph."

The other step was to build a formidable multinational corporation that employed the largest—and most internationally diverse—cadre of Islamic diplomats, publicists, scholars, and clerics ever assembled. Their institution-building resembled the Roman Catholic response to the Reformation: infrastructure, education, and hierarchy. There was no Ottoman equivalent of the Roman Inquisition to protect against religious schism. But there was sustained bureaucratic, infrastructural, and educational professionalization akin to the agenda set by the Council of Trent, the Holy Congregation of Propaganda Fide, and the Society of Jesus. The Ottomans centralized their administration and transformed religious affairs.[5] They sent imams, built houses of worship, and established seminaries, training institutions, and university faculties across the empire. Istanbul did not encourage the violent uprising of Muslim minorities living outside its borders because it could not offer them military assistance.[6] Instead, it granted asylum to millions of Muslim refugees fleeing repression. This development fueled internal demand for religious services within the empire's borders.

Ottoman rulers proved that a fatally dismembered *political* sultanate could still be a vitally energized *religious* caliphate, operating in a variety of legal and political contexts, and not only under Muslim sovereignty or the rule of religious judges applying shariʾah. At each juncture, the caliphate demonstrated a capacity to distinguish between shrinking political duties and a growing spiritual role. A French diplomat described how the caliph had opened a vista upon hundreds of millions of Muslims "on the three continents of the old world and the archipelago of Oceania."[7] The caliphs mirrored their papal counterparts in Rome, who in moments of political defeat created scores of new dioceses and cardinal positions to cultivate new constituencies and protect old ones from undesired influence. Overseeing the spiritual lives of the faithful at home and abroad became the House of Osman's last stand. The further European armies ventured, the more they galvanized Ottoman leadership of the free Sunni Islamic world that was not yet under European domination. Even after the empire was whittled down to the imperial core of Anatolia and Arabia, Istanbul was the sole regime to resist Western occupation and domination. The caliphate became a metonym for Islamic independence and a magnet for religious solidarity. Soft power, not military might, was its chance to stave off obsolescence in the modernizing world. The late caliphs understood the possibilities of this sympathy and cultivated Pan-Islamic leadership domestically and abroad.

In the grander historical scheme, the institutional subordination of Islam and the state's absorption of religious functions had already been under way for over three centuries. The novelty of nineteenth- and early twentieth-century Pan-Islam, then, lay in its unprecedented institutional expression. The concerted challenges to Ottoman Islamic hegemony—and Istanbul's responses—helped to eliminate the remaining temporal powers of religious authorities. The bureaucratization of Islam during this time of imperial competition catalyzed the differentiation of administrative roles for religious and political authorities—a revolutionary development. Following the Ottoman lead, the British and French empires also subordinated religious authorities to modern state bureaucracies. They centralized waqfs in their territories, placed education under state control, and implemented the rule of law by replacing shariʾah courts with a justice ministry.[8] The Ottoman courts had already ceased to apply the infamous *Hudud* punishments (such as amputation and stoning), including in the conservative Arabian Peninsula. The new civil and criminal courts imposed by Europeans limited the jurisdiction of shariʾah judges, who were educated in public institutions, to cover only matters of personal status, religious endowments, and family law.[9] Collectively, shariʾah judges trained tens of thousands of imams across the Middle East and North Africa, building mosques and establishing new religious authorities with local reference points, under a new rule of law.[10]

Entire swaths of new Ottoman legal code were cribbed from French commercial and maritime law. Nationalist leaders from the faction of Young Turks applied additional pressure that shifted the caliphate's focus away from hard politics and toward the spiritual realm. They started by placing the imperial ulema in service of the state's secular arm, and they completed the transfer of temporal powers to the nonreligious side of the house when they abolished the sultanate.

There is scholarly consensus about the Ottoman Empire's protracted *political-military* decline, but the last caliphate's *spiritual* viability and institutional legacy are underappreciated. The historian Adeeb Khalid writes that "Ottoman Islam occupies a black hole in the historiography of modern Muslim thought"—that is, the experts are uncertain which laws apply.[11] Pan-Islam was not taken seriously because it was a grandiose institution closely associated with a political regime in decline. That universe of Islamic scholarship and piety is dismissed as the quixotic attempts of propagandists to paper over a disintegrating empire—or as power-hungry rulers who usurped the role of ulema and raided the coffers of religious foundations (*evkaf*).

The caliphs can be accused of religious manipulation but not neglect. The Ottoman state dedicated a growing share of its budget to projecting a global *ritual* influence through religious education and the governance of Islamic prayer. The caliphate's spiritual borders already far exceeded its jurisdictional reach. At home and abroad, the caliph's imperial prerogatives became merely *symbolic*. Abdülhamid wrote in his memoirs that even if the Europeans "succeeded in destroying our temporal power, our spiritual power can never be eliminated."[12] His policies reinforced the principle of spiritual leadership without political sovereignty. The reorganization of the Evkaf Ministry and the professionalization of religious personnel provide a glimpse of coexistence with non-Islamic government within and across national borders.[13]

My original archival research and new historical accounts provide evidence that compel a reassessment of Ottoman religion policies.[14] Traditional authorities were politically defeated, but this bred a division of labor—civilian oversight, in other words—and not just one-sided domination. Evidence I gathered in Ottoman archives demonstrates how the nineteenth-century sultan-caliphs augmented support for traditional religious institutions.[15] As the Ottoman historian Kemal Karpat put it, the "stark reality of European imperial ambitions" shook off earlier "indifference" to the roles of caliph.[16] They improved the religious infrastructure of the empire, afforded wider access to religious services, and imposed more professionalism—and less cronyism—within the ulema. The Ottoman ulema issued hundreds of fatwas monthly to reconcile Islamic piety with the realities of modernizing society. The caliph continued to support the

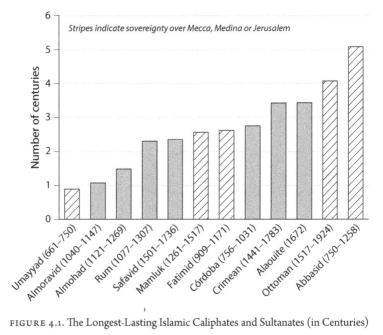

FIGURE 4.1. The Longest-Lasting Islamic Caliphates and Sultanates (in Centuries)

maintenance of Islamic holy sites and extended Ottoman spiritual leadership over nearly the entire Muslim world. This set of policies gave concrete expression to the empire as an international Islamic service provider in tune with the secular rule of law. By virtue of their longevity, bureaucratic expanse, and geographic breadth, the Ottomans dominate the annals of historic caliphates (see figure 4.1).

God's Shadow on Earth

In Ottoman lore, the insignia of the caliphate—Muhammad's cloak, hair from his beard, and the sword reputed to belong to the first caliph, Omar—were surrendered by Abbasid rulers after the sixteenth-century conquest of Baghdad. Ottoman rulers did not make use of the reliquary for three centuries—that is, not until the loss of Egypt (1819) and Algeria (1830) to British and French influence. Like Rome's doubling down on the Church's legitimacy with baroque cathedrals, saints, miracles, and relics, Istanbul made use of bells and whistles to defend the caliph's legitimacy. Rather than being pulled in the austere Wahhabi direction, the nineteenth-century caliphs conjured majestic mosques and doled out pomp and ceremony. Monumental houses of worship were built for public admiration, including Istanbul's Nusretiye Mosque (1826) and Ortaköy Mosque (1853) and Aksarayda Valide Mosque (1871). Caliphs went so far as to recognize the miracles of local holy figures and canonized them as saints—anathema to Wahhabis—in addition to augmenting their own history with the stuff of legend. In an alliance with the Iranian shah, another target of Wahhabi puritanical rage, Sultan Mahmud II (1785–1839) even agreed to share the title of Caliph (1823).[17] Mahmud II was the first to universalize the traditional *bai'a* of allegiance to the caliph as an opening benediction at Friday prayer across the empire. He also had the mosques and waqfs in Arab lands fitted with Arabic-language plaques commemorating the Holy Name of the Caliph.

Enactments of Ottoman continuity with a distinguished past were intended to compensate for the regime's real and perceived shortcomings. The military motif of the caliphate's leadership was crucial to resisting sectarian challenges and maintaining religious legitimacy. Mahmud arranged to be ceremonially girt with Omar's Sword in the fifteenth-century Eyüp Sultan Mosque in Istanbul. He assumed the title of Ghazi (holy warrior), and referred to his troops as Trained Victorious Soldiers of Muhammad.[18] In reality, the cavalry was never on its way—not to Tunisia, nor Sumatra, Egypt, or India, where Muslims had all appealed for military aid.[19] Instead, what detractors derided as Ottoman apocrypha are a classic illustration of what the historian Eric Hobsbawm has called the "invention of tradition."[20] The Ottoman historian Selim Deringil describes the usage of "manifest official fiction" as "an ancient tradition in Islamic court panegyrics."[21] Beforehand, no Ottoman sultan made much of the caliph title after it was seized in Baghdad in 1517.[22] Even personally pious sultans wore the mantle lightly.

Article 3 of the 1876 constitution set the stage for the rule of Sultan Abdülhamid II (1876–1909). It declared that "The Exalted Ottoman Sultanate Possesses the great Islamic Caliphate" and named the sultan the Protector of Islam.[23] Abdülhamid instructed that his title of Commander of the Faithful precede his status as Sovereign of the Osmans.[24] He also changed the name of Istanbul, on coins, to "Abode of the High Caliph." A sketch of the proposed bridge spanning the Bosphorus captures the atmosphere (see figure 4.2). The bridge was never built, but Abdülhamid did the most of anyone to upgrade religious infrastructure, including the Hamidian Star Mosque (Yıldız Hamidiye, 1886) on his new palace grounds (see figure 4.3). It was the first mosque to be named for a living sultan in 270 years—in other words, the first since the generation of warriors who conquered Constantinople.[25] The anniversary of his accession to the throne became a public holiday celebrated on the scale of the Prophet's birthday.[26] Abdülhamid II gave his private life "an appearance of devout austerity" and observed Islam with "discreet ostentation."[27]

FIGURE 4.2. Proposed Kandilli-Rumelihisarı Bridge, Istanbul (1900)

FIGURE 4.3. Hamidiye Mosque and Minaret in Yıldız, Istanbul (1890)

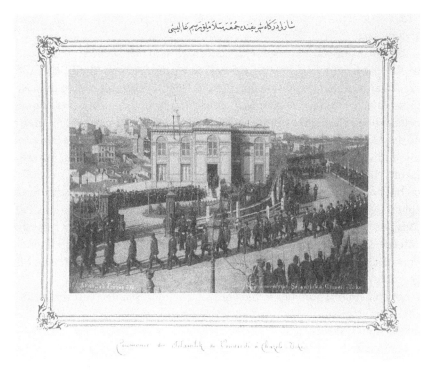

شارلردكاه شريفنده جمعه سلام ملقىريم عاليبى

FIGURE 4.4. Friday Selamlık procession on Yıldız Palace grounds, Istanbul (1890)

Selamlik

Another criterion for serving as caliph of all Muslims was to act as the Imam Salat, ceremonially leading Friday prayers (*Cuma selamligi*). Those were the sultan's only public appearances aside from special occasions like the end of Ramadan. The ritual was central to affirm the reigning consensus for Abdülhamid. The caliph proceeded to his eponymous mosque in a French-made carriage, "between a wall of steel" (see figure 4.4).[28] Observers described the columns of "Albanian house guards in livery, their spears glinting in the sun, who escorted the imperial [entourage] while a military band struck up the *Hamidiye*, the musical salute to the Sultan," and foreign dignitaries watched from a dais.[29] The carriage ride to visit the Holy Relics mausoleum at Topkapı was even more elaborate: "300 carriages bearing his harem and entourage traveling on roads 'covered with a thick white sand.'"[30] As Deringil puts it, Abdülhamid "pushed the 'holy personage' title further than any of his predecessors."[31] The Yıldız Hamidiye Mosque, for example, included not only more ceremonial space than prayer space but also a supplemental two-story structure with a special platform for the sultan that "went beyond the prerequisites of architecture."[32]

Ottoman popular Islam stood in stark contrast to the ascetic Wahhabi sect, which had recently allied with al Sauds in eastern Arabia. The British and French argued that the Ottomans could not legitimately rule Mecca because they were not Arab. The Osmanlı dynasty lacked Qureyshi roots, which British-allied Hashemites happened to satisfy. That line of argumentation annoyed Muslim populations that had never been Ottoman subjects but now found themselves under British, French, Dutch, or Italian colonial government.[33] Indian and Indonesian Muslims represented a major audience for Istanbul precisely because their lack of a shared ethnic background with Arab contenders added to their potential solidarity with the "Caliph of (all) the Muslims" (see figure 4.5).[34] While Abdülhamid was not of Arab or Qureyshi descent, Istanbul had a cheeky retort to the European obsession with bloodlines. The *State Almanac* made note of something better: he could trace his genealogy, by way of Noah, all the way to Adam and Eve.[35]

Abdülhamid II communicated with Islamic motifs aimed at several audiences simultaneously. His sense of "showmanship was specifically designed for the non-Turkish element" abroad.[36] The historian Caesar Farah describes a receptive audience among Muslims worldwide: "Since the majority of Muslims were forced to pledge allegiance to their Christian European overlords," Farah writes, "Muslim sentiment [spontaneously] gravitated . . . towards the Caliph."[37] In the case of Austria-Hungary, Hamza Karčić writes, "the spiritual bonds between Bosnian Muslims and their Caliph in Istanbul were not completely severed by the occupation of Bosnia."[38] Abdülhamid also found supporters in India, where the Khilafa movement later inspired migration and foreign fighters, and in parts of Syria, Palestine, North Africa, and even the East Indies and South Africa. Early on, Indian pamphleteers backed the sultan's claims that "the sovereign of the Turks is looked upon by the vast majority of Her [Majesty's] Muhammedan subjects as the vice-regent of the Prophet, and the recognized religious head of forty millions of Her subjects."[39]

Well-timed archaeological discoveries also aided the Ottoman legitimacy war against Arab challengers. One memorable episode of stagecraft as statecraft involved the miraculous uncovering in northern Iraq of an original pair of the Prophet Muhammed's sandals. The footwear was found among the possessions of a dervish who descended from the Abbasids—providing a direct link to the last Arab caliphs. A caravan carried the Prophet's sandals from Diyarbakir in the southeast all the way to Topkapı Palace to join the Prophet's battle standard and beard hairs. The festive eleven-day journey was followed breathlessly in the press as the sandals made their way across Anatolia and finally to Istanbul by boat. It was reported that miracles occurred along the way:

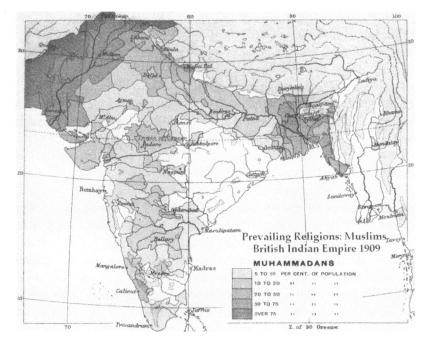

FIGURE 4.5. "Prevailing Religions: Muslims: British Indian Empire (1909)"

"The River of Amasya stood still when the carriage carrying the sandals crossed a bridge."[40] A public holiday was proclaimed on the day they arrived in Istanbul. Awaiting the sandals upon a dais were the grand vizier, the Council of State, ministers, representatives of the ulema, and other state officers. "The Grand Vizier solemnly placed the box containing the sandals upon a special carriage driven by four horses. Fifty men carrying torches and 50 special guards all praying and calling 'Ellah-ü Ekber.'" After Friday prayers, the sultan had a private audience with the sandals.

Technology

The caliphs did not rest on their relics and ceremony, however. Another way around European-controlled borders and waters was to go under and over them with a new telecommunications cable—including one along the floor of the Red Sea. Unlike their papal contemporaries, mid-nineteenth-century Ottoman sultans were early adopters of printing, postal, and telegraph services and other new media of the time. Steamships, the telegraph, photography, and passenger rail travel all enhanced Istanbul's virtual and physical connections with the far reaches of the empire. They deployed Samuel F. B. Morse's telegraph and Thomas Edison's wax cylinders to broadcast fatwas. The telegraph allowed authorities to communicate ceremonial undertakings and to receive reports from (and govern) the farther-flung provinces and to strengthen their connection to the Hejaz. The Red Sea cable reached the cities of Jedda and Mecca and plugged Istanbul into local goings-on: "The Sharifs could not act in secret."[41] It also helped support the complicated bureaucracy developing along the Red Sea coast in Medina, Jedda, Mecca, and Taif. The wireless telegraph brought minute-by-minute coverage of the opening session of a new Ottoman parliament to the farthest corners of the empire, the first time such events were broadcast with live commentary.

The regime also made avid use of a Muslim press and readership, which became a "vector for the aspirations and claims of the Islamic world," from Russia, Afghanistan, and India to Egypt and North Africa.[42] Abdülhamid did not merely publish and distribute Ottoman editions of the Prophet's sayings (*hadiths*) and the Qur'an. Pro-Ottoman pamphlets appeared under the byline of the local Ottoman-appointed rais (grand mufti), or Sheikh-ul-Islam. It was customary for newspapers to refer to Abdülhamid as the Shadow of God on Earth and the Father of All Islam, as well as "Patron of Justice, Learning, Literature, Art, War, &c."—what one contemporary author called "The transposition of Jihad from the battlefield to the broadsheet." [43] Low-cost photographic printing allowed believers of modest means to own a portrait of their caliph (see figure 4.6). An incredulous British diplomat cabled home in 1908: "To pious Moslems inside and outside of Turkey," the "long string of high-sounding names . . . have a ring of reality and serve to magnify the spiritual prestige of Abdul Hamid, the Victorious, the Lord of the two Continents and two Oceans, &c."[44]

Sacred Custodianship

Another criterion for the authority of the caliphate was custodianship of Mecca and Medina—the single most effective tool to reinforce Istanbul's spiritual authority. When the sharif of Mecca offered his allegiance to the empire centuries earlier, he gave the Ottoman sultan "the keys of Mecca and Medina and transferred to him the custodianship of the Sacred Cities."[45] No sultan-caliph ever returned there, but because of the sacred, sentimental, and historical connection to the Prophet and his entourage, sovereignty over the Hejaz was the "jewel in the crown of the exalted Caliphate."[46] Taking good care of the holy cities was a sure way into the heart of the global Muslim community (umma). The "pulpits of Mecca and Hejaz have the supremacy over all pulpits of the world," as one British diplomatic memorandum read. In other words, the colonial rulers believed that "when [sermons] mention anyone as the

FIGURE 4.6. Portrait of Sultan Abdülhamid II (1890)

Caliph all the people must recognize him."[47] Mahmud II was the first sultan to ceremonially retake possession of the keys of the holy Ka'bah and to resuscitate the title of custodian of the two sacred cities of Mecca and Medina— Khadim-ü 'l-Harameyn—three centuries after Sultan Selim.[48]

After Mahmud came Sultan Abdülmecid I (1839–1876), in the late 1850s, who subsidized 98 percent of the Hejaz's overall budget and exempted it from tax and conscription requirements. He also spared it from Istanbul's centralization of the judiciary everywhere else in the empire.[49] Sultan Abdülmecid reconstructed the Prophet's mosque in Medina (1860) and renovated the house where the Prophet lived with his wife Aisha.[50] By controlling Mecca and Medina, Ottomans retained ownership of the hajj—one of the five religious requirements of every able-bodied Muslim. The pilgrimage to Mecca gave them the chance to reach Muslims from the world over every year. By 1880, the two most-represented nationalities among the 93,250 annual pilgrims were British and Dutch subjects.[51]

The sultan's annual shipment of gifts to Mecca and Medina—a supplement to budgetary appropriations—was borne by a caravan of camels "in gilded livery" and sent off by cheering crowds. The caliphate and the office of Sheikh-ul-Islam became a spiritual lighthouse to guide an Islamic community in distress while promoting a stark alternative to Wahhabism. The annual Ottoman hajj delegation pitched two ceremonial tents on the hills of Arafat and Mina, where the caliph's annual message was pronounced. A memorandum to government ministers asserted that custodianship of Khadim-ü'l-Harameyn constituted one of the sultan's four pillars of the state.[52] Fostering Islam in its birthplace was a winning strategy, and the nineteenth-century caliphs would restore Islam's holiest sites, Mecca, Medina, and Jerusalem, including the redecoration and gilding of the Dome of the Rock mosque in Jerusalem. Mahmud's successors expanded upon his gestures and asserted custodianship of *all* Islamic holy sites, whether Sufi, Sunni, Salafi, or Shi'a. The scope of Ottoman ambitions represented the umma in all its diversity and complexity. That included repairing and maintaining not only the Ka'bah (see figure 4.7) and the mosques in Medina, but also the shrines in the Shi'a-majority cities of Karbala and Najaf, including the family tombs of the fourth caliph, Ali, who is especially revered by Alevis.[53] They restored the tombs of three companions of the Prophet and those of saints in southern Iraq.[54]

The most audacious Pan-Islamic public works project was the construction of the Hejaz Railroad, a holy railway linking central Ottoman lands to the pilgrimage cities of Arabia. Mass transportation options already linked the world's Muslim population to some of the empire's religiously and economically important cities. The caliph's embrace of rail contrasted with the views of his colleague in Rome: the pope had called railroads *chemins d'enfer*, making a French pun on the rhyme of the words for "hell" and "steel." In total, Abdülhamid nearly quadrupled the length of imperial railroads (see figure 4.8). There were 6,500 kilometers of rail when he took office (1876), 14,395 kilometers twenty years later, and 23,675 kilometers by the time he left office in 1909.[55] They conveyed the umma to the empire in modern railcars to admire the renovated attractions and pilgrimage sites. Abdülhamid announced that only funds raised from fellow Muslims would be used to lay the rails, limiting European assistance to German engineering advice. The first stretch of rail was ceremonially laid during the sultan's jubilee celebrations.[56] European diplomats "watched warily as Sultan Abdülhamid, in a brilliant political stroke, initiated the building of the Hejaz Railway," Leon Carl Brown writes. The plan was to extend the rail lines started at Damascus all the way to Mecca and Medina.[57]

FIGURE 4.7. The Ka'bah, Mecca (1900)

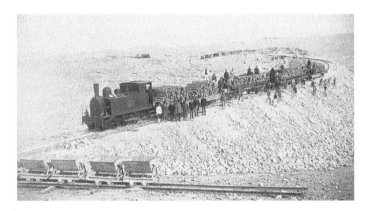

FIGURE 4.8. Hejaz Railroad, Jordan (1902)

While the railroad was a hugely successful branding exercise by Abdülha-mid, it was no mere vanity project. It verified Ottoman claims upon the caliph-ate while easing the fulfillment of hajj by Muslims in Asia and the Indian sub-continent.[58] Rapid transit reduced a four-month desert journey to a few days. It was billed as a geographical "hyphenation" (*trait d'union*) connecting the near eastern provinces and bringing "Muslims of Asia in proximity to their caliph."[59] It also conveniently allowed the Muslims of Siberia and the Russian Empire to get closer to the vital centers of Ottoman Islam—Damascus, Bursa, Istanbul, Medina. Hercule Diamontopulo wrote that "previously, one had to exert great efforts and rely on the aid of Bedouin tribes to penetrate the vast areas practically unknown [to outsiders] before rail."[60] Eight years later came the inauguration of the line from Damascus to Medina—a total of 1,448 kilometers. Intended to reach Mecca, the railroad never got past Medina. During the Second Constitutional Period (1909–1913), financial support for the project dried up. The rails were targeted for destruction during the Arab Revolt of 1916, in part because they diverted lucrative traffic from the British-controlled Suez Canal.

Secularization through Bureaucratization

These Islam-oriented public policies were not entirely novel: they signaled the strategic revival of an earlier Ottoman tradition. The codification of Islamic law and the formation of the Ottoman legal establishment—including the standardization of madrassa curriculum—had been taking place since the sixteenth century.[61] Over time, the religious establishment was subordinated to the sultanate in what was known as the Ottoman-Islamic synthesis. Mehmed II (1432–1481), who conquered Constantinople, decreed that one specific legal school of Sunni Islam (*madhab*) would be followed: the Hanafi school of Islamic law. Generations of ulema served as salaried bureaucrats in medieval Damascus and incorporated their scholarly organization into the state.[62] Historians have identified the period of the Second Empire (1580–1826) as formative in the process known as confessionalization and the experience of subordination to new political institutions.[63] The process of the First Imperial Bureaucratization—what scholars call *Sunnitization*—paralleled the Counter-Reformation taking place several thousand kilometers to the west. Suleyman the Magnificent (1520–1566) tried and failed to centralize religious education but succeeded in creating the Sheikh-ul-Islam position and Islamic catechism-style religious manuals were introduced for the lay public.[64] It was around this time that Ottoman theology first elaborated the caliphate as an enduring ideal.[65] Nonetheless, even the standardized Islamic apparatus was not monolithic.[66] Civil and criminal law not only followed the principles of the Hanafi school but also borrowed from other legal schools and was applied to Muslims and non-Muslims alike.[67] This was done in consideration of the Hanbali bastions in Baghdad and Damascus, and in deference to the preferences of the Sheikh-ul-Islam.[68]

Other aspects of the nineteenth-century caliphs' leadership roles at home and abroad, by contrast, were new. Historically, internal legitimacy always derived from an independent ulema. In extreme cases in past centuries, displeased ulema had the power to depose sultans.[69] The new policies reversed those roles and applied a bureaucratic framework to religious life. It was only beginning with Sultans Mahmud II (1808–1839) and Abdülmecid I (1839–1876) that the Ottoman state achieved direct control over existing religious structures. The period had much in common with revolutionary France and nationalist Italy, both of which also dissolved religious corporations (in 1791 and 1861). First, Mahmud nationalized the equivalent of "church lands"—the religious foundations of the empire—and created the Evkaf Ministry (1826). In 1839, he absorbed the Sheikh-ul-Islam and all institutional personnel into the expanding civil bureaucracy, ending that office's history as an independent entity.[70] Bringing the country's principal cleric into the Council of Ministers could be seen as elevating religion to an affair of state, but it was a move of containment. The state-ification eliminated the counterpower of the ulema by taking over their judicial and educational activities.[71] According to the historian Halil Inalcik, the Ottoman state went "farther than any previous Islamic state in asserting the independence of state affairs and public law vis-à-vis the religious law."[72] As a matter of practice, the sultan named the Sheikh-ul-Islam with only the "nominal concurrence of the Ulema."[73] The Sheikh-ul-Islam became a mere government employee, financially dependent on the state. Three office-holders who exceeded their mandate were executed for dabbling in politics.[74] The "conflict between state law and the shariʾa," Inalcik writes, "overlaid a political social struggle among the bureaucracy, the *ulema* and the ruling military class."

This marked the full subordination of religious affairs under civilian rule for the first time and the Muslim world's first bureaucratized clergy.[75] At the start, the Evkaf Ministry had a poor reputation. Characterized as "generally incompetent and thoroughly corrupt," provincial officials were said to have "laid their greedy hands" on nearly all religious foundations and allowed mosques to fall into ruin.[76] Within a decade of its creation, the ministry had gained control over most of the evkaf, and the number of independently held foundations fell from hundreds of thousands to around 1,000.[77] Many scholars have concluded that nationalization destroyed the evkaf system, centralizing all revenues while setting aside only 10 to 15 percent of these funds for religious activities.[78] Western analysts painted a similarly dire picture at the time: "The reformers, who are uprooting religion . . . have utterly destroyed the independence of the Turkish Church."[79] One contemporary observer described the status of imams as "subordinate to the civil authorities, who exercise over them the power of diocesans."[80] The economic historian Timur Kuran writes that the Evkaf Ministry's revenues were squandered on imperial parades, new palaces, and foreign debt. He views the nationalization of evkaf as a major reason for what he calls the "Great Divergence" in Ottoman development.[81]

Recent work by Ottoman historians has added nuance to this view. One side effect of the ulema's hierarchical positions dependence on state authorizations was the "maintaining of high standards and credentials."[82] It is inaccurate to portray Pan-Islam as a project built on the backs of a docile, co-opted ulema. Birol Başkan, for example, found evidence of ample employment "opportunities for religious scholars within new educational establishments."[83] Murat Akgündüz discovered "regular financial contributions and distribution of *evkaf* revenue by the state to support seminaries and religious scholars."[84] The state continued to employ a large number of ulema as teachers in the new schools.[85] As Serif Mardin has argued, the ulema's "swift displacement" meant that "religion became more of a field of specialization than a pervasive social function" and, as such, provided intellectual space to examine "the role of religion in society."[86]

Nevertheless, there was great variation in the lived experience of Islamic subject-hood in the Ottoman Empire administration, which was not exactly the same as a worldwide network of dioceses and seminaries. Although a major administrative centralization, from easternmost Anatolia to the Fertile Crescent, had been launched, religious localism often prevailed—for example, in Palestine, Syria, and Tunisia, where Ottomans did not customarily send their own muftis to work. There were also Sunni revivalist movements in the scholarly hubs of Baghdad and Damascus, but their efforts seldom reached beyond the traditional imperial borders. Other traditions—such as Sufi and anti-Sufi—also coexisted.[87] Although the ulema were the "guardians of scriptural authority," and while they agreed upon the Sunna (and in their denunciation of Shi'ism and other heterodoxies), they were frequently at odds with one another.

In response, Shail Marayam writes, sultans were flexible administrators: they employed a "variety of administrative patterns" in the provinces that allowed quasi-independent local rulers where appropriate.[88] These accommodations furthered their perpetual pursuit of what historian Karen Barkey calls "the art of the possible and the negotiation of difference between the center and political periphery in religious affairs."[89] The codification of shari'ah based on Hanafi law produced the standardized *Mejelle* code covering "mainly economic and procedural matters."[90] Judges and legal training also took into account Hanbali and Maliki traditions in Arabia and North Africa. Ottomans exercised a light touch in Tunisia, a vassal state with wide latitude for self-government where the bey nominated his own muftis, qadis,

sheikhs, and imams.[91] Despite the formal predominance of Hanafi jurisprudence, it was the task of Ottoman judges "to establish coherence and harmony and avoid handing down contradictory judgments."[92] For diplomatic
reasons, the Islamic framework they propagated following the Tanzimat reforms (1839–1871) were influenced by European Enlightenment ideas, such
as religious toleration. During its brief but groundbreaking tenure, the late
Ottoman religious hierarchy and bureaucracy interacted with modernizers
and traditionalists—and with a wide range of Islamist, Sufi, Shi'a, Maliki, and
Hanbali adherents.

Infrastructure, Education, Hierarchy

The institutional response to non-Muslim rule over Muslim minorities and
the arrival of Christian missionaries reciprocated and mimicked European
influence. The Ottoman strategy consisted mainly of eliminating administrative and religious vacuums. The government laid down religious infrastructure, education, and hierarchy across the empire where none had existed in
standardized form.[93] With the extension of registries and central control
over the provinces, every new settlement was mandated to have a religious
school, a mosque, and a public water well—usually an imperial waqf. This was
a natural extension of Istanbul's effort "to restore its authority over the provinces, and to produce a reformed and centralized system of provincial
administration."[94]

   The bureaucracy grew dramatically during the nineteenth century, with
multiple overarching sources of religious authority, including the Ilmiyye
(ulema), the Sufis, and the sultan.[95] Mahmud II built an official residence,
Bab el Fetvahane, for the new state council in charge of publishing fatwas
(see figure 4.9).[96] There were eleven kinds of madrassas teaching holy law,
including regional variants. On a daily basis, subjects of the Ottoman shari'ah
courts encountered the thousands of Istanbul-trained judges (qadis)—often
via Arabic interpreters—and their deputies (naïbs), who ruled on the personal status questions that fell under shari'ah law.[97] Observers reported in
the mid-1890s that it seemed "at every mosque there is an Imam"—in other
words, there were around 11,600 imam-preachers on the payroll.[98] Above the
rank of imam-preachers were a roughly equal number of *muderris* (1,000),
above whom ranked three levels of muftis, qadis, and naïbs at the Vilayet,
Sancak, and Kaza levels of Ottoman administration (see table 4.1).[99] Muder-
rises lectured on religious obligations and were members of the ulema.[100]
Muftis issued fatwas and legal rulings, but were not physically present in all
of the empire's provinces.[101]

FIGURE 4.9. Bab el Fetvahane, Istanbul (1904)

Territorial losses in wars against European powers were partly compensated, demographically speaking, by receiving repeated expellee and refugee flows from the Russian Empire into Istanbul and across Anatolia. The Ottoman Refugee Code of 1857 encouraged population transfers, and arriving families received public land exempt from tax or military service.[102] More than 5 million Muslim refugees arrived between 1856 and 1914, including 1 million in a three-month period in 1877 (see figure 4.10).[103] Together with the loss of land, this dramatically increased the proportion of Muslims in the Ottoman Empire (see figure 4.11).[104] The sultans, though suspicious of Russian-speaking refugees, adopted assimilative policies, aiming to foster loyal and useful subjects.[105] New regulations called for a mullah and a mud-walled mosque in each village populated by refugees.[106] For the duration of the 1880s, authorities imposed obligatory prayer and religious education for refugee children. The construction of permanent mosques, schools, and military barracks followed.

Assimilation policy targeted the entire imperial population, not just newly arrived refugees. From all sides of—and within—the empire's shrinking bor-

TABLE 4.1. The Institutions of Ottoman Islam

Statutory Personnel and Institutions	Number (estimated)
Caliph	1
Sheikh-ul-Islam	1
Sheikhs*	5
Muderris*/teachers	1,000
Grand mufti*	1
Chief Qadi*/Judge	1
Qadis*/judges and muftis*	3,500
Naïbs/deputy judges	2,000
Imams/preachers	11,000
Muezzins/hafizlers	160,000
Madrassa students	12,000
Mosques	50,000
Qur'an schools	1,700
Waqfs	100,000–300,000
*Part of ulema/Ilmiyye	

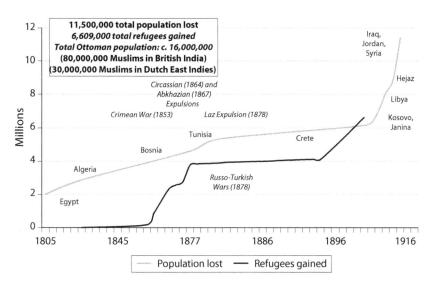

FIGURE 4.10. Ottoman Populations Lost and Muslim Refugees Gained, 1805–1920

ders, threats were perceived to emanate from nationalists, Russian-speaking refugees, Islamists, and foreign missionaries and were only amplified by an "underlying current of doubt about the loyalty" of non-Turkish Muslims.[107] In an effort to retain control over Palestine, Transjordan, Iraq, Aleppo, Beirut, and the Hejaz, the nineteenth-century caliphs pioneered modern "communal

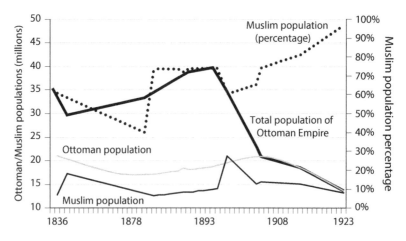

FIGURE 4.11. The Unintended Islamization of the Ottoman Empire, 1836–1923

worship, religious instruction, and publication of sacred texts" (see table 4.2). The message was tweaked only slightly for each constituency: current residents, former subjects, and Muslims under European rule. The Ottoman state school system was extended to Transjordan, and Abdülhamid II posted village preachers (köy imamlari) to every rural Syrian town where Muslim children attended foreign-run schools.[108] The provinces were dotted with uniform mosques (see figure 4.12). Between 1895 and 1915, the state restored and renovated mosques up and down the border. The Evkaf Ministry financed the construction of new "mosques for immigrants, paid for imams sent to teach Islam to various tribes, and other religious activities."[109] The ministry performed repairs—and affixed the sultan's name on a plaque—on 4,000 mosques, madrassas, lodges, graves, and shrines from Istanbul to Jerusalem and Benghazi to Salonica.

Rising Spending

The empire had prior experience keeping religious rivals at bay. The central government historically encouraged local ulema to enforce Sunni practices centuries earlier, for example, by establishing Friday mosques in sparsely populated settlements in areas known for heterodoxy.[110] But the nineteenth century marked a meaningful change in quantity and quality. Internal consolidation led to the deployment of more ulema and the construction of more madrassas in the villages, the amplification of shari'ah courts, and the restoration of thousands of mosques. This was overseen by a hierarchy of provincial and regional titles and levels of administration, including seven-

TABLE 4.2. Religious Education: Ottoman Empire, 1839–1915

Year	Location	Ottoman Institutional Response
1839	Empire	Mahmud II mandates primary education in local religious schools and mosques, employing ulema as teachers (under the Evkaf Nazareti)
1854	Empire	The Sheikh-ul-Islam creates new schools to train religious judges (Muslimhane-i Nuvvab, Medresetü'l-Kuzât)
1866	India	Deoband seminary built in India (Darul Uloom)
1880	Empire	The Sheikh-ul-Islam leads curriculum reform in the Mekteb-i Mülkiye and all Muslim schools of the empire
1889	Arabia	Educational establishments opened for sons of Arab sheikhs (Harbiye)
1890	Empire	Abdülhamid II founds the Dar-ul-alim to develop the "Arabic language and religion . . . and to facilitate their teaching to the Muslims' children"
1894	Mecca	Oumm Institute created by Jamal al-Din al-Afghani
1894	Empire	Religious rules, obligatory prayer for the sultan, and courses on the Qur'an, shari'ah, and Islamic history introduced to teachers' schools (Mekteb-i-Sultani)
1896	Arabia	Special classes (Mülkiye) opened for the education of sons of Arab sheikhs
1903	Empire	Education Ministry training for state bureaucracy increases religious instructional hours
1909	Empire	Creation of predecessor organizations to İmam Hatip Okulari/Lisesi
1913	Empire	Reorganization of medreses (Daru'l-Hilafeti'l Aliyye Medresesi; Medreset ül-Mütahassisin; Medreset ül-Eimme ve'l-Huteba)
1913	Medina	Cornerstone laid for new Islamic university
1913	Jerusalem	Medrese-i-Kulliyah established to train religious leaders
1914	Istanbul	Istanbul: "Theological Medrese of the Great Khalifate"

FIGURE 4.12. Mosquée du Pacha, Algeria (nineteenth century)

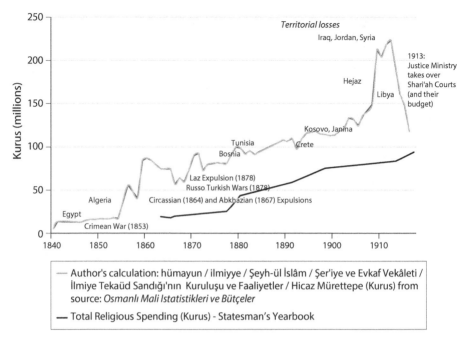

FIGURE 4.13. The First Defeat and the Ottoman Response:
Religious Affairs Budgets, 1840–1926

teen grades of religious officials. Between 1850 and 1921, Eugene Rogan explains, "government Ulama were placed in bureaucratic careers and civil administration" around the empire, and not only in religious affairs. By the end of the nineteenth century 34 percent of all ulema had formal roles in non-Ilmiyye institutions.[111] They also built mosques in rural towns and sent religious instructors to work in the countryside, "imitating the Europeans by dispatching Hanafi missionaries to the Bedouin to preach the Word of God."[112]

To convey the relationship between the dynamic of defeat and spending on spiritual self-defense, I created a religious spending index based on records of budget-line expenditures on religious foundations (evkaf), shari'ah courts (Seriye), ulema (Ilmiyye) and sheikhs, and the subsidies to Mecca and Medina (Hejaz) (see figure 4.13).[113] The sum of that activity approximates the total expenditures on religious infrastructure and education that underpinned the caliph's religious legitimacy. According to a statistical almanac of the era, evkaf expenditures rose steadily from the early 1860s until World War I. Overall, religious spending per Muslim subject increased by approximately 20 percent. Despite the empire's financial troubles and the amounts spent on debt servicing, Ottoman administrators always found the resources to "dispatch men to instruct Muslims in the tenets of Islam."[114] Barnes shows that the sultans' policy "allowed for the spread of religious foundations throughout the empire" to counter foreign missionaries and Islamic rivals.[115]

Even when government budgets began to shrink in the late 1880s, religious affairs spending kept growing.[116] When viewed as a share of state spending, the allocation to religious affairs—education, training, mosques, the holy sites, and hundreds of thousands of employees—fluctuated between 4 percent and 5 percent of total spending.[117] Of the nearly 50 million Kurus in spending on religious affairs in 1909, around 15 percent funded sheikhs and the fatwa council, 10 percent went to train imams and qadis (*Medresetü'l-Kuzât*), 10 percent paid the salaries of muftis, and 40 percent was invested on waqfs and holy sites. This sum did not include the cost of the Holy Railroad, which required the expenditure of another 65 million Kurus annually. After Abdülhamid II was dethroned in the 1908–1909 revolution, religious spending rose further during the Second Constitutional Period (1909–1913).[118] The 1909 constitutional reform was even "more Islamic than the 1876 original," with new references to shari'ah and Hanafi jurisprudence (fiqh) as "a major source for new legislation."[119] Even while other departments shrank in the midst of World War I, the government increased staffing on the fatwa council (Fetvahane) from twenty to twenty-eight member-sheikhs in 1916.

Education

Schools

Mahmud II was the first modern sultan to mandate primary education in religious schools and mosques.[120] The Ministry of Education (1856) was created to oversee *medreses* and schools to train religious judges.[121] Mahmud's building spree was not limited to religious education. He also built thousands of state schools and began a process of cross-fertilization by placing Islamic instruction alongside secular curriculum. The number of state-run primary schools (*iptidai*) rose from around 200 to 4,194.[122] These were still far outnumbered by the 28,596 primary schools run by the ulema.[123] But they signaled a major novelty: one-stop national curriculum and imam training, augmenting the traditional courses *with classes about nonreligious subjects.* Supplemental religious education and imam/teacher training were frequently injected as a measure of inoculation.[124] Whereas in 1874 there were no religion courses in professional schools, two decades later the Qur'an, shari'ah Islamic history, and ethics were mandated.[125]

The new educational establishments were also intended to shield the empire's vulnerable populations. Benjamin Fortna argues that there was "little that Istanbul could do to redress . . . usurpations of Tunis by the French in 1881 and Egypt by the British the following year." However, "education provided a means for Ottoman action on Ottoman soil."[126] Many schools, Birol Başkan writes, were deliberately located in areas where there were "large concentrations of non-Muslims or where foreign missionary schools were particularly active."[127] The historian Eugene Rogan describes a situation that remained out of control into the mid-1890s, especially among "tribesmen in the Ma'an region," who were unaccustomed to practicing Islam: "The government, competing for the souls, minds and bodies of its subjects, had to provide the services which they forbade missionaries to deliver."[128] The governor in Damascus added in his reporting to Istanbul in 1898 that "Latin and Protestant foreign missionaries [were] opening unlicensed schools and educating uncivilized Arab Muslim children devoid of Islamic beliefs." Like the sixteenth-century Bavarian dukes who requested Jesuit assistance, Abdülhamid II and his successors "sought to check all inroads by foreign missionaries among the Muslim population . . . and to inculcate religious values as a means to reinforce attachment to the Caliphal Ottoman state."[129]

The focus of this renewed religious enthusiasm was kept tight. Textbooks of the era asked students, "Why do we love the Sultan? Because he is the Caliph of the Prophet, according to the testimony of three hundred million Muslims."[130] Classes took time for prayer and taught students how to recite the benediction of the sultan-caliph.[131] The medreses were reformed again in 1913–1914, this time divided into separate vocational schools for preachers and mosque functionaries. A new division in the Sheikh-ul-Islam's offices for sermons and preaching soon began to plan for recruitment. After World War I, the number of the empire's schools with a religious endowment fell from 325 to 250.[132] In the early twentieth century, the territories of Syria and Iraq had 570 Ottoman government schools, with 30,500 students, many of whom were subsequently matriculated in institutions of higher education in Istanbul.[133] Literacy rose tenfold, from 1 percent in the year 1800 to 10 percent in 1900.[134] Around the turn of the century, there were 1,025 religion teachers (out of 3,613 registered teachers in the empire) who taught at 1,700 Qur'an schools.[135] Medreses (madrassas) had an additional 12,000 students enrolled. Archival documents from 1906 reveal that British diplomats conceded that Abdülhamid had "exerted himself tirelessly to spread education, non-liberal and narrow in type though it be," and that, as a result, "a large percentage of the poorer classes of Moslems can now read and write."[136]

International Faculties

In the Second Constitutional Period, Serif Mardin has observed, the new government engaged in "a positive rebranding of the *ulema* and their institutions."[137] From the eighteenth century onwards, the divisions (*riwaqs*) of Al-Azhar University in Cairo were organized as residential colleges based on students' region of origin: Upper Egypt, Blue Nile, Damascus, Turkey, India, and Indonesia.[138] On the British subcontinent, "Indian Mohammedans . . . knew very little about the Ottoman Sultan."[139] The Deoband seminary Darul Uloom was built in India (1866) in response to the deposing of the Mughal emperor by the British several years earlier.[140] After several failed uprisings, Indian Muslims expressed Pan-Islamic (and anti-British) sentiment by offering financial support to Istanbul.[141] For the Arab populations of the empire, Abdülhamid founded the Dar-ul-alim (1890) in Istanbul to develop the "Arabic language and religion . . . and to facilitate their teaching to Muslims' children."[142] He opened special programs for the sons of Arab sheikhs and created schools to train ulema in most large cities.[143] There were fully equipped Ottoman medreses for Arabic speakers in Cairo, Damascus, and Aleppo, as well as curriculum in Ottoman Turkish in Bursa and Adrianople. Students training to become imams, clerks, teachers, or preachers received free lodging and bread and soup rations.[144] Abdülhamid also founded a college "for the training of missionaries who were dispatched in batches to the furthest corners of Islam."[145] In the early twentieth century, theology and Islamic law were taught in Ottoman educational institutions in Damascus, Aleppo, Bursa, and Adrianople. Istanbul was itself a burgeoning capital of Islamic scholarship. Islamic educational establishments in the Ottoman capital enrolled between 15,000 and 20,000 students, half of whom were studying shari'ah law. This was more or less comparable, in the aggregate, to Al-Azhar in Cairo, which boasted 11,095 students.[146]

In 1913, Istanbul completed reforms of medrese education across the empire. The government also created three major international centers of Islamic learning: the Theological Medrese of the Great Caliphate in Istanbul, the Medrese-i-Kulliyah in Jerusalem, and the new Moslem University at Medina—to be overseen by a central committee in Istanbul but administered by a committee in Medina.[147] The Ottoman sheikh Abdul Aziz Shawish is reported to have said in 1914 that the Theological Medrese of the Great Caliphate was a "training place for the *ulema* of the whole Islamic world, to rival and eclipse Al Azhar"—which was itself busy training imams for service in the occupied Muslim territories of the European empires.[148]

Hierarchy: Islamic *Propaganda Fide*

The late caliphs built on an earlier tradition of religious envoys. Sultan Abdü-laziz had sent some to South Africa and Brazil. Abdülmecid sent a qadi to the Cape of Good Hope to teach and assist the Muslim community of the Cape Malays. In Nablus, by the mid-nineteenth century, Istanbul exerted "growing control over ulema appointments." Top-ranking administrative posts were being filled "by direct appointment from either Istanbul or the province's *wali* . . . weakening the power of the old local governing elite"; only six of the forty-seven ulema in Nablus had studied in Nablus itself. For decades, Caesar Farah writes, "swarms of picked emissaries went forth, bearing to the most distant parts of Islam the Caliph's message . . . of deliverance from the menace of infidel rule."[149] British occupation of Egypt decreased the influence of Al-Azhar in Syria, helping tip the scales in favor of the Ottoman sultan's influence in that country. On the other hand, the Muslim world had begun to look to Istanbul as Muslim rulers fell under the sway of European colonial powers: "Only after 1871 did Ottoman envoys meet with a positive, though limited response."[150] Hasan Kayali writes that "administration of the provinces of the Fertile Crescent had to be improved to preclude the possibility of European aggression"; as a result, İstanbul sent some of its ablest administrators to the Fertile Crescent as governors."[151] In the 1870s, Istanbul made an offer to federate the Muslims of the Maghreb, the Middle East, and India under a Tunisian ally.[152] Ultimately, however, Istanbul provided a safe haven for failed anti-European resistance movements across North Africa and Arabia. Two well-known figures in the historical struggle for Algerian independence sought asylum during the French occupation.[153] After a "desperate struggle to prevent French conquest of Ottoman province of Algiers," Abd al Qadir (1808–1883), the Algerian emir and anticolonial hero, went into exile in Ottoman Damascus in 1847.[154] Decades later, Sheikh Abdelhamid Ben Badis, an Islamist thorn in the side of the French, received asylum in Istanbul. Senusiya fighters from Libya were also welcomed following the Italian invasion.[155]

Other intellectual leaders of failed military resistance movements against European occupiers—such as Jamal al-Din al-Afghani (1839–1897) and Abd al Rahman al Kawakibi (1849–1902)—naturally gravitated to the safety of sovereign Ottoman cities like Istanbul and Damascus.[156] A cadre of leading figures played the role of powerful cardinals at court, holding together a fraying empire and fulfilling a leading ministerial role at a time when the offices of the Sheikh-ul-Islam and the Evkaf Ministry had been hollowed out. They were significant international Islamic activists, authors, and charismatic leaders on behalf of Ottoman Islam. Abdülhamid II ratcheted up outreach efforts. It was not exactly equivalent to the wave of Catholic diocesization like the 126

TABLE 4.3. The Pan-Islam Caliphs, 1808–1918

Ottoman Sultan	Pan-Islamic Activity
Mahmud II (1808–1839)	1826: Evkaf Ministry; Fetvahane (fatwa council); the Sheikh-ul-Islam is brought into government; the caliph role of the sultan is reinforced
Abdülmecid I (1839–1861)	1860: Rais-ul-Islam positions are created outside the empire; Tanzimat reforms; Refugee Commission
Abdülaziz (1861–1876)	1876: Constitutional Article 3 declares a High Islamic Caliphate
Abdülhamid II (1876–1909)	1880: Shari'ah Council
	1886: Reorganization of religious curriculum; sultan appoints cabinet to support his religious supremacy worldwide
	1894: Position of Sheikh-ul-Islam of the British Isles established
	1900–1908: Hejaz Railroad connects Baghdad, Damascus, and Medina
Mehmed V (1909–1918)	1911–1918: Teşkilat-ı Mahsusa (special advisers) dispatched to Africa
	1913: Formalization of all religious instruction (medreses); missionaries countered in Transjordan

bishop's mitres and dozens of cardinal's rings doled out under Pope Pius IX. But in an attempt to make his Islam policy more plural and representative— and more resistant—among his remaining subjects, Abdülhamid diversified the background of the major hierarchs of Ottoman Islam.[157] He sent religion emissaries to Java and established ties with Sufi brotherhoods in East Africa and Indonesia. Missionaries traveled to Chat, Abyssinia, Somalia, and Zanzibar, and the government sent preachers to China, where it aimed to train ulema and imams who could counteract their "colonial overlords."[158] Centers were set up in Tunisia, Shanghai, and Java, modeled on the Pan-Islamic Society in London.[159] Representatives of Muslims from India, Afghanistan, and Central Asia were encouraged to form a pro-Istanbul Islamic league in 1877.[160]

The British Empire was a prime target of Abdülhamid's program to use envoys on behalf of religious standardization and Pan-Islamic unity.[161] He opened new consulates in Calcutta, Peshawar, Karachi, and Bombay.[162] In India, local dignitaries were appointed to the position of honorary consuls.[163] Abdülhamid sent an Arab emissary to meet the Moroccan sultan in 1880 to expand the Ottoman footprint there and seal an alliance against France.[164] Envoys traveled to Cairo in 1882 to counteract the British irritant coming between the caliph and devout Egyptians.[165] Turkish and Arab emissaries were sent throughout India and Russia "for propagation of the faith." In the East

Indies, they concentrated "on reinforcing the faith of Indonesian Muslims in Islam [but took care] not to preach anything that could be interpreted as seditious by the Dutch."[166]A decade into Wilhelmina's rule, Abdülhamid spoke out in favor of "the project to send a delegation of Arab notables from Batavia to salute me, their Caliph," saying it "would create an excellent impression in the whole world and show how strong the ties are that unite all Muslims."[167] The caliph wrote in his memoirs: "It is sad to see so many Muslim peoples in the hands of the Christian empires. All that is left is the Ottoman Empire, a mere 20 million believers—but despite all of that, all Muslims look towards Istanbul."[168]

The efforts transcended simple survival mechanisms or lofty rhetoric. Late Ottoman strategies allowed them to compete with rival empires.[169] Abdülhamid did his best to ensure that outcome with his kitchen cabinet of ministers of Islamic affairs to cover the empire (see table 4.4).[170] He identified a range of dignitaries who enjoyed good reputations, co-opting public luminaries to sing his praises against European encroachments in Arabia and North Africa. An Indian 'alim (a member of the ulema) was responsible for the southern shore of the Red Sea and India.[171] Amir Abd el-Malek al-Din promoted a Pan-Islamic message in North Africa.[172] In Libya, Ottomans nurtured a relationship with the Senusiya tribe (1835–1911), who helped defend North Africa, the Sahara, and the Hejaz. In 1886, the sultan was received into the order of Senusiya, and in 1898, he was acknowledged as caliph by the Senusiya sheikh, who sent his official representative to Constantinople.[173] The outsourcing to a new clerical corps independent of the traditional hierarchy was critically important. The ulema were increasingly multilingual, conversant in German, French, Greek, Armenian, Italian, Persian, Arabic, and Turkish.[174] In several respects, this development shares similarities with the Holy Congregation of Propaganda Fide, in that they were tasked with defending and propagating Ottoman Islam worldwide. They were also the result of a stovepipe maneuver reminiscent of Rome's cultivation of the Jesuits and the Propaganda Fide to play similar roles outside the normal channels.

The sultan had another method to attract talented advisers. He identified potential Pan-Islamic challengers to his authority, invited them to Istanbul, and hugged them tight. Abdülhamid drew on a new, empire-wide pool of advisers, secretaries, and "functionaries who were removed from the bureaucratic power struggles in Istanbul." (Perhaps for the same reason, he had a personal security battalion composed only of Arab recruits.) The circulation of this group of advisers, publicists, and scholars led some to observe that "the ministries were still a hunting-ground for Turks but the Palace has fallen entirely into the hands of the Arabs."[175] In this way, notable leaders were frequently "coopted by forced residence," including the (Hashemite) sharif of Mecca, Hussein bin Ali, who spent

TABLE 4.4. Hierarchy: Abdülhamid II's Cabinet of Sheikhs

Name	Region	Accomplishments
Abulhuda al-Sayyadi	Empire-wide	Head of all tariqah sheikhs; author of 212 publications (Cairo, Istanbul, Beirut); sharif status; "*naqib al ashraf*, head of the Prophet's descendants" (1873); Sayyadiyya of Rifa'iyya, Rawwas, Ahmad al-Rifa'i, and Sufi orders
Abd al-Razzaq al-Bitar	Syria	Pro-Ottoman scholar; publicist and biographer of Abdülhamid II
Hamza Zhafir al-Madani	North Africa	Son of founder of Madaniyya Order; recommended strict observance of Islamic obligations, reading of Islamic texts, and proselytizing; chief of Madaniyah dervishes (Tripoli and Algeria, headquarters in Istanbul); established multiple madaniyya tekkes; oversaw gatherings in the Yıldız Hamidiye Mosque; allied with Sanussiya in Libya, Egypt, and the Hejaz; became confidant of sultan
Hasan Izzet	Syria	Brought to court by Abulhuda; more inclined toward Syro-Arab interests than Pan-Islam; favored German alliance; mastermind of Hejaz Railroad and secured concession from Germany
Jamal al-Din al-Afghani	Empire-wide	Follower of Muhammed Abduh; forced to leave (1871–1895); offered services to sultan, after offering same to Great Britain
Muhammad Rashid Rida	Empire-wide	Combined Pan-Islamic, Ottomanist, and modernist tendencies; believed the caliphate had a crucial role to play in the modernization of Islam, the maintenance of Islamic links, and resistance to the European imperial tactics of divide and rule; used the Damascus mosque to preach "preservation of religion based on Muslim embrace of modern knowledge"
Abdullah Quilliam	British Empire	Convert appointed by the caliph and Queen Victoria; Shaykh-ul Islam of the British Isles (1894)
Abu Bakr Effendi	South Africa	Appointed by Abdülhamid II; from Erzerum

sixteen years at court in Istanbul before finally challenging the caliph, with British encouragement. This challenge entailed some active rabble-rousing in former Ottoman territories, but this added to Abdülhamid's allure. For example, when a "Mahdi appeared under Anglo-Egyptian rule," a Syrian courtier (who had predicted that the sultan would rule until the Mahdi arrived) announced that "Muhammad Ahmad could not be the mahdi because he was in revolt against his . . . rightful [Ottoman] sovereign."[176]

Abulhuda al-Sayyadi

Originally from Aleppo, Syria, Abulhuda (1850–1909) had Sufi lineage and early in his life laid claim to sharif status as "*naqib al ashraf*, head of the Prophet's descendants." However, shortly after Abdülhamid's installment, Caesar Farah writes, Abulhuda "ingratiated himself with the Sultan" by bringing him "a personal message" that he had received in a dream from the Prophet. He was named to the court in 1876. Valued for his knowledge of the Arab world's religious institutions, Abdülhamid made Abulhuda the head of all *tariqah* sheikhs, and a de facto minister of religious affairs for Arab Muslims of the empire.[177] His position at court, simply put, was to "urge his fellow Arabs to acknowledge his Sultan's claim to the universal caliphate." During the 1880s, Abulhuda was said to have placed the sultan's agents "in every important *tekke* and *madras* of the Empire" and to "act as a link with the sheikhs of Syria and Arabia." Asked to write and publish religious and Sufi works, he authored 212 books and booklets (mostly in Arabic) that were distributed in Istanbul, Beirut, and Cairo between 1880 and 1908; most of them were devoted to defending Abdülhamid's "absolute authority as the legitimate Caliph of all Muslims."[178]

Hamza Zhafir al-Madani

Son of the founder of the North African Madaniyya Order, Sheikh Zhafir (1847–1903) concentrated on promoting Ottoman Islam in the areas under French and British control.[179] Zhafir was responsible for "maintaining strict observance of Islamic obligations and the reading of Islamic texts,"[180] and as the leader of the *madaniyya* dervishes in Tripoli and Algeria, he was given a home near Yıldız.[181] Three *madaniyya tekkes* were established in Istanbul, which served as headquarters for operations to influence sheiks of various orders. Zhafir's emissaries are said to have won recruits among Algerians employed by the French. Serif Mardin writes that in Barka the efforts of Sheikh Zhafir linked up with the Senusiya resistance, with colonial encouragement. Zhafir did the same in Egypt and the Hejaz.[182] Finally, he oversaw gatherings in the new Yıldız Hamidiye Mosque and became a close confidant of the sultan. He had the Ertugrul Lodge constructed a short distance from Yıldız as the symbol of Pan-Islamism; his own tomb was later placed there. Critics mocked "The Sheikh Zafirs, the Abul Hudas, the Afghanis, the Husseins, and multitude of others who claim to exert influence over the Muslim element."[183] But scholars have found that the use of tariqah sheikhs, in particular, "to strengthen ties between the Ottoman center and restive Muslim communities in the provinces" was effective; many Sufi brotherhood leaders, they note, enthusiastically preached loyalty to the caliph and, moreover, "had a greater influence in the everyday life of the Muslim population than did the ulema."[184] In addition to setting up the rais-ul-Islam system, such arrangements helped Ottoman soft power reach well beyond the empire.

Jamal al-Din al-Afghani

Jamal al-Din al-Afghani's (1839–1897) increasingly popular notions of Pan-Islam were given real-world meaning when Abdülhamid II—playing Ben-Gurion to al-Afghani's Herzl—began to adopt them as a program "reaching across state borders to impact on all parts of the Muslim world." Al-Afghani favored a "movement of Muslim liberation from European rule" but had a difficult relationship with Istanbul, where he was not welcome for nearly twenty-five years (1871–1895).[185] Amira Bennison writes that the solutions he proposed to Abdülhamid were geared toward "reviving the religious connection between Muslims."[186] He held that the caliphate had a crucial role to play in the modernization of Islam, the maintenance of international Muslim networks, and "as a means of resistance to European imperial tactics of divide and rule."[187] Al-Afghani's efforts included the promotion of Ottoman Islam within associations, lodges, clubs, and societies to whip up support for the Pan-Islamic project. He also realized the power of newspapers, which he used to great "international impact." Al-Afghani's long-term efforts are credited, for example, with moving Indians in the British Empire to help fund the Hejaz Railroad (1900–1908) and to lend their political support to the Ottomans in the Balkan Wars (1910–1912). The role of Indian public opinion may have been greatest during the interallied occupation of Istanbul (1918–1923), at the height of discussions of the caliphate's fate, which reinforced the British decision *not* to abolish the caliphate.[188]

Abdullah Quilliam

The appointment of a sheikh-ul Islam of the British Isles was comparable to the pope's decision to send envoys to enemy territory in northern Europe after the Reformation. Abdülhamid II and Queen Victoria officially made Abdullah Quilliam (1856–1932) (and received him as) an Honorary Consul of the Ottoman

Empire in 1892. Quilliam was a temperance activist and solicitor who was attracted to the wholesome society he observed while visiting Morocco; he converted to Islam and created the English Islamic Association in Liverpool (1889). Quilliam's association came to the attention of the Ottoman ambassador in London in 1890, leading Abdülhamid II to send Quilliam a telegram thanking him for his proselytism in Great Britain. Yahya Birt argues that Ottomans had in mind the recent experience of Bosnia-Herzegovina, which they had lost to intra-Sunni sectarianism stimulated by European empires.[189] The rais-ul-Ulema (grand mufti) system that developed in the Balkan states as a formal delegation of powers, however, was never applied to Quilliam. He was understood to be the leader of "an Ottoman *millet* in reverse." This may have also been a sop to Indian Muslims, for whose consumption Quilliam operated a printing press and edited a periodical that was included as a flashy supplement to the "well-established *Anjuman-i-Islam*" in London, led by Maulvi Mohamed Ibrahim.

Turkish Nationalists

After the definitive loss of its last toeholds in the western Balkans and North Africa, Turkish nationalists sent Abdülhamid II into exile and then proceeded to guide his successor to double down on his Pan-Islamization agenda. The nationalist Committee on Union and Progress prized away the administration of justice and education from the sultan. The Young Turk coalition rebranded and repurposed these institutions in the national interest. Sultan Mehmed V (1909–1918) took the empire a further step toward Islamic standardization and professionalization. The summary deposing of Abdülhamid II and replacing him with Mehmed V suggested the office's innate fallibility; the Shadow of God could simply be shooed away. Nonetheless, it was carried out according to lineage and succession. The Sublime Porte was doing what their contemporaries in southern European nation-states did to the Catholic Church: taking Islam out of the temporal realm with the later prospect of granting it autonomy within the *spiritual* domain—that is, in the organization of religious exercise and self-perpetuation.[190]

The Young Turk government proposed a complete restructuring of Ottoman foreign policy to adapt to the new reality that the state had no territory left in Europe. The solution to the "crisis of international isolation," he suggested, was "Islamization and nationalization of Ottoman foreign relations, with a focus on Asia." They argued that the previously neglected Muslim populations in Asia would be "the basis of Ottoman survival and revival." Cemal Aydin writes that the Young Turks "emphasized the sadness that Ottoman defeats in the Balkan wars had caused in the hearts of Muslims in India, Egypt,

Afghanistan, Algeria, Morocco, and Tripoli." Ultimately, they refused to "separate the institution of the Caliphate from Turkey's foreign policy."[191]

The regime of the Second Constitutional Period made one last-ditch attempt at Arab propaganda with a new intelligence unit (Teşkilat-ı Mahsusa).[192] These shock troops countered the French, British, and Italian empires with Islamic unity propaganda through the 1910s.[193] After the Ottoman defeat in the Balkan Wars, the Italian invasion of Tripolitania (1911–1912) was seen as an opportunity "for decisive action against European encroachment . . . to preserve for ourselves what remains of our dignity."[194] Acknowledging that it stood no chance in a direct confrontation with the Italian navy, Istanbul instead sent military advisers to Tripoli to help organize national resistance alongside the Sanussiya tribe.[195] The Teşkilat-ı Mahsusa unit helped "keep the Italians in their coastal beachheads" on the Libyan coast, though not for long.

Encouraged by the new Ottoman regime, Sheikh Abdelhamid Ben Badis returned from Istanbul to Algeria in 1913, settling in the city of Constantine and teaching at the Sidi Qammouch Mosque.[196] Taking advantage of a house of worship "that escaped state control" under French rule, Ben Badis founded a movement of "free mosques" that rejected colonial oversight. This turned out to be a precursor of the Algerian independence movement—whose germ was incubated in Istanbul.[197] The concerted harassment of European empires would likely have continued had the First World War not begun. However, as the conflict brewed, Aydin notes, Ottoman officials cited the "liberation of colonized Muslim lands" as a goal of the war.[198]

The shift away from temporal authority and toward spiritual power became irreversible, ironically, when the sultan-caliph declared a holy war against the Triple Entente. A shared list of enemies made natural bedfellows of Abdülhamid and Kaiser Wilhelm of the Second German Reich (1880–1914). They consummated the military alliance with an exchange of homes away from home: a chalet for the kaiser near Yıldız Palace and an Ottoman mosque complex (and cemetery) in Berlin for the sultan. In 1906, Abdülhamid and Wilhelm offered assistance to North African anticolonial leaders to help them dispose of the French presence in the Maghreb.[199] Propaganda leaflets in Arabic were distributed in France calling for loyalty and obedience to the sultan-caliph.[200] In 1914, Istanbul joined World War I alongside the German Reich.

The fatwa ruling for jihad against Great Britain and her allies called upon the more than 100 million Muslims living in European territories to overthrow their colonial masters.[201] On the one hand, the call for jihad against European empires (except Germany, which encouraged the jihad for its own reasons) vindicated those who had predicted political interference from Istanbul.[202]

But the scattered response to Istanbul offered proof of the caliphate's *political* irrelevance, annihilating the myth about "the terrible things that would ensue in all Islamic communities outside of Turkey" should the sultan-caliph invoke holy war against the Triple Entente: "He invoked it, and nothing happened," wrote one journalist. Instead, "in France, the Moslem Indians and Moroccans continue to fight the Kaiser; in the Levant, the Egyptians redoubled their efforts to put the Caliph-Sultan out of business; in the Hejaz the Grand Sharif of Mecca revolted against him."[203] The call fell flat because it was out of step with the spiritual influence that Istanbul had been peddling for the previous century and also because of the apparent hypocrisy of the regime's alliance with Christian Germany.

The Ottoman holy war gave Europeans political coverage to shatter the emergency glass and seize the gavel of religious authority. They proceeded to smash four centuries of Ottoman rule in Islam's holy cities and beyond.[204] The Ottomans lost control of the remaining pillars of their legitimate religious authority, without which the Prophet's relics risked being reduced to collector's items. The British proceeded to help remove their custodianship of Mecca and Medina and control of Jerusalem, as well as the Arab provinces of Iraq, Syria, and Lebanon. They supported Hussein bin Ali's attack on the Ottoman garrisons of Mecca. To formalize the break, the British took over paying the salary of the Sharif of Mecca. The British crown had done the same thing in the early 1530s with the former Roman Catholic hierarchy in England and Wales.

As with the Catholic Counter-Reformation, the defeat elicited a transformative institutional supernova. Sultan Vahdettin's response to the rising pressure on the imperial rump was to pivot to his constituencies further east, which were unmistakably outside his literal temporal jurisdiction.[205] Even as the empire crumbled, Istanbul did not give up its religious mantle, neither figuratively nor literally: it refused to hand over the Prophet's effects to Hussein. Even after they lost Mecca, the Ottoman governments selected a new "legitimate" Mufti of Mecca and "bundled him south to assume his position of supreme religious authority." Much like the Hejaz Railroad, however, the substitute mufti never got farther than Medina. There he sought to "blunt Hussein's appeal" by engaging in "rivalry to Hussein's regime in Mecca."[206]

Despite that crucial loss, the overall effect of Ottoman international mobilization had the effect of shielding them from British aggression and warding off gratuitous hostility on several occasions—for example, during the 1875 Balkan Crisis and upon the construction of the Hejaz Railroad.[207] Despite their shortcomings, the sultan-caliphs represented a more dignified option for many Muslims living under European rule than following the lead of London, Moscow, Paris, or Rome in Islamic affairs. Regarding British designs on Islam's holiest cities, Indian Muslims told British authorities that they were "not likely to look on unmoved when the Prophet's shrine at Mecca and his tomb at Medina have become the objective points of foreign aggression." Support for Istanbul aligned with Indian religious scholars' skepticism of the Arab autonomy movement. Without the glue of Ottoman Islam, they feared that "foreigners would swallow it whole and nothing would remain of [any] Islamic state."[208] Then they articulated the critical division between the caliph's spiritual and political roles that had been emerging for the previous century. "We are the strongest link in the natural alliance between our Queen and our Caliph, *between the temporal power in India and the spiritual power that radiates from the Bosphorus.*"[209] There was melancholy at the coordinated assault upon their symbolic figurehead.[210]

Even Muslims in Siberia annexed by the czar shared "a close affinity with all of their Ottoman brothers" thanks to the efforts of Pan-Islam. There was also genuine "popular support for the caliphate in opposition to European expansion."[211] In 1908, "telegraph reports of the opening of the Ottoman parliament" occasioned an "outpouring of enthusiasm" among Siberian Muslims: "'It was as if the wireless telegraph bound their hearts together' with their co-religionists in the Ottoman empire."[212] Along with the printed matter, these less tangible new media perfectly illustrated the power of "imagined community."[213] During the Yemeni revolt, rebels severed the telegraph wires, leaving Istanbul in the dark. One contemporary observer concluded from the incident that "Yemen is too far from Constantinople to be governed from there."[214] But even neighboring territories—and eventually Turkey itself—were receding from the sultan-caliph's *political* control. This is how it was possible, Cemil Aydin explains, that "while dreaming to save India from the British rule, the Ottoman State could lose Western Thrace just fifty miles from its capital city."[215] Like the papacy's survival of the death of the Papal States thanks to outside pressure, the international support movement had kept the British from putting an end to it. This extended the caliphate's life by at least five years. Despite scattered pro-Ottoman uprisings, little could be done against the designs of Turkish nationalists.

After World War I, the military hero and future head of state Mustafa Kemal (1881–1938) met with Sultan Mehmed VI Vahdettin (1861–1926) in Yıldız and gave him the chance to stay on as sultan, if he would help stave off the British who were occupying Gallipoli. However, Vahdettin "detested the [Turkish] nationalists," British diplomats reported, "and wouldn't accept the deal. He refused to accept loss of temporal power as a fait accompli, and still hoped to reverse the nationalists." In January 1920, the Committee on Union and Progress set up a new Pan-Islamic association called Mouvahidin. A memorandum written to Lord Curzon claimed that the society, located in Sivas but with large bases of support in Egypt, Syria, and Iraq, had published "proclamations addressed to all Moslems of which nearly a million copies have been distributed," and had already "sent several dispatches to Egypt, Syria, etc. in order to coordinate a cohesive Islamic community."[216] Twelve cities under British control hosted Mouvahidin centers: Damascus, Homs, Baalbek, Cairo, Tanta, Reshid, Haifa, Aleppo, Zor, Baghdad, Najaf, and Kuwait City.

The Treaty of Sèvres (1920) abolished the Ottoman Empire, but awkwardly left in place two power centers.[217] The first was French-occupied Ankara, a small central Turkish town with around 5,000 inhabitants that was the seat of the new national government and the political capital. The second was the caliphate in Istanbul, under occupation by the British. The sultan dissolved the Ottoman Chamber of Deputies, and the Sheikh-ul-Islam issued a fatwa declaring Kemal's nationalist forces infidels.[218] Mustafa Kemal's supporters responded with a "contrary *fetva*, drawn up by the nationalist *Müftü* of Ankara" and signed by 250 of his colleagues.[219] Kemal immediately called for a Grand National Assembly to be seated in the new national capital of Ankara. Its first session took place less than two weeks after the last chamber's dissolution. Fifty of the 300 delegates elected were Islamic clerics.

In Ankara, Mustafa Kemal trumped the Osmans' religious card: he outlined the religious ceremonies to precede the opening of the assembly: "Reading of the Koran and Sunna, sheep would be sacrificed, a hair from the prophet's beard and his reputed standard would be borne in procession, prayers would be offered for the safety of the Sultan and Caliph."[220] Kemal assembled with deputies at the Hacı Bayram Mosque for prayer on April 23, 1923, before joining a "procession led by a cleric carrying a koran on lectern ... to the cries of *Allahuekber*." His first public proclamation was to "swear in the name of god and the prophet that [we are not] rebels against the Sultan and Caliph. We want to save our country from the fate of India and Egypt."[221] After composing the whole scene, Kemal sent a telegram to Sultan Vahdettin pledging the assembly's loyalty. Kemal had out-Ottomaned the House of Osman.

By the time the Republic of Turkey was established, rival empires had already deprived the caliph of some of his most precious and defining attributes—safeguarding holy cities and military independence. In one defeat after another, he had lost every major holy city and large Muslim population of the once-mighty empire: Kairouane, Sarajevo, Jerusalem, Damascus, Mecca, Medina, Bursa. Even Istanbul itself fell, first to the British and then to Turkish nationalists. At the start of the new legislative year, the first of March 1924, the Turkish National Assembly administered the coup de grâce. Atatürk oversaw the appropriation of all imperial property and exiled the descendants of the Osman dynasty, which had ruled the empire for more than 600 years. He replaced the Evkaf Ministry with the new Department of Religious Affairs,

FIGURE 4.14. A fallen locomotive that once pulled pilgrims on the Hejaz Railroad, built by the Ottoman Empire

withdrew accreditation from the religious school system, and completely extracted ulema from the government.[222] On March 3, 1924, the night of Law 431's approval, Dolmabahçe Palace was surrounded by military and police. Caliph Abdülmecid II and his royal family members were paid 10 million Kurus in British currency before they left for Switzerland; they would later settle in Paris and Nice.[223] The glorious Ottoman caliphate ended in ignominy, fleeing Istanbul on a night train to Switzerland, never to return.

Conclusion: The Legacy of Pan-Islam

From the time it declined to intervene militarily to its development of cross-border activism, the caliphate began to resemble something less than a literal empire. It became an international entity in defense of Islam and offered

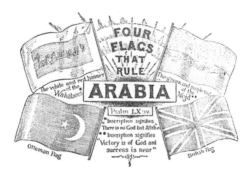

FIGURE 4.15. "Four Flags That Rule Arabia" (1900)

asylum for persecuted Islamic minorities. Jacob Landau argues that its inability to defend Muslims militarily, despite the World War I fatwa, "triggered a shift in the meaning of jihad": from armed resistance to engendering Islamic solidarity through good works. Missionaries spread the good word while the Red Crescent Society (1868) cared for wounded soldiers and assisted the settlement of Muslim refugees in the empire.[224] In this process, the caliph was becoming, like the pope, a moral voice to be reckoned with—but one that nation-states could safely ignore if raison d'état called for it. This was not a case of straightforward decline, but of transmogrification.

The religious bureaucracy grew spectacularly, employing more than 150,000 civil servants in Islamic affairs by the end of the nineteenth century.[225] The Ottoman Empire was not Islamized; instead, Islam was Ottomanized.[226] The lamb lay down with the lion, in the sense tha the lamb was was *inside* the lion. The modernizing state ended the sultanate itself one century after the sultans brought the Sheikh-ul-Islam under state control. Yet Caliph Mehmed VI still recited opening prayers of benediction for the Grand National Assembly. The assertion of religious authority led to the bureaucratization that ultimately acted as a model for the nation-states that followed the end of empire.[227] When Turkish nationalists ended the caliphate itself (1924), dozens of new national ministries of Islamic affairs inherited the Ottoman model of legal subordination and spiritual monopoly.

The unceremonious abolition of the centuries-old institution, however, also threatened the division of labor between the civil and religious spheres. The processes of differentiation under way were thrown into confusion by the decapitation of the spiritual authorities. This situation created disempowered and disenfranchised religious-cultural groups across the realms of former Ottoman influence, each with extensive religious grievances vis-à-vis the modern states that followed the end of empire. When control over the Islamic center of gravity—Mecca and Medina—shifted from the House of Osman to the Saud dynasty, modern Pan-Islam changed dramatically with it. The decision to leave the caliphate defunct while allowing Saudi Arabia to act as its de facto successor placed the Muslim-majority nation-states that emerged from the old empires in an uncomfortable position. As one scholar writes, the region has witnessed ever since a "prolonged transnational ideological struggle among Muslims over the best regime."[228] The Saudi-Wahhabi alliance spread a religious orthodoxy inimical to the Ottoman model of adaptation, which had followed the lead of local custom, co-opting local eminences and budding religious toleration. Turbocharged by the chance discovery of oil beneath the sacred Hejaz, the Muslim World League (Rabita) and other Saudi waqfs spent hundreds of *billions* of dollars in the twentieth century on Islamic education, mosques, and branch offices—whose official mission was to "propagate the faith."[229]

The indelicate handling and ultimate failure by European empires to address the Eastern Question contrasts with their more cautious navigation of the Vatican's parallel experience in political limbo. The Great Powers viewed the pope as a bothersome obstacle to their political destiny but never precipitated his disappearance. Chronologically and thematically, the issue of what to do with the caliph in Istanbul tracked the Roman Question and what would become of the pope in the nation-state era. As the next chapter explores, the nineteenth-century quarrel with Rome was unlike either the Protestant Reformation or the European takeover of ex-Ottoman populations, where one religious leader was being substituted for another. Nineteenth-century European nation-states started jettisoning the *ancien régime* for modernity and republican institutions. Much like *Atatürk*'s attitude toward the caliph, European statesmens' concern was with their *domestic* realm and their own cultures: defeating the Church meant secularization in the name of liberal consolidation—at home.

The Nation-State Era

5

Nation-State Catholicism

THE IRON STATUE of the scientist-monk Giordano Bruno anchors one of Rome's liveliest piazzas, known as the Campo de' Fiori. Stained by a century of rain, Bruno is gazing downwards from atop a pedestal turned away from the Vatican that sentenced him to burn at the stake in that very spot in 1600. Upon the anniversary of his execution in 1888, government ministers unveiled Bruno under the clarion calls of municipal trumpets on Pentecost Sunday, surrounded by hundreds of Masonic flags (see figure 5.1). A mob of nationalist Italians invaded a nearby Catholic seminary, chanting "Death to the Priests, Down with the Vatican, Long Live Bruno," before marching under protection of the new royal paramilitary police (*carabinieri*).[1] An Italian senator riled up the crowd beside a burbling fountain in the piazza, shouting "These clear waters cannot wash the stain of the crime that the Priest of Rome committed against the life of Bruno."[2] Statues of popular martyrs—Joan of Arc in flames was another favorite—were erected around Catholic Europe in the late nineteenth century to announce a new political order. Twenty-first century market-goers and tourists may see Bruno's statue as a moody tribute to humanist values. The men who had his likeness cast, hauled into place, and fixed in marble, however, were implanting a specific reminder for future generations: never again Church rule.

Whereas defeat of the Roman Catholic Church in the 1500s was delivered by reformed churches beyond international borders, an enemy *within* inflicted the Second Defeat: the nineteenth-century nation-state. The Vatican's much-reduced post-Reformation authority had been besieged on its own turf before. Renaissance scientists, Enlightenment philosophers, divine rulers, and religious wars all did their part, at different speeds and with a variety of institutional outcomes.[3] For the nineteenth-century Church historian William Shea, the nation-state culled the "sad fruit" of the Reformation.[4] It was the French Revolution and the subsequent spread of constitutionalism, however, that gave rise to a new kind of polity and a new breed of nondynastic ruler: *statesmen*. In the

FIGURE 5.1. Inauguration of the statue of Giordano Bruno, Rome (1888)

decades that followed Louis XVI's head hitting the basket, modern statesmen transformed Catholic Europe into something unrecognizable.

Until the early 1800s, the pope appointed every grand elector (*Kurfürst*) in the Holy Roman Empire, and prior to Italy's annexation, he governed millions of citizens in the Papal States.[5] Given the papacy's historical role in conferring (and withdrawing) political legitimacy and its historical function as an international court of arbitration, the significance of the late nineteenth-century turning point in the resolution of state-church relations can hardly be overstated.[6] There were more Catholics in the world than any other faith group—growing from 106 million to 266 million between 1800 and 1900—but that did not guarantee home rule in the cradle of Roman Catholicism.[7] This was not a sudden development: the tectonic shift was centuries in the making. But the Vatican's ambitions finally outstripped its deterrence resources—the armies and alliances that had kept it from being overrun.

In 1870, the Vatican sat helpless and encircled by the military forces of unifying Italy. The popes had considered Rome home since Charlemagne, perhaps even Constantine. Unlike during the last nationalist assault in 1848, no deus ex machina from neighboring Catholic superpowers saved the Papal States.[8] As a result, public affairs fell into the hands of anticlerical Catholics in one nation after another—France, Spain, Italy, Germany—all of whom appeared bent upon "the complete dechristianization of the whole civil and political order."[9] This transition imposed heavy short-term costs on the ritual life of religious believers and the Church itself, measured in lost authority and operational freedom and seized property and wealth. Every major nation-state "openly set at naught the temporal claims of an infallible Papacy." In one prescient formulation, an observer wondered whether "the Pope might become 'the Director-general of the humanitarian forces in the world.'"[10]

Polities governed by canon law became an endangered species, viable only in tiny duchies and principalities like Lichtenstein and Monaco. Every other European government crippled Roman Catholic institutions and their sociopolitical force. They also sought to preclude Catholicism's resurrection— religious authorities experienced it as the age of "state omnipotence."[11] Church-state relations in modern Europe are usually presented as the outcome of three possible models: an established national church with an official religion; a cooperative arrangement with state oversight; or strict separation with minimal support or interference.[12] The nineteenth-century secularization of Catholic nation-states in Europe, however, shared more commonalities than differences. Practicing Catholic fellow citizens came to be viewed as a national minority that pledged loyalty to a foreign capital: the Vatican.

National governments asserted a public monopoly over education, cleansed schools of Church teachings and personnel, expelled Catholic orders, shuttered thousands of parishes and dioceses, invalidated the sacrament of marriage, and introduced civil divorce. To establish preeminence over the civilian realm of national life, they nationalized Church property and imposed restrictions on tax-exempt organizations (see figure 5.2).[13] The path toward egalitarian citizenship and religious pluralism was paved by state jurisdiction over family law, gender roles, and youth education. This was the process of state-church differentiation of the secular spheres that has been identified by systems theorists like Talcott Parsons and Niklas Luhmann. New civil codes and constitutions overruled Church law and eliminated centuries of privilege. Saint Peter's sword became a strictly ceremonial object, and the Catholic hierarchy—bishops, apostolic delegates, nuncios, and cardinals—became subject to the oversight of hostile governments.

The most internally destabilizing—and unintentionally transformative— restriction was the state's hostile takeover of the nomination of priests, bishops, and cardinals. Of course, states had long sought to control episcopal appointments. The government approval of clerics had been around since the eleventh century, but nineteenth-century Nation-State Catholicism had new guises—Josephism in Austria, the civil constitution of the clergy in France, and Caesaro-Papism or Regalism in Spain, Portugal, and Italy. States placed the local hierarchies into political receivership and interfered with "the inter-

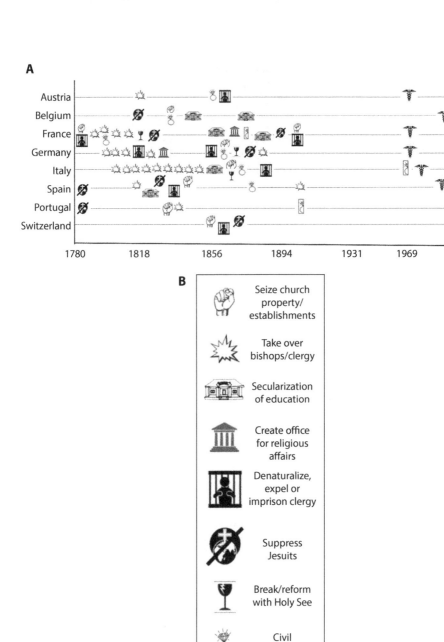

FIGURE 5.2.1 AND FIGURE 5.2.2. The Church's Encounter with the
Nation-State, 1780–2000

TABLE 5.1. Nineteenth-Century State Offices for Church Oversight

Nation-State	Religious Affairs Ministry
Germany	Prussian Religions Ministry, Religionsangelegenheiten
Italy	Ministry of the Interior, Ufficio per le confessioni religiose
France	Ministry of Justice and Religion; Ministry of the Interior and Religious Exercise, Bureau Central des Cultes
Spain	Ministry of Education and Science; Ministry of Grace and Justice, Despacho de Asuntos Eclesiásticos
Austria	Ministry of Education and Religious Exercise, Religionangelegenheiten
Belgium	Ministry of Justice, Direction générale de la Législation civile et des Cultes

national government of the Church by increasing control over the choice of men."[14] Administrative oversight was replaced by new offices for religious affairs, located within ministries of interior or justice (see table 5.1). The Church had never experienced such a demotion through the modern mechanisms of state bureaucracy. Daily humiliations living under majority-Catholic rule thus made the Church's experience even more difficult than in Anglican, Lutheran, or Orthodox lands.

The dark political horizons provoked countermeasures in an area where the Church could act more decisively: the professionalization and centralization of its infrastructure, training, and hierarchy. The reluctance to accept national borders radiated outwards from the Vatican, with "the spiritual sovereignty of the Pope crossing the artificial boundaries separating the States of the far flung international community, in order to reach every man, woman and child of the Catholic persuasion, whether in Catholic or non-Catholic countries."[15] Papal envoys sent to report on the new spiritual desert described a lack of priests, in both quantity and quality, from southern Italy and Spain to Prussia. Rome increased the centralization and homogenization of the national hierarchies.[16] Just as it had done during the Reformation, the Church compensated for losses in Europe with institutional growth in its less established geographical and demographic markets.

The Church used such spaces—as well as the growing Catholic presence in the Americas—to accelerate overseas operations and to multiply dioceses worldwide. Its habit of operating as a minority helped create a new bureaucratic class within the Church that was different than the rest. In the language of civil-military relations established by Samuel Huntington, it marked the opening decades of modern civilian control over Catholic religious hierarchies. However, it was being done in a highly *subjective* manner, with excessive interference. Ultimately, the regulatory destination in state-church terms was a soft restoration, a new deal under *objective* civilian control. This entailed more than mere toleration: also required were the right to infrastructure, education, and hierarchy and the restoration of delegated activities—in other words, the license to educate and train. The following account unpacks the institutional adaptation that produced that outcome in five national contexts: France, Spain, Germany, Italy, and the Papal States.

France

With a population of nearly 40 million, France was the largest Roman Catholic nation. France considered itself the "eldest daughter" of the Church, but for over 700 years it had tried the patience of her Mother Church. French sovereigns inflicted schisms, papal kidnappings, destitutions, deportations, and other indignities.[17] France had always been an enthusiastic steward of Church institutions: it had provided some of the most important religious orders over the millennia, from Benedictines to Sulpicians, and was second only to Italy in cardinal nominations. Church influence in France and French influence in the Church dropped sharply, however, after the Revolution. The Declaration of the Rights of Man and of the Citizen (1789) eliminated the clergy as a class apart within the state, stripping them "of their spiritual dominance, their religious monopoly and political privileges."[18] All Church property was nationalized, and clergy were made into civil servants. The initial intention of the Jacobins—named for the former Couvent de Saint Jacques they occupied near the University of the Sorbonne—was to fashion a national French church, forcing all clerics to take a loyalty oath to nation, king, and the rule of law. The unintended effect, the historian Noah Shusterman argues, was to "give the counter-Revolution . . . a popular base that it had never had." A schism arose between the "constitutional church" and the "refractory church." Priests who refused the oath, Shusterman writes, "lived hidden in the countryside . . . giving the mass clandestinely to packed houses on Sundays, while constitutional priests celebrated the Mass in empty churches."[19]

Church historians report what happened next as a period of "the vilest acts of tyrannical government."[20] In 1792, the revolutionaries traded Christ for the Republic. They introduced a new calendar to mark the Era of the French, replacing the Gregorian calendar in use for two centuries. There followed a massive reduction of dioceses and bishops from which France's role in the Church would never recover. French revolutionaries reduced the corps of bishops by 30 percent—from 130 to 83—and limited dioceses to 67, or one per administrative state *département*. Another innovation was their application of revolutionary notions of popular will to the Church hierarchy. They mandated that parish priests and bishops be elected by popular vote.[21] And with absenteeism now expressly forbidden, priests and bishops had to live within their diocese.

While he was still around, King Louis XVI vetoed all "laws restricting their activities, deportation, executions," but once the monarchy was suspended, the National Assembly decreed the banishment of all dissident (*réfractaire*) priests. Unmarried priests were considered suspect, and 3,500 priests were forcefully married off (and thereby exempted from deportation).[22] The refractory church refused the National Assembly's authority in religious matters: they claimed that only Jesus Christ could grant "essential church jurisdiction." Some historians draw a direct line "from the civil constitution of the clergy to the civil war," noting that the Vendée revolt "broke out along the dividing lines that the disputes over the civil constitution of the clergy had revealed."[23] In the event, the state met the uprising with mass exile and executions. Thousands of clerics were deported by ship, and Christianity was temporarily banned in 1793. The suppression of the Vendée uprising foreboded the coming era of state terror under the "Cult of Reason and the Supreme Being" (see figure 5.3). In 1795, it was decreed that "no one may practice any religion without first obtaining a certificate of submission to the laws of the Republic."

Paris-Rome

The first French Empire under Napoleon is remembered for partially restoring the place of Rome and the Church in post-Revolutionary France with the 1801 Concordat with Rome, which the sociologist José Casanova calls the "blueprint" for all subsequent treaties with the Church.[24] Napoleon's civil code and the reestablishment of Pope Gregory XV's twelve-month calendar in 1806 signaled France's return to the international community. Before that, however, the French military spread revolutionary zeal and destruction to its south, leading to the occupation of Rome and the establishment of the first Roman Republic (1798–1799)—around the same time as Napoleon landed in Cairo. A French general tracked down the reactionary Pius VI in Tuscany and "conducted him to Parma, then across the Alps, to Briançon, and subsequently to Valence, where, overcome by his sufferings of mind and body, the old man died."[25]

The 1801 Concordat subjected the Church to "vexatious supervision and humiliating regulations," and Napoleon's invasion and occupation of Rome devastated the local curia and episcopate.[26] A state-approved catechism was distributed to all French dioceses, which were modestly increased in number from the Jacobin period.[27] Bishops were guaranteed a generous state salary, but Napoleon reserved the right to name all bishops and archbishops (to be confirmed by the pope).[28] The bishops, in turn, named priests who were certified and salaried by the French government: the country's 42,000 parish clergy were reduced by over one-third, to 27,000, and made to subsist on poverty

FIGURE 5.3. "Abbé Francois Nicolas under the Gun" (1793)

wages.[29] Despite its drawbacks, Rome's 1801 "compromise" with its French nemesis is seen as having preserved the Church's unity. Without it, "the separation of the French Church from Rome would have become, without a doubt, an accomplished fact."[30] This is borne out in Napoleon's first batch of episcopal appointments, which balanced twelve constitutional bishops with sixteen holdovers from the *ancien régime*.[31] In his remaining thirteen years, only a dozen or so of Napoleon's choices for bishops were denied canonical investiture by the pope.[32]

Nonetheless, within a few years of the Concordat, Napoleon threatened to move against the Papal States unless the pope realigned his foreign policy and appointed Frenchmen to one-third of the seats in the College of Cardinals.[33] The pope's refusal triggered the formal annexation of the Papal States—the French tricolor replaced the papal flag atop Castel Sant'Angelo—and Napoleon declared Rome an "Imperial Free City" in 1809. The emperor's birthday was proclaimed a day of public celebration, observed even by St. Peter's Basilica (1809–1810), and prayers on behalf of the French First Family were ordered up in Roman churches.[34] Napoleon also emancipated the Jews, abolished the Roman Inquisition, shuttered convents and monasteries, and expelled all Roman clergy "who refused an oath of loyalty to the French Empire." In all, fifteen bishops and 900 priests swore the oath; nine bishops and 500 priests refused.[35]

For the rest of the nineteenth century, the Church's fortunes in France depended largely on the regime in power. Some things drifted back toward the previous state of affairs: Rome's influence on nominations rebounded as ultramontanism grew and Gallicanism faded (1840–1870). The number of dioceses was expanded to ninety from sixty-seven, and local demand helped raise the number of parish priests to 36,600 by the mid-nineteenth century.[36] The number of diocesan priests peaked in the early years of the Second Empire and declined steadily until the interwar period.[37] The Italian nationalists' establishment of the Second Roman Republic (1848) was built on the French precedent set fifty years earlier, but the French redeemed themselves with the Church by repelling Italian nationalists and restoring Pius IX's rule in Rome.

Other things, however, would never be the same. Diocesan priests were bureaucratized and made into civil servants for the first 115 years of the Republic. The state did not regulate religious doctrine, but closely monitored all communication, controlled appointments to church positions, and oversaw the administration of religious associations.[38] The clergy's ability to provide spiritual services to the steadily increasing French population suffered as a result: the proportion of priests per person fell from one per 300 citizens at the time of the Revolution to one per 660 one century later. Church construction fell

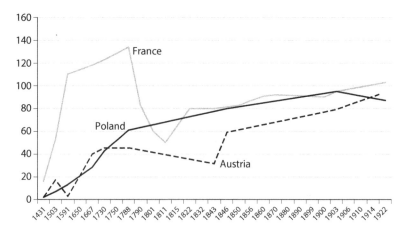

FIGURE 5.4. Bishops from Austria, France, and Poland, 1431–1922

behind: in 1856 Paris, 38 parishes served 1.2 million people, which amounted to just one-third of earlier capacity.

State control had an impact on the socioeconomic origins of French church leadership. Before 1789, all bishops were nobles; only half were noblemen in 1830, and just 4.5 percent in 1880. Nor would France ever again have as many bishops or cardinals in Rome (see figure 5.4). Catholicism was subjected to a new regulatory state and was one of four religions recognized by the new Administration des cultes (with Lutheranism, Calvinism, and Judaism). Of the four, only Catholicism was authorized for "public exercise," but new laws strictly governed everything from ringing church bells to requesting permits for public processions and the *déplacement* of the Holy Sacrament.[39] When Louis Napoleon became Emperor Napoleon III (1852–1870), he reached an agreement with the Church. His reign was culturally more attuned to traditional Catholic mores. For example, state prosecutors defended public morals against subversive poets and novelists like Flaubert and Baudelaire.[40] But the emperor frustrated the Church's requests for military relief from the successful Italian nationalist onslaught in the 1860s. In that sense, the Second Empire (1852–1875) was scarcely different from the Third Republic that followed (1875–1940).[41]

The Third Republic (1875–1940)

The definitive divorce took place between 1880 and 1906, more than a century after the Revolution. The republican government shared concern about the Church's restored role under the Second Empire, especially in the education system—one of the few themes that "an otherwise factious" coalition could agree upon. In the words of Prime Minister Léon Gambetta, a national hero, "The enemy is Clericalism." Authorities aimed to "eliminate all traces of ecclesiastical influence from the machinery of government" and to "check and repress the Church . . . in all her efforts to influence the people in political affairs . . . and doctrines inimical to the republic."[42] Worried about the Church's traditionalist influence, the Republic targeted the autonomy that Rome had clawed back after the French Revolution. A long roster of public institutions figured on the agenda of the secularization campaign: "Schools were made undenominational, public prayers were abolished, participation of the army in religious processions was forbidden, divorce was legalized, hospitals secularized, exemptions of ecclesiastics from military service suppressed, religious communities and sectarian schools partly abolished."[43]

Jesuit institutions were banned (1880), the press was freed (1881), divorce was legalized (1882), and all publicly funded religious education was abolished (1886).[44] The "government feared that clergy who objected to Civil Constitution would use local dialects to influence ignorant peasants against the Republic" and so sought to regulate the "language and content of catechisms and sermons."[45] Using local dialects, in theory, allowed one to "speak politics from the pulpit without being understood by the civil authorities." The Fallières directive of 1890 instructed churches in non-French-speaking departments to use only French-language materials.

When Church-state conflict flared up, the state always wound up on top. In 1892, an archbishop circulated a pastoral letter "voicing resentment at being forced to marry in church only those who first obtained a certificate of civil marriage from the City Hall," and he criticized the notion that "the sentence of a lay tribunal could break the knot on which heaven's blessing descended." The French minister of justice and of religions sued him for writing a letter of a "collective nature" and with "political character."[46] Authorities condemned the archbishop and four bishops for abuses and censored the letter.[47] More anti-Church laws were passed over the last decade of the nineteenth century, until finally all male and female orders were prohibited, 14,000 Catholic schools were closed, and diplomatic relations with the Holy See were broken off. The French laws spurred an exodus of 30,000 religious employees—the largest such outflow since the failed revolutions of 1848.[48] Despite the persecution, the republican revival in the 1890s nonetheless attempted to "reconcile the Church with republican imperialism." Bishops named priests from a list preapproved by the government (*double investiture*).[49] The appointees were reminded that "Bishops' powers are exclusively of a spiritual order, and these powers are measured with the strictest economy."

Another Catholic epistle placed a wedge between Church and Republic after the French president paid a state visit to King Vittorio Emanuele III of

LA SÉPARATION
Séparons-nous. - Je garde vos biens.

FIGURE 5.5. "The Separation: 'Let's separate—I'll keep your property'" (1905)

Italy. Pope Pius X protested such legitimation of the rulers of "occupied Rome" in a letter sent to all the Catholic powers, writing that "the heads of Catholic nations owe especial deference to the supreme pastor of their church." This was especially true, Pius wrote, given France's "large representation in the sacred college of cardinals" and its vocation as "the protectorate of Catholic interests in the Orient." The letter is credited with precipitating the 1905 law of separation and making it easier to break with Rome.[50] The 1905 law forced the Church to reorganize as an *association cultuelle*, along the same lines as Judaism and Protestantism. The public budget for diocesan buildings was transferred to museums and fine arts, and the Ministry of the Interior was placed in full control of religion policy (see figure 5.5). "The so-called separation was concluded so that the state received all of the seized property of the church but ceased all payments for the maintenance of the clergy and spiritual establishments."[51] It was not a legal contradiction for the state to hold on to Church property. The 1789 decree that all houses of worship were the property of the nation was never repealed. For this reason, "it [would] have been unduly generous to hand this property over to the clergy" in 1905. The state stopped paying Church salaries and revived the Revolutionary practice of mandatory inventories of Church property in 1906. This encountered popular resistance in western French cities as it prepared to sell off parsonages to the highest bidders, turned churches into music halls, or placed them at the disposal of any association of worship recognized under the 1905 law. The toll upon believers was so serious by that time that, in what was surely an exaggeration, estimates of practicing Catholics were as low as 5 million out of a population of 42 million.[52]

Spain

As elsewhere, Napoleon's invasion plunged Spanish pastoral authority into confusion and introduced a brutal phase of civilian control and intentional neglect. Bishops who mysteriously vanished or died were not replaced: by 1813, a majority of Spanish dioceses were unoccupied.[53] King Ferdinand VII (1784–1833) seized church properties, dismissed religious officials who refused to swear an oath of loyalty, and banned the Society of Jesus; the Jesuits were briefly welcomed back until seventeen Jesuit priests were killed in Madrid riots (1835). Next, Queen Isabella II (1830–1904) nationalized the entirety of Church holdings (1837) and froze all priestly ordinations.[54] Twenty bishops who disobeyed were exiled or imprisoned. When the Church sat down with the government in 1851 to negotiate a new concordat, forty dioceses still lacked a bishop.[55] From this disadvantaged position, the Church "renounced [a] 'substantial portion' of property" and the state "maintained the right to appoint to bishoprics and benefices." Theological faculties in universities were replaced with six national seminaries. (Spanish bishops, under Madrid's thrall, refused Rome's suggestion of a single central seminary in Escorial.) The state undertook to maintain parish clergy and church buildings and allowed a limited revival of male orders (including Jesuits).

In Spain, the division of labor—the hard-won separation of temporal and spiritual—took the following form. The state had control over academic coursework in the seminaries, while the bishops oversaw trainees' "way of life and devotion."[56] A major insult was delivered to the Church when Amadeus of Savoy—the son of Vittorio Emanuele II of Italy, "the man who robbed the church"—briefly served as king of Spain (1868–73). Amadeus dissolved all Church corporations and seized its land, libraries, archives, and artwork. Jesuits were permitted to teach but only in civilian dress, not in their black soutane. Two bishops were named to the Spanish parliament (Constituent Cortes), and the state tried to impose a civil service oath of allegiance on all bishops and clergy; all but the two Spanish bishops refused it.

One consequence of the elimination of religious corporations was the clearing away of internal competition and the centralization and professionalization of the Church's educational offerings. Bishops representing the centralized Church dominated the realm of religious educational oversight "to verify conformity of education to Catholic teaching," relatively free of the rivalry of brotherhoods and clerical orders. In 1869–1870, the Spanish state granted toleration to Protestants and instituted civil marriage.[57] The government hoped to create "a free church in a free state"—as the Italian statesman Camillo Cavour put it. It declared "illegitimate" the children of any couple who were married only in the Church. With the restoration of the Bourbon monarchy, King Alfonso XII (1874–1885) recognized the legality of Church marriage and declared Catholicism the state religion.[58] Liberal ministers remained influential over the next fifty years, until the Second Spanish Republic and civil war.[59] No bishops were appointed for long stretches, and religious properties were destroyed in a single week of anticlerical activism. The Spanish Civil War (1936–1939) claimed the lives of 283 nuns, 2,365 monks, and 4,000 parish priests (see figure 5.6). In the mid-1700s, 65,000 priests ministered to Spain's 10 million inhabitants. Two centuries later, by comparison, there were only 25,000 priests for over 30 million Spaniards.[60]

Germany

The German hierarchy rebounded from the Napoleonic invasion thanks to post-Revolutionary French absenteeism in Rome. In the aftermath of Napoleon's invasion, the Vatican paid close attention to Bavaria and Rhineland,

FIGURE 5.6. Republican female fighters besiege a monastery in Madrid (1936)

home to millions of Catholics. In 1817, according to the Bavarian agreement, the state funded all bishoprics, the *Domkapitel*, and theological seminaries. The king named bishops, and the pope granted them "canonical institution." Bishops were allowed to have "free interchange with Rome" and were given "oversight of beliefs and values" in state schools. German bishops and cardinals slowly improved their position internally within the centralized Church, as shown by agreements in the 1820s that restored Church provinces in Cologne, Prussia, Hanover, and Württemberg and placed additional *suffragen* bishops in regional hubs. Episcopal nominations were subject to the review of local rulers, who could exclude undesirable candidates.

According to the Breslau (Wroclaw) model pioneered by Frederick the Great of Protestant Prussia, a Jesuit university was founded with two faculties of theology, one Catholic and one Protestant. The same was done in Bonn, Württemberg, Tübingen, Würzburg, and Hesse-Darmstadt (1831). Publicly funded state universities were unique in having Catholic theology faculties, but they had difficulties keeping them staffed. Shortages of Catholic professors at all seventeen German universities were ascribed to a lack of qualified applicants. Acute state-church conflicts emerged at times—for example, over mixed-marriages in Prussia, which decreed that children were to be raised in the religion of the father. When the archbishop of Cologne audaciously defended the Church's position against that practice, he was imprisoned (1837). The same happened with the archbishop of Gnesen-Posen (1839).[61] In the 1840s, Prussian authorities created a Catholic division within the Kultusministerium to oversee religious education.[62] Catholic faculties of theology were still in publicly funded state universities, however, and in 1866 the Prussian religions minister reconstituted a Catholic affairs department.

When the king of Prussia became emperor of a unified German empire in 1871, the new state absorbed the Catholic populations in Bavaria and the Rhineland. His prime minister, Otto von Bismarck, eliminated the Catholic department inside the Prussian religions ministry. Relations with Rome took a quick turn for the worse. Within a year, after a public feud between Pius IX and Bismarck, Germany expelled all foreign Jesuits and severed diplomatic relations with Rome.[63] An 1872 law suppressed the Jesuit order and subjected all Catholic schools to expanded state inspections.[64] The May Laws (Maigesetze, 1873) criminalized the performance of Mass and the delivery of last rites, required clergy to hold a university degree, and placed all seminaries under state supervision; nearly half were closed within five years.[65] The state asserted the right to veto any clerical appointment that "might imperil public order" and abolished Roman interference in disciplinary measures of the German Catholic Church.

The term *kulturkampf* (1873) comes from the free-thinker Reichstag deputy who intended to wage "the struggle of modern progress against [the] medieval un-culture" of the Catholic Church. In a demonstration of the Church's political toxicity at the time, the largely Catholic Zentrum Party was told to establish its independence from clerical influence. In a letter from a party leader to a priest in Posen, the party dutifully instructed the Church, "Do not send us any more petitions to the Reichstag." In Church-state relations, the kulturkampf led to another crisis of investiture—"the struggle with the Pope over the appointment of Catholic bishops and clergy." For a decade following unification, Bismarck battled the Catholic Church over Rome's appointment of bishops and clergy. The state reserved the right to veto nominations that threatened public order, leaving nine of twelve Prussian dioceses without bishops and 1,400 parishes with no priest. Secret Masses were celebrated in the woods, as had once been the practice during the Reformation.[66] The May Laws also created a court to judge the "illicit exercise of church office." The court sentenced around 2,000 church employees to be fined, dispossessed, imprisoned, expelled, or denaturalized. The Congregations Law progressed, and in 1875 Germany abolished religious orders, ending all state subsidies to the Catholic Church. A civil ceremony was made mandatory for marriage, and clerics who resisted the laws were imprisoned or removed.

Catholic states with a long Josephist tradition, like Bavaria, were familiar with several of the powers that Bismarck seized for the Prussian government.

Despite the privations of liberty and property, "Bismarck discovered that against the *intangible resistance* of Rome his Krupp guns were powerless."[67] More importantly, Bismarck recognized that the Vatican could be a useful wedge against their common adversaries—namely, the secular Catholic governments of France, Italy, and Spain—and he reestablished diplomatic relations with Rome in 1882. The "Iron Chancellor" came out publicly against the new Italian nation-state, in favor of "retrocession to the Pope of the entire city of Rome, which would thus become an independent pontifical territory, enclosed within the kingdom . . . under the guarantee of all European powers"—displacing the Italian government from its new capital. He said the pope could temporarily seek haven in Germany: "His departure will be the signal for civil war and insurrections . . . [to] ruin the Italian monarchy." Bismarck even pursued Catholic powers' agreement to "guarantee the uses to which the Pope may put his spiritual independence" (which Italians, however, interpreted as simply "a means of [German] coercion on the Holy See").[68] Bismarck abrogated the anti-Catholic laws one by one—the Culture Exam (1883), the Royal Court for Church Affairs (1886), the Expatriation Law (1890)—and finally he approved a law to pay reparations to Jesuits (1891).

This did not put an end, however, to the political interference in Church affairs. In 1891 Prussia, "in every part of the monarchy the crown has reserved to itself control over the election of bishops and priests."[69] Catholics grew used to perpetually understaffed parishes, even though one-third of the population was Catholic. The Weimar Constitution (1919) granted greater rights to Catholic communities as corporations of public law. That enabled the gradual restoration of autonomy in the administration of Catholic institutions—from hospitals to orphanages and religious education. Nonetheless, a century after Weimar, one lone Catholic university survived within German borders, in the Bavarian city of Eichstätt-Ingolstadt.

Italy

The first attempt at Italian unification failed when Austria and France came to the aid of the pope. They conquered Piedmontese troops and the short-lived Roman Republic (1849), and the pope was allowed to return. Forced to postpone the national Risorgimento, the constitutional monarchy in Piedmont under Carlo Alberto implemented its own liberalization. The Siccardi laws (1851) restricted Church land purchases, abolished residual medieval clerical privileges like its separate justice system, and set about reducing the clergy's immense wealth (see figure 5.7). Within the next several years, the Italian scholar Angela Pellicciari writes, thirty-five religious brotherhoods were suppressed, including Franciscans, Dominicans, and other monastic orders,

FIGURE 5.7. Monument to the Siccardi Law abolishing the Ecclesiastic Courts, Turin (1853)

affecting 5,500 individuals altogether. When unification succeeded a decade later, the Siccardi laws were extended over the entire kingdom.[70] The persecution and purges had an immediate and devastating impact upon tens of thousands of priests, monks, and nuns—as well as upon the millions of those who made use of various Church institutions and services.

Catholicism was officially maintained to be "the sole religion of the State" in the Kingdom of Italy of the 1860s, but it was transformed into a state religion. Between 1860 and 1865, the Ministry of Public Instruction closed 82 seminaries, in some cases depriving towns of their only educational establishment. In 1864, observers recounted (in a curiously passive voice), there were "43 bishops exiled, 20 bishops imprisoned, 16 bishops deported and 16 dead." A bishop was reportedly imprisoned for fourteen months for having skipped out on a royal visit to his diocese, and dozens of bishops and cardinals were put on trial in southern Italy.[71] A cardinal was said to have been arrested for refusing to sing *Te Deum* for King Vittorio Emanuele II. In 1866, the king abolished all religious corporations and seized their property. The government saw the seminaries as anti-state "nests," and in 1866 it shut down all seminaries in several regions.[72] There was heightened scrutiny and regulatory inspections of all primary and secondary classes being offered by Catholic seminaries.[73] Adding insult to injury, the new Italian government "devoted a great part of the property confiscated from the monastic establishments to the cause of public education"—which was staunchly secular and patriotic in nature.[74]

In a speech on the Roman Question, the diplomatic architect of Italian unification, Camillo Cavour, vowed to eventually make Rome the national capital while promising that "there shall be no interference with the Pope's spiritual independence."[75] Nonetheless, royal consent was henceforth required for any bishop or archbishop, and nearly half of all dioceses in that decade had no bishop—108 of 227—owing to royal denials.[76]

When the Italians finally invaded Rome in July 1870, they became the latest wave of infidels to vandalize the city. The nationalist soldiers deconsecrated the Colosseum and the Pantheon (pre-Christian structures that had been converted into churches) and took over the papal residence, the Quirinale Palace, as well as Jesuit headquarters. The cloisters and Monte Casino were seized as national property and turned into new state schools—whose curriculum eliminated religious education.[77] To this day a sizable number of former monasteries and seminaries that were never returned to the Church still serve as Italian public buildings.[78] A parliamentary leader declared war "upon the Catholic preponderance in the world with all of our means." Official organs of the Revolutionary Party in Italy wrote solemnly that in the case of a great European war, "it would be exceedingly difficult for the Pope, his Court, and the Roman clergy to escape with their lives from Rome."[79]

The unilateral Italian Law of Guarantees (1871) provided a take-it-or-leave-it package deal: personal protection, an annual grant of several million liras, and tax-exempt use of the Vatican, Lateran palaces, and the Castel Gandalfo summer palace.[80] Despite the infringement upon organizational autonomy, article 9 of the law affirmed "the Sovereign Pontiff is entirely free to exercise all the functions of his spiritual ministry."[81] Article 13 gave the pope sole authority over seminaries, academies, colleges, other Catholic education and cultural institutions in Rome and area dioceses "without interference from the scholastic authorities of the Kingdom."[82] Within six months of the law's promulgation, Pius IX successfully nominated over 100 bishops.

Nonetheless, state intimidation did not disappear. Upon the death of Pius IX in 1876, "several battalions of Italian infantry surrounded the great square of St. Peters . . . to assert the rights of the Italian Government."[83] Spontaneous pro-Church demonstrations—for example, to protest the statue of Giordano Bruno, and to accompany the transportation of Pius IX's body—were tolerated by the government.[84] In 1877, a bill aimed at "correcting clerical abuses" was introduced; it threatened imprisonment and fines for "any minister of religion who abuses his office so as to offend against the institutions or laws of the State and perturbs the public conscience or peace of *families*."[85] The government resisted politicians' calls for a raid on the Vatican in March 1888, but it blamed deadly riots in turn-of-the-century Milan on a Vatican ploy "to overthrow the House of Savoy in favor of a republic which might pave the way to a restoration of the temporal power of the Pope."[86]

The Papal State's Resistance to the Nation-State

At first, the Church hierarchy harbored fear and resentment following the wave of anticlerical violence, imprisonment, expulsions, and expropriation. After being removed from their traditional roles, Church officials faced a dilemma: Should the clergy recognize the new institutional reality by running for office and participating in parliament? Or should a volunteer army be drafted to defend the papacy by any means necessary? A contemporary observer worried that "Europe is *on the verge of a great war* in which the Roman Catholic element may find itself arrayed not only against Protestant countries, but also against Catholic Governments." An attempt was made on German chancellor Bismarck's life in the town of Bad Kissingen (1874) when a disgruntled Catholic citizen of the German Empire shot him as a protest against anti-Church laws, but failed to mortally wound him. A short-lived international armed resistance by an international Catholic volunteer force delayed the Italian invasion of Rome for a brief spell. For the most part, however, the Church weathered the Second Defeat as a one-sided *cultural* war (*kulturkampf*)

TABLE 5.2. Ecclesiastic Officials in National Parliaments (*Annuaire Pontificale*), 1907

Austria	21 clerics elected to the House of Representatives
	23 bishops sit ex officio in the House of Lords
Belgium	17 clerics elected to the National Constituent Assembly (1830)
France	2 abbés elected to the Assemblée Nationale (1907)
Germany	1 cleric elected to the Reichstag; 25 clerics elected to state parliaments (1907)
Holland	3 clerics elected to the Riksdag (1907)
Luxembourg	5 clerics elected to the Chambre des Députés (1907)
Portugal	11 bishops and cardinals sit ex officio in the Senate
Piedmont	1 bishop sits ex officio in the Senate; 39 clerics elected to Parliament (1848)
Spain	11 archbishops elected to the Senate; 16 archbishops sit ex officio in the Senate (1871/1876)
Switzerland	1 archbishop elected deputy in the Bundeshaus (1892)

waged by the modern state, and Catholic religious leaders gathered the institutional strength to respond in kind.

Political Participation

There was tentative ex officio political participation in national parliaments and constituent assemblies, but few Church officials ran for parliament (see table 5.2). In pre-unification Italy, the royal House of Savoy named bishops to serve in the Piedmontese senate, where they defended the interests of the Church (and its clerical courts) against attack and expropriation (for example, the Siccardi laws of 1851). After Piedmont annexed, conquered, and bargained its way to a unified Italy in 1860, seizing the Papal States along the way, the clergy departed all public offices in protest. The national revolutions strengthened the hand of reactionaries in the Church and weakened reformers.[87] The early nineteenth-century debate over the wisdom of priestly celibacy, for example, was displaced by the refusal of popes of the mid-1800s to recognize Italian unification and to prohibit political participation—under penalty of excommunication.

The papacy remained oriented toward temporal power and political rule in the face of national states' secularization attempts. The Vatican refused the "usurpation of pontifical rights and sovereignty" and rejected the legitimacy of liberal nation-states. "Men were never all equal," one Church defender wrote confidently: "The first principle of 1789 is false."[88] The *Syllabus of Errors* (1864) condemned modernism, liberalism, religious freedom, the idea of progress, and the separation of church and state.[89] A growing list of excommunicated Catholic statesmen was nailed to the doors of Roman basilicas. One widely circulated tract declared belief in "liberalism" to be an excommunicable sin. The encyclical *Non Expedit* (1868) forbade voting under penalty of excommunication. Voting, according to Pius IX, was the moral equivalent of "swearing approval of the spoliation of the Church, of the sacrileges committed, and of anti-Catholic teachings."[90]

The Pope's Fist

When Pope Pius IX declared holy war against unified Italy and asked believers to join the final battle for Rome, the Catholic civil war moved beyond the realm of politics and took kinetic form. This turned out to be Rome's last meaningful gesture toward temporal political ambitions. Thousands of irregular "Papal Zouaves" answered the call to support the pontiff's last stand against Giuseppe Garibaldi's Red Shirts. They managed to delay Italian nationalists' invasion of Rome by several years. Newspapers reported that the Church was "proud of her gallant defenders, prouder still of her newly made martyrs."[91] The pope's raising of an army declared "his determination in regard to the Temporal Power. He will not give it up, He will fight for it with all his strength and with every weapon." Nearly 20,000 Zouaves—also known as *Papalini*, or "The Pope's Fist"—volunteered to defend Rome against Italian nationalists (1861–1870). These men, who hailed from across western Europe—Flemish, Alsatian, Irish, German—and North America, were "considered heroes in their own Catholic circle," newspapers reported at the time. The largest single national contingent, 3,100 men, arrived from the Netherlands (out of a Dutch Catholic population of about 2 million). The volunteer soldiers were legendary for their "heroic devotion" and for "leaving the field strewn with their glorious slain."[92] One soldier's journal describes the feeling: "We are fully recompensed for all we have undergone by the satisfaction of knowing that we have done our duty, the pride of having served the Holy Father, and the edification of having witnessed so many holy and happy deaths, which really make one quite long to become a martyr. . . . I am half sorry that I was not left on the field. . . . Another time I hope I shall not come out of the fight at all."[93]

The international military volunteers gave the pope breathing room during a critical period (1867–1870). The Zouaves guarded the Vatican when Pius IX fell seriously ill, creating a security buffer that allowed the consideration of holding a conclave while the current pope still lived, to guard against the danger "of a Garibaldian attack on Rome during an interregnum."[94] The Zouaves' major military contribution came in the fall of 1867, when they joined French troops in routing the Italian forces at Mentana, twenty-nine kilometers northeast of Vatican walls. This was their first time using deadly new *chassepots* (bolt-action rifles), which left behind more than 800 dead Italians, compared to only 200 "Catholic martyrs." The French author Victor Hugo dedicated a

FIGURE 5.8. Pope Pius IX blesses papal Zouaves in St. Peter's Square, Rome (1870)

poem to the Italian nationalists whose "brows were split by Zouave bullets," portraying the pope, unflatteringly, as someone who "preaches the righteousness of Howitzer [artillery guns] and says at the end of prayers: 'Now, slit their throats, my Holy Zouaves!'"[95] By holding off the Italian advance and successfully defending Rome, the volunteer soldiers scuttled Italian plans to relocate their capital from Turin to Rome, forcing it to settle midway, in Florence, instead. The Zouaves' efforts permitted the pontiff, who recovered his health, to convene the First Vatican Council (1869–1870) until it was interrupted by the invasion of Rome. After the pope's formal surrender, thousands of Zouaves gathered in St. Peter's Square for a final blessing before dispersing to their various countries of origin (see figure 5.8). Pope Pius granted the assembled volunteers a full pardon for any and all personal sins, valid for three generations. And he publicly excommunicated everyone who was involved in the Italian "occupation" of Rome.

The First Vatican Council

It took time for the Vatican to find its footing in the new geopolitical terrain. Like the Council of Trent before it, the First Vatican Council attempted to close the destructive debate over the pope's place in the Church and the world. The first to be held in St. Peter's Basilica, Vatican I formulated the papal response to the nation-state era. The meeting embodied the ambitions of the Ultramontane revival: as the Church historian John O'Malley writes, Vatican I made a "solemn and defiant statement against that century's Liberalism," rooted in a conviction that "liberty, equality and fraternity were not a panacea but a recipe for carnage and chaos."[96] It sought to provide a definitive answer to the challenges that Catholic monarchs made against papal claims—including, for example, two centuries of Gallicanism (and one century of its German variant, Febronianism). National governments had always exercised control over episcopal appointments, but Vatican I stood up to new republican governments. The papacy asserted that episcopal appointments were a matter of privilege, leading to new crises of investiture.

This was the chance to assert papal infallibility once and for all: the pope's power "to pronounce that a teaching is of divine and apostolic faith" with absolute, unquestionable, and unmistakable authority.[97] The assertion of papal primacy did not represent a direct political threat to European states. It was aimed at bishops who faced political pressure or who otherwise exhibited independent tendencies, warning them not to stray from the Roman line. Provinces and hierarchies were scrutinized so as to eschew indigenization, or what Vatican I termed "domination by the congregation's country of origin."[98] Despite parallels with the sixteenth century, Ultramontane sympathizers could never conjure the Church of the Inquisition.[99] The religious leadership meted out no punitive acts of violence; its judiciary had no enforcement mechanism. There were no major violent aftershocks after Rome fell, no reprise of the thirty-year war or significant military struggle. The Vatican employed a variety of strategies to oppose liberal nationalism, but it did not choose the route of political participation either. It pragmatically adjusted its sights from temporal to spiritual authority through the reinforcement of churches and priests, educational institutions, and religious hierarchy.

Infrastructure

So long as the Roman Question remained open, Rome feared nationalist infiltration and manipulation of the episcopal and cardinal corps. The vulnerability to political interference pushed much of this activity abroad, outside the heart of Catholic Europe. Two Counter-Reformation institutions played a key role: the Congregation de' Propaganda Fide and national colleges. Ironically, the Church had greater freedom to operate within the bounds of Anglican, Calvinist, and Lutheran regimes than in most Catholic countries.[100] The number of clergy per citizens in Sweden and Denmark in 1903 was luxurious compared to Catholic Europe, which had one priest per 150 Catholics; Norwegian Catholics had one priest for every 64 believers. All Scandinavia, however, was

home to fewer than 12,000 Catholics. In the Netherlands, Calvinism was abolished as the state religion (1798), and unification with Belgium (1815–1830)
temporarily brought a Catholic majority: the Dutch hierarchy was reestablished in 1853.[101]

Reeling from national government controls in Europe, the 700 or so attendees of the First Vatican Council called for a massive standardization of
infrastructure, educational institutions, and Church hierarchy across international borders. The Church strengthened its religious education networks and
internal hierarchies in order to help resist the onslaught from nineteenth-
century statesmen. The result was a building boom across Europe as communities "restored churches, rebuilt chapels, re-opened monasteries and organized schools."[102] The gradual demise of temporal power fostered the creation
of new institutions of infrastructure, education, and hierarchy to recover control from the nation-state—and to fend off competing religions and other
modern ills.[103] Pius IX helped establish hundreds of new religious congregations, transnational enterprises, networks of schools, hospitals, orphanages,
asylums, and penitentiary experiments.[104] Most significantly, he invested 29
archbishops and 132 bishops during his papacy. The relative growth of "national" positions in the hierarchy compared to religious infrastructure and
educational institutions reveals a new geographic strategy that had an unintended consequence. The episcopate and the College of Cardinals were
opened to new influences from the outside world as the Vatican sought to
evade and escape decentralizing designs.

Education

Rome also turned to the same Reformation-era tool of priestly education that
the Church had used to survive in Lutheran havens like Germany, Switzerland,
and the Netherlands. They developed new national seminaries within the confines
of property still under their control in Rome. For the first time, a majority-
Catholic country not under foreign occupation received its own college.
France, which was a sixteenth-century haven for the English College in Douai,
came full circle three centuries later when Pius IX established a French College
in Rome (1850). New national colleges in Rome were meant to insulate clerics
from the interference to which governments in majority-Catholic contexts
ceded in the late nineteenth century.

The crux of the spiritual self-defense strategy was to "address the poor quality of education and priest shortages that had worsened since the end of civil
service for the Clergy." Leo XIII (1810–1903) established the Spanish College
(1892) in the context of "diminished quality of studies in Spain" and to shelter
priests from the political volatility of late nineteenth-century Madrid, where

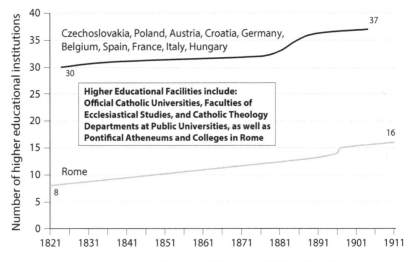

FIGURE 5.9. Roman Catholic Establishments of Higher Education in
Nineteenth-Century Europe

anarchists had bombed religious processions. From 1894 to 1969, the Spanish College occupied the palazzo adjacent to the Collegio Germanico, the first place to harbor and train foreign priests in Rome. A Holy Congregation for Universities, *Congregatio studiorum* (1870), was created as a centralized mechanism for oversight of Catholic universities worldwide. Some of the national colleges worked in conjunction with the Gregorian University, and the former Collegio Romano (1551) was chartered as a pontifical university (1873). Training seminaries had ground to a halt across much of late-nineteenth-century Europe and needed to be rebuilt so as to cultivate the next generation of clergy.[105]

All told, the number of pontifical atheneums, colleges, and universities in Rome doubled over the course of the nineteenth century, from eight in 1821 to sixteen in 1909. The number of universities, faculties of ecclesiastical studies, and Catholic theology departments at public universities across the rest of Europe increased by nearly 25 percent, from thirty to thirty-seven (see figure 5.9).

Hierarchy

The Italian Law of Guarantees that served as the post-invasion framework agreement between the Italian state and the papacy permitted the pope to remain in the Vatican. He was allowed to appoint local bishops, and he successfully nominated 102 Italian bishops between October 1870 and May 1871.[106]

The following year this agreement fell apart, and the pope instructed dozens of Italian bishops and mitered abbots *not* to submit the nominating bulls to the Italian government. By 1875, out of ninety bishop nominations submitted to the government, only 28 were approved.[107] As a result, half of Italian dioceses remained vacant for the duration of the Roman Question (1871–1929). This effort to insulate the major national hierarchies from political interference by anticlerical forces differed from the strategy during the Reformation, when the more endangered territories received more institutional attention and bishops were widely distributed to form an offensive line.[108] Over the course of the nineteenth century, by contrast, Italy added eighty bishops while the entire rest of the world contributed only seventy-six.

The Vatican also chose, however, to increase cardinal appointments in Church-friendly countries. Being under political siege in Italy, France, Germany, and Spain would spur the Church to definitively diversify the College of Cardinals. This led to the further globalization of the College between 1800 and 1900. Between 1846 and 1878, Second Empire France received sixteen new cardinals, Restoration Spain received twelve new cardinals, and Germany received only four. That, too, was the fruit of the sixteenth century: far-flung missions and colonies were appointed cardinalates where the aggressive Catholic nation-states could not interfere. In England, Catholics received full citizenship and emancipation in 1829. Their nineteenth-century numbers in England, Wales, and Scotland steadily grew from around 100,000 to 2 million. The British crown's restoration of the Catholic hierarchy in England and Wales (1850) and in Scotland (1878) was followed by increases in the arrival of priests.[109] Remarkably, despite being implanted in what could have been inhospitable terrain, the growth of Catholic clergy in Great Britain perfectly tracks the population growth (see figure 5.10).

Catholic organizations labored to expand in *minority*-Catholic countries—including the United Kingdom (1850), the Netherlands (1853), and Scandinavia and across the Protestant New World in the United States—which all recognized the clergy and the clerical status of bishops.[110] In France, a major missionary organization known as Holy Works for the Propagation of the Faith was established in Lyon, near the Swiss and German borders. In 1827, a similar missionary organization, Istituzione Leopoldina, was formed in Vienna, with imperial blessing. The relative growth of positions in the hierarchy compared to religious infrastructure and educational institutions reveals an implicit geographic strategy and its unintended consequence. As the hierarchy sought to evade political control that could infiltrate decision-making in the Church's centralized Roman institutions, the episcopate and the College of Cardinals were opened to new influences from the outside world—especially voices from minority-Catholic contexts.

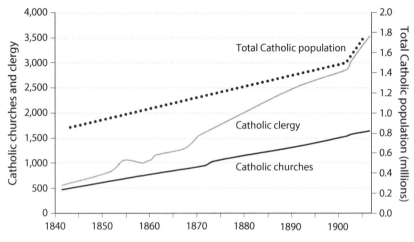

FIGURE 5.10. Roman Catholic Churches and Clergy in England and Wales, 1840–1910

Resolving the Roman Question:
A New Deal on Via della Conciliazione

The possible breaching of Vatican walls posed an existential question: How was the papacy and its continuity of succession to be preserved? In an increasingly inhospitable heartland, Pius IX formed a committee of cardinals to determine whether it was "better to go." If flight from Rome was their determination, where could he "have freer links with all the Churches of the world"? A parliament of bishops was convened outside Rome, and rumors circulated that the Holy Father would soon depart from the Vatican.[111] Belgian and German bishops offered the pope sanctuary, and the government of the United Kingdom put its Mediterranean fleet—and a palace on the island of Malta—at Pius's disposal.[112] The Roman Question persisted because the doctrinally unreconstructed pontiff declined to relocate to friendlier climes and instead dug in behind Vatican walls. This was not a satisfactory outcome for either side. The pope's decision seemed to be to "retire into a dark fastness as the 'Prisoner of the Vatican,'" to snipe at the Italian government in pursuit of his own political sovereignty.[113]

Paradoxically, the argument for returning to the pope a modicum of political power was to restore the integrity of his spiritual authority. Operating under the Italian Law of Guarantee made "Papal communications with the Episcopate subject to the control of Italian authorities," denying the pope the sovereignty and dignity as Supreme Head of the Church. In the earlier search for solutions, the Roman curia had sought out negotiations with the new governments in majority-Catholic states to recover earlier privileges. But they found that governments tended to ignore previous concordats.[114] The treatment engendered resentment and enduring suspicion and left unresolved an underlying contradiction.

The Holy See perceived an existential threat: Pius IX believed that the nationalists were not only targeting "its legitimate temporal authority" but also seeking "the complete elimination of the Catholic religion's very power of salvation."[115] Later popes described Italian unification as "the extermination of the religion of Jesus Christ."[116] After the invasion of Rome in 1870, an eyewitness wrote evocatively, "The Bronze Gate of the Vatican was shut. . . . The gilded and painted coaches of the cardinals utterly vanished. No more processions of the Bambino . . . no more carrying round of the *Pontefice Massimo* on the *Sedia Gestatoria*, the swinging of the giant fans of peacocks' plumes."[117] From the perspective of many traditionalists, the absence of "a Pope-King"— that is, one without temporal authority—implied that the Church existed under state control.[118] Without temporal power, the Church historian Jean Carrère argued, "The ship of St. Peter would either be put at the service of the victors or risk being dashed to pieces."[119] Church leaders who resided in nation-states with official Catholicism were considered to be a captive leadership.[120]

The Vatican's subtle change in approach occurred by degrees as the popes engaged in nuanced, loss-cutting behavior over time. Pius IX suspended the king's excommunication and allowed for a chaplain to grant him absolution and last rites. He did not wish eternal damnation upon him, but nor would he allow a religious funeral to be held in a Roman cathedral. He also forbade bishops and cardinals from attending Mass while the Italian king lay in state at the desacralized Pantheon.[121] Leo XIII (1878–1903) did not stop vigorously condemning the religious toleration under Italian rule as false doctrine.[122] But the new political reality elicited a key concession in Leo's *Immortale Dei* (1885), namely, that toleration of non-Catholic religions might prevent worse evils. Allen Hertzke argues that Leo began a "long *rapprochement* of the Church to the 'new things' of the world," culminating in the encyclical *Rerum Novarum* (Of Revolutionary Change, Rights, and Duties of Capital and Labor, 1891), which urged the Church to formulate compelling answers to the industrial era's downsides, such as "untrammeled capitalism, child labor, mass suffering, and Marxist revolutions."[123] Leo stated his support for a "vast reconciliation between Religion and Civilization, between Church and State, and between the Papacy and Italy." In 1897, he said the conflict was creating the unhappy situation of "forcing Italians to choose between being good Catholics and being good Italians."[124] Leo's reconceptualization cast the Church in a quasi-civic role, as a utility of public good.

Turn-of-the-century liberal Italy, however, was not in a conciliatory mood. It celebrated the silver anniversary of "liberation from papal tyranny" and declared a national holiday on the date of Rome's conquest. Seminaries were subject to regular inspections and the prime minister proudy used the word "persecution" to describe his Catholicism policy. He declared it the duty of freethinking Masons everywhere to combat the pope as an enemy of Italy.[125] A parliamentary deputy argued that it was time for the country's "pious endowments and religious institutions" to disappear and "make way for brotherly civilization among peoples."[126] The 1901 Cocco-Ortu memorandum prohibited meetings or gatherings in churches for anything other than explicitly religious ceremonies.[127]

The Italian prime minister, Francesco Crispi (1893–1896), had been an instrumental figure in the Risorgimento, and he continued to spar with Leo XIII throughout the 1890s. Crispi made a telling prediction: "Material power eludes [the pope] and it would be a virtue if he had the wisdom to forget about it. The greatest statesman of Italy will be the man who solves the 'Roman Question.'"[128] The papal prohibition against voting in secular elections began to erode soon thereafter, and *Non Expedit* was formally reversed in 1919. This marked acceptance of the idea that Catholics had a separate sphere of political engagement as *citizens* of Italy—or of one of the dozens of Catholic nation-states—and not of the Vatican. This did not mean the pontiff now accepted liberal democracy, except, perhaps, as a means to an end, like a tram car. Indeed, wherever possible in Catholic countries, "the Church sought state privilege and . . . limitation of the rights of non-Catholics."[129] But the Church officials who arrived for the next conclave came with an open attitude to the Roman Question; in the words of one Belgian cardinal: "Forgive your enemies."[130] The overture to Catholic political participation, together with the growing influence of cardinals and bishops outside of France, Germany, and Italy, accelerated the Vatican's reconciliation with the Italian kingdom. The 1922 conclave elected Pius XI, and he pronounced his inaugural *Pro Urbi et Orbi* blessing from the external loggia of St. Peter's—for the first time since the Italian army seized Rome in 1870, foreshadowing an openness to accommodation.[131]

The articulations of a new universal mission statement evolved to justify the necessity of a sovereign Catholic state and to make it as acceptable as possible to European neighbors. Church authorities said that their "mission lies in the sphere of the spirit, over which the civil State has no jurisdiction, and extends to all nations and states." They argued that "for the Pope to be anyone's citizen or subject would destroy his essential character."[132] The radical corollary was left unspoken: that *the Church no longer claimed jurisdiction over the realm of the civil State.* At the 1922 conclave, it was evident to those in attendance that political instability in Catholic Europe had provoked significant shifts in the personnel staffing key Church institutions. Witnesses described an early push to consider a non-Italian as pope so as to avoid "an impasse between the two Italian parties"—the constitutional cardinals and the dissident cardinals. Ultimately, an Italian cardinal was elected as pope Pius XI, who would "heal the breach" and accept the Church's defeat by the Italian state.

The leader of Italy who rose to power at the same time as Pius XI, the Duce, Benito Mussolini, saw a chance to consolidate his political support by resolving the Roman Question. There were 20 million practicing Catholic subjects to woo.[133] After several years of negotiations, the 1929 Lateran Accords between the Italian kingdom and the Vatican re-created the 1,000-year-old Papal States on a small parcel and formally restored the pontiff's temporal powers as the sovereign civil ruler of a Vatican city-state. The net result was a 100,000-fold reduction of the Church's temporal realm, from the 4 million hectares controlled by the Papal States in 1850 down to the 44 hectares of Vatican City, around the size of Manhattan's Central Park. It was reported that some in the Vatican "dreamed of a rather wider kingdom, reaching to the sea by a strip of land ... permitting the Holy See to have its window freely open to the whole world." What might have been a seaport—a *Porto della Conciliazione*—however, was downgraded to a *via* (street) after the Italian government denied the Vatican access to the sea. The pope's subjects declined from 2.5 million citizens—a bit smaller than Ireland at the time—to a handful between 1,000 and 2,000 church officials and their families, who it was thought would dwindle over time to only 100 to 200 people. Pius XI confirmed the Holy See's transition to a purely spiritual force, saying: "I have no desire to have subjects."[134]

On June 7, 1929, Swiss Guards "marched out of the apostolic palace and took possession of the territory ceded by Italy and mounted guard at its frontier."[135] The bronze doors that had been closed "in mourning for the loss of the Pope's temporal power" were thrown open again nearly sixty years later (see figure 5.11). News accounts capture the mood: "The Pope is again an independent sovereign ruler, as he was throughout the Middle Ages, through his temporal realm," one paper reported. "Long live Pius, our Pope and King."[136] Pius XI said of the 1929 Accords that they "restored God to Italy and Italy to God."[137]

Conclusion

Following the Lateran Accords, the pope expressed the Church's "wishes to remain extraneous to all temporal disputes between nations and to international congresses convoked for the settlement of such disputes—unless

FIGURE 5.11. Via della Conciliazione, Rome (1929)

specially asked to do so by the contending parties."[138] While the clergy pledged
to avoid overtly political acts, they reserved the right to encourage civil society
groups, such as Catholic Action, to do so in furtherance of their causes. Governments installed no new loyalty requirements, although it was unlikely that
a stalwart Ultramontane would be installed in any large diocese in Europe or
North America. The agreement with the Italian kingdom also included a
clause requiring Italian bishops to take an oath pledging loyalty to the king and
reserved the right for the government to veto parish clergy.[139] The truth was
that, as one scholar wrote with palpable *schadenfreude* in the *Harvard Theological Review*, "there is now no such thing as a Catholic country—a nation whose
life, laws, and civilization are formed on Catholic lines. . . . Catholicism has
become an individual attitude, and ceased to be a corporate fact."[140]

The pope clashed with rulers over public education and the civil recognition of religious marriages (and vice versa).[141] This proverbial struggle between Peter and Caesar was itself the path to compromise, toward organizational autonomy. As Casanova put it, the papacy "exchanged transnational
spiritual claims for the protection of its temporal sovereignty at home."[142]
Despite the losses, the papacy reaped the benefits of loyalties it had cultivated
earlier. A pro-Vatican petition gathered an astounding 5 million signatures—

likely the largest single act of transnational political mobilization to that date. More followed, including transnational press campaigns, meetings, and congresses organized along the lines of international Catholicism. A massive fund-raising operation revived and expanded the practice of paying Peter's Pence and raised millions of dollars every year. In Germany, Catholic citizens made a collection to pay the fines of bishops and religious employees, boycotted state-employed preachers, and held their own lay prayer services. The cross-border activity was interpreted by some as "evidence of the faith in the supernatural nature of the Church and her mission."[143] Public sentiment compensated for the legal defeat, reinforced by the advent of the telegraph and photography, which helped stitch together a global Catholic population around the Vatican's spiritual leadership.

This illuminates another paradox. Other than a handful of visits to nearby Church events, Pius IX never again left Church grounds. Yet, as a North American contemporary wrote, the Vatican "never had greater influence than since it has been deprived of territorial sovereignty": "Jubilees, pilgrimages, ceremonies in St. Peter's, exhibitions, even a conclave. The Pope writes whatever he pleases, has his own diplomatic corps, guards and court."[144] "The continually growing moral greatness of the Papacy rises from the mystic isolation in which the spiritual father of all the faithful lives in the heart of the Christian world. The sublime irony of history! This spoliation would be regarded . . . as the very cause of an increase in the power of the Holy See."[145] The international demand for papal blessings reached its highest level in 150 years.[146] So long as they were willing to accept the unpleasant reality that nation-states were there to stay, the surge of activity "gave Popes the sensation, hardly felt since the Counter-Reformation, that they led a mighty revival of religion." The experience elicited greater sympathy for the pope among Catholics: "It made the Pope stronger." As the religion came "face to face . . . with centralizing governments . . . people began to look to a court of appeal outside the state." The positive spin on a negative situation proved rewarding. "The bureaucratic and symbolic reach of the papacy," the American historian John McGreevy writes, "came in response to expanded governmental authority in nation-states."[147]

The total breakdown in relations was followed by a triumphant return to civil society, in a new guise. The clarity of positions emerging from twentieth-century agreements placed the religion under *administrative* oversight, moving the situation of Catholic hierarchies closer to civilian rule—and away from political control—through relocation to the bureaucratic sphere. The centralizing state rewarded the Church's turn-of-the-century professionalization by granting it administrative and tax privileges and state recognition. The national hierarchies of the Catholic Church were given the necessary licenses to manage the souls of their own flock—a soft restoration, by way of the re-introduction of autonomous spaces, such as schools under contract. In each national context, Church-affiliated organizations made up thousands of associations: shelters, asylums, children's homes, homes for the poor, technical schools, maternity centers, museums, boarding schools, sanitoriums, and so on. As evidenced in a papal encyclical nearly a century later, a new citizenship status came to take the place of what were once the Church's earthly governing ambitions.[148] By that time, the papacy again enjoyed near total sovereignty to name bishops across the globe.

A new era was born, free of state interference or the need for government consent for the appointment of bishops and priests or the regulation of clergy's communication with the Vatican. The voices critical of Pius XI for signing the Lateran Accords called him a "simpleton duped by European statesmen and a traitor to the Church" because he "surrendered the Church's 1,100-year-old destiny of meaningful temporal rule."[149] One century after its creation, Vatican City remains the world's smallest nation-state. Diplomatic recognition from the rest of the world followed relatively late (see chapter 10). However, the agreement resolved the issue of temporal power in a highly symbolic way, granting dignity in defeat with the ultimate face-saving gesture. Vatican City offered a focal point for the religion's statehood, an elegant earthly resolution to the burning question of papal authority and sovereignty on earth.

The secular revolutions in nineteenth-century Europe were sometimes followed by a strong religious revival within a generation, leading to brief periods of restoration. Although France and Spain had introduced civil marriage and divorce in the nineteenth century, for example, their monarchs, Louis XVIII and Charles X, reversed these developments and restored the Church as the official state religion once more. This meant sacrificing women's rights and participation in the public sphere. It was more common for women to march in political demonstrations in late 1880s Rome than it was in the 1950s. Spanish women lost the right to divorce for another forty years, and women in Italy would not again be allowed to divorce until 1973. The counterrevolutionary periods restoring a religious role in public life also forfeited the hard-won religious toleration achieved during fleeting republican moments in the nineteenth century. State hegemony eventually arrived and stayed. By the 1980s, even Spain and Italy had again liberalized their state-church regimes to grant full recognition to several non-Catholic religions.

The extreme phase of Nation-State Catholicism culminated in a settlement with peaceable relations: governments conducting oversight and regulation of the Church's partially recovered spaces of autonomy. This facilitated the reintegration of the culturally alienated portion of the population into the nation via religious community, contributing to the consolidation of democracy during periods of political strife over religious authority. In many ways, the European process of removing and co-opting the Church served as the model for disparate nation-states, including mid-twentieth-century Turkey and the countries of North Africa. The top-down control of Nation-State Islam in Turkey and North Africa in the twentieth century and early in the twenty-first century shared characteristics with the organization of religion in nineteenth-century western Europe.

6

Nation-State Islam

IT IS OFTEN FORGOTTEN that before the Turkish republic became ada-
mantly secularist, it first struck a deal to preserve the caliph as the head of state
and spiritual leader. For two years, Mustafa Kemal Atatürk allowed the court
to remain in Dolmabahçe and Yıldız Palaces in Istanbul. Once he tired of the
rivalry and ambiguity of a two-headed executive, Turkey expelled the lot of
them, thereby demolishing the last pillar of the *ancien régime* in the Islamic
world.[1] The Sunni Muslim world changed forever when they left Istanbul on
March 4, 1924. The relative theological and spiritual unity projected by the
Ottoman caliphate, which was imperfect at its apex, had no chance of surviv-
ing twentieth-century fragmentation into dozens of independent states. Despite the universality of Islam and the indivisibility of the umma, there was no
longer a unifying caliph. After the last caliph left Istanbul, no international
Islamic figure would again enjoy enough consensus to receive the pledge of
loyalty or benediction during the Friday prayer of Muslims the world over.
Without spiritual leadership to guide politics, religion was left to the Muslim
statesmen who followed in the footsteps of their Catholic counterparts in
Latin Europe.

For the vast majority of the world's Muslims who lived *outside* Turkish borders, the abolition of the caliphate was a formality that simply confirmed a new
nationally oriented reality. The British, Dutch, French, and Russian empires
had already done everything to eliminate the caliphate's traces—and to prevent its survival as a spiritual figurehead—while they were occupying powers
in the Middle East, North Africa, India, and Indonesia. North African nationalist movements that resisted French occupation in the early twentieth century
found it useful to fold spirituality into their repertoire of revolt against imperial
rule—for theological, "psychological and sociological reasons."[2] Although
religious authorities helped clear out the Europeans, the ulema failed to reclaim any majority-Muslim lands for Islamic rule. They were outmaneuvered
by secular Muslim leaders who declared new states—sometimes explicitly
godless socialist republics—that left no place at the table for nonstate expres-

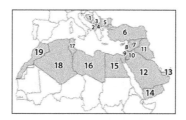

Country	Islamic or Religious Affairs Ministry
Bosnia	Ministry of Justice
Albania	Superior Shari'ah Council
Kosovo	Ministry of Culture, Youth and Sports
Macedonia	Ministry of Culture
Bulgaria	Ministry of Culture
Turkey	Directorate of Religious Affairs
Syria	Ministry of *Awqaf*
Lebanon	Fatwa Council
Israel	Ministry of Religious Services
Jordan	Ministry of Religious Affairs and *Awqaf*
Iraq	Ministry of Religious Affairs and *Awqaf*
Saudi Arabia	Ministry of Religious Affairs
United Arab Emirates	Department of Islamic Affairs and Charitable Activities
Yemen	Ministry of *Awqaf* and Guidance
Egypt	Ministry of *Awqaf*
Libya	Ministry of *Awqaf* and Islamic Affairs
Tunisia	Ministry of Religious Affairs
Algeria	Ministry of Religious Affairs and *Awqaf*
Morocco	Ministry of Habous and Islamic Affairs

FIGURE 6.1.1 AND FIGURE 6.1.2. Post-Ottoman Administration of Religious Affairs
(Twentieth century)

sions of Islam.[3] Before the national independence of nearly two dozen majority-Muslim states across North Africa, the Arab world, and the Balkans, a juridical revolution introduced by Ottoman authorities and then colonial occupation had reduced the responsibilities of religious leaders. That earlier experience of modernization facilitated the transfer of legal and judiciary powers from Islamic authorities to the new governments.[4] Secular Muslim rulers asserted the new states' monopoly over religious affairs by establishing national Islamic hierarchies under civilian oversight. The lone exception was Morocco, which unified the spiritual and political roles of the king in its 1962 constitution—but it too created a religious affairs ministry under nonclerical rule (see figure 6.1).

As with the Church in the nineteenth century, when there was no longer any country governed by Roman canon law and, briefly, no sovereign Papal State, the twentieth-century majority-Sunni countries experienced their own phase of state omnipotence. National politicians uniformly endeavored to co-opt religious scholars and monopolize the organization of religious exercise.[5] There is a direct parallel between the nineteenth-century "constitutional bishops" and the twentieth-century muftis of the republic. Echoing the European experience of the Catholic Church, the statesmen suppressed religious orders, seized their property, and took over the appointment of imams and ulema. Some statesmen were more pious or nostalgic than others, but ultimately none tolerated *independent* religious competition during a sensitive moment of national political development.[6]

On the one hand, the two polities of Rome and Istanbul could seem to be heading in different directions. The Roman papacy-monarchy weathered centuries of conflict with secular governments and had its powers gradually stripped by rival empires and monarchies. The Ottoman sultans, on the other hand, were primarily secular rulers who gradually arrogated to themselves the spiritual powers inherent to their dual role as caliphs. Analogously to the nineteenth-century majority-Catholic nation-states of western Europe, the sultans gradually took over control of education, justice, and, ultimately, oversight of religious exercise from the office that, until then, had been supreme religious leader and chief of the scholarly caste of ulema. The sultanate took on the spiritual powers by appropriating the nominating authority for the religious hierarchy and regulating prayer spaces, religious charities, and, finally, religious training and education. The ulema were already reduced to the role of overseeing ritual unity and family law, with prayer, polygamy, repudiation, and inheritance under their jurisdiction. Istanbul established the bureaucratic precedent for this differentiation—that is, the policing of the separation of secular and religious roles through new bureaucracies for Islamic affairs.

This made it easier for Islam to be systematically subordinated to the all-powerful nation-state, which asserted control over the spheres of justice, education, and religion.[7] Instead of promoting loyalty to a far-off ruler in the Friday prayer, the scholar Bryan Turner writes, Nation-State Islam became a "megaphone for the propagation of the [national-] Islamic synthesis."[8] An all-powerful state in the majority-Muslim context was just as shocking a concept to the religious hierarchies and traditions as the experience of Nation-State Catholicism was for the Roman Catholic Church. Some of the policies could be traced back to the French Revolutionary repertory, part of what historians have termed a top-down secularization across the Islamic Middle East that removed clerics from public institutions and abolished holy days,

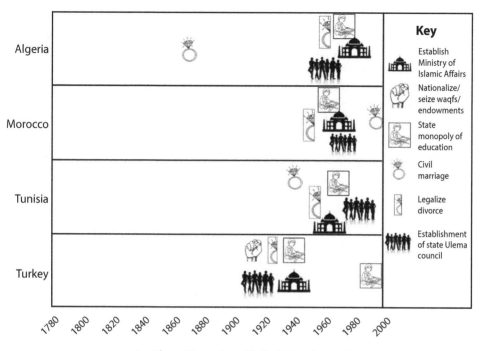

FIGURE 6.2. Islamic Encounters with the Nation-State, 1780–2000

privileges, and titles.[9] The postcolonial nation-states removed religion's remaining privileges in the realm of personal status as well (see figure 6.2).[10] Professionalization of the religious sphere allowed states to come to an accord with a community of believers in the unprecedented context of independent nation-state-hood. The institutions perpetuated their capitulation until it was internalized in the leadership corps' institutions of training and elite reproduction.

Nation-State Islam

The First Phase of Nation-State Islam (until 1980)

As with Nation-State Catholicism in nineteenth-century Europe, the final political disempowerment of Islamic leadership was carried out not by "infidels" but rather by the hand of their own religious ilk. No Muslim government dared prohibit Islam outright, although some came close to doing so through a combination of repression and neglect.[11] Successive leaders ceded to the temptation to bend Islamic institutions to their political aims. The new regimes treated the clergy as one more class with unearned privilege whose spell had to be broken. They found that many believers were willing to trade national secular rule and economic modernization for ancestral religion. In some cases, the ulema participated in their own transformation and reinvention for tactical purposes of survival or to preserve their dignity.[12] Overall, the nation-state era signaled the *second modern defeat* of Sunni Islamic religious authorities after their humiliation at the hands of Christian empires.

While Islam was acknowledged as the majority religion and shari'ah cited as a source of legal inspiration in a majority of the nearly four dozen majority-Muslim nation-states, Islamic leadership was stripped of all temporal authority— sometimes including the most basic acts related to matrimony and burial. It was rare for the state to allow private Islamic spaces outside the home, that is, there was little to no civil society. Secular courts adopted Western legal codes and further reduced the powers of religious courts.[13] Ruling elites competed to put the remaining religious establishment at their service.[14] The regimes preserved Islamic activities that could be drafted in support of the raison d'état.

During the first phase of Nation-State Islam, religion was treated as a matter of public order and was administratively located within the Ministry of the Interior. Top law enforcement officers oversaw appointments to clerical office and exercised a state monopoly over prayer spaces and religious education, which was coordinated with mandatory public education to include "curriculum based upon technical and scientific rather than religious knowledge."[15]

It made no difference to the traditional ulema and *imamat* whether they had been co-opted (or fired) by a hereditary monarch or by an elected president of the republic. In either case, there was a new sharif in town across the new nation-states of the post-Ottoman region. Each ruler claimed temporal and spiritual preeminence. In Morocco, King Hassan II (1929–1999) was Emir al-Mu'mimin (Commander of All the Faithful); in Turkey, Mustafa Kemal had the moniker of Ghazi; and Tunisian president Bourguiba and Algerian president Ben Bella (1916–2012) were known as chief mujtahid and chief mujahid, respectively. Some of these statesmen rendered Islamic homages in appearance more than in substance. In that sense, they were the anticlerical mirror of latter-day Islamists who said they viewed democracy as a tramcar, getting off at their desired stop when they no longer needed it. Mustafa Kemal Atatürk conducted an elaborate prayer ceremony before inaugurating the Grand National Assembly in Ankara; the Algerian Front de Libération Nationale (FLN, Front for National Liberation) adopted the language of holy war (for example, calling their fighters *mujahadin*) to defeat French occupation; and the Tunisian president, Habib Bourguiba, even defended the Islamic veil as a "symbol of national identity."[16]

During the first phase of Nation-State Islam (1950–1980), religion policies were used to consolidate rule, but lacked great urgency. Official Islamic iden-

TABLE 6.1. Islam in Twentieth-Century Arab Political Development (Dessouki, 1987)

1. The state eliminates independent sources of finance for religious foundations (awqaf or habous), which are made dependent on public budgets and resources.
2. The national government exerts control over internal religious organization through administrative reorganization and structural change.
3. Religious schools are integrated into national governmental systems of education. Governments establish alternative institutions to replace traditional offerings.
4. The shari'ah courts are abolished, and their jurisdiction is absorbed by a unified system of courts.

tity offered one instrument against *other* potentially roiling subnational identities. With many other priorities in a developing economy, governments rarely dedicated large budgetary resources to Islamic affairs during the first phase of centralization and consolidation. Nation-states rhetorically and symbolically Islamicized the public sphere but provided imperfect territorial coverage and loose oversight of education and hierarchy.

A government's commitment to Nation-State Islam might also be measured by the number of imams it could train or the spread of approved religious education and mosques where citizens could hear Friday sermons from a licensed preacher. An unintended legacy of neglect in the region, according to Faïza Tobich, was "the fading of the intellectual superstructures which regulated religious knowledge."[17] Tobich argues that the net effect was "the state became the only producer of juridical norms and the only actor with the legitimacy to change it."

Nonetheless, there was significant national variance in terms of the budget and political attention allocated to Islamic affairs. Not all ministries of Islamic affairs were created equal. My comparative analysis of primary sources on budgetary spending and infrastructure revealed two national-administrative echelons of religious affairs expenditures: first, Morocco and Turkey, and below, Algeria and Tunisia. From the 1960s onward, Muslim prayer leaders in Morocco and Turkey were consistently better funded, and had far more mosques per person, than either Tunisia or Algeria. In 1980, Morocco and Turkey had one mosque for every 800 to 900 citizens, while Algeria and Tunisia had one for every 3,800 citizens. In many cases, the growth of state Islamic bureaucracy followed a traumatic moment of violence: for example, the execution of former Turkish prime minister Adnan Menderes in 1960; a machine-gun attack on the Moroccan king's outdoor reception in 1974; and in the 1980s, an Islamist commando's assault on Tunisian forces in Gafsa and the Bab al Oued riots in Algeria. As Sebastian Elischer writes, institutional preparedness and density in the 1960s and 1970s determined whether or not regimes had ready defenses against the spike in transnational Islamist activism in the 1980s and 1990s.[18] States that downplayed religion by having fewer mosques and keeping them padlocked most of the day left their citizens more vulnerable to the cross-border proselytizing of the Muslim Brotherhood and Salafist movements.

The Second Phase of Nation-State Islam (post-1980)

The second major growth spurt of the twentieth century occurred between 1980 and 2000 and came in response to *external* threats that had begun to make their way inside. The formal creation of a ministry of Islamic affairs (or its equivalent) lighted a path to Islam's "soft restoration" under civilian rule. There were simultaneous movements toward religious professionalization, standardization, and bureaucratic expansion—in other words, toward Islamic infrastructure, educational institutions, and hierarchy.[19] The proximate cause was Great Britain's withdrawal from the Gulf region in the mid-1970s, which ignited the rivalry between Iran and Saudi Arabia. This area of the Muslim world came into its own, religiously and in terms of national sovereignty, with the Iranian Revolution of 1979. When the Westernized shah was overthrown by an Islamic movement led by the Ayatollah Khomenei, a new day dawned for religious utopianism—and for political Islam in particular.

Amid a Sunni leadership vacuum and with no new caliph since 1924, Iran grabbed the empty helm. The revolution coincided with the start of the Islamic fifteenth century: Tehran's example represented "a dawn of possible renaissance for all Muslims" because the previous century of European colonial domination was "considered by many Muslims as the worst of Islamic history."[20] The Shi'a confession formed a small minority of global Islam (12 to 15 percent), but Iran's was the only political system in the Islamic world where religious leadership stood atop secular politicians, not the other way around—although Morocco came close. Tehran began to spread revolutionary Shi'ism, which Saudi Arabia evaluated as an existential threat. Like the Safavids and Ottomans 500 years earlier, religious revolution in the Persian Gulf raised the Sunni world's defenses and led to the definition and institutionalization of its own practices so as to prevent unwanted inroads. Attempts to export the Iranian Revolution, in particular, elicited a Saudi counterpunch.

Saudi Arabia's position in control of Mecca and Medina emboldened it to act as the de facto caliphate, and it used institutions like the Muslim World League (Mecca, 1962) to project its power. Riyadh had Ottoman-size ambitions and in some ways managed to surpass Istanbul's former influence, worldwide, thanks to evolving technology and its lucrative energy reserves.[21] The

Saudi kingdom spent billions on propagating Salafi Wahhabism, casting their shadow over the spiritual lives of scores of millions of Muslims. Their influence over global oil markets gave them the power to distribute tens of millions of Qur'ans, train tens of thousands of religious scholars and students, and steer thousands of officials to institutional positions, from the sub-Saharan to the Subcontinent. This escalated into confrontation with the other postcolonial governments over time: since "Salafis oppose all forms of nationalized Islam . . . tensions between national religious authorities and Salafis are reported everywhere."[22]

The Kingdom of Morocco exerted control over Islam within its borders by divine right, whereas the Republic of Turkey did so in the name of the people; both were better prepared than Algeria and Tunisia to resist Saudi influence. The spread of audiocassette and satellite video technology rendered previous censorship measures obsolete, making ideas harder to contain. Seizing physical copies of contraband or arresting leaders was less effective, since their sermons could survive their own detention or demise. New technologies created virtual borderless spaces for religious expression in the last quarter of the twentieth century. Satellite television beamed in Islamic messaging over the heads of national governments. The technology represented an exponential development over the newspapers, journals, and books that had circulated for centuries: alternative theologies and competing schools of law could be received by rural, remote populations where illiteracy prevailed.

In weak states or areas where religious foundations were not governed with close attention, Saudi Wahhabism found its way in. The preemptive Soviet invasion of Afghanistan (March 1980) triggered an armed resistance supported by Saudi Arabia and the anti-Communist Cold War powers. The Iran-Iraq War (1980–1988) provided the next battlefield for the Sunni-Shi'a conflict. Libya and Algeria, initially favoring Iran in the conflict, were put in a position of countering Saudi religious propaganda. Morocco and Tunisia supported Iraq and accepted Saudi largesse while hoping not to be overwhelmed by it. Not satisfied with the influence of its home-trained clerics globally, Saudi Arabia began building all-expenses paid seminaries and universities abroad that produced tens of thousands of graduates. The Muslim Brotherhood leadership it harbored in Mecca and Jedda also promoted Islamist political programs that were waiting out the secularist moment of Nation-State Islam. The rise of Islamist political parties led to mass incarceration and exile in Morocco, Tunisia, and Turkey. Concern over Riyadh's exportation of revolutionary ideology peaked when it embraced violent extremists during the 1980s. Wahhabi activists fomented Tunisian extremism and the Algerian civil war hoping to dislodge the state-sanctioned Islamic leaders, whom they considered to be socialist or pagan.

Iranian attempts to export their Islamic revolution—and the Saudi reaction it provoked—helped drive the second consolidation of Nation-State Islam. They raised the antennae and hackles of national governments across the Sunni world, where decades of neglect had left a vacuum. In the early 1980s, for example, 60 percent of Algerian prayer spaces had no trained imam. The entry of external threats into domestic politics led states to seek greater control and increase investment in religious institutions and personnel to fill the domestic vacuum.

In the second phase (1980–2000), state institutions targeted those influences, principally emanating from transnational Salafism and the Muslim Brotherhood (Ikhwanism) and from revolutionary Libya and Iran. Governments went from suppressing Islamic identity to embracing a grand act of religious impersonation. The Islam policies of the four nation-states under consideration—Algera, Morocco, Tunisa, and Turkey—followed distinct national paths during the postcolonial era in pursuit of similar goals.[23] What they all had in common was the gradual replacement of independent Islamic authorities with civil bureaucracy. They shared the common challenge of a wave of Salafi clerics who "began to challenge the conduct of autocratic leaders in the Arab world." There were suddenly as many ministries of religious affairs, departments of religious endowments, and offices of the Grand Mufti as there were new nation-states.[24] Each office, with its budget, personnel, and licensing of all religious life, replaced the roles of the old caliphate—and undermined any notion that Islam was a decentralized religion without a clergy. The Turkish Directorate for Religious Affairs continues to be held close, in the prime minister's own offices, while the Moroccan Ministry of Habous abuts the royal palace, the only ministry located on royal grounds. Tunisia's grand mufti sits in the prime minister's office.

These states approved immutable laws and constitutional clauses regarding religion's place. The ministries sent a strong signal that only the state may mix religion and politics. The "20th century appropriation of the state apparatus . . . harmonized Islamic legal schools" in each national context. Religious rulings were "no longer left to this or that *faqih* (judge) who presented himself as the source of legal and legitimate authority."[25] By monopolizing the resources for public prayer and religious education, ruling on what was religiously permissible, and standardizing specific rituals and omitting others, Islamic affairs ministries constructed a network of norms and services to mediate the citizen-believer's relationship to the umma and the divine. This national filtration system regulated everything religious, from literature and prayer spaces to education and leadership.

Turkey

After Independence: The State's Stranglehold on Islam (1922–1946)

The clocks at Dolmabahçe Palace are set to 9:05 a.m., the time of day that Mustafa Kemal—who was by then known as Atatürk, father of the Turks—died there on November 10, 1938.[26] Atatürk's austere gaze, under a furrowed brow, greets visitors to each room of frilly imperial splendor. But lingering a bit longer in the Besiktas neighborhood, if you wind up the road past the W Hotel, to Yıldız Kiosk, you will sense the ghost of Abdülhamid II, riding his open carriage to the Yıldız Hamidiye Mosque. Today the two phantoms coexist uneasily, Cain and Abel separated by a two-kilometer stretch of Bosphorus. Atatürk did not start out with anti-Islamic intentions so much as he recognized early on, as Şükrü Hanioğlu writes, how a "Turkified version of Islam could serve as a useful vehicle for advancing Turkish nationalism."[27] This was never far from his considerations, first as a parliamentarian and later as prime minister and president. Hanioğlu observes that Atatürk "wished to tame Islam's power, harness it to his own program of reform, and exploit it to raise the moral standard of the masses." Atatürk appeared aware of the disadvantages of leaving a spiritual void and the imminent possibility of an Arab caliphate. Mohamed Samin Khan observes that many of the national revolution's leaders did not support abolishing the caliphate and "favored an evolutionary constitution on the model of England"—which preserved its monarchy as a symbol at the head of state and as leader of the national Church.[28] The US ambassador described Atatürk as a mixture of Martin Luther and John Wycliffe, the dissident fourteenth-century Catholic priest who translated the Bible into Middle English and challenged the imperial papacy and the monastic orders.[29] In a 1923 speech in Konya, while still under the caliphate, Kemal told a crowd that, "to be a *hodja*, to bring religious truth to the people, one need not wear a spiritual robe."[30]

In the early 1920s, Kemal fused Robespierrean and Napoleonic approaches and grafted a Turkish nationalism onto a stripped-down administrative structure of Ottoman Islam. He retained the caliph as figurehead so long as he still had value to the republic. The first taste of Atatürk's unique blend came before the proclamation of the Turkish republic, when the Grand National Assembly substituted an Islamic *shura* council and voted to install Abdülmecid II (1868–1944) as caliph.[31] The 1923 constitution removed the clerical monopoly on marriage licensing, but retained other symbolic roles for Islam, including the caliph at its head, within the new republic. With the abolition of the caliphate in March 1924, however, the Turkish republic began to nationalize Islam. It did away with the Sheikh-ul-Islam and the Evkaf Ministry. Religious affairs were overseen by a new administrative unit in the prime minister's office, the Presidency of Religious Affairs (Diyanet İşleri Reisli, or Diyanet).[32] This was in stark contrast with the cult of Atatürk being exhibited in public imagery, portraiture, statues, and so on.[33] Nurulla Ardiç writes that sheikhs, muftis, and imams were vetted for friendliness to "the nation" and Atatürk's goals.[34] The shari'ah court system was eliminated, and all Islamic affairs were transferred to the new department. Article 1 gave the Grand National Assembly the right to codify and apply the laws of shari'ah.[35] The country's 454 theological seminaries and all "institutions of scientific instruction" (including medreses) were placed under the Department of Public Instruction.[36]

Turkish nationalists neither executed the sultan-caliph—as French revolutionaries did their King—nor murdered his family, as Russian revolutionaries did to their czar and his family. Nor did they dig a symbolic moat around Yıldız Palace—a Vatican-type solution debated during the interwar period—to allow the figurehead to reign another day. The appeal of running a Turkish caliphate was outweighed by officials' perception of traditional religious authority as monolithically reactionary.[37] Instead, Mustafa Kemal Atatürk announced to the Turkish Grand National Assembly that the new Turkish generation would be raised with a "free conscience."[38] The Grand National Assembly seized Yıldız Palace as national property and forced the last caliph and his entourage of 1,500 courtiers into permanent exile. Doing away with the institution of caliphate, they made it impossible for the House of Osman to return to a position of spiritual authority. The republic also banned the call to prayer in Arabic, suppressed all religious orders and education, changed the national alphabet, and prohibited religious clothing associated with the old religious hierarchy, which they allowed to die out from attrition. The nationalization and rerouting of religion for state interests was so thorough that the state even set up "halal" pig farms.

Collective prayer on Fridays was allowed to continue in the Turkish republic, but conditional upon omitting the name of the former Ottoman caliph. As quickly as the Hagia Sofia had been converted from a church to a mosque in 1453, the Grand National Assembly seized it and converted into a national museum in 1923.[39] The Arabic and Ottoman Turkish languages were retired; using a new alphabet script ensured that any Anglo-Arab efforts to communicate with Turkish believers in the old languages would meet a dead end. The decision also rendered useless the classical education of theology graduates.[40] Mustapha Kemal's bride accompanied him on his travels in European-style clothes and without a veil. This was as shocking in the 1920s as Turks found it eighty years later to see their first lady *in* a headscarf.

Atatürk kept open a handful of İmam Hatip schools and allowed for a small cadre of several thousand future imams and theologians.[41] All ulema were removed from government office and forbidden to wear special dress.[42] Decrees followed that eliminated all spiritual houses (*tekkes* and *zawiyyas*) and all religious orders.[43] The 1926 (Swiss-imported) civil code amended the constitution to remove all civil powers from the clergy. In 1928, articles 2 and 26 were removed from the constitution.[44] Islam was no longer the state religion, and the Grand National Assembly no longer had the responsibility to uphold shari'ah law.[45] The erstwhile Pan-Turanism (Turkish imperialism) of the Ottoman era became something more like a Turkish nationalism that was increasingly hostile to any remnants of the Islamic establishment. Atatürk's motto became "There Is No Religion, Just Nationality: My Turkishness Is My Religion."[46]

Gradually, muftis and imams became "propaganda merchants for the national cause": the Diyanet instructed them to "pray for the wellbeing and the felicity of the nation and republic." Following the restrictive laws, officials began closing religious schools, stopped hiring replacements for retiring faculty, and gradually wound down the religious institutions, faculties, imams, and preachers. Personnel dwindled from 7,500 in 1927 to just over 1,000 between 1930 and 1950 (see figure 6.3).[47] It took fifteen years to purge all traces of Islam from public education: by 1938, no schools offered religious instruction.[48] The Diyanet's largest growth spurts occurred in the immediate aftermath of military coups (1960, 1971, 1980), lifting the Diyanet budget to a new de facto spending floor. The ratio of employees hit an all-time high in 1989—fifteen Diyanet employees per 10,000 citizens, or five times the 1950 ratio.[49]

The First Correction: The Growth of Nation-State Islam (1950–1980)

A modest number of elementary Qur'an courses had quietly survived during the republic, but no imams or preachers were being trained by İmam Hatip schools in the 1930s.[50] That did not do away with demand for religious services, however, and grievances were aired against the state because of insufficient leadership at prayer time and at funerals.[51] Legislators debated whether one of the reasons "children no longer paid any attention" to their parents might be the absence of religious education.[52] According to the legal historian and doyenne of Diyanet studies, Iştar Gözaydın, "the absence of clergy legitimated state intervention in the organization of religious life as a public service."[53] Atatürk's death and the end of World War II opened a new phase in state-Islam relations.

The 1946 elections marked the "downfall of single party (CHP) rule and the end of the religious reforms."[54] The victorious Democratic Party's support "came from the deeply religious parts of the public across Anatolia," Amir

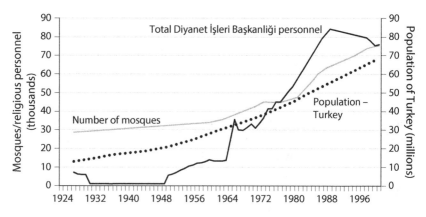

FIGURE 6.3. Turkey: Official Mosques and State-Employed Religious Personnel
(Diyanet), 1924–2000

Teheri writes.[55] Once in power, the Democratic Party authorized Muslim schools to reopen. Optional religion classes were reintroduced to public schools in 1949, after sixteen years of absence, and many parents chose this option.[56] Within a year, "religious classes in primary schools became regular parts of the curriculum and compulsory."[57] This time, parents needed to request in writing in order for their children be released from the obligation, which virtually none did. The head of the Democrat Party, Adnan Menderes, emerged as the leader of this new majority. There is little evidence that Prime Minister Menderes personally strived to overturn Turkish secularism: electoral considerations motivated his actions as much as religious conviction. In 1950, he lifted Atatürk's ban on the public call for prayer in Arabic and ended arrests of those praying in Arabic.[58] The state faculties of divinity at Ankara and Istanbul were reopened in 1950, for the first time since 1933.[59] A new budget line was allocated to hire a dean, eight professors, fifteen docents, and twenty-nine research assistants. Scholar Howard Reed reported in the mid-1950s how the modern divinity faculty was designed anew, having been "established on the basis of profiting from the errors of the past," and worked "to produce religious savants and well informed men of religion." The Institute for Islamic Research, which had been temporarily resuscitated under Atatürk, was formally revived and placed under the oversight of the Faculty of Letters in the University of Istanbul. The İmam Hatip schools—religious high schools—reopened in 1951.[60] Hundreds of Qur'an study groups were authorized by the Diyanet.

The new prime minister declared to a befuddled parliament in February 1951 that "paying salaries to religious employees using state funds does not

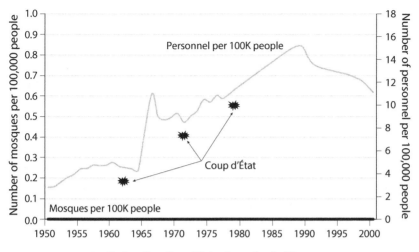

FIGURE 6.4. Turkey: Post-Coup Hiring Spurts by the Diyanet, 1950–2000

contradict Laicism." In 1953, seven years after the first multiparty election, teaching of the Qur'an was made obligatory in schools.[61] A 1956 note from the US embassy in Ankara described the emerging regime: "Turkey is the contrary of a secular state."[62] The country was divided into 500 counties with 500 muftis, and the number of preachers and mosques rose sharply in the 1950s, from 18,000 to 34,000 (see figure 6.4).[63] The government also encouraged "private initiatives to build mosques and set up of centers of religious instruction."[64] Fifteen thousand mosques were built during ten years of Democrat Party rule (1950–1960).[65] In addition to compulsory religious education encouraging more pilgrimage to Mecca, one of Prime Minister Menderes's last acts was to oversee the establishment of high Islamic institutes.[66]

The military generals—constitutionally empowered as guardians of secularism—ultimately judged that Menderes was too much of a religious populist.[67] Tensions increased between the government and the Republican People's Party (CHP). In May 1960, the military removed Menderes and accused him of "exploiting religion for political purposes and infringing the constitution."[68] They hanged him the following year. Despite the renewal of religious education options, however, fewer than 1 percent of Turkish primary and secondary students were enrolled in an İmam Hatip school at the height of his rule.[69] The generals continued along the same trajectory, with the next government continuing the boom in mosque construction.[70] Endowed with new impetus to create a viable container for Islamic expression, Levent Tezcan writes, the Diyanet moved from using a "technical language to one of religious content."[71]

The agency went on a three-year hiring spree that nearly tripled the number of employees, to around 35,000. The Ministry of Education increased its paid religious instructor positions from 666 in 1964 to 1,005 in 1968.[72] The next politician to bring Islam into the electoral campaign was Suleyman Demirel (1924–2015), a fixture in Turkish politics who served as prime minister seven times.[73] When he was deposed in a 1971 coup, the military claimed that it was to crush leftist terrorists. But it was clear that Demirel's rapprochement with Islamist groups had also hurt his standing with the armed forces. Finally, Necmettin Erbakan (1926–2011) reintroduced Islamic discourse overtly and lastingly to Turkish politics. In 1970, he founded the National Order Party, which was renamed the National Salvation Party (MSP) after yet another coup. Erbakan was part of a movement of businessmen and publicists who advocated a "Turkish-Islamic Synthesis."

During this period, religious education became a political football. The military government passed a law (1971) placing all Qur'an schools under state control. They also closed the middle school grades of İmam Hatip schools, cutting three years from the curriculum.[74] After Erbakan's brief term as prime minister five years later, Turkey increased its inventory to 350 İmam Hatip schools, enrolling 200,000 students.[75] In the mid-1970s, the MSP participated in three coalition governments, during which it continued to promote İmam Hatip schools. They were reclassified as general high schools, and in 1976 the schools began admitting girls.[76] Prime Minister Demirel was "overthrown a second time as prime minister in 1980" after he "formed a coalition that included the National Salvation Party under Necmettin Erbakan."[77]

The Second Correction (1980–1997)

Chronic political instability in Turkey relativized the urgency of the Islamist challenge. In 1979 alone, there were 1,126 politically motivated murders, but no record of religiously motivated killings. After the 1980 coup, the military governed until 1983, and it engaged in the harshest campaign of political repression in the history of the republic: 1.7 million people were listed as suspect; 650,000 were jailed; 517 death sentences were handed down (49 were executed); 388,000 travel bans were issued; 30,000 activists were forced into exile; 14,000 citizens were denaturalized; and 600 associations were banned.[78] The constitution was also amended to prohibit political parties from challenging the Diyanet's status or calling for its abolition.

The largest effort to reverse infrastructural deficits and ensure basic coverage of the national territory and professionalize a cadre of Islamic experts in the republic's employ took place after the 1980 coup. The number of mosques—which had risen more or less in line with the population—grew sharply from 1982 to 1985 (see figure 6.4). The ratio of mosques to citizens reached its most favorable point ever in 1988—when there was one for every 857 citizens.[79] Religious culture and moral education for two hours a week, taught by certified graduates of the divinity faculties, were introduced as a mandatory class for all students from fourth grade through the end of high school (1982).[80]

The liberalization and modernization agenda pursued by Prime Minister Turgut Özal (1983–1989) helped initiate a set of "cultural and social changes" that allowed for the flowering of a traditional Islamic middle class.[81] His policies modestly loosened the regulations governing religious and other civil society organizations and allowed for some venting of steam. Özal brought religion back into the public sphere and "returned religion to public respectability."[82] This liberty extended even to Necmettin Erbakan's party, which had renamed itself again—now it was the Welfare (Refah) Party (1983–1996)—marking "the first time [that] a political party declared itself to be founded on Islamist ideology."[83] The government directed increasing resources to countering the party's influence by doubling down on religious education, whose content it could influence by opening more İmam Hatip schools. The government reduced barriers to enrollment by permitting graduates to take university entrance examinations in any field, not just theology. The number of students enrolled in İmam Hatip middle and high schools reached an all-time high of 500,000, as did the number of religious personnel employed by the state. Diyanet employees outpaced population growth, going from three religious civil servants per 10,000 citizens to twelve in 1980.[84]

Thanks to the new influx of İmam Hatip graduates, the Diyanet gradually became more professionalized—and the Ankara bureaucracy became more ideologically diverse. Iren Özgur writes that, in 1995, 68 percent of Diyanet personnel (and half of all new public-sector hires) had a diploma from an İmam Hatip school.[85] While the governing parties fretted about expanding Islamist networks, the Diyanet pushed back and issued fatwas against the 1993 headscarf ban. In its judgment, "covering the head is a religious commandment and any decision against it is an infringement on religious rights."[86] Erbakan's Welfare Party rose steadily—from 7.2 percent in 1987 to 11 percent in 1991, to its 1996 victory in the general elections with 21.3 percent of the national vote.[87] This made religious voters more confident about reintroducing Islamic specificities in the public sphere, like headscarves and alcohol restrictions. A new era of struggle ensued between Islamists and Kemalists for the levers of Nation-State Islam: the Diyanet and the İmam Hatip schools. Erbakan resisted increasing general mainstream education from five to eight years, which eliminated religious middle schools and devalued a high school degree in theology.

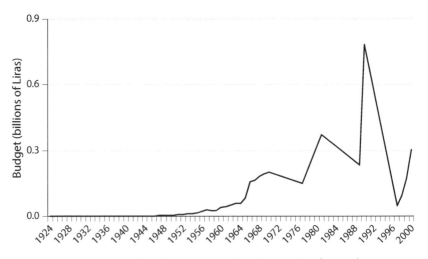

FIGURE 6.5. Turkey: The Directorate of Religious Affairs (Diyanet)
Budget Allocations, 1924–2000

The Welfare Party was accused of stuffing the Diyanet with 6,000 party members.[88] In fact, the personnel-to-citizen ratio decreased under its watch—as did the Diyanet budget relative to the growing population.

The Third Correction (1997–2001)

That equilibrium changed abruptly at the end of the century. The "postmodern" coup (called so because it was carried out with threats rather than force) that induced the most dramatic shifting of gears since the 1950s took place at the end of the century. The Welfare Party's success was a shocking development for the convinced Kemalists who made up most of the traditional political class. In 1997, "angry military chiefs gave Erbakan an unvarnished warning" in the form of an eighteen-point plan.[89] It may have also been the republic's last rearguard effort to preserve the Kemalist orthodoxy. The fourth military intervention (the postmodern coup against the Welfare Party–led government) ensnared a variety of religious dissidents. The CHP-led coalition that took over following Erbakan's exit, Özgur writes, was "fearful of . . . numerous closet 'reactionary' imams on its own payroll."[90] In their view, the growth of religious education outside mainstream public schools and the rise of İmam Hatip graduates in the civil service significantly *overcompensated* earlier secularizing measures. The trends were portrayed as part of a coordinated and politically motivated effort to infuse new Turkish generations with religious values.

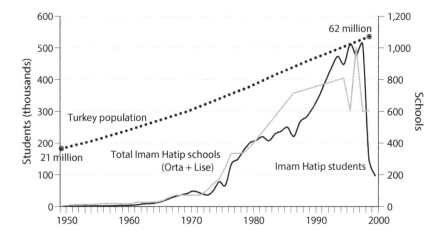

FIGURE 6.6. Turkey: İmam Hatip Schools and Students, 1950–2000

The new regime centralized the Friday sermon to ensure content control and aimed to sever the pipeline of religious education to religious personnel. The 1,000 or so spots available for the Higher Ilahiyat School of Professions program were dramatically insufficient given the number of officials employed by the Diyanet (54,476). Other basic deficiencies were revealed: in 1998, only 3.76 percent of Diyanet officials had received any kind of higher religious education.[91] To encourage young people to choose secular schools, new laws prevented İmam Hatip graduates from attending any university program other than theology: their grade point average was automatically reduced by 80 percent.[92] This was to implement the National Security Council directive to scale back İmam Hatip enrollment "to accommodate only students who genuinely wished to become clerics."[93]

The government also introduced eight-year compulsory mainstream public education, which resulted in the shutting of İmam Hatip middle schools (sixth to eighth grades) and a sharp decline in high school students down the line. The number of students in İmam Hatip Lisesi, which had doubled from 1987 to 1997, suddenly fell, from 511,502 in 1997 to 64,534 in 2002–2003 (see figure 6.6).[94] The gradual shortage of reliable Friday preachers contributed to the use of recorded sermons on cassette tapes produced in Ankara instead of actual human beings. As a percentage, İmam Hatip schools never enrolled anywhere near a majority of Turkish high school students: 1.2 percent in the 1950s, 2.6 percent in 1965, 8 percent in 1985, 10 percent in 1997, and 1.5 percent in 2003.[95] The number of schools rose from 715 to 1,500 between 1987 and 1997 and then fell to 400 in 2003. Meanwhile, the proportion of

Qur'an students enrolled in part-time courses increased from 400 per 100,000 in the late 1980s to twice that one decade later.[96]

The period opened feuds that resonated for decades afterwards: between Kemalists and followers of Fethullah Gülen—who was prosecuted in 1998 and fled to the United States—and between Kemalists and Islamists, whose culture clashes began to permeate the public sphere. The headscarf ban was first implemented after the coup, leading to controversies on campuses and in the Turkish parliament.[97] The next dramatic change of gear came with the arrival of Recep Tayyip Erdoğan and the AK Party (2002–present).

Morocco

Pre-Independence (1912–1956)

In his study of religion in Morocco, the distinguished anthropologist Clifford Geertz described French colonialism (1912–1956) as having reinforced a "symbolic framework of religio-political legitimization" around the person of the sultan. The occupiers "carefully preserved religious structures in order to ensure stability [and made] use of religion to structure public life," he wrote, and they had definite opinions about who should occupy the structures.[98] Loyalty to Islamic religious authority helped rally the national independence movement, and a unified national identity threatened France's hold on the country. The French kept their options open both inside and outside the Moroccan protectorate. British statesman Lord Curzon noted in diplomatic correspondence that French investment in North Africa did not keep the foreign minister from visiting Turkey for pan-Islamic talks ("I cannot imagine a greater danger to the peace of the world than a division between French and British Islam," Curzon wrote, "of which I do not think that I am fanciful in seeing the omens already above the horizon. On his recent return journey from Syria, M. Picot, the French High Commissioner, and no friend of ours, went out of his way to visit Mustapha Kemal at Sivas.") In Morocco, the French resident general pursued a strategy that emphasized competing identities and practices, seeking to contain the eighteen-year-old Moroccan sultan Mohammed V (1909–1961) upon his accession in 1927. The Moroccan nationalist movement was inadvertently strengthened in reaction to some of these policies, such as a decree granting an array of new rights to Berber communities (known as the *Dahir Berber*, 1930).

The French subsidized the folkloric *zawiyyas*, which were out of the sultan's control, and supported various expressions of ethnic Berber identity.[99] The centuries-old *zawiyyas* had strong local roots, charismatic leaders, and membership in the tens of thousands. Nonetheless, Mohammed V gradually asserted himself as a natural religious-political authority in the royal cities of Meknes and Fes. A revolutionary atmosphere prevailed across North Africa after World War II, with nationalist stirrings in Tunisia and Algeria spreading to Morocco. As was happening elsewhere in the European-occupied Muslim world, the Moroccan "'repertoire of contention' intertwined Islam and anti-colonial political protest, while forging a popular conception of Moroccan national identity . . . that conflated *umma* and *watan* (nation)."[100] This community had a natural leader in the sultan.

In diplomatic cables that have recently been declassified, the US consul, William Stokes, detailed how the French resident general reversed his "much-advertised policy of avoiding any interference in religious institutions" and adopted a more activist stance.[101] As the nationalist movement gained momentum, the French restricted Islamic gatherings. Fearing unrest from large crowds, they discouraged travel to the traditional end-of-Ramadan Eïd in the capital city of Rabat, threatening to suspend the operating license of any bus company that carried prayer-goers. Soon thereafter, in 1953, France called for the dismissal of the many scholars who spread "hateful propaganda" (Moroccan nationalism) at Qarawiyin, "one of the great centers of Islamic theology."

They also tried to tamp down ambitions for national independence by generating popular demand for Mohammed's abdication. The influence of Mustafa Kemal's Turkish spin on French *laïcité* can be seen in what happened next. The (briefly successful) bid to remove the man who united the national and religious spheres was an effort to disentangle Muslim faith from Moroccan identity—so that French occupation could continue. Three decades earlier, Kemal had abolished the Ottoman sultanate while retaining the position of caliph, which he put to a vote by the parliamentary *Mejlis*. The French resident general then convened a Congress of Religious Brotherhoods without inviting the sultan. *Le Monde* reported at the time that the "religious brotherhoods of Morocco [were] forming a coalition against the Sultan," while Mohammed V accused French officials of helping "circulate petitions calling for his abdication." The French audaciously announced new "ground rules for selecting a new sovereign" of Morocco and held an election for the new position of "Chief Imam" of Morocco.[102] The results were announced by the Pasha of Marrakech to an audience that included hundreds of tribal leaders: Mohammed V was outvoted as spiritual leader by his uncle, Mohammed Ibn Arafa. The uncle immediately signed a decree giving up the sultan's traditional legislative monopoly in favor of a "French and Moroccan committee to exert legislative powers" and took on reduced, symbolic functions of religious leadership—very

FIGURE 6.7. Morocco: Sultan Mohammed V, with son Hassan II (1950)

much like Abdülmecid II in 1923 Turkey. The French exerted "severe pressure compelling the ulema to sign the *bai 'a* recognizing the new Sultan," the consul reported. The "Ulema [were] coerced into signing these petitions."[103] And just like that, Mohammed V lost his high religious authority, which was invested in the new chief imam. The French bundled off Mohammed V and his family to Corsica and then Madagascar (1954). This was a historic step: it marked the first time in Morocco that spiritual and temporal powers were formally sepa-rate.[104] Given the conditions of the separation, however, its validity was doubtful.

After Independence (1956–1970)

Mohammed V returned from exile in November 1955 to reclaim his political and religious authority and to oversee the French departure from Morocco. One month later, his inaugural government created the country's first ministe-rial department for Islamic affairs.[105] Clifford Geertz writes that the sultan enjoyed an unusual position, there being "[no] other new nation in which the hero-leader of the revolution and independence was as engulfed in religious authority, over and above the political, as Muhammed V was in Morocco in 1956."[106] He crowned himself King Mohammed V (1956–61) and granted the ulema oversight of the personal status code and family law according to the Moroccan rite. Although the sultanate did not traditionally enjoy a monopoly over all religious foundations (known in Morocco as *habous*), the kingdom inherited control over the nationalized *awqaf* from the French protectorate, bringing all public habous under central control.[107] These included major centers of Islamic education: Qarawiyin at Fez, Youssefia at Marrakech, and El Mukharage El Elmi at Tangier and Meknes. The ulema were officially recognized and organized into the Grand Council of Ulema at Fez, with regional branches in Tangier, Marrakech, and Meknes. From 1956 onwards, Franck Frégosi and Malika Zéghal write, the monarchy "consolidated a framework of rule in which Islam and Arabic identity remained important pillars legitimating the post-colonial state."[108] It pushed back against the resistance of traditional brotherhoods which contended that Moroccan nationalism was a forbidden innovation.

By fortune or design, Hassan II's (1961–1999) day of investiture—the Fête du Trône—fell on the same day as the abolition of the Ottoman caliphate thirty-two years earlier. The 1962 constitution enshrined him as Emir al-Mu'minin (Commander of All the Faithful). Patrick Gaffney describes the claims of prophetic lineage as a kind of "mystical patronage amounting to divine right."[109] The king's duties included shielding his subjects from local and external influences and preventing the emergence of any rival religious authority. This was accomplished using the familiar tools of state-building. The government chartered an Islamic affairs administration, nationalized religious endowments, and standardized religious education.

The Moroccan state grew fast between 1962 and 1976. Starting from a rudimentary bureaucratic infrastructure, the state's prefectures and provinces tripled, from 15 to 47, and the number of civil servants rose nearly tenfold, from 55,000 to 500,000.[110] Part of this growth included the new Dar al Hadith (Hadith Council) and more university departments of Islamic studies. The Qarawiyin University, which had a tradition of operational independence, was endowed as a royal foundation. In 1963, new faculties of the university opened in the provinces, in order to break up the religious sphere.[111] Frégosi and Zéghal write that Hassan II thereby "prevented [ulema] from building too strong an 'esprit de corps,'" which might have counteracted the influence of the royal court (*Makhzen*).[112] In 1968, the king created thousands of Qur'anic schools to "fight illiteracy . . . and prepare young people to enter the school system."[113] The number of Qur'an schools doubled from 13,000 in 1973 to 25,600 in 1979. The new institutions produced "graduates en masse," some of whom eventually rose to the level of official ulema.[114] At the time, there were 20,481 employees in the Ministry of Religious Affairs, but only around 250 Friday preachers.[115]

The 1970s Hothouse: Growth under Pressure

A 1971 memorandum from the prime minister's office describes a major initiative to rationalize the oversight of Moroccan Islam: a mosque census.[116] A team of three dozen agents in state-issued automobiles combed the kingdom. The memorandum "estimated that there are around 100,000 constructions in the Kingdom which fit in the chosen definition for our working unit—the mosque," which included zawiyyas. The structures were either licensed or closed; the number of edifices that the Ministry of Habous defined as mosques was reduced to 20,000. Amid signs of disloyalty, Hassan II thus increased care to keep control over the religious field, confronting a "popular Islam" that attracted the unemployed and those let down by the national education system.[117] Louis-Jean Duclos notes that Hassan also led the reorganization of the ulema councils.[118]

Between 1972 and 1976, the Shabiba al Islamiya, a violent group, staged periodic uprisings and attacks before being shut down.[119] In 1973, the leader of another Islamist movement that emerged, Abdesselam Yassine, asserted himself as the anti-Emir. He impudently published a series of open letters to King Hassan and created the group Al Adl wal Ihsane.[120] Much like Fethullah Gülen in Turkey, Yassine was a longtime state employee. Whereas Gülen was a Diyanet preacher, Yassine was an inspector in the Ministry of Secondary Education. His first moment of defiance came by declaring that the ulema's oath of allegiance was invalid and that King Hassan II was illegitimate. Christiane Souriau notes that the king's rivalry with the leader of Al Adl wal Ishane "took an unexpected turn when Yassine openly praised the Iranian Ayatollah, who claimed spiritual hegemony over the entire Muslim world."[121] This coincided with the rise of an electoral challenge from Islamists. The platform of the Al Istiqlal Party (1976–1983) attempted to marginalize the official state ulema by creating new degree programs (1979) for religious clerics outside of the usual state controls and opening theology specializations in university literature departments.[122] The regime's popularity was unsteady: in 1979, the general secretary of the Ulema League openly criticized "le régime du pouvoir en Islam" in a ministry periodical.[123]

The government responded to the general challenge with Moroccan-accented Islamic mobilization. For example, Hassan II organized a massive Green March for 350,000 participants brandishing flags, royal portraits, and small Qur'ans to walk to a Spanish-occupied city in western Sahara.[124] He also addressed deficiencies and threats within the three institutional worlds: infrastructure, education, and hierarchy. New zoning restrictions limited mosque construction by private citizens or local city councils. Mohamed Tozy describes how the government streamlined mosque construction permits to

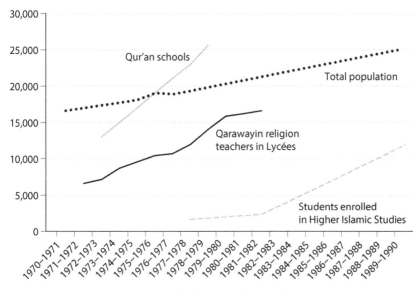

FIGURE 6.8. Morocco: The Rise in Religious Affairs, 1970–1990

direct them toward more *mosquées cathédrales*: large, transparent structures "located in an open space, easy to access and therefore inspectable."[125] In the year that Al Istiqlal came to power, the Ministry of Islamic Affairs was given its formal charter and statutes (1976). A new training service was created within the religious affairs ministry, which, Tozy notes, was "the first time that the administration acknowledged the need to formally train clerics."[126] The government also created thirty-nine institutes of Islamic education. The number of employees in the growing Qarawiyin complex of educational institutions rose from 6,600 high school teachers of religion in 1972 to 16,613 in 1982 (see figure 6.8). Mohamed Al Ayadi writes that the king placed the ulema in charge of defending the authority of "state fundamentalism"—erudite and knowledgeable—against oppositional "integralism," which the king called "intolerant and fanatical."[127]

Growth under External Pressure: Shielding (1980–2000)

The 1980s inaugurated a new era and a new Moroccan-Islamic vision to resolve the Arab world's problems.[128] Iran's revolution gave King Hassan II the opportunity to emerge from the shadow of the Egyptians, Hashemites, and Sauds. As the only Sunni *religious* leader who was also a head of state, Hassan was a natural choice to chair the Al Quds Committee for Jerusalem from 1979 to 1986.[129] As Louis-Jean Duclos writes, Hassan's status strengthened the "international recognition of the Moroccan King as leader of the Muslim Community."[130] Hassan helped create the Organization of the Islamic Conference—forty-two members strong, headquartered in Mecca—which replaced the Arab League as the new center of power after Egypt's peace deal with Israel. A royal order (*dahir*) in 1981 formalized fourteen regional ulema councils and chartered the Ulema High Council, presided over by the king. Looking for them to rally around his leadership, Hassan urged the ulema to stop fulminating, Christiane Souriau writes, "about naked women, wine and movies" and to "start taking more political positions."[131]

Unregulated Islamist preaching continued to expand in the large cities, however, and religious groups fought back against royal leadership with a series of "disturbances known as the Troubles" starting in 1984. As Geoff Porter writes, "Hassan II blamed supporters of [Iranian ayatollah] Khomeini, as well as Socialists and Zionists, for inciting the riots."[132] In the mid-1980s, however, it was Sunni Islamists who took advantage of new audiocassette technology and recorded portable sermons. These tapes were immensely useful to the *prêcheurs libres* (unauthorized preachers) who operated under the government's radar. Geoff Porter writes that, "in the 1980s, the Moroccan king embraced 'tradition' anew."[133] To counter the religious dissidence, "Qarawiyiin students once again [became] part of the social life of the medina" for the first time since national independence.[134] Hassan brought religious matters large and small—from relations with the Organization of Islamic Cooperation (OIC) to religious education in mosques—under his own direct oversight.[135]

In 1980, the Ministry of Habous and Islamic Affairs was created to oversee all organization of religious exercise.[136] There were 20,481 religious affairs employees; 1,775 imams who could perform the Friday sermon and 5,361 five-prayer imams, who were increased to a total of 6,500 during the month of Ramadan.[137] For the first time, the ministry had a five-year plan (1981–1985) and a national commission in parliament. The number of "religious centers" and preachers was outpacing population growth and catching up.

The Ministry of Habous and Islamic Affairs was restructured between 1979 and 1984, and the number of official mosques in the kingdom increased by 25 percent, from 19,000 to 25,000.[138] Hassan "intensified regulation of Islamic activities in local mosques . . . [and] more than doubled the number of regional councils responsible for overseeing sermons . . . and the performance of rituals by local religious leaders." Dale Eickelman sees this expansion of the regional council network as an attempt to "'limit the potential for developing an oppositional Islam.'"[139] In 1984, the kingdom increased regulations on mosque construction, requiring formal permission from the Ministry of Habous and Islamic Affairs (again). The state moved to block the *prêcheurs libres* from illicitly preaching and distributed a weekly sermon template to state preachers. A new class of "religiously trained civil servants" emerged "to supervise the mosques, monitor the [radicals], and make sure that . . . sermons [comply with national] religious authority."[140]

Students matriculating in higher Islamic studies increased nearly fivefold in the space of a decade, from 1,638 in 1978 to 2,223 in 1982 to 11,834 in 1992. The number of religious educational institutes increased by 50 percent, from thirty-nine in the late 1970s to sixty-three in 1991.[141] Around the time of the Gulf War, during Saddam Hussein's siren call for Islamic uprising, the Moroccan ulemas "regularly intervened in the political discussion," just as they had after the Iranian Revolution (albeit in favor of Iraq at the time).[142] By 1982, there were twelve departments of Islamic studies operating in the political capital; there were also three higher Islamic education institutes in the city of Fez alone. Geoff Porter relates statistics from the Ministry of Higher Education between 1984 and 1994 showing that "departments of Islamic Studies became the largest departments in the Humanities Colleges." In 1999, the Qarawiyin University's four faculties accounted for roughly 8,000 students.[143] Construction began on the grand Hassan II Mosque complex in Casablanca in 1996. In the decade before the ascendance of Mohammed VI to the throne (1999), the ground was being prepared for his ambitious religious reforms.

Algeria

Before Independence

In the years leading up to the nationalist uprising, mobilization for Algerian independence was spearheaded by the country's religious leadership. As early as 1931, the Association of Muslim Algerian Ulema promoted an Arab-Islamic national identity, supported religious education, and encouraged the use of the Arabic language instead of French.[144] In 1952, the association revived an old grievance and demanded the "strict application of the 1905 French law" on *laïcité* and the "liberation of the religious sphere from the control of the French administration." It sent a formal letter of protest to the French prime minister in 1953, complaining of the "unjust" treatment of Islam, which was "denied the same freedom granted other religions."[145] A slogan of the era mocked French policy: "Authentic Islam belongs to God, but Algerian Islam belongs to Caesar."[146] The independence movement relentlessly pursued the separation of Islam from the French colonial state. President Ahmed Ben Bella (1916–2012) and his staff were aware that pro-religious sentiments were widespread, and they viewed Islam as a primary

FIGURE 6.9. Algeria: The Mosque in La Place du Gouvernement, Algiers (1955)

element of Algerian identity. The Front for National Liberation (FLN) declared alcohol illegal for Muslims and enlisted party members to enforce public fasting during Ramadan in 1954. The Association of Muslim Algerian Ulema joined the war for independence in 1956 and formally merged with the FLN.[147] The revolutionary government never implemented the religious leaders' demand for separation between Islam and state. As Achi Raberh writes, "Long after Algerian independence, Islam in the country was almost completely guided by the state."[148] The first independent president, Ahmed Ben Bella, made concessions to religious actors but never let go of the reins: instead, Islam became Algeria's de facto official religion. Over the coming decades, the state took control of religious affairs and effectively nationalized religion. It alone authorized mosque construction and issued the Friday sermon to imams, whom it trained, appointed, and salaried. The Ministry of Religious Affairs built up a bureaucracy to oversee waqfs, religious training, and the recruitment of civil servants (see figure 6.9).[149]

The Growth of Nation-State Islam: Re-Islamization during the 1970s

Although traditional religious authorities were pleased by the recognition of Islam as the religion of state in the 1963 constitution, they were disturbed by the constitution's simultaneous recognition of religious freedom.[150] All forms of religious education, including part-time Qur'anic instruction, were placed under the Ministry of Religious Affairs and required prior authorization. Fatefully, in 1964 the regime's Algiers Charter placed the country on the "Socialist path" and disengaged the Algerian state from Islam.[151] In an effort to garner support from religious elements for the socialist policies being put forward by the government, a leader of the Association of Muslim Algerian Ulema was named minister of waqfs. Once installed, he declared that "Islam is a socialist religion, it is a religion of equity."[152] Franck Frégosi writes that the pressures of observant Muslims' opinion "were strong enough to force Ben Bella to accept the adoption of a Resolution providing for a conservative family code."[153] Just before the coup that removed him from power, Ben Bella formally prohibited the Islamic associations that he came to see as a threat to national security.[154]

His successor, President Houari Boumedienne (1965–1978), tried to co-opt religious sentiment by throwing the weight of the central state behind it. Boumedienne promoted a reformist, progressive, and above all anticolonial religious heritage, introducing a period that has been called the confessionalizing of Algerian political institutions.[155] Whereas French occupation had favored the *zawiyyas*, Boumedienne denounced the Sufi imams as charlatans and seized their printing presses, accusing them and other brotherhoods of Moroccan influence. The president ordered portraits of the religious folk heroes Ben Badis and Abd el-Kader to be displayed in all Algerian classrooms. The small number of madrassas were inventoried in the 1960s, and the government established the national Higher Islamic Council (1966) as the sole authoritative body to issue religious legal decrees (fatwas). Algiers then nationalized all religious foundations (waqfs) and incorporated them into the new Ministry of Traditional Education and Religious Affairs (1966). Imams were granted civil servant status three years later.

The symbolic concessions to Islamic sensibilities piled up. The official day of rest was shifted from Sunday to Friday, and various measures were taken "to establish the obligatory nature of the Ramadan fast." Pork farming was criminalized, and the sale of alcohol to Algerian citizens was restricted.[156] In 1968, the ministry oversaw a public morality campaign during which its enforcers tore down vines in the country's wine-producing regions. The national agrarian revolution was defended in religious terms.[157] The 1973 National Charter included a rule permitting references to Islamic law within the civil code.[158] The 1976 constitution made the head of state swear upon the Qur'an to "glorify the Islamic religion" and included an article that no future amendment could alter the principle of the state religion. An amendment added the requirement that the head of state be Muslim.[159] Moloud Belkacem, an influential minister to the president for religious affairs in the 1970s, helped establish Islamic institutes in large cities. He was especially attuned to Islam's "civilizational" role in Algerian society, especially the mosque and the madrassa. Belkacem professionalized Qur'anic education, granted teachers civil servant status, and created regional training centers for them. These moves belied growing tensions "between the defenders of 'genuineness' and those of 'modernity,' between a State-established law and religious law."[160] The same constitution reserved all "general rules in the field of personal status and family law" exclusively for the parliament.[161]

Multiparty Politics and the Path to Civil War in the 1980s

When Chadly Benjedid (1929–2012) became president in 1979, he tried to leverage religious fundamentalists against his opponents on the left. President Benjedid reversed Boumedienne's course and initiated an opening to the brotherhoods—the tariqat and *zawiyyas*—and tried to point them against the Salafists, whose counterassault against Iran's Shi'a revolution could be felt internationally. The ministry consolidated its hold on waqfs. This was a last-ditch attempt to ward off the gathering Islamist storm by pandering to *other* religious conservatives. The government published the Cultural Charter (1981) stating that "Islam shall not be considered contrary to the social (or Socialist) Revolution nor as something to be kept outside of the Revolution."[162] Amid an influx of Wahhabi literature, 1980 was a turning point, a time when Algerian Islamism "expanded beyond the tight circle of mosques and found its place in the street" as a contentious political force aiming to bring about Islamic rule.[163] The 1982 Family Code unraveled Algeria's two-decade-old progressive laws: for example, it institutionalized polygamy and denied wives the right to apply for a divorce unless they gave up all claims of alimony.[164] But in 1984 the Justice Ministry abruptly codified secular family law, removing it from the realm of shari'ah courts.

The newly appointed minister of religious affairs (1981) declared his intention to improve the distribution of trained imams in the country's 5,000 mosques. He emphasized the social and cultural role of mosques and pointed out that 3,000 of them, or 60 percent, did not have adequate personnel.[165] The FLN-led government updated and expanded religious education for all ages at around the same time.[166] In the early 1980s, the ministry had 5,183 employees, including 2,881 imams; only 592 of these were licensed as Friday-mosque imams. All religious schools were incorporated into the public education ministry after a transition of three years.[167]

President Benjedid approved a five-year plan to build new mosques and Qur'an schools in each of Algeria's 160 *daïra* territorial units, plus new Islamic cultural centers in each of the country's 48 states (*wilayas*).[168] He announced the construction of eighty-eight new mosque complexes in Oran and Algiers and laid out a systematic approach to religious education. A separate minister of *religious* education was temporarily established, and religious studies became a university discipline that required students to acquire a license degree to be hired as a religion teacher.[169] The first Islamic theology faculty was opened in Algiers in 1982, followed by one in Constantine and Oran in 1984. Another reform created a high school specialization in Islamic sciences (alongside humanities, sciences, and technical), inaugurating five such specialized *lycées* in each of the wilayas. Benjedid also introduced regulations requiring all imams to possess a state diploma and to receive a formal appointment by Algiers. A 1981 decree expanded the number of imam training institutions from one to thirteen and transformed the Institut des sciences islamiques into a national theology institute.[170] In 1984, the government created the University of Islamic Studies, named after Emir Abd el-Kader (Constantine). A 1986 decree inaugurated a new university diploma in Islamic sciences.

The target audience did not appear to be persuaded by these official efforts. It was around this time that the antigovernment Islamic Salvation Front (FIS) emerged "to protest the brutal repression of the Islamist movement." A rally of 2,000 Islamists, including the movement's future leaders, took place at the University of Algiers. They issued a rival charter (1982) accusing the government of "atheism [and] judeo-masonic conspiracy" and called for the "total application of Shari'ah law."[171]

The urgency to address infrastructural deficits put Algeria at the mercy of the Pan-Islamic force on offer: Saudi Arabia. To make up for the lack of trained personnel, the ministry opted for a short-term stopgap and "authorized 'independent' imams who escaped state oversight," but who would be allowed the use of the state pulpits.[172] Algerian students earned tuition scholarships at the University of Medina in Saudi Arabia, where they were subjected to intense Wahhabi propaganda.[173] The Institut de sciences islamiques in Algiers (1983) was staffed almost entirely by former students of the University of Medina and became a center of Wahhabi proselytism. In 1985, the education ministry announced its intention to shore up national Islamic knowledge—12,000 specialists would be trained within the next fifteen years—but it was too little too late.[174]

In 1988, the government inadvertently worsened the chaos with the decision to liberalize requirements for civil society organizations. The political pluralism that followed bred direct conflict between radical political Islam and left-wing secularization. The 1988 Bab al Oued riots in the nation's capital—the "culmination of a decade of confrontation between Islamic movements and the government"—led to hundreds of injuries and thousands of arrests.[175] State control continued, but it coexisted with a more conservative independent Islam, which in some ways was "more influential than official Islam between 1989–1992."[176]

The FIS received direct support from the Saudis, but it also made ample use of networks of hundreds of independent imams and thousands of new "free mosques" across Algerian towns and cities.[177] Myriam Aït-Aoudia reveals how free mosques escaped official control through a regulatory loophole. The state could only inspect mosques that were fully built and operational, so religious communities took care to leave them partly unfinished and under construction. Officially, on the eve of civil war, there were 7,111 completed mosques and 1,962 under construction, and an additional 2,148 were counted as "empty mosques."[178] Unofficially, estimates of ungoverned religious spaces were even higher. Most imams active in them were aligned with the FIS, constituting a network with the power of political mobilization. The state began cracking down on the previously tolerated religious opposition movements as a countervailing force to leftist student organizations.

An analogous situation was taking place in the educational realm. A government census in 1989 counted 2,251 Qur'an schools attached to mosques, plus another 514 that were being run independently.[179] One education official said in an interview that "there were only three genuine Islamic specialists in the country and they were all trained in Saudi Arabia." The inspector general of the Ministry of Religious Affairs said in an interview that "they returned to Algeria in the 1980s and 1990s to teach, and to Islamicize Algeria. They believed that we were a pagan state, their mission was to change this." Despite the flurry of activity, at the end of the 1980s the courses of study had little academic content and were more Arabic language instruction than anything else.[180] The government's socialist preferences were impossible to miss: one of the religious affairs ministry's tasks was to "explain and spread Socialist principles of social justice which constitute an essential element of Islam." Collectively, this did little to stave off the rising tide of the FIS.

The Worst-Case Scenario: Civil War in the 1990s

In 1989, a bill was passed that reformed the constitution and allowed the FIS to charter a political party. Michael Driessen writes that this was seen in hindsight as an "ill-conceived electoral process" because the party's statutes violated a constitutional ban on religiously inspired political parties.[181] In June 1990, the FIS party ran in its first local elections, winning 54 percent of the vote, against the ruling FLN's 28 percent. Ahmed Mahiou and Jean-Robert Henry write that Algeria thus had the distinction of being "the first Arab country to have an Islamic political party achieve electoral success in a democratic polity." The FIS declared its objective as the restoration of the caliphate and named its principal inspirations as "Iran, Saudi Arabia and Sudan."[182] The party's "fiery young orator," Ali Belhadj, called for the implementation of shari'ah law.[183]

The FIS party ran in the following year's national elections, whose results were annulled once it became clear that the Islamist party had won. The first signs of an armed Islamic reaction manifested on campuses, which were hotbeds of debate over the merits of Shi'ism, Wahhabism, the Muslim Brotherhood, and the Soviet war in Afghanistan. Instances of violence at universities in Constantine and Oran escalated, ultimately setting off a civil war that left as many as 200,000 Algerians dead. Over the course of the 1990s, eighty-six imams were murdered, and a brigade from the Armed Islamic Group (GIA) ambushed and killed a senior religious affairs official in 1995.[184]

Cautious Restoration: The Early Bouteflika Years

In an attempt to reassert state control over the religious sphere after the worst fighting was over, the Higher Islamic Council was created for religious interpretation (*ijtihad*) adapted to the Algerian context (1996). A truce was established in 1997, followed by presidential elections the following year that produced an interim regime of reconciliation. The fact that leftist currents had returned to power after the horrors earlier that decade suggested that Islam could remain a factor of discord. The new government reduced the space dedicated to religion in schools and looked for a new approach to avoid the pitfalls of the 1980s. A senior religious education official described the process in an interview: "We wanted to have one interpretation for all of the country's schools, so we oversaw an overhaul of our textbooks. The 1998 reform revised all educational texts—removing chapters that were no longer relevant or that contained interpretations which were criticized for various reasons."[185] From then onwards, Algerian religion teachers were required to study for three to five years at the university level before being placed in primary, middle, and high schools. Imam training was later modeled after a similar approach, depending on which of four roles a teacher fulfilled in the mosque.[186] The Ministry of Religious Affairs faced the gargantuan task of "reintegrating the organically-built mosques" and pairing them with a state-trained imam. Under "civil harmony legislation," armed Islamist groups were allowed to surrender with immunity or significantly reduced sentences. The conflict was over but not gone: 150 Algerians were killed in attacks during Ramadan 1999.[187] When President Abdelaziz Bouteflika was elected that year, he changed many things but retained the same minister of religious affairs from the first postwar government; this minister remained in office for nearly two decades, until 2014.

Tunisia

In the nineteenth century, Tunisia enjoyed a tradition of relative religious independence preceding the French protectorate, thanks to an independent (Husaynid) state that held its own within the Ottoman Empire.[188] As happened elsewhere in French-occupied North Africa, Tunisian religious institutions helped mobilize anticolonial movements. The sheikh who founded the Democratic Constitutional Rally (Destour Party) in 1920 was a Zeitouna graduate influenced by Pan-Islamic figures of the previous century. Decades of French rule weakened the system of traditional religious education in favor of modern schools. In the late 1920s, many Tunisians sent their children to French schools, at a roughly equal rate to the number in traditional kuttab schools.[189] The state was infused with religious touches. The first leader of the Tunisian General Labor Union (UGTT) was the son of a Zeitouna president. At midcentury, despite the popularity of the Franco-Tunisian baccalaureate program, 40,000 students still attended a traditional kuttab for secondary school, and 14,000 pursued higher education at the Zeitouna, which had a faculty of 500.[190]

After Independence: Bourguiba Unleashes
His Inner Atatürk (1950–1980)

While he was still an up and coming nationalist leader in the late 1920s Habib Bourguiba (1903–2000) defended the headscarf as a symbol of national identity. When he became state president, however, Habib Bourguiba of the late 1950s was better known as an anticlerical fan of Mustafa Kemal.[191] The president-mufti shut down the 1,000-year-old Islamic faculty of Zeitouna, personally unveiled girls in countryside photo-ops, and declared two of Islam's five religious pillars to be optional for Tunisians. Authorities padlocked the country's mosques save for fifteen minutes before daily prayers.[192] He seemed to be locked in competition with another modernizer, Egyptian president Gamal Nasser (1918–1970), for Atatürk's legacy. Bourguiba abolished the monarchy in Tunisia and ensured that the constitution would not proclaim Islam as the state religion. He neutralized potential opposition coming from the ulema or their student supporters by entirely nationalizing the religious infrastructure.[193]

In the interest of accuracy in official documents, Bourguiba traded the Islamic year marking Mohammed's emigration to Medina for the common era marking the birth of Jesus.[194] Within months of national independence, Bourguiba implemented legal reforms that removed every scintilla of authority from religious leaders. Ulema were viewed not so much as a political threat as a threat to the president's version of Tunisian national identity. Malika Zéghal writes that Bourguiba's arrival signaled "a death warrant" for "professional men of religion" and for mainstream piety in Tunisia.[195] First, he focused on the institutions that could potentially compete with his rule: he dissolved the shari'ah courts and the Ministry of Awqaf, so that waqfs would "pass entirely into the state's budget."[196] All religious affairs policies, "from the treatment of civil servants to the preservation of mosques, were decided upon in the national assembly." In 1958, when Bourguiba demoted the Islamic faculty at Zeitouna to the status of an academic department of the new University of Tunis, a public corporation under the authority of the Ministry of Education. Religious instruction in the new Tunisia emphasized Islam's humanistic and socialist sides and warned against religious formalism.[197]

During his time in power, Bourguiba issued numerous "influential pronouncements" that served as de facto religious dispensations from various Islamic religious requirements. He viewed the state as the guarantor of Islam and said that if the state "were ever in danger, political necessity must take precedence over religious rituals."[198] In the realm of personal status, the regime abolished polygamy, legalized abortion, raised the minimum age for marriage, and substituted civil divorce for religious repudiation.[199] Abdelwahab Bouhdiba notes President Bourguiba's personal war on the month of Ramadan: in 1960, he recommended that working people give up the Ramadan fast and work efficiently "for the battle against economic underdevelopment."[200] He went to great lengths to demonstrate that fasting during Ramadan should no longer be considered obligatory. Jennifer Noyon describes "his televised downing of a glass of orange juice during daylight in the month of Ramadan, saying that fasting decreased productivity in a modernizing society."[201] He told Tunisians to get "authorization to break this fast . . . if it risks endangering your health or interrupts the activity which is your means of living."[202] Regarding headscarves, in one film clip from the era, Bourguiba tours the countryside and ceremoniously removes the veils off of the women who greet him. Abdelwahab Bouhdiba remarks that Bourguiba's "distaste for traditional dress" extended to men as well: "Turbans have disappeared from the traditional teachers of religious knowledge in our secondary schools. Sheiks wear European dress and the majority of them go uncovered."[203] During the Eïd at the end of Ramadan in 1964, the president recommended that indigent Tunisians forgo sacrificing actual lambs. Regarding Muslims' duty to perform the hajj pilgrimage, Bourguiba encouraged pilgrims to settle for the tombs of local saints.[204] Sami Hanna found that in the late 1960s the "socialist experiment" had led to the "intentional abolition of religious education from Tunisian schools."[205]

Over a period of ten years, "the structures of national religious life were brought under control of the political party in power."[206] Employees in the Office of the Imam were renamed "preachers" and given broader speaking responsibilities:

"lectures and courses on subjects of national interest" under party supervision. Many new mosques were built to be community centers where masses could assemble. A new department of religious affairs (1967) was created in the prime minister's office to coordinate state religion policies.[207] This included oversight of mosque construction, religious instruction, and the training and appointment of *agents de culte*.[208] President Bourguiba relied on the precedent set by Egyptian President Nasser in order to expand the public religious sphere.[209] He timed his weekly radio addresses for Thursday so that what he said could be echoed in mosques on Friday.[210] "What system?" he asked once. "I am the system!"[211] Seeing how Nasser had named himself chief imam in Egypt and how the Moroccan constitution named Hassan II Emir al-Mu'minin, Bourguiba appropriated the role of official interpreter of religious law of the republic. Malika Zéghal notes that he was undaunted by his lack of training in religious law: "By virtue of my responsibilities as head of state" Bourguiba declared himself to be the "supreme *mujtahid*."[212]

In the mid-1960s, Abdelwahab Bouhdiba reports, "Tunisia gives the impression of becoming increasingly deaf to the call of the muezzin, and more and more attentive to the blast of the factories. . . . Productivity and yields [were increasingly] substituted for prayer or meditation."[213] The Tunisian president had decreed that Ramadan and hajj, serious religious obligations—40 percent of a Muslim's core duties—were optional. Within a short period, the number of *non*-practicing Muslims skyrocketed, especially among those under age thirty-five.[214] The "supreme mujtahid" shifted his attitude in the late 1960s after Islamic movements emerged "looking to preserve a threatened identity" and questioning many of the hallmarks of Tunisian secularization. The emblematic leader of the Islamist opposition, Rachid al Ghannouchi, articulated the dissident views of a large plurality of Tunisians who felt alienated from an abruptly secularized state, notwithstanding Bourguiba's pious gesticulations. "Islam is not only about spiritual teachings and orientations," Ghannouchi said. "It also has a distinct doctrine, law, set religious practices and views about humans and society." He judged that "Bourguibism went against the religious sentiments, beliefs and values of the masses."[215]

In the last decade of a thirty-one-year reign, Bourguiba paid increasing attention to "authentic Islam"—with mixed results. He engaged in "constant solicitation of religious references to justify the government's various positions."[216] At the time, the nonstate "Islamist discourse was apolitical," and mostly concerned with "re-valorizing Islamic rituals and symbols." He tolerated an informal network of sheikhs and their disciples who "preached in mosques and high schools" and created the Association to Preserve the Qur'an (1968).[217] Both the network and the association, however, had unintended consequences: the Islamist movement began to "escape the regime's oversight." The former ulema slowly "regained control over parts of the education sector and judgeships."[218] Bourguiba empowered an "arabo-Islamic current" within his own party that raised the prospect of applying shari'ah prescriptions at the party congress (1971).[219] To keep up, the regime "launched into a policy of progressive re-islamization."

Ever attuned to Islam's symbolic value, Bourguiba gave an annual "major religious address" (*mouled*) in Kairouan. He closed down nightclubs during Ramadan and engaged in a "campaign of repression against wine and liquors." An administrative memorandum forbade marriage between Muslim women and non-Muslim men (1973). Alcoholic drinks could no longer be sold after 8 p.m. in bars and cafés, and they were banned from sale during religious holidays.[220] Bourguiba began to sound like an Islamic scholar-statesman: "The presidential regime in western democratic countries has deep roots within Islam. . . . The President is simply the supreme commander, the Imam whose election results from the vote of a national community."[221]

This statement hints at the other way Bourguiba tried to keep up with the Islamizing landscape: he adorned his policies with religious trimmings and rhetoric. He renewed the Directorate of Islamic Affairs under the prime minister (1970). In an about-face from a decade earlier, authorities started encouraging "citizens to complete their religious obligations" within the managed framework.[222] A minister of state declared the government's determination "to disseminate an education based on the true and original values of Islam."[223] The Ministry of Education wanted classes of religious instruction to inspire a "spiritual atmosphere" in order not only to make students "memorize and thoroughly understand quranic texts" but also to "stimulate a love for the Qur'an."[224] The Tunisian capital also played a visible role in international organizations to make a domestic political point about Islamic leadership. Tunis hosted the headquarters of both the Arab League (1979) and the Palestinian Liberation Organization through most of the 1980s. The regime mustered the enthusiasm to celebrate the much-diminished Zeitouna University's thirteen centuries of existence (1979). The main item on the policy agenda was to extend the state's coverage of the religious scene across Tunisia. This would require the centralization and standardization of a landscape desperately lacking in prayer spaces and institutions of religious education. Violence occasionally shattered the illusion of control: in 1980, a Libyan-trained Islamist commando of 300 fighters besieged the Tunisian town of Gafsa, attacking the army barracks, the national guard, and a police station.[225] Several years later, an Ennahda supporter assassinated the sheikh of Zeitouna in the Kram neighborhood of Tunis—a brazen assault on the notion of President Bourguiba as supreme mujtahid. In 1986, the government moved religious affairs from the prime minister's office to the Interior Ministry.[226]

Co-opting Islamism: Undoing the Undoing (1987–2000)

Zine El Abidine Ben Ali (1936–2019) replaced Habib Bourguiba as president in a "medical" coup d'état in November 1987 and immediately demonstrated his readiness to broker a reconciliation of religion and state.[227] He granted amnesty to hundreds of MTI (Mouvement de la tendance islamique) militants and members of the Islamic Liberation Party and freed Rachid al Ghannouchi (1988) from prison.[228] Ben Ali extended a hand to one of the cofounders of the Ennahda Party, reopened Zeitouna University, restored the office of secretary of state for religious affairs, delegated his own brother to implement an Islamic banking system, and began interrupting regularly scheduled radio and television programming to broadcast the call to prayer. Ben Ali increased the number of pilgrims going on the hajj, undertook an Omra pilgrimage himself, restored the Islamic calendar on official documents and national currency, and decreed the official use of Arabic within the administration. He opened each public speech with "In the name of God the Clement and Merciful" and frequently ended with a *sourat* from the Qur'an.[229] Islam was not made the official state religion, but the "increasingly ostentatious daily practice of political leaders suggested the opposite." Soon thereafter, the prime minister issued an administrative order that all cafés and restaurants were to remain closed during the month of Ramadan and asked hospitality workers to "discourage through persuasion any Tunisian Muslims who come to restaurants to eat or drink."[230] A national pact was signed that proclaimed a commitment to Tunisia's "specifically Arab-Islamic values." In 1989, the Center for Islamic Studies opened in Kairouane, and the Islamic faculty of the Zeitouna was restored in its "former structures and responsibilities." After thirty years as part of public state education, the Zeitouna began offering degree programs to deliver traditional four- and seven-year diplomas.[231]

Once President Ben Ali's regime formalized its monopoly over Islam—as he put it, "only the State may provide for the flourishing (*épanouissement*) and spread (*rayonnement*) of Islam"—a confrontation with the Ennahda Party was inevitable.[232] Extending control over the landscape required a state crackdown across Tunisia and occasioned the disappearance of Islamist leadership into decades of exile or prison.[233] Between 1990 and 1992, "a cycle developed including episodes of agitation and some violence by Islamist partisans, widespread arrests and government repression" during which 8,000 suspected Ennahda supporters were arrested.[234] The government hired an additional 400 religious affairs officials (*agents de culte*), increasing its corps from 9,000 to 9,400, and major funding was released for the improvement of mosques.[235]

In 1992, Ben Ali created the Ministry of Religious Affairs (see figure 6.10), charged with applying state policy in the religious sphere and protecting spiri-

FIGURE 6.10. Tunisia: The Ministry of Religious Affairs, Tunis (1992)

tual values.[236] The number of bureaucrats within the ministry would increase by 50 percent during the 1990s, to 13,000.[237] The ministry oversaw construction, inventory, maintenance, and use of the country's 5,000 mosques. Ben Ali was eager to keep his Islamist adversaries from occupying the religious spaces he created—as had happened to Bourguiba in the late 1960s—and so mosques were closed outside of prayer times and remained off limits whenever a state representative was unavailable to supervise.

The confrontation between forces could be seen as a rehashing of the post-independence cleavage: the Ennahda Islamist movement as the "genealogical product of a section of the Zeitouna Ulema," and Ben Ali as the "logical consequence of Bourguiba."[238] President Ben Ali "considered himself to be a kind of Caliph—the safe-keeper of country and religion." In reality, the Ministry of Religious Affairs had little presence outside of the large cities. His legacy is as contested and controversial as that of Bourguiba: Ben Ali stands accused by secularists as having "paved the way to a narrower and more rigid identity within Tunisian society."[239] His education policy, however, received the opposite criticism. Drawing "perverse lessons of previous reforms," it swung to the other extreme: the laicist, anti-Salafi textbooks seemed to be "a Bourguibian strategy to secularize Tunisian society."[240] Despite the veneer, the ensemble of religious affairs policies was weak. In reality, the Zeitouna's graduating classes decreased from an average of 1,000 per year in the 1980s to fewer than 100 a year in the late 1990s. Religious affairs became one more part of the repressive policing apparatus. The mosques were listening posts to aid the vain attempt to defeat growing political opposition to Ben Ali's rule.

Conclusion

There is disagreement as to whether the first phase of state Islam precipitated the gathering storm of Islamism or held it at bay. On the one hand, the religion scholar Jocelyn Césari says that the *state* "has been a central if not the primary agent in politicizing Islam."[241] She finds that institutionalization spurs religious conflict because it created incentives for Islamic political parties and makes space for religious violence.[242] Césari blames postcolonial states for including Islam within the nation-building project, saying that the "homogenization process led to a politicized narrative of religion . . . [that is,] Political Islam." She argues that the "institutionalization [of Islam] is correlated with the politicization of Islam, e.g. the existence of Islam-based political parties and religious-based political violence."[243] Kristen Fabbe notes the paradox of bureaucratizing Islam while simultaneously secularizing and asks if this is not just "the complete relegation of religious institutions and elites to state authority?"[244]

In reality, the homogenization processes had begun under Ottoman and then European rule. Since the turn of the century, well before national capitals got into the act, waqfs and madrassas were already centralized by Istanbul, London, and Paris. The modern political Islam was born in the leadup and aftermath of the abolition of the Ottoman caliphate. Nation-State Islam succeeded best in taking root when it cultivated connections to national religious traditions, as in Morocco and Turkey. Rather than seed the ground, however, many postcolonial states imposed an era of austerity upon Islamic life. They closed seminaries and theology faculties and defunded Islamic personnel and education. The standard liberal critique of state Islam is that "regimes sought to control the functions of religion" as part of an "overall drive to establish hegemony over society and expand its powers and controls."[245] As Robert Hefner put it, "The Qur'an speaks in favor of no such modernist leviathan."[246] But there was no leviathan, in fact. Islamic institutions withered away. According to Malika Zéghal, "religious symbolism was used against leftist opponents and to preempt Islamists who waved a Wahhabi yardstick."[247] Official religion as ritual practice became hollowed out, stultified, and chronically underresourced. As Jakob Skovgaard-Petersen puts it, the "state-building reforms of Middle Eastern Islam . . . did serious damage to the roots of religious authority."[248] The neglect threatened the transmission of religious traditions from one generation to the next. Millions of citizens could not get married or buried the way they had done for generations.

Insufficient numbers of mosques, imams, preachers, and teachers had long-term consequences for national security. Sebastian Elischer has shown with his research on Islam in Africa that "states that chose institutional regulation as their primary strategy prior to the emergence of Saudi Arabia as a major international player . . . successfully undermined the spread of political and jihadi Salafism in later decades."[249] The existence of adequate prayer spaces and religious guidance cannot guarantee any particular outcome. But the absence of Islam as part of everyday life in neighborhoods and schools led those who sought a pious life to embrace foreign sources—in some cases, under the sway of the Muslim Brotherhood or Saudi Wahhabism—who operated in different contexts and perpetuated an overtly political agenda. These were not hypothetical influences upon national citizens: Algeria suffered years of violent civil war, and Tunisia supplied a stream of fighters in jihadi conflicts worldwide. In terms of their internal domestic security, Morocco and Turkey, on the other hand, experienced mostly foreign-born (European) security threats relating to Islamic extremism.

Did twentieth-century official Islam stimulate its own competition in the form of political Islam? Or was the state just binding Islamic institutions to the national rule of law? There is no way to tell, because instead of serious investment, presidents and prime ministers built a flimsy, two-dimensional religious universe that was heavy on policing and light on spirituality. This skeletal form of official Islam would prove insufficient to face the twenty-first-century challenges presented by al Qaeda, Islamic State, and the immigrant diasporas that formed a religious minority abroad. Seen in this light, governments had an opportunity to leverage the material advantages of statehood in an ongoing conversation about the place of Islam in modern societies. The challenge lay in fostering a landscape of religious institutions so that citizens had options to lead a full religious life—without having to equate piety with political opposition.

The Era of Believers without Borders

7

Catholicism in the United States

THE 50,000 BELIEVERS and handful of clergy in the original thirteen colonies carved a small Catholic niche in a world that was otherwise increasingly hostile to the Roman Church. The American revolutionaries granted the tiny minority of US Catholics religious liberties that were suspended for many of their European counterparts after the French Revolution. They could assemble freely, own property, and make appointments to Church offices without government interference.[1] With Benjamin Franklin's recommendation, John Carroll—whose brother signed the Constitution—was named the country's first bishop of Baltimore in the same year he founded Georgetown University (1789). The purchase of Louisiana and Florida from France and Spain doubled the American Catholic population.[2] The young republic did not become a major Catholic power, however, as a result of its appetite for territory. Its status as a twentieth-century Catholic powerhouse arose from the American economy's thirst for foreign labor. As rural Europe emptied out between 1820 and 1920, the United States absorbed 15 million immigrants from majority-Catholic countries—in other words, nearly one of every two immigrants arriving on American shores had Catholic origins.[3] Much as the conquest of the New World helped offset the loss of northern Europe after the Reformation, nineteenth-century mass migration extended a lifeline to the Vatican during the southern European revolt that ended clerical privilege and wiped the Papal States off the map.

The United States was a land of opportunity and danger for all sides of the conflicts that were roiling late nineteenth-century Europe. Working-class movements and agricultural populations displaced by industrialization were joined by dissidents who had been excluded from their native political systems. Each year hundreds of thousands of Catholic immigrants entered the United States during a global pitch of political violence emanating in their countries of origin (see figure 7.1). Across the Atlantic, Anarchists and socialists traded blows with European governments in a cycle of intrigue, repression, and revolt. In the United States, a First Amendment oasis where over 100

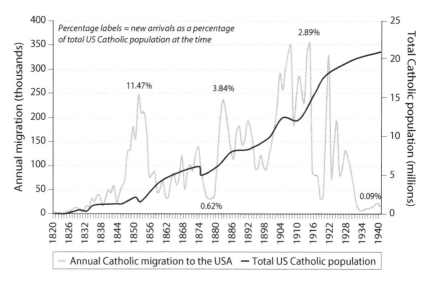

FIGURE 7.1. Annual Catholic Migration to the United States, 1820–1940

Christian sects were actively organized, believers might fall away from the Church and embrace one of the many rival faiths or ideologies.[4] The growing US community also threatened Rome's control of the global Church. Rome placed bishops on a short leash to curb excessive dispensations from Church requirements, also known as the heresy of Americanism. The country remained under the supervision of the Propaganda Fide and a single apostolic delegate long after the end of the missionary era.

For the Protestant-led American nation, the sudden emergence of a Catholic plurality was a dramatic plot twist. When Roman Catholics surpassed the booming Methodist community in 1890 and became the largest single religious group in the United States, an editorialist wrote that anyone making that prediction a century earlier "would have deserved a place in a lunatic asylum."[5] Within decades of that milestone, one in every five American citizens was Catholic by birth (20 million), and several states had an absolute Catholic majority.[6]

Why would this be considered a defeat, from the standpoint of the Church? A transatlantic population transfer granted the chance, after all, to avenge the defeat of colonial Catholic powers on US territory. The problem for the Church, however, was that the unanticipated movement of millions of believers created an infrastructural deficit of unprecedented scale in America, at a time of unmatched catastrophe in Europe. The US minority community grew at the peak of class conflict—a period when the existential Roman Question was embodied in the Social Question (1848–1948) and the Italian war on the

Papal States (1860–1929). Reeling from the consequences of nationalism and industrialization, the Church simultaneously made a frantic effort to build up its own capacity while also trying to prevent the immigrant diaspora from becoming a conduit for its enemies' agendas.[7] Without adequate tutelage, Church leaders feared that the masses were vulnerable to "gullible causes" and superstition.[8] The American city was the Catholic Church's third modern nemesis, after Lutheranism and the nation-state.

American Catholics were prominently represented in industrial-labor conflicts and union organizing, and they were overrepresented among those afflicted by social ills. They were singled out for blame in the press for the violence during the 1877 railroad strike and the 1886 Haymarket riot in Chicago. The community suffered disproportionately higher rates of mortality and incarceration. News reports of the era evoke neighborhoods awash with "neglected children and victims of the drink plague."[9] Competing national hierarchies and rival governments vied to assume moral, intellectual, and religious leadership of the Catholic masses—or at least prevent their defection to enemy camps. The cast of European fugitives influential in American civil society ranged from Johann Bapst, a Swiss Jesuit who escaped civil war and fostered Catholic life and universities in New England, to Errico Malatesta, an Italian publisher who spread violent anarchist ideology in immigrant communities in New Jersey.[10] The terrorists who answered the anarchist call either were nonbelievers or had explicitly renounced Church membership.[11] But because of the perpetrators' ethnic origin, few plots were entirely free of certain latent associations.[12] For decades, newspapers reported regularly on political violence committed by assailants with Catholic-sounding surnames (see table 7.1). The United States became a crucial node in the international anarchist conspiracy to assassinate heads of state in a campaign of public terror. The reputation of the Church suffered indirect damage by personal implication of large numbers of Catholics in such "notorious evils."[13]

The same factors that contributed to the Protestant majority's wariness catalyzed action by Church leaders, who presented themselves as the best rampart against ideological and moral ruin—that is, against anarchism, socialism, and alcoholism. After an Italian immigrant from New Jersey assassinated the king of Italy in 1900 and a second-generation Catholic of Polish origin from Chicago assassinated the president of the United States in 1901, the US government took immigrant integration and the lack of religious infrastructure more seriously. Working in tandem with US authorities, American clergy created civil society organizations and educational institutions to counteract the lure of the saloon and the gambling den.[14] The highest reaches of government embraced the role of American citizens in the Catholic hierarchy in immigrant

TABLE 7.1. International Terrorism Tied to Catholic Perpetrators, 1874–1933

Date	Location	Attack	Assailant(s) and Country of Origin
1874	Bad Kissingen, Germany	Assassination attempt on Otto von Bismarck	Eduard Kullmann (Germany)
1878	Naples, Italy	Assassination attempt on King Umberto I	Giovanni Passanante (Italy)
1893	Paris, France	Bombing at French Chamber of Deputies	August Valliant (France)
1893	Barcelona, Spain	Bombing at Liceu Theater, killing thirty	Santiago Salvador (Spain)
1894	Lyon, France	Assassination of President François Carnot of France	Sante Geronimo Caserio (Italy)
1894	Rome, Italy	Assassination attempt on Prime Minister Francesco Crispi	Paolo Lega (Italy)
1897	Mondragón, Spain	Assassination of Prime Minister Antonio Cánovas del Castillo of Spain	Michele Angiolillo (Spain)
1897	Rome, Italy	Assassination attempt on King Umberto I	Pietro Acciarito (Italy)
1898	Geneva, Switzerland	Assassination of Empress Elisabeth of Austria, wife of the Austro-Hungarian emperor	Luigi Lucheni (Italy)
1900	Paris, France	Attempted assassination of the shah of Persia	Francois Salson (France)
1900	Monza, Italy	Assassination of King Umberto I	Gaetano Bresci (Italy)
1901	Buffalo, NY, USA	Assassination of President William McKinley	Leon Czolgosz (Poland)
1902	Brussels, Belgium	Assassination attempt on King Leopold II of Belgium	Gennaro Rubino (Italy)
1905	Paris, France	Assassination attempt on King Alfonso XIII and President Émile Loubet of France	Mate Morral (Spain)
1908	Lisbon, Portugal	Assassination attempt on King Carlos I and Crown Prince Luís Filipe of Portugal	Alfredo Costa (Portugal)
1913	Madrid, Spain	Assassination attempt on King Alfonso XIII	Rafael Sanchez Alegre (Spain)
1920	New York, NY, US	Bombing on Wall Street, killing thirty and wounding two hundred	Mario Buda (Italy)
1933	Miami, Florida, US	Assassination of Mayor Anton Cermak of Chicago and assassination attempt on President Franklin D. Roosevelt	Giuseppe Zangara (Italy)

integration, overruling the Church's own governance plan and choosing its own domestic interlocutors.

The account that follows aims to resuscitate the memory of this turning point as the catalyst for the professionalization and Americanization of the US Catholic Church. The key moment came in 1908 when Rome removed the United States from the Propaganda Fide Congregation for missionary lands and US bishops gained their own national hierarchy. The evolving goals of this process are reflected in the changing patterns of clerical supply: from the wholesale importation of priests from Europe to a *collegio* system in which American priests were trained in Europe, to the method of Trent, in which a seminary in every diocese trains priests and recruits bishops *locally*. The statistics reported in this chapter's figures quantify the institutional growth spurts of churches, priests, schools, seminaries, delegates, bishops, and cardinals that followed. The slow acknowledgment of a community's permanent status abroad in 1908, along with the creation of the Vatican city-state two decades later, were two important steps for overcoming Catholics' foreignness in the United States and the native resistance it elicited. Within a generation, most US priests were US-trained, and it was then only a matter of decades until the episcopate and the College of Cardinals were integrated in reverse by influential American-born clerics in the 1950s and early 1960s. The reaction to integration failures and political violence in the diaspora, in other words, generated the feedback mechanisms that later transformed the Church in Rome.

Foreign Catholicism

Bishop John Carroll had a minimalist understanding of Rome's influence in the United States, believing that "it is only in necessary spiritual things that a foreign power has control."[15] The country's first new cathedral—the National Shrine of the Assumption in Baltimore—shared the same architect of the US Capitol Building; its design expressed comity with the environment and confidence in the nascent American republic (see figure 7.2). In contrast with the postrevolutionary era, international involvement grew throughout the nineteenth century. After the massive wave of Catholic migrants, the American missionary operations of the Propaganda Fide covered thirteen provinces and over sixty bishops. This was around one-third of its global activities, but no prefect of the Congregation ever learned English or visited the United States.[16] From the perspective of American authorities, mass migration and freedom of expression transformed the assimilation-oriented Catholic faithful from the early 1800s into an inward-looking community by the turn of the century. Rome appointed one Italian cardinal after another as the apostolic delegate—the most senior papal representative.[17] Contemporary observers remarked on

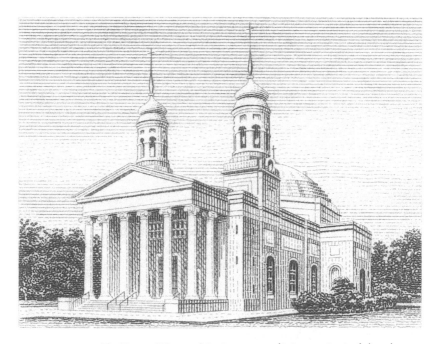

FIGURE 7.2. The National Shrine of the Assumption (Baltimore Basilica) (1806)

each delegate's "ignorance of the language, of the feelings and of the manners and customs of this country."[18]

The Vatican's efforts at asserting influence over US Catholic life from Rome were accompanied by the activities of Catholic hubs across western Europe, from Leuven in Belgium and Lyon in France to the German cities of Mainz and Regensburg. More than a dozen European missionary orders independently established US operations.[19] Laymen chartered institutions to support national emigré communities by sending mother-tongue priests and teachers to the United States, all while their representatives lobbied Rome to reward their communities abroad with collars and miters (see table 7.2).[20] A member of the German parliament named Peter Cahensly worried that, in the United States, "immigrants and their descendants who forget their language likewise forget their religion and their country."[21] Cahensly argued that "American bishops should belong to the nationality composing the majority of Catholics residing in any particular dioceses."[22] Part of his concern was no doubt rooted in Ireland's domination of the American episcopate, two-thirds of whom were of Irish descent.[23] He founded the Archangel Raphael Society for the protection of German emigrants in the United States, saying, "All we desire is to have the German, the Slav, the Italian, and the Frenchman under the care of a priest of his own nationality."[24]

TABLE 7.2. European Organizations Supporting Catholics in the United States in the Nineteenth Century

Organization Name	City
Pontificia Opera della Propagazione della Fede (1822)	Lyon
Leopoldinen Stiftung (1840)	Vienna
St. Raphaelsverein zum Schutz deutscher katholischer Auswanderer (1871)	Mainz
Priests of the Pious Order of St. Charles (1906)	Rome
Orelato della migrazione	Rome
Santa Congregazione "de propaganda fide" (1622)	Rome
Azione Cattolica	Rome
Christopher Columbus Missionary Institute (1890)	Rome
Missionary Congregation of St. Charles Borromeo (1895)	Rome
Opera Bonomelli (1900)	Cremona

Catholic associations identified foreign solutions for each of the areas most critical to religious discipline: more "national" bishops and more religious schools overseen by local priests.[25] Frequently, the approval of one or another European capital was necessary to appoint "invariably foreign national Papal Delegates, Bishops and Cardinals" and even "to approve school curriculum proposed by American school boards" as being fit for Catholic children.[26] Another Church scholar "urged all foreign groups . . . to cultivate as fully and as long as possible the language and customs of their respective homelands."[27] Some leaders preached the incompatibility of Catholic faith and American citizenship, arguing that naturalization "should be delayed until the immigrants gained more numerical strength and . . . converting all America to Catholicism might be realized."[28] More realistically, it may have reflected the expectation that there would be a significant amount of return migration to Europe from the United States, and that this would pose the threat of "Protestantism, tuberculosis, alcoholism and anarchism" traveling from American cities to the European provinces.[29]

While foreign influence was being institutionalized in US Catholic life, a newfangled ethnic pride was paraded before a startled Protestant majority. The public expressions of communal pride contrasted sharply with the early days of the republic: this was not your founding fathers' Catholicism. The Church appealed to Catholic immigrants' nostalgia with bells and music and the smell of incense to bring denominational contrasts to the fore.[30] Leaders encouraged believers to engage in visible acts of communitarian identity, such as restricting one's diet during Lent and avoiding meat on Fridays. Catholic organizations also began to defend their collective identity against Protestant domination of the public and educational spheres.[31] They raised objections to mandatory public education, criticizing "the philosophically absurd and historically false notion that the adolescent belongs first to the State and second to his parents."[32] It was reported in the early 1890s that "in many cases throughout the Union, priests have refused absolution to parents sending their children to the public schools."[33]

Archbishop John Hughes of New York, who oversaw the construction of New York's cathedral, worked with Irish Catholic newspapers to generate immigrant support for church schools and opposition to advocates of temperance and abolition.[34] Despite being the fourth archbishop of New York, Hughes's positions were less "American" than those of his predecessors at the beginning of the century. He shared the pope's view that "fast steamers have made New York one of the nearest dioceses to Rome."[35] The city had become home to the largest Church edifice in the Western Hemisphere: the 100-meter spires of St. Patrick's Cathedral were a dominant feature of Manhattan's early skyline. The new cathedrals towering over American cities contrasted mightily with the more down-to-earth Baltimore cathedral, which contemporaries likened to a "temple of reason." By comparison, St. Patrick's and St. Nicolas Kirche in New York and the Cathedrals of the Holy Cross in Philadelphia and Boston were straight out of Gothic Europe (see figure 7.3). The ambition to keep immigrant communities in the Church, in other words, formed part of a broader effort to prevent their disappearance into the American landscape.

Early accusations of clannishness among old world Catholics was nurtured by the tendency of early immigrant generations to self-segregate and avoid intermarriage. Religious tolerance of other sects or religions was doctrinally impossible. At a time when all higher authorities were directly appointed from Rome (see figure 7.4), the Baltimore Catechism restated Church doctrine that only "higher authorities," not state representatives, could grant or dissolve the sacrament of matrimony.[36] Critics perceived Catholics' rejection of majority society and their tendency to self-segregate when they availed themselves of civil society—for instance, creating professional organizations for economists, philosophers, historians, accountants, lawyers, journalists, writers, war veterans, pharmacists, and so on.[37] Like the Catholic Centennial parade held on Fifth Avenue under copious amounts of bunting and festooned with American flags in 1906, these demonstrations of participation in civil society appeared to be typically American displays of community pride and religious patriotism. But given the unreconstructed illiberal views of the Church at the time, there was room for skepticism.

Political Catholicism

The international debate over the fate of the Papal State vividly illuminated possible contradictions between US citizenship and Catholic beliefs. After failing to create a republic in 1848, the Italian founders of the Risorgimento

THE NEW ST.PATRICK'S CATHEDRAL.
Fifth Avenue. New York.
CORNER STONE LAID AUG. 15TH 1858, BY HIS GRACE JOHN, ARCHBISHOP HUGHES.
Extreme length 334 ft. Width of Nave, 96 ft. Height of Nave, 108 ft. Height of Spires, 334 feet.

FIGURE 7.3 [TRIPTYCH OF 7.3.1, 7.3.2, AND 7.3.3]. St. Patrick's Cathedral (New York City),
St. Nicolas Kirche (New York City), and Cathedral of the Holy Cross (Boston)

FIGURE 7.3 (*continued*)

changed tack and pursued unification as the Kingdom of Italy, successfully annexing the Papal States but temporarily placing its political capital in Florence (1861). Italian nationalists stopped short of invading Rome and delayed moving their political institutions from Florence to the Eternal City. For years, Catholics worldwide lived with the threat that the new Italian government would sack the Vatican and declare Rome their capital. Indignant at Garibaldi and the Red Shirts and the violation of papal authority and sovereignty, the Vatican called for holy war. An international volunteer force rose up during the 1860s to defend Rome: the papal Zouaves.

FIGURE 7.3 (*continued*)

Their military contribution took place mostly at the margins, but they added vitality to a grim moment for the Church. For the first time, that energy came from the Catholic immigrant diaspora in North America. A former brigadier general in the Union Army served as the informal recruitment officer for the war effort in the United States.[38] He placed announcements for how to enlist or make donations and lobbied bishops to help the effort.[39] A Catholic periodical

FIGURE 7.4. Illustration from *Saint Joseph Baltimore Catechism: The Truths of Our Catholic Faith Clearly Explained and Illustrated: With Bible Readings, Study Helps, and Mass Prayers* (Baltimore, MD: Catholic Book Publishing, 1964).

reported receiving "a great many letters" from veteran officers and soldiers from both sides of the Civil War who volunteered for service in the pope's army. An American businessman visiting Rome donated millions to the pontifical treasury.[40] Contingents of American fighters departed from the port of New York with the blessing of local leaders. One ship chartered by an organization called American Aid to the Pope carried several hundred foreign fighters to join the army of His Holiness. The archbishop of New York City—the future Cardinal John McCloskey—held a special mass in St. Peter's Church in February 1868 to bless a group of 130 soldiers on their way to Rome. "I call you Soldiers of the Cross," McCloskey told them, "taking your departure from our American shores ... to go forth animated ... with chivalrous sentiments of Catholic faith and piety, to offer [your] lives for the sake of our common Holy Father."[41]

It is not known exactly how many American Zouaves sought adventure or martyrdom in Italy, but the US consul in Rome received enough requests for information "concerning the possibility of forming companies in the United States for the purpose of entering the Papal army" that he cabled the State Department for advice.[42] The assistant secretary of state replied "that by act of Congress the enlistment of citizens for services in foreign countries was forbidden."[43] The foreign fighter phenomenon led to the first coordinated moni-

FIGURE 7.5. A contingent of North American papal Zouaves, New York (1868)

toring of national borders for citizens seeking to travel abroad to fight, leading
to prohibitions and travel restrictions. Foreign fighters returning to the United
States were not prosecuted, but thousands of Dutch Catholics were denaturalized by the Netherlands in 1870. The total foreign fighting force of around
18,000 provided the edge defending Rome from invasion at the crucial battle
of Mentana in 1867.[44] They also guarded the pope and the curia while they
convened the largest gathering in Church history, the First Vatican Council,
which adjusted Church policies for the nation-state era (see figure 7.5).

The willingness to martyr oneself for a foreign prince was the most extreme
expression of Catholics' deviation from the American political mean. While the
Roman Question was open and the pontiff fought for survival, Catholics' views
of democracy, authoritarianism, and religious violence tended to differ from
those of the rest of US society.[45] American Catholic leaders toed the Church line
without fail, even after Pope Pius IX (1792–1878) excoriated liberalism and
democratic institutions.[46] The historian John McGreevy writes that American
Catholicism of the era officially repudiated "modern civilization, freedom of the
press, individual rights, freedom of religion," and was officially intolerant toward
Protestants, Jews, and liberals.[47] Rome also demanded belief in the antiscientific
notion of immaculate conception (1854) and in the antiliberal *Syllabus of Errors*
(1864). Bishops of the period worried that the US-born faithful would embrace
democracy and the separation of church and state.

After the Italian defeat of Rome, Pius IX continued to call for war against
the heretics and for his own restoration to temporal power. Thousands of US

Catholics who judged temporal power as necessary to preserve the Vatican's spiritual independence protested in the streets against the holidays and symbols of liberal Italy—the latest breed of pagan to vandalize the Eternal City.[48] The *North American Review* editorialized that the pope "could not be the creature, the slave, or the subject of any one empire, kingdom or republic, but an independent sovereign, free, in his own house."[49] Italian-American churches did not permit memorial services to be held upon the death of Vittorio Emanuele II, the Italian king who conquered Rome. They and their Irish counterparts also declined to hold memorial services for his two royal successors, Umberto I (1844–1900) and Vittorio Emanuele III (1869–1947).

As for the representative of the Propaganda Fide, Cardinal Francesco di Paola Satolli (1839–1910) argued that removal from temporal rule was the prelude to removal from spiritual authority: after "the Papal States are blotted from the map of Italy," he said, "Catholicism itself will be uprooted from the soil."[50] The first act of the Catholic Congress of the United States "protested to the world that the Pope is not free in his own episcopal city." The group called for the US government to take a firm stand "against the wrong inflicted on Catholicity." The first archbishop of Minnesota argued for the "civil princedom of the Pope."[51] A prominent Irish-born monseigneur in New York wrote: "The mighty question forces itself on the attention of the Old World and the New. All nations who possess a considerable minority of Catholics, cannot help being interested in a subject which so deeply moves the Catholic conscience."[52] The United States never altered its diplomatic relations with the Italian kingdom, however, on account of Catholics' feelings. The State Department recognized Italian sovereignty over the whole peninsula and commended its government's liberalizing agenda.[53]

Meanwhile, Catholics were publicly lambasted as antimodern, antidemocratic, uncivilized, alien, hostile, and unassimilable.[54] The nativist know-nothing movement took the Church hierarchy at its word: Roman Catholicism was foreign, hostile to American values and an obstacle to immigrants' assimilation. The movement conflated religious extremism, criminality, and integration problems: it fused theological and populist anti-immigrant and anticlerical sentiment.[55] The well-known promoter of the telegraph, Samuel F. B. Morse, accused European governments of "subsidizing religious missions and the immigration of Catholics" for the "subjugation of the United States."[56] By midcentury, the Know-Nothing Party claimed the loyalty of eight governors, 100 congressmen, the mayors of Boston, Philadelphia, and Chicago, and thousands of local officials.[57] The Know-Nothing presidential candidate received 22 percent of the popular vote in 1856.

Public debate was rife with stereotypes: resentment grew over the cost of supporting Irish-born paupers and other foreigners in the almshouses and prisons.

The New York State Assembly voted to restrict corporate ownership of Church property on the grounds that Catholic priests were "generally foreigners, educated in the most absolute doctrines of Papal supremacy."[58] Enemies of the Church imagined "the supreme influence of the Catholic priests over the mob, ripe for riot or excess of any kind."[59] In reality, clerics were more likely to find themselves on the receiving end of mob violence. Johann Bapst was tarred and feathered in Maine, and the papal nuncio evaluating midcentury Catholic communities in the United States was forced to flee a violent mob of anticlerical liberals in New York. Caricaturists published vignettes deeply skeptical of Catholics' integration into American politics. One caption read, "Religious freedom is guaranteed, but can we allow foreign reptiles to crawl all over U.S.?," and showed a Roman Catholic alligator devouring the dome of the US Capitol Building.[60] A general consensus grew, James Anthony Froude wrote in 1879, that "if America does not conquer Romanism, Romanism will certainly conquer her."[61]

Disputes over the pope's temporal powers and the appropriate role of European organizations in American Catholic life negatively impacted the Church's relationship with US Protestants. Supporting Rome required overlooking its antidemocratic attitudes and behavior. In the 1890s, for example, Pope Leo XIII condemned the separation of church and state and the notion of adapting Church doctrine to modern society—in other words, the heresy of "Americanism."[62] A magazine cover caricatured the pope climbing through a ballot box to tear down the constitutional amendment against religious establishment with provocative statements posted behind him—for example, "All Catholics must make themselves felt in daily political life," and "Penetrate wherever possible in the administration of civil affairs" (see figure 7.6). The largely anticlerical Protestant majority in the United States was joined by liberal Italian politicians who targeted immigrant public opinion, rebutting the Church's arguments in speaking tours and publications in US Catholic periodicals. In 1901, an Italian member of parliament, Roberto De Cesare, accused American bishops of parroting "the doctrine of the most violent Intransigents" by affirming that temporal power was necessary to the spiritual power of the pope.[63] American Catholics' moral support of Rome continued to put them at odds with their Protestant neighbors over other issues, such as US neutrality during World War I and the rise of fascism.[64] Neutrality in the war was also supported by some active emigrant aid associations.[65]

Political Violence

The most significant clashes involving immigrant communities of Catholic origin had nothing to with religious ideology, Catholic practices, or Roman sympathies. The same American liberties that protected religious activity also

AT IT AGAIN!
Through the Ballot-box to the Constitution.

FIGURE 7.6. "At it again! Through the Ballot-box to the Constitution" (*Puck*, 1885)

FIGURE 7.7. Dynamite attack in the French Chamber of Deputies, Paris (1893)

harbored anarchist and socialist movements. Thanks to mass migration, the United States became home to around 10 percent of the world's 300,000 anarchists, but authorities turned a blind eye to incitement to class revolution in speeches, periodicals, and books. In the context of violent attacks on European parliaments, theaters, and public gatherings, European governments and the Vatican alike were exasperated by American toleration of anarchist enclaves. In 1890s Europe, anarchists were being incarcerated en masse and attacked by police, sometimes indiscriminately, and set before firing squads, garroted, and guillotined. The United States was a safe haven far from the prying eyes of the political police and acts of repression in France, Italy, and Spain.

Le Petit Journal

TOUS LES JOURS
Le Petit Journal
5 Centimes

SUPPLÉMENT ILLUSTRÉ
Huit pages : CINQ centimes

TOUS LES VENDREDIS
Le Supplément illustré
5 Centimes

Quatrième Année   SAMEDI 25 NOVEMBRE 1893   Numéro 157

LA DYNAMITE EN ESPAGNE
Explosion d'une bombe au théâtre du Liceo à Barcelone

FIGURE 7.8. Bombing of the Liceu Theater, Barcelona (1893)

Combined with technological advances like the telegram and the steamship, immigrant-driven radicalism produced major international incidents. Another critical development was the miniaturization of firearms and explosives, which revolutionized terrorism and marked the democratization of mass murder. The first innovation was the American-made, five- to seven-shot pistol that allowed for accurate rapid-fire shooting. The other was a Swedish industrialist's invention of dynamite, whose explosive punch, capable of killing dozens, could be packed into a suitcase small enough to fit under a seat.[66] Both weapons gave attackers the element of surprise. Sticks of dynamite allowed "a very small number of unscrupulous fanatics to terrorize the entire human race," as one journalist observed, and handguns heralded an era of successful assassination attempts.[67] The three US-linked anarchist assassins used a US-manufactured five-shot Smith and Wesson and fatally struck their victims with multiple bullets, more than terrorists of any other national background.

The Italian communities on the East Coast followed the political repression of workers' movements in Italy with rapt attention. Paterson, New Jersey, was known as Silk City because of its booming textile industry, and it was packed with political refugees who fled Italy and joined the wave of labor migrants with textile-related skills in the 1880s. Paterson's workers came from an area of Italy that had experienced significant worker unrest, and the same was true for the anarchist communities of Barre, Pennsylvania, and Tampa, Florida.[68] Around 15,000 of Paterson's inhabitants were of Italian origin at the turn of the century (15 percent), and it was estimated that one-quarter of them held anarchist sympathies. There was a booming Italian-language anarchist press: nearly half of all Italian households in the city subscribed to an anarchist weekly.[69] They brought anticlerical attitudes and habitually low church attendance with them from northern Italy, held anarchist meetings in competition with Sunday Mass, and refused last rites; one prominent citizen registered his son's name as Lucifer.[70] For the first two generations, Paterson's Catholics were served by a single church.[71]

They also thought of themselves as Italian activists, not as participants in American politics.[72] Unlike in Europe, the movement operated openly and freely in the United States. Paterson and West Hoboken were hotbeds of violent Italian anarchism in New Jersey. They set up their foreign-language newspaper and book publications, formed associations, held meetings, issued statements, and hung out regularly at bars. Anarchists hosted speakers and held debates in saloons like Tivola and Zucca's and Tua's, and they convened large meetings, sometimes with over 1,000 attendees, where they openly "plotted to kill the crowned heads of Europe."[73] They were actively exporting the same extremist ideology to old world politics, providing, for example, nearly half of all donations to a publication called *Volontà* in Ancona, Italy.[74] Italian diplomats started filing reports in 1885 on the "proliferation of anarchist associations" in New York, Philadelphia, Chicago, Boston, San Francisco, and Paterson. Cables were sent to the Italian Foreign Ministry in Rome whenever leading anarchist intellectuals visited the emigrant communities.[75] As one scholar has noted, "Paterson made good society shiver and was a point of reference for terrorism investigators worldwide."[76] Italian intelligence agents helped foil a transatlantic assassination plot against King Umberto in 1888, and on another occasion, in 1892, they stopped anarchist instigators from traveling back to Italy to foment worker uprisings.

In 1897, however, the Italian anarchist Michele Angiolillo—who had also spent time in Paterson—evaded their defenses and traveled to Madrid, where he assassinated the Spanish prime minister with an American-bought repeating handgun.[77] The anarchists who sought refuge in New Jersey commented to US reporters, "We were driven out of Italy by the oppressions that were heaped upon us. The laws of Italy are a mere sham. . . . Here we have been treated fairly."[78] A future assassin wrote home upon arriving in the United States: "Here we are free to express our opinions. The police respects us, we can write what we want in our newspapers and citizens of every social class have the same political rights."[79] The publications that were shut down in Italy reopened their presses in New Jersey, "for distribution in the US and to be sent clandestinely to Italy."[80] As Turcato puts it, they "consciously [gave] voice to Italian anarchism whenever that voice was choked in the homeland."[81] The weekly newspaper *La Questione Sociale* (1894–1908) had good circulation in Italian communities, growing from 3,000 to 4,000 around the time of Errico Malatesta's editorship (see figure 7.9).[82] Malatesta appreciated the relative freedoms of the United States in comparison to Europe. "We must profit from the circumstances," he advised, "to create a force that can come to the aid of our cause."[83]

Anarchists responded in print to a raft of illiberal legislation in Rome, including laws that dissolved workers' associations and suspended freedom of the press and freedom of assembly. The Italian government suspended the voting rights of nearly 1 million voters "suspected of harboring progressive ideas" and sent hundreds of political prisoners to island prisons without due process.[84] The indignation of activists frequently boiled over into violent confrontations: at least 300 died between 1891 and 1894 during the repression of the Fasci Siciliani.

A post-amnesty wave of political refugees from Italy into the US in the late 1890s included Gaetano Bresci, a silk worker who had spent two years on the island prison of Lampedusa and was classified as a dangerous anarchist by the Italian government. He was released in 1896 and left for the United States for a job in a silk mill. He married a non-Italian, native-born American woman,

FIGURE 7.9. Editorial offices of *La Questione Sociale* in Paterson, New Jersey (1900)

had a child, and was considered well integrated into US society. Bresci har-bored resentment, however, for his political exile.[85] He joined the anarchist community in Paterson and became a regular of the association behind *La Questione Sociale*. Bresci was among the many outraged by the Italian govern-ment's militarization of the confrontation with working-class protesters. Bread-tax protesters in the streets of Milan were attacked by the Italian army; the royal government broke down barricades in May 1898 with cannons and mortar rounds, killing hundreds (estimates range from 300 to 800).[86] The prominent Lithuanian-Jewish anarchist Emma Goldman wrote an essay my-thologizing the moment in which Bresci first learned of the events in Milan:

"The wives of the peasants had gone to the palace of the King, held up in mute silence their emaciated infants. And then the soldiers fired and killed those poor fools. Bresci's mental eye beheld the defenseless women and innocent infants of his native land, slaughtered right before the good king."[87]

Bresci may have been personally radicalized into action by one of the key personalities in Italian anarchism who visited the United States: Errico Malatesta. Malatesta was invited to Paterson, New Jersey, to serve as editor of *La Questione Sociale* after escaping from an island prison near Sicily in early 1899. He spoke with Italian-American groups and oversaw publication of activist literature alongside the periodical. On a small stage adorned with black-and-red flags at Tivola and Zucca's Saloon in West Hoboken in November 1899, Malatesta publicly debated anarchist strategy with Giuseppe Ciancabilla, who had recently created a rival newspaper supporting a more individualist approach. Ciancabilla drew a revolver and shot and wounded Malatesta in the course of their otherwise intellectual confrontation, as though to prove his point.[88] The audience was mostly of Piedmontese and Tuscan origin—the regions where the unified Kingdom of Italy located its first two capital cities before capturing Rome—and also included Germans, Poles, and Spaniards.

The following year, King Umberto decorated the general who had overseen the "pacification" of Milan and named him a senator. Incensed, Bresci purchased a five-shot handgun at a Paterson shop in February 1900 for $7 and several months later bought a one-way ticket to Le Havre. In July 1900, he fired four rounds at King Umberto I in Monza, near Milan, the culmination of "two decades of political activity by a group of anarchist textile workers" in New Jersey.[89] In response to the crowd's cries that "You killed Umberto!" he shouted back: "I didn't kill Umberto, I killed a King" (see figure 7.10).[90] *La Questione Sociale*'s offices in Paterson may have served as headquarters of the group behind the plot to kill Umberto.[91] Malatesta was fingered in the New York press as the mastermind, but authorities treated the crime as an individual act and not as a conspiracy.[92]

After Umberto's assassination, some small changes were made in New Jersey: authorities confiscated the black-and-red flags at anarchist saloon hangouts.[93] The anarchist press glorified the assassin in editorials, commissioned sculpted busts of his likeness, and composed protest songs in his honor. *La Questione Sociale* printed 15,000 copies of a special issue honoring Bresci.[94] The head of the benevolent association of which Bresci was a member told a journalist that "most of Paterson's Italians are Anarchists . . . if there will be an end to kings in Italy, it is a good thing."[95] At a meeting of nearly 1,000 anarchists, held in order "to show that the Italians in Paterson had no connection with the plot," one Italian-language speaker after another nonetheless expressed "satisfaction" with the king's death: "we made no plot, but our motto is death to all

FIGURE 7.10. Gaetano Bresci assassinates King Umberto in
Monza, Italy (1900)

Kings."[96] The United States served as a base for counterrevolutionary activities, unwittingly hosting and exporting anarchist propaganda and terror.

The *New York Times* wrote in 1900 that "if Bresci had been a native born
American, he never would have done what he did."[97] But one year later, President William McKinley was assassinated by a second-generation Polish-
American anarchist.[98] Leon Czolgosz was a twenty-six-year-old natural-born
citizen who was baptized and brought up in the Roman Catholic faith in Detroit, where he "attended parochial school and was devoted to his church" and
worked as both an apprentice blacksmith and in a rolling mill job. He formally
renounced his Catholic faith roughly a decade before he killed the president.[99]
Inspired by the Paterson cell, Czolgosz subscribed to anarchist and socialist
periodicals and joined an anarchist club that met above the saloon owned by
his parents.[100] *Harper's Weekly* reported in 1901 that he was "mesmerized by
the assassination of King Humbert I of Italy, obsessively rereading accounts
he had clipped from the newspaper."[101] Resolved to commit a copycat act,

FIGURE 7.11. Leon Czolgosz assassinates President William McKinley in
Buffalo, New York (1901)

Czolgosz boarded a train to Buffalo, where President McKinley was visiting.
He waited for the right moment at a public event before approaching the head
of state with his revolver wrapped in a white napkin (see figure 7.11).

Catholic groups active in civil society took care to distance themselves from
the violent acts. St. Patrick's Cathedral in New York announced a special prayer
to be read in all churches of the diocese for the speedy recovery of President
McKinley in the days before he died.[102] In the days afterwards, conservative
Italian Catholics condemned the attack by a man who had forsaken the
Church. The United Italian Societies met at Tammany Hall "to express a sentiment of unanimous sorrow." Csolgosz was "vigorously denounced by the Italian
residents of Jersey City and Hoboken," who held memorial services for the

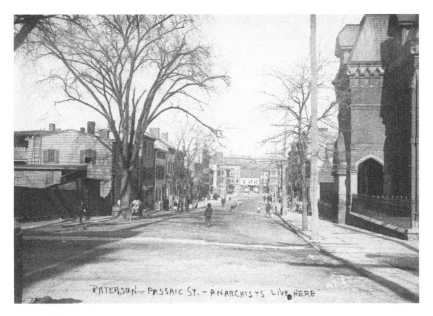

FIGURE 7.12. Paterson, New Jersey: "Anarchists Live Here" (1900)

president. At meetings of the Catholic Union in Chicago and Philadelphia, priests and lay leaders gathered to "deplore the shooting of President McKinley," and statements were issued rejecting any connection of the act with the Polish people of the United States.[103] The *Chicago Tribune* wrote that "Czolgosz, the assassin, does not find any of our foreign contingents in this country ready to admit that he is one of their number."[104]

Restricting Borders and Alcohol

It was difficult to avoid the connection between this new lawlessness— including the gravest political crime imaginable—and the arrival of millions of Catholics, whose numbers had doubled from 5 to 10 million in the preceding twenty-five years.[105] The sudden visibility of immigrant-origin communities coincided with a wave of anarchist attacks in majority-Catholic Italy, Spain, France, and Poland. A diffuse perception of threatening young men of Catholic origin spread in the streets of New York, Philadelphia, and Boston.[106] This atmosphere was captured in popular cultural works like the best-selling *Revolt of the New Immigrant*.[107] A 1901 editorial in the *New York Times* observed that "the most Catholic countries in Europe, Italy and Spain, namely, are those in which anarchism is most rife and has taken on its most ferocious and inhuman forms"—and that "the Protestant countries are those that are freest from the disease." Would it be wise "to conclude from this," the newspaper asked, "that Catholicism is a breeder of anarchist assassination?"[108] Foreign diplomats worried in outgoing cables "that the criminals and assassins who recently acquired a sad fame all belonged to 'a certain nationality.'"[109] A newspaper article noted that "dynamite is obtainable by any Italian laborer employed in building work. How can we find such men before it is too late?"[110]

In the wake of President McKinley's death, restrictive practices were put in place to stem the flow of ideologically radicalized migrants.[111] Whenever possible, authorities intercepted anarchists at the border and deported them to their point of departure.[112] Congress added more restrictive laws after anarchists assassinated King Umberto and President McKinley, but authorities acknowledged "the difficulty in spotting" them "if they don't declare it."[113] An international treaty signed in 1902 placed the burden on the Italian government to prevent anarchists' international travel.[114] Ultimately, anarchist organizations preyed upon "the influx of cheap labor" from Germany, Italy, and Poland, which also represented the three largest nationalities among the 360,000 immigrants entering the United States annually.[115] The Restriction Acts of 1921 and 1924 singled out Polish and Italian nationals for dramatic quota reductions.

The temperance movement marked another call for majority society to reclaim public spaces and urban spaces that had been invaded by new immigrants. The campaign to ban alcohol frequently mixed with anti-Catholic rhetoric at election time.[116] It targeted working-class drinking habits and was couched as an effort to protect vulnerable women and children from violence and poverty. Advocates claimed that 80 percent of social degeneracy was "the direct result of intemperance."[117] The historian Lisa McGirr describes the "total suppression of distillery, saloon, brewery and bar" as "an attempt to secure Protestant value orientations in the nation." The Anti-Saloon League (1895) included the Methodist, Baptist, Presbyterian, and Congregational Churches, but not the Catholic Church (which preached voluntary abstinence and temperance), although Cardinal James Gibbons supported the constitutional ban.[118] The political connection between saloons and Catholic-origin immigrants was reinforced by revelations of the role played by anarchist bars in Paterson and Hoboken, where Gaetano Bresci cultivated his extremist views and Errico Malatesta held forth in debates held under black-and-red flags. The family of Leon Czolgosz owned the bar in which the plot to assassinate a head of state was hatched. These dens of iniquity—the unregulated spaces of the immigrant neighborhoods of New York, Hoboken, and Chicago—constitute the link between restrictions on alcohol and the war on terror and criminality among Catholic-origin migrants.

Presidential Intervention

The United States had inadvertently become an exporter of global terror and a hub for extremist propaganda. Policy solutions were not limited to better policing of the borders and more orderly cities. Upon taking office following McKinley's death, President Theodore Roosevelt used his first major address to deny any social or economic aspect to what he described as a *political* assassination. Roosevelt refused to see any omen of class warfare.[119] He declared that the assassin was "a malefactor and nothing else. He is in no sense, in no shape or way, a 'product of social conditions.'"[120] However, the violent anarchist scourge compelled authorities to become more aware of the ideologies and individuals circulating in American cities.

US authorities had made the hypothetical link between political radicalization of young Catholic men and the absence of any religious guidance or education. Church educators and the benefactors of American Catholic life agreed that public schools had failed to produce "God-fearing men who are a safe member of society."[121] The *New York Times* asked in an editorial if it might not be the "lack of proper religious instruction and obedience to the rules of the Church which explain the criminal?"[122] Perhaps, one editorialist mused, Catholic youth in America needed to be taught their culture and religion of origin as a vaccination against ideological extremism. An Italian religious scholar wrote that only "the voice of the bishops" could "illuminate those who might be seduced by the socialistic utopias."[123] As the German politician Peter Cahensly put it, either the immigrant "remains true to the faith" or he "becomes the pupil of Anarchists and Socialists."[124]

Apart from conducting a repressive crackdown against the anarchist scene, President Roosevelt recognized an ally in the Catholic Church. While it had been no great friend of American democracy, the Church was locked in an existential war with the same enemy forces. Pope Leo XIII viewed socialism as a gateway to godlessness. In his very first encyclical, he inveighed against socialism's errors and affirmed that "the only real way to prevent the effects of growing anarchism is religion."[125] Too many American Catholics had succumbed to political extremism or suffered social ills that Church participation might have assuaged. Roosevelt is credited for reducing tensions with the minority community. He requested Cardinal Gibbons's advice on military chaplaincies and the filling of Catholic posts in the US-occupied Philippines.[126] One of Roosevelt's first acts was to dispatch a delegation led by Governor William Taft to personally congratulate the pope upon his jubilee celebration and address US intentions to protect Catholic religious life in the new territories recently acquired in the Spanish-American War.[127]

The European churches at first played a critical role in filling the gaps and providing an infusion of institutions and personnel. Over time, it became increasingly awkward for ecclesiastical matters to be "uncontrolled by Americans or in America," in the words of Rome's critics, "and instead managed in a foreign country, by a foreign power, for political purposes."[128] That criticism accelerated the professionalization of the US clergy. Authorities pursued a long-term goal as well, granting accreditation to Catholic educational institutions. One of the assassination's main consequences was therefore not just the importation of more priests but the development of religious schools and seminaries on American soil.

The most visible change in US policy, however, was signaled by the president's courting of Cardinal James Gibbons. In so doing, the US government valorized and promoted the American branch of the Roman Catholic Church but rejected its oversight by the Propaganda Fide in Rome. By making Cardinal Gibbons into a nationally prominent figure, the government snubbed the apostolic delegate—the Italian cardinal who had been the resident papal envoy to the United States since the early 1890s. Gibbons, by contrast, was the first US-born member of the College of Cardinals and was instrumental in "Americanizing" the Church while serving as archbishop of Baltimore. He began to appear alongside President Roosevelt at major speeches on behalf of temperance, and another time he joined the president's carriage to attend an address to working-class miners (see figure 7.13). Later that decade, Gibbons hosted then-US president Taft at the inauguration of the Catholic Summer School of America in 1909.[129] By embracing the American cardinal over the Italian one, two US presidents endorsed the Americanist school that Gibbons represented.

Rome Was Not Built in a Day

In the short term, the first item on the agenda was to import priests from abroad, a step that the US government supported by facilitating clerical visas. The dramatic increase of clerical visas granted by the US Department of State to Catholic priests from European countries accelerated in the aftermath of the two assassinations. The number of priests granted entry rose from around 200 annually in 1899, 1900, and 1901 to 1,400 in 1906 before leveling off at around 800 per annum (see figure 7.14). This could appear counterintuitive. If Italian immigrants were committing a wave of terrorist attacks worldwide, why would the American government send for more Italian priests?

American officials began to appreciate the role of the cultural and religious institutions that supported immigrant-origin Catholic communities.

FIGURE 7.13. President Theodore Roosevelt and Cardinal James Gibbons in
a friendly exchange (date unknown)

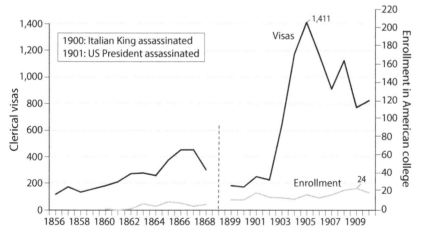

FIGURE 7.14. Clerical Visas to the United States and Enrollment in
the North American College in Rome, 1856–1910

TABLE 7.3. Milestones in US Catholic Church History, 1784–1893

Year	Milestone
1784	John Carroll appointed prefect-apostolic of the Church in the New Republic
1789	Carroll appointed first US bishop; Carroll establishes Georgetown University
1791–1822	St. Mary's Seminary, the first Rome-approved seminary, established
1793–1820	Dioceses created in Louisiana, Baltimore (first US archbishop), New York City, Boston, Philadelphia, Bardstown, Woodstock, Florida, Richmond, and Charleston
1806–1822	Construction of the National Shrine of the Assumption (Baltimore Basilica)
1838–1850	Dioceses created in Texas, the Californias, Savannah, and New Mexico
1875	First US cardinal, John McCloskey
1878	Catholic University of America, the first official Roman Catholic university in the United States, established in Washington, DC
1893	Cardinal Francesco di Paola Satolli named apostolic delegate
1908	US is removed from the Sacred Congregation of the Propaganda Fide; establishment of national US Roman Catholic hierarchy

The new emphasis on the Catholic Church in the aftermath of the McKinley assassination and the subsequent political crackdown confirmed the overlap of religious values and anti-anarchism. US churches were starting from a point of deeply inadequate personnel because parishes had expanded faster than priests could arrive or be trained to lead them (see table 7.3). The same was true for the educational realm: Catholic populations were growing faster than religious schools could be established to educate them. It also applied to the realm of church hierarchy—bishops and cardinals—who had yet to catch up with representatives in the episcopate, the curia, and the College of Cardinals compared to Catholic populations of similar size.

Two popes were particularly influential in reconciling the new reality of permanent migration with the imperative to standardize and centralize. Pope Pius IX (1846–1878) demonstrated a steady preoccupation with building religious infrastructure, education, and hierarchy for diaspora Catholics. The number of dioceses expanded throughout the nineteenth century: Pius IX oversaw the establishment of 29 new archbishoprics, 132 episcopal sees, and thousands of schools worldwide. By the end of his papacy, the spiritual lives of 10 million Catholics living in the United States were attended to by 14 archbishops and 63 bishops—second only to Italy—plus 5,750 priests, 5,589 churches, 500 convents, 700 colleges, seminaries, and academies, and nearly 2,000 parish schools (see figure 7.15).[130]

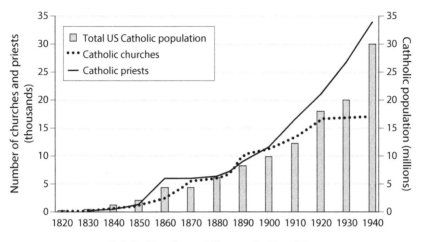

FIGURE 7.15. Catholic Churches and Clergy in the United States, 1820–1940

The Fifty-Year Wait: Clergy and Prayer Space

It was immediately clear that religious authorities would need to cater to specific nationalities. Before the end of the nineteenth century, New York had the third-largest German population after Hamburg and Berlin. Catholic institutional options included "the full panoply: orphanages, asylums, homes for destitute children, nursing homes, and three hospitals." New York's Archbishop Michael Corrigan calculated that between 1890 and 1900 he had opened new buildings—schools, churches, and seminaries—at the rate of one every two weeks, for a total of more than 250 major buildings in all. The late-nineteenth-century archbishop of Chicago, Patrick Feehan, holds the parish-opening record, with 140 edifices constructed during his tenure.[131] Nonetheless, a persistent infrastructural deficit remained. There were only 250 Italian-speaking churches in the United States in 1918. In Italy, there were 55,263 churches: one for every 500 Italians. In the United States, there was one for every 50,000 Italians.[132] The Catholic Extension Society was founded in 1905: within two decades, it had built new churches in over 2,000 hard-to-reach areas of the country, especially in the West. The society sponsored the Chapel Car of St. Anthony, which carried a priest around the Midwest on rail and by motorcar; it unfolded to become a platform with a pulpit and an altar.[133]

Imported Priests

The immensity of the US territories always posed a geographic challenge: how to cover vast dioceses with a small troupe of clergy. A missionary report from the Propaganda Fide described a difficult situation in 1841: the bishop of

Bardstown, New York, arrived without money or housing in a diocese several times the size of France. In Mobile, Alabama, the bishop lacked ornaments and breviaries; students in Cincinnati could not write relatives in Europe because they had no money for postage.[134] Adding western territories to the country's vast expanses and "scattered districts" began to stretch Church resources so thin that it became a "struggle to supply priests and churches." Later, the "benevolent assimilation" of Puerto Rico and the Philippines under US jurisdiction would make the problem more acute.[135]

Rome and Church city-hubs in Europe responded: in one fifty-year period (1840–1890), fewer than 500 priests in service became a force of 9,000 priests (see figure 7.16). A new "transnational clerical economy" emerged to save the day: male religious orders and congregations (for example, Benedictines, Vincentians, Franciscans) provided trained priests for the immigrant Church. National hierarchies in the countries of origin competed to send their own men, exporting thousands of priests into immigrant communities.[136] In Baltimore, the first hub of American Catholicism, the community rose from 25,000 to 350,000. In that same time span, Jesuits and other orders reinforced and replenished the city's 25 priests to form a clerical corps of 160 who manned 150 churches under the authority of seven bishops (in 1832).[137] In one five-year period in New York (1837–1842), 38 churches and 40 priests nearly tripled to 120 churches and 102 priests.[138] Between 1820 and 1850, the number of Catholic churches nationwide increased from 124 to 1,124; this figure doubled in the next decade and rose to 12,000 by the turn of the century. The ratio of the faithful to available prayer spaces improved markedly, going from seven churches for every 10,000 Catholics in 1850 to twelve in 1890.

At first, American Catholics received pastoral care from an almost entirely foreign clerical corps. Only 150 of 1,141 priests in 1850 were native-born Americans.[139] The United States continued to import an average of 250 priests annually between 1856 and 1868. In 1869, nearly half of the country's 3,505 priests were German-speaking. Irish priests were prevalent in some states, like Minnesota and New York, where two-thirds of priests were from Ireland. The importance of linguistic and cultural barriers was apparent when Italians were served by Irish or German churches; some German and Irish priests learned Italian to minister to the latest arrivals in the early twentieth century.[140] The surplus of Irish clergy allowed Ireland to export large numbers of priests to staff the burgeoning dioceses. There was significant "need of American priests for the Italian missions."[141] Compared to Italy proper, where there was one priest for every 370 Italians, the US parish average was one for every 1,500 Catholics. In New York, each Italian priest was theoretically responsible for the spiritual life of 12,000 Italian Catholics.[142]

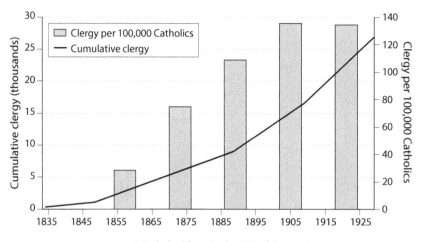

FIGURE 7.16. Catholic Clergy in the United States, 1835–1925

The number of clerical visas issued annually spiked to 1,000—with a high of 1,400 granted in a single year (1905). The ratio of clergy to the faithful improved for a century, going from one priest for every 2,000 US Catholics in 1850 to one for every 870 Catholics in 1900, to 750 in 1930 and 630 in 1940.[143] In 1920, Catholics made up 24 percent of the population in the eastern United States, but out west, home to one-fifth of American Catholics, they were a small minority of only 7.5 percent of the local population.[144] In all cases their pastoral care took place thanks to imports, not the American training of priests—a dependency that would not relent until the mid-twentieth century. In 1916, one-fifth of parishes used exclusively non-English languages (German, Italian, Polish, French) in confession, alongside the Latin Mass, and 28 percent of parishes used both a foreign language and the English language.[145] During the postwar period, there was a 21 percent increase in the Catholic population but only a 10 percent increase in the number of priests.[146] (In 1960, the priest-to-Catholics ratio declined for the first time in nearly a century, to one for every 770.[147])

The 100-Year Wait: Schools and Seminaries

The birth of new generations spurred the growth of enduring institutions, not only to proselytize to the majority society, as the Propaganda Fide Congregation was formally chartered to do, but also to socialize native-born Catholic children. The Church, governments, and revolutionary movements all agreed that many young men were ripe for recruitment by extremists (and religious conversion). The Irish bishops were open to working with public school systems, whereas the Germans leaders worried that their flock would lose the

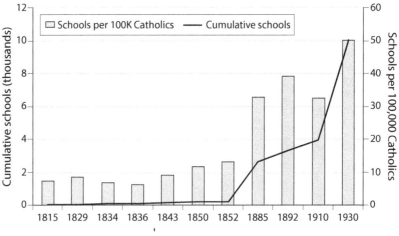

FIGURE 7.17. Catholic Schools in the United States, 1815–1930

faith along with the language. The bishops who assembled at the first Balti-more synod recommended establishing schools in connection with churches, but this was an unfunded mandate.[148] Tuition costs were prohibitive, leaving tens of thousands of young Germans and Italians with only a public school education and no religious formation whatsoever.[149] Bishops accepted public taxpayer support for Catholic schools, even after public school systems began developing in the 1830s and 1840s. In one arrangement in Minnesota, the arch-bishop sold a parochial schoolhouse in financial difficulties to the board of education for a symbolic sum if they agreed to keep and pay the same teach-ers.[150] They reached an agreement to hold no religious services and teach no religion and to remove all crucifixes and "emblems of Catholicity." A catechism class was taught after hours as a voluntary, separate offering. The Church ob-jected and declared the arrangement to be in "direct violation of the last coun-cil of the Roman Catholic hierarchy."[151]

This led to an awkward situation in which the state government of Min-nesota concluded a deal with the Holy Congregation of Propaganda Fide in Rome to shape a schooling model 5,000 miles away, reinforcing nativists' views of a remote-controlled community and the Catholics' erosion of state-church barriers.[152] The combination of public demand and local financial pres-sures elicited more resources from Rome to help build schools.

The first tuition-free Catholic high school for boys opened in Philadelphia in 1890. The next decades were critical, as the roughly 4,000 schools in opera-tion in 1900 grew to 10,000 by 1930. In other words, religious educational cov-erage of the national Catholic population started to keep pace with births and the arrival of new immigrants (see figure 7.17). To give a sense of proportional-

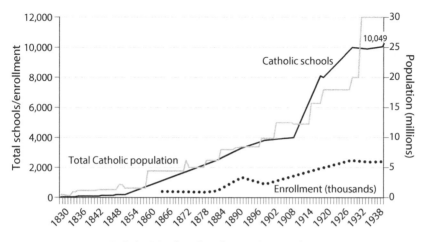

FIGURE 7.18. Catholic Schools and Students in the United States, 1830–1940

ity with Catholic demography, the ratio improved from seven religious schools for every 100,000 Catholics, to fifty schools per 100,000. The Boston diocese alone counted more than 50,000 students in religious institutions, from primary school to the university level (Boston College).[153] In 1900, around 900,000 students were enrolled in over 400 Catholic primary and secondary schools across the United States. In 1916, around one-third of parishes (just under 6,000) had their own schools, and the number enrolled rose to more than 1.5 million.[154] Fifteen years later, there were 4.5 million elementary school students and another 1 million in Catholic high schools (see figure 7.18).[155]

From the Import Model to the Collegio Model

The issue of educating the next generation of the faithful differed from the task of providing trained clergy who could minister to them. Whereas schoolchildren needed to be taught on-site, clerics in the missionary context could be brought to a majority-Catholic setting for seminary training. There was one single seminary, in Baltimore, whose training was recognized by Rome in 1822, thirty years after its establishment. One seminary could not suffice to train clergy to minister to the millions of Catholic immigrants arriving in the United States.[156]

The challenges necessitated action: the first American bishop, John Carroll, recommended ordaining "as many as can be trusted to receive them, though they may not have studied all the Treatises of Divinity, provided they know the obvious and general principles of moral Theology."[157] Archbishop John Hughes of New York granted accelerated ordination after six months of study of ecclesiastical sciences. The abbreviated seminary experience led to calls by some bishops to make better use of the Catholic University of Louvain: "A few good missionaries educated in Belgium scattered through our dioceses would leaven the whole mass."[158] Even as US seminaries grew in quantity and quality—three- and four-year courses of study, including philosophy and theology, were offered by the 1850s—bishops could still withdraw seminarians for emergency ordination if necessary.

Reports of a situation spinning out of control reached the pope via missionary hubs in European cities and the Holy Congregation of Propaganda Fide. There was an unsustainable "dependence on recruiting European priests" throughout the United States, and the bishops' annoyance with the behavior of "unfit immigrant priests" had become a feature of church life.[159] Church authorities in Ireland were pressured to introduce screening procedures "to eliminate the unfit" before leaving for the United States, and they added a predeparture training course on American culture at the Royal College of St. Patrick's.[160] The papal nuncio sent to investigate American Catholicism in the early 1850s, Cardinal Gaetano Bedini, suggested developing an American college in Rome as the long-term solution to the lack of priests. It would be "the single most important thing," he said, "that would satisfy every desire, achieve every purpose and would give the greatest enthusiasm to America." Bedini foresaw many advantages in a dedicated college. First, the "Roman Catholic spirit would be assured among priests and people," he argued, citing the record of other national colleges in Rome as proof. Second, the college would "facilitate and encourage vocations to the priesthood" because the number of American seminaries was not sufficient."[161] The pope immediately endorsed the idea and, the North American College in Rome opened its brass doors in 1857, joining a long list of national seminaries, including English, Armenian, Belgian, Bohemian, Canadian, Scottish, Spanish, Germanic, Greek, Irish, Maronite, Polish, and Portuguese colleges (see figure 7.19).

American Catholics demonstrated a collective lack of enthusiasm for the North American College in Rome.[162] The first class comprised only twelve students from eight US dioceses. The US bishops, who were never won over by the college, sent few students to be ordained there, often preferring to send students to Louvain in Belgium for their European training. During its first decade (1859–1869), the entering class of the North American College averaged only five recruits per year; average matriculation rose to sixteen per year in 1899–1909, and to twenty-five per year in the following decade. At this rate, they had difficulty affecting the pastoral experience of 12 million American Catholics around the turn of the century. The North American College also did little to weaken the influence of the thousands of priests who continued to arrive in the United States on clerical visas.

FIGURE 7.19. North American College in Rome

FIGURE 7.20. St. Mary's Seminary in Baltimore (1851)

Despite the end of the reign of the Propaganda Fide, US priests were slow to take on the habit of attending American seminaries. Hundreds of active priests were not full members of any American diocese. Hundreds of others arrived in the 1920s and 1930s from dioceses in large Italian cities but remained affiliated with their bishops in Italy. More were sent from a new pontifical college for Italian emigrants in Rome, under the direction of the bishop for Italian emigration. As a result, US-born Italian-American Catholics attended "national parishes run by immigrant clergy with close juridical and cultural ties to Fascist Italy and with weak ties to American dioceses."[163] Since Italian-Americans did not send their young men to American seminaries, this state of affairs continued (see figure 7.20). Only 10 percent of the 1,164 priests ordained in Chicago between 1903 and 1939 were of Italian descent. Of the 2,013 graduates of the major seminary in Brooklyn between 1820 and 1944, only 34 had Italian parents. In Boston, 1,519 priests were ordained between 1884 and 1945, but only 20 of them were of Italian descent. (Irish-Americans were overrepresented among nuns and priests even after losing their internal majority in the early 1900s.)[164]

From the Collegio Model to the Diocesan Seminary Model

The tepid reception of the North American College in Rome planted doubts in the Vatican about the Americans' overall fealty. In preparation for the meeting of Propaganda Fide officials and the US bishops, one from each ecclesiastical province, the Jesuit theologian Cardinal Johannes Franzelin prepared a massive study (*poenza*) in which he traced the problems of the "unruly priesthood" of the American Church. He described "inadequate seminary training" and subjected the four US diocesan seminaries "to a severe appraisal."[165] He altogether ignored the seminaries maintained by individual Catholic orders. Franzelin recommended the implementation of the Council of Trent's model of the diocesan seminary in the United States. Each of the eighty-odd dioceses, he said, or at least every ecclesiastical province, should sponsor a seminary.

The religious orders had already begun to establish institutions of higher education and seminaries. By the mid-nineteenth century, the United States had become home to the largest single Jesuit community outside of Rome: more than 1,000 Jesuits would help establish nearly one-quarter of all Catholic colleges and universities in the country.[166] The era when Jesuits automatically manned the frontispieces of Catholic education, however, ended with the papal suppression of the order under pressure from the monarchs of France, Portugal, and Spain (1773–1814). The establishment of universities was similarly delayed, despite calls to improve the quantity and quality of Catholic higher education in the United States.[167] In 1900, there were twenty-five Jesuit colleges in the United States, usually including a high school, and sometimes established before any state university.[168] On the other hand, as the Jesuit superior in the Missouri Province asked: Why do so many Catholics attend non-Catholic universities? The two answers given were Catholic aspirations for social mobility and the weaknesses of Catholic schools. The seven-year cycle of Catholic education was mismatched with four-year high schools and four-year universities.[169]

The Vatican established its flagship Catholic University of America in 1885.[170] There were 130 Roman Catholic institutions of higher education by the year 1920 (not including seminaries). That accounted for around one in every eight US institutions, with 3,600 faculty dispensing instruction to 30,000 students. Dozens of these Catholic colleges and universities had an enrollment over 300; four had around 1,000 students (Holy Cross, Boston College, Fordham, and Notre Dame), and seven other universities enrolled 1,500 to 5,000 graduate and professional students.[171] By 1930, there were an additional thirty-two Catholic colleges and universities, tripling the overall student population in Roman Catholic higher education to 105,000—around 10 percent of all Americans enrolled in university.[172] In 1966, the United States hosted a total of 454 diocesan and religious seminaries (high schools and colleges) with 5,036 clerical and lay faculty, and there were 120 classic Tridentine seminaries based in a diocese.[173]

The 150-Year Wait: Hierarchy

My analysis of episcopal records distinguished four distinct waves of Roman Catholicism's hierarchical expansion into the Americas: 1511–1673, 1777–1830, 1830–1870, and 1880–1930. The Propaganda Fide established five apostolic delegations in North America between 1784 and 1874 and two in the half-century thereafter. There had already been bishops, archbishops, and cardinals from the Americas since the seventeenth century, but they hailed from branches of national hierarchies in the European colonial powers (England, Spain, France). Baltimore served as the nineteenth century's American Catholic capital and the country's only archdiocese. In 1791, Bishop John Carroll convened twenty-two priests for the first of seven diocesan synods that would meet over the course of the next century, during which three plenary councils of US bishops were also held in Maryland.[174] In terms of institutional weight, the Papal States' sixty-eight dioceses were overtaken by eighty-five US dioceses in 1850.[175] At Baltimore's Second Plenary Council in 1866, thirty of the forty-seven bishops in attendance were foreign-born. The absence of Americans from the College of Cardinals became an issue of contention since the immense Plenary Council "has not one single representative at the seat of their Church."[176] After Rome established a space for itself in the United States, it needed to start making room for the United States in Roman institutions. That changed soon thereafter, proving that the seminaries and the episcopate were not a one-way street (see figure 7.21). The door that the pope opened from the Vatican to the United States also entered into his court. In 1875, John McCloskey became the first American appointed to the College of Cardinals.

Catholicism in America or American Catholicism?

During the country's long missionary period, many American Catholics sought greater independence from the Church in Rome. That group included nonbelievers who wanted to be free of their Catholic roots as well as

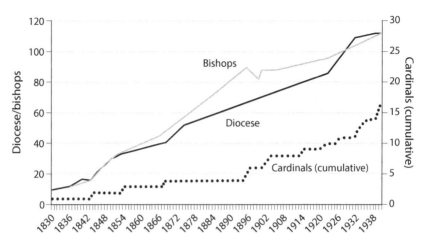

FIGURE 7.21. Roman Catholic Dioceses and Cardinals in the United States, 1830–1940

institutional actors who wanted an American church that could exercise full diocesan powers. That was the hope of Bishop John Carroll, who wanted to "remove Protestant jealousy of foreign jurisdiction" over things like the appointment or removal of Church leaders "at the pleasure of the Propaganda or any other tribunal out of the country."[177] US bishops preferred early on to be empowered as credible interlocutors for American public officials without having to check back with Rome for every little thing—in other words, they wanted to become a national hierarchy capable of making its own adjustments to local conditions. Before testifying at a trial in Massachusetts in 1830, for example, a bishop refused special treatment and insisted on swearing his oath upon the usual King James Bible of the Church of England.

One of the thornier questions was whether or not to end the state of exception under which the American Church operated. Absent a national hierarchy, US bishops operating under the Propaganda Fide could remove priests at their pleasure, but under canon law a priest held "his position during life or good behavior." Canon law also permitted parish priests to nominate their own bishop—which would have been a significant departure from the procedure under the Propaganda Fide. There was frequent conflict between American prelates and officials in Rome over the naming of bishops and archbishops— in one particularly suspenseful case in San Francisco the candidate was accused of "modernism."[178] The generation that decisively pushed back against Rome, however, arrived in power when native-born Americans were named to leadership positions and accumulated decades of experience in Church governance. Having an intuitive link with the native-born diaspora gave them greater freedom to reject foreign influences on the American Church.

In 1884, James Gibbons, archbishop of America's "primatial see" of Baltimore, presided over the country's Third Synod. It included archbishops, bishops, abbots, and at least 800 prelates and priests in all and, except for the First Vatican Council in 1870, was the largest council convened since Trent.[179] Gibbons was chosen to lead the meeting instead of the usual Italian envoy of the pope, who sent a life-sized portrait to sit in his place in Baltimore. The Baltimore Catechism that was issued from the summit unified American Catholicism under a standardized doctrine that remained in use for a century. Pope Leo XIII's conservative ideas helped American church leaders articulate what sort of demands they wanted to make upon American laws and society. Gibbons's efforts included trying to improve the Church's relations with all major social movements.[180] As the first US-born member of the College of Cardinals, he resisted Roman influence on behalf of a realist "Americanism," which only arose in earnest after the termination of Propaganda Fide status (see figure 7.22). During the 1910s, Gibbons spoke out forcefully against German and Irish campaigns to manipulate the naming of bishops to their political and linguistic-national-cultural advantage. He also opposed using European foreign languages in Church services and was credited for having "defeated a determined movement to introduce permanent foreign influences into the life of America."[181]

Tension between US Catholic leadership and Rome returned over the desirability of public education and "national" control of institutions by the countries of origin. After the Propaganda appointed a blatantly pro-German archbishop in Wisconsin in the 1890s, Archbishop John Ireland, in a reflection of the growing consciousness of the new US Catholic perspective, articulated the local resentment of European interference. The *New York Times* reported his petition to the pope to complain about districting foreign immigrants along national lines. He expressed his "indignation and mortification" that "Catholics' religion is made the occasion of insolent foreign intermeddling" and sarcastically told a journalist, "We may soon expect a cablegram announcing that the Prussian ambassador has claimed in the name of the Kaiser the right to veto our appointments to a dozen of Episcopal Sees in the United States. So long as the Church in America is fit only to be portioned off to the care of foreign countries, why would not any foreigner . . . ask for a piece?"[182] To eliminate the accusations that priests, bishops, and cardinals represented a foreign government, the American Church needed to be removed from the direct control of the Roman curia.[183]

Conclusion

At the height of the anarchist terrorist threat, the United States was still treated as a missionary land under the supervision of the Holy Congregation of Propaganda Fide. The domestication of American Catholicism required first the

FIGURE 7.22 [TRIPTYCH OF 7.22.1, 7.22.2, AND 7.22.3]. [7.22.1]: John Carroll, SJ, first US-born bishop (1789); [7.22.2]: John McCloskey, first US cardinal (1875); [7.22.3]: James Gibbons, first US-born cardinal (1886)

end of the community's temporary, missionary status. Worry about political violence helped hasten its transition to permanence. American authorities were preoccupied with the restless working classes and the rise of trade unionism, and they worked with the Church to counter extremists. All things considered, the US government preferred a Catholic centennial parade to the socialist May 1 celebration. The Vatican formally brought the American church out of the Propaganda Fide and into its own national hierarchy under canon law in 1908. Pius X's bull *Sapienti Consilio* placed the Church in the United States on a basis of equality with those of Italy, France, and Germany. The United States was no longer regarded by the Holy See as missionary territory.[184]

The new status of the American Church allowed bishoprics to continue growing at unprecedented speed, and archbishops were no longer required to submit parochial school plans—nor candidates for bishop or cardinal—for preapproval via the Propaganda. The US Society of Jesuits marked the moment with the creation of a new periodical: *America*. The US Church became its own master, relatively speaking, at the peak of social-political tensions in the first decade of the new century. It would take two more generations before the number of churches and priests responded proportionately to demographic needs. It took until the interwar period for there to be sufficient Catholic schools and educational institutions.[185] Decades later, American Catholics finally found their place in the College of Cardinals. The pope's unusual delay in lifting the American Church's Propaganda Fide status led to a flourishing of missionary arms and orders of the Church in the United States—many of which were far ahead of Rome in terms of local adaptation. In 1833, after two centuries of operations in Maryland, Jesuits had already stopped reporting to their European provinces and set up permanent shop in the United States.[186] The expansion of Jesuit and other universities catering to waves of Catholic immigrants spurred Rome to establish its own academic faculties under direct control.

Acknowledging American Catholics' permanent presence as a minority and, later, accepting the minimalist Lateran Accords resolved major obstacles—both occurred on dates of Rome's choosing—and allowed for the gradual diminishment of the Roman Question in US politics. The creation of the Vatican city-state did not make a huge splash in the United States, but together with the 1908 exit from the Propaganda Fide, the two most extreme obstacles to Catholics' political and social integration—the pope's temporal powers and foreign control of American religious institutions—were considered settled. The communitarian features gradually ceased to arouse controversy or fear as "political suspicions of Catholicism began to wane."[187] Senior US Church officials were now more likely to come from the United States over time,

FIGURE 7.23. St. Mary's Seminary, Class of 1919

FIGURE 7.24. Catholic elementary school class, United States (1930)

marking the country's normalization within the central hierarchy. And the "stove-piped" leadership from mission central in Rome could now be replaced with a set of locally rooted institutions: chaplaincies, bishoprics, rectorates, dioceses, and cardinalates that collectively acknowledged the permanent nature of the American Catholic community (see figures 7.23 and 7.24).

That is also what gave the American Church a voice in centrally governed institutions like the episcopal synods, the curia, and conclaves of the College of Cardinals—the bodies that set policy and selected popes. An examination of class photographs from the North American College in Rome provides an interesting illustration of the emergence of a US Church. The American flag made its first appearance hanging in the background of the portrait of the class of 1903, and it got progressively larger every year until it filled the entire background.[188] It was this Americanized Roman Catholic hierarchy that negotiated a growing space for the United States in Rome. The US experience helped the Church stage a partial recovery from the dispossession of the French Revolution and its aftershocks across the old continent. It also led to significant institutional adaptation and mission transformation: the focus on the United States enhanced the internationalization and professionalization of the Holy See. The addition of American bishops and cardinals activated a feedback mechanism within the Church's own global institutions and later helped define a new role for the Roman Church vis-à-vis democracy and pluralism and its place in international politics.

8

Islam in Europe

THERE WAS NO INTERVAL between the mid-twentieth-century collapse of European overseas empires and the influx of millions of labor migrants and hundreds of thousands of refugees.[1] Much as the United States did for the Catholic countries, western Europe societies presented a mixed blessing to the states of the majority-Muslim world. Postcolonial Europe offered an economy to absorb the unemployed as well as political liberties for dissidents. The growing pains of rapid modernization and economic dislocation wracked postcolonial South Asia (India, Pakistan, Bangladesh), North Africa (Algeria, Morocco, Tunisia), Asia Minor (Turkey), and the Indian Ocean (Indonesia). Shielded by the sea and empowered by new European freedoms of expression and association, the individuals and groups whose countries of origin had no space for them reemerged on the northern shores of the Mediterranean. Against expectations that the guest laborers and refugees would eventually return home, they and their families settled in Europe and continued to arrive in the late 1900s and early 2000s. The Muslim communities of Europe grew from 500,000 in the 1950s—0.1 percent of the general population—to around 30 million, or 8 percent, by the 2020s (see figure 8.1). More than three of every four European Muslims traced their ancestry to zones of former imperial influence. It would prove more straightforward to govern 80 percent of all Muslims worldwide as colonial subjects than to have 2 percent of the world's Muslims as citizens.

Their integration was forestalled by European reluctance to bring Islam into national institutions, leaving Muslims without adequate infrastructure and religious education and exposed to the crosscurrents of the postcolonial Middle East. Despite the earlier acquaintance of host and guest, albeit in reversed order, the twenty-first-century Muslim experience with European institutions found no useful policy models in the history of rule in British India, Dutch Java, Austrian Bosnia, or French Algeria. The goals that Europeans pursued at the time to simplify their lives as colonial powers, against the wishes of most of the world's Muslims, later complicated their lives at home as countries of immigration. In particular, European Muslims felt the consequences of the imperial powers'

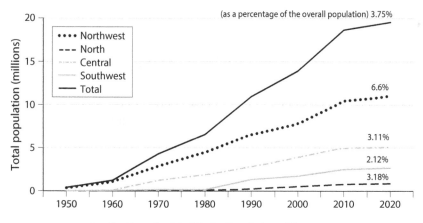

FIGURE 8.1. The Growth of the Muslim Population of Europe, 1950–2030

weakening of the Ottoman caliphate and installation of Wahhabi Sauds as custodians of Mecca and Medina. In the absence of any Islamic equivalent to the Lateran Accords, which resolved the issue of temporal sovereignty for the papacy, the distinction between temporal and spiritual oversight became a muddled site of competition for political-religious influence.

Sunni Muslim groups based in Doha, Riyadh, Algiers, Rabat, and Ankara created multiple missionary congregations and religious outposts to provide services to the European diaspora. First, the Pan-Islamic brotherhoods under political suppression in the majority-Muslim world survived in European civil society organizations, where they preached resistance to the imperially engineered international order and advocated religious rule. Second, the European powers invited the Saudi-based Muslim World League to set up full-service mosques and salaried imams in major cities and to distribute Qur'ans and religious literature. Third, the religious-political activism took place beyond the juridical reach of homeland institutions. That stimulated efforts by Morocco, Turkey, and Algeria to provide their emigrant communities with Islamic services in western Europe.

Diaspora Muslims were exposed to Pan-Islamic crosscurrents that were closely guarded against in the ancestral homelands: from political Islam to revolutionary Shi'ism and Wahhabism, to national dissident groups like Kaplançis in Germany, the Armed Islamic Group of Algeria (GIA) in France, and the twenty-first-century transnational networks al Qaeda and the Islamic State. Believers abroad slipped through the fingers of Islamic authorities in the countries of origin, lost to atheism, militant jihadism, or "Sheikh Google." The contradictions built into this approach became unsustainable in the mid-2010s, when citizens and long-term residents of Europe streamed *out*, to fight

Western-backed armies in Syria and Iraq and settle in the short-lived Islamic State.[2] The political violence raised the stakes of competition for intellectual and ideological leadership across the generations. To counter religious extremism, European governments searched for interlocutors and religious service providers who endorsed peaceful cohabitation with the non-Muslim minority.

Through this combination of circumstances, the settlement of Muslims in Europe came to represent the third modern defeat for organized Islam, and the latest exogenous shock to centralized religious authority. The religious capitals had an interest in formalizing links of spiritual patronage as their emigrants became other countries' citizens and temporal ties weakened. Any attempts to do so were doomed to failure, however, in the absence of any acknowledgment that the communities were permanently settled in Europe. To be accepted as interlocutors and granted full religious freedom, the branches of international Islamist movements and the sending states of North Africa and Turkey needed to undergo the equivalent of 1908, when Rome allowed for an independent US hierarchy by removing it from the centralized control of the Propaganda Fide.

European Muslims faced the classic jurisprudential dilemmas that ulema had considered for centuries. For example, which rules applied to Muslims outside of majority-Muslim lands? For the purposes of Sunni jurisprudence (fiqh), was western Europe defined as a place that required a war footing (dar al harb) or as a home for Islam (dar al Islam)? The gradual acknowledgment that the diaspora was no longer part of a missionary community and lived as a *permanent minority* would permit European Islam to act as a locally owned and operated, fully licensed branch endowed with a degree of decision-making authority. This administrative-theological transformation went to the heart of the host society's understanding of the separation of religion and politics. The change in location and status of authority made the difference between local governance and remote control—between centrally appointed and locally cultivated leadership. It had concrete implications for the recruitment and training of religious officials, from prayer leaders (imams) to interpreters of religious texts (ulema).

Political Violence

At first, immigrant communities in Europe were used by first-generation dissidents as an operational base for spectacular terrorist attacks elsewhere—for instance, in New York, Paris, Washington, Casablanca, and Djerba between 1993 and 2003. Then these communities became principal targets in their own right, in Paris, Brussels, London, and Berlin from 2004 to 2020 (see table 8.1). Most of the terrorists were fallen-away Muslims who had been born or raised

TABLE 8.1. International Terrorism with Ties to Muslim Countries, 2004–2016

Date	Location	Attack	Assailant(s) and Country of Origin	Number of Victims
March 11, 2004	Madrid, Spain	Bombing in Atocha Railway Station	Jamal Zougam et al. (Algeria)	192 dead; 2,050 wounded
July 7, 2005	London, United Kingdom	Bombing in public transport system	Mohammad Sidique Khan et al. (Pakistan/Jamaica)	56 dead; 784 wounded
June 30, 2007	Glasgow, United Kingdom	Car ramming attack at Glasgow Airport	Bilal Abdullah and Kafeel Ahmed (Iraq/India)	1 dead; 5 injured
March 2, 2011	Frankfurt, Germany	Shooting in Frankfurt Airport	Arid Uka (Kosovo)	2 dead; 2 injured
March 11, 2012	Toulouse and Montauban, France	Weeklong shooting of French Army soldiers and children/teacher from a Jewish school	Mohammed Merah (Algeria)	8 dead; 5 injured
May 24, 2014	Brussels, Belgium	Shooting at Jewish Museum of Belgium	Mehdi Nemmouche (Algeria)	4 dead; 0 injured
January 7, 2015	Paris, France	Shooting at *Charlie Hebdo* offices, followed by a two-day siege and shooting at a Hypercacher kosher supermarket	Saïd and Chérif Kouachi et al. (Algeria)	17 dead; 20 injured
February 14, 2015	Copenhagen, Denmark	Shootings at a cultural center, railway station, and the Great Synagogue	Omar Abdel Hamid (Palestine)	3 dead; 5 injured
November 13, 2015	Paris, France	Bombing outside the Stade de France and shootings at a Bataclan concert and cafés and restaurants	Abdelhamid Abaaoud, Salah Abdeslam, et al. (Morocco)	137 dead; 413 injured
March 22, 2016	Brussels, Belgium	Bombings at Brussels Airport and Maalbeek Metro Station	Ibrahim El Bakraoui, Najim Laachroui, et al. (Morocco)	35 dead; 340 injured
July 14, 2016	Nice, France	Truck ramming attack on the Promenade des Anglais during a Bastille Day celebration	Mohamed Lahouiaj Bouhlel (Tunisia)	87 dead; 434 injured

(continued)

TABLE 8.1. (*continued*)

Date	Location	Attack	Assailant(s) and Country of Origin	Number of Victims
July 24, 2016	Ansbach, Germany	Bombing near the entrance to the Ansbach Open music festival	Mohammad Daleel (Syria)	1 dead | 15 injured
December 19, 2016	Berlin, Germany	Truck ramming attack at the Breitscheidplatz Christmas Market	Anis Amri (Tunisia)	12 dead | 56 injured
March 22, 2017	London, United Kingdom	Car ramming attack on Westminster Bridge	Khalid Masood (United Kingdom)	6 dead | 49 injured
April 3, 2017	St. Petersburg, Russia	Bombing in St. Petersburg metro on day of President Vladimir Putin's visit	Akbarzhon Jalilov (Kyrgyzstan)	16 dead | 64 injured
April 7, 2017	Stockholm, Sweden	Truck ramming attack into crowds along Drottninggatan (Queen Street)	Rakhmat Akilov (Uzbekistan)	5 dead | 14 injured
May 22, 2017	Manchester, United Kingdom	Bombing at Ariana Grande concert in Manchester Arena	Salman Abedi (Libya)	23 dead | 800+ injured
June 3, 2017	London, United Kingdom	Van ramming and stabbing on London Bridge	Khuram Butt (Morocco), Rachid Redouane (Libya), and Youssef Zaghba (Pakistan)	11 dead | 48 injured
August 17, 2017	Barcelona, Spain	Van ramming attack on La Rambla	Younes Abouyaaqoub (Morocco)	15 dead | 131 injured
August 18, 2017	Turku, Finland	Stabbing at the west corner of Market Square	Abderrahman Bouanane (Morocco)	2 dead | 8 injured
September 15, 2017	London, United Kingdom	Bombing at Parsons Green Underground station	Ahmed Hassan (Iraq)	0 dead | 30 injured
March 23, 2018	Carcassonne and Trèbes, France	Shooting and car hijacking	Redouane Lakdim (Morocco)	5 dead | 15 injured
May 29, 2018	Liège, Belgium	Stabbing during temporary prison leave	Benjamin Herman (Belgium)	4 dead | 4 injured

in western Europe without formal religious education, radicalized in a mael-
strom of old world conflict and new world disappointments.[3] Belgium and
France were both targets and incubators of five military-style attacks on European citizens: nearly 200 were murdered in Toulouse, Brussels, and Paris between 2012 and 2016.[4] A Frenchman killed four at the Jewish Museum in Brussels.[5] Three Frenchmen killed the editorial board of *Charlie Hebdo* and
shoppers at a kosher supermarket in January 2015.[6] After two French-Algerian
brothers murdered twelve in the newspaper's editorial office, the Algerian minister for religious affairs said in an interview that "the *Charlie Hebdo* attack is a
Franco-French problem. The perpetrators may have Algerian origins, but they
never spent any time in Algeria, never attended Algerian mosques or any
qur'anic schools in Algeria—or elsewhere. The Algerian people are immunized against these temptations and aware of the dangers of the instrumental-
ization of Islam."[7]

The sensational acts contributed to a view of Muslims as a potential fifth
column and revealed their communities as the object of extraterritorial influence. Yet they were also clearly the product of Western societies. Islamists in
Europe were monitored but free to associate, assemble, and circulate their
publications. In the aftermath of attacks, investigators asked the same set of
questions that detectives posed in Paterson, New Jersey, after the assassination
of the Italian king in 1900. How could the offending ideology spread so virulently and so unchecked? A city councilor from Molenbeek, the Brussels
neighborhood of the cell that attacked Paris and the Brussels airport, wondered, "Why did the government allow Saudi Arabia, with its simplistic and
binary vision of Islam, to finance mosques and imams, and to exercise a near-
monopoly on French translations?"[8] Just as late nineteenth-century European
governments were incredulous that American authorities permitted hornets'
nests of assassins to flourish without intervening, so the Moroccan, Tunisian,
and Turkish governments could not fathom why western European countries
allowed groups with names like the Caliphate State and the Great Eastern
Islamic Raiders Front to freely assemble (see figure 8.2).

Anti-Islamic sentiment in Europe was also fueled by the de facto foreign
control of Muslims' religious life. There was ambiguity regarding the spiritual
intentions of temporal rulers, and vice versa. Like the Italians in the early
twentieth-century United States, Muslim-origin communities combined a
variety of traits, leading to a greater incidence of delinquency and overrepre-
sentation in prisons. This reinforced their paradoxical image as vectors of disorder *and* communal conservatism.[9] Turkish leaders campaigned against assimilation as a "crime against humanity" and encouraged Turks to "integrate
in their host countries while retaining their own values."[10] In an interview in
Ankara, Turkish education ministry officials illuminated their understanding

FIGURE 8.2. The unofficial French "Foreign Legion" in Syria (Facebook, 2016)

of diaspora: "Our obligation continues even in the case of naturalization. If they are born to a Turkish mother and father, then we accept they are still Turkish people and that it is our duty regardless of their nationality." The number of teachers sent from Turkey will not diminish over time, they said, because "in the third generation they still speak Turkish."[11]

Similarly, officials in Rabat treated the preservation of Moroccan identity as a matter of national security. Morocco had faced a severe crisis since the 2004 murder of Dutch filmmaker Theo van Gogh by a member of its diaspora, a second-generation Moroccan-Dutch citizen. Within a bit more than a decade, dozens of Moroccans residing abroad (MRE) plotted and joined attacks on Casablanca, Madrid, Paris, and Brussels. "Moroccan nationality is inalienable," a counselor to the king said in an interview, and applied "to individuals and across generations. If you are of Moroccan origin, you can be prosecuted in Moroccan courts."[12] In another interview, the Moroccan minister of Islamic affairs predicted that: "Even the 4th generation will remain Moroccan—it is a refuge for identity and nostalgia and self-defense. It must be managed in a positive way and without fear."[13]

All receiving countries limited migration and implemented measures to improve integration outcomes, for example, by revising citizenship policies and introducing new standards for family reunification and marriage visas. France expelled 166 Islamists in the decade following the terrorist attacks of September 11, 2001, and in the year after the November 13, 2015, attacks in Paris

The New Editors

FIGURE 8.3. "The New Editors" (*Daily Mail*, 2015)

the French Interior Ministry used emergency powers to close one mosque every two weeks on average.[14] After the Paris attacks, there were moves across Europe to close down Salafi mosques, including those with no links to violence or terrorism.[15] A court sentenced a French mother to two years' imprisonment for wiring money to her jihadi son in Syria. France began targeted assassinations of its own jihadi nationals at war in Iraq and Syria.[16] The Italian government stepped up its pace of deporting religious extremists to around ten per month.[17] After an attack with a hijacked truck in Berlin in 2016, the German government began deporting extremists at a rate of three per month.[18] Authorities across Europe arrested hundreds returning from the war zone of the Islamic State and came down hard on residents and citizens they considered to be *potential* foreign fighters, seizing their passports and identity cards and sometimes resorting to preemptive incarceration.

In surveys taken in 2016, one in five Dutch and French voters supported closing all mosques.[19] Claiming to defend women's rights and toleration toward gays and Jews, Dutch and French populists surfed on fear of Islam, and discontent with the European Union, asylum policy, and the common currency. Far-right political parties found new success in Sweden, Norway, Finland, France, Germany, Hungary, Italy, Denmark, Poland, the United Kingdom, and the Netherlands. Religious rights that were supposed to be guaranteed by national

FIGURE 8.4. "A Breeding Ground for Terrorists" (Molenbeek, Belgium, 2015)

constitutions were restricted in a tit-for-tat with countries of origin. Some political parties opposed building mosques until Saudi Arabia permitted churches to be built. Measures taken to, for example, ban the wearing of the headscarf, burka, and burkini, limit the height of minarets, or ban them altogether said more about host-state anxiety than actual trends. Despite annual EU statistics showing that right-wing and ethno-national terrorism was more frequent and more lethal, it seemed to many that while not all Muslims were terrorists, all terrorists were Muslim.

Professionalization

The periodic incidents of violence over two decades (1995–2015) drew the attention of public authorities to the local and national organization of Islamic prayer and education. Furthermore, each terrorist attack and security crisis in the majority-Muslim world damaged Islam's local reputation as an organized religion and made its foreignness less acceptable to European governments. The crises of European combatants' departure for Syria and the attacks in Paris, Berlin, Brussels, London, Manchester, and Nice accelerated domestic policy reform.[20] The first and most urgent issue was the low quantity and quality of religious infrastructure—the mosques and imams. The number of western European mosques and prayer rooms rose from around 100 in 1950 to a projected 15,000 in 2030, and the number of imams to a projected 8,000 to

10,000. Despite the creation of prayer spaces and the arrival of foreign clerics, the ratio of prayer space and leadership across western Europe was still two to three times lower than in Turkey or Morocco—one for every 3,000 believers instead of one per 1,000. There were shortages of religious personnel in classrooms, prayer spaces, hospitals, and prisons.

In 2012, a Moroccan official said in an interview, the 500,000 students of Moroccan background in Spanish schools "would normally require 400 teachers but right now only have fourteen" to teach language and culture.[21] Imams were hardly present in European penitentiary systems, where prisoners from a Muslim background sometimes made up an absolute majority. Outside of the United Kingdom, there were few Islamic schools or seminaries in Europe. In many countries, fewer than 15 percent of practicing imams were estimated to possess any formal training, and those who did had been trained somewhere else.[22] Governments in their countries of origin would never leave citizens so unequipped and vulnerable to nonstate actors. "Some young French Moroccans say we're sellouts," one imam said, "but these are people with no knowledge of either religion or French law. We remind them that Islam requires taking into account the local context, and that therefore fatwas can neither be imported nor exported."[23]

In the first decades of the twenty-first century, there was new growth in religious services for citizens abroad: through the Turkish-Islamic Union for Religious Affairs (DİTİB) and its French branch, the Coordinating Committee of Muslim Turks in France (Comité de coordination des musulmans turcs de France, CCMTF), via Turkey; the Grande Mosquée de Paris (GMP), supported by Algeria; and also by the National Federation of French Muslims (Fédération nationale des musulmans de France, FNMF), the Rally of Muslims of France (Rassemblement des musulmans de France, RMF), and other associations affiliated with Morocco.[24] Such federations succeeded thanks to support from the country of origin—and, at first, to the hosts' receptiveness to them.[25] Consular imams were always best positioned to receive residence permits—they had a nearly perfect approval rate.[26] The French signed agreements with Algeria, Morocco, Tunisia and Turkey to invite contingents of language teachers and imams.[27] In 2015 alone, 300 government-paid imams were distributed across a wide cross-section of French mosques: 150 from Turkey, 120 from Algeria, and 30 from Morocco.[28]

Over time, theological questions that were once referred to ulema councils in the countries of origin began to be addressed by theologians based in Europe. The transition began from reliance on imported clergy and personnel who were exported as-is from foreign capitals between 1970 and 2000 to a system tailored to new permanent religious realities. The 2000s introduced a new phase in the professionalization of religious training. Sending governments took steps to become less foreign in choosing personnel, using European languages, adapting the training of religion teachers, coordinating the training of imams, and adapting religious content—such as school curricula and Friday sermons—to the new national context. The next advance was the specialized faculties and seminaries in the country of origin, the equivalent of the Roman national collegio system. And finally, with the passage of time, the earlier missionary objective turned to one of socialization: propagating religious traditions across *generations*. The last step has not fully taken place: the sanctioning of the establishment of schools and seminaries with full ordination abilities, or the twenty-first-century Islamic version of the diocesan model from Trent. There is no way to fast-forward this process or to substitute the corresponding process of institutionalization.

Turkey in Germany and Europe

Infrastructure and Education

Turkey was the first of the four countries to sign bilateral guest worker accords. At the time of the raising of the drawbridge, in 1973–1974, around 750,000 Turkish guest workers were residing in western Europe.[29] In the early twenty-first century, it was estimated that 5 million people of Turkish origin lived in the countries of the European Union, half of whom were still citizens of Turkey—and an additional 10 million "related people" lived in other countries abroad. Together these communities increased Turkey's potential religious audience by nearly 20 percent, but they were also the most vulnerable to dangers related to political dissidence overseas.

Some imams had been sent along with guest workers in the 1970s, but the clerical supply increased after the 1980 coup d'état, when religious activity in the diaspora caught the attention of the generals.[30] The Diyanet opened its first office in West Berlin in 1982, the year of Turkey's new military-drafted constitution, and soon started sending imams according to a 1984 bilateral accord with West Germany.[31] In the view of a member of an opposition group at the time, "Diyanet's objective at the beginning was simply to prevent any organic Turkish civil society from taking root."[32] The agreement gave Ankara a monopoly on clerical visas for all imams of Turkish nationality in Germany and in 1984 inaugurated a Department of Foreign Affairs, which was responsible for mosques and prayer leaders abroad.[33] The first customized exports came in 1985, when İmam Hatip schools were created in eastern Turkey especially to staff international DİTİBs.[34] In the mid-1980s, the Directorate of Religious Affairs (Diyanet, or DiB) in Ankara paid the salaries of 75 imams in the Netherlands, whose number rose to 140 by 2011.[35] In 2014, the

Diyanet employed 150 imams in France and 970 Turkish imams in Germany. The number of full-time DİTİB employees in Germany grew to 1,170 in 2019; another 1,161 DİTİB volunteers taught weekend religious courses.[36] Hundreds more were sent across Europe to replace preachers who were cycled out after their multi-year stay abroad.[37] In an effort to raise the vocational quality of the pastoral services, Ankara agreed to extend imams' residency in Europe to five years (from four). "To keep them there any longer," the official said, "would create administrative and psychological problems."[38]

Turkish state Islam was the dominant actor among the diaspora, reportedly accounting for two-thirds of Turkish mosque attendance in Belgium and one-half in France.[39] Mosques and prayer spaces were absorbed or constructed and incorporated as wholly owned subsidiaries. The Diyanet in Ankara owned the deed of most prayer spaces abroad, officials said, because local associations faced trouble securing their own bank loans.[40] There were other ways in which Ankara did not let go, institutionally. For example, the Diyanet president frequently exercised his ex officio role as honorary chairman of all DİTİBs worldwide to influence executive board meetings in Europe.[41] In the early twenty-first century, Recep Tayyip Erdoğan encouraged a large array of civil society organizations to cultivate ties abroad, alongside state agencies. He was energized by the European diaspora, which resembled his electorate: religious conservative descendants of rural Turks. Erdoğan engaged the diaspora with civil society groups like European Turkish Democrats (EUTD) and through the activities of his own foreign aid agencies. The number of Turkish associations registered abroad rose from around 1,700 in 1993 to over 5,000 associations, many of them cultural-religious in nature, in the early 2010s.[42] One-third of the Diyanet's 3,000 western European mosques were located in Germany and 15 percent were in France.[43]

Like its predecessors, the Diyanet kept an eye on diaspora groups attracted to other Islamic movements—not just violent jihadists but also the adherents of the Islamic service movement directed by the former Diyanet imam living in Pennsylvania in self-exile, Fethullah Gülen. Committees of Turkish parliamentarians regularly visited Germany to hear the main complaints of the expanding European diaspora. But unlike its predecessors, the Erdoğan regime applied steady pressure to improve the integration of European Turks. The vice president of the Directorate for Turks Abroad said in an interview in Ankara that "we always got the same message from the European communities: there are not enough teachers and not enough imams. We will do anything, within our mandate and international law, to protect the diaspora's identity and culture."[44]

The Diyanet pursued these objectives with a steady supply of Turkish Islam. Their goal was to staff mosques as if they were in Turkey. "We'd like to

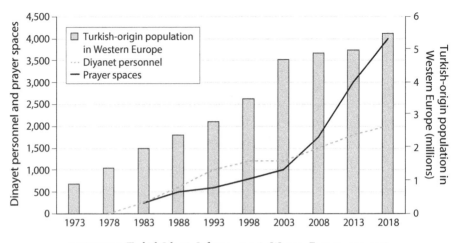

FIGURE 8.5. Turkish Islamic Infrastructure in Western Europe, 1973–2018

have three employees in each of Germany's 900 prayer spaces, i.e. 2,700 employees" (see figure 8.5).[45] Officials insisted that they no longer centrally distributed Friday sermons, but they acknowledged that they made a database with texts available to state imams.[46] Schoolteachers were sent separately from imams, increasing from 1,100 to 1,850. In 2015 in Germany, over 50,000 students were enrolled in weekly Islamic religious education at one of 500 schools in eleven states (*Länder*).[47] Around two dozen Turkish mosques received permission to create extracurricular boarding schools in France and Germany.[48] Before the 2016 coup attempt, many German Länder invited DİTİB's participation as a sole or cooperating partner in organizing Islamic education. This was a change from DİTİB's former refusal to participate in any project they did not lead or own, and a respite from Germany's avoidance of negotiating directly with DİTİB—which resumed after 2016.[49]

The domestic pressures on European governments led to the goal of reducing the number of imams sent by Ankara. The Diyanet president said in an interview, however, that proper training was much harder than Europeans thought.[50] In a 2010 document, the two countries indicated "a strong desire to 'Frenchify' the religious personnel by nominating French citizens of Turkish origin for service in France, now trained in Turkey" and the "progressive reduction of personnel on loan from Diyanet and the increase of religious personnel trained in France, beginning in 2014–2015."[51] The model shifted to centralized training in Turkey in the International Theology Program, away from the political pressures of European governments to adopt a collegio model. The "EU wants to train imams but they don't have the institu-

FIGURE 8.6. Islamic theology students from Germany at the University of Marmara, Istanbul (2009)

tions to do it," one religious scholar said, whereas "we have the institutions here in Turkey to try."[52] The program was originally established for German high school graduates, who were given lodging and a stipend. Turkish citizens completed coursework in Ankara, while German citizens went to the University of Marmara (see figure 8.6).[53] Thousands of foreign students, almost all of them European, enrolled in the coursework, with the expectation of academic recognition for the program in Germany under the Bologna process. In addition to producing ten years of graduating classes, Turkey also offered graduate scholarships in theology. When the German-Turkish students returned to Germany, the Diyanet vice president said, "there is no language problem, they know German culture, and they are much more integrated than our imams." By 2016, there were sixty Turkish-origin graduates of the program who were employed in DİTİB's German mosques. They were paid by Ankara but did not have the same civil servant status as DİTİB imams.[54]

Tridentine Seminary

In separate interviews, members of the Turkish parliament from ideologically distinct political parties said some version of: "In Germany there are dozens of theology faculties but not a single Islamic one!" A nationalist MHP politician suggested that "these have to be realized via interstate negotiations. Maybe a Turkish university should be founded in Germany," an issue discussed in parliament.[55] As of the early 2000s, there was little Turkish Islamic theology taking place on European campuses, which, as AKP deputy Talip Küçükçan noted in an interview, "created a gap between the Muslim immigrants and the state."[56] At first, Turkey's preference was to hire some of the several hundred Turkish theology graduates living in Germany to teach religious education.[57] The Diyanet also allocated funds to finance two chairs in Islamic theology at Frankfurt's Goethe University, within the Protestant Theology Department.

In 2011, the Diyanet opened an İmam Hatip school in Strasbourg: the Yunus Emre lycée. It was modeled on its esteemed Catholic, Protestant, and Jewish counterpart schools in town. Open to all, including non-Muslims, the school was intended to serve as a feeder into a new faculty of theology in Strasbourg. In 2013, the German foreign ministry worked with the Diyanet to offer preparatory classes in Ankara and Bursa.[58] The French embassy in Turkey wrote to the Diyanet to propose cooperation on a university theological faculty in Strasbourg, modeled on the Goethe University arrangement in Frankfurt.[59] Turkey and France held ministerial-level meetings in Ankara in 2011 to discuss the format—a faculty and an institute or center—and curriculum and pedagogy.

The *faculté de théologie islamique* (Ilahiyat Fakultesi) in Strasbourg started a five-year curriculum for a diploma from Istanbul's divinity faculty. But ultimately it was denied university accreditation and needed to decamp. DİTİB still intended to reopen at Hautepierre, where they acquired a set of buildings in the Strasbourg suburbs, 2,000 kilometers northwest of Istanbul, 1,000 kilometers west of Vienna, on five acres of surface area—"the largest Muslim site in Europe" and a tantalizing space of Turkish-European Islam to come. The German education ministry, meanwhile, sponsored the creation of "centers for Islamic theology" (2011–2021) at five universities (Tübingen, Münster, Osnabrück, Frankfurt/Main, and Erlangen-Nürnberg) that had a collective enrollment of over 2,500 young German Muslim men and women by 2019. These programs would not produce imams, who would still largely be Ankara-trained, but would form the future intellectuals and interpreters of German Islam.[60] After the trial period with renewable (federal) funding, the centers presumably would blossom into full-scale theology faculty departments. The Belgian DİTİB announced a plan to streamline "a number of small-scale private initiatives that offer Qur'an lessons into a complete course of education for teenagers," intended to evolve into an "imams' institute." The Brussels spokesperson said that training imams was "not like growing tomatoes! You can't just say, 'We are going to invest €100,000 and then one year later we have three imams.'" In 2017, he said he expected the first cohort of Turkish-Belgian imams to be ready after "five or ten years."[61]

FIGURE 8.7. Turkish President Recep Tayyip Erdoğan meets in Ankara with Turkish association leaders from Strasbourg, France (2015)

In Pursuit of Integration

Predeparture preparations were improved for imams and their families in the early 2000s. One former senior Diyanet official and DİTİB president in Germany said in an interview that Europeanization could mean "cutting hateful passages in texts, for example, as we did in Denmark," or "it can also mean institutions, university chairs, and the like."[62] In 2009, a Europe-wide Diyanet office was established in Brussels with thirty theologians who would be engaged "to primarily target Turks living in Europe.[63] Denominalization, however, meant changing who had the power to hire and fire: "In Bavaria, they decided to hire our teachers to teach religion five years ago, who then had to resign from the Turkish education ministry and began teaching in German." DİTİB imams began delivering German-language sermons in 2010, but specified that preaching would not only be in German but bilingual. "Turkish is important for our youth not to be alienated from their culture," the Diyanet president said. But they dropped the insistence on Turkish-language Islamic education. "We will interact with German Muslims in the way we now interact with African Muslims," an official said in an interview—that is to say, as an entity unto themselves. Turkish-German Muslim leaders said, "We make all our own decisions here. Most of the time Ankara isn't even aware. Religion officials come from Turkey, which pays their salaries directly. That's all."[64]

The Turkish ambassador to Germany lamented Islam's infrastructural deficiencies as well as German attitudes, but nonetheless expressed optimism

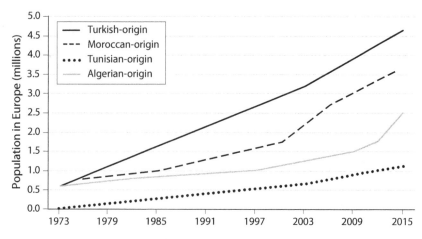

FIGURE 8.8. The Growth of Moroccan-, Algerian-, Tunisian-, and Turkish-Origin
Populations in Western Europe, 1973–2015

that "Germany will change so that there is the rule of law in all domains, so religion can be fully lived out and experienced."[65] The former DİTİB president said: "If we want legal status, then we must understand the system correctly. Once you decide to stay here for the duration, then you have to get to know Germany's uniqueness."[66] This shift from the emphasis on "Turkishness" alone marked the concrete passage to dar al Islam.

Erdoğan's chief adviser, Ibrahim Kalin, described the pursuit of an agenda against both extremism *and* assimilation. Kalin said in an interview in Ankara that "it would be rather tricky to banish foreign influences altogether. We want these communities to integrate and to abide by the law, vote, invest, etc. But we also want them to maintain their cultural heritage. It's fine if you define 'German-ness' or 'Frenchness' by language and law, but when you go beyond that, then it has racist overtones. I mean, the third generation in Germany speaks better German than Turkish!"[67] Or, as the DİTİB representative in Strasbourg asked in response to criticism of its plans for Hautepierre, "Doesn't France have French high schools and cultural centers abroad?"[68] Both arguments support the recruitment of German-born imams. One thing seemed certain to Ali Kizilkaya, the Islamrat president in Berlin: "The longer equal rights are delayed here, then the more the Germans strengthen the hand of the political extremes. They are not doing themselves, or us, any favors."[69]

In turn, the Turkish government did itself no favors in the aftermath of the July 2016 coup attempt when it engaged in a large-scale purge and persecution of Gülenist plotters (and a number of innocent bystanders). The ensuing confrontation with Austrian, Belgian, Dutch, and German authorities may have accelerated the transfer of responsibility—and semi-autonomous religious communities—to locally incorporated European-Turkish communities. DİTİB went through some administrative processes to become a membership-based organization, but German and other national authorities demanded a clean rupture with the government of President Erdoğan. The Diyanet reported on Gülenist activities in more than three dozen countries to a parliamentary committee, including more than a dozen in Europe. Turkish comportment in the diaspora had crossed a line with host countries, even though it was largely consistent with earlier crackdowns (e.g., on Islamist or Kurdish groups) that Europeans ignored. This reinforced Erdoğan's identity as the perpetual victim of double standards.

Morocco in France and Europe

By 2007, half of all Moroccan households had firsthand experience with international migration.[70] The number of Moroccans living in Europe doubled between 1998 and 2018, to around 4 million, 40 percent of whom held dual nationality. The largest group (38 percent) lived in France; 24 percent lived in Spain, 14 percent in Italy, 11 percent in Belgium, 7 percent in the Netherlands, and 6 percent in Germany.[71] In studies of mosque attendance among North Africans, Moroccans were among the most active. In France, experts estimated that they accounted for nearly half of imams, for most hajj pilgrims, and for most mosque administrators.[72] It was a dramatically insufficient institutional landscape, however, compared to the homeland. In interviews, officials frequently volunteered that diaspora communities requested help: "The community wanted to have religious institutions inspired by Moroccan Islam to transmit across the generations," according to one royal adviser. "They say things like, 'We don't want to be taught by Wahhabis or Iraqis—or by Sunnis who have lived too long in the company of shi'a,' etc."[73]

One official who had split his time between Paris and Rabat said that the "rise in religious observance in the third generation . . . no matter what, will eventually reach us."[74] The phenomenon of "indoctrinated" Moroccans visiting from Europe in July and August and proselytizing Wahhabi or Shi'a Islam—leading to conflict with the families and communities—was one oft-repeated concern.[75] Officials estimated that tens of thousands of Moroccans in Belgium and elsewhere had converted to Shi'a Islam—which was virtually nonexistent in Morocco because of strict controls since 1979.

In Barcelona, a newspaper quoted an unnamed Moroccan intelligence agent saying that groups in Spain were plotting to destabilize the Moroccan monarchy by financing subversive actors in Morocco. One of the ways Rabat responded was to build a large new mosque to counter Salafi influence in

Barcelona. An adviser to the interior minister explained in an interview in Casablanca that "religion policy is conceived as defense policy, with the aim of keeping Moroccans in the Moroccan rite, and not, say, Wahhabism." In his view,

> They're Muslim whether we like it or not, and if they get the religion bug and receive no orientation, they can stumble upon dangerous things. There were 600 Moroccan prayer spaces in France, and there were only two state-paid Moroccan imams. Meanwhile, dozens of imams from Morocco were being hired by Saudi Arabia, Libya, and other countries.[76]

In the years leading up to the Molenbeek cell's attacks in Paris and Brussels, Belgian officials found that 15 percent of imams active in the country were itinerant, passing from one country to the next on tourist visas and thus completely unknown to them.[77] The creation of an al Qaeda affiliate calling itself Moroccan was especially galling (Groupe islamique combattant marocain, GICM). The terrorist group postured as Islamic warriors and set their sights, first, on reconquering the *reconquistas* in the Madrid bombings of March 11, 2003. In response to the Casablanca bombings and the murder of Theo van Gogh in the following year, the ambassador to Berlin said, "We were just shocked by the crimes being committed by those who did not know their own origins."[78]

Infrastructure

The Religious Affairs Ministry recognized the need for a European framework and became more engaged under a new minister. The Moroccan ambassador to Germany, Omer Zniber, summarized the approach to the European diaspora: Morocco aimed, he said, for "neither indifference nor interference."[79] Rabat lent a helping hand to mosques and associations starting in the late 1970s in the Netherlands and in the mid-1980s in France. For decades afterwards, it maintained ties with the major Moroccan-origin federation in each country (the Federación Española de Entidades Religiosas Islámicas in Spain, Rassemblement des musulmans de France in France, Associazione musulmani d'italia in Italy, and the Zentralrat der Marokkaner in Germany).[80] Starting in 2008, the Ministry of Habous received a budget of 12 million euros to support associations that proposed religious projects in Europe. This was supplemented by one-off special projects, such as the Grande Mosquée Mohammed VI de Saint-Étienne.[81] The Ministry of Habous and the Hassan II Foundation coordinated the European deployment of imams and private donations worth many millions more.[82] Benjamin Bruce reports that the Makhzen sent 25,000 Qur'ans to France in 2011 and arranged for the delivery of small gifts for prisoners.

Ambassador Zniber described diaspora outreach as "a colossal endeavor." In the first decade of the twenty-first century, the number of Moroccan general consulates in Europe tripled to more than sixty.[83]

Imams

During the missionary phase, there were two official sources of Moroccan-trained imams: the Ministry of Habous and the Hassan II Foundation. One official described a deficient selection process in preceding years: "We were sending ignoramuses."[84] The logic of recruitment changed from being based on patronage or seniority to cultivating promising candidates.[85] "We can only fight radicalism by proposing structured alternatives and proposing knowledge—we carefully choose the people we send." The Hassan II Foundation required a master's degree and language proficiency in the destination country. It was sending not just "clerics," according to a spokesperson, but "people who are open to a multitude of perspectives."[86] The adviser to the religious affairs minister said that: "RMF in France would contact us and say we need X number of imams for Y number of mosques. The COEM [Council of Moroccan Ulema in Europe] might then say they need 100 imams. On average, we send 250 to 300 every year to Europe, mostly for reciting the Qur'an during Ramadan."[87] Several years later, during Ramadan in 2015, a total of 514 preachers and imams were sent (217 of them to France).

In 2017, Morocco sent thirty imams to Spain plus an additional 300 preachers during the month of Ramadan.[88] There is plenty of room for growth—there are only 600 Moroccan mosques in France—but European host societies have mixed levels of enthusiasm for the solution.[89] The Dutch, for instance, have never been eager to revisit the agreement signed with Morocco to send an official delegation of thirty imams on four-year terms.

Education

Moroccan religious education has been described by native scholars as "an impenetrable citadel and permanent shelter for the construction of the Moroccan's very sense of self."[90] In 1990, the Hassan II Foundation exported the first Arabic language and Moroccan culture courses, taught by a delegation of 108 teachers.[91] Like Cardinal Bedini encountering the sorry state of Roman Catholic educational institutions and ignorance among the clergy in the United States in the 1850s, envoys were moved to action by what they encountered in Europe in the early 2000s. The former Moroccan ambassador to Spain described what he found during a visit to a mosque and cultural center that had requested embassy funding:

There we were in twenty-first-century Madrid, and there was one row of girls staring at the wall, and a separate row of boys who practiced writing the Qur'an on wooden planks. They didn't have regular notebooks, so they couldn't measure their own progress over time. I asked the teacher why, and he said that was how he had learned. *That* is what we want to change.[92]

Citing the approximately 75,000 students in Moroccan-sponsored Arabic courses across Europe (roughly 20 percent of their potential audience), ministry officials aimed to raise diaspora parents' awareness of the importance of teaching their children a religious and national identity.[93] Ahmed Abbadi, general secretary of the Mohameddiya League, said: "Our youth in Europe are being bombarded with information by the minute; they need to be trained, in terms of ethics and values, pragmatically. Who is going to define the spirit of Islam for centuries to come?"[94]

The Hassan II Foundation coordinates with the Moroccan education ministry to organize competitions and exams for Arabic language teachers being deployed to Europe; one official winked and referred to the "armada of 500 Arabic language teachers" sent across the Mediterranean. Several hundred additional teachers were sent by other ministries—including the ministries of higher education, training and research, and habous and Islamic affairs.[95] Nearly three decades after the 1994 agreement on the Program for Arab Language and Moroccan Culture to support extracurricular education in Spanish regions, Moroccan officials were still trying to implement it.[96]

Toward a Collegio System

The first steps away from a system of exported imams and toward a collegio system was to create a training cycle to prepare Moroccans from the community abroad to become imams and *mourchidates* (spiritual guides). In the early 2000s, agreements were signed between the ministries of education and Islamic affairs to "allow children of the Moroccan community abroad to study Muslim canon law" at the University of Rabat.[97] This initiative evolved into a major innovation: the Mohammed VI Institute for Imam Training, located on a large campus in the nation's capital. In March 2015, the institute opened its doors for the first 700 students from France and five countries in West Africa.[98] The director explained why students were separated by nationality: "Islam's strength is that it adapts to all eras and cultures. So the Institute's pedagogical approach is tailored to the expectations and hopes of each country. The Malians, the Ivorians, the Guineans or the French are not all living the same historical and cultural situations and they face different challenges."[99] At a meeting with the king in the summer of 2014, the RMF leader formally

FIGURE 8.9. French foreign affairs Minister Laurent Fabius and Moroccan Islamic affairs minister Ahmed Toufiq signing an imam exchange agreement in front of King Mohammed VI and President François Hollande (2015)

requested that places be reserved in the new institute. The first class from the "French College" had fifty students, all of whom were selected by the Union des Mosquées de France.[100] The agreement signed by the French foreign minister and the Moroccan minister of habous restricted enrollment to dual national Frenchmen of Moroccan origin (see figures 8.9 and 8.10). "We recruited bi-nationals to keep it simple," an official explained, and to avoid diplomatic incidents with countries that also had professional imam training.[101]

Toward the Tridentine Seminary

Speaking in Strasbourg in 2011, the French-Moroccan leader Abdellah Boussouf said: "We need European imams, French imams, Italian imams, Dutch imams, and we need training here in Europe and not over there."[102] Brussels was in fact the first choice for the Institut Mohammed VI, not Rabat. In an interview in Rabat with Ahmed Toufiq, the minister of Islamic affairs explained that at first "we discussed the possibility of creating a training center for imams in Brussels with [the French interior minister]—but one that would be for all of Europe. We want to help European Muslims escape the tunnels of virtual preaching online."[103] There is ongoing Moroccan cooperation with imam training programs at universities in Belgium, the Netherlands, and Germany, and exploration of the same in France (see figure 8.9).

A royal decree created another major Islamic institution in Brussels, the Council of Moroccan Ulema in Europe (COEM), legally incorporated in Belgium in 2009. Ahmed Abbadi, the general secretary of the Mohameddiya Foundation, said in an interview in Rabat that the COEM addresses a basic vacuum: "People need responses to concrete issues. French and German Moroccans teach us about context, and we teach them about text."[104] The group

FIGURE 8.10. French Imams studying at the Mohammed VI Institute meet with French senators in Rabat, Morocco (2016)

of theologians and imams within the COEM was the answer to the void that had favored the Islamist perspectives sponsored by the Gulf countries. Another COEM official in Brussels said in an interview that "the *Maliki* rite always takes the local situation into consideration, which is why the COEM, and not the Ulema Council in Morocco, will respond [to local questions]."[105] Officials described the ambition to have a common European policy in similar terms to the Turkish DİTİB, which had opened a Brussels headquarters several years earlier. Imams in Europe, in the words of one COEM member, "need a special jurisprudence that defines the relationship between institutions because legal decisions vary over time."[106] For example, earlier jurisprudence that ruled *against* Moroccans' naturalization in European countries or voting in European elections was reversed in the late 1990s. In 2011, the first Italian "synod" of Moroccan imams was convened in Rome: seventy-one imams arrived from the regions around Turin, Milan, Bologna, and Rome and "were presided over by the senior 'alim of Brussels, Tahir Tijkani."[107] Nonetheless, the COEM struggled to become a permanent installation.

Identity on Behalf of Integration

In the early 2000s, the government recruited Moroccan Europeans to return to help develop Moroccan administration, including that of Islam. Embassies were asked to provide lists of potential candidates for return. Six of the thirty-six members of the Consultative Council for Moroccans Residing Abroad

(CCME) were religious professionals: imams, theologians, and mosque administrators in Amsterdam, Rome, Madrid, and Frankfurt. The CCME's general secretary said in an interview that "Morocco refuses to interfere: these are federations made up of Moroccans but who act in a European context."[108] A ministry official in Rabat referred to the RMF leader in France as "a Moroccan from over there [France], not a Moroccan from here." He articulated this concrete distinction: "With respect to the Moroccans around the world who recognize the king as the Commander of the Faithful as a spiritual reference, obviously, we don't 'respect' national borders—just like the Dalai Lama for Buddhists or Rome for Catholics. But on the question of political sovereignty, our administration clearly stops at the border."[109] The director of a royal foundation said: "When we sent imams or teachers, some Europeans said we were trying to hold on to the umbilical cord, but if the community is well integrated, that is the best guarantee against any indoctrination—from the Moroccan state or otherwise."[110]

The MRE minister agreed, arguing in an interview that "when they know their identity, they integrate better. It helps salve the immigrant's inferiority complex."[111] Some scholars were chosen on the basis of their knowledge of local dialects and languages of communities abroad. In Ambassador Omar Azziman's view, "Islamic history should not be portrayed in pink, but gray, like in reality." And in order to do so, he said, "you have to be there—to give them a leader who can show how to work in new ways, because otherwise they will just reproduce what they know, fifty years later in the heart of Europe. That is why we send imams during Ramadan and organize talks that reinforce our legal school and views."[112]

Algeria in France and Europe

In the early twenty-first century, France was home to 2 million Algerians who shared an intimate colonial history. The direct sea link from Algiers to Marseille was easier than the path to many remote wilayas. The second generation of Algerian-French that emerged in the 1980s and 1990s experienced some outreach, but Algerian GDP and economic growth were less dependent on their own diaspora compared to Morocco and Turkey. With its gas and oil reserves, the Algerian economy had less need for the hard currency of workers' remittances from Europe and so did not engage for Moroccan or Turkish style outreach. With regard to Islamic leadership, moreover, Algeria started with the most meaningful home-court advantage outside Cordoba. The jewel of French Islam, the Grande Mosquée de Paris, was handed over to Algeria by the French government in 1981 as a sort of prefabricated Islamic archdiocese. But the diaspora was a politically sensitive domain after the Algerian government canceled elections won by Islamists in 1990; a civil war ensued, leading to the death of as many as 200,000.[113] The GMP received subsidies from the city of Paris, but its main support came from Algiers and international donors.

Algeria's successive nomination of *recteurs* of the Grande Mosquée who also held political roles in Algiers sparked an administrative showdown with the French interior ministry. An exchange of threats and promises was followed by the pioneering nomination of a French citizen—a medical doctor and religious scholar, Dalil Boubakeur—in 1992. This occurred decades ahead of other countries, which have still not "domesticated" their leadership. Boubakeur was considered a major improvement on the nuncios before him. During his more than twenty-five-year reign at the *Grande Mosquée*, the centerpiece of Algerian Islam abroad, the foreign ministry official responsible for Algerians abroad said in an interview, "The labor migrant who stayed in France remained attached to his faith, and the GMP shined its light across all French regions," inspiring Algerian Muslims in England and Germany to solicit similar federations and support.[114] Boubakeur's prominence accelerated the accommodation of certain aspects of French Muslims' religious lives.

At moments of political violence and uncertainty in the Muslim world— and among French Muslims—Boubakeur took on the role of a national archbishop, similar to James Gibbons amid the terror attacks stemming from "Catholic" Europe under the presidency of Theodore Roosevelt. Boubakeur reassured an anxious public about terrorism and religious diversity (see figure 8.11). Even when outpaced or outvoted by his ideological or ethnic-national rivals—in terms of mosques, imams, congregants, or delegate votes in the Council of the Muslim Faith (CFCM)—the rector of the GMP enjoyed the kind of treatment reserved for the Vatican envoy—that is, as unofficial dean of the Islamic corps. Under three successive presidents—Jacques Chirac, Nicolas Sarkozy, and François Hollande—Boubakeur was the go-to leader for symbolic functions, whether or not the GMP won CFCM elections. His reassuring qualities had historical roots—his father and grandfather held the same leading role at the GMP before him when the mosque was under French oversight. The GMP continued in this way even after the naturalization of Algerians in France, thanks to Boubakeur's French citizenship status and the confluence of French and Algerian interests in containing Islamist movements.[115]

But Algiers was also being cautious regarding the diaspora population, aware that dangers to its rule lurked within. As the French ambassador to Algiers said in an interview, "Algerians know better than anyone about the boomerang effect" from not properly screening imams.[116] Algeria extended the right to vote to Algerians abroad in 1995—the same year Armed Islamic Group (GIA) terrorists first targeted civilians in Paris—with eight parliamentarians representing them. The participation of 800,000 or so voters in France, out of

FIGURE 8.11. Dalil Boubakeur, recteur of the Grande Mosquée de Paris, with French president Jacques Chirac, Paris (2004)

an Algerian electorate of 21 million, provoked controversy during the campaign season. Algerian diplomats were scrutinized for their use of consular resources to combat abstention or prevent the Islamist penetration of the diaspora vote. The minister of religious affairs came to the Grande Mosque de Paris, where he told Algerian imams to use their Friday khutba before the April vote to "raise the awareness of Algerian voters" about the upcoming election.[117]

French interest in the development of Algerian Islam peaked during two waves of political violence. The first began with the 1994 Airbus hijacking and GIA bombings, and the second peaked with the shooting sprees and suicide attacks in the mid-2010s. Officials on both sides of the Mediterranean were keenly aware that some Algerian nationals figured among high-ranking Islamic State (ISIS) leaders, and that young men of Algerian descent committed murderous attacks in France and Belgium between 2012 and 2016.[118] The Algerian position was that the radicalization of young Frenchmen was a French problem, but they could not stand idly by. The Algerian religious affairs budget devoted an additional 4 million euros to religious associations abroad.[119] The Supreme Islamic Council (HCI) in Algiers established a national foundation for diaspora mosques and religious activities with the aim of providing neighborhood centers to teach Arabic and the Qur'an to the "children of the Algerian communities abroad." Its first cultural center was in Paris.[120]

Lingering in the "Propaganda Fide"?

Algerian authorities began transferring training and personnel to France, but these clerics continued to occupy an in-between space, with neither definitive rupture with the government in Algeria nor definitive acceptance by and institutional equality within the French republic. When the minister for religious affairs was asked to characterize his vision of Algerians abroad, his reply came without hesitation. "We need to pursue the Russian model. Muslims in Russia feel Russian; the only difference is their religion. There, you can be a useful citizen and a useful Muslim. I have always said to our community abroad: serve France in order to serve Algeria."[121]

In an interview at the foreign ministry office for Algeria's diaspora, an ambassador explained that it took time "to shift mentalities from one in which 'Algerians had only left temporarily' to the reality, thirty or forty years later, of a significant Algerian population permanently abroad." He continued, "We decided to consider them part of the 'national community' and not the diaspora. There are many success stories in politics and the society of elites in Europe, and we want to include them in our work." He described how to reach them with positive messages about Algeria: "We try to get to young people with activities during the summertime rush, June through September, and on religious holidays when many Algerian nationals return."[122]

The Algerian minister of Islamic affairs, Bouabdellah Ghlamallah (1997–2014), said in an interview: "We don't try to impose or dictate our views elsewhere, nor do we allow others to do that. We do not want Shi'ites and Wahhabis influencing our religious life."[123] Ironically, Algeria intervened abroad to preserve the principle of *non*-intervention in others' internal affairs. "We have an expression," one ministry official said, referring to the ferries in port waiting to depart for France, "that Marseille is the forty-ninth wilayat."[124] The diaspora's impact was always felt internally—Algerian imams were explicitly prohibited from engaging with trade unions or French politics in general. Ghlamallah expressed dismay at the spread of politicized religion by others, which had led, he said, to the bizarre phenomenon of "fanatical European women converts who wear the *niqab* claiming they are the real Muslims and saying that we're fake ones!"[125]

Regarding Algerian outreach to the estimated 20 percent of French prayer spaces in their network, Ghlamallah explained: "We try to do everything in coordination with the Grande Mosquée."[126] Algeria's eighteen consulates form

FIGURE 8.12. Dalil Boubakeur with Mohammed Aïssa,
Algerian Minister of Religious Affairs, Paris (2015)

the largest diplomatic network in France and continues to grow.[127] A summit
of general consuls in 2014 announced the "intensification and reinforcement
[of] cooperation between the Grande Mosquée and the Algerian civil society
organizations that administer prayer spaces in France." When Ghlamallah's
successor, Minister Mohammed Aïssa (2014–2019), convened imams about to
leave for France in 2015, he stressed "the necessity to consolidate the Muslim
religion amongst our 2.1 million strong *émigré* community, and to preserve the
national reference in this domain."[128] The religious affairs ministry announced
an agreement "to update (*assainir*) the *Grande Mosquée*'s administrative status"
by turning Muslim sites on French territory into waqfs under his ministry's
oversight. *El Moudjahid* reported that "an Algerian association will be created
to register all mosques established and built by members of the Algerian community abroad in order to 'legally preserve them and prohibit selling them or
deviating from their mission.'"[129] There was a side benefit too: Minister Aïssa
predicted that Algerian imams in France would "contribute to the *Accalmie*"—
an atmosphere of calm—and noted that the number of French converts to
Islam had doubled from the previous year.[130]

Since the appointment of Dalil Boubakeur to lead the Grand Mosquée of
Paris, Algerian Islam policies have scarcely run afoul of the official religious-
political line in France. Interior ministers have raised or lowered the GMP's
profile over the years, depending on the consultation strategy vis-à-vis Moroccan

and Turkish mosque federations, as well as those representing Islamist and other nonstate movements.[131] Boubakeur reassured the public by denouncing what he called *Islam des excités* after 9/11. A decade later, however, he caused a stir when he remarked that France needed more Islamic prayer spaces, and he aggravated some by suggesting that empty churches be used for the purpose. The bottom line was that Algerian officials claimed jurisdiction purely in the realm of "spiritual" influence—*religious* affairs were administered by an entirely separate ministry from *diaspora* affairs—although this was not easy to distinguish from the outside. The appearance was a hard sell: the same consular network that endeavored to protect Algerian Islam used the same mosques to mobilize some of the same people to vote in Algerian elections. That was less striking in the case of Roman Catholicism because the questions of permanence as a minority had been resolved. Nonetheless, Algerian officials did not see themselves as trying to influence French Muslims within the *French* political system—except positively, by helping them integrate.

Algerian consular authorities progressively delegated administrative oversight of these imam–civil servants to the recteur of the Grande Mosquée. But it would not be the Algerian imams in France who elected the next recteur, just as Irish priests in the United States had no say in who their bishops were until 1908, when the diaspora exited the Propaganda Fide and was no longer considered a "missionary" community. Boubakeur's successor was chosen, officials said, in a selection process overseen by the religious affairs ministry in "close cooperation" with the Algerian interior ministry and the French embassy to identify "the most adept candidate." There was a stubborn reluctance to spin off the religious institutions and relinquish control to local proxies when only a fraction of imams in France had formal training.

Imams

In 1995, the French interior ministry encouraged the Al-Ghazali Institute in Paris to explore "in-house training" so as to phase out the importation of imams.[132] The method of providing imams partially evolved from wholesale importation into a collegio model to a Tridentine seminary model (building local seminaries in Europe). "European Islam is barely in its third or fourth generation, so there is no established model yet," the minister explained. "But we have been pursuing the Russian model there to set up institutions for training imams that work."[133]

The Al-Ghazali Institute became operational but was unable to provide training from the ground up so long as neither Algiers nor Paris accredited it to provide a complete course of study. It remained limited to an "arrival seminar" to be taken only after two or more years of theological studies—under

FIGURE 8.13. The Al-Ghazali Institute recruitment stand at the annual Bourget conference for French Muslims (2018)

the watchful eye of an inspector general detailed from Algiers.[134] In the meanwhile, the French asked Algerians to identify candidates sufficiently in advance and to commit to their continuing education during their service in France.

The Import Model

A contingent of 120 Algerian imams serve abroad in four-year rotations, with thirty departing annually.[135] In some years, the group is larger: in 2010, the ministry sent fifty-two imams and an unspecified number of (female) mourchidates on missions of "orientation, education and culture."[136] Another 100 imams, religion teachers, and Qur'an reciters serve during Ramadan each year.[137] The ministry also sends speakers to visit communities in Europe year-round.

Ghlamallah noted that the French interior ministry requested more Francophone imams, to expand upon the existing agreement.[138] Beginning in 2011, a predeparture training course was coordinated between the Algerian Ministry for Religious Affairs and the French embassy: "First, they improve their French language skills with an intensive course at one of the Algeria's five instituts

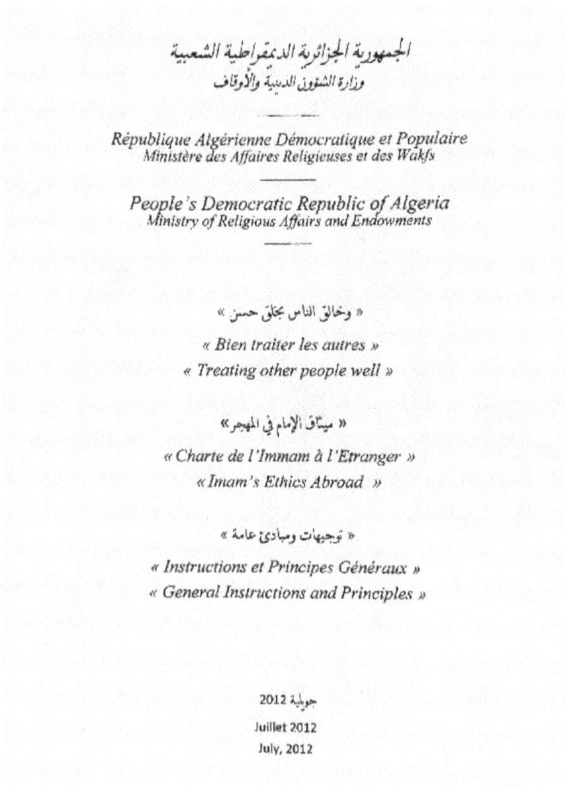

الجمهورية الجزائرية الديمقراطية الشعبية
وزارة الشؤون الدينية والأوقاف

République Algérienne Démocratique et Populaire
Ministère des Affaires Religieuses et des Wakfs

People's Democratic Republic of Algeria
Ministry of Religious Affairs and Endowments

« وخالق الناس بخلق حسن »

« *Bien traiter les autres* »

« *Treating other people well* »

« ميثاق الإمام في المهجر »

« *Charte de l'Immam à l'Etranger* »

« *Imam's Ethics Abroad* »

« توجيهات ومبادئ عامة »

« *Instructions et Principes Généraux* »

« *General Instructions and Principles* »

جويلية 2012

Juillet 2012

July, 2012

FIGURE 8.14. Cover of guide for imams abroad, Algiers (2012)

français," the French ambassador explained in an interview.[139] "Europe needs Algerian imams, and European citizens have confidence in our imams," the minister of religious affairs told a 2014 management seminar for religious affairs directors, announcing new programming and one-year language courses. "We will train imams and teach them the languages they need to work in Europe. They are known for their moderation and for carrying with them an authentic Islam where religion is attached to the nation."[140]

The director general of the national community abroad said, "On the religious front, with the aid of the Grande Mosquée de Paris, the imams who leave for France are well-trained and are increasingly bilingual."[141] After arrival, they have "continuing professional education" and complete their training at the Al-Ghazali Institute at the GMP to improve their French language skills, learn about French law, and become familiar with the secular (*laïc*) nature of the French republic (see figure 8.14).[142] However, a senior official who covered North Africa at the foreign affairs ministry in Paris said that the "training program for the imam delegations has been a failure from the French perspective" because of insufficient predeparture language training. "We really need to improve language abilities by promoting more intensive French courses" that will "complement the existing 'civilizational' introduction of one week."[143]

French authorities encouraged the development of twelve regional dar al imam—Algerian religious seminaries where imams can fulfill part of the prerequisites for service in France. "Algerian imams receive extra training because they are serving a community that is not rooted in the national administrative and political system."[144] Algeria encountered the same built-in problem to the import system as other sending countries: by limiting imams to a single, nonrenewable four-year term, they exposed themselves to criticism that a constantly renewing foreign corps of imams was unlikely to be able to help others with "integration" issues. A group of French mayors addressed a letter to the Algerian minister of religious affairs requesting that he extend the terms, to which Ghlamallah replied: "We see the service in Europe as a temporary rotation. The imams are there to *serve* the immigrants, not to *become* immigrants."[145] The ministry published a "Charter for Imams Abroad"—a kind of Baltimore Catechism—that encouraged inclusive attitudes toward fellow Muslims and reminded imams of the "rights of other people and their feelings."[146] The charter stated that shari'ah preserved the principles of "democracy, coexistence and tolerance" and called for acting "within respect of other people's opinions." It further explains that "Islam calls for integration in society while preserving the cultural identity and religious specificity," while cautioning that "Muslims are called to protect mosques from distortion that might affect its holiness or derail it from its religious and social path" (see figure 8.15).

From a Collegio Model to a Diocesan Seminary?

There has been an attempt to transition to a collegio model in which French citizens would come to Algeria for several years of training before returning for service in France. An agreement based on a French interior ministry proposal to explore the possibility of a one- to two-year study cycle in Algeria for French students to attend the Université Abdel-Kader was proposed in June 2013.[147] The religious affairs minister said in an interview: "I proposed to the French, on numerous occasions, [that they] send us the young Franco-Algerians, and we will give them the training here that you don't have available there: a two-year program. We offered them funded spots for French students in our institutions, but they have not accepted it yet."[148] The Ministry of Religious Affairs announced a new doctoral program and a new faculty for imams along with six new planned training institutes, in addition to the sixteen existing institutes.[149] He also suggested that Algeria was prepared to skip the collegio

FIGURE 8.15. Ayman Mazyek, chairman of the Central Council of Muslims in Germany, with Chancellor Angela Merkel and President Joachim Gauck (2015)

step: "The invitations still stand, but it would be preferable to do it in France." Al-Ghazali's diplomas were not officially recognized by French universities for over twenty years, and enrollment grew only modestly—imam and chaplaincy training classes in Paris's Fifth Arrondissement consisted of around forty students.

In late 2014, the French interior ministry signed a cooperation agreement with Al-Ghazali and ten French universities—"requested by Algeria to help fight Islamic radicalization." "The times have changed," Interior Minister Cazeneuve told *Le Figaro* newspaper during his visit to Algiers to discuss the accord. "France is not saying what the theological training should be," an adviser added. "France is going along with a holistic strategy to strengthen the general preparation of imams."[150] The Ministry of Religious Affairs and the Grande Mosquée promoted Al-Ghazali in order to achieve recognition by the Sorbonne.[151] To attract the best theologians, preachers, and teachers, they announced that henceforth Algerian mosques in France would include housing for imams and teachers.[152]

In an indication that this had been a subject of discussion between the Grande Mosquée and the Ministry of Religious Affairs, the longtime legal counsel (and new Rector) of the GMP, Chems-Eddine Hafiz, said: "The French government needs imams who truly master theology. There should be a real competition to become an imam. *I have been trying for years to place more training centers in France.* . . . A religious voice is necessary in any counter-jihad plan."[153] This is a reminder that the most effective movement against foreign priests in the United States did not come from "secularists" but from American bishops defending their turf and fighting for independence. The federation leaders claim that decisions are made independently. But they are still net recipients of Islamic solidarity, not funders of it, and the power to hire, fire, approve curriculum, and so on, still resides abroad.

At the January 2015 graduation ceremony for the imams leaving to serve the Algerian diaspora, the religious affairs minister charged them with "protecting Algerian Islam from the destructive ideas that are ruining the image of Islam in the West."[154] Bidding them farewell from Algiers, he expressed hope that "Algerian imams who serve in the GMP mosques will immunize our national community abroad, and brush away all of the dirt and dust to reveal the true face of Islam." Four days later, as the imams settled in Paris, two brothers—the radicalized, orphaned sons of an Algerian couple who moved to France in the 1970s—stormed the offices of the satirical newspaper *Charlie Hebdo* and unleashed a hail of bullets with Kalashnikov rifles, killing twelve journalists and editors, they said, for having blasphemed the Prophet Muhammed. The brothers had slim chances during their French upbringing of receiving substantial religious education or of encountering trained religious professionals, let alone an Algerian imam—the ratio of imams to Muslims of Algerian background is around 100 times smaller in France than in Algeria. The Al Ghazali Institute of the Grande Mosquée de Paris announced a three-year training program in three national annexes (Lille, Marseille, and Les Mureaux), starting in 2020.[155] Nearly two centuries after the first French naval vessel disembarked at the port of Algiers, Algerian Islam is still circling France, waiting for permission to land.

Tunisia in Europe

Tunisian migration to Europe has always been on a different scale than the other national groups: there were around 1 million Tunisians in Europe (75 percent of them residing in France) at the time of the Jasmine Revolution (2011). Morocco and Algeria had a population of 10 million to 12 million in 1960, whereas Tunisia had only around 4 million. While each of these three states more than tripled in size, Tunisian presidents pursued progressive education and family policies that reduced pressure on the job market and led to less labor migration.[156] Tunisians abroad therefore represented a relatively large proportion of the country's small population of 11 million in 2011.

Using a nonviolent coup to take power in 1988, Zinedine Ben Ali affirmed that "it is the State alone" that could organize the practice of Islam.[157] As he sought to rationalize Islamic education and Qur'anic recitation, the religious affairs Minister dispatched a delegation of imams, preachers, and teachers to give lectures and religious courses in Europe. The minister urged them to preach "moderation, tolerance and the principles of dialogue and peaceful cohabitation which are among the main specificities of the Islamic religion."[158]

The main reason for intervention abroad was that the regimes of Bourguiba and Ben Ali each ordered thousands of arrests in the Islamist milieux, creating a stream of ideological exiles fleeing the country. They were not all firebrand preachers: many were intellectuals who earnestly sought to reconcile Islam and democracy. They kept Tunisian Islamism alive while repression reigned at home. When asked about the Tunisian suicide bomber in Djerba (2013), Tunisian officials "hastened to point out that the bomber had spent several years" in Europe.[159]

The engagement of the diaspora was taking place at the same time that Italy's young Muslim federation hosted Rachid al Ghannouchi's first visit within a year of the January 2011 revolution.[160] By the time of the presidential and parliamentary elections in 2012 and 2014, Ghannouchi had expanded his campaigning to include Spain and France. In all, seven Tunisian party leaders campaigned in France in 2011. Of the 400,000 Tunisian voters allowed to vote at French sites in 2011, more than one-third chose Ennahda.[161] In an interview, the Tunisian president, Moncef Marzouki, formerly exiled in Paris, explained that during the transition period "I do not give much thought to Tunisians abroad—that's not a priority for us. The situation is extremely difficult right here. We have political, economic, and security crises."[162] He had one eye on the television in his office: Islamist fighters had just taken over the airport in Tripoli. There was a huge difference in the scale of the problem that Tunisia faced—tens of thousands of potential ISIS recruits—compared with a handful of Euro-Tunisian terrorists. Tunisia was fighting an active, small-scale resistance within its borders: in the previous two years, the country had sustained raids on the interior ministry and a presidential convoy, as well as assassinations of major political figures; in the year that followed, there were two paramilitary attacks on civilians—one at a museum and one at a beach resort.

The minister of religious affairs said in a 2014 interview that "we don't have the means to build mosques right now, but we try to send preachers during holidays—for the second and third generation abroad."[163] Tunisians stood out on account of their disproportionate involvement with the Islamic State, including the rejected asylum seeker who hijacked a truck and killed twelve in central Berlin, and a refugee who murdered three churchgoers in in Nice in 2020. In May 2017, the new minister of religious affairs, Ahmed Adhoum, had contacted fifteen Islamic centers in European countries to offer preachers and imams during Ramadan.[164] The minister said that religious affairs attachés would "fill the gaps in religious communication with Tunisian residents abroad. We need to break with the traditional religious discourse towards our citizens abroad and revive the spirit of exegesis (ijtihad) that is necessary to equip and arm young generations against extremist thought and radicalization."[165]

Conclusion: Islam in Europe or European Islam?

In an interview, the Turkish ambassador to Germany, himself the son of a dual national, proudly quoted the Turkish president Recep Tayyip Erdoğan: "Turkey is no longer a country that doesn't take care of its emigrés."[166] Some of his fellow Turkish-Germans, however, wanted to be free of any foreign government's attention. Increasingly, parliamentary representatives in European countries with large Muslim minorities began to push for detachment.

European governments justified their rejection of foreign offerings with the refrain that Sunni Islam is not hierarchically organized and has no clergy. Islam has had no preeminent clergy since the end of the caliphate, but it does have the national clergies of the states that followed. Nonetheless, nonhierarchical religions like Protestantism (1905) and Judaism (1807) were accommodated and fit into the structures of the republic. As one of President Emmanuel Macron's future ministers wrote in 2016, "We must impose a Concordat-like set of rules . . . and cut all religious ties with foreign countries."[167]

Whereas Europeans feared Islamization, the majority-Muslim countries additionally feared dilution. The Moroccan minister recounted that the "French government ministers told us, 'Don't interfere,' to which I replied: 'Are you happy with the current state of things? *Vive la laïcité* and all the rest, but religion is still there.'"[168] The Algerian minister of religious affairs recalled "being told in the late 1990s that they wanted an 'Islam *de* France,' and I told them then, as I tell them now, that Islam is Islam."[169] The leader of a major Turkish-Germany federation, the Islamrat, said, "It's an open secret that the authorities here want a Euro-Islam, an easy-care Islam."[170] When the Diyanet president was asked in an interview whether there could be such a thing as "Euro-Islam," his answer was unequivocal: "No. Islam is Islam. Its sources are Qur'an and the sunna." Nevertheless, "when times change," he continued, "religious interpretations also change."[171]

In reality, none of the governments had an interest in selflessly promoting European or French Islam alone. The centers of Islamic religious authority aimed to cultivate, administer, and preserve ties with their followers after losing direct political power over them. They had religious rites to preserve— within Algerian Islam, Moroccan Islam, Turkish Islam, and so on—and governments sought legitimate viaducts to convey their national spiritual services abroad. Their national brands were already difficult to protect on a global marketplace, and their international religious outreach expanded well beyond Europe.

The extent to which foreign governments remained involved in the religious lives of their former citizens and diasporas reflects the unsatisfactory efforts to fill this vacuum of religious services for citizens and their descendants. The former sending countries' experience administering religious life—with considerably greater state resources for religious affairs spending at their disposal—made a good match for European countries where Muslims lacked the funds and states lacked the legal mechanisms to build their own. The imams arriving from Morocco, Algeria, and Turkey in the 2010s hoped to bring order to a situation that had veered dangerously out of control.

Decades after acknowledging Muslims' permanent presence, European governments still entertained the enduring ideal of a liberal Euro-Islam in their own image—for example, the Polder Mosque in the Netherlands, or the egalitarian mosque in Berlin. But they fetishized the notion of "Euro-Islam" at their own risk, since it required managing the political paradoxes of diverse societies and adjusting to new realities elsewhere. As the minister for MREs said in an interview: "We know that this Facebooking and Twittering generation can easily take on more than one identity—two, three, even four. . . . Tens of thousands of Moroccans take on European citizenships every year."[172] It is what Bernard Lewis argued was already under way in 1990, when he observed that immigrants in Europe were "bound by a thousand ties to their country of origin [and yet] inexorably . . . integrating."[173]

Given the high stakes for countries of origin and host societies, it was surprising that there were not more trained religious personnel in circulation. When the ministers of religious affairs were queried as to why the numbers of religiously qualified staff in European host societies were so paltry, they responded with mirthless smiles. Ahmed Toufiq, the Moroccan minister of Islamic affairs and habous (2004–), said that "in Europe they won't let us send any more imams than we already do. I asked!"[174] Similarly, the education ministry official in Ankara said, "It is not nearly enough. We would send 10,000 teachers if they permitted it."[175] The notion that the better acquainted one is with one's cultural roots the more immunized one is against transnational Islamist movements was a point consistently made by Moroccan and Turkish officials but frequently lost on their Dutch and German counterparts.

The French government authorized young men to be "trained in those countries that fight against jihadi terrorism" so long as they fulfilled a series of specific requirements: being Francophone, obtaining a diploma in legal and civic education from one of twelve French universities, and holding a degree in Islamic studies.[176] Even Marine Le Pen, heiress to the Front National franchise and a critic of foreign influence upon French Islam, paid a campaign visit to the sheikh of Al-Azhar in Cairo after the *Charlie Hebdo* massacre in 2015—not to a Muslim leader in France.[177]

Islam Councils (1990–2020)

In order to integrate Muslims as individual *citizens*, regardless of religious belief or practice, governments have convened summits of community leaders. Simultaneously, interior ministries in Europe have fast-tracked the development of indigenous, Europe-based Islamic institutions—even while foreign governments continue to dominate state-Islam forums and are invited to send more imams and religious envoys. Anouar Kbibeche, who became CFCM president in the tumultuous mid-2010s, observed simply that "no cases of radicalization have taken place in a mosque."[178] A former interior minister in Berlin agreed; in a report, he wrote: "Radicalization takes place outside of Mosques at special meeting places, in prisons and through virtual contact," he said, as more and more citizens lived out of the reach of the "religious capital cities" of Sunni Islam.[179] In Germany, Islamic extremists were not known to frequent DİTİB mosques.[180] As the Salafi strain of Sunni Islam grew in popularity among tens of thousands of young European Muslims, governments enhanced dialogue platforms with Muslim leaders of civic and religious organizations.

Sponsored integration courses for religious professionals proliferated, and dozens of imams, civil servants, and teachers graduated annually from multiple programs in Paris, Strasbourg, Aix-en-Provence, and Lyon. In 2015, all 1,800 imams in France were assigned an obligatory educational program of 130 hours of classes over one year.[181] The government invested another 1.5 million euros in sundry imam-integration projects.[182] Some of the young imams trained in France were offered contracts by their country of origin, "which may reassure French mosques but does not remove any of the implicit dependence."[183] The leader of the Institute for European Human Sciences, one of the few places in France that trains imams, said that when CFCM and CRCM elections are held, "it is clear that mosque leaders vote according to the nationality of the imam whom they invite."[184]

Rejecting the Foreign Funding of Islam (2015–2020)

The scale and intensity of the religious outreach from the countries of origin led some European states to repudiate the religious offerings of foreign governments entirely.[185] The 2015–2016 terror attacks in the United Kingdom, Belgium, Germany, France, and Spain pushed some already skeptical parliaments in Austria, Norway, and France to reject foreign funding of Islam. Legislation was passed to block the transnational economy of foreign imams—partly out of fear of their own vulnerability to right-wing populism. A Dutch parliamentary inquiry demanded to know "why are any Imams whatsoever being imported?"[186] These efforts were a reprise of the period from 1875 to 1925 when European empires governed most of the world's Muslims and severed ties to the Ottoman Empire in order to substitute their own preferred religious hierarchy. A 2015 law regarding Islam in Austria directly echoes the creation of the Independent Islamic Community of Austria (iGGÖ) following Vienna's annexation of Bosnia-Herzegovina one century earlier. On both occasions, Austria intended to cut off Turkey's influence over its Muslims, first from Istanbul and then from Ankara. Since these countries lacked adequate religious infrastructure, they willingly leapt into the dark, trusting that somehow a Muslim corps of religious leadership would emerge. (Belgium and Austria had administrative regimes that allowed for the public financing of religious communities.) In the twenty-first century, it was not Saudi Arabia lurking beyond the vacuum but, for example, al Qaeda and the Islamic State, as well as their virtual social media universe. The first director of Fondation pour l'Islam de France (2017) had a starting fund of 5 million euros to pursue "the goal of helping French Islam become autonomous, in funding and in its approach" to religion. "The Islamic State's strategists do not hide that they want to throw our country into civil war," he said.[187]

Despite calls at the highest levels of the German government for Turkey to relinquish control over the country's 1,000 mosques and imams, Berlin and Ankara still cooperated on a technical level to ensure that imams and teachers arrived to staff language classes and carry out religious duties. Moreover, in the years following the Austrian *Islamgesetz (Islam law)*, Turkish officials said in an interview, Austria still received imams from the German branch of DİTİB.[188] In reality, there were a few training programs for Islamic professionals in Europe—a hodgepodge of taxpayer-sponsored programs and private initiatives in public universities. Islamic schools or seminaries were still rare in the early twenty-first century in Europe. Only the United Kingdom had a significant number of them.[189] One of the very few Islamic secondary schools in France was on the island of Réunion in the Indian Ocean; others included the Averroes in Lille (2003), al Kindi in Lyon (2006), and La Réussite in Seine-Saint-Denis (2001). At the lower levels, France's Islamic education system developed relatively quickly. France's inventory went from twenty Muslim educational institutions in 2009—crèches and primary and secondary schools—to thirty-one in 2010, forty in 2013, and sixty-three in 2015.[190] In the Netherlands, the number of Islamic educational establishments grew from two in 1988 to six in 1989, to thirteen in 1990, to forty-eight in 2015. Around two dozen Turkish mosques received permission to create extracurricular boarding schools in France and Germany. Three EU countries now teach Islamic religion—theological courses, not the history of religion—in public school; Austria has 350 such teachers, and Belgium and Spain have around 150 together.[191]

The German states avoided having separate confessional schools but opened their public schools to Islam by offering religion classes on an equal basis to the other recognized communities.[192] This has been institutionalized on the *Land*-level in eleven out of seventeen states—all of which have a substantial Muslim minority.[193] An increasing share of the nearly 1 million school-age children of Muslim origin in schools across the country will have the option of state-sanctioned weekly religious education in public schools just like the other recognized faith communities.[194] Federal authorities announced a new *Islamkolleg* (2020) in Osnabrück, a publicly funded Islamic college to reduce dependence on foreign-trained imams. The DİTİB announced the creation of its own training academy in Dahlem, a two-year program that will graduate thirty imams per year, and a handful of other smaller initiatives.[195]

To achieve autonomy as a national branch—if Islamic education was to be a tub that stood on its own bottom—the training of imams, teachers, children, and students of the community had to be subsidized. To reduce reliance on foreign powers to pay salaries and costs, plans that had been set aside for decades were dusted off, for example, collecting taxes on halal meat and other Islamic services, such as pilgrimage (hajj) or burial.[196]

Obstacles to a Historic Settlement

The absence of a single unifying institution within international Islam—a role honed by the papacy at the height of Catholic migration in the late nineteenth and early twentieth centuries—is inconvenient for state-Islam relations but not the end of the story. There could always be multiple agreements with different religious authorities and international religious NGOs. Other religious communities did not have their ideological networks scrutinized, as has happened with Islamic associations' trustees, or faced a demand that they form an *Einheitsgemeinde* (a single, united community) and prove their democratic representativeness. After all, most European citizens do not recognize any spiritual authority of the pope, because they are Protestant or Orthodox Jewish or atheist, even as milestones in the relationship between the state and the Catholic Church remain significant for the many who do. The recognition of multiple Christian denominations has been the price of peace since the seventeenth century.

The early communities struggled to detach themselves administratively but made symbolic efforts to fit in. Local church architects were hired to build landmark mosques that departed radically from their donors' usual styles.

Take the case of three large-scale projects undertaken by Saudi Arabia, Morocco, and Turkey, respectively: Paolo Portoghesi's Moschea di Roma (1995) opens onto a spacious cobblestone piazza with loggias, a sleek cascading staircase, and a large fountain, its low profile blending into the Roman hills; Portoghesi's Mosquée de Strasbourg (2009) looks like a planetarium ready for liftoff; and the German architect Paul Böhm's Kölner Moschee (2014) resembles a sleek modern art museum (see figure 8.16).

Despite such superficial concessions, there was ever greater discomfort in European capitals with homeland Islam.[197] The countries of origin stayed involved because their national politics were still impacted by their citizens' religious and political lives abroad. While providing religious assistance, consulates were keeping tabs on Islamist and autonomist networks, from Kurdish groups from southeast Turkey to Polisario supporters from western Sahara. Numerous misunderstandings have ensued between the former sending states and the host societies. Morocco moved to defend its cultural, linguistic, and religious traditions by creating centers for Moroccan culture in major MRE cities in the early 2010s. European governments, however, took these projects as proof of Morocco's intentions to stymie local integration efforts. The deputy minister for MREs wearily related the Europeans' stonewalling of his repeated pleas to promote what they considered to be a troublesome "culture of origin," delaying necessary permits and circumscribing activities. A European ambassador in Rabat recounted the reaction: "Everyone took a deep breath—this again? Why is there this primordial desire for them to stay Moroccan, all the way to the eighth generation, in, I don't know, Stockholm?"[198] Back in Morocco, Ambassador Azziman explained how he illustrated the case for his European interlocutors: "I tell them that we fell behind on religious questions. As a result, Moroccans were trained and taught by other movements. Then we were struck by the attacks in Casablanca—by a Salafi who came from Europe, not from Morocco!"[199] Basic miscommunication about this mission of cultural inoculation led, for instance, to Moroccan religious affairs advisers being expelled from Spain for unauthorized spying activity. Just as Turkey's consular network had previously been used against the AKP's ideological forebears (for example, the Milli Görüs movement) to try to prevent their legitimation in Europe, 2016–2017 saw the systematic use of the Diyanet and consular networks in Europe to track Gülenists. Turkish attachés were expelled from Belgium, the Netherlands, and Germany.[200]

Lateran Accords, Islamic style

Notwithstanding the proliferation of minor bilateral accords, there have been no formal treaties with foreign Islamic authorities wherein they renounce political claims on diaspora and the state reciprocally recognizes the spiritual

FIGURE 8.16 [TRIPTYCH OF 8.16.1, 8.16.2, AND 8.16.3]. The grand mosques of
Rome (1974), Strasbourg (2009) and Cologne (2014)

sovereignty of the holy leadership. There was a flurry of recognition and coordination to formalize the state-Islam relationship in the decade following 9/11, to shield European Muslims from religious ideologies emanating from the Gulf region. But European countries did little else to facilitate Muslims' religious lives or to integrate them into existing state-church structures. The whole process of consultation has been overshadowed by a deep-rooted suspicion of the religious services offered by national governments in the countries of origin, depriving young Muslims of legitimate Islamic arguments that they could wield against extremist ideas.

In the absence of a caliphate, the de facto transnational leadership fell to the Custodian of the Two Holy Mosques. For European Muslims, as for Sunnis worldwide, it was impossible to avoid the radiating influence of Saudi Arabia—a bottomless source of free Qur'ans, imams, and monumental mosques named after members of the Saud dynasty. But Saudi Arabia could not claim to speak on behalf of most Muslims—it was too strict for some and not strict enough for a small but perseverant few. Within a few years of the appearance of Muslim settlements in western Europe, the Mecca-based Rabita (Muslim World League) opened offices "for the propagation of the faith" in the outskirts of Brussels, Vienna, London, Paris, and Rome. Pan-Islamist Wahhabism and the Muslim World League poured tens of millions of dollars annually into the construction of mosques in Europe and were the first official Islamic interlocutors in Belgium, Spain, and Italy.[201] The Rabita's general secretary, always a highly placed Saudi prince, visited the missionary territory—Spain, Belgium, France—on annual ceremonial visits. In Jeddah, a university faculty dedicated to the study of Muslim minorities fed its own research into policy recommendations for the budding non-caliphate.

Nonetheless, the legitimacy of Saudi custodianship was undermined in the eyes of Islamic purists (*takfiri*), who objected to their toleration of the Shi'a minority and the US military presence in Saudi Arabia after the 1990 Gulf War, among other issues. Saudi hegemony ended after 9/11 when it lost the confidence of its Western interlocutors and its international charities were closed or restricted. Other religious centers were preparing their own transition to local operations. Also streaming into the vacuum, to counter the political Islamists, were the several key players of Nation-State Islams. As the Muslim World League secretary general's visits decreased, those of the Diyanet president and ministers of Islamic affairs in Algeria and Morocco increased. This undercut the image of independence but was part of the transition to symbolic religious jurisdiction: the Moroccan king was a holy figure, as well as Commander of the Faithful for Maliki Muslims in Africa and Europe, not just *intra muros*. That was the recognition sought by the countries of origin: spiritual power divorced from temporal political claims.

The vacuum allowed for the spread of politicized Islamic religious education and prayer leadership and ultimately created the conditions for political violence to ferment. European countries were attacked by the same networks that threatened regime stability and security in Algeria, Morocco, and Tunisia. The vice president of the Hassan II Foundation said in an interview in Rabat: "Some countries are very sensitive and keep asking us, 'Why do you send us chaplains? Why are you sending us imams?' We explain that we are above all trying to protect the community. We say that if you are able to protect them, go ahead and we will withdraw. But if you cannot, it is not a good idea to let nature take its course because the risks are enormous. Someone needs to protect them."[202] Diplomats in European embassies in Ankara and Rabat embraced policy solutions that gave more space to their influence. As one official said in an interview, "We must be realistic: maybe the mythology of assimilation in Europe is taking a hit, but I prefer to have Moroccans in Europe who return to Islam within a framework established in cooperation with Morocco than to rest on grand principles and let all of those people go off the rails."[203]

There was increasing recognition that the constituents of foreign religious authorities included a diaspora of citizens and their descendants. Institutional solutions were beginning to take shape for them, marking the passage towards European *Islams*. The spiritual realm of the modern Muslim state included an extraterritorial piece comprising millions of citizens of the EU abroad. This hastened the articulation of the transition of Europe's status from dar al harb to dar al Islam. Such views were far from unanimous. As an adviser to the Moroccan minister for Islamic affairs said in an interview, some European partners "seemed to have always had a problem with us and think we have a hegemonic agenda. But for us, religious action is spiritual, not political."[204] For the religious centers of authority, cultivating, administering, and then maintaining ties after the loss of temporal power required that the future religious capitals—Moroccan, Turkish, Algerian—resemble Rome, Copenhagen, Canterbury, Wittenberg, Lorde, or Regensburg today, with multiple, overlapping spheres of influence within a global community.

9

Nation-State Islam versus the Islamic State

ON THE FOURTH DAY of Ramadan in the Islamic year 1435 (July 2014), a former US prisoner of war and recent theology doctoral student at Saddam University strode up to the *minbar* (pulpit) of the medieval Great Mosque of al Nuri in Mosul, Iraq's second-largest city. A crisp online video documented the man in Abbasid-black robes calling upon Muslims to make *hijra*—return migration—to the new Islamic State. Barring that, he exhorted them to wage violent jihad upon infidels wherever possible. He spoke with the authority of a quadruple-barrel name of Salafi and Prophetic pedigree—Abu Bakr al Baghdadi al Husayni al Qureyshi—and declared war on the postcolonial borders of the greater Muslim world. Like Martin Luther 500 years earlier, he articulated grievances with a corrupt religious hierarchy. "Your rulers," he intoned, using Saudi Arabia as a stand-in for the Sunni world, were complicit with the "plots and schemes" of infidels to further carve up the map and "remove Allah's rule from this earth."[1]

In addition to broadcasting gruesome online executions of locals and foreigners as part of the Islamic State's holy war, its well-funded leaders stood up a functional bureaucracy and minted license plates and its own currency. An unofficial map purporting to show the designs of the coming caliphate circulated widely online, another act of provocation toward national sovereigns across the Middle East and North Africa (see figure 9.1). Two generations after King Hussein's abortive declaration in Mecca (1924), and one generation after the Shi'a Revolution restored Islamic rule in Iran (1979), al Baghdadi became the world's best-known pretender to the mantle of the Prophet in the cradle of Sunni Islam.

Within weeks of the Mosul sermon establishing the Islamic State, the leaders of 126 official and nongovernmental Islamic institutions—including the sheikh of Zeitouna University, the mufti of Jerusalem, the leader of the Nigerian Fatwa Council, and eminences from Al-Azhar and Qarawiyin Universities—

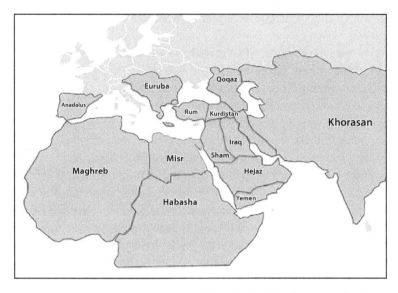

FIGURE 9.1. The Twenty-First-Century "Caliphate" of the Islamic State (2015)

fired back a heavily footnoted open letter to the would-be caliph. Addressing him by his civil title and given name without the added plumage, the international guild effectively served notice to "Dr. Ibrahim Awwad Al-Badri" to cease and desist operating a caliphate without a license. Like the Council of Worms refuting Luther's Wittenberg theses, the official representatives and scholars from Egypt, Turkey, Dubai, Palestine, Tunisia, Indonesia, Sudan, and France, laid out the Iraqi's twenty-four errors, including: "It is forbidden to issue fatwas without . . . the necessary learning requirements; To oversimplify matters of Shari'ah; To ignore the reality of contemporary times; To kill the innocent; To declare people non-Muslim; To harm . . . any 'People of the Scripture' [Jews or Muslims]."[2]

The scholars and officials were united in support of the rule of law over competing interpretations of Islamic jurisprudence (fiqh). The last two lines drove home a nation-state-friendly message: "Loyalty to one's nation is permissible in Islam," and "Islam does not require anyone to emigrate anywhere."[3] The would-be caliph was outgunned by the hundreds of diplomas arrayed behind the letter, which were the tip of a broad geopolitical, military, and ideological alliance against the Islamic State. The hodgepodge of ulema—listed phonebook-style at the end—underscored the lack of a single repository of Islamic authority. The absence of such an interlocutor has prevented resolution of what European colonial powers called the Eastern Question. The missing caliphate had left the basic premise of state legitimacy open for debate. In other words: should Islamic resources be mobilized in service of the state, or vice versa?

At the turn of the twenty-first century, nearly half of the world's Muslims lived in states where Islam was the official, established religion. This was wholly the case for those living in the former Ottoman area, across regime types and ethnic groups. Religious exercise remained subject to a state monopoly, and there were no private Islamic spaces permitted to exist outside the home—that is, there was no religious civil society. Since the end of the Cold War, there had been breakthroughs in religious professionalization and soft restoration of some traditional ritual roles for Islamic leaders, but they hardly compensated for the earlier evisceration of religious institutions. The various compromises, large and small, made by national governments made it impossible for the purist guardians of the takfiri flame to condone the nation-state format. The dour Iraqi theologian in the black turban offered a simple solution, but his merciless and contextless shari'ah justice did not have wide appeal, and the Islamic State regime was offensive and unattractive to all but a tiny share of Muslims worldwide.

Like Martin Luther, however, Abu Bakr al Baghdadi had a valid point about the degenerated state of the clergy and religious scholarship in many corners of the realm. As could be seen the world over, bureaucratization of state Islam was no guarantee of service quality. In certain countries, half of the imams were appointed by virtue of memorizing the Qur'an, whereas others were the fruit of patronage networks. Even if there was little appetite for al Qaeda or ISIS, their charismatic mahdis drew attention to state weaknesses in the Islamic arena—and to the caliph's empty seat. The twentieth-century secularist governments had not left behind conditions that could reproduce an ulema and imamat. Their unprepared successors had to fend off basic interrogations of their very purpose and legitimacy. Al Baghdadi's unforeseen ascent was the latest reason to stop making Islamic affairs policy inside national police ministries and start improving their quantity and quality.

Institutional Growth

Spring revolutions swept through the region during a decade of unprecedented open elections (2002–2012). Political Islamist parties rose to their peak visibility and power in Turkey, Lebanon, Gaza, Iraq, Tunisia, Egypt, Libya, and Morocco. Two inflection points indicate a new appraisal of Islamist challenges, when antisectarian tactics and professionalization benchmarks aligned with those of the Council of Trent. These reappraisals interacted with different national scenarios. Morocco and Turkey (2002–2004) experienced it before Algeria and Tunisia (2011–), but the physical and spiritual contiguity of the

Sunni Arab and Turkish states exposed them to the same succession of ideological assaults—first Ikhwanism on audiotape, then Salafism and Shi'ism via satellite television, and finally al Qaeda and the Islamic State online. Their reality was that if they did not standardize and spread religious education and the training of imams, muftis, and ulema against an array of politicizing influences, they risked becoming factional tools or channels of influence for external agents. An international Salafi movement tried to nudge public practices and opinion toward a fundamentalist Islamic order. In that atmosphere, the declaration of an ISIS caliphate in Iraq and al Shams (the Levant) deeply spooked states in the region.

To hold off a rising tide of defections of religious (and therefore political) loyalty, governments raised a counter-reformation effort reminiscent of sixteenth-century Rome's protection of its traditions and interests. Nation-State Islam thrived under all shades of government, and its growth outpaced that of any other bureaucracy, extending coverage over the entire national territory and frequently beyond it. Governments in Turkey and across North Africa devoted growing resources to Nation-State Islam in the first decades of the twenty-first century. After 2011, across the board, per capita Islamic affairs spending rose by more than 60 percent (see figure 9.2). The countermovement empowered an army of clerics to educate and defend the faithful against twenty-first-century religious fundamentalism. Algeria, for example, decided to include in all new mosques an imam training seminary (dar al imam) and a Qur'an school for children.[4]

In each post-Ottoman land, newly endowed ministries of religious affairs improved the national religious corps under civilian oversight to shield a specific brand of Islam. Each became a *spiritual* defense ministry for the post-9/11 and post-ISIS world at home and abroad. In some respects, the bureaucracies grew into mini-Leviathans. Repression still played an important role in religion policy: authorities closed down bookstores, dismissed insubordinate imams, and prohibited unlicensed Qur'an courses. But after years of playing whack-a-mole—imprisoning unregistered clerics and raiding unapproved religious schools—governments shifted to long-term planning and invested in institutional breakwaters to improve the quantity and quality of religious affairs. A typical Islamic affairs ministry's activities included responsibility for the country's inventory of mosques; the training, employment, and quality control of imams and other mosque employees; the foundations (waqf) and charity (zakat); public education campaigns (spreading literacy and prophetic hadiths); and Islamic broadcasting—religious channels broadcasting in the Arab world increased by 50 percent between 2011 and 2014 (religious education falls under the ministry of education).[5]

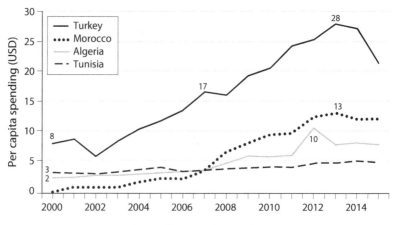

FIGURE 9.2. Islamic Affairs Spending per Capita, 2000–2014

Depoliticization

Why do Islamic affairs ministries persist—even exponentially increase—whether democrats or Islamists take power? The main reason, articulated in my interviews with Islamic affairs officials, was to achieve *depoliticization*—in other words, to avoid fitna (religious strife) within the national community. Nation-State Islam was wielded against political and religious extremisms, regionalisms, and other splinter movements.[6] Governments did not Islamicize the public sphere in service of divine conquest or a theocratic endgame. Rather, they preempted and co-opted hostile takeovers by strengthening schools, mosques, seminaries, and faculties to act as a buffer from the ground up. These institutions would thus be better able to compete directly with non-state actors who had filled a twentieth-century vacuum—the brotherhoods that were active domestically and abroad.

Such a benign reading of Nation-State Islam challenges the predominant understanding of Islam's return to the public sphere. Indeed, the state was frequently accused of politicizing religion selectively. The scholar Nathan Brown quotes an imam who "observed wryly . . . , 'If I endorse the constitution, that is not political. But if I oppose it, that is political.'"[7] Indeed, much of the political science literature has expressed the view that providing more resources for Nation-State Islam simply created more flunkies spouting more propaganda. The contemporary official mosque has been portrayed as a "regime mouthpiece" by Quintan Wiktorowicz, a specialist in Islamist movements, and the political scientist Stathis Kalyvas described the ulema as "servile to power." Jocelyne Césari singles out official imams as a contributing factor to religious radicalization and violence. Prominent scholars of the previous generation like Bernard Lewis and Elie Kedourie dismissed institutionalized religion as just another clumsy tool in the arsenal of state repression. The economic historian Timur Kuran blamed the Ottoman nationalization of waqfs for the Muslim world's divergent economic success in the contemporary world. For law professor Noah Feldman, the end of independent ulema stripped the Middle East of its autonomous bases for civil society; waqfs and wisemen could no longer serve as a counterweight to executive power.[8]

On the other hand, to portray disestablishment and establishment as Manichaean alternatives does not capture the reality of religious regulation. Meir Hatina has argued that official ulema have been done a "historical injustice" by the pantheon of Middle East scholars who "depicted ulema as religious mercenaries in the service of heretical regimes."[9] The analogy with state-military relations is apposite here. The point of having civilians sit atop the military sector, as one scholar writes, is simply to "subordinate [it] to the larger purposes of a nation, rather than the other way around. The purpose . . . is to defend society, not to define it. While a country may have civilian control . . . without democracy, it cannot have democracy without civilian control" (see table 9.1).[10] The work of religion scholars Ann Marie Wainscott and Michael Driessen has illustrated the role that religious regulation has played in nation-state consolidation in Muslim contexts.[11] After all, as Dale Eickelman writes, "Muslim politics *is* the competition . . . over the interpretation of symbols and control of the institutions that produce and sustain them."[12]

State oversight of Islam is depicted as uniformly heavy-handed and pro-regime. In each case discussed here—Algeria, Morocco, Turkey, Tunisia—the state-sponsored mosques and imams were indeed at some point put to work, alongside other public servants, to quell a political crisis at various moments—for example, to urge public calm during riots; to discourage separatism and generally promote the institutions of the state (such as getting out the vote); or to defuse material threats, such as helping put down a coup. In Algeria, a police car stood vigil outside each Friday-sermon mosque every week, as much to keep an eye on worshipers as to protect them from others. In Tunisia, which has considered punishing those not fasting during Ramadan, ulema have insisted that "the state had the duty to supervise social morality."[13]

The following sections present evidence that underneath that surface, however, the ministries and directorates of religious affairs seemed earnest in their attempts to provide politically neutral religious services in a highly charged environment. Scholars like Sultan Tepe caution against models that "reduce state-religious relations to the one-dimensional interaction of control or contestation."[14] Variation was expressed through an array of tools to fine-tune the bureaucratic machinery. Whether that amounted to illegitimate control or legitimate protection was in the eye of the beholder.

TABLE 9.1. Objective Civilian Control in the State-Religion Relationship

Balance	Equilibrium of "the authority, influence and ideology" of religious and nonreligious groups (Huntington 1966)
Professionalism	"The principal focus is the relation of the [clerical] corps to the state"; "professionalization renders them politically sterile and neutral" (Huntington 1966)
Nationalization	The shift from small, decentralized [religious] services to large standing bureaucracies; national control replaces private control; Islamic authorities are a public corporation or under the oversight of a government agency

Explaining National Variation

To examine the question empirically, this chapter gathers in one place the religious spending and infrastructure of four countries in the early twenty-first century: Turkey, Morocco, Algeria, and Tunisia. Each case examines (1) the impetus for policy change in the national context; (2) the growth of infrastructure, education, and hierarchy; (3) the ways in which each country enforced the monopoly; (4) the degree of religious pluralism; and finally, (5) the future of the country's ministry or directorate of religious affairs. The accounts are based on interviews with current office-holders, diplomats, and policymakers, including three ministers of Islamic affairs with a combined experience of fifty years at the helm of national religious affairs. There is variety in the timing of the rehabilitation of the Islamic establishment and the related reorganization of each nation's ministry or directorate of religious affairs. Turkey and Morocco outspent Algeria and Tunisia in the Islamic affairs sector two-to-one in both per capita spending and as a percentage of GDP and the national budget. This was reflected in levels of religious education, the different numbers of schools and students, the duration of compulsory courses, and the job prospects of graduates. These measures give an indication of the strength of Nation-State Islam; it is harder to gauge the strength of opposition Islamists, however, since some operate underground.

Morocco and Turkey

Morocco and Turkey undertook their major reform *before* the Arab Spring of 2010–2012, overhauling administration, personnel, and content in the aftermath of Morocco's transition from Hassan II to Mohammed VI (1999–) and Turkey's from CHP to AK party rule (2002–). King Mohammed and Prime Minister Erdoğan set about restoring Islam in public spaces on multiple fronts simultaneously, reforming religious law and suppressing religious

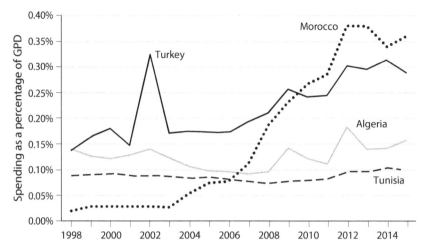

FIGURE 9.3. Trajectory of Spending on Nation-State Islam in Turkey and North Africa as a Percentage of GDP, 1998–2015

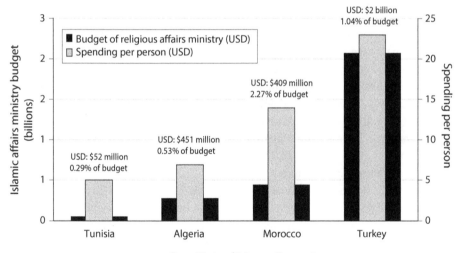

FIGURE 9.4. Cross-National Mosque Comparison, 2017

brotherhoods. Despite Turkey's reputation as a secular republic, it led in overall spending per person and in spending as a percentage of the government budget (see figure 9.3). Morocco led in spending as a percentage of GDP.[15] Morocco and Turkey also had 50 to 60 percent more mosque "coverage" than the other two— their mosque-to-citizen ratio was one per 1,000 believers—and they also received more hajj visas per capita from Saudi Arabia (see figure 9.4).

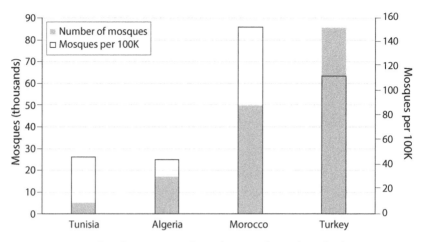

FIGURE 9.5. Spending on Nation-State Islam in Turkey and North Africa, 2016

Algeria and Tunisia

Algeria's and Tunisia's twentieth-century leaders were known for their secular-authoritarian credentials. Many held progressive and postcolonial views of Islam that ranged from contemptuous to cynical. The genuine professionalization push came later, after the Arab Spring (2011), and logically had less to build on during the subsequent crises. Ali Abootalebi argues that when state ideology was "weak and fragmentary" and the "oppositional Islamic trend" was strong, there was less state intervention in religious institutions and an "increasing reliance of the state on the religious establishment to counterbalance anti-regime Islamist movements."[16] This matched up with twentieth-century patterns in the timing of chartering a full-scale ministry of religious affairs and a significant national budget line. Algerian and Tunisian administration of religious affairs lingered longer in the interior ministry before being transferred to an Islamic affairs ministry, and the historically low levels of Islamic affairs spending persisted over time (see figure 9.5).

Twenty-First-Century Turkey: Erdoğan the Restorer

Religion policy in Turkey has been a constant source of partisan rancor. There were seventy-five years of cycling between anticlerical coalitions and democratic corrections, with longer and longer intercessions between military coups.[17] Large majorities in Turkey disapproved of the headscarf ban but also disapproved of shari'ah law. After decades of marginalization, party name changes, and the imprisonment or exile of its leaders, the fortunes of the

Justice and Development Party (AKP)—a political Islamist formation—rose under new leadership. Secularist assertiveness was at a peak in turn-of-the-twenty-first-century Turkey: Friday sermons were centralized, women who wore headscarves were prohibited from higher education and political life, and political manipulation led enrollment in religious schools to plunge by 90 percent.

The main impetus for the improvement and professionalization of Nation-State Islam in Turkey came from the rise of the AKP. Its leader, Recep Tayyip Erdoğan—the charismatic former mayor of Istanbul and also a former political prisoner, with a headscarf-wearing wife—reintroduced faith into public life. Erdoğan pronounced himself an Islamic Democrat—to suggest he had no different intentions than the Christian Democratic parties—and referred to himself as the "imam of Istanbul."

The AKP inherited a weakened set of religious institutions. Secularist governments had both centralized and reduced the bureaucratic capacity of the Directorate of Religious Affairs. Both the Diyanet and İmam Hatip schools were in a sorry state owing to a hiring freeze that had been in place since 1990. In 1998, only a handful of Diyanet officers had received a degree in higher religious education. The shortages extended to the basic infrastructure: as of 2004, more than one-quarter of mosques (23,000 prayer spaces) lacked any state employees whatsoever and thus had no one to oversee maintenance or preaching. This was at a time when an estimated 20 million citizens attended Friday sermons, up from 10 million two decades earlier. The February 1996 coup's targets included religious education. An emblematic measure was the use of a coefficient to penalize grade point average so that İmam Hatip students could attend university only by committing to religious studies, a field with limited employment opportunities. "The [secularists] virtually paralyzed the entire education system just to end İmam Hatip schools," Erdoğan said.[18]

Erdoğan's legacy will be his restoration of religious rights for the Sunni majority. Nonetheless, Alevis and Orthodox also did better under the AKP than under previous republican regimes. Neither they nor the Armenian Church nor the Jewish community, however, always felt warmly welcomed or equally treated. The party of Erdoğan never made headscarves or mosque attendance obligatory, but it pushed Islam back into institutions and forced the retreat of the Kemalist-republican synthesis. While he served as prime minister (2003–2014), Erdoğan pursued a less overtly ideological platform than the previous Islamist who tried governing—his mentor, Necmettin Erbakan—in order to form an electoral coalition with nationalist forces. During that decade, Erdoğan expertly sewed together alliances with a broad range of ideological families, including nationalists, Islamists, and followers of the exiled imam Fetullah Gülen. First as prime minister and then as president, he shepherded his allies to the negotiating table with the European Union, with the armed Kurdish resistance (PKK), and with minority Alevi leaders—and rallied them against ISIS. In the 2000s and 2010s, Erdoğan cranked up the Diyanet muezzin's volume to drown out the siren songs glorifying jihad being broadcast by Gulf Arabs and Saudis and to counter the messages of both al Qaeda and ISIS, which took direct aim at Erdoğan and the Republic of Turkey.

Since taking power, one focus of the AKP was to overcome the republic's original sin of abolishing religion from the public sphere by restoring religion to its "rightful" place.[19] In many cases the party reintroduced basic religious freedoms—for example, allowing marriages to take place in a mosque or permitting headscarves in public institutions.[20] A chief party ideologue, Ahmet Davutoğlu, declared, "This is an era of restoration," an expression that Erdoğan adopted.[21] A peaceful transition of power to the former opposition had unmistakably taken place, a major event for the normalization of an Islamist party in a parliamentary democracy.

The beginnings were relatively modest: in 2004, Erdoğan said that "while attaching importance to religion as a social value, we do not think it right to conduct politics through religion or to attempt to transform government ideologically by using religion."[22] The AKP entered a period of what Shadi Hamid calls "soft Islamization"—something far from the "implementation of sharia."[23] But where does the needle land on the dial? According to the Islamist daily *Yeni Akit*, the Diyanet under the twentieth-century secularists "had become too 'technical' but is now infused with spirit."[24] It also received an infusion of more suitable employees: in 1998, only 3.76 percent of Diyanet officers had received higher religious education, but this number tripled within a decade.[25] A 2010 law restored the Diyanet to its earlier protocolary status under the early days of the republic, raising the religious affairs director from fifty-first to tenth in the line of succession and restoring the position's diplomatic standing—"as Atatürk intended," in the words of the deputy prime minister Bulent Arinc.[26] The Diyanet was formally granted the powers "to study the legal aspects of and express opinion on draft acts, bills, decrees, and other laws sent to it by the Prime Minister's Office," as well as to monitor, assess, and, if necessary, destroy "inaccurate" religious texts—powers enjoyed by the Ottoman office of Sheik-ul-Islam, upon which the directorate was first modeled.

Infrastructure

Per capita, Turkey outspends the North African countries in this study when it comes to religious affairs spending. As a portion of GDP, it is outdone only by the Kingdom of Morocco. From 2008 to 2018, the Diyanet's budget and personnel spiked upwards, from an overall budget of 553 million liras in 2001

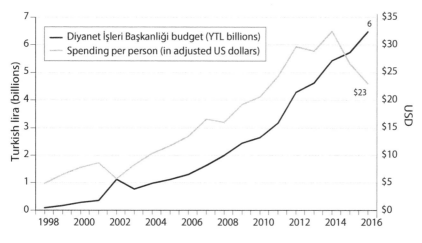

FIGURE 9.6. Turkey: Religious Affairs Spending per Capita, 2000–2016

($335 million) to 5.95 billion liras ($2.14 billion) in 2016, making it the seventh-largest ministry. The GDP doubled that decade, but the Diyanet budget qua-drupled (see figure 9.6). "We received some support from the previous gov-ernments," the Diyanet's vice president said in an interview, "but perhaps the AKP government simply understands us better."[27] The budget for religious affairs became as large as the ministries of foreign affairs, energy, culture, and tourism combined.[28] The Turkish government has said that the increase in spending was almost entirely associated with the cost of personnel, which grew from 75,000 to more than 140,000, including tens of thousands of religion teachers for the country's growing İmam Hatip enrollment. Many of the posts were seconded to other ministries. Nearly 75 percent of Diyanet personnel had a college degree, and fully 13 percent had a graduate degree.[29] Imams, who accounted for three-quarters of all Diyanet employees in 2003, were managed alongside thousands of religion teachers, leaving the directorate's Ankara headquarters overwhelmed. In 2013, that ratio had declined to around half of Diyanet employees (see figure 9.7). The proportion of imams per 1,000 citizens rose from 1.1 to 1.6.

Mosques

Press reports regularly cite mosque construction as evidence of the AKP's plan to re-Islamicize Turkey. Opponents saw the government's decisions—for ex-ample, keeping Turkey's 86,762 mosques open twelve hours a day and furnish-ing them with chairs—in an uncharitable light.[30] This was not Islamization so

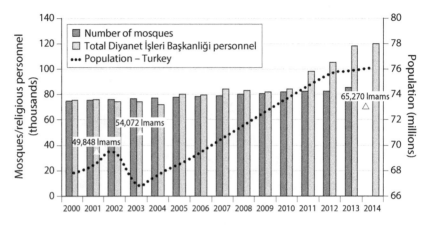

FIGURE 9.7. Turkey: Mosque Construction and Religious Affairs Hiring, 2000–2014

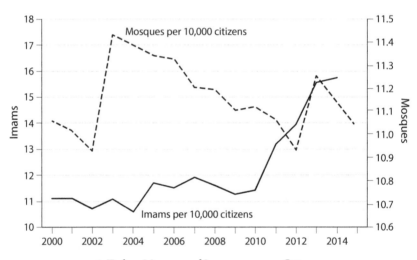

FIGURE 9.8. Turkey: Mosques and Imams per 10,000 Citizens, 2000–2015

much as state-ification; ultimately, it was a centralizing initiative. If there was demand, Erdoğan reasoned, why push prayer-goers into the hands of nonstate actors? Both the hiring at the Diyanet and mosque construction increased in absolute terms (see figure 9.8). The ownership deed of any newly constructed mosque in the country was transferred directly to the Diyanet rather than to the foundation or donor that built it.[31] The sheer number built under Erdoğan's first ten years in government was an impressive 17,000.[32]

There was ample evidence that Erdoğan sought to use mosques to transform Istanbul's soul, from its skyline to its urban center. The mega-mosque that he had built on the Asian hills of Istanbul in his home neighborhood of Camlica—with minarets higher than those on the (Ottoman-restored) Mosque of the Prophet in Mecca—could hold 30,000 prayer-goers.[33] Erdoğan's own presidential complex includes a mosque that can hold 3,000 worshipers. He and his appointees generally encouraged the construction of mosques in universities and private schools and required future İmam Hatip schools to be built with a prayer space.[34] The planned mosque in Taksim Square irked secularist opponents even more than the monumental mosque in Erdoğan's old neighborhood. The mosque in Taksim was accompanied by Ottoman-style barracks and a commercial center in place of the square where the Turkish left had defined itself. The police-led clearing of Gezi Park in 2013 was the Kemalists' noble and tragic last stand.

An examination of the data, however, reveals a less dramatic reality: mosque growth did not even keep up with demography. While mosque construction was a centerpiece of AKP rule, the numbers reflect continuity with previous governments, not rupture. In the history of the Turkish republic (see figure 9.8), there has always been one mosque for roughly every 1,000 citizens, and that proportion did not change during AKP rule. The boom in state-led construction did not alter the proportion of mosques per 1,000 citizens—in fact, the proportion shrank. In 2002, the ratio was 1.09 mosques per 1,000 people. After fifteen years of Erdoğan in power, the ratio decreased to 1.03. Many of the new buildings were large mosques, so the footprint or holding capacity of new mosques was relatively larger. Nonetheless, the 2016 ratio was the same as it was in 1981.

Education

The AKP introduced a number of changes and restored other elements to the educational system. One of their first acts was to introduce a course on the Qur'an and the Prophet from fifth to twelfth grade. The education ministry distributed new Qur'ans and textbooks and set its sights on undoing some of the previous regime's restrictions.[35] Ahmet Kuru describes many of the basic changes, including the lifting of a ban on teaching the Qur'an to students under twelve years of age.[36] The most dramatic adjustments occurred with regard to the İmam Hatip schools. The AKP decreased the discriminatory İmam Hatip grade point average coefficient and began building the schools that were missing because of the previous governments' interferences. For the first decade of the twenty-first century, there were only around 500 İmam Hatip schools. Following the 2010 reform, they were joined by 1,100 more İmam Hatip middle

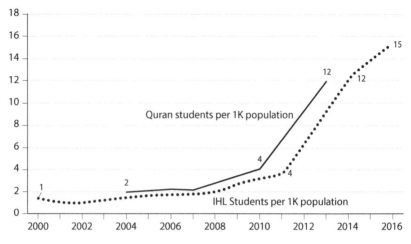

FIGURE 9.9. Turkey: Religious Education Enrollment in İmam Hatip
and Qur'an Courses, 2000–2016

schools.[37] In 2012, the AKP implemented a new education system. Known as
"4 + 4+4," it extended mandatory schooling to twelve years divided into three
levels; the law also reinstated the middle school level of İmam Hatips.[38] The
number of schools doubled within five years, and enrollment rebounded from
85,000 in 2003 to 1.1 million in 2016 (evenly split between the middle schools
and high schools) (see figure 9.9). After this dramatic growth, the İmam Hatip
schools accounted for 11 percent of Turkey's 29,000 middle and high schools
and a similar proportion of students. (In France in 2017, by contrast, around
16 percent of students attended confessional schools.)

Liberal or Conservative?

The journalist Cafer Solgun wrote in 2013 that the muftis and imams of the
republic were "propaganda merchants for the national cause" who were instructed to "pray for the wellbeing and the happiness of the nation."[39] Critics
such as the academic Ahmet Erdi Öztürk say that the Diyanet supports "an
explicitly ideological political agenda at the behest of the ruling party."[40] There
was little evidence of overt partisan usage of the Diyanet, but its pro-state
stance and dependency naturally align it with whoever is in government—
secularist, military, or Islamist. Its every policy proposal was regularly scrutinized for signs of religious influence. As an article in *Vatan* put it, was the
Diyanet "the subcontractor for the AKP's social engineering project"?[41] The
Diyanet's most controversial involvements in politics—such as sending a text
message to all 65,000 imams to resist the 2016 putsch; or taking stands against
Kurdish separatism, Gülenist machinations, and Armenian genocide resolu-

tions; even discouraging labor strikes—were not clearly conservative or liberal, Islamic or secular.[42] In the absence of Islamist rule during the 1980s and 1990s, however, the Diyanet acted much the same: it combated the expansion of Kurdish nationalism, revolutionary Shi'a Islam, and the beaming via satellite of revolutionary Sunnism. One may criticize these actions as political interventions, but they have long been Turkish policy.

The doyenne of Diyanet studies, Iştar Gözaydın, observes that "Kemalists and Islamists imagine very different societies, but they use the same tools. . . . The directorate today is used to shape the current government's vision of society and family and to prevent moral decay or the influence of foreign religions."[43] In many ways, the Diyanet under the AKP defied existing stereotypes of Islamist views and pursued a reformist agenda with regard to women's issues and Alevism. Diyanet cadres appointed to leading positions in the first decade in AKP rule came from the reform-minded Ankara School of 150 or so theologians whose emblematic project was the rewording and adjusting of religious language to the historical context and "the current requirements of the age." They aimed to reduce the thicket of over 200,000 hadiths in the Diyanet's archives—all of the sayings attributed to the Prophet—to a smaller set of 30,000 "accurate and incontestable" hadiths in a six-volume publication.[44] Supporters called this "Turkish Islamic liberalism" and applauded the government's efforts to create a "literature free of misogyny," also noting in its monthly magazine that the Diyanet reflected a "growing emphasis on individualism."[45] But Turkish liberals were unconvinced and mocked what they called a cynical, cosmetic maneuver by the AKP: "Look, we threw out all the bad hadiths. . . . Now let us into the European Union!"[46]

Other traits of the Diyanet under AKP rule, however, raised the ire of conservatives who resented the party's populism and compromises. This critique came not only from ISIS and al Qaeda but also from within Erdoğan's own political camp. On some issues, the journalist Pinar Tremblay writes, "pious Muslims were vocal on social media about their deep resentment about how non-Islamic" the AKP's initiatives were.[47] For example, these Muslims did not approve of the government's proposal to allow the reopening of the orthodox Christian Halki seminary in 2013, and they looked askance at the Diyanet's proposal to reopen historic churches and its general defense of Christian missionaries' right to preach their faith in Turkey.[48] The newspaper of the old Erbakan wing of the party, Mili Gazete, was a severe critic of the Diyanet's efforts and worried openly about a plan "to destroy and eliminate Sunnism in Turkey" and create an "Islam without Islamic jurisprudence and shari'ah."[49] The Diyanet leadership was therefore seen as a group of accommodationist stooges—as a cabal of "Native Orientalists, academics, and 'open-minded' professors" who replaced the esteemed "Sunni scholars" of yore. One Mili Gazete columnist wrote that the AKP cynically "exploited religion" and that its "phony services bring dishonor." For Mehmed Şevket Eygi, the Diyanet leadership's thesis of "historical context" meant that "there was no longer religion, just a moderate, light, domesticated and diluted Islam."[50]

While most Muslim citizens' religious liberties increased under AKP rule, the soft restoration did not bring the same rights revolution to those who did not subscribe to Hanafi Sunni Islam. Ottoman Turkey's non-Muslim population before the republic was once as high as 40 percent, but it was reduced to 0.2 percent in 1923 after a century of imperial conquest, independence movements, and population exchange.[51] Despite the common slogan that Turkey was "99%-Muslim," its nominally Muslim population was highly diverse. In total, 35 to 40 percent of the population did not identify as Hanafi Sunni Muslim. That included millions of Twelver Shi'a, millions of Nusayri/Alawites, and tens of millions of Kurds and Alevis. A majority of Kurds were Sunni but followed the Shafi'i rather than the Hanafi school of jurisprudence.

The experience of the heterodox Alevi group was mixed. Alevi groups had a more liberal stance than the government on many aspects of religious practice in houses of worship and in lived experience. The Diyanet president said that "we don't categorize Alevis outside Islam."[52] While Alevis asked for equal treatment, they made no uniform demand for the legal recognition of cem houses (cemevis) as places of worship, nor for other forms of institutional engagement. The AKP shared its predecessors' view that Alevis should pray in mosques, but in 2003 the government replaced the word "mosque" with the more inclusive "place of worship." Alevism was debated in 107 separate parliamentary sessions between 2002 and 2012.[53] "With this 'unifying' Sunni Islam, Alevis were effectively excluded from the Kemalist vision of an ethnically diverse, yet religiously united, Turkish nation."[54] Meles were hired as imam preachers and as dedes (Alevi wisemen) who were sent to Europe for the Turkish Alevi living there.[55] Nonetheless, the number of cemevis for Turkey's 10 million Alevis grew from 106 in 2002 to 400 in 2013.[56] The 2012 educational reform included a provision to allow Alevi (and Christian) students to organize their own religious courses in public schools. Information about the Alevi faith was placed in religious textbooks, and the government considered placing more Alevi dedes on the state's monthly payroll. Cemevis were still considered "cultural centers" and thus were ineligible for the free water or property tax exemption that mosques, churches, and synagogues all received. However, a potentially landmark ruling in an Istanbul district court in 2017 required the Diyanet to cover electricity costs for cemevis, just as it did for other houses of worship. It was upheld by the European Court of Human Rights, and the cemevis ceased paying utility bills.[57]

Gender relations was another area where AKP policies ran afoul of traditionalist Muslims. Defying easy categorization as religious extremism, the party's "soft Islamization" did not require women to shut themselves away in the home or to cover themselves fully when outside. As Recep Tayyip Erdoğan claimed, "We have lifted the pressure on our daughters."[58] He used a speech to the Organization of Islamic Cooperation (OIC) to call out majority-Muslim countries for sexist practices that limited women's prospects. "The logic that believes a woman should only be at home, or keeping women away from science, knowledge, political life and social life is wrong," he told the Islamic delegates. "Do not lock women up," Erdoğan exhorted, recommending instead that women "be fully included in employment and decision-making mechanisms."[59]

Shortly after the AKP's first Diyanet president took office, he appointed the first female mosque counselors in the history of the republic.[60] Women employees within religious affairs more than doubled, from 1,257 in 1991 (99 percent of whom were Qur'an course teachers) to 2,715 in 2013. Fourteen percent of all Diyanet employees were female, compared to an average of 9 percent in other ministries. The Diyanet encouraged women to attend mosques and to learn about Islam. President Erdoğan told religion officials that "a mosque is empty without our women's grace and dexterity."[61] It was under AKP rule that a theologian, Beyza Bilgin, became the Diyanet's first woman preacher, and all mosques were ordered to set aside space in the main area for women: to comply, "15,000 mosques immediately created a woman's section."[62]

In 2013, when the AKP lifted a decades-old ban on women wearing the headscarf in state institutions as part of a package of reforms that the government said were meant to improve democracy, it was not an unambiguously conservative act.[63] In İmam Hatip schools, more than half of the general studies teachers (55 percent) were female, as were 45 percent of the religion teachers. Thanks to the elimination of headscarf bans, by 2011 female students outnumbered male students in both İmam Hatip schools and Qur'an courses. Four female AKP lawmakers wearing headscarves were elected to parliament, which they entered to applause—in contrast with the hostile slow clapping that evicted the elected deputy Merve Kavakçı, also wearing a headscarf, fifteen years earlier. One of the three female mayors elected for the first time in 2014 was the AKP politician Fatma Sahin of Gaziantep. Shortly after the appointment of a new Diyanet director—the fourth in sixteen years—the Diyanet's first female *murakips* (religious auditors) were hired. In 2018, a woman was appointed deputy director of the Diyanet.

Enforcement of the Monopoly

Ultimately, the Republic of Turkey's return to Islam was hardest not on women or ethnic minorities but on its own religious rivals, who were neither the Kurds nor the Alevis nor traditional religious extremists. Instead, the challenge took the form of an opaque movement that embodied the most dangerous rival of a majority-Muslim state: a set of informal networks that amounted to a parallel religious affairs directorate. The AKP and followers of the charismatic imam Fethullah Gülen once shared a common cause—removing the Kemalist-nationalist deep state, reducing the threat of a military coup, and reelecting Erdoğan. The crash between the AKP and the Gülen movement was a slow-motion collision of the two former dissident groups that elapsed between 2012 and 2016.

The Gülenists' network of educational establishments was useful to conservative Islamists in Turkey throughout the 1990s. The Hizmet movement, as it preferred to be called, provided a haven for the pious-minded at a time when religion was being driven out of the public sphere by a strictly secularist elite. The movement expanded via 2,000 independently owned educational institutions in 160 countries, and then through civil society organizations. In Turkey, Hizmet followers did not dare register as a political party or even as a simple cultural or charitable organization. Even if it was an educational and charitable network, its leader was a learned Islamic scholar (Hoca Effendi) who challenged Erdoğan directly. As Fethullah Gülen said in a newspaper interview, "Nothing is being done to eliminate the grave problems facing the country's educational system. We have enough mosques, many of which are empty, but not enough schools."[64] Cemal Usak, vice president of the Journalists and Writers Foundation, said in an interview:

> My religion cannot be involved with the state or with power. The state means power. [The Diyanet] may seem big and large, but it is without spirit! The mosque is important, but it is official. The Diyanet can only control what is inside the mosque. But a majority of religious activity is outside the mosque. Religion is lived outside the mosque. It is liberal, individual, and social.[65]

The Diyanet's strategic plan for 2012 to 2016 (announced in 2010) spelled the end of carte blanche for Gülen. His institutional activities both inside and outside of Turkey came into direct conflict with the new legal mandate of the republic's religious affairs directorate. By late 2012, Hizmet schools were being pressured to close, and in 2013 the aftermath of the Gezi Park confrontations led to the dismantling of their popular test prep courses (Dershanes). The Hizmet and AKP traded escalating blows: the supporters of Gülen infiltrated the highest levels of government and exposed security and corruption scandals, while the government targeted suspected supporters in every sector and industry. In 2014, Erdoğan said, "They have entered our institutions over the past 35–40 years and infiltrated everywhere. Now it is time to comb them out, within the law."[66]

The confrontation culminated in the failed coup d'état of July 2016. A four-year ideological purge across Turkish institutions followed, during which an estimated 100,000 citizens were detained and 150,000 lost their jobs, including many who were found guilty by association.[67] An ideological purge across Turkish institutions followed: 21,700 Ministry of Education officials were fired, and 21,000 private school teachers were suspended; 1,000 private schools linked to Gülen were converted to public schools, 40,000 new teachers were hired, and 1,500 university deans were forced to resign (some were later rehired).[68]

The Hizmet was best known for running schools and dormitories, not mosques. The state agency, department, or ministry *least* affected by the purge was the Diyanet, though it was criticized retrospectively, *après-coup*, for having allowed Gülenism to spread. Some commentators accused the movement of having "usurped Diyanet's decision-making mechanisms," leading to "40 years of occupation [by the] Fetullah Gülen Terror Organization."[69] Only around 1,000 Diyanet employees were purged in the aftermath of the coup, out of 120,000—a low figure compared to the education ministry, where one-third of teachers lost their jobs.

A year after the coup attempt, the Supreme Board of Religious Affairs issued a report on how to reintegrate Gülen's millions of followers into the Diyanet fold.[70] Diyanet president Mehmet Görmez told journalists that Diyanet officials reviewed 80 books and 670 hours of Hizmet-related audiovisual recordings and that "all sections contradicting Islamic faith and belief were ascertained, one by one. Announcements were then issued to explain why these were wrong."[71] Görmez said that the movement was a "parallel Diyanet," a "fake Mahdi movement" rather than a religion, and that the Gülenists had "tinkered with the religion's genetics" and drawn citizens away to "something else instead of attending Friday prayers."[72]

Achieving Semi-Autonomy

What does soft restoration look like? One former senior Diyanet official described contemporary Turkey in an interview: "Today is a normalization—our attempt to reckon with the past."[73] Insofar as the party attempted to use social engineering via legislation to produce a more religious society—more headscarves, Qur'an courses, and İmam Hatip schools—the result was only a faint echo of an Islamic state, not tantamount to the revival of the caliphate. A typical restoration of Ottoman-era laws was a loosening of the requirement to notify officials of a religious marriage. Imams could bring the certificate to the municipality on their own within fifteen days of the ceremony. There was no large demand for religious-only marriages—only around 1 percent of all marriages in 2016, officials estimated—and similarly, only 1.8 percent of couples marrying opted for a civil ceremony alone.[74] The measure allowed the Diyanet to maintain control where rival religious figures—specifically, unofficial imams, perhaps using unofficial spaces—performed marriages without notifying officials at all. This was illustrative of the dual nature of soft restoration: it simultaneously built a framework and set the limits. Relatedly, the Diyanet issued a fatwa against underage marriage in 2016.

The Diyanet was targeted by a broad range of opposition perspectives—from Kemalist to Kurdish to Gülenist—attacking the state's control of religion. When the Kurdish People's Democratic Party (HDP) crossed the threshold of 10 percent and threatened Erdoğan's majority in 2015, its campaign manifesto promised: "The Religious Affairs Directorate will be abolished, the state will take its hands off of the area of religion and belief, and religious and belief-related duties will be left to society and believers."[75] The columnist and professor Sahin Alpay wrote, "The Religious Affairs Directorate has to be taken out of the state structure if Turkey is ever going to consolidate liberal democracy."[76] Ahmet Kuru has argued that "Diyanet should become an autonomous entity with a budget supplied by religious foundations, instead of through government funding. A board of trustees should be responsible for appointing its president, not the government."[77]

Erdoğan's principal adviser, Ibrahim Kalin, acknowledged in an interview that "some propose abolishing [the Diyanet], but this is not a viable option—nor is it something that a vast majority of Turkish people would approve of."[78] Indeed, in surveys 90 percent of the "very religious" declare full confidence in the Diyanet. Numbers for general popular support range from 72 percent who trust the Diyanet in 2007 to 84 percent, several years later, who replied in a survey that the "Diyanet should be kept in the constitution." Half wanted things to stay as they were, 40 percent favored the equal recognition of all religions, and 8.7 percent wanted no mention of secularism in the constitution.[79] A report on the Diyanet's future status in the Turkish constitutional system declared that the "ideal" would be the "abolishment of the Presidency," but that it was practically impossible in the short run.[80]

In 2004, Diyanet president Ali Bardakoglu stated that the "Directorate of Religious Affairs is an autonomous institution, which makes use of its freedom." He told Diyanet employees, "I hope that I am the last director to be *appointed*" to the position he occupied. Those present applauded and shouted back: "You would be the last appointed and the first *elected* director."[81] Almost a decade later, Diyanet president Mehmet Görmez said, "Diyanet should be independent and autonomous in terms of religion and scholarship, if not exempt from administrative oversight."[82] Meanwhile, Ibrahim Kalin said: "We are working on internal revisions for internal organization of Diyanet, such as the election of muftis."[83] Improvements were made in "an attempt to enhance the administrative autonomy of Diyanet." There is evidence of trends toward devolution, decentralization, and, eventually, electoral systems that express a shura-like consensus. The Diyanet president was chosen by the Religion Supreme Council (Din Üst Kurulu): 120 theologians, members of the Higher Council of Religious Affairs, and regional muftis select three candidates; the Council of Ministers then chooses one of the three and proposes his appointment to the president of the Republic. Other moves toward devolution included the presence of a Diyanet mufti in each of 81 provinces and the drawing of 900 districts.[84] Responsibility for the Friday sermon was delegated to commissions within those regional mufti offices, and soon thereafter they were given a role electing the Supreme Religious Council.

In response to testimony heard by parliamentarians that the "Diyanet should either be abolished or become autonomous," Diyanet representatives told lawmakers to simply look east to Iran "as a bad example where Mullahs have become too powerful."[85] The Diyanet was too useful: it was a key institution that produced and spread a counternarrative—for instance, by deploying 700 preachers to prisons, where "radicalization can spread."[86] Islamists were in an odd position: "Some of us used to refer to Diyanet as a treasonous organization and called for its abolition." But "if it were removed, there would be fitna" (intracommunal strife), and "the mosque communities would be pulverized under the destructive millstone of miscellaneous groups."[87]

The religious rhetoric and test balloons launched by the AKP hinted at a potential for more severe religious rule—from a bill targeting adultery in 2002 to talk in 2017 of removing the principle of secularism from Turkey's constitution. But the party's attempts to remodel society in an Islamic image were circumscribed. There was no equivalent to the Kemalist state's imposition of a dress code, no return to Arabic script, no talk of reviving a ministry for shari'ah law. There were alcohol and advertising restrictions familiar to anyone who has visited the United States. The pious and paternalist ambiance was off-putting to many secularists but did not always translate into legislative action. President Erdoğan's opposition to abortion, for example, shared by the Diyanet president, was never inscribed in law. One of the most controversial items concerned the reversion of the Hagia Sofia Museum to the status it enjoyed as a mosque between 1453 and 1923. The complex had been open for prayer since 1991, but in 2016 the Diyanet assigned a permanent imam who led Friday prayers and held services for Ramadan and Laylat al Qadr holidays. The reversion was completed with fanfare in 2020.

Sultan Tepe asks the underlying question: is the Diyanet "seeking to tame religious practices . . . or is it expanding traditional religious practices by using the state's power?"[88] On the one hand, the AKP is post-Islamist, what the

Turkish liberal Mustafa Akyol has called simply Erdoğanism. It zeroes in on political enemies regardless of their piety. The religious generation that the AKP aimed to raise, however, did not sprout overnight.[89] After two decades, only 28 percent of Diyanet employees were graduates of an İmam Hatip school. In 2017, only 17 percent of respondents to a Diyanet survey reported having ever read the Qur'an in Turkish translation, while 45 percent said that they got their religious information from the Internet. As one of the Diyanet presidents under AKP rule told a secular columnist in an interview: "The failure of the previous regime's attempt to raise a Kemalist generation serves as a warning, because social engineering usually produces unexpected results: you might plant barley but get sunflowers instead."[90]

Mohammed VI's Morocco

The main impetus for the professionalization of Moroccan Islam came from a need to fill the vacuum at home and abroad, two fields where traditional Moroccan religious actors were being routinely outspent and out-influenced by oil-rich competitors. The uniformity of the Sunni religious ritual (*unité de rite*) is frequently credited with ensuring the kingdom's stability. "All of the political parties recognize the fact that the Commander of the Faithful is the center of our religion and our politics," Ahmed Toufiq, the minister of Islamic affairs, said in an interview. "That is Moroccan identity."[91] Namely, only the king may join politics and religion—not political parties, and not imams, who were excluded from office-holding. The political realms are distinct but not separate. This was still being reinforced as the minister spoke.

Despite a reputation for an iron-fisted security policy, Hassan II bequeathed a surprisingly disorderly religious scene to his son. Friday prayer attendance was estimated at nearly one-third of all Moroccans, but when Mohammed VI became king in 1999, half of all mosques—many of them improvised spaces in shantytowns—completely escaped government attention.[92] Eight out of every ten imams had no formal training.[93] Within the kingdom, no single institution had a monopoly over religious-legal opinions. Dissident ulema issued fatwas criticizing the government's "silence" following the US invasion and NATO occupation of Afghanistan. Hundreds of Moroccans defied authorities and traveled to fight the coalition; seventeen landed in the US military prison on Guantanamo Bay.[94] Mohammed VI's first years as king were scarred by terrorist attacks in Casablanca and Marrakech and the rising domestic popularity of political Islam. The arrest and public trial of Zaccarias Moussaoui, the Frenchman of Moroccan origin, in the United States raised the specter of a terrorism threat associated with Moroccans Residing Abroad (MRE). For Islamic affairs officials, Moussaoui was the tip of a submerged danger: extremists of Moroccan origin seduced by Salafism while living abroad, and who willfully rejected or were ignorant of the king's religious authority.

The investigatory aftermath of 9/11 exposed an underlying chaos within Moroccan Islam and confirmed that religion policy would be one of the new regime's central challenges. Hakim el Ghissassi, an adviser to Minister Toufiq, said that the international context was defined by "religious radicalism and a profusion of contradictory opinions which threaten Moroccan cultural unity. That is the urgency behind the spiritual protection of Moroccan citizens and modernization of religious affairs (*champ religieux*)."[95]

Mohammed VI was the first king born into a modern Moroccan nation-state. He was not only "Commander of the Faithful, Supreme Representative of the Nation, symbol of its unity, guarantor of its perpetuity and continuity of state, vigilant of the respect for Islam and the constitution," but was also a "constitutional, democratic, and social" monarch.[96] For followers of the Maliki school of Sunni Islam, he was the Prophet's heir and the Shadow of God, reaffirmed annually in an elaborate public demonstration of clerical loyalty (*bai'a*), as described by a journalist: "Rows of figures in traditional hooded white Moroccan robes advance in unison under the blazing sun to where the King, surrounded by his courtiers, is seated on a black pure-bred horse shaded by a burgundy parasol."[97]

The future Mohammed VI was enrolled in a Qur'anic school at an early age and was attentive to his role as Emir al-Mu'minin. His counselors encouraged this by identifying Islamic affairs as an area ripe for reform, and one where investing more resources could have a significant return.[98] Hakim el Ghissassi writes that Mohammed started by firing 150 of his father's key advisers and officials, replacing the "old network" to instill a new "professionalism."[99] Mohammed ordered Minister Toufiq to circulate four memorandums in June 2000. Nineteen provincial ulema councils were chartered and placed under royal tutelage. "To limit the flowering of political Islam," Mehdi Belhaj Kacem writes, mosques were ordered to remain open longer.[100]

Moroccan institutionalization of Islamic exercise followed a familiar pattern of gradually transferring religious matters from the Ministry of the Interior—primarily a policing administration—to the dedicated Ministry for Religious Affairs. Religious Affairs is one of four sovereign ministries whose occupants are directly appointed and who may not belong to a political party. Along with the Holy Qur'anic presses, it is the only ministry physically located on the palace grounds in Rabat. By choosing to name an amiable history professor and former national librarian as his minister of Islamic affairs, the king drew a contrast with the stern Islamic jurist whom his father had chosen. Toufiq avoided using the word "reform," saying that he preferred to use *tanzyl*, an "ancestral" term meaning "placing in context."[101] With a friendly but firm demeanor, he supported the king's campaign over the next two decades to slowly gain control of the country's mosques and imams. In a newspaper interview, he justified the increase in mosques and ulema councils in a larger context: "The Moroccan ulema's religious authority (*machiakha*) has a long and noble history during centuries of fusion with the Commander of the Faithful, which forged Moroccan identity and specificities—it is what preserves the country in the rite of the Sunna and of the Jama'a, unambiguously sealed in the Maliki rite."[102] Toufiq helped coordinate a royal monopoly while security services broke up al Qaeda and other Salafi cells.[103]

In the midst of these reforms, the king told *La Médina* magazine: "We cannot know the real problems of the populations we'd like to help without getting close to them."[104] In this context, proximity meant filling the vacuum with trained imams to head off political extremism. A fistful of sand requires a tight grip, and the king issued an early disclaimer: "There will be no democracy for non-democrats."[105] Before legislative elections in 2002, the ministry undertook a nationwide confiscation of books and audiocassettes. The government began annual print runs of 1.5 million copies of the Qur'an and organized prize competitions for expert and artistic recitation. For those who did not read, 800,000 recordings of *al Mos'haf al Mohammadi* were distributed in mosques across the kingdom.

Mohammed VI's first son was one week old when terrorists struck Casablanca in 2003, perhaps adding extra weight to his conscience as he set about reconfiguring national security policy more comprehensively than his father had ever done. That year, the king reminded the country of his constitutional role unifying religion and politics in a series of addresses. His most dramatic gesture was to follow through on the reform of the personal statute code (*Mudawana*), which had stalled since the early 1990s.[106] New legislation reformed the code and the Islamic affairs ministry. The unprecedented empowerment of the Moroccan Ministry of Habous and Islamic Affairs followed, which quickly had the fastest-growing—and the tenth-largest—budget out of twenty-one ministries. A new mosques directorate centralized the multiyear planning of a national mosque inventory and oversaw preaching and "sensitivity training" in coordination with local ulema councils. Another new directorate for traditional education regulated Qur'anic schools. Eighty new laws were passed in the space of eight years (2004–2012).[107] Hakim el Ghissassi described the overhaul of the *champ religieux* in historic terms for the state-Islam relationship: "We have 'desacralized' religious acts by drawing borders around the religious field."[108]

Spending on imams and mosques spiked upwards in the years after the Casablanca attacks and the involvement of MREs in terrorist acts in Amsterdam and Madrid (see figure 9.10). The Islamic affairs budget rose from the equivalent

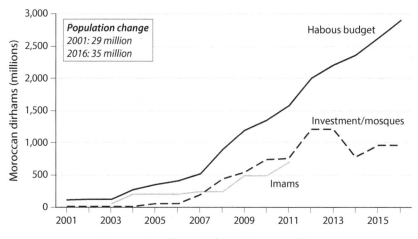

FIGURE 9.10. Morocco: Spending on Habous, Mosques, and Imams, 2001–2015

of less than $1 per person in the early 2000s to $13 per person in the early 2010s. A second growth spurt for religious affairs took place in 2011, similar to the one in 2004. The brewing unrest of the Arab Spring was ominous: while security deteriorated in Egypt, Tunisia, Iraq, Syria, and Libya, self-immolations spread across the region and a local "February 20" movement sought political reforms and garnered international attention. In 2011, supplemental imam training was announced for 44,600 imams, overseen by 1,426 ulema and following a curriculum designed by the Conseil supérieur des ouléma. Continuing religious education was built into the program.[109]

In an interview in Rabat, Minister Toufiq said, "The growth of the religious sector's budget has no equal in any other sector. From 2012 to 2013, it was raised several hundred million, from DH [dirham] 1.54 billion to DH 1.88 billion. Then if you include [other sources], it reached DH 4 billion. It is more and more each year, more than the budget of some armies! We were able to be persuasive that this intervention is necessary."[110] Another 8 percent increase followed in 2015–2016, bringing Islamic affairs' share of the national budget from 0.19 percent at the turn of the century to 3.1 percent in 2016, equivalent to the Ministry of Justice. Nonetheless, the habous ministry accounted for only 2 percent of all new public-sector positions between 2007 and 2013.

Infrastructure

The lion's share of the Islamic affairs budget was dedicated to maintaining the country's mosques.[111] A new policy kept houses of worship open extra hours during the day and after the final prayer for "preaching and the struggle against illiteracy and ignorance." Less than half of Moroccans could read and write when King Mohammed VI arrived in power. Another of Toufiq's first programs was a massive literacy campaign enrolling 2.7 million Moroccans (mostly women) in thousands of mosques nationwide from 2000 to 2017.[112] Provincial ulema councils selected associations and individuals to implement the literacy campaign, growing the corps of 242 teachers and advisers to nearly 6,000 in 2014; literacy rates rose to nearly 70 percent. The ministry aimed to establish mosques in each neighborhood of every city and village. The number of prayer spaces in the late 1990s stood at 24,000 mosques, and that figure more than doubled in the next twenty years. The Moroccan state planned to "close the doors" to extremism, Avi Spiegel writes, leading to "the most dramatic increase in the construction and oversight of state-run mosques in the country's history."[113] The budget for the construction, restoration, and maintenance of mosques grew from DH 6 million in 2004 to DH 910 million in 2011 (see figure 9.10). By 2011, there were 35,000 mosques, and in 2019 the government counted over 52,000 mosques; two-thirds of the recently built mosques were financed with voluntary donations.[114] Ministry officials said that they had achieved the desired ratio of one mosque to every 1,000 faithful, and they still aimed to build one for every 700 believers in the Friday sermon mosques. They reached even higher mosque density in the most heavily populated areas: 4.5 mosques per 1,000 citizens. Sixty percent were large, state-owned mosques (*grandes mosquées*). The rest were small- and medium-sized spaces operated by the local community and funded by the ministry. Their combined surface area added up to 8 million square meters, making them the most prevalent man-made structures on Moroccan soil after residential homes.[115]

In 2003, the ministry counted only 9,000 imams who were accredited by the local ulema council and salaried by the state. Following the religious reforms Hakim el Ghissassi said, "If we want to name an imam and to accredit him, there is now finally a process."[116] After 2005, the imam profession was bureaucratized: imams would no longer be nominated by a sheikh or teacher in a traditional Qur'an school or mosque, but instead follow a standard ministerial procedure. Their numbers rose to 33,000 in 2005, to 38,700 in 2008, and to 46,000 in 2011.[117] The total number of part- and full-time employees in all departments at the Ministry of Habous reached 116,000 in 2018.[118] Around 25,000 of the 67,633 mosque personnel were authorized to sermonize in one of the country's Friday prayer mosques.[119]

Education

The Ministry of Education reformed the high school curriculum in 2007 with the goal of creating "independent, open, and balanced" students guided by four sets of values—Islamic, modern identity, nationalist, and human rights.[120]

There were 12,811 Qur'an schools in the year 2013, a number that expanded to 16,800 in 2016.[121] Another 12,000 khutbas and 300 madrassas offered traditional education. There was a systemwide supply problem, however: only 18 percent of imams had formal training. Nearly half (45 percent) were appointed simply because they had memorized the Qur'an. The ministry started a one-year ministerial training course open to graduates holding a *licence*, and it has trained hundreds of imams annually.[122] Between 2004 and 2012, the budget for imam training rose from around $6 million to more than $75 million. In addition, the government spent $200 million to "upgrade" the training of 45,000 current state-employed imams.[123] In 2006, the ministry produced a "training manual for imams, laying out the principles of Moroccan Islam." It set up nearly 1,500 centers to "educate those 'responsible for the supervision of (religious belief and practice).'" Another 1,300 "super imams" were tasked with "preserving the fundamentals of Moroccan Islam."[124] At graduation ceremonies, Minister Toufiq told newly minted imams to "promote attachment to the religious and national constants in the country as their primary mission."[125]

Cognizant of the ubiquity of satellite signals, the government went to great lengths to physically reach the faithful in Morocco's vast rural mountainous and desert expanses. Rural areas were assigned 1,500 trained religious supervisors. A new corps of 750 imam trainers was responsible for small towns and remote villages. Dozens of motorcycles were made available to allow imams and mourchidates to reach the faithful in the country's south.[126] Thousands of mosques were equipped with a televisual system for preaching and distance-training in rural areas, such as in the country's sparsely populated southwest, to give them "coherent information and training."[127] In its first ten years, the program trained 1,600 new prayer leaders.[128]

Ulema Training

The Dar al Hadith al Hassania was recalibrated in August 2005 to train the next generation of ulema. The ministry's mission statement was to train ulemas who are "capable of interacting with the diverse sources of human knowledge, qualified for scientific and civilizational dialogue with their counterparts from other religions."[129] The curriculum used to train imams and religious scholars was heavily revised.[130] An ulema charter was formalized and enhanced by the *Mithaq al ulema*. The pact "renews responsibility of Ulema in religious training with two goals: to secure dogma . . . and the basis of shari'ah. We can only preserve our identity and guard against the risks of isolation and alteration through a judicious understanding of our religion," the king said in Tetouan. "That is why we consolidated our promotion of religion with the Ulema Charter which guarantees the Kingdom's spiritual security and the preservation of Moroccan Islamic identity."[131] New university courses in Islamic studies came online, as did new professors of fiqh and shariʾah. Conditions for students were improved, including the awarding of larger scholarships: nearly 25,000 students received significant subsidies. In 2016, five historic madrassas and the Dar al Mouaqquit in Fez were reopened. The number of Moroccan ulema in the Conseil supérieur des ouléma reached 600 in 2018.

Enforcing the Monopoly

After the minister of Islamic affairs reportedly pressured the president of the ulema council to give a US-friendly speech at a post-9/11 ecumenical ceremony held in a church, an official sheikh accused the ministry of heresy. The United States and its allies had "diabolical policies," he said, and the ulema had "the obligation to speak out when something is wrong, and to pronounce fatwas if need be . . . no matter what the current Religious Affairs Minister says."[132] The ministry fought back against such independent-mindedness among religious authorities and reminded any newspapers that had published unauthorized fatwas against the NATO coalition that "nobody and no group has the right to issue fatwas apart from the body of Ulema."[133]

The Casablanca attacks of May 2003 crystalized Mohammed VI's decision to institutionalize the ulema.[134] Security services discovered dozens of "potential" bombers in four other cities, and 2,300 individuals were imprisoned. Local ulema councils continued to increase, from 18 in 2004 to 82 in 2012. Beginning in 2006, the Conseil supérieur des ouléma distributed 50,000 copies of the *Guide for Imams, Preachers, and Sermon-Givers* and asked graduates to sign a pledge to respect it.[135] Nearly 42,000 imams participated within its first two years. The imams' local ulema council grants accreditation, while the national ministry offers "occasional guidance" and texts. In special cases, the Conseil supérieur des ouléma may oversee production of a single approved sermon to distribute in all mosques across the country. But in general, Ahmed Toufiq said in an interview, "we provide a guide to trace the outlines of the speech. We explain our expectations to all of our preachers, which doesn't mean there are not rare deviations."[136] The fear of deviation tended to rise during the month of Ramadan, when the government frequently banned after-hours prayers.[137]

Targeting Mosques and Qur'an Schools

"If we become aware of anything that jeopardizes neutrality" taking place in any of the smaller mosques, Toufiq said in an interview, then "we take over the mosque and integrate it into our administration."[138] In 2002, the government closed thirty makeshift prayer spaces.[139] In 2006, the ministry announced an emergency program to eradicate inappropriate prayer spaces, shutting down thirty-three unlicensed Qur'an schools.[140] In 2008, the Ministry closed the Qur'an schools, religious association and Internet site run by a theologian who had authorized child marriage.[141] The imam of al Hamra in Casablanca was prohibited from preaching after saying that the king's fatwa council (*majlis al ifta*) was irrelevant.[142] The ministry reminded citizens that "any fatwa which does not come from the Superior Council of Ulemas" was simply an opinion.[143] The ministry fired 1,500 Qur'anic teachers in 2011.[144] It also closed Shi'a religious schools and ended relations with Iran.[145] When phase two of the renovations of 11,000 mosques "in danger of collapse" led to the closure of 1,200 prayer spaces, the Islamist Party of Justice and Development accused the ministry of delaying their reopening.[146] The ministry identified 461 mosques being constructed without the necessary licensing and ordered the buildings' seizure or demolition.[147]

Firing Imams

In my interview with Minister Toufiq, he said, speaking of imams, that "you will be recalled if you make a mistake or suddenly change religious ideology. But out of 20,000 Friday preachers, someone is fired only every two or three months."[148] According to a report by Haim Malka, however, the ministry dismissed 765 imams for incompetence in 2009, and an additional 34 imams were dismissed for violating the ban on participating in political events.[149] In 2011–2012, imams protested against the ministry's centralization of sermons.[150] In 2014, a court sentenced a Salafist preacher to one month of prison for having declared a Moroccan politician to be an apostate.[151] In a Friday prayer, an imam openly accused Prime Minister Abdelilah Benkirane's government of causing rises in food prices and electricity and water bills. After a Fez imam was banned from preaching after "vigorously criticizing the Mawazine festival, especially the presence of half-naked artists—with reference to Jessie J and her famous shorts," the imam welcomed the ban "as an honor for him before God." Commenting in a newspaper interview, Minister Toufiq said that "the Friday sermon follows a certain form established by the Sunna of the Prophet. The Imam Guide has all the details. An imam can discuss general topics but cannot attack a person or a particular event."[152]

Pluralization

Mohammed VI "exhorts the ulemas to inscribe their jurisprudential efforts . . . in the international context of Moroccan treaties and conventions."[153] For women, Hakim el Ghissassi writes, religion in Morocco "has undergone considerable transformation," with their role being institutionalized for the first time "in Ulema councils and mosques."[154] In 2004, the king appointed the first woman to the Islamic Scholars body and also advanced the mourchidate program at Dar al Hadith al Hassania. They recruited women under forty-five years of age, who were reportedly paid more than twice as much as male imam-preachers. This led to the remarkable occasion of a female mourchidate preaching her khutba before the king and Emir al-Mu'minin himself.[155]

The Amizigh/Berber minority population concentrated in the northern Rif region suffered a stigma of rebelliousness. They had briefly enjoyed autonomy in the 1920s, under the French Protectorate. Relations with the Moroccan crown worsened into a state of near–civil war shortly after independence (1958). There were some tendencies within the diaspora movement based in Spain, the Netherlands, and France toward autonomy-mindedness, and Morocco sought to nip that in the bud in Europe too.[156] In 2003, upon the privatization of radio and television in Morocco, a public service station was preserved in order to "guarantee the respect of religious values and other elements that constitute Moroccan identity," including the Amizigh language. The 2011 constitution also increased Amizigh linguistic rights.

As the centennial of long-lost independence neared, protests followed a dramatic incident involving a civil servant and the tragic death of a fishmonger. Months of unrest followed in and around al Hoceima in 2017. The movement's leader was Nasser Zafzafi (1979–), the charismatic grandson of a government minister during Rif independence, who accused Rabat of misrule and neglect.

Zafzafi also attacked the government for issuing un-Islamic fatwas and predicted the government imams would "lead Morocco into a bloodbath." State mosques and imams were mobilized to defuse the situation. The Islamic affairs ministry asked imams to "deliver a Khutba [sermon] accusing the disgruntled youth of promoting sedition and division." The ministry circulated a text ("Security is a blessing") to the eighty imams employed in and around al Hoceima that reclaimed the legitimate religious ground. The ministry rebuked the protest movement for its own un-Islamic behavior: "Nothing in religion allows or justifies the destruction of property."[157] The imam-preachers reminded prayer-goers that "Morocco enjoys calm and security, unlike other countries in the region." The sermon continued: "This does not mean there is nothing wrong, but the true believer does not send off anonymous messages on the Internet, nor become unduly inflamed, nor focus solely on what doesn't work. . . . It is necessary to avoid Fitna." The sermon ended by accusing the leader of providing "a portal for shiism."[158] With the country's mosques thus deployed to combat dissidence in the Rif, any truce was over.[159] When Nasser Zafzafi challenged the crown's religious authority by interrupting the imam during a Friday sermon, he was tried and sentenced to twenty years' imprisonment.

Integrating Islamists

The Moroccan state has sought to prevent the opposition from using religion as an instrument of political mobilization. Simultaneously, however, it has integrated political Islamists into formal politics—on the condition that they recognize the king's religious authority. In the 1990s, while Islamists fought a violent insurgency with the Algerian government and faced crackdowns in Tunisia and Libya, Islamists in Morocco were integrated into parliamentary politics. As reports of headscarf wearing increased, the most important Islamist faction, the Justice and Development Party (PJD), rose in the polls.

The warning shots of the Arab Spring were heard in the streets of Moroccan cities in 2011. Mindful of the attention received by the February 20 movement, King Mohammed VI proposed a constitutional referendum, derived from a commission of experts, and submitted it for public approval that summer. Even though there was no mechanism for MREs to vote in regular elections, an exception was made and special ballots were organized for the diaspora. As a result of the new referendum and constitution, reference to the king's "holy" character was dropped, but his role as Commander of the Faithful was maintained.

The PJD won parliamentary elections in 2011 and formed a coalition government, remaining in parliamentary politics long enough to have its own corruption scandals, losses, and comebacks. Was this more about absorption than substantive democratization? Some argue that "the PJD became another co-opted opposition party," which had the unintended effect of "giving . . . other radical groups traction they would not have had if PJD's independence were more assured." However, it is unclear how any loyal opposition party could be considered anything but co-opted.[160] Only the king may define the role of religion in the public sphere, so any religion-based party must be careful not to overplay its hand.[161] The party accepted the national slogan: "God, Homeland, King" as the price of entry. In my interview with Minister Toufiq while the PJD was in its first year of government, the question of the party's influence on religion policy was raised. "The PJD never does anything without consulting first," Toufiq said, pausing to raise his brow to make exaggerated eye contact over his glasses frame, and then repeated "never."[162]

Moroccan ulemas' proximity to the state makes it "impossible for the ulema to condemn outright all Islamists" and yet it also makes "Islamists wary of attempts to co-opt them."[163] Francesco Cavatorta and Fabio Merone have studied Moroccan attempts to "delegitimize and co-opt extremists by reaching accommodations with well-known jihadi-salafi sheikhs."[164] For example, King Mohammed shocked observers by pardoning a group of jihadi-salafi preachers, including Mohammed al Fizazi, who had been sentenced to thirty years in prison after the 2003 Casablanca attacks. The king attended Friday prayers at a Tangiers mosque led by al Fizazi, who delivered a televised sermon.[165] In 2011, another Salafi leader was invited to help "isolate traditionalists from participation in the *20 février* protests." Al Fizazi endorsed the royal constitutional amendments in July 2011 and "urged his followers to vote for the 'best party' that 'respects Islam.'"[166] Salafis also entered Moroccan public religious life through the side door, establishing NGOs that agreed to prioritize Maliki doctrine over Wahhabism.[167] This marked an achievement in terms of co-optation: "Moroccan Salafis have publicly declared that they accept the monarchy and are not seeking to restore the Caliphate." Al Fizazi went on record to say that Morocco had lived under the same monarchy since the twelfth century and that the Commander of the Faithful was in fact a "protection against secular political projects."[168]

One group missing from Morocco's strategy of inclusion was Al Adl wal Ihsane. Hassan II's perennial enemy, Sheikh Yassine, had his internal travel restrictions removed by Mohammed VI. Yassine recognized the king as sultan but not as the religious leader. From the perspective of the Moroccan state, "al Adl is perverse—Yassine claims to be representing Moroccan Islam. He wants to be Caliph in place of the Caliph. He has a problem with the dynasty and wants to replace the King. He is delirious, in a dream state."[169] Some mosques defied the monarchy by eulogizing Sheikh Yassine of al Adl after his death. Al Adl activists claimed that there was "never any doubt that religion would be present in Moroccan rule. The question is whether other competing expressions of Islam could also be allowed to influence such rule."[170] Some sort of deal with al Adl might have offered a way out, but recognizing their existence risked a schism in the umma because it would legitimize contestation of the monopoly.

Maintaining control meant maintaining street credentials and nodding to or enforcing some orthodoxies. This took the form of prison time for a sixteen-year-old whose wall graffiti replaced "King" with "Football" in "King, God, Country." There were also news reports of an eighteen-year-old sentenced to one year of prison time and a fine of 1,000 euros for having "harmed the holy character of Mohammed VI" after posting a "disrespectful cartoon" on Facebook.[171] A twenty-two-year-old was punished for declaring, "There is no god but Mickey Mouse."[172] The same government that brought Elton John hosted Yusuf al-Qaradawi and multiplied religious broadcasting. Two new Islamic television stations and Radio Mohammed VI expanded under the religious affairs ministry's supervision.[173] One decade into the king's reign, broadcasting and satellite television were still more important than social media: television was the main source of information for two-thirds of eighteen- to twenty-four-year-olds. Despite the presence of Moroccan preachers on state television networks, however, citizens held the remote control.[174]

The state continues to assert its control in this realm—for example, by arresting a journalist who illegally broadcast video reportage from the Islamic State.[175] Such repressive tactics are less relevant in an online age. Under the old regime, a government could place someone under house arrest and successfully isolate that person's ideological influence. Today their sermons or videos remain Internet-accessible, for eternity, regardless of their physical fate in this world. The government assessed that up to 1,000 fighters had departed for Syria to volunteer for the Islamic State.[176] It was reported that around one-third were later imprisoned under anti-terrorism laws.

One of the policy goals that Minister Toufiq set for himself remained elusive: "Convincing other religious actors that the religious field must remain politically neutral."[177] In 2014, Mohammed VI issued a royal decree prohibiting employees of the Ministry of Religious Affairs from participating in any political activities or publicly expressing support for political or trade union causes.[178] On the other hand, twenty years after Mohammed VI's accession, Morocco had the highest density of publicly funded religious personnel per capita in the region and dedicated the highest share of GDP to religious affairs. As the minister said in an interview, "Our reforms don't date from the so-called Arab Spring; we are the only country in the world with the institution of Imarate-el-Mu'minin that truly lives up to its name."[179]

Algerian Islam in the Twenty-First Century

The main impetus for change in Algeria was applying lessons learned after the formal end of the civil war. Faced with new challenges—Al Qaeda in the Islamic Maghreb (AQMI), the Salafist Group for Preaching and Combat (GSPC), the Islamic State (ISIS)—the Bouteflika presidency entered the twenty-first century on better footing after a devastating decade of canceled elections, military coup, and civil war. It continued its agenda of reconciliation and consolidation while remaining determined to incorporate or suppress Islamist elements. The religious infrastructure is relatively underdeveloped: in 1989, there were only 856 instructors and 6,899 trained religious affairs personnel for a country of over 25 million. In a region where religious identity and authenticity are the currency of statehood, the Democratic and Popular Republic of Algeria has its own style of Islamic engagement. The state's outer limits of toleration for religious activism are unmistakable, and the message is delivered with the confidence of victors in the fifteen-year civil war against insurgents that only officially ended in 2004. The Algerian state, in that sense, approaches religion policy from a position of strength. One religious affairs ministry official put it like this in an interview: "We beat the army of the French empire and you don't think we can handle these ragtag Islamists?"[180]

President Abdelaziz Bouteflika skillfully limited the prospects of the legal Islamist party by drawing it into his coalition starting in 1997.[181] The Islamists accepted compromise on religious education, family law, and their goal of an Islamic state, and in return the government ended emergency law. Their agenda of "more Islam" was adopted by the new and improved Ministry of Religious Affairs (MARE) under Bouabdellah Ghlamallah (1997–2014). The Algerian state "declared its commitment to a national Muslim identity . . . as a national duty which is to be accomplished by the Algerian state." This commitment mirrored a growth in religiosity: in 2002, 50.1 percent of Algerians reported weekly mosque attendance, a proportion that increased to 63 percent in 2009.[182] The ministry's powers were broad, including the mandate to "eliminate sources of erroneous understanding of Islam" and to "regulate all forums for Islamic thought and exchanges with the Islamic world."[183]

Ministry officials attributed the country's civil war in the 1990s to the proliferation of untrained prayer leaders who fostered the conditions for violent jihadi sympathies. During the civil war, according to the inspector general at the ministry, Mohammed Aïssa, "eighty percent of those who took up arms against the state left school very early. We lost 200,000 lives and $200 billion." After that, he said, "we decided to prevent any instrumentalization of religion by parties, unions—or by the government itself." He said that his job required him to constantly defend against "pseudo-sheikhs"[184] The state revisited religious education policy, renationalized mosques, and redesigned imam training. Security conditions finally allowed state imams to return to the mosques; during the 1990s, ninety-six state imams had been assassinated. "After ten years," Aïssa said, mosques were now able to defend themselves spiritually— "although there is of course still some residual [backlog]," he added.

Officials at the religious affairs ministry worried most about foreign influences—especially of "religious practices imported from Saudi Arabia, Afghanistan and Iran."[185] Two decades after the civil war, Algeria experienced the return of Salafism. When asked to define the ministry's strategy against the expansion of Islamism in general, a senior adviser to the minister referred to institutes that train Algerian imams. Inspector General Aïssa, who would shortly become the minister, stressed that a key failing of theological training in the 1980s was that it attracted the weakest students who had done poorly in middle school. "The students got to know the Islamic part very well, but they did not have much intellectual power." This was a recipe, he said, for producing potential extremists: "There was an ideological invasion, and many students embraced the Muslim Brotherhood's ideas."[186] He cited another Algerian vulnerability: "Wahhabi influence against our national revolution spread further through satellite television and clandestine networks of distribution of propaganda CDs." To avoid a repeat, Maliki-style dress codes were enforced against Middle Eastern incursions.[187] As Minister Ghlamallah said, "Our imams should dress the same as our grandfathers and ancestors from Algeria and not from elsewhere."[188]

But there is still work to be done. One official stated, "With all the mosques that we have in Algeria, we even have problems finding imams who are adapted for the Algerian context!"[189] Another warned that "the Islamic community is bathed in an ocean of tears and blood because of political fatwas calling for discord."[190] During Ramadan and summer vacation time, periods when more unofficial preachers came into circulation, Minister Ghlamallah reminded the public that "consulting foreign preachers or imams is not in the interests of the Algerian citizen; these fatwas from foreign sources do not correspond to Algerian reality. Citizens should instead refer their questions to members of the existing scientific council in each region (Wilaya) for any explanations or religious guidance."[191]

Infrastructure

The Ministry of Religious Affairs experienced a renaissance in 2009 after a cabinet reshuffling made it one of the most visible posts in the government. Spending surpassed 1990s levels (circa US$160 million) for the first time in 2008, then continued to grow to $420 million in 2012 before settling at an operating budget of around $300 million (25 to 30 billion dinars) later that decade (see figure 9.11). The total number of ministerial employees rose from 24,000 in the year 2000 to 34,000 in 2014.[192] Within a decade, each of Algeria's forty-eight wilayas had an Islamic cultural center, and every four shared a dar al imam training institution. The 1968 proposal to create an axis of grand mosques in Algiers, Oran, and Constantine, after being delayed by civil war, came to fruition fifty years later. The ministry constructed a new five-building headquarters with 219 offices at a cost of 220 million dinars.[193]

Mosques

But first, into the early 2000s, the ministry had to retake control of mosques that had escaped state control and assign them a state imam.[194] The MARE's Inspector General described two goals: ensuring that "Algerian mosques be immunized against extremist ideologies," and eliminating the nonstate competitors (because "Shari'ah says that it is fitna [religious strife] to divide the community with a competing mosque").[195] Despite the overall growth of mosques in Algeria between 1989 and 2015, from 11,221 to 17,500, Algeria's ratio of mosques to citizens remained low after national independence: only one for every 2,300 people.[196] The future minister said assuredly, "We do want to have 1,000 per mosque—and yet at the same time we want to . . . enhance the importance and visibility of large neighborhood mosques."[197] It can be a struggle

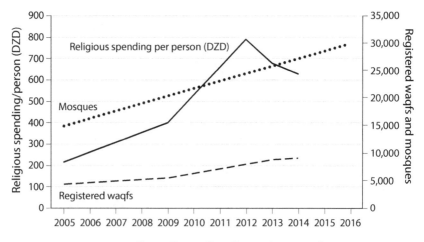

FIGURE 9.11. Algeria: Twenty-First-Century Institutionalization
of Religious Affairs, 2005–2016

to reach some of the prayer spaces tucked away in the impassable Casbah of Algiers or the Sahara, where the state's presence is minimal. There was confidence that large *mosquées pôles* (flagship mosques) were the solution for discord. Inspector General Aïssa said:

> We want to avoid the multiplication of prayer spaces; we feel it is better to have fewer but larger *grandes mosquées,* with well-trained imams. We even had to demolish a number of prayer spaces that were illegally transformed into mosques to spread Salafism in the 1990s.[198]

A senior mosque inspector said in an interview that he favored "prohibiting small prayer rooms" altogether, "because that is where the problem starts."[199] This explains the official emphasis on establishing a flagship mosque in every wilaya and a training mosque in each province (daïra), where imams would be given practical experience.[200]

The Grande Mosquée of Algiers, the Djamaa el Djazair, was another multiyear construction project on an area nearly the size of Vatican City.[201] Two more grand mosques were planned: one in Mascara with a capacity for 10,000 worshipers and 500 cars in its garage.[202] And another grand mosque in the wilaya of Annaba will have room for 8,000 prayer-goers, a Qur'an school, a library, and a number of other structures.[203] In an interview, the director of religious affairs for Oran described the 100,000-square-foot grand mosque that would accommodate 14,000 prayer-goers: "Small mosques do not capture the spirit of Islam. In order to really bring people together, you need one single voice—whether it's sermons on Friday or at holiday time."[204] As a senior

FIGURE 9.12 [DIPTYCH OF 9.12.1 AND 9.12.2]. Ministry for
Religious Affairs and grand mosque projects, Algiers (2016–2020)

official at a state agency in Oran said in an interview, "Once the grand mosque
and Islamic center are up and running, even Moroccans will come visit!"[205]

The need to fill the map with new mosques led to a large public works
program.[206] In 2014, there were a total of 17,000 mosques, with 4,000 under
construction, in addition to roughly 3,000 religious lodgings. In the coastal
city of Oran, the number of mosques grew from 250 to 713 and one new grand
mosque in the space of fifteen years. The national capital of Algiers is served
by 670 mosques for Friday sermons for a population of 8 million.[207] Each request for mosque construction passes through a council of four advisers of the
local wilaya's mosque foundation. Aside from the grand mosques, the Algerian
state has relied largely on private benefactors to build small and medium-sized
mosques. These non-state construction projects are transferred to the ministry
and then registered as waqfs. "We have them cede us the deed so it becomes
a public waqf. Otherwise they could just say, 'Hey, it's my mosque and I will
preach whatever I please.'"[208]

In addition to all of the construction, the ministry went to great lengths to
create an accurate inventory of existing mosques. In the year 2000, the ministry had completed 26 percent of its grand mapping project; in 2014, it reached
80 percent, and the inventory was slated for completion in 2019.[209]

FIGURE 9.13. A Mosque under construction in Oran, Algeria (2014)

Imams

Authorities aim to have multiple employees present in each mosque to fulfill various roles: preaching (*imam-khatib*), teaching Qur'an courses (*muderes*), calling to prayer (*muezzin*), and managing the administrative aspects (*qayyim*). The ministry assigns seven employees to each of the grandes mosquées, some of which accommodate up to 20,000 prayer-goers. The medium-sized mosques (*moyennes*), with capacity up to 4,000, receive three to four civil servants. The neighborhood prayer room gets one or two civil servants. "All employees have to have a certain minimum religious education before the mosque can open its doors," Minister Ghlamallah said in an interview.[210] The inspector general stressed in an interview, however, that these were ideal numbers and not the current reality.[211] There are varying educational requirements for the different levels of employees: while a senior employee (*cadre supérieur*) must have at least a university degree (*licence*), the muezzin and the maintenance workers just have to be able to recite at least half of the Qur'an from memory.

In the early 2000s, Minister Ghlamallah called attention to a dramatic deficit of imams across the country: "There are only 22,000 imams and Algeria needs another 22,000 to fill the void."[212] After years of a practice of hiring only 30 to 40 new employees, in 2006 President Bouteflika authorized 500 new hires per annum.[213] The personnel goals of his successor, Mohammed Aïssa (2014–2019), were to reach at least 75,000 permanent civil servants so as to put "five permanent agents in each medium and large mosque." The 2010s saw a vast improvement. By 2013, recruitment efforts were "adding between 2,000–3,000 new mosque staff each year."[214] Two years later, there were 53,000 civil servants, including 30,000 imams working in 20,000 mosques. Even if the ministry reached the goal of 75,000 employees, its officials would be a much smaller corps than, for example, the Ministry of Health (100,000), and just one-tenth the size of the education ministry (750,000). "Even if the training mosques (*mosquées d'application*) are supervised by the best imams," Aïssa said, "there are still young people joining terrorist groups or who have vile behavior when they step outside the mosque." That, he said, was why the ministry's challenge was "to raise the level of the imam so he can assume a critical role of both awareness-raising (*sensibilisation*) and guidance."[215]

Public Schools

The Ministry of Education redefined the role of public education by aiming to "give students an awareness of their belonging to a historic, collective, common and unique identity, officially consecrated by Algerian nationality—as a unifying factor for the Algerian people."[216] "We are the first in the Arab world to have reformed Islamic education," Aïssa said in an interview, "because of our history."[217] Qur'anic verses and hadiths were removed from schoolbooks— "to avoid the confusion of literary and divine texts"—and shari'ah was no longer offered as a separate track in high schools. Aïssa suggested that the ministry considered ending all Islamic education in public primary and secondary schools but parents were unwilling to send their children to study religion in mosques so soon after the country's civil war—moreover, the mosques did not have the staff. Students in the country's roughly 18,000 schools were instead given two hours of mandatory Islamic education, from the first year of primary school to the third year of secondary school.

Inspector General Aïssa recommended expanding religious curriculum to include "'shocking' topics, such as Jihad and the Islamic State." Aïssa said, "We believe that if you keep students from certain topics, then the extremists will say the state is imposing a false Islam."[218] Critics accused the education ministry of spreading Salafi tenets, but the teachers were being trained to counter such influences. The government introduced weekly continuing education requirements for the country's 4,200 religion teachers (out of 96,000 schoolteachers). The education ministry also added a 400-hour module to the required certification of religion teachers and tripled the number of religion education inspectors to 30 between 2009 and 2014. The number of teachers still lagged behind, however. The inspector general at the education ministry explained that "we need 5,000 new teachers. We already had 2,000 teachers, and another 2,200 were recruited among university graduates" (to teach subjects other than Islam). In 2011, the Ministry of Religious Affairs detailed a large group of employees to the Ministry of Education, including 122 secondary school teachers.

Qur'an Courses and Schools

The 1990 law on associations in Algeria changed registration requirements for religious education, and authorities scrambled to bring "Qur'anic schools into line" in order to "prevent extremist thinking from finding its way into Algeria."[219] Qur'an study arrangements were sometimes very informal, and teachers were often volunteers. Minister Ghlamallah called for the "unification of the methods of teaching the Qur'an: this reform is motivated by realism and moderation . . . to preserve the unity of Muslims in general and Algerians in particular."[220] The number of Qur'anic schools grew consistently, from 1,345 in 1999 to 2,360 in 2013, an increase of 57 percent. In 1989, there were 4,024 Qur'an classes, including 2,251 offered at mosques. By the mid-2010s, the majority of the country's mosques (more than 10,000) offered Qur'anic education.[221] Ghlamallah said that Qur'an courses were especially useful to offer during the summer, when students can "recite the Qur'an and be saved from idleness in the streets, which is the source of all evil."[222] By 2014, Oran counted 770 Qur'an schools, 135 of which were connected to a mosque; half of the 28,000 students enrolled in Oran's Qur'anic education were under the age of six.[223] During my visit to one of Oran's new neighborhood mosques, the imam—who had served in prayer spaces around Oran since 1972—demonstrated how the youngest students learn to write verses with a bamboo brush and ink based on burnt wool. When the words were correctly executed, the student could wash the tablet clean. Whence the parental question upon a child's return home from Qur'an course: "So, did you erase your board today?" (see figure 9.14).

Imam Training

In the early 2000s, the country was producing tiny numbers of imams—ranging from as few as a dozen to a hundred annually.[224] Minister Ghlamallah said in a news interview that "with regard to Imams, training is the only thing that counts. The first step is to invest in better training for imams . . . so they can adapt to society's developments."[225] Inspired by a program for general teacher training (dar al alim), the Ministry of Religious Affairs created twelve

FIGURE 9.14. Religious affairs officials with tablet and brush at the Abu Bakr Issadek
Mosque in Oran, Algeria (2014)

regional institutions (*dar al imam*) and one national branch that offered standardized imam training between 2004 and 2015. The director of the dar al
imam in Mohammedia said in an interview that enrollment varies from 100 to
200 students in each branch and that students are typically recommended by
their mosques and *zawiyyas*. After two years of training and memorization of
the Qur'an (three years if seeking a higher level of certification), they face a
competitive review.[226] The program of study requires higher-level imams who
will also teach Qur'an courses to master the theme of "toleration within Islam"
and to complete a thesis on political, economic, cultural, or social problems
in the contemporary world. The examination to become a principal inspector
includes sections on "fanaticism and extremism in the past and present" and
"the proclamation of heresy and its danger to religion and society."

The Ministry of Education reported that 800 new imams were trained nationally in the early 2010s, and it set the goal of increasing the graduating class
to 2,000 per annum by the end of the decade. In terms of professionalization,
a religious affairs official said in an interview, "the imam of 2014 is a world away
from the imam of 1980—there is a higher level of education, higher aptitude,
and greater patriotism."[227] Religion policy expanded its focus to also include
more Algerian women—especially mothers raising children in a religious

lifestyle—not just the usual target audience of young men. In Oran, the number of women enrolled in religious studies at mosques increased from just 40 in 2004 to 8,790 in 2014. Nationally, 200,000 women were enrolled in Qur'an courses, ranging in intensity from six to thirty hours per week. In 2002, 150 women graduated from Algerian universities with training to become a mourchidate. They had the same rights as imams and could rise, through promotion, to higher positions, such as principal mourchidate and female inspector. There were also four female deputy directors, and women made up 40 percent of the religious affairs ministry's workforce.[228] Minister Ghlamallah welcomed hundreds to a national meeting on training women held at the principal dar al imam in Mohammedia neighborhood of Algiers.[229]

Enforcement of the Monopoly

Regarding the sensitive topic of the Friday sermons, officials said in an interview that "we assign imams to mosques, but they are autonomous."[230] Ghlamallah said that "every imam is free to write his own sermon, so long as it is done in an educated manner."[231] Public employees in each region and province reviewed the content of sermons before they were delivered on Fridays.[232] Another official suggested that the review might occasionally suggest topics that advance government policy. "On a recent Friday," he explained, "we asked the imams to discuss the recent teachers' strikes. We didn't name any names, but we spoke about how it's tough on the kids who have nothing to do when there's no school. But this provoked an angry reaction from the teachers' unions. Usually we ask them to talk about something like Earth Day, or the importance of voting."[233]

Firing Imams

According to the Algerian penal code, only authorized imams may lead prayer. Anyone caught preaching without a license must pay 200,000 dinars (US$2,782) and faces a prison term of one to three years.[234] If imams do not demonstrate their "respect for the national religious framework," one official said, "they won't be inducted into the corps of imams."[235] In an interview, Minister Ghlamallah explained that when he arrived,

> we removed around 100 imams who had been trained abroad during the 1980s and 1990s. We told them to find another profession because we did not want to have anyone who was compromised by terrorism—by way of fatwas, accommodation or other types of complicity. They were not included in the general amnesty.

Since then, he said, "it is rare for imams to be fired; the administration always knows the person before he is hired. Even when they are working on a voluntary basis without pay, they do so under contract."[236] "While not every imam is under inspection at all times," officials said,

> this does not mean that we do not know what is happening in mosques. Sometimes we hear things from worshippers and sometimes from inspectors. If imams make serious mistakes they will be sent to the disciplinary committee. We do not control imams—well, we control some of them. It is a conditional control. I do not impose ethical controls. However, the abnormal behavior of an imam can be detected.[237]

Nonetheless, because of stricter hiring requirements, "we have fewer and fewer cases of ideological discipline."

Since 2001, it has been illegal for imams to allow political activities in mosques.[238] The inspector general recalled a disciplinary case from the imams council in which he issued a stern warning against an imam to stop talking politics in the mosque.[239] "There can be no partisan discourse," Aïssa said, "no defense of any party ideology. No calling for voting a specific way. I cannot accept an imam who belongs to a political party."[240] The Islamist National Salvation Party (MSP) accused the ministry of harassing imams who were friendly to their political formation. Michael Driessen describes a "string of public spats" between the party and the ministry, ranging from whether certain public ordinances were in keeping with shari'ah law to disagreements over education reform, family law, mosque administration, imam promotions, and "electoral positioning."[241] In an embarrassing 2010 incident, five imams refused to salute the flag or to rise during the national anthem. They were not fired, but they were no longer allowed to preach on Fridays. As Inspector General Aïssa put it, "They disrespected the sacrifices of the martyrs of the revolution, the greatest war of liberation in the twentieth century."[242]

Salafism

With mosques lacking proper staffing, there were fears that they would become "venues that could be exploited to propagate extremist ideas and beliefs."[243] Officials estimated that there were several dozen Salafi mosques in operation at any time, many of which were legally operating under restrictions.[244] The Algerian government denied permission to a Salafi party to hold its annual convention (something Tunisia tried unsuccessfully to do with Hizb-ut-Tahrir). When the government "announced its determination to better control mosques and reduce the influence of other Islamic trends," a wave of closures of "unauthorized prayer spaces" followed.[245] The religious affairs ministry suspended fifty-five imams who were "close to the Salafi movement" and active in mosques in Algiers. Aïssa said that they "swore allegiance not to Algeria but to foreign parties," and that whenever they receive instructions from the ministry, the Salafis "requested the permission of sheikhs in Mecca whether to follow them or not!"[246]

According to a 2003 decree, "the distribution of the Holy Qur'an and religious books and works in all mediums is subject to the agreement from the Ministry of Religious Affairs and Wakfs."[247] This allowed the ministry to announce the "monitoring of bookstores, the standardization of the calls to prayer, and a ban on 'roquia' [usually referring to exorcism] and 'hidjama' [magic practice] and all sorts of practices that derive from charlatanism," as well as "systematic monitoring of books, CDs and cassettes of a religious nature at ports, airports, and the borders." On average, several hundred books were rejected as "subversive" by the ministry's national reading commission, out of around 7 million books imported annually. Algeria imposed importation licenses on copies of the Qur'an, religious books, and cassettes, and licenses were refused to all material containing "calls for violence, terrorism, extremism, divisive jurisprudence, heretical doctrines, anti-Sufism, political edicts, or a 'culture of hatred.'"[248] There was an ambient competitive spirit. In August 2013, a well-known "television sheikh" sued the religious affairs minister for defamation after an exchange of public insults.

The ministry opposed Salafis' calls for prosecuting those who did not fast during the month of Ramadan, saying that it "had no legal basis." The Salafis' deviations from Algerian religious customs were scrutinized, and the minister "denounced the behavior of radical Salafists" who observed the sunset with their naked eye, instead of following the announced times, and who "broke the fast 7 to 8 minutes before the call of the Muezzin." In 2010, while awaiting the creation of a high fatwa council (haut conseil de la fatwa), the ministry launched online fatwas "to avoid excesses that are contrary to the fundamental principles of Islam, and the transcontinental fatwas; its primary goal is to block the path of fatwas that damage Islam and Muslims and to end the imbroglio confronting young people because of fatwas spread by satellite television."[249]

Despite the actions taken against Salafism, one university professor said in an interview that MARE's great error was to try to "return to the sources," because that inadvertently let Salafis inside the ministry. Some ministerial discourse did seem rooted in the paranoid style of the extremist competition. In one instance, Minister Ghlamallah referred to "the Christian-Zionist infiltration which is trying to take root in Algeria" and evoked shadowy "campaigns of evangelization and calls for Algerians to convert to Judaism . . . to destabilize and divide the Algerian people."[250] But such remarks were not the style of his successor, Mohammed Aïssa. In response to the US Department of State's admonishments on religious freedoms in Algeria, Minister Aïssa said: "If they want to accuse us of defending Islam and our historic traditions, then let them."[251]

Soft Restoration

Facing the problem of imams who did not report their marriage ceremonies to the state in the 2010s, the ministry reminded imams that ceremonies were not valid without a certificate from the city hall. The state, interestingly, did not go so far as to forbid certain "qualified imams" who were not employed by the state from performing religious marriages. But the ministry found a compromise: it issued official registry books to imams where they could inscribe the marriages and thereby keep records with which to update the state. During Ramadan 2013, Minister Ghlamallah declared that those who did not observe the fast were committing a "grave sacrilege"—a comment that was seen as an attempt to cozy up to Salafis. In 2015, even after the death of twenty-five people in riots in Ghardaia, Minister Aïssa took pains to convey that the state was not at war with Salafism per se. "Extremist Salafist thought" was responsible for the worst of it, he said, which was different from "national Salafist thought, which does not destroy the country."[252] There was an increase in trials put on for show, in an apparent attempt to appease radicals. For example, there was "increased public discipline for individuals who have denigrated Islam; prison terms for disrespecting the Qur'an, or soldiers who smoked cigarettes during Ramadan." Yet Minister Ghlamallah also continued to toe a fine line, expressing his disapproval of any attempt to punish people for not fasting during Ramadan. "Don't ask me about violating Ramadan's sanctity—the Algerian constitution guarantees freedom of belief. Ask those who arrested them."[253]

Pluralization

The Algerian Ministry of Religious Affairs has actively protected its monopoly to ensure that only approved religious content will find public expression. In an interview, the minister spoke of "other sects" active in Algeria and of their right to religious freedom. Should any of these movements "have destabilizing effects, and stop being a good guest, then we intervene with the aid of imams."[254] In interviews, officials spoke wistfully of the Jewish and Christian communities that thrived in Algeria before the arrival of European colonists in the nineteenth century. Most of the country's Jews and Christians fled in the 1960s, following the French departure, leaving only a few thousand Roman Catholics and a couple of dozen Jews. While a handful of historic buildings and sites were preserved, tensions with France and with Israel ensured there was little overt sentimentality and no official expectation that these minorities would return. The grand synagogue of Oran was turned into a mosque, and the grand cathedral of Oran became a public library. A half-century after Algerian independence, the religious affairs minister made a gesture of reconciliation and called for a reopening of synagogues and churches. He encouraged the rediscovery of Algeria's pre-Islamic roots—"Algeria had Jews before it had Muslims, after all," he said in the interview—and recognition of its ecumenical public sphere before the rise of Islamist movements. In the 1970s, it was not unusual to find instructors of Christian background who were responsible for teaching Islam. The short-lived effort to reopen synagogues was called off after a flare-up in the Arab-Israeli conflict. The desire to avoid irking reactionary elements still outweighs the impulses toward toleration.

The Future of the Ministry

In many ways, Algerian Islam is still recovering from the trauma of civil war. In interviews, officials said that mosques were built with excessive zeal during the 1990s, and with no provision for ensuring the ability to oversee or staff them. Two decades later, mosques were still missing staff. For example, the deficit of *imams instituteurs* throughout the Sahara region had left mosques in Souk-Ahras with no imams; after thirty-nine departures, there were insufficient imams for the 122 mosques of the wilaya.[255] The result was the kind of vacuum that officials take seriously; Wahhabism tends to take the place of nothingness. Ghlamallah said:

> Our current shortage [of ulema] is due to the infernal period of the early 1990s. . . . Before, there were local muftis who were not centralized. It is only when our ministry tried to return to the sources—Malikism, spirituality, and Sufism—that mosques were finally able to defend themselves.[256]

Opponents of the ministry level the reciprocal accusation that the government politicized the space even with anodine efforts to get out the vote, by "exhorting Algerians to carry out their duty as citizens in the next elections."[257] Some referred to the state's preachers as *Les Imams CCP*, a reference to the national bank account from which their paychecks were drawn. The ministry did not hesitate to mobilize mosque preachers to urge public calm during the riots in Bejaia that followed budgetary austerity measures. It issued "urgent instructions to preachers to use their Friday sermon to warn worshipers against *Fitna* (divisiveness) and to refrain from anything that might harm the country's peace and stability," and they intimated that the protests were un-Islamic. Minister Aïssa said that his priority was "the preservation of the nation through the protection of national religious references founded upon the Maliki rite." "Algeria must be immunized against the contagion of instrumentalizing religion for political ends" and avoid the attempts to destabilize it "that stemmed from the Arab Spring."[258]

To this end, the ministry intended to deploy regional fatwa councils and a new Islamic jurisprudence (fiqh) authority. Nostalgic for "the great role played by *zawiyyas* to eradicate fitna in the 1990s," the ministry also announced the establishment of a centralized zawiyya federation in 2016.[259] There was an official recommendation to use the *zawiyyas* against Wahhabi influences. Official were also seeking better uses for the country's thousands of waqfs—the number of religious foundations rose from 5,500 in 2009–2014 to 9,119 in 2017. Many of these were nonprofit establishments that provided lodging for imams.[260]

The inspector general for religious affairs even envisioned the possibility of creating a Mufti of the Republic. "We don't want what people to imagine a man with a white beard up on a minbar who declares this or that licit or illicit," Aïssa said.

> That concept doesn't exist anymore in the modern Islamic world. I envision a national interdisciplinary academy of some kind. . . . This body could address the questions that people have questions about and where unified religious rulings are called for. . . . The Mufti of the Republic will be the one who announces these decisions to the public.[261]

Despite the fact that it is "nearly impossible to stop the development of a sect that claims to follow the Qur'an and reaches people through its satellite channels and internet," the Algerian state will keep trying, because it has to.[262] There is no question of disestablishment; as Ghlamallah put it: "Mosques represent religion in Algeria. Those who wish to dissociate mosques from the state want us to renounce the essential mission to shore up the state, and they want to spread anarchy and acts of terrorism."[263]

Tunisia in the Twenty-First Century

The main impetus for change in Tunisia arrived with the 2011 revolution, which exposed the deep-seated state-Islam cleavage. For all of its proud secularism in the twentieth century, it was the country's political Islam party, Ennahda, that emerged as the largest single party in postrevolutionary Tunisia: it received 89 of 217 seats in the National Constituent Assembly, three times the size of its closest competitor.[264] The Tunisian landscape was also a strong wellspring of support for Salafi movements. As one minister put it in 2016, "After the fall of the regime, we discovered the alarming situation that was buried underneath the surface . . . we went through a major crisis with Salafi currents. . . . We suddenly found ourselves face to face with jihadi and knowledge-based types [of Salafism]—a world we knew nothing about. They started to move within the society and institutions, both officially and unofficially."[265]

Given the Ennahda Party's own recent history of repression, the first postrevolutionary governments were ambivalent about policing religion. The coalition of three parties (Troika) intended to "correct the religious landscape" after five decades of autocratic secularist rule and to achieve "the coexistence of democracy and Islam."[266] The landmark 2014 constitution, which passed by a vote of 200 to 16, marked an impressive compromise in that direction: Article 6 protects religion and guarantees freedom of religion and the neutrality of mosques.[267] After years of marginalization under the old regimes of Bourguiba and Ben Ali, when "the police ran the mosques," a corps of religious professionals was summoned to take charge. After the revolution, imam appointments previously handled by the Interior Ministry were transferred to the Ministry of Religious Affairs. The majority leader of the National Constituent Assembly said in an interview that "we need to carefully choose the men who will be preaching every day—we can't let just anybody do it. There should be a certification process and a public examination for Friday preacher to make sure imams and sermons are in concordance with Tunisian values."[268]

But given the lack of earlier institution-building, and the razed-earth Islam policies of twentieth-century national leaders, Tunisian religious life was resistant to the arrival of professional civil servants. The revolutionary government's religious affairs ministers faced insubordination from all sides—including from within the government—and demands that the state intervene more, less, or differently. (As the president of the republic defended women who wore the niqab, a group of deputies submitted a bill to ban the outfit in public places.) Unlike Algeria or Morocco, the minister's authority was shared with the Mufti of the Republic—an office created under the previous regime. As analyst Haim Malka concluded in a recent report, "No single actor can determine religious policy. . . . Tunisia's Islamic identity . . . will remain contested."[269] While this could be interpreted as more democratic—or anyway less monopolistic—the overall effect was abdication.

The Tunisian religious affairs ministers lacked the stability of their counterparts in Morocco and Algeria, who were substantial power brokers with control over large budgets and remained in place for fifteen to twenty years. They also lacked the authority of Turkish Diyanet presidents, who had minimum four-year terms. In the first six years after the revolution, the Tunisian ministry changed hands *every year*. One minister had to resign for criticizing the spread of Saudi Wahhabism. Opposition parties accused the ministry of absentee-ism—in other words, for a basic "failure to run mosques and Qur'anic schools in the country."[270] But its difficult task was made nearly impossible by the fact that it had the *smallest* of all ministerial budgets. Oversight of the Islamic in-stitutions presented an immediate dilemma for an administration determined not to repeat the behavior of the *ancien régime.*

Three party leaders agreed in interviews that they are reluctant to intervene in Islamic life in the country. Each also acknowledged that intervention was inevitable, and that there should be a technocratic Ministry of Religious Af-fairs to do so. A strong ministry would help keep Islam policy out of the hands of political parties or security professionals. Mondher Belhadj, the policy di-rector for the Nidaa Tounes Party, said in an interview, "We need mosques to be independent and neutral; we need to train imams in a new way without becoming imams ourselves. It's a delicate task made more difficult by the cur-rent Wahhabi wave."[271] The Tunisian president Moncef Marzouki (2014–2016), a former human rights lawyer and political dissident who spent four months in prison before fleeing abroad in the 1990s, said in an interview:

> The government used to control the mosques, so secularists are reluctant to say that the state should control religion. But if we leave society to itself, the Salafis would try to take over. A democratic state and society has to control this, but one cannot behave like the Ben Ali regime![272]

In another conversation, Sahbi Attig, an Ennahda Party leader in parliament who spent eighteen years in prison, said, "The Religious Affairs Ministry will always be under the government's oversight to keep mosques impartial, out-side the control of any political party. It would be chaos if the state pulled out. You would get Salafis or Hibz-ut-Tahrir."[273]

The immediate aftermath of Tunisia's Jasmine Revolution, when Islam was almost entirely unregulated, provides a glimpse of life without an effective religious affairs ministry. Early on, the ministry signaled that "not all religious activities of unauthorized groups will be restricted. Those which do not di-rectly challenge the ministry . . . will be permitted because they are a result of a Revolution that claimed plurality and tolerance."[274] The vice president of the revolutionary transition, Yadh Ben Achour, said in an interview that "everyone took advantage of the newfound freedom."[275] Minister Munir Tlili in 2014 described a situation of "anarchy, where some people misunderstood the meaning of freedom."[276] The number of mosques that were seized in the after-math of the revolution during the period of lawlessness reached 1,100 in No-vember 2011, while the number of mosques experiencing "administrative prob-lems" was twice that; in sum, nearly half of all houses of worship were under "unreliable" oversight.[277]

FIGURE 9.15. Tunisia: The Minister of Religious Affairs and the
Mufti of the Republic inaugurate a new mosque, Tunis (2016)

The government was loath to use a heavy hand. Among the mosques under
siege was the historic Zeitouna Grand Mosque, which was declared "independent" by an unofficial imam, who asserted his right to "directly manage [the
mosque's] own funds [and avoid] state oversight of religious education." For
two years, the ministry was powerless to prohibit his sermons—even after he
called for sentencing artists to death. Similar to Salafis in Algeria who broke the
Ramadan fast ostentatiously early to defy the Ministry of Religious Affairs, the
mosque challenged the authority of Tunisia's ministry by announcing competing prayer times, leading "a number of mosques to move forward *al Isha* prayer
and delay the *al Sobah* prayer."[278] The former chairman of Zeitouna University
recalled in an interview that the Salafis' "goal was to torpedo the Tunisian religious reformist school completely. . . . I was shocked by the vicious onslaught
against us and by the absence and disintegration of the State."[279]

The ministry initiated an inventory of the country's mosques and took
stock of the hundreds of prayer spaces in the hands of Salafi extremists. Within
six months, the first minister after the revolution "rolled back Salafi mosques
through persuasion, pressure and legal action, and reasserted control over
1,000 mosques."[280] "In about 50 cases, we have called on the Justice Ministry
to step in and resolve the issue."[281] The minister of religious affairs said in an
interview in 2014 that "we have a soft approach, we get in touch with the religious leader, eventually involve ministries of interior and justice and the local
governor. But the police never enter the premises: we do not want a violent
solution."[282] Even after the initial period of anarchy had passed, however, the
ministry had diminished capacities of either dissuasion or repression. In
May 2017, "the Ministry still [had] no legal framework and [was being] run
with decrees and memos; it [had no] computer system to administer its 19,000
employees."[283]

Infrastructure

President Ben Ali's government had started a process in the 2000s, prodded along by the 2002 Djerba synagogue bombing, of holding national Qur'an recitation contests and filling the days of Ramadan with 150,000 religious activities and a thirty-part religious television series.[284] The post–Ben Ali governments immediately increased the means available to religious affairs: the 2014 budget of around $53.7 million was significantly higher than the $41.5 million that the Ben Ali regime spent in its last year. But as a percentage of overall government spending, Ministry of Religious Affairs expenditures under Ben Ali had already decreased from 0.46 percent of the national budget in 2001 to 0.24 percent in 2010. The postrevolutionary governments maintained a similar rate of spending: after five years in power, there had been only a 0.29 percent increase in total allocations for religious affairs. The 2017 budget of 99.8 million dinars (approximately $41 million) was nearly unanimously approved.[285] The 2018 budget assigned slightly more to religious affairs: 105.3 million dinars (around $42.4 million).[286] The whole government's budget of 35.85 billion dinars represented a total spending increase of nearly 5 percent on the previous year—but the share of religious affairs spending remained at just 0.29 percent of total spending. When measured as a fraction of GDP—a rate that in total was only one-half of Algeria's and one-third of Turkey's and Morocco's—spending on religious affairs increased to 0.11 percent (up by 0.02 percent) before falling again to 0.09 percent in 2014.

Mosques

After the 2011 revolution, the Tunisian government faced a similar task to Algeria's after its civil war, albeit on a smaller scale: it had to win back mosques from revolutionaries. In Tunisia, around 1,100 mosques, out of 5,100, escaped official oversight. (In Algeria, the figure was 10,000 out of 15,000.) The ministry did its best to prevent mosques from being used for political activities. It reasserted control of mosques at a quick pace, around eight to twelve a week.[287] Each year the ministry claimed to have halved the number of uncontrolled mosques, from a height of 1,100 in 2011 down to 58 in 2015.[288] In addition, a period of sustained construction had begun five years before the Jasmine Revolution, in 2006, and it continued for at least six years afterwards (2017). Altogether, the ministry added around 1,700 new mosque structures. Fewer than 200 mosques were built between January 2011 and May 2014, but then over 500 were added in 2015–2016, and 1,000 more in 2017, for a national total of 5,817.[289] The relative amount of prayer space in Tunisia thus increased drastically, but remained much lower than in the rest of the region. In 2016, there

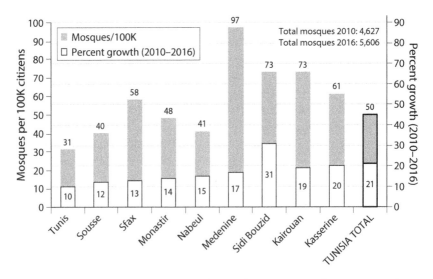

FIGURE 9.16. Mosque construction in Postrevolutionary Tunisia (2010 versus 2016)

was roughly one mosque for every 2,000 Tunisian citizens (whereas there was one for every 1,000 Turkish citizens). It was possible to see exactly where the government had concentrated its mosque-building efforts, such as Tunis and Bizerte (see figure 9.16). Two other heavily affected cities, Medenine and Sidi Bouzid, were similarly known for the presence of "unruly mosques" in an area where a large majority voted for Ennahda over the secularist party.[290] Despite the growth, authorities are still making up for lost ground: only Medenine approximated the golden ratio of one mosque to 1,000 of the faithful.

Imams

Tunisian officials have also acknowledged "a crisis with imam-preachers."[291] The corps of imams grew slowly from 9,000 employees in religious affairs in the late 1980s to 13,000 in 2005. The modest investment in a shari'ah institute and imam training centers was measured in the hundreds of thousands, not millions.[292] Imams were required to have a Zeitouna diploma and pass a public exam. Only 15 imams were recruited in 2006. The pace picked up just before the revolution, when 150 graduates were recruited by the ministry in a single year.[293] By 2014, there were 18,000 imams, including 3,000 Friday preachers.[294] Imams still had no formal bureaucratic status as civil servants, so they were not being paid except for "some pocket money." Between 2018 and 2020, an Ennahda-linked American NGO (Center for the Study of Islam and Democracy) was contracted to provide training to more than 1,000 imams in ten

Tunisian regions.[295] In an interview, the minister said, "They are not really civil servants—they receive a bonus at the end of the month. They are religious employees without fixed salaries or social security; we hope to raise their salaries soon and transform them into civil servants."[296]

Education

In 2012, after more than fifty years, education resumed at Zeitouna University. The number of students enrolled in 1956 had been on the order of 14,000, whereas in the 2010s it rarely exceeded 1,200, including foreign students. Ennahda was accused of "blocking initiatives to create qur'an schools," yet "civil society has reacted vigorously on each occasion to block initiatives" to create an adequate system of "full-time religious education and qur'anic schools independent of [the] public education" ministry that would be controlled and monitored by the Ministry of Religious Affairs.[297] The Mufti of the Republic said in an interview: "We need a training seminary so imams and preachers can carry out their scientific and religious roles."[298] Plans were being developed for an Institut supérieur de théologie. Additionally, an imam training center was in preparation with the education ministry, to be built in Kairouan. The Ministry of Religious Affairs signed an agreement with its Moroccan counterpart in 2012 to receive a three-year pilot program "rehabilitating imams, training preachers, and establishing local ulema councils." (The ministry sent forty-three imams for training in Morocco.)[299] Additionally, it authorized continuing education for ninety-nine selected imams to help "bring rationality to religious discourse."[300]

Enforcing the Monopoly

The International Crisis Group noted in a report that with the repression of Ennahda under President Ben Ali, "the Salafi phenomenon—quietists and jihadis alike—gained ground in Tunisia."[301] It was difficult to say whether there was a markedly different Islamization trend when Ennahda came into government, or whether government policies amounted to an attempt to stave off the threat coming from Salafi activists. In President Marzouki's inaugural address, he proclaimed a unifying message: "I am the president of the Niqabis, the Veiled, and the Secularists." In the new Tunisia, mosques would be open for more of the day, and the new coalition stopped the practice whereby "imams had their sermons handed to them."[302] In my interview with President Marzouki, he described the gradual diminution of "a soft conflict" between secularists and Islamists: "They accepted the state and human rights: we extracted that from them! From time to time we have to give them something.

Society itself is getting more religious. For five decades, this was an authoritarian state—a dictatorship."[303]

The Ennahda-led coalition (2012–2013), however, found it hard to formulate a new Islam policy that would please all constituencies. One group of imams accused it of importing Wahhabism, and another accused it of using Ben Ali's tactics of repression. The former thought the state was too reluctant to enforce its religious monopoly—either out of fear or respect for Salafis—while Islamists further to the right accused it of inadequate respect for Wahhabis. In its first year, the government approved three Salafi groups and Hizb ut-Tahrir, an international movement calling for an Islamic caliphate, as legal political parties. It also registered hundreds of new Salafi charities and schools and "allowed radical preachers from the Gulf and Egypt to go on speaking tours around the country."[304] It invited Salafi personalities to provide input on the state's religious institutions. The government permitted one of them, Abou Iyadh al Tounsi, to preach openly in Tunis. The leader of Ennahda was recorded in a charm offensive with members of Ansar al-Sharia that came off badly on YouTube. Ennahda politicians were portrayed as Salafi apologists who acted as a gateway to more extreme ideologies. The ministry, it was said, was trying to "import Wahhabism to Tunisia."[305]

The government thought it could control Ansar al-Sharia just as Ben Ali had aimed to control Wahhabis. President Marzouki recalled in an interview:

> I told the Salafist sheikhs that we wanted them in the framework of the democratic state. Ennahda and Ghannouchi really tried with Ansar al-Sharia. We knew that they were against Ben Ali, but now we wanted them to support human rights. We weren't naive, but we were wrong to think we could divide them.[306]

The reluctance to intervene, the religious affairs minister Mounir Tlili said, was rooted in awareness of the recent past:

> Before, there used to be dictates on what subjects to discuss for the benefit of the government. Since the revolution, there have been no such orders given. But we have organized visits across the country to open a dialogue with our preachers and imams, to speak about solidarity, unemployment, morality. We teach them to love their work and their country, but without being severe about it.[307]

Successive religious affairs ministers have struggled to distinguish the ministry's behavior from that of the *ancien régime*. Minister Tlili insisted in an interview that he did "not engage in domination, coercion, and control"; instead, "we deal with preachers as cultured people and scholars . . . who command

FIGURE 9.17. The new Tunisian Ministry of
Religious Affairs, Tunis (2016)

respect . . . as free, responsible people. The era of regime dictates is long gone, when sermons served political and partisan ends." Ironically, the new regime's formulation of religious freedom in article 6—guaranteeing religious liberty and freedom of conscience—closely resembled article 5 from the Bourguiba-era constitution (1959). Public order regulations were resuscitated from the age of Bourguiba, and "the imams . . . were forbidden to talk about anything people cared about . . . [like] corruption [and] unemployment."[308] Successive postrevolution ministers invoked the same powers that they had abhorred when they were deployed by the Ben Ali regime. To regain control over Zeitouna University, for example, the government used the Ben Ali–era laws of 1988 and 1994 that gave the ministry control over "the appointment and firing of religious employees, and maintenance of the mosques."[309] At one point, the government banned public prayer.[310]

The minister of religious affairs introduced new regulations covering preachers' sermons, and like its *ancien régime* predecessors, the ministry soon began arresting unlicensed preachers, monopolizing fatwas, and struggling to assert state control over the country's mosques after the chaotic years of transition (see figure 9.17).[311] It, too, cited Bourguiba-era clauses to try to prevent a radical Islamist party from holding its annual convention. When fifteen soldiers were killed in a battle with al Qaeda insurgents two weeks after the Islamic State caliphate was declared, the ministry fired any Tunisian imams who refused to pronounce prayers for the soldiers who died. It also closed at least twenty mosques (including "all 'outside ministerial supervision' or 'where we have confirmed that our soldiers' death was celebrated'") and shut down "television stations, radios and internet sites spreading messages of takfir and jihad."[312]

The revolution coincided with the start of the Syrian civil war, which became a magnet for Islamist fighters. The opposition parties accused Ennahda of facilitating passports so that young Tunisians could "go for a Turkish vacation." Tunisian authorities remained alert for would-be combatants looking to make their way to Syria/Iraq and Europe and confiscated the passports of tens of thousands they accused of seeking violent jihad abroad—while missing thousands of others who made it abroad.[313]

Crackdown on Salafis

Political pressure quickly pushed Ennahda and its partners to wage not merely ideological but also actual military war on violent Islamist extremism. Ennahda's approach began to change in September 2012 after hundreds of Tunisians attacked the United States embassy to protest a film ridiculing the Prophet Muhammad. That same week, Ansar al-Sharia fighters overran the US consulate in Benghazi, Libya, killing four Americans, including the ambassador. The Ennahda Party completed its metamorphosis into the representative of state legitimacy and turned on the Salafis it formerly tolerated. The minister directly faced down the Salafi leader of Ansar al-Sharia, Abou Iyadh al Tounsi, who had preached that "Muslims should fight an 'infinite battle' to defend Islam."[314] The minister of religious affairs, Noureddine Khadmi, responded with a half-hour sermon broadcast over mosque loudspeakers: "It is totally forbidden in Islam to kill ambassadors or anyone who is sent from another country."[315]

In May, al Qaeda–linked fighters laid siege to the home of the interior minister, killing four guards. The final straw was the Islamists' militarization. Ansar al-Sharia clashed with army troops in western Tunisia and was blamed for the atmosphere that led to the assassination of two secular opposition leaders. Ansar al-Sharia was declared a terrorist group and banned in September 2013, more than a year and a half after the January revolution.[316] The martyrs of the Tunisian revolution now include not only Chokri Belaïd and Mohamed Brahmi, gunned down by unknown assailants in 2013 but also the scores of Tunisian soldiers who were killed by Ansar al-Sharia sympathizers in the years that followed. The regime's turnaround was not swift, but it was decisive.[317] In an interview, President Marzouki said, speaking of Ansar al-Sharia, "We discovered how stubborn they are. They don't want the country to be democratic. I deeply regret it. It means killing and arresting people, but I have to defend this state."[318] The al Qaeda network singled out the Tunisian government for "imposing restrictions on preaching and for monitoring the movement of Ansar al Sharia members."[319]

Abdeljalil Ben Salem was promoted to religious affairs minister in 2016 but was fired within months after an excess of candor before a parliamentary committee. "The reproduction of terrorists and extremism is due to the Wahhabi school," he told Tunisian deputies, "whether in good faith or not. This school of thought produces nothing but extremism," and he demanded specific reforms from the Saudi ambassador.[320] Ben Salem was dismissed for violating the "principles and constants of Tunisian diplomacy," and his final ministerial statement avowed his "respect for all strands of Islam and commitment to the Islamic traditions of Tunisia."[321] His successor, Ahmed Adhoum, suggested that he would also hew to a national framework for Islam, saying that he accepted the position with "patriotic fervor."[322] Echoing Ben Ali–era officials, he said that his administration would promote the Kairouane school as a "prominent beacon" of Maliki jurisprudence, which was known for "encouraging exegetic efforts while rejecting extremism and dogmatism."[323]

President Marzouki said with pride that Tunisia has always been a tolerant country, one that has welcomed Jews and Christians and has "no room for any form of extremism." He recounted having been pressured by the religious affairs ministry not to sign the UN convention recognizing religious pluralism, "but I signed it anyway and sent it to the United Nations. And we guaranteed rights in article 6. Everyone is happy with the constitution."[324] The constitution aimed to establish mutual toleration of believers and nonbelievers, making the state the guardian not only of religion but also of freedom of belief and conscience. Despite article 6, however, the taxpayer-supported national Mufti still incarnates the Sunni character of the state's Islam—just as the Ministry of Religious Affairs does not administer any non-Sunni mosques or imams. In a situation where minority taxpayers do not receive religious services, there is a direct parallel with the Turkish Diyanet's "bias" in favor of the Hanafi Sunni majority, although the country's many atheists and Alevis also help fund the directorate.

Conclusion

Tunisia is different from the other countries in the region: it is smaller; it does not have a hegemonic military; and unlike the Egyptian Freedom and Justice Party or the Turkish AKP, the Tunisian Ennahda has nowhere near a majority of votes.[325] The birthplace of the Arab Spring appears to offer a tantalizing third way for Islamist participation in the democratic process: a Goldilocks outcome between electoral majoritarianism and antidemocratic militarism. In the context of their discussion of the existence of multiple secularisms, political scientists Alfred Stepan and Juan Linz write about the concept of a civil state (*dawla madaniyah*) versus a religious state and cite their May 2011 interview with Rachid al Ghannouchi and Tunisia's future prime minister, Hamadi Jebali, who "spoke extensively of the political imperative of a 'civil state.'" In 2012, Stepan and Linz wrote, "Tunisia became the first Arab country in more than three decades to receive a ranking of 3 or better for political rights on the 7-point Freedom House scale."[326]

However, divergent attitudes toward Islam reveal deeper discord about political fundamentals. Polarization is one of the most evident characteristics in a landscape of Rashomonic proportions. The only thing secularists and Islamists agree on is the role of the state: it should evangelize their set of values and keep the other side's extremists in check. They may also agree on the need for a politically neutral religious broker for Tunisian Islam. Interviewees of all political stripes found it scandalous that in 2017, six years after the revolution, nearly 20 percent of the country's mosques remained without an imam. The minister of religious affairs, whose official mission includes "popularizing religious precepts" and "combating hate speech," said, "Despite the budgetary increase, we have limited means to oversee speech in 5,817 mosques and prayer spaces of the Republic."[327] There are an estimated 500,000 Friday mosque attendees, and the politicization of Friday sermons has reportedly persisted for years. As the intellectual Hedi Yahmed put it, "So long as mosques are lawless zones, fighting terrorism will remain a slogan, a chimera."[328] The minister testified to the National Assembly in 2017 that "all mosques are now under control" and that "any imam who does anything illegal or who compromises his neutrality will be removed."[329]

Nonetheless, basic security remained problematic. In 2017, there were continuing acts of aggression against the ministry's imams and preachers. According to a trade union of imams, there were more than 1,000 attacks on imams; 1,300 political and partisan speeches were delivered at mosques; and 6,000 complaints were filed by imams and worshipers to express their anger over inflammatory speeches and attackers' behaviors. In 2016, it was estimated that "there were at least 300 radicalized imams who refuse our way of life, our perceptions and our faith."[330] The minister said that "it is not easy to recuperate these mosques when the new imams we recruit receive death threats from the former imams, and fear for their life."[331] He added, "Conservative religious groups have taken control of several mosques without official approval," and he deplored "the forcible expulsion of imams."[332] The minister told journalists that "chaos, problems and dissent" in Tunisian mosques were leading to abstention by the faithful and the demoralization of imams; he spoke of "daily resignations and the absence of training for the new imams." "The problem," he said, "lies in adequately forming mentalities and training imams who are capable of delivering a moderate discourse."[333]

Noting that his ministry was one of the poorest, the minister referred to reliance on "interstate cooperation" to defend the Maliki rite. In an interview with the author, the Mufti of the Republic lamented the irony that Tunisia needed "to reimport the Zeitounian model from Morocco and Algeria."[334]

Nonetheless, in a poll conducted for the International Republican Institute (IRI), Tunisian respondents ranked religious institutions as being among the least corrupt institutions.[335] The Tunisian political scientist Noureddine Eloui has pointed out that "the real battle over who runs mosques and who should take charge of religious affairs" is between those who favor "private groups" and those who favor the state.[336] Yassine Essid writes that "the Grand Mufti of the republic [should be] more than enough" to satisfy the desire for Islam in public life. As for the organization and maintenance of places of worship, Essid asks: "Why not simply entrust them to the Ministry of Local Government? Islam, which should be a strictly private matter, has in fact no 'affairs,' . . . and does not need a minister."[337]

Many elites profess a desire to separate mosque and state, but their dilemma, as the Tunisian scholar Mohammed Haddad points out, is that "if you liberate the mosques from state administration then half of them will become Salafist overnight."[338] Any institutional solutions are also subject to turf battles between the minister, ministry employees, the Grand Mufti, and other major institutions like al Zeitouna and the faculty in Kairouane. One association of imams lobbied for an independent elected authority that would "administer mosques to appoint, dismiss, and monitor imams' sermons and religious lectures in mosques."[339] Another proposal was to revive Zeitouna's oversight of a network of mosques and preachers.[340]

While one side cherishes the milestones of secularism, the other side experiences bans, denials, and humiliation. The dearth of resources explains why the state has been catching up and playing "whack-a-mole" with Salafi mosques and preachers. Some argue that it was an error of the Bourguiba administration to close the historic Zeitouna University in the 1950s, attributing the rise in radicalism to such moves. The Mufti of the Republic said in an interview: "Bourguiba made a mistake when he put Zeitouna University in sleep mode, because he created a vacuum. . . . Secular terrorism chased out religious culture in this country and gave way to religious terrorism—it's a sickness. We need balance in society."[341] He told another interviewer that "the trigger for terrorism under Tunisian skies was when President Bourguiba made women take off their headscarves."[342]

The vacuum of religious dignity and institutional autonomy had practical consequences.[343] As Rachid al Ghannouchi argued in a 2014 speech: "He who sows dictatorship, reaps the Islamic State."[344] Young people sought information about religion on satellite channels and the internet. Despite ministry promises that the "total control of all mosques" was just around the corner, dozens of mosques eluded state oversight for years after the revolution.[345] In April 2017, the government announced that it was "working to exercise full control over all mosques without exception."[346] As one commentator put it, because of its share of responsibility in "anarchy in the mosques after January 14," Tunisian society bore partial responsibility for the birth of ISIS. Tunisia was the largest per capita exporter of foreign fighters to Syria and Iraq. Until 2015, mosques around the country allegedly continued to act "like travel agencies for Syria and Iraq."[347]

During the interview in his office in 2014, President Marzouki kept one eye on a television silently broadcasting images of masked men from ISIS in black uniforms taking over a Libyan airfield, and he gestured toward the screen several times in the course of the conversation, saying: "Those problems are my main concern."[348] Speaking one month before al Baghdadi emerged in Raqqa, Marzouki dismissed discussion of a unifying figure for the umma: "There is no way to achieve the dream of a caliphate. That has mainly a political purpose. But under the caliphate there are the same political trends that work against the caliph himself. In Morocco, [there are] different Islamist movements, even though there is a type of mini-caliphate. This is true even in Saudi Arabia, where the king is everything. There are the same problems everywhere. Despite these kings' religious role."[349] He was prescient about Libya as a source of instability but underestimated how attractive the ISIS caliphate would be for hundreds of thousands across the region. In July 2014, the Islamic State was declared; months after that, the Bardo Museum and a beachfront in Sousse were attacked by Tunisian ISIS supporters who had trained in Libya, killing dozens.[350] Another one of those who swarmed out of Libya in the aftermath of the overthrow of the president was radicalized in an Italian prison and rejected for asylum in Germany before he pledged allegiance to al Baghdadi as caliph, hijacked a truck, and drove into a Berlin crowd in December 2015, killing twelve.[351]

Professionalization and Religious Identity

Opinion surveys suggest that governments have succeeded in the short term in reducing the superficial incompatibilities between religious and national belonging. Despite the high extent of state intervention in Morocco and Turkey, more than 90 percent of Moroccans, Tunisians, and Turks reported in a 2015 survey that they felt free to practice their religion; only 2 to 4 percent felt "not free at all." Slightly more Turkish respondents thought that Turkey would be *worse* off separating religion and state (40 percent versus 37 percent)—presumably because of the fundamentalist forces they feared the freedom of deregulation would unleash. At three-to-one, the proportion in Tunisia was higher (62 percent to 19 percent). On the one hand, 97 percent of Turks affirmed that "everything in the Qur'an is accurate and timely," and nine out of ten respondents in both Turkey and Tunisia agreed that "the Qur'an has correctly predicted all the major events that have occurred in human history" and that "Islam is the only true religion." But Turks and Tunisians were far less likely than others to prefer the Qur'an as the source of civil or criminal law.[352] Only around 10 percent of Turks wanted shari'ah law. By contrast, in Morocco, where shari'ah is interpreted by a national ulema council presided over by the King and Commander of the Faithful, 82 percent preferred shari'ah law (perhaps because they already had it in some civil realms).

Tunisian respondents were paradoxical: they were 15 percent more likely to believe in the importance of separating religion and politics than Algerians and Moroccans, but 10 percent *less* likely to support equal rights for all religious groups. Their intolerance was higher than average in both directions: Tunisians also had the highest proportion of respondents in favor of banning the face veil (84 percent). In a country where half claimed to frequent mosques while half did not, equal measures (20 percent) thought that religion and Islamic texts should *either* be "completely absent" *or* "form all foundations" of policy and lawmaking.[353]

In Algeria, the Arab barometer found that 90 percent agreed that government "should implement only laws of the shari'ah," but 30 percent thought that democracy and Islam were compatible.[354] Close to two-thirds stated that "men of religion should have an influence on decisions of government"; a vast majority said that they felt Muslim above all (70 percent), followed by 20 percent who felt primarily Algerian and 6 percent who identified as Arab. Asked about their social or geographical identity, however, only 12 percent chose the "Islamic World." A slight majority believed that women were required by Islam to wear the hijab; fewer than half (42 percent) believed that "Islam requires non-Muslim rights be inferior." Tunisians and Turkish citizens were far likelier to allow the possibility that non-Muslims were going to heaven. Around two-thirds of Turks and Tunisians supported equal rights for other religions.[355]

Counterintuitively, the relative number of mosques decreased under AKP rule, and so did the number of Turkish citizens saying that they felt "Muslim first," from 64 percent in 2001 to 39 percent in 2013; meanwhile, the number of those saying that "above all" they felt Turkish rose from 34 percent to 44 percent.[356] Another survey comparing opinions in 2018 and 2008 found that fewer respondents described themselves as religious (51 percent versus 55 percent), and there was an even steeper drop-off in the number of those who said they were "strictly religious." In the same survey, the number of atheists and nonbelievers increased from 2 percent to 5 percent.[357]

Governments' efforts to lessen the incompatibility between Islamic faith and citizenship may be credited for the uptick in patriotism. The risks of disestablishment—removing Islam from government ministries—included giving an opening to the many revolutionary nongovernmental religious organizations (Hezbollah, Hamas, Shi'a proselytizers, ISIS) that stood ready to fill any vacuum. Authorities warned citizens against the dangers of frequenting "parallel" structures. Warnings were issued in Tunisia against the "parallel hajj," in Algeria against "parallel fatwas," and in Turkey against a "parallel Diyanet." To revisit the two pairs from the beginning of the chapter—Algeria-Tunisia and Morocco-Turkey—what was the relationship between the strength of Nation-State Islam and support for Salafism or the Islamic State?

One consequence of the "absence of an organizational gatekeeper in the Islamic sphere," the religious scholar Sebastian Elischer explains, was that "the state missed the opportunity to establish steering capacity in the Islamic *milieu*."[358] Where governments did not adequately nationalize the practice of Islam, the state was at best extraneous and at worst an obstacle to citizens' religious sentiments. There were tens of thousands of young men across the region who felt no national loyalty and attempted to make hijra (emigrate) to the Islamic State. Governments with strong Nation-State Islam, Elischer points out, reaped dividends from a state apparatus that was built up in the 1980s and 1990s, when Saudis first expanded transnationally and satellite dishes became widespread. In his study of sub-Saharan Africa, he writes that those "states that chose institutional regulation as their primary strategy *prior* to the emergence of Saudi Arabia as a major international player in the mid-1970s successfully undermined the spread of political and jihadi Salafism in later decades."[359]

By a similar logic, the survival of the Middle East state system depended on intact Nation-State Islam. In other words, rather than viewing state involvement with Islam as either theologically predetermined or the blunt instrument of social control, it was possible to see it carving out a new role for the imam in the modern state. Each of the Sunni post-Ottoman states found it necessary to oversee and control Islam, a pattern that was reinforced by democratization. There was some attendant increase in autonomy within certain realms, all while religious employees remained state employees. They were civilians, even if their position occasionally called for (or permitted) ceremonial garb. The next step would be toward semi-autonomy: elected muftis, ulema, and so on. After peaking in the period 2010–2015, religious affairs spending began to settle down again. This was not exactly government by shari'ah law, but rather religion overseen (*encadré*) by state law—the gilded cornice that frames a living tableau.

Embracing Spiritual Power

10

Out of Office:
Rejoining Civil Society

THE PLACE OF RELIGIOUS communities in the nation-state has been determined by three modern crises. The meaning of Catholic and Islamic religious leadership changed in response to the threats and defeats dealt them by rival empires, nation-state governments, and the challenge posed by having large numbers of believers beyond borders. Facing the loss of executive powers over ever larger numbers of followers, they transformed their mission. They became beacons, advocates, and religious service providers for flocks outside their legal jurisdiction.[1] This required ceding political-administrative control over the faithful. It also intensified the focus on performing spiritual oversight across jurisdictional borders by other means. Religious institutions adapted, under duress. The professionalization process provoked by political defeat allowed organized Catholicism and Islam to survive in the nation-state order as recognized entities. Thanks to more training and larger bureaucracies, they became better positioned to operate across borders as well. Counterintuitively, this process reinforced their operational shift from the temporal to the spiritual realm.

Despite its disastrous encounter with the modern state in the nineteenth century, the Roman Catholic Church arrived at a peaceful cohabitation by the turn of the new millennium. The watershed decades of the twentieth century that produced Vatican City independence and the Second Vatican Council were a historic turning point. Since then, Rome has neither tried to reinsert clergy into national governments nor sought to recover the executive powers it once enjoyed. The creation of Vatican City resolved a fundamental issue of papal sovereignty and offered state authorities and believers a face-saving way out of their confrontation over the temporal power of the pope. When the Church got forty-four hectares and reparations in exchange for its recognition of the Italian kingdom in 1929, it began construction on a new grand boulevard—the Via della Conciliazione—that allowed international traffic to and from St. Peter's Cathedral once more.

The Church never got back the Colosseum or the Quirinale Palace in Rome, but it recovered other properties and its status as a recognized religion across Europe—albeit one that excluded its previous role ex officio in the political process. In the 1980s, a papal ban eliminated the lingering phenomenon of cleric-legislators in national parliaments. The population of Vatican City as a political entity has not exceeded a thousand or so citizens since its creation. As a spiritual enterprise, however, it cultivated an effective global network containing immense national diversity and doctrinal consistency that balanced centralized control with greater autonomy for its national hierarchies. European states granted Church officials control within community institutions, but like any other civil society association, its internal rules and veto points end at its outer walls. All this was possible because the vanquishing of the pope's temporal power left the papacy in place. The Church avoided the caliphate's fate because the papal seat remained filled. A sovereign Catholic prince has enforced God's rule on his patch of earth for the past ninety years.

The cause of contemporary disarray within Sunni Muslim religious authorities is not Islam's inherent lack of hierarchy or clergy. The Ottoman caliphate flourished as a spiritual project during its final century. It was a proud, independent empire at a time when the rest of Sunni Muslims lived under European domination. Istanbul abandoned efforts to reclaim lands formerly under its control and pursued spiritual dominion over fellow Muslims instead. Religious authority crossed boundaries, but political influence was governed by *realpolitik*. Across North Africa, the Balkans, and the future nation-states of India, Pakistan, Bangladesh, and Indonesia, scores of millions of followers inserted the caliphs' names into Friday prayers. European empires undercut and disbanded the existing religious infrastructure in their occupied territories in the Middle East and North Africa because they did not want Istanbul influencing their subjects. Istanbul could neither offer military assistance to Islamic uprisings nor persuade Muslims to wage jihad against the Western powers. This underscored the caliph's irrelevancy as a political leader. However, it belied the success of the *spiritual* caliphate as a transnational project.

The French scholar Louis Massignon argued for an Islamic city-state as a remedy to the Eastern Question, writing in 1920 that a caliphate was an essential element of the international order. "Islam requires there be somewhere on earth a Muslim sovereign, absolutely free [and] dependent on God alone, who maintains the written rules and punishes the illicit ones." The way to achieve this would have been to preserve the caliphate as an Eastern counterpart to the recently created League of Nations, crowned by a consensually selected chief religious authority.[2] Massignon thought that "Muslims need not become the Caliph's subjects but may desire to pray for him," and he believed that the caliph's powers would be "neither legislative nor judicial." He would have "temporal power of execution" on his own land, however, and he would "lead the public prayer and publicly enforce respect for the law."[3]

If Massignon were around today, he would lament the twenty-first-century absence of such an Islamic polity, the nonexistence of even a pint-sized state. No government anywhere on earth exercises God's law on earth according to the Sunna and Qur'an alone. In the century since the last caliphate, contenders have jostled for regional hegemony—Saudi Arabia, Iran, and Turkey most recently—without broad consensus or formal recognition. The postcolonial nation-states built infrastructure, educational systems, and hierarchies of state Islam for their citizens and for diaspora populations abroad. An international network of stately mosques project their ideological and religious worldviews from Los Angeles to Laos.[4] For decades, geopolitical blocs led by Washington and Moscow contained the splintering of the post-caliphate, relegating Islamic activists to the nongovernmental margins. Then the ejection of the Soviet Union from Afghanistan by Islamic holy warriors tore open the seam. Western governments supported and celebrated the Soviet retreat from Central and Eastern Europe and Central Asia. But a race for religious hegemony has ensued, posing ever more urgently the issue of Islamic temporal sovereignty (see table 10.1).

The Twenty-First-Century Custody Battle

As guardian of Islam's two holiest cities since the 1920s, Saudi Arabia has laid claim to being the natural interlocutor for Muslims' issues worldwide—ranging from the fate of immigrant-origin minorities in Europe to the discussion of Jerusalem's future. Visitors to the Saudi court are told to use the title Custodian rather than King. The al Sauds have used their extensive financial resources to influence global piety and Islamic public opinion.[5] For four decades, they built mosques, published Qur'ans, and trained and sent imams to serve in Muslim communities around the world. By 2002, the royal family had financed around 1,500 mosques, 210 Islamic centers, 2,000 Islamic schools, and 202 colleges worldwide. Within the space of three decades, they had spent an estimated $150 billion on schools, mosques, and Islam-related causes in Muslim-minority countries.[6] Every year since 1984, the King Fahd Complex in Medina has printed tens of millions of Qur'ans, translated into twenty languages.[7] Saudi Arabia was an imperfect substitute for the Ottomans as the main Propagator of the Faith. Religious fundamentalists rejected the various compromises that the al Sauds made in the name of nation-state-hood: they tolerated religious imagery, permitted Shi'a, and entered military alliances with non-Muslims against other Muslims. Despite its Wahhabi bona fides, it was a regime that could be portrayed as violating Islamic rules. Moreover, the al

TABLE 10.1. The Missing Caliphate: Twenty-First-Century Global Contenders

	Islamic Rule	Sovereignty over Holy Sites	International Network of Mosques/Imams	Defend Muslims with Arms	Military Independence	Qureyshi Descent	Number of Criteria Fulfilled
Islamic State of Iraq and Al-Sham (2014–2019)	x			x	x	x	4
Royal Kingdom of Morocco		x	x			x	3
Kingdom of Saudi Arabia	x	x	x				3
Al Qaeda				x	x		2
Republic of Turkey			x		x		2
Gulf Cooperation Council States	x			x			2
Hashemite Kingdom of Jordan		x				x	2

Sauds were not personally of Qureyshi descent. The ability of a national religious hierarchy under Grand Mufti Abdulaziz al Sheikh (1999–) to project a de facto worldwide spiritual caliphate was vastly restricted after fifteen Saudi nationals killed nearly 3,000 civilians in New York, Washington, DC, and Pennsylvania in the al Qaeda attacks of 2001.[8]

The closing bracket of one era overlapped with the opening of another historical parenthesis: the lifting of the Cold War fog revealed that the custodial seat was proverbially vacant. Each would-be Islamic hegemon bred malcontents who rejected the compromises of inhabiting the nation-state system. There was broad regional dissatisfaction with the postcolonial custodians of the Middle East, especially those in charge of Islam's holiest sites in Mecca and Medina and the Al-Aqsa Mosque complex in Jerusalem. The Palestinian-Israeli conflict and the US-led invasion of Kuwait in the 1990s were small-scale wars with relatively low casualties, but they presaged the end of an order. The kiss of death was delivered to Saudi Arabia by leaders in Western capitals when the kingdom was made to quarter 500,000 American soldiers.[9] The Hashemite Kingdom of Jordan—heir to Hussein bin Ali—may have inadvertently affected its own claims by ending its war with Israel and becoming a major ally of the Western powers. Islamists portrayed nation-state rule as the equivalent of losing hundreds of millions of believers and saw these rulers as snuffing out God's rule on earth.

New challengers like ISIS, al Qaeda in Iraq, and al Qaeda in the Islamic Maghreb later thrived thanks to the pruning back of Saudi influence after the September 11, 2001, attacks, and the military fronts opened against Ba'athist regimes in Iraq and Syria (2003–2013). The United States, partnering alternately with the former British and French empires, used military force to dislodge rulers in the former Ottoman provinces of Iraq, Libya, and Kurdistan (2003–2018). The executions of Saddam Hussein and Muammar Qaddafi, two Sunni leaders who held caliphal pretensions and kept jihadist militancy in check, paved the way for Islamist parties to take power in Iraq and Libya, enabled Shi'a expansion in the region, and gave al Qaeda and then the Islamic State a foothold in both countries.

For a short time, the ISIS leader Abu Bakr al Baghdadi had several advantages over earlier pretenders, including territorial sovereignty in the heartland of early Islam and claims of tribal lineage linking him to the Prophet Muhammad. Al Baghdadi told his audience, "You have tried all secular regimes . . . and now is the era of the Islamic State."[10] One of the criteria to identify worthy candidates for caliph, aside from having moral probity and physical and mental integrity, is whether he governs territory where Islamic law is enforced. Al Baghdadi was the only Sunni Arab leader who confected a polity where "the Qur'an is the only source of legislation, laws and the constitution."[11] He defied the international order, Olivier Roy explains, by asserting that "Syria is not for the Syrians and Iraq is not for the Iraqis. The Islamic State is a state for all Muslims."[12] He linked together dozens of disconnected "emirates" that offered their oath of loyalty (bai'a) in 2014 and 2015. ISIS attracted some 30,000 foreign irregulars, while tens of thousands of others were blocked from traveling to join the fight (see figure 10.1) (As a proportion of their respective populations, Pope Pius IX mobilized three to five times as many Catholic irregular soldiers in defense of Rome against the Italian nationalists in 1860s.) This was the largest such influx of Muslim foreign fighters on behalf of Islamic rule since 1980s Afghanistan under Soviet occupation.[13] As Bruce Riedel writes, ISIS "challenged the legitimacy of every Muslim leader, especially the current custodians of Mecca and Medina."[14]

The leader of al Qaeda, Ayman al Zawahiri, considered al Baghdadi to be an impudent upstart and a scourge upon his cause. Al Zawahiri reminded him on Telegram that "the entire leadership and all al Qaeda's branches and millions more" had already pledged allegiance to the founder of the Taliban in Afghanistan, Mullah Muhammad Omar, as Mujahid; Mollah Omar had "created the first true Islamic emirate since the fall of the Ottoman Empire a century ago."[15] But Mollah Omar had no Qureyshi heritage and had not been heard from since hightailing it out of Kabul on a Harley-Davidson as US troops closed in after 9/11. Al Qaeda's violence was sporadic and spectacular, whereas ISIS was realizing a caliphate on earth. In a 2017 essay, Hamza bin Laden, the twenty-eight-year-old son of the deceased al Qaeda founder, kept his eyes on the prize and painted his target on Saudi Arabia. He accused the kingdom's founder, King Abdelaziz bin Saud, of colonial-era treason:

> Bin Saud broke the agreements he made with the Ottoman State, to which he had pledged allegiance. He paved the road from Kuwait for the British Crusader [to impose] hegemony on the Land of the Two Holy Mosques. He betrayed the ummah and pleased the English [knowing this would mean] fighting the Ottoman State and enabling the English and their allies to occupy the homelands of the Muslims.[16]

After the fall of the ostentatiously (and only lately) pious Saddam Hussein regime to Shi'a majority rule, the disintegration of Libya, and the death of Osama bin Laden, there was an opening for a defiantly independent Sunni Arab figure capable of making war on the current world order, restoring the Sunna to political rule, and, as William McCants and Shadi Hamid write, pursuing the "goal of erasing the borders separating Arab countries."[17]

Al Baghdadi's puritanism recalled the style of the last audacious challenger of Saudi Islam: Juhayman al Utaybi, who led the 1979 siege of Mecca. Al Utaybi and al Baghdadi both stemmed from the pre-Islamic Qureyshi tribe and viewed the house of Saud as un-Islamic and ripe for overthrow. ISIS did not view Sauds or Ottomans as legitimate Islamic rulers because neither fully enforced shari᾽ah and none of their sovereigns had Qureyshi origins. The Islamic State leadership had the bitter flavor of Sykes-Picot in their mouths, but unlike Osama and Hamza bin Laden—who frequently evoked the "humiliation tasted [by the Muslim world] for the last 80 years"—they were not nostalgic for the Ottomans. Malise Ruthven writes that, instead, they were "nurtured by the myth of preco-lonial innocence." ISIS "tweeted pictures of a bulldozer crashing through the frontier between Syria and Iraq, announcing—triumphantly—that they were destroying the 'Sykes-Picot' border."[18] In their view, the caliph's seat had been empty for 1,000 years.[19] Will McCants writes that "some Islamic prophecies of the End Times say a man descended from the Prophet will one day rule as ca-liph," and Abu Bakr al Baghdadi claimed to fit the bill.[20] Olivier Roy points to the "strand in messianic Islam," predicted by several hadiths, that foresees "the restoration . . . of the true Islamic state under Shari᾽ah law and governed by a ca-liph, a Muslim sovereign who claims authority over all Muslims."[21] Observers noted al Baghdadi's attention to costume, set, character, and "his command of the symbols and iconography of medieval Islamic history," which evoked the Abbasid caliphs who preceded Ottoman rule.[22] He entreated "Soldiers of the Khilafa" within Islamic State's "global wilayas" to rise up wherever "mosques are desecrated and sanctities are violated [or] Muslims' rights are forcibly usurped," naming nineteen countries and regions of the Arab-Muslim world in particu-lar.[23] At its height, ISIS controlled a swath of territory the size of the United Kingdom, with a population of 6 million to 9 million individuals.[24]

Abu Bakr al Baghdadi promised—prematurely, in the event—that ISIS would bring an "end to the humiliation of life under the Sa'ud family," accord-ing to a July 4, 2014, report in *al Taqrir*, and would finally "fully implement shari᾽ah law."[25] After centuries in the position of insurgents against Ottoman rule, the Wahhabi-Saud alliance had to defend its own revolution with state institutions. The irony could not have been lost on them when ISIS "pointed out that al Saud, being not of *Quraysh* descent," did not qualify as caliph and needed replacing.[26] Riyadh recognized that ISIS's "first and fundamental enemy is Saudi Arabia."[27] Part of the problem was al Baghdadi's potential ap-peal: one survey suggested that 92 percent of twenty-five- to thirty-year-olds in Saudi Arabia agreed that "ISIS conforms to the values of Islam and Islamic law."[28] Two days after al Baghdadi declared a worldwide caliphate, the Saudis deployed 30,000 troops along the border with Iraq; ISIS forces arrived within sixty miles.[29] Al Baghdadi's fortunes soured in 2017 when the Islamic State was militarily destroyed by a mix of Syrian, Russian, Iranian, American, Kurdish, and Turkish air and ground forces. Al Baghdadi suffered the same fate as his brief caliphate before the decade's end.

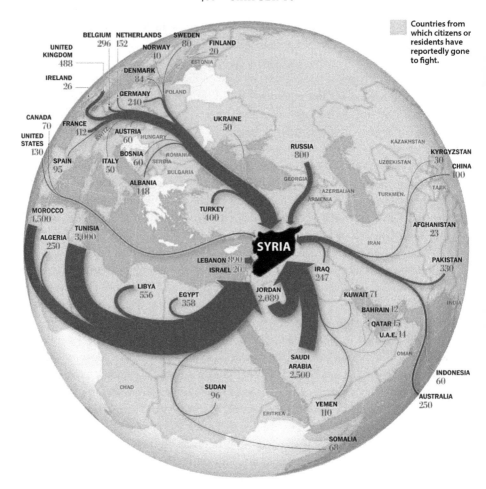

FIGURE 10.1. Foreign fighters in Syria and Iraq (Soufan Group, 2016). Figures for fighters from Western Europe are from the International Center for the Study of Radicalization's high estimate category. All other numbers are from the Soufan Group. Per-country fighter estimates determined from a date range of December 2013 to October 2014. Cream-colored countries are those from which citizens or residents have reportedly come to fight. Small numbers of fighters are also reported to have come from Bangladesh, Chile, Ivory Coast, Japan, Malaysia, Maldives, New Zealand, Philippines, Senegal, Singapore, and Trinidad and Tobago. These countries are not shown because they are off the map.

Meanwhile, the purveyors of Nation-State Islam were busy establishing themselves as legitimate religious actors. As Shadi Hamid and Peter Mandaville noticed in their study on *The Geopolitics of Soft Power*, a number of governments began to engage in "transnational religious propagation," sometimes to promote their favored religious interpretations, and at other times to ensure their own survival.[30] A large-scale opinion survey gauging the atmosphere of religious authority found that in Morocco the most trusted national religious figure was Mohammed VI, by a long shot. In Turkey the Diyanet president came second to a well-known traditional scholar, and in Tunisia the top two figures were also state-affiliated religious leaders. The same survey found, however, that transnationally President Recep Tayyip Erdoğan was the most trustworthy transnational religious leader among all ten nationalities polled—Turks, Moroccans, Tunisians, Egyptians, Palestinians, Jordanians, Saudis, Kuwaitis, Qataris, and the Emirati. Erdoğan's personal approval ranged from 10 to 20 percent, placing him well ahead of the 5 to 8 percent for the famous Islamist scholars Yusuf al-Qaradawi and Rachid al Ghannouchi—and under 2 percent for al Baghdadi.[31] How did the head of state of the Kemalist Republic of Turkey come to enjoy such cross-cutting esteem among Muslims in the Middle East and North Africa?

Turkey Abroad in the Twenty-First Century

Restoring Ottoman Pathways

The end of the Cold War created international opportunities (and threats) for Turkish Islam. New ethnic and religious coalitions were made possible by the loosening of Communist rule in China and the collapse of the former Soviet Union. The Balkan Muslim community that had been abruptly ripped from the Ottoman umma in the early twentieth century was beckoned to rejoin the community. In the 1990s, only 3.7 percent of Bosnians completing Islamic studies abroad chose to do so in Turkey, while ten times as many went to Saudi Arabia. To counter Wahhabi influence, the Diyanet set itself an ambitious agenda to publish and export religious "classics" and textbooks in dozens of languages.[32] The Diyanet began to offer competitive scholarships in religious studies courses taught in Turkish and English. Students from the Balkans, Eurasia, and Africa were given grants to study in Turkey's İmam Hatip religious schools, Qur'anic courses, and postgraduate and doctoral programs.[33] By 2010, the number of Turkish-trained alumni in circulation in the Balkans had reached 10,000.[34]

One of the chief ideologues of AKP foreign policy, Ahmet Davutoğlu, was a mild-mannered academic who served as foreign minister and prime minister in the 2010s. Behlul Özkan conveys Davutoğlu's argument that Turkey's borders were "geopolitical errors that separate Islamic communities from one another." The Ottoman Empire was felled not by "our separation from the Balkans," Davutoğlu believed, "but from the [majority-Muslim] lands of the Middle East."[35] While serving as foreign minister, he vowed that "between 2011 and

2023, we are going to meet again with our brothers in those territories from which we retreated and which we lost between 1911 and 1923."[36] This was indicative of Turkey's soft power agenda, not its upcoming schedule of foreign invasions.[37] Turkey sent humanitarian aid, not missiles, to Gaza, and it set up mosques, not military bases, in the Balkans—even after Muslim boys and men were massacred. When the Turkish military finally intervened in Syria, it did so to *preserve* its borders with Syria and Iraq. To do otherwise risked opening another Kurdish front. While ISIS blasted dirt barriers, Davutoğlu waxed poetic: "We will shatter the state of mind that Sykes-Picot created for us."[38]

In addition to the Turkish Cooperation and Coordination Agency (TİKA), the foreign aid agency that wielded a billion-dollar budget, another prong was the Yunus Emre Institute (YEE) cultural diplomacy network. YEE opened its first three offices in Sarajevo, Tirana, and Damascus, and in the subsequent decade it expanded its cultural diplomacy to 83 partner universities and 135 affiliated organizations in sixty countries around the Balkans, Central Asia, western Europe, the Middle East, Africa, and South America (2007–2017).[39] In a newspaper interview, the YEE director said that he aimed to "conduct Turkey's public diplomacy and other elements of what we call soft power" in 100 countries by 2023. "Especially in the Islamic world," he said, "many are hopeful toward Turkey. People who learned Turkish and come from various countries such as Sudan, Afghanistan, Germany and Serbia . . . [say they] want to work with us and . . . need Turkey."[40]

Well before the arrival of the AKP in power, Ankara had begun to enhance its international profile thanks to what Kerem Öktem describes as an array of "non-conventional foreign policy instruments, religious and educational networks [and] popular culture."[41] The AKP augmented the Diyanet's foreign activities and developed a multifaceted approach. The relationship with the diaspora was formalized when Erdoğan announced the creation of a new agency, the Presidency for Turks Abroad and Related Communities (Yurtdışı Türkler): "Our Government places special importance upon our citizens living abroad. . . . It is necessary to professionalize and institutionalize our interests."[42] Baser Bahar writes that Turkey, projecting influence westward, beyond the 8 million Balkan Muslims, "broadened its diaspora" and definition of the nation to include not only the 5 million to 6 million Turkish citizens in Europe and the Middle East but also "relatives and kin groups [such as] Azerbaijani, Kyrgyz, Kazakh, Uzbek and Turkmen groups," which amounted to "200 million kin and related communities."[43] The government of Recep Tayyip Erdoğan also laid claim to the tens of millions of followers of the Muslim Brotherhood who were orphaned after Brotherhood leadership was imprisoned and scattered by the al Sisi regime in Egypt in 2013. When calculated in these terms, the "greater" Turkish-led community of believers has a demo-graphic weight closer to that of the Arab populations around the world—which outpaced the Turkic peoples by the 1980s.

Defender of the Faith

An important part of these operations was the system of de facto national colleges for Turkish Islam abroad. In addition to the faculties in Marmara and Ankara, for example, the Union of International Muslim Scholars opened the Istanbul International Islamic University—which was intended to compete directly with Al-Azhar in Cairo. A pet project of one Diyanet president was the elaboration of a Department of International Islam and Religion Studies at 29 Mayis University in Istanbul, where instruction was offered in three languages (Turkish, Arabic, and English) to students from all over the world—from the Middle East to the Caucasus to the Balkans to North Africa.

The Diyanet created a new foundation to endow foreign projects, the Türkiye Diyanet Vakfı (TDV), and expanded its activities to 300 regions in 79 countries. In its first decade, according to the organization, it convened over 200,000 meetings, conferences, panels, and symposiums, mostly in Central Asia and Africa, and gave financial support to mosques and schools.[44] During the month of Ramadan, the Diyanet sent "hundreds of thousands of religious officials to various countries, from Crimea to Mongolia."[45] Turkey built dozens of monumental mosques in the early twenty-first century—in Romania, Bulgaria, and Hungary and "from Somalia to Kazakhstan"—including a 30-million-euro project in Albania that would be the largest in the Balkans (see figure 10.2).[46] The Diyanet enjoyed a de facto monopoly on Islamic education in Bulgaria by agreement with the local directorate for religious denominations. The TDV also "established a broad network" of dozens of schools in Kazakhstan, Azerbaijan, and Kyrgyzstan, where the Diyanet developed religious curriculum with Osh State University.[47] In addition to the activities of the Diyanet, TDV, TİKA, YEE, and Yurtdışı Türkler, beginning in 2007, the government organized the Eurasian Islam Shura, a series of summits for mufti councils from fifty countries. The Diyanet also convened an annual council of Balkan Muslim leaders, and since 2012 has organized another for European leaders. There was little doubt as to Turkey's signaling of availability for global Islamic leadership. On the occasion of certain state visits, the Turkish presidency had soldiers wear Ottoman-era period costumes while he donned a suit and tie (see figure 10.3).

The Diyanet's international activities extended to the Gulf region and Latin America and also reflected a renewed interest in sub-Saharan Africa (Cameroon, Mali, and Somalia, for instance).[48] The Foreign Affairs Ministry opened

FIGURE 10.2. Great Mosque of Tirana in Albania under construction (2017)

eighteen new consulates and twenty-three new embassies on the African continent between 2005 and 2017. Turkey established a small military base in Somalia to house several thousand troops, and it leased the Sudanese island of Suakin in the Red Sea, a former outpost known as the Ottoman "gateway to Africa." To "reanimate the ancient Umrah route" for Turkish pilgrims, TİKA restored the Hanafi and Shafi'i mosques and a historic inn on the island and planned to reinstate departures by boat to Jeddah. Erdoğan compared the project to the general spirit of AKP rule as a retort to the excesses of Kemalist secularism: "Like us shaving our beards, we will rebuild and reconstruct in such a way that, like a shaved beard, it will regrow much more abundant."[49]

Leadership Vacuum

The Turkish capital emerged as one of a handful of plausible candidates for militarily independent Sunni states in the twenty-first-century Muslim world. Erdoğan projected himself as a new champion of Muslims worldwide, one moment proposing a Muslim seat upon the United Nations Security Council and at another defending Chinese Uighurs.[50] One of the Turkish leader's favored sayings was "Only Recep Tayyip can do it." Erdoğan made explicit reference to the wrongs of European empires: "Let no one misinterpret the silence

FIGURE 10.3. Turkish president Recep Tayyip Erdoğan receiving
Palestinian president Mahmoud Abbas, Ankara (2015)

that dominated this region for almost a century." Erdoğan's references to the
"missing century" and the "silent century" were a mantra-like lamentation for
the abolition of the sultanate and caliphate. In his 2011 Cairo speech, Erdoğan
said: "Just as Mecca, Medina, Cairo, Alexandria, Beirut, Damascus, Diyarbakir,
Istanbul, Ankara are each other's brothers . . . so are Ramallah, Nablus, Jericho,
Rafah, Gaza and Jerusalem . . . these cities' brothers and our brothers."[51] All of
those cities were once Ottoman, and Turkey still pays to maintain historical
cemeteries in them and in thirty other countries. Visiting Tunisia in early 2012,
President Abdullah Gül told reporters that after its postrevolutionary liberalization of religious exercise, Tunisia was like a second Turkey and could be
another role model.[52]

Despite the successful outreach in the Balkans and Central Asia—and Jerusalem—there has been no Ottoman *reconquista* of Arabia. The majority-Arab populations to its south, in North Africa and the Gulf countries, were the last pieces to be severed from Istanbul in the Treaty of Sèvres. But one century later, local populations were slow to warm to Turkish leadership. The Turkish state's relationship with Islam was considered "problematic" by key constituencies—and not just by the supporters of Fethullah Gülen or Islamic State extremists. In a TESEV opinion survey of Arab League states, several explanations emerged for why Turkey was still not the obvious leader of the pack. One was that "it is not Muslim enough" (23 percent), and another was that "it has a secular government" (13 percent).[53] The final nail in the republican caliph's coffin, however, came from Turkey's "relationship with the West," which 17 percent cited as reason to exclude Turkish leadership, placing opponents firmly in the majority.

That was after the prime ministerial period; Erdoğan's second decade as president and head of state, in Cankaya, may have shifted those numbers downwards. Turkey's leadership role was arguably reinforced after Western democracies looked away from the Rabi'a Square massacre in Cairo (2013), and Erdoğan also channeled Sunni sensitivities to the selective Western intervention in the Syrian war. In accusing the Syrian religious affairs ministry of harboring "people intent on dividing the Muslim community," he was referring to the influence of Shi'a Iran.[54] He also condemned Egypt's grand sheikh for supporting the coup d'état. "History will curse the Al-Azhar Imam as it cursed the religious intellectuals in Turkey before," the Turkish president said.[55] After Cairo fell and Doha experienced diplomatic isolation from Saudi Arabia and the Gulf Cooperation Council (GCC), Istanbul became the de facto capital of the movement. The city headquartered the international Muslim Brotherhood after 2013, serving as the host country for conferences that gathered thousands of theologians from over 100 countries.

Erdoğan's steadfastness earned the respect of major figures within the world of Muslim Brotherhood. He received public pledges of loyalty—almost like a bai'a—from Yusuf al-Qaradawi and Rachid al Ghannouchi. Ghannouchi, who founded Tunisia's Ennahda Party, stated that the "AKP carried Turkey to the heart of the Ummah after . . . a century [on] history's margins."[56] Al-Qaradawi, the movement's elder and spiritual leader, actually took to calling him Sultan.[57] In a speech in Istanbul, al-Qaradawi said:

Thank you, Turkey, for aiding Syrian refugees and defending the cause of Gaza and Jerusalem. Who can make war with Sultan Recep Tayyip Erdoğan? He became the Muslim world's defender fighting in the name of

Islam and the Qur'an and shari'ah. He stands firm in the faces of tyrants to tell them no.[58]

Turkey was the only Western ally that rejected the status quo of custodianship of Islam's holy sites—in Mecca, Medina, and Jerusalem—by Saudi Arabia and Jordan. A Diyanet mufti called the Saudis a "disgrace for Islam," and said, "Our ancestors gave the descendants of the Prophet exemption from military service and from paying taxes, paid their living expenses and built a railroad of thousands of kilometers!"[59] Turks could not conceal their prickliness toward Arab leadership. They resented their haughtiness and ingratitude—and their intolerance. When the Saudi grand mufti called for all churches on the Arabian Peninsula to be destroyed, the Diyanet president spoke out against him. Diyanet officials also downplayed Sunni-Shi'a divides. "It is important for Turkey to stand above sectarianism. . . . Not taking a side in the Sunni-Shiite scheme is good for Turkey and to the benefit of all Muslims in the region."[60]

Another leader who decided to do something about that empty caliph's seat was Abu Bakr al Baghdadi, whom Turkey viewed as an upstart usurper. Graeme Wood says that, when ISIS threatened that "the march of the Mujahidin will continue until they reach Rome," they meant Byzantium, the former eastern Roman empire. (Al Baghdadi also referred to "Constantiniyya" rather than Istanbul, as if to ignore the Ottoman chapter entirely.)[61] ISIS targeted Turkish citizens with attacks in Syria and Turkey and produced Turkish-language videos calling for Erdoğan's assassination. The Diyanet president told a journalist, "The declaration of a Caliphate by ISIS has no meaning in the Islamic world."[62] The audacity that ISIS displayed by using the seal of the Prophet on its flag, Mehmet Görmez said, "brings more injury to Islam itself than anything else, it is self-inflicted harm by its ignorant followers."

Turkey's international leadership of the Palestinian national cause can be seen as a proxy for protecting the holy site of al Haram on the Temple Mount in Jerusalem. Erdoğan treated the mosque and minaret in the compound as politically up for grabs. One of the last Ottoman acts was to gild the dome of Al-Aqsa. Nearly a century later, TİKA and the Diyanet combined forces to place a new crescent ornament atop the dome. In 2009, Erdoğan denounced the Israel-Gaza war and walked out of a debate in Davos, Switzerland, with Israeli statesman Shimon Peres.[63] He returned to a hero's welcome of thousands from supporters in Istanbul. Erdoğan picked another public fight with Israel by supporting a flotilla to break the blockade of Gaza—including a ferry from the Mavi Marmara fleet in Istanbul that had a fatal confrontation with Israeli special forces.[64]

In 2014, both Davutoğlu and Erdoğan spoke of the need to "defend" the Al-Aqsa Mosque in Jerusalem. Davutoğlu referred to rule by the Ottoman

TABLE 10.2. The Turkish Republic's Gestures toward Jerusalem, 2004–2016

Rebuilding Nabi Musa site between Jerusalem and Jericho location of Moses's tomb

Building a sports stadium in the At-Tur neighborhood on the way to the Mount of Olives

Refurbishing the archive of Ottoman and Muslim documents at Al-Aqsa

Providing a water tank for worshipers at the Dome of the Rock

Rebuilding the Muslim cemetery at the foot of the eastern wall of the Temple Mount

Funding archaeological salvage excavations on the Street of the Chain in the Old City

Doing restoration work on al Quds; replacing the golden crescent on top of the Dome of the Rock

Supporting Our Heritage Foundation in preserving and renewing the Ottoman legacy in al Quds

Opening a TİKA branch office in Ramallah to oversee sixty-three projects in Jerusalem from 2004 to 2014

Spending $40 million between 2006 and 2016 on refurbishing forty-six mosques and seventy apartments, as well as furnishing hundreds more apartments near the al-Aqsa compound

Incorporating the image of Al-Aqsa Mosque alongside the holy cities of Mecca and Medina in the TV station logo of Turkey's religious affairs directorate

TİKA providing Turkish flags on the Temple Mount and along the way to it.

TİKA printing hundreds of thousands of booklets in Turkish, Arabic, and English about seventy-six Muslim historical sites and buildings in the Al-Aqsa compound

---

sultan in an address and concluded that "*Al-Quds* [Jerusalem] will be our cause for eternity." Like the Algerian ministry official who said in an interview that "on est chez nous à la Mecque" ("Mecca is our home too"), Erdoğan said in a speech, "The *Masjid al-Aqsa* is not only a shrine for Palestinians, but is the shrine of all Muslims. Nobody can turn to a Turk and say '*al-Quds* is not your cause.'"[65] When Diyanet president Mehmet Görmez received a delegation from the International al Quds Institute, he said, "If Jerusalem is calling for help, then every Muslim has to heed this appeal."[66] Görmez became the first Turkish religious leader in more than a century to chant in Arabic in the Al-Aqsa Mosque.[67] Under Görmez, the directorate added Jerusalem as an official station on the Turkish hajj route to Mecca, and Erdoğan rallied Turks to increase their visits to Jerusalem above the 26,000 visits being made each year.[68] The Turkish-Israeli agreement that settled the Mavi Marmara incident guaranteed TİKA access to Gaza to develop projects (see table 10.2).

The Turkish scholar Burhanettin Duran has noted "an emerging discourse of common Islamic civilization."[69] Erdoğan singled out what he said was Western hypocrisy: "Europe's universal ideals have been trampled. Europe has been silent during the Syrian crisis. . . . Silent for decades on the Palestinian question . . . [and now again] concerning the Iraqi question. This silence will dig wounds that are hard to salve in the consciences of the peoples of the Middle East."[70] At one point, Erdoğan held an incongruously outward-focused victory speech after his party won Turkish local elections: "I thank my brothers in Palestine who saw our victory as their victory. I thank my brothers in Egypt, the Balkans, in Bosnia, in Macedonia, in Kosovo and in all the cities in Europe who celebrate our victory. My suffering brothers in Syria. . . ."[71] He even thanked the Indian, Pakistani, and Bangladeshi volunteers of the Khilafa movement who kept Great Britain in check after World War I: "You protected the new Turkey's struggle for Independence."

As the only Turkish official authorized to wear religious ceremonial garb, the Diyanet president makes a different impression than other ministers of religious affairs in their suits and ties. Despite his Sheikh-ul-Islam-like role in Turkey and its related communities, he has the status of a deputy minister in the eyes of the outside world. This hit home when the Diyanet head announced his intention to meet with Pope Benedict XVI, only to learn that the pope "only conducts face-to-face meetings with presidents or ambassadors."[72] This gets to the core of why some will never accept Turkey as leader of the umma in its current constitutional form: the head of religion is not the head of state.

Turkish officials do not exclude the possibility of serving as an overarching guardian. Republican institutions now cover the old Ottoman paths while incorporating new channels along routes established by Saudi religious diplomacy (for example, sub-Saharan Africa and western Asia). The Türkiye Diyanet Vakfı fulfilled many roles that Saudi Arabia used to do. For example, when floods hit Bosnia in the mid-2010s, Turkey paid the salaries of Bosnian imams and restored mosques and religious buildings.[73] In 2017, Turkey helped rebuild Syrian mosques—reopening fifty-six out of sixty damaged mosques in time for Ramadan—and sent 400 imams to Syrian towns.[74] The Diyanet has of course never laid claim to an international caliphate—indeed, the Turkish republic helped block the appointment of any successor to the last caliph, Abdülmecid II (1868–1944). But there are signs that the government's position on this is softening. Ninety-five years after the Grand Turkish Assembly voted to abolish the caliphate, the government commissioned a survey asking citizens what they wanted. Fifty-four percent replied affirmatively when asked whether "Islamic countries need international religious leadership similar to the papacy."[75] The survey and its public funding fed rumors that a referendum might be held on the "Caliphate Question." The issue was still alive politically. An AKP parliamentarian called for a Vatican-like administration of the Hejaz by Muslim countries during the hajj season. This recalled a similar proposal by a prominent Turkish theologian who sought international funding for his effort to turn Mecca into an autonomous zone. His Islamic Vatican was based on a Saudi plan to administer the Hejaz via an international Muslim committee.[76]

The Diyanet president Mehmet Görmez said in 2015, "For years, our citizens have been asking 'If there is a Pope in the Vatican, can there be this kind of union for Muslims too?'" He started his reply by observing that "people's worlds are intertwined and distances have shortened," and he did not dismiss the idea out of hand.[77] But there were conditions to be met. When musing about the ISIS declaration of a caliphate, Görmez said, "It is natural for Muslims to search for ways of acting together again in unity and brotherhood as Islamic community, [but] heads do not unite unless hearts unite first. If we can ensure a union of hearts then that union you speak of will take place by itself, God willing."[78]

Despite the Islamist credentials of Erdoğan and the AKP, there is international resistance to state-led Turkish Islam. Erdoğan's historic visit to Cairo after President Hosni Mubarak's departure previewed the limits of Turkish appeal when Erdoğan endorsed secularism to a bewildered group of Ikhwan politicians.[79] The Turkish president also faces the challenge of emulating a spiritual caliph who is nonetheless in close military alliance with not one or two crusader states, which might be considered unlucky, but more than thirty of them. To take Turkish diplomacy as one measure of its orientations, in one critical period of the mid-2010s, an analysis of sixty official visits shows that the Turkish government made twenty-four high-level foreign trips to countries within the former Ottoman Empire, ten to former recipients of Ottoman Pan-Islamic services, and twenty-five to fellow NATO countries. This pattern confirms Turkey's position as a bridging state, the metaphorical and literal link across the Bosphorus between Asia and Europe. But the reality of thick ties to Western countries leaves Turkey vulnerable to charges from Islamists that it is a Western stooge. To his street credit, however, Erdoğan was the only NATO statesman outside of Eastern Europe who had spent time as a political prisoner.

The Diyanet's religious activities have focused predominantly on the needs of Hanafi Sunni Muslims, and thus in some ways it has been less ambitious and more majoritarian than its predecessors. Görmez has sought to reassure the public, however, that Turkey does not seek to impose its rituals on anyone: "The concept of *Istanbulian* Islam as suggested by [Erdoğan] refers to the possibility of many conceptions of Islam existing at the same time . . . a view of Islam that . . . does not ignore the sociological reality of Islam shaped by local and regional dynamics."[80] That is not the behavior of a regime looking for takfiri approval: the Turkish government is pursuing something both narrower and more moderate.[81]

While Erdoğan unapologetically appealed to Turkey's Ottoman heritage, he seemed to be nudging other leaders to acknowledge more explicitly their own international roles and responsibilities. This could explain the inspired idea to place himself and Angela Merkel in the pair of golden thrones built

FIGURE 10.4. German chancellor Angela Merkel with Turkish president Recep Tayyip
Erdogan at Yıldız Palace, Istanbul (2015)

for Abdülhamid II and Kaiser Wilhelm II (see figure 10.4). He had no intention of moving into Yıldız: he built his own palace outside the city.[82] The
elements of theater, bombast, setting, and architecture all help define the
moral—and intangible—role that the Turkish leader is asserting for his republic. The policy implications of the Ankara caliphate are ethereal: sending
aid to Gaza, receiving Muslim refugees, building mosques around the globe,
building up Istanbul as a center of Islamic scholarship. Added up, these efforts
are the distillation of soft power projection, on the model of the Küçük Kainardja treaty 150 years earlier. They seek no more or less than similar recognition for Turkey as a legitimate spiritual guidepost for the diaspora—and related communities. The school system of twenty-first-century Turkey again
offers instruction in Ottoman Arabic script. The former Turkish ambassador
to India said in an interview that Indian Muslims had queued up outside the
embassy to express their concern for Erdoğan's health and safety after the
2016 coup attempt.[83] Turkey's global role gained a harder edge when, in the
late 2010s, Erdoğan deployed the Turkish military: once to the Levant, when
the Syrian civil war spilled over the Turkish border; and again, in a confident
power projection upon old Ottoman stomping grounds, in the early 2020s in
North Africa during heightened instability in postwar Libya.

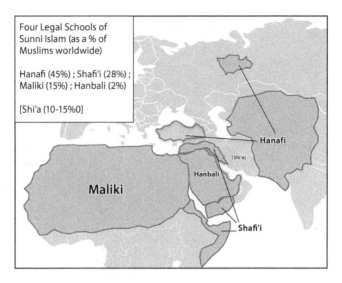

Four Legal Schools of
Sunni Islam (as a % of
Muslims worldwide)

Hanafi (45%) ; Shafi'i (28%) ;
Maliki (15%) ; Hanbali (2%)

[Shi'a (10-15%0]

Hanafi

[Shi'a]

Hanbali

Maliki

Shafi'i

FIGURE 10.5. A stylized geography of Sunni Islamic jurisprudence

Fatwas and Phosphates from Morocco

Morocco responded analogously to similar pressures, but the Moroccan sovereign had greater continuity with a unified religious-political past, and his job title gave him organic legitimacy in a transnational role. The king had three official portraits—as military leader, as political sovereign, and as Commander of the Faithful (Emir al-Mu'minin) covering all those who practiced the Sunni Maliki rite. That included 35 million Moroccans at home and another 4 million to 5 million Moroccans residing abroad. There are millions more Maliki Muslims in West Africa, sub-Saharan Africa, and the Gulf region, allowing Morocco to triangulate in opposition to Wahhabism and Shi'a Islam. In addition to the specific Ash'arite and Maliki rites, Morocco is a regional exporter of Sufi brotherhoods (tariqat). The city of Fes, for example, is "a reference point for millions of Senegalese and Malians who make pilgrimages to the founder's mausoleum—which is an abomination for the Wahhabis." That extensive international outreach was given metaphorical life by King Hassan II, who said that "Morocco is like a tree whose nourishing roots run deeply in the African soil, and which breathes thanks to its foliage that rustles in the winds of Europe."[84] The relationship was reciprocal: in the following generation living abroad, young candidates for Moroccan training said: "We feel close to the Islam that is taught in Morocco, an open Islam . . . that is shared by the whole Maghreb and West Africa" (see figure 10.5).[85]

FIGURE 10.6. King Mohammed VI kisses the Qur'an with Malian leaders (2014)

King Mohammed VI has made periodic African tours, attending Friday sermons in major mosques in Mali, Costa de Marfil, Guinea, Gabon, Senegal, and Côte d'Ivoire and distributing tens of thousands of free Qur'ans printed by his royal foundation (see figure 10.6). When he traveled in the Sahel to reinforce his leadership role within regional Maliki Islam, he wore his traditional robes and was received by clamorous crowds. The kingdom also deployed eminent Moroccan ulema to give talks in European and sub-Saharan mosques.

Upon completion of the Moroccan-sponsored grand mosque of Dakar, officials told a Spanish newspaper that "Morocco will contribute to renovations in the entire Sahel-Saharan region so as to never again leave an open field for extremist ideologies."[86] In the 2010s, the kingdom signed accords to cooperate in mosque administration and religious education there and beyond, with Tunisia, Kuwait, Senegal, Mauritania, Côte d'Ivoire, Gabon, and Indonesia.[87] Hakim el Ghissassi explains that "the Emirate of the Faithful does not seek regional or international political hegemony. It is based on a culture of pragmatism. Beyond territorial borders, it operates on a spiritual level to keep and consolidate ties with those who pledge their allegiance to it or feel close to it."[88] In 2017, Mohammed toured Gulf and Arab countries—breaking the Saudi-led blockade of Qatar. "By betting on religious diplomacy and not just security policy," Lahcen Haddad writes, Morocco was "hoping to forge an alliance of moderate spirituality to offer young believers a real alternative to the jihadist discourse."[89] (The minister of Islamic affairs pleaded with politicians not to speak of "religious diplomacy" because of its manipulative connotations.[90]) In 2016, the Moroccan king received family members of Moroccans killed in terrorist incidents committed by fellow Moroccans residing abroad in Brussels and Paris—more evidence that their enemies organized transnationally too and needed to be confronted.

The centerpiece of Moroccan policy was the Mohammed VI Institute for imam *mourchidines* and *mourchidates*, which was expanded in 2014 to train imams from Côte d'Ivoire, Guinea, Gabon, Libya, Maldives, Mali, Nigeria, Tunisia, and western Europe. Governments were solicited to submit slates of students—there was no individual application process. By 2018, the institute had 1,400 foreign students matriculated in its three-year program, and it planned to recruit another 600.[91] Sixty alumni imams were already employed in mosques around France, which sent fifty students each year. The largest contingent in the annual graduating classes came from Mali (around 25 percent); 10 percent came from Guinea, 5 percent from Tunisia, and 5 percent from France.[92] Between 2015 and 2019, the institute produced a total of 4,300 African and European graduates.[93]

On-site workshops with electrical and seamster equipment are set up to simultaneously train the imams as electricians and tailors, to reduce financial pressures on them when they return home and to avoid any need for stipends from conservative wealthy benefactors in the Gulf region. Besides promising to train hundreds of imams annually and build thousands of housing units in Mali, the king also, for example, announced that he would build a processing plant in Mali for phosphate destined exclusively for the African market. These efforts were complemented by the Mohammed VI Foundation for African Ulema (established in Casablanca in 2015), which had 120 members in thirty countries with a combined population of over 300 million Muslims. Prominent ulema from Burkina Faso to Nigeria came to pay their respects and pledge their *bai 'a* to the king as Commander of the Faithful.[94] Even the royal airline supported this agenda; it made Casablanca into a hub for the rest of the continent and added dozens of new routes between 2018 and 2020.

Algeria Abroad

In an interview, the Algerian minister of religious affairs described tensions with Morocco in western Europe and West Africa. In the latter, there was open rancor regarding the Sahel and the western Sahara: "Morocco considers the Sahel its backyard, but it can only retain access to it by occupying the western Sahara."[95] The longtime standoff between Algeria and Morocco over occupation and refugee camps had an aspect of religious competition in that the Sahel region offered a gateway to sub-Saharan Africa, where there are more countries under Moroccan religious influence. The ministry in Algiers chartered the League of Ulema, Preachers, and Imams of the Sahel and created a headquarters for the *secrétariat général*. "We all share the Maliki rite, readings, calligraphy, Sufism, and dogmatic approaches. They ask us to intervene and help organize preachers and general training," said the minister. "It's our contribution to their national cohesion. We offer a moderate religious discourse to combat terrorism."[96] Religious leaders from Mali, Niger, Burkina Faso, Mauritania, and Algeria convened in 2014 on a "mission to promote peace against radicalism and narco-terrorism in the Sahel-Saharan region."[97] By the time of its seventh workshop in 2018, the permanent members had expanded to include Libya, Nigeria, and Chad, plus Senegal and Côte d'Ivoire as honorary members (see table 10.3).[98]

Religious affairs officials and faculty from Nigeria, Mauritania, and Sudan are trained in Algiers or benefit from ministerial advice there. The ministry broadcasts a Qur'anic radio station that reaches eight countries across the Sahel, and it offers thirty scholarships annually to attend a dar al imam and become a "made-in-Algeria imam." Algeria established a special training institute in the southern Tuareg city of Tamanrasset, with courses of study lasting three or more years and offered in French and Arabic; ministry officials say the institute is producing graduates.[99] The competition between the Algerian League of Ulema, Preachers, and Imams for the Sahel and the Moroccan Mohammed VI Institute for Imams illustrates how sometimes multiple spiritual jurisdictions overlap—for example, Mali sends imams to both Algeria and Morocco. Tunisia is also under Algerian tutelage: "We have been offering assistance to the Tunisians, who had no proper religious administrative structure before the 2011 revolution," noted the ministry official. "So we have been offering

TABLE 10.3. Overlapping Influence in Funding and Expertise for Mosque Construction, Imam Training, and Religious Studies

Country	Legal School	Presence in Europe	Presence in Asia and Africa
Algeria	Maliki	France, Belgium, Spain (for example, Grande Mosquée de Paris)	Mali, Niger, Burkina Faso (for example, Ligue des Ouléma du Sahel)
Morocco	Maliki	France, Belgium, Spain, Netherlands, Italy (for example, Conseil des oulema marocains pour l'Europe)	Mali, Senegal, Nigeria, Côte d'Ivoire (Ivory Coast), Gabon, Guinea-Bissau, Tunisia
Turkey	Hanafi	Germany, France, Netherlands, Belgium, Austria, Balkans (for example, DİTİB)	Kazakhstan, Kyrgyzstan, Tajikistan, Turkmenistan, Uzbekistan
Saudi Arabia	Hanbali	Austria, Belgium, France, Spain, United Kingdom, Italy (for example, Muslim World League)	Bangladesh, India, Indonesia, Kenya, Malaysia, Pakistan, Philippines, Senegal, Sudan, Tanzania
Gulf Cooperation Council states	Hanbali	France, United Kingdom, Netherlands, Ireland (for example, European Council for Fatwa and Research)	North Africa

our services for inspection, training, zakat, and waqfs. The Tunisian minister specifically requested Algerian documentation that we believe they are using to organize the entire administration of religion in Tunisia."[100] (In 2017, Tunisia also signed eight agreements and memoranda of understanding with Saudi Arabia.[101])

Twenty-First-Century Feedback for Rome

Pius IX evaded national clampdowns and institutional interference from nineteenth-century European rulers by creating dozens of new dioceses and cardinals in Propaganda Fide countries, including for immigrant communities that had begun to settle en masse (see figure 10.7). The nineteenth-century dioceses that were created in missionary lands (including the United States until 1908) thus at first reinforced centralized control over clergy and hierarchy, since the pope had direct oversight of the Holy Congregation of Propaganda Fide. Many of the bishops who attended the First Vatican Council in 1869 were Europeans who returned by steamship from sojourns in the Catholic provinces. The historian John O'Malley recalls that Vatican I enshrined

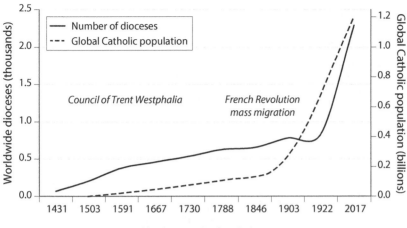

FIGURE 10.7. Worldwide Growth of Catholic Dioceses, 1431–2017

papal infallibility and codified laws forbidding Catholics from participation in "any non-Catholic religious service, even weddings and funerals."[102] Before the end of the Propaganda Fide, Charles Morris writes, the "Vatican took an ever stronger hand in the appointment of American bishops."[103] To outside observers, the long arm of Rome that sought standardization and control—from the size of seminarian bedrooms and the ratio of latrines to the curriculum taught in Church schools worldwide—appeared to be endowed with new strength.

However, Morris writes, it was also true that "Rome was riddled by factions that the Americans ... played to their own advantage." When Vatican pronouncements conflicted with American bishops' good judgment—such as papal fulminations against free speech and freedom of religion, or rallying against the Italian state—the bishops, "with great deference and humility, simply ignored them." He concludes that the "American Church developed a wonderful skill at picking its own path between American patriotism and loyalty to the Pope."[104]

After Rome acknowledged the permanence of the US Catholic minority and ended the missionary status of the American Church in 1908, the subsequent waves of appointments vastly increased the volume of Church operations and decision-making taking place outside Rome and Europe. After reaching a historic high of seven dioceses per million Catholics in the early 1600s, the ratio steadily declined before it settled into the twenty-first-century ratio of two dioceses per million worldwide. But at the same time, my research revealed, the number of non-Italians tapped for the cardinalate tripled: 63 were appointed between 1800 and 1850, and 171 from 1850 to 1900.[105] The College of Cardinals was enlarged to make space for newcomers of increasingly diverse geographical origins, including many from former colonial territories, the so-called "third world cardinals."[106] The twentieth-century popes made appointments that were proportionate to the new global distribution of Catholics. By the 1960s, the share of Italian cardinals had fallen by half.[107] The seats created for European-born representatives of Rome who were sent to the Catholic periphery were gradually turned over to the local descendants of Catholic immigrants.

As in previous periods, Catholic minorities living in majority-Protestant countries received preferential treatment and had a higher ratio of episcopal and cardinal appointments. In its first hundred years in the College of Cardinals, for example, the United States received the same number of cardinals (thirty-seven) as Spain, a founding member of the college.[108] Countries like Brazil, Mexico and the Philippines that in 1910 were at the *bottom* of the top ten Catholic populations worldwide now ranked first, second, and third just one century later.[109] In the twenty-first century, Latin America, Africa, and Asia continued to be underrepresented in the College: they accounted for more than two-thirds of the world's Catholics but provided fewer than one-third of the cardinals.

As new, large national hierarchies under canon law were created, they escaped day-to-day management from Rome. Only 27 of the 111 voting cardinals were Italian when the first non-Italian pope in 450 years took office: the Polish cardinal Karol Wojtyla (Pope John Paul II, 1978–2003). Ironically, the growth of the hierarchy outside of Europe was originally intended to reinforce *Roman* control at a time of political persecution by late nineteenth-century Catholic governments. But together with the unforeseen mass migration, these positions set the stage for unanticipated feedback on the Roman authorities. Personnel and ideas from the "new world" were exported back to the old curial structures (see figure 10.8). The share of cardinals from Europe changed from more than nine out of ten under Pius X (1903–1914) and Benedict XV (1914–1922) to five out of ten one century later. This helped create the conditions for the modernizing reforms of the Second Vatican Council, and fifty years later, the election of a pope from "the ends of the earth." Francis I (2013–), an Argentinian cardinal born Jorge Mario Bergoglio, was chosen by a college that was nearly two-thirds of non-European origin (62.6 percent).

Geography was not the only relevant dimension of representation. Benedict XVI referred to the College of Cardinals as "an orchestra, where diversity—the expression of the Universal Church—competes with something superior: concordant harmony."[110] During the papacy of Francis, the curia and episcopate were frequently compared to a hospital ward. As the magazine *Catholic Insight* put it, the archbishops named by Pope Francis were

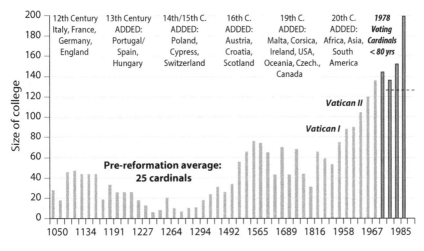

FIGURE 10.8. The Size of the College of Cardinals, 1050–2010

"drawn disproportionately from communities that are in pain."[111] The French scholar Danièle Hervieu-Léger has argued that the Church revived other techniques from an earlier era—hierarchical appointments and the use of sainthood to beatify role models from the developing world—to tie the Church's periphery to the center.[112] This strategy started at the bottom: the student body of seminarians in the United States, once strictly of European heritage, began to reflect the ethnic diversity of the greater US Catholic population. According to the *Official Catholic Directory*, more than one-third of US seminarians had Asian-, African-, or Latino-American backgrounds at the start of the twenty-first century.[113]

Under the Influence: The Second Vatican Council

The expansion of the electorate to encompass the new Catholic diaspora had concrete policy consequences. The universal Church could claim for the first time to operate globally, on all continents, and it planted the seeds for growing diversification. The lessons of Vatican I still taught that "Catholics were not only forbidden to pray with those of other faiths but also indoctrinated into a disdain or even contempt for them," and the "Holy Office . . . still enforced civil disabilities against members of other churches and religions."[114] The 1953 concordat with Spain revealed an inconsistency: Rome favored a strictly confessional state where Catholics were in the majority while fervently arguing for the principle of religious freedom wherever they were in the minority.[115]

The Second Vatican Council was convened in 1959, with meetings and votes held between 1962 and 1965. As John O'Malley has written, Vatican II "took account of the world outside the church."[116] But "the truly revolutionary aspect," theologian Mark Massa argues, was to "recognize that pluralism was, in itself, a profoundly Catholic value," and part of "the history of Catholicism itself."[117] The Catholic diaspora identity forged in the United States helped drive the Vatican's reconciliation with the contemporary world. The Church scholar Manlio Graziano points to the "increasing presence of US personnel at the top" of the hierarchy, as well as the progressive influence, beginning with the acknowledgment of laborers' rights in *Rerum Novarum* (1891) and culminating with Vatican II.[118] The historian David Hollenbach argues that the Jesuit priest John Courtney Murray's "distinctly American accent" had considerable influence on discussions at Vatican II.[119] Murray brought to Rome his conviction of the "wisdom embodied in US institutions," Hollenbach writes, "including first amendment protections of religious freedom."[120] In his own words, Murray believed that the "concern of the government" is to maintain "minimum standards" of public order, whereas "the vocation of the church" is "working for . . . the fullness of virtue and the totality of the common good."[121] Murray was just the tip of the US delegation to Rome. Half of all international experts invited to Rome came from the United States, in addition to 246 US bishops, all of whom brought with them what Graziano calls "their 175-year experience of separation between Church and state."[122] Most crucially, Murray begot a lineage of ideological successors who saw "no fundamental contradiction between liberal democracy and Catholicism."[123]

Back in the 1920s, the US government and foreign policy establishment reacted stoically to the creation of the Vatican city-state, viewing it as an internal Italian affair. The State Department seemed eager "to avoid any religious controversy" that might violate the wall between church and state in the United States and declined to acknowledge the Lateran Accords.[124] When asked about it by a journalist, Secretary of State Henry Stimson professed ignorance of the agreement and said that he had never considered the question. A typical view held that "the dictator of Italy stands with the Pope in making august guarantees . . . to the apprehension of all those throughout the world who are not Roman Catholics." The accords were called a "blow to religious and scholastic freedom in Italy and the rest of the world."[125] These views might have never changed without the associated reforms of Vatican II, leading to the diplomatic recognition of the Vatican city-state (see figure 10.9).

Is the See Half-Empty or Half-Full?

The 1960s marked a historic rupture for many Western regimes, but there may be greater continuity in the Second Vatican Council's acts than it is credited for. Critics disliked everything about Vatican II, from the elimination of Gre-

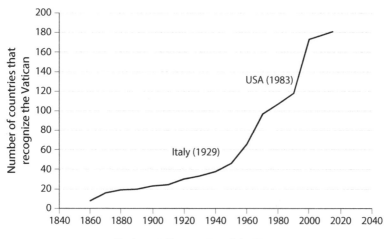

FIGURE 10.9. Diplomatic Recognition of the Vatican, 1860–2015

gorian chants to the introduction of the vernacular and the expanding role of lay men and women in the Holy Mass.[126] Some scholars suggest that such distillation of ritual was common: "Through the Roman rite's simplification, the liturgical feature is restored back to its previous condition."[127] Nonetheless, as John O'Malley acknowledges, the decree on ecumenism "signaled a change of 180 degrees, so much so that a small minority during and after the Council denounced it as heretical," and it spawned dissident factions openly defiant of the pope.[128]

Within weeks of the council's conclusion, Mark Massa writes, a Baltimore priest founded a liturgical protest movement against the council, with the support of thirty US bishops.[129] Many of their dissident views (and traditional forms of celebrating Mass) had been Church policy from 1570 to 1961, and some Vatican II laws were proximate to heresies condemned by earlier popes.[130] Within a year, Manlio Graziano writes, "thousands of US Roman Catholic priests and nuns asked Church officials to laicize them."[131] Some adherents of *Sedevacantismo* ("empty see"–ism) claimed that Pope John XXIII and every pope thereafter were illegitimate and that the papal throne was vacant. There have even been a handful of parallel popes (usually called Gregory XVII).[132] French archbishop Marcel Lefebvre is one prominent example of a Church dissident who straddled the border between disobedience and heresy for decades. Lefebvre did not rise to the level of anti-pope, but he declared the new Order of the Mass (1969) to be "a striking departure from the Catholic theology."[133] His critical stance presented a thorny challenge after he founded his own seminary in Valais, the Roman Catholic heartland of the Swiss Alps, and established seminaries in five more countries. Within several years of its creation, Lefebvre's Society of St. Pius X (1970) had dozens of satellite offices around the world and boasted nearly 500 priests and four bishops. Lefebvre was summoned to the Vatican and invited to desist. He would not, and in 1988 John Paul II excommunicated the archbishop, along with the bishops he had illicitly ordained.

John Paul kept liberalizing tendencies in check with the aid of his prefect of the Congregation for the Doctrine of the Faith (and successor), Joseph Cardinal Ratzinger, who was a walking billboard against compromise. "It is the hallmark of truth that it is worth suffering for," Ratzinger told a delegation of US bishops in the mid-1980s. John Paul added, "We are the guardians . . . of something that is not merely the best among many, but the one and only true path to salvation."[134] The post-conciliar crisis, however, was the Church's worst in centuries. Between 1970 and 2000, as many as one-third of personnel left the fold—roughly "100,000 priests in the world (and possibly even many more nuns)," according to Graziano—a hemorrhaging made worse by secular trends that slowly emptied the pews they served.[135]

The Benedictine-Franciscan Revolution

A half-century after Vatican II, the first two popes of the new millennium further upended the status quo. The first of these, Benedict XVI (2005–2013), heralded a conservative revolution. Coming from the heart of the curia, he had spent years guarding against permissiveness toward homosexuality, women's ordination, and liberation theology. Vatican II, so far as he was concerned, contained "fabricated liturgy." While still a cardinal, Joseph Ratzinger was known for rereading the corpus of Vatican II in a traditional light, to curtail excessive freedom. He chose for his papal namesake the Patron Protector of Europe, whose order's austere motto was "Pruned, it grows again."[136] In the sixth century, with the Roman Empire in its last throes, Saint Benedict (Benoît) built religious communities separated from the rest of society. The new pope's conservatism reached far back: Benedict reintroduced two long-lost institutional possibilities to the modern papacy. First, he established the reversibility of excommunication *without penance* when he restored four bishops who had been punished for disobedience and preaching retrograde views. The implication was that a heretic or schismatic who rejected papal authority could yet receive a papal pardon in his lifetime. Second, Benedict's surprise resignation after a seven-year term demonstrated that popes did not serve at the pleasure of God for life and could remove themselves if they no longer felt up to the task.

The election of Francis (Cardinal Jose Maria Bergoglio) in 2013 brought a member of the diaspora to the apex of the Church, half a world and half a millennium away from the mores of his immediate predecessor. John O'Malley calls his election "the end of an era—and perhaps the beginning of a new one."[137] As the first pontiff not to have personally experienced Vatican II, Francis is "free of the battles and memories" from the council. Moreover, the cardinal electors, by choosing an Argentinian national, paid homage to Latin America as a prize territory to be defended against Evangelical expansion. It was rumored that "US cardinals had a 'major political role'" in his selection, helping channel votes toward Bergoglio.

When President Barack Obama traveled to Vatican City, he brought a box of fruit and vegetable seeds for Pope Francis—an analogy wrapped in a simile. The box, divided into nine compartments, was crafted with timber from the original St. Mary's Seminary of Baltimore, founded in 1791. St. Mary's was the first US seminary that the Vatican authorized to ordain priests (in 1822). The final layer of meaning—the wrapping—was that Paul III, who initiated the Council of Trent that led to diocesan seminaries and the modern priesthood, was the same pope who recognized and charged the Jesuit order with battling Protestantism in 1540. The election of a Jesuit cardinal archbishop from a New World diocese was a missive in a bottle that reached shore "from the far ends of the earth," as Francis said in his acceptance speech, nearly four centuries after the founding of the Jesuit society.[138]

The pope did not choose as his namesake the Spanish Saint Ignatius, founder of the Jesuits, but rather the Italian Saint Francesco of Assisi, who famously gave away all his possessions. The Italian scholar Fabio Benincasa dubs Francis the "social Pope," a descriptor that plays on his social media presence and attention to the poor. Francis has used his global platform to extract the Church from political squabbles and return it to its core activity: purveying salvation and aiding the poor.[139] The first post–Vatican II pope opposes "mixing spiritual and temporal powers" because, he says, it always "means subjecting one to the other." Francis's view is that "the religious element should never be confused with the political one."[140] He thereby takes things further than the Second Council document *Gaudium et Spes* (1965), which states that priests should be the source of "spiritual light and [spiritual] nourishment"— not political advice. *Gaudium's* description of "the layman's own distinctive role" is open for interpretation.[141] Ought the "political engagement of Catholics," for example, be directed toward "a different agenda than the clergy?"[142] Or should it be used to persuade Catholic legislators to reject bills that bishops dislike? In answer to whether Europe's "Christian roots" should be formally acknowledged, Pope Francis says, "Yes, and Christianity has the duty of watering [these roots], but in a spirit of service as in the washing of feet. Christianity's duty for Europe is that of service."[143]

With these words, Francis hinted at the restoration of an earlier division of labor, predating even the fourth-century deal between Theodosius and

Constantine. As some scholars have argued, Christianity was originally anti-political because Jesus preached that his "empire is not from this world" and did not seek worldly power.[144] In the words of an adviser to Pope Francis, the current Holy Father rejects the "idea of activating a Kingdom of God on earth . . . including [through] a [political] 'party.'"[145] "Church doctrine is not to be employed as a weapon," the pope has said, "but as a source of pastoral vitality." A church "that 'does' little in practice, while incessantly 'explaining' its teachings, is dangerously unbalanced."[146] An analysis of hundreds of papal appointments confirms that Francis has prioritized pastoral experience over doctrinal purity in his major personnel decisions. And as the Vatican adage goes, personnel is policy.

The Role of Demography

These political debates and theological disputes will be resolved by demographic developments. Globally, Roman Catholicism's share of Christianity has remained constant for 500 years. Two arguably illiberal positions that survived Vatican II—the pro-natalist policies against contraception and abortion—can be seen in light of a demographic race that has allowed Catholics to outnumber Protestants by a factor of three to one, from when Christianity claimed 140 million souls in 1800 to the more than 2 billion of Christian heritage today (see figure 10.10). This growth was enabled by the spread of Catholicism in high-fertility developing countries, and it is how Catholics have also retained their share of global population at around 17 percent over the last fifty years.

One consequence of the Church's successes in new territories was the inevitable internal demographic overtaking by Catholics outside the traditional heartland. In 2010, 81 percent of all Catholic baptisms and 70 percent of priestly ordinations were performed outside the United States and Europe.[147] One-third of the world's 1.285 billion Catholics lived in Africa and Asia and less than one-quarter in Europe. (One-half lived in the Americas.) Vatican Council II was impossible without the United States, but not all feedback from the periphery is progressive.

In *The Young Pope*, an artistic rumination on the Vatican's inner circle, film director Paolo Sorrentino speculates on what would happen if an American cardinal became pope and restored the severity of inquisition and prohibition. Three of the four cardinals with the highest reported number of first-round votes in the 2013 conclave came from the "new world" (Argentina, Canada, and the United States).[148] It is reasonable to anticipate such a "Pius XIII" from the diaspora in this century or the next, but he is likely to come from another hemisphere. The African continent recently led population growth among all Catholic regions, increasing by nearly 20 percent from 2010 to 2015.[149] In the

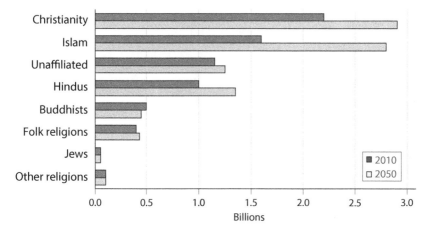

FIGURE 10.10. The Demography of Global Religions in the Twenty-First Century

last 100 years, the Catholic population of sub-Saharan Africa grew from 1.9 million to more than 130 million. In addition, vocations were booming across the continent. When enrollment in a Catholic seminary in southeastern Nigeria reached more than 1,100 in 2015, it became the world's largest.[150]

A seasoned Vatican observer described the contingent of African bishops at a 2014 synod on the family as "conservative on matters of sexual morality, especially gay relationships," and unafraid to "insert themselves into the conversation." A liberal cardinal reportedly worried aloud that African bishops "should not tell us too much what we have to do."[151] Such tensions between blocs were the natural dynamic of a growing college whose cardinals lived in very different contexts. By 2013, 19 percent of cardinals hailed from Africa and Asia, roughly half as many as their share of the overall population would merit based on proportion alone. On the other hand, the extension of the cardinalate outside Europe may have been a twentieth-century anomaly. One analyst predicts that the growth of the Catholic population outside of Europe is likely to "proceed faster than the 'de-Europeanization' of the College."[152] Francis made nearly eighty appointments to the college in his first seven years, during which time the share of voting cardinals from outside Europe—Asia Pacific, sub-Saharan Africa, and Latin America—grew measurably (from 9 to 15 percent, 9 to 13 percent, and 17 to 19 percent, respectively), while the overall share of cardinals from Europe and North America decreased (from 52 to 42 percent and 12 to 9 percent, respectively).[153] The outcome will determine the path taken: to what extent will global Catholicism, in its myriad contexts and experiences, be reflected within the episcopate and the College of Cardinals, and what does that imply for a Third Vatican Council in a future era?

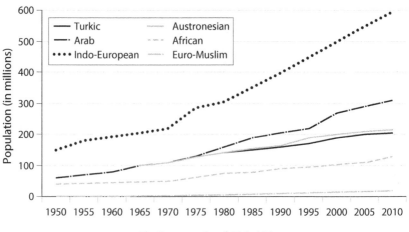

FIGURE 10.11. The Demography of Global Islam, 1950–2010

A potentially significant shift in its geographic concentration and ethnic composition has also occurred within Sunni Islam over the last 300 years. As a result of successful Islamic conquest and conversion, the Arab proportion of the world's Muslim population decreased from one-third in 1700 to one-fifth in 2020 (see figure 10.11). Today's Arab League territories are roughly twice as populous as the Turkic peoples of Anatolia and Central Asia—70 million to 35 million in the mid-twentieth century. The Turkic peoples were overtaken by Austronesians (the peoples of Indonesia, Philippines, Madagascar, Thailand, and Taiwan) in the mid-1980s. The Arab League territories contained 320 million people in 2010, compared to 220 million Austronesians and 200 million of Turkic origin.[154] These population numbers and the religion's origins in the Arabian peninsula lead most to presume that Arab spiritual leadership and custodianship of the holy sites will prevail for the foreseeable future. The change in the ratio of Muslims to Catholics worldwide over the past thirty years is striking. In 1970, there were 554 million Muslims and 666 million Catholics.[155] By the Great Jubilee of 2000, Islam counted 1.2 billion adherents and Catholicism almost 1.1 billion. In 2025, 1.3 billion Catholics (out of 2.1 billion Christians) will find themselves living in a world with 1.8 billion Muslims.[156]

You've Been Denominationalized!

It was only once the Vatican had been restored to self-government and diplomatic recognition that it was possible to reduce the salience of secular-religious cleavages within Western Christendom. By contrast, the vast majority of the Islamic faithful have no Sunni Muslim authority to look to and no fully recognized religious communities in most of the Western countries where they live as a minority. They lack what the religious studies scholar Jose Casanova calls "the freedom to enter or not to enter the public sphere" that gives individuals greater choice to maintain either "more privatist or more public identities." Disestablishment, Casanova says, is what allowed the Catholic Church to become a "voluntary religious association," a free church, catalyzing the transformation "from a state-oriented to a society-oriented institution."[157] The term "Roman Catholic" lost its geographical connotations once the political capital of the Church no longer lay within the jurisdiction of the city of Rome. Unpredictably, this occurred just a few generations after the belligerent First Vatican Council, and one decade after the Spanish concordat denied toleration to non-Catholic groups.

As Stathis Kalyvas has shown, the politicization of religious identity is frequently rooted in the deprivation of fundamental rights by modern nation-states. It does not matter that Sunni Muslims were never in the minority, sociologically speaking, in the parliaments of Turkey or Tunisia, or that Roman Catholic men technically never left power in Italy or France. For the better part of a century, those secularizing regimes treated Islam and Catholicism like an antique nuisance being promoted by an old guard to block modernity and progress. Nonstate actors were the greatest beneficiaries of this vacuum and the flagging legitimacy of Nation-State Islam.[158] As Mustafa Akyol wrote too tentatively, "Islamism in Turkey is at least partly an unintended consequence of Kemalism which created a vacuum that a radical Islamism of a foreign origin could fill."[159] As a corporate body, the Church's experience with the state was catastrophic. It was stripped of its property, its leaders were imprisoned, exiled, or worse, its organization was removed from the ministries of education and justice, and so on.

After this history of appropriation and exile, what sort of reparations do states owe religious authorities? Soft restoration facilitates the reintegration of a culturally alienated portion of the population into the nation via religious community. To accept the state is to swear not to subvert the state's laws and civilian leadership, but accepting civilian rule is more than toleration. Civilian oversight of the military is commonly accepted as a necessary condition of democratic rule. It has also been the key element of consolidating democracy during periods of political strife over religious authority. Semi-autonomy has allowed the space to create infrastructure, education, and hierarchy and restore religious licensing, education, and training. The late political scientist Alfred Stepan's concept of "twin tolerations" is helpful to understand the dynamic of where the relationship between church and state has landed. In a civil state, Stephan writes, rather than being governed by a fear of repression or the desire to reintegrate society, "religion respects democratic prerogatives—the people are sovereign, and they make the laws. Yet a civil state also respects some prerogatives of religion and its legitimate role in the public sphere."[160] Where you have both types of toleration, "religious authorities do not control democratic officials who are acting constitutionally, while democratic officials do not control religion so long as religious actors respect other citizens' rights." Stepan hastens to add that there are "multiple secularisms, i.e. many different patterns of relations among the state, religion, and society" that are compatible with the twin tolerations.[161]

This is similar to the normative argument that John Locke made on behalf of an institutional design that encourages political neutrality and the principle of mutual non-interference. In his *Letter Concerning Toleration* (1689), Locke counsels a division of labor that Stepan would recognize: "Ecclesiastical authority ought to be confined within the bounds of the church [and not] in any manner be extended to civil affairs," just as church affairs "are removed out of the reach of the magistrate's jurisdiction." Locke describes the undesirable outcome when civil-religious relations are biased by factionalism—that is, when the "civil magistrate [is] inclined to favor one church and to put his sword into [that church's] hands" so it could "chastise the dissenters as [it] pleased."[162] Indeed, contemporary autonomy means "being run by duly constituted Catholic authorities," as Douglas Laycock writes, and not being run by "legislators, administrative agencies, labor unions, disgruntled lay people, or other actors lacking authority under Church law."[163]

Once Church authority was no longer the law of the land, the tables were turned. Getting permission back from the state to teach and preach became Rome's priority, signaling the shift from a mission of providing minimal religious services to building up a self-sufficient religious community, able to educate its own clergy and its own children within the Church. Catholic and Muslim cross-border influence became characterized by suzerainty, a kind of halfway house on the way to complete sovereignty/restoration with formal gestures of courtesy to previous rulers. Instead of "bringing about the ruin and end of the Church," as one observer wrote in 1923, "the spoliation [was] the very cause of an increase in the power of the Holy See."[164] In the aftermath of state domination, Church leaders had many important corporate privileges restored.In most of the world, the Church does not pay land taxes on its significant properties; its receipt of charitable donations is not subject to withholding; in many jurisdictions, its clergy have civil powers to license marriages; it is protected from antidiscrimination law in its hiring, and it carved out other exemptions in labor law; and it is licensed to provide social services and establish institutions of education, worship, and advocacy.

The modern secular state leaves wide latitude for independent internal practices and for civil society to thrive for hundreds of millions of Catholic citizens. The situation of Catholic education is surprisingly strong in France, which has a slightly smaller number of citizens with a Catholic background than the United States. Nearly 2 million French students (16 percent of the total) were enrolled in 8,700 Church-run schools, which employed over 200,000 teachers and professionals in 2018. Germany, home to around half as many Catholics as France, has 325,000 students enrolled in 750 Church schools, of which 250 are segregated by gender. The hospitals administered by the main recognized churches provide most of the beds in many areas of the country. Most public schools in the German *Länder* offer weekly religion class, taught by a Church delegate who submits curriculum in advance to the state educational authority.[165] Italy has more than twice as many Catholics as Germany but fewer full-time students in Church schools: 275,000, less than 4 percent of the total, are enrolled in 2,400 Catholic schools. Spain has the highest twenty-first-century enrollment share, with around 1.4 million, or 20 percent of all students, studying in 2,700 Catholic schools.

To take the United States as an example, twenty-first-century American Catholics are the largest single religious group, with 17,650 houses of worship. Additionally, the US Conference of Catholic Bishops manages 5,400 elementary schools, 1,200 high schools, and 225 universities and colleges with over more than 6 million students and 200,000 teachers and professors. It also oversees 550 hospitals serving 90 million patients, as well as other charitable institutions—orphanages, shelters, museums—that served 9 million people in 2013. In recognition of these critical functions, a significant amount of US federal funding flowed to Catholic charities.

There is still sharp debate over the Free Exercise Clause of the US Constitution's Establishment Clause regarding the "jurisdictional limits on courts' authority to adjudicate issues of religious import."[166] That is the realm, for example, where a "ministerial exception" to employment law allows churches to hire according to discriminatory criteria. This could be considered a key aspect of privacy from government—a *Roe v. Wade* guaranteeing self-control over the religious body. The trick was arriving at consensus—intra- and intercommunity—about where one jurisdiction ended and the other began. The intervening variable, Casanova suggests, is Catholics' internalization of "the teachings of Vatican II in a way the Council fathers may not have anticipated, . . . facilitating 'do it yourself' or 'selective Catholicism.'" Once the Church accepted that it "can no longer legislate public morality," he writes, it abandoned old models of Catholic political mobilization—one of the many "unintended consequences of having entered the modern sphere."[167] Casanova admires the subsequent "reticence of the bishops to present authoritative Catholic solutions" to policy problems and who instead offered up "Catholic normative tradition as the basis for public debate." Such traditions, Casanova writes, "should have the same rights as any other normative tradition to enter the public sphere as long as they play by the rules."[168]

Feedback on Global Institutions

The experience of global Catholicism and international Sunni Islam with the modern state has been taxing. In the space of fifty generations, Roman Catholicism went from being the predominant religion of the European continent and the British Isles in the year 1500 to being the *official* religion of just 0.22 percent of the European population in 2015. By the time Pope John Paul II took office, only his city-state and the sovereign territories of Andorra, Lichtenstein, Malta, and Monaco still professed Catholicism as the religion of state. Of twenty countries that legalized same-sex marriage in recent years, nine were majority–Roman Catholic; all allowed abortion to save the life of the mother.[169] The mighty Roman despot became an ontological afterthought. As the last will and testament of French president François Mitterrand ambiguously phrased it, "Une messe est possible" ("A mass may be held").[170] Making peace with a constitutional nation-state is a slippery slope: when hadiths are culled and the Latin Mass ceases to be, are these still the same religions? Oliver Rafferty notes the persistence of the view in some clerical circles that canon law must take precedence over civil law. But if real power was wielded, it no longer had *executive* aims. The pope, whose predecessors fought so hard to retain temporal power and obtain nation-state status, acts like the powerful chairman of the world's largest NGO.

Upon inspecting the ledgers, Islamic leaders might hesitate to follow the Catholic Church's model of doctrinal adjustment and accommodation to the nation-state and modern world. Catholic clergy have not kept up with the growth of the flock. While the global number of Catholics grew by over 10 percent between 1990 and 2013, to 1.285 billion, the number of priests grew by only 3 percent in that time.[171] For the first time ever, in the 2010s, the absolute number of priests in the world—around 415,000—fell slightly (by 136). This was reflected in worsening ratios of clergy to the faithful. The worldwide corps of bishops kept growing (5,304), as did permanent deacons (45,255), and so did the number of diocesan priests—but populations grew faster.[172] The situation was most dramatic among the diaspora in the developed world. Ordinations in the United States fell from an annual high of 1,050 in the mid-1960s to around half that number fifty years later.[173] The 57,000 American priests of 1985 fell to fewer than 40,000 in 2015. "For many Americans," Maria Cristina Fiocchi wrote in 1989, "volunteerism and a multitude of self-help programs take the place religion used to occupy."[174] The political scientists Robert Putnam and David Campbell found that 60 percent of non-immigrant Catholics in the

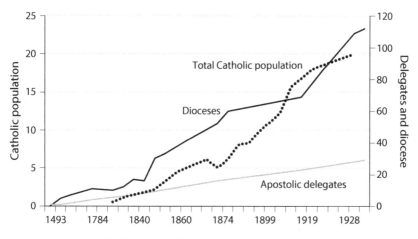

FIGURE 10.12. North America: Dioceses versus Apostolic Delegates, 1493–1940

United States were not observant of their religious traditions.[175] Weekly church attendance fell from around 40 percent of US Catholics in the 1980s to under one in four in 2014.[176] The Pew Center found that one-third of Americans raised Catholic no longer describe themselves as Catholic, meaning that 10 percent of all Americans are *former* Catholics.[177] On the other hand, Graziano observes, "even if 'only' one-third (or one-tenth or one-twentieth) of Catholics regularly attend Church . . . no other organization on Earth is able to mobilize on a purely voluntary basis, so many people so often."[178]

Some blame the emptying pews and seminaries, ironically, on the Church's single greatest attempt to increase its public appeal in the nation-state era— the Second Vatican Council (see figure 10.12). The historian Philip Gleason suggests that Vatican II had something to do with the decline because it eliminated the Latin liturgy and "weakened traditional practices like confession and fasting." Gleason argues that Vatican II "introduced uncertainty and confusion of what it means to be Catholic." The religion went from being a tightly wound combination of "creed, cult, and discipline" to something "etherealized," closer to ethnicity. One consequence for the religious vocations was the loss of "a great deal of social prestige."[179]

As with the institutions of the Counter-Reformation, it is impossible to know whether losses would have been worse *without* Vatican II. A pre-conciliar Church report took a more sociological approach and suggested that the weakening of organized religion was being driven by other changes in society. Foremost to blame was "the 'economic miracle' in post-war [Europe]." This development "favored the growth of materialism, even among country people who previously furnished the greater part of [the priesthood]."[180] Despite the Cold

War, a survey of dioceses showed that more than half of respondents chose "materialism and secularism" as the main reason for the decline in vocations, followed by "unfavorable parental attitudes."[181] The Church also faulted "parents and educators" for not asserting their inherent authority. Nothing was being done to stem "the growing demand for freedom among the young," who were being tempted by modern stimuli, including "literature, an atmosphere of sensuality and eroticism, the cinema, television, and illustrated papers."[182]

In the words of David Hollenbach, American Catholic leaders needed to convince "Protestants and secular shapers of US culture to get over their fears that Catholicism was a threat to US political institutions" and convey that Catholics did not believe it was "the role of the state or government to reach decisions about religious truth."[183] The Second Vatican Council, a long-distance, unilateral concordat, amounted to a pact with modern states that was duly ratified by Church representatives: the resounding vote in favor of the document formalizing religious toleration was 2,000 to 70 (see figure 10.13).[184] This was the final turn that helped Western states stop worrying about the politicization of Catholicism and start to love Catholics. In the United States, Catholics adapted from a position of strength: since the end of World War II, there had been more of them in the United States than the next six denominations combined.[185] Catholics' total population share grew to 23 percent at the turn of the new millennium.

The election of John F. Kennedy as US president (1960) benefited from the zeitgeist in Rome, helping Kennedy's reassurances of separation to ring true as he became the first Catholic to break through to the summit of the state. Accepting the separation of church and state in the United States turned the Roman Catholic faith into a religious denomination—with the same legal status as any other.[186] Despite the relative decline in ordinations, mass attendance, baptisms, marriages, and schools, Catholic institutions were robust in comparison to other communities' religious institutions.[187] In absolute terms, there were nearly twice as many seminarians in the United States in 2013 than there had been in 1978.[188] Priestly ordinations had stabilized, and some of the other shrinkage was a correction for the twentieth century's exponential growth of US Catholic institutions; from the perspective of losing the faithful, the shrinkage should have been much greater. The Second Vatican Council introduced a new solution for the recruitment shortages: enlisting laypeople in parish life. For example, 40 percent of all permanent deacons in the world are now from the United States, even though it is the only country in the world with more priests than Italy.[189]

Undermining traditional religious authority rarely had the intended effect in the short term and could be disastrous over time. Europeans provoked a century of political Islam. Rulers of Muslim countries who deprived genera-

FIGURE 10.13. Second Vatican Council (1963)

tions of religious freedom and knowledge allowed extremist recruiters to thrive on a supply of young people who never learned their own religion's holy books. In the twenty-first century, the United States lost to the mujahidin in Afghanistan and the Mahdi army in Basra, inadvertently paving the way to al Qaeda and ISIS. Governments that gave in to the temptation to break the glass and seize the emergency hammer of religious authority were left with a pile of shards in one hand and a blunt instrument in the other. While it is frequently argued that Islam is fundamentally incompatible with liberal democracy, neither Wahhabism nor ISIS can be described as essentially Islamic. They are modern fundamentalist movements that moved into vacuums created by Western empires and their successors.

It is easy to be distracted by the measures taken to defend religious turf in a proprietary way. No authority structure, however, would be expected to lie down and accept displacement: neither the angry pope who learns that Catholic children in the United States will attend public school nor the angry twenty-first-century director of religious affairs in Ankara when he gets word of gender-egalitarian mosques beyond his control in Germany. On the other side, taking the *illegal* discourse framework at face value can unduly legitimize the wholesale appropriation of a religion by a terrorist group. Cardinal Archbishop Timothy Dolan said that the dynamic was familiar: "The Irish Republican Army claimed to be Catholic, they were baptized and they had a Catholic identity. But what they were doing was a perversion of everything the Church stood for."[190] The French scholar Florence Bergeaud says that the main challenge posed by the Islamic State and its ilk "is an intellectual one. Radicalism affects manners, food and religious norms. That won't be ended by closing the borders or by buying it off with millions of Euros, but only by depoliticizing the question of Islam."[191] Bergeaud may be too hasty, however, in adding that "this has nothing to do with how the religion is structured and organized." This book has assembled a body of evidence to argue the contrary: depoliticization has everything to do with how the religion is structured and organized.

Waiting for Soft Restoration

What can be restored to reanimate Islamic civil society, as Catholic associations have done? Ridwan al-Sayyid argues, not entirely helpfully, that it is an "illusion to [think] that it is at all possible to use Islam as a ruling system," but that it is "also an illusion to think that social and political elites can ever be separated from religion."[192] The Tunisian scholar Mohammad Haddad has revived the early twentieth-century thought of Muhammed Abduh, who preached that returning to tolerance was more urgent than secularization per se. Haddad stakes out a clear position of what there should *not* be: "an international Islamic organization responsible for issuing fatwas," or a "religious man appointed to become the great representative of Muslims." Religious heritage is too different from one nation to another for such notions. Nonetheless, Haddad's stated objectives sound a lot like the Catholic landing point described earlier: an end state of depoliticization where "religion is in no way used to serve the state's interests, nor vice versa." His goal of "integrating religion in the general social movements" of the Muslim world even resembles the notion of soft restoration.[193] Moreover, the recent commitment of major Islamist parties around the Middle East and North Africa to participating in mainstream politics, John Esposito, Lily Zubaidah Rahim, and Naser Ghobadzadeh write in *The Politics of Islamism*, "signals an important transformation [away] from the simplistic focus on the compatibility or incompatibility of Islam and democracy."[194]

What other structure, aside from an activist, dispassionate state, can provide the conditions for this transformation to take place peacefully? On the need for theologically trained imams, one religious scholar compared imams to state-licensed pharmacists: "You don't just let customers rifle through the medicine cabinets." Whenever governments zealously eradicated a religious-cultural past, they weakened Islamic institutions to the point of inviting foreign intervention. This has occurred in a historical period when key issues of sovereignty, democracy, and theology remain highly politicized in the international Sunni Muslim sphere. Paradoxically, the protective structure of a government ministry makes pluralist outcomes more likely. Assuming that a durable Islamic caliphate will not reemerge during the nation-state era, the multiple *centers* of religious authority will continue developing into emirates or something resembling mini-caliphates, forming a constellation of spiritual lights orbited by communities at varying distances. Given how much autonomy states have taken away from Islam, there is plenty for governments to restore.

Policy areas where states can initiate the soft restoration include religious education and life-cycle rituals related to births, marriages, and funerals, such as licensing clergy to perform circumcisions at home and in state hospitals, giving imams civil powers to officiate marriages on behalf of the state, and permitting burial without a coffin.[195] But it also raises the specter of other privileges, such as allowing parents to place their children in religious education before age twelve, accrediting the religious affairs ministry to certify religious schools, or permitting elected representatives to pass laws limiting alcohol distribution or restricting public morals.

Whereas other authors attribute the rise in religion's salience to the insidious efforts of the nation-state, this book has argued that Islam's position in the public sphere has been politicized so long as the "Eastern Question" first posed by the European empires remained open. Against the barrage of Islamicization from the outside world—arriving by plane, satellite, and internet—nation-states, with their awkward bureaucracies, worked to preempt (and sometimes to co-opt) outside attempts to win over believers' loyalties. They aimed to create a politically neutral, professional civic corps of religious professionals under civilian rule—in effect, national ministries of religious affairs. A religious-institutional complex is a public utility for believers and also acts as a beachhead against ideological and religious rivals. In much of the Muslim world, religion policy is an area where governments still justify top-down control. The traditional Sunni religious authorities who have survived the transition to the modern state have declared that one must follow the law of the nation-state. But they might also feel that the present cost of survival is barely tolerable.

One policy implication is that governments leave their religious communities underserved and unprotected at their own peril. In the same way that allies in the NATO defense treaty were encouraged to spend 2 percent of GDP on defense budgets, governments with contested religious borders find it expeditious to spend at least 0.5 percent of their GDP on religious affairs to produce professional clerics and construct enough prayer spaces to satisfy demand. The status quo in the Islamic world arguably contributed to social and political stability, but it has been disastrous for religious pluralism and religious toleration. There is a distinctly pre–Vatican II air to the Islamic concordats that define contemporary state-Islam relations. The lack of soft restoration measures for Islam in North Africa, Turkey, and western Europe left religion in the realm of security policy. This prevented the blossoming of relations with Islamic scholars who could make the religion relevant to a given population of believers. Robert Hefner writes that, in the absence of anything approaching community-wide consensus, there was a splintering of religious authority and "an intensification of debates over Islam's social meaning and the authorities by whom it was to be defined." The destabilization of religious hierarchies unleashed "competition over the interpretation of religious symbols and control of the institutions that produce and sustain states."[196] Trained scholars are today up against a mix of internet and television preachers, Islamists, and ulema.[197]

Rome resisted pressures to remove territories from the Propaganda Fide for as long as it could. But within generations of establishing dioceses, archdioceses in the United States, whether in Birmingham or Boston, had the same degree of self-government over episcopal and clerical appointments, educational curriculum, and other key decisions as did the archdiocese in majority-Catholic Brescia or Bavaria. Similar stresses prompted the institutional devolution of multiple systems of Nation-State Islam—independently operated by ministries of religious affairs in Algiers, Ankara, Rabat, and so on. These largely national Islamic communities are the concrete legacy of British and French strategies to divide the umma into manageable bits. An analogous Islamic sequence of events to the Catholic experience as a migrant minority would professionalize mosques and religious education while building a corps of imams and ulema, culminating with the recognition of Europe as part of dar al Islam—not as missionary or enemy territory. That change would lead to the appointment of native-born members from the new world minority—trained under locally accredited auspices—to positions of responsibility and leadership to replace the previous export-grade services. What originated as a foreign branch controlled by a religious capital city abroad would metamorphose into a nationally run franchise, easing its overall acceptance by skeptical majority societies.

In the past two decades, Turkey, Morocco, Algeria, and other centralized spiritual communities undertook limited measures in this direction vis-à-vis their Austrian, Belgian, French, German, Italian, and Spanish communities. Feedback from increasingly diverse local experiences—through personnel, travel, migration, and media—flows into the religion's nervous system. Over a century ago, the Ottomans invited notable religious scholars and personalities from the Balkans, Central Asia, the Levant, and the Maghreb to serve as courtiers and high-level administrators in Istanbul. Before that, the Vatican recruited northern Europeans and North Americans to take positions in the curia. The path of the Roman Catholic Church over the past sixty years—from Vatican II to Pope Francis—was decisively influenced by diaspora Catholics. Muslims living in western Europe have already pushed centers of Islamic authority on a very different course than their original trajectory, and feedback through institutional globalization will increase in the coming century.

When reforms do occur within minority communities abroad, they can reach the Islamic affairs ministries in the countries of origin, as Alevi and Berber groups in the Middle East and North Africa have enjoyed more recognition thanks to diaspora pressure and foreign government support from western Europe. But there is no Islamic administration with global reach for modernizers to feed back into—no place for the role played by Yıldız Palace in the time of Sultan Abdülhamid II. The closest approximation is overseen by Saudi Wahhabis, who have long seemed impervious to the dynamic of feedback because their fundamentalist aims are intentionally insular and retrospective. But in 2020 the Muslim World League announced that Saudi Arabia would relinquish control, for the first time, of a major mosque abroad. Complete control over the administration of the grand mosque of Geneva, built in the late 1970s, would be handed over to a locally appointed council, with an elected president, fifty years after its creation.[198] Could that mark the formal start of a "diocesization" process for international Islam akin to that experienced by the Catholic Church? The semi-autonomous space for religion could be seen as having the benefit of lending legitimacy to the nation-states of the Middle East and North Africa.

It is still common to treat any hint of religion's official return like the restoration of oppressive political opponents. But if the cycle of secularists' terrorization of religious orders giving way to jihadi terrorism is not to repeat ad infinitum, then credibly neutral experts must build institutions behind constitutional firewalls.[199] Such efforts to build up the corps of religious professionals are necessary for a successful civil-religious relationship in the majority-Muslim world. The Middle East and North Africa began to democratize only after the departure of European armies in the mid-twentieth century. The map of this region still resembles an earlier era of political development akin to nineteenth-century Europe—a patchwork of secularizing and confessional regimes that created democratic institutions without fully empowering them. The tension at its heart was whether and how to protect the state monopoly on religion and the formal supremacy of the majority religion, Islam.

It is a bitter irony that the European-occupied populations in the Middle East missed out on the religious-institutional evolutions, painful as they were, of the European nineteenth century. During an interview on my final trip to North Africa for this book, a French consul general evoked the recent visit of Pope Francis to Morocco as an optimistic note upon which to depart for his next diplomatic posting. In the garden behind his office, a statue of the legendary French governor Maréchal Lyautey stood within the compound's walls, moved from its previous pedestal on the Place du Gouvernement. The consul called up YouTube on his portable phone and let the video play: Pope Francis sat smiling alongside King Mohammed VI while they listened to an interfaith concert overlaying the Islamic call to prayer with the Catholic *Ave Maria* and, finally, with the Jewish *Shema*.[200] The ancient Hebrew incantation wafted over the heads of the two sovereign religious rulers and above the twenty-first-century rafters of the auditorium in Rabat and through the Samsung, the ambiguous legacy of the oldest monotheism echoing in the walls of the heavily guarded consulate: *The Lord is our God, the Lord is One. Blessed is the name of His glorious kingdom for ever and ever.*

Algeria

1515–1830	Ottoman Algeria
1830–1962	French Algeria
1954–1962	Provisional Government of the Algerian Republic
1962–Present	People's Democratic Republic of Algeria

France

1500–1589	House of Valois
1589–1792	House of Bourbon
1792–1804	French First Republic
1804–1814	House of Bonaparte, First Empire
1814–1815	Capetian Dynasty
1815	House of Bonaparte, First Empire
1815–1830	House of Bourbon
1830–1848	House of Orleans
1848–1852	Second French Republic
1852–1870	House of Bonaparte, Second Empire
1870–1940	French Third Republic
1940–1944	Vichy France
1944–1946	Provisional Government of the French Republic
1946–1958	French Fourth Republic
1958–Present	French Fifth Republic

Germany

1438–1740	House of Habsburg
1742–1745	House of Wittelsbach
1745–1806	House of Habsburg-Lorraine
1806–1813	Confederation of the Rhine
1815–1866	German Confederation
1867–1871	North German Confederation

1871–1918	German Empire
1919–1933	Weimar Republic
1933–1945	Nazi Germany
1945–1949	Allied-occupied Germany
1949–1990	Federal Republic of Germany/German Democratic Republic
1990-Present	Unified Germany: Federal Republic of Germany

Italy

1437–1556	House of Habsburg
1556–1805	Foreign domination
1805–1814	House of Bonaparte
1861–1946	House of Savoy
1861	Unification as Kingdom of Italy
1922	March on Rome and rise of Mussolini
1943	Overthrow of Mussolini
1946–Present	Italian Republic

Jerusalem

1250–1517	Mamluk Period
1517–1917	Ottoman Empire
1917–1948	British Mandate
1948/1967–Present	Division between Jordan and Israel

Mecca

1382–1517	Mamluk Period
1517–1916	Ottoman Empire
1916–1924	Kingdom of Hejaz
1924–Present	Saudi government

Morocco

1500–1554	Wattasid Dynasty
1554–1603	Saadi Dynasty
1603–1627	Succession War
1627–1659	Reunified rule
1659–1663	Dila'i interlude
1666–1957	Alaouite Dynasty—Sultans of Morocco/some Spanish rule/treaty with Ottoman sultan
1912–1956	French Mandate

1912	Installation of Moulay Yusuf
1927–1953	Mohammed V
1953–1955	Mohammed Ibn Arafa
1957–Present	Alauoite Dynasty: Kings of Morocco
1956–1961	Mohammed V
1961–1999	Hassan II
1999–Present	Mohammed VI

Spain

1516–1700	Hapsburg Spain
1700–1868	House of Bourbon
1870–1873	House of Savoy
1873–1874	First Spanish Republic
1874–1931	Restoration of Bourbon Dynasty
1931–1939	Second Republic of Spain
1939–1975	Rule of Franco and reestablishment of the Bourbon monarchy
1975–Present	Parliamentary constitutional monarchy

Tunisia

1500–1574	Hafsid Dynasty
1574–1705	Ottoman Tunisia
1705–1881	Husainid Dynasty
1881–1956	French Tunisia
1956–1957	Kingdom of Tunisia
1957–2011	Republic of Tunisia
2011	Jasmine Revolution
2011–Present	Parliamentary system

Turkey

1299–1922	Ottoman Dynasty
1299–1453	Rise of the Ottoman Empire
1453–1550	Growth of the Ottoman Empire
1550–1700	Transformation of the Ottoman Empire
1700–1827	Stagnation and reform of the Ottoman Empire
1827–1908	Modernization of the Ottoman Empire
1908–1922	Dissolution of the Ottoman Empire
1922–1924	Republican Caliphate
1923–Present	Republic of Turkey

The Papacy

The Reformation Era

1513–1521	Leo X
1522–1523	Adrian VI
1523–1534	Clement VII
1534–1549	Paul III
1550–1555	Julius III
1555	Marcellus II
1555–1559	Paul IV
1559–1565	Pius IV
1566–1572	Saint Pius V
1572–1585	Gregory XIII
1585–1590	Sixtus V
1590	Urban VII
1590–1591	Gregory XIV
1591	Innocent IX
1592–1605	Clement VIII
1605	Leo XI
1605–1621	Paul V
1621–1623	Gregory XV
1623–1644	Urban VIII
1644–1655	Innocent X

The Era of Enlightenment and the Scientific Revolution

1655–1667	Alexander VII
1667–1669	Clement IX
1670–1676	Clement X
1676–1689	Innocent XI
1689–1691	Alexander VIII
1691–1700	Innocent XII
1700–1721	Clement XI
1721–1724	Innocent XIII
1724–1730	Benedict XIII
1730–1740	Clement XII
1740–1758	Benedict XIV
1758–1769	Clement XIII
1769–1774	Clement XIV

The Era of National Revolutions

1775–1799	Pius VI (deposed by Second Roman Republic)
1799–1800	Interregnum
1800–1823	Pius VII
1823–1829	Leo XII
1829–1830	Pius VIII
1831–1846	Gregory XVI

The Era of the Roman Question and Mass Migration

1846–1878	Pius IX
1878–1903	Leo XIII
1903–1914	Saint Pius X
1914–1922	Benedict XV

The Era of Reconciliation and Reaction

1922–1939	Pius XI
1939–1958	Pius XII

The Denominational Era and Restoration

1958–1963	Saint John XXIII
1963–1978	Paul VI
1978	John Paul I
1978–2005	Saint John Paul II
2005–2013	Benedict XVI
2013–Present	Francis

The Caliphate

Ottoman Sultans since 1500

1497–1508	Al-Mustamsik
1508–1516	Al-Mutawakkil III
1516–1517	Al-Mustamsik
1517	Al-Mutawakkil III
1517–1520	Selim I
1520–1566	Suleiman I
1566–1574	Selim II
1574–1595	Murad III
1595–1603	Mehmed III

1603–1617	Ahmed I
1617–1618	Mustafa I
1618–1622	Osman II
1622–1623	Mustafa I
1623–1640	Murad IV
1640–1648	Ibrahim
1648–1687	Mehmed IV
1687–1691	Suleiman II
1691–1695	Ahmed II
1695–1703	Mustafa II
1703–1730	Ahmed III
1730–1754	Mahmud I
1754–1757	Osman III
1757–1774	Mustafa III
1774	Treaty of Küçük Kainardja
1774–1789	Abdülhamid I
1789–1807	Selim III
1807–1808	Mustafa IV
1808–1839	Mahmud II
1839–1861	Abdülmecid I
1861–1876	Abdülaziz I
1876–1876	Murad V
1876–1909	Abdülhamid II
1909–1918	Mehmed V
1918–1922	Mehmed VI (Vahdettin)
1922–1924	Republican Caliphate
1922–1924	Abdülmecid II

Supreme Leaders of the Islamic Revolution (Iran)

1979–1989	Ruhollah Khomenei
1989–Present	Ali Khamenei

Limited Caliphates

2001	Omar Mohammed (Mollah, Taliban regime)
2014–2019	Abu Bakr al-Baghdadi (caliph, Islamic State regime)

GLOSSARY

'Alim (**pl.**, *ulema*): Muslim scholar recognized as having specialist knowledge of Islamic sacred law and theology.

Alaouite: the ruling dynasty in Morocco, named after the Imam Ali (also called Sharifian).

Alawite: A sect of Shi'a Islam in the Levant that identifies as a separate ethnic and religious group.

Alevi: A mainly Turkish offshoot of Shi'a Islam, reverent of Imam Ali and liberal in practice.

Ansar Al-Sharia (alt., Ansar al-sharia): Tunisian Salafi Islamist group created in April 2011 that seeks to establish Islamic rule; designated as a terrorist group in 2013.

Archbishop: The chief bishop responsible for an archdiocese.

Archdiocese: A higher-ranking diocese of greater size or significance, ruled by an archbishop.

Auto-da-fé: The ritual of public penance for condemned heretics and apostates that took place during the Spanish and Portuguese Inquisitions.

Awqaf: See *waqf.*

Bai 'a: (Ba'yat) An oath of loyalty to an emir or religious ruler.

Bey: Turkish title given to governors and leaders of the Ottoman Empire.

Bishop: A senior member of the Roman Catholic clergy who is typically in charge of a diocese and empowered to confer holy orders.

Bishopric: A diocese or region of the Church governed by a bishop.

Caliph: Chief Muslim civil and religious ruler who is viewed as the successor to the Prophet Muhammad.

Calvinism: A theological system developed by John Calvin and his successors that emphasizes justification by faith alone and the doctrine of predestination.

Canon law: Ecclesiastical laws, set by papal pronouncements, that organize and regulate church activities, from sacraments to clerical roles.

Cardinal (cardinalate): A leading dignitary of the Catholic Church who is nominated by the pope and is a member, together with other cardinals, of the College of Cardinals.

Cemevi: A house of gathering and prayer in Alevi Islam.

College: See **seminary**.

College of Cardinals: The chief ecclesiastical body of the Roman Catholic Church, endowed with the responsibility of electing and advising the pope.

Colony: A territory, area, nation, or country under partial or full political control by another country and occupied by settlers from that country.

Condominium: A political territory over which multiple sovereign powers have formally declared equal ownership and whose administration or governance is their joint responsibility (for example, Anglo-Egyptian Sudan).

Constantinople N.B. (alt., Istanbul): Capital city of the Roman, Byzantine, and Ottoman Empires; named after the Christian emperor Constantine. The interior of the city walls was known as Istanbul, which became its formal name in 1923.

Curia (in Rome): The papal court and government of the Catholic Church.

dar al harb (lit., abode of war): Territories where Muslims are in the minority or lands that are not ruled by Islamic law.

dar al ifta: A fatwa council.

dar al Islam: Majority-Muslim territories or lands ruled by Islamic law.

Deacon (in Catholic, Anglican, and Orthodox churches): An ordained minister of an order ranking below that of priest.

Diocese (see also bishopric): An ecclesiastical district under the pastoral care of a bishop; the spiritual adumbration of the old territorial governing unit (*civitates*) in the Roman Empire.

DİTİB (Turkish-Islamic Union for Religious Affairs): The European branch of the Diyanet, and one of the largest Islamic organizations in Germany.

Diyanet (Diyanet İşleri Baskanligi/Directorate of Religious Affairs): An official state institution established in 1924 that has acted as the successor to the Sheikh-ul-Islam since the abolition of the Ottoman caliphate.

Eïd (Arabic): Eïd ul-Fitr is a Muslim festival and feast marking the end of the fast of Ramadan; Eïd ul-Adha is the festival marking the culmination of the annual pilgrimage to Mecca and commemorating the sacrifice of Abraham.

Emir (alt., Amir): A Muslim military commander or holder of high office (Emir al-Mu'minin is the Commander of the Faithful).

Emirate: The rank, lands, or reign of an emir.

Episcopate: Collective body of all bishops of the Catholic Church.

Fatwa (Arabic; Turkish, *fetva*): A ruling on a point of Islamic law given by a recognized authority.

Fiqh (Arabic): Islamic jurisprudence providing insight into divine law.

Fitna (Arabic): Communal strife that is usually theological but can also be political.

Gallicanism: Doctrine calling for the separation of the French Church from the papacy.

Gülenists: Followers of an Islamic transnational religious and social movement led by the Turkish preacher Fethullah Gülen (also known as the Hizmet movement).

Habous: See *waqf*.

Hadith: a tradition or saying that incorporates teachings from the Prophet Muhammed.

Hajj (honorific title, *hajji*): The pilgrimage to Mecca; a mandatory religious rite that all Muslims must carry out at least once in their lifetime, unless they are physically or financially incapable of doing so.

Hanafi: One of the four schools of thought of religious jurisprudence within Sunni Islam.

Hanbali: One of the four schools of thought of religious jurisprudence within Sunni Islam.

Hejaz (Hijaz): The Holy Land of Islam, a region centered on Mecca and Medina and comprising most of present-day western Saudi Arabia.

Hizb ut-Tahrir: Transnational movement founded in 1953 in Jerusalem that seeks the restoration of the caliphate.

Holy Congregation (Sacra Congregazione): A Vatican administrative unit equivalent to a government ministry.

Holy Congregation of Propaganda Fide (Sacra Congregazione de' Propaganda Fide): Roman congregation founded in 1622 to centralize missionary work.

Holy See: The government of the Roman Catholic Church led by the pope.

Hussein: The given name of the grandson of the Prophet Muhammad, and the third shi'a imam; inspired derivations such as Husseini, Husseyni, and Husaynid.

Hussein bin Ali (Husseini [adj.]): The House of Hashemite, which traces descent in the male line to Fatima, daughter of the Prophet; for generations provided the Grand Sharif of Mecca, Father of Ali (Hejaz), Feysal (Iraq), and Abdallah (Jordan); distinct from Husseyni family of Jerusalem; also distinct from Hussainid.

Imamat: The office or region ruled by an imam.

Jihad: A personal struggle or holy war.

Ka'bah: The sacred building at the center of the al-Haram mosque in Mecca and considered to be the holiest site of Islam.

Khutba (Turkish, *hutbe*): Friday sermon.

Kulturkampf: Conflict between civil governments and the Roman Catholic Church over the control of education and ecclesiastical appointments, usually in connection with secularization campaigns.

Mahdi: A Sunni leader prophesied to restore peace and justice; or, in Twelver Shiite Islam, the last of the Twelve Imams who is destined to reappear.

Maliki: One of the four schools of thought of religious jurisprudence within Sunni Islam, with a large presence in North and West Africa.

Makhzen: The royal court and members of the political establishment in Morocco.

Manshur (*mansur*): Ottoman document, sealed and signed, approving appointment to office.

Medrese (Arabic, Madrassa): A religious school.

Mitre: A tall, pointed headdress worn by bishops in official ceremonies as symbols of office.

Mourchidates: Female spiritual guides in Islam.

Muezzin: Mosque official who chants call to prayer.

Mufti: A Muslim legal expert who gives rulings on religious matters.

Mujahid (Pl.: Mujahidin): A Muslim who engages in (usually armed) jihad.

Nuncio: A papal ambassador, typically of cardinal rank, accredited to a foreign court or government.

Mujtahid: Someone who interprets religious law (sometimes, a Qadi).

Osman (House of): The Ottoman Dynasty.

Papal Zouaves: An infantry force formed in defense of the Papal States in the mid-nineteenth century.

Parish: A local church community with its own church and priest or pastor.

Protectorate: A state that is partially controlled and protected by another government.

Qadi (alternative spelling: *kadi*): Judge of a shari'ah court whose decisions are based on Islamic religious law.

Qur'an: The central religious text of Islam, taken by Muslims to be the literal word of God; the sacred book containing the divine principles of Islam, the Sunna (the practices of the Prophet and his companions), and the *hadith* (words and acts).

Rais-ul-Islam: The title of a grand mufti or leader who served as the locally appointed religious authority under the Ottoman caliphate and under the rulers of some Arab states.

Ramadan: The ninth month of the Islamic calendar, observed by Muslims worldwide as a month of fasting to commemorate the first revelation of the Qur'an to Muhammad.

Regency: A period of time in which a country is ruled by a regent substituting for a monarch.

Risorgimento: An ideological and literary movement that stirred the national consciousness of the Italian people and led to a series of political events that freed the Italian states from foreign domination and united them politically.

Sahel: The geographic region of Africa south of the Sahara, stretching from Senegal to parts of Mauritania, Mali, Burkina Faso, Niger, Nigeria, Chad, Sudan, and Eritrea.

Salafism: A transnational religious-political ideology based on a belief in "physical" jihadism and the Salafi movement; the reform branch seeks to bring society back to what adherents believe to be true Sunni Islam.

See: See **diocese**.

Seminary: Educational institution that provides edification for students in scripture and theology and prepares them for careers in ministry, clergy, or academia.

Seyh-ul-Islam (Sheikh-ul-Islam): The senior Ottoman jurist who issued legal opinions (fatwas).

Shari'ah: Islamic religious law derived from the Qur'an and the hadith.

Sharif: Traditional Arabic title typically given to Muslim rulers, magistrates, or religious leaders.

Sharifian: Relating to a descendant of Muhammad through his daughter Fatima; also relates to rulers of Morocco since the Sultanate of Ismail ibn Sharif (1672–1727).

Soutane: Full-length garment worn by Catholic and Protestant clergy.

Sublime Porte: The Ottoman court in Istanbul.

Sultan: Title used by sovereigns in Muslim countries.

Suzerain (suzerainty): A sovereign or a state exercising control over a dependent state that maintains a degree of autonomy.

takfiri: A Muslim who declares another Muslim to be an apostate.

Ulema (sing., *'alim*): A body of Muslim scholars recognized as having specialist knowledge of Islamic sacred law and theology.

Ultramontane: Clerical political notion within the Catholic Church that advocates supreme papal authority.

Umma: The global Muslim community.

Vicar: A representative of a religious community within the Roman Catholic Church.

Vicar apostolic: A Roman Catholic titular bishop who administers a territorial district that is not organized as a diocese.

Waqf (*Vakfı*; pl., *evkaf; awqaf, habous,* mortmain property): Religious foundations or inalienable charitable endowments under Islamic law; acquired by donating a building, a plot of land, or other assets for religious and/or charitable purposes with no intention of reclaiming the assets.

Wahhabism (eighteenth century, Abd-al-Wahab): An austere form of Islam that insists on a literal interpretation of the Qur'an; allied with ibn al-Saud and Saudi Arabia.

Wilaya: A subnational administrative region or state.

Zakat: Obligatory payment made annually under Islamic law on certain kinds of property (used for charitable and religious purposes).

Zawiyya: Islamic school or monastery, or Sufi lodge, in North or Northwest Africa.

INTERVIEWS
(2011–2019)

INTERVIEWS ARE LISTED here by position, whereas in the text, remarks from interviews are frequently ascribed to the officeholder who spoke them. This list is intended to facilitate quick identification of the relevant institutions and organizations consulted by the author without indexing them by name. An asterisk (*) indicates that more than one interview was conducted with the respondent.

Algeria

Interviewee	Employer, Place of Interview
Diplomatic Attaché to the United States	Ministry of Foreign Affairs, Washington, DC
Director General	Ministry of Foreign Affairs, Institute for Diplomacy in International Relations, Algiers
Director	National Community Abroad, Ministry of Foreign Affairs, Algiers
Director	Dar al Islam, Algiers
Director, Religious Studies	Ministry of Education, Algiers
Bishop	Chapelle de Santa Cruz, Oran
Senior Priest	Notre Dame d'Afrique, Algiers
Ambassador to France	French Embassy, Algiers
Deputy Chief of Mission	French Embassy, Algiers
Second Counselor	French Embassy, Algiers
Director	*Algérie News*, Algiers
Inspector General	Ministry of Endowments and Religious Affairs, Algiers
Chief of Protocol	Ministry of Endowments and Religious Affairs, Algiers
Director of Legal and Cooperation Studies	Ministry of Endowments and Religious Affairs, Algiers

Minister	Ministry of Endowments and Religious Affairs, Algiers
Director of Qur'anic Studies	Ministry of Endowments and Religious Affairs, Algiers
First Counselor	US Embassy, Algiers

France

Interviewee	*Employer, Place of Interview*
Chief of Staff to the Secretary General	Ministry of the Interior, Immigration and Integration Department, Paris
Director	Ministry of the Interior, Central Bureau of Religious Affairs, Paris
Adviser to the Director*	Ministry of the Interior, Central Bureau of Religious Affairs, Paris
Head of Algeria Desk	Ministry of Foreign Affairs, Paris
Counselor for Religious Affairs*	Ministry of Foreign Affairs, Paris
Chief Adviser	Ministry of the Interior, Central Bureau of Religious Affairs, Paris
Prefect	Seine Saint Denis, Paris
Deputy Prefect	Department of Antony, Paris
Mayor	Montfermeil, Paris

Germany

Interviewee	*Employer, Place of Interview*
Head	Federal Ministry of the Interior, German Islamic Conference, Berlin
Head	Federal Ministry of the Interior, Integration, Berlin
Head*	Ministry of Foreign Affairs, Public Diplomacy, Berlin
Chief of Staff to State Minister	Ministry for Migration, Refugees, and Integration, Berlin
Member of Parliament	Bundestag (FDP), Berlin
Adviser to the Minister	Federal Ministry of Justice, Berlin
Adviser on State-Church Law	Federal Ministry of Justice, Berlin
Adviser to the Minister*	Ministry for Integration, North Rhine Westphalia, Berlin
First Counselor*	German Embassy, Rabat
Ambassador to Morocco	German Embassy, Rabat

Chairman (2009–2012)	DİTİB, Turkish Embassy, Berlin
Ambassador to Turkey	German Embassy, Ankara
Members and Former Members	German Islamic Conference, Berlin
Chairman	Koordinierungsrat der Muslime, Islamrat, Berlin
Federal Co-Chairman*	Alliance 90/The Greens, Berlin
President*	JungMuslimAktiv (JUMA), Berlin
General Secretary	Avicenna-Studienwerk, Berlin
President	Zahnräder
Professor of Islamic Theology*	University of Osnabrück, Osnabrück
Head of Speeches and Publications	Federal Ministry of Finance, Berlin
Deputy Representative of the Council	Evangelical Church of Germany, Representation to Germany and the European Union, Berlin
Project Director	Wegweiser Mentors for Refugees
Representative for External Relations	Sehitlik Mosque in Neukölln, Berlin
Adviser to the Ambassador of Germany	Turkish Embassy, Berlin
First Counselor*	Turkish Embassy, Berlin
Imam and Association Director	Neuköllner Begegnungsstätte, Berlin (mosque and cultural center)
Foreign Policy Adviser to Member of Parliament (Social Democratic Party)	European Parliament, Berlin
Former EU Ambassador to Turkey, Tunisia, and Libya	European Union, Berlin
Former German Ambassador to Algeria and Morocco	Federal Ministry of Foreign Affairs, Berlin

Italy

Interviewee	*Employer, Place of Interview*
Ambassador	Moroccan Embassy, Rome
Former Minister	Ministry of the Interior, Rome
Director	*Arab News*
Deputy Minister	Ministry of Foreign Affairs, Rome
Deputy (Partito Democratico)	House of Representatives, Rome
Former Prime Minister and Interior Minister	Ministry of the Interior , Rome

Adviser	Ministry of the Interior, Rome
Vice Director	International Affairs Institute, Rome
Professor of Political Sociology	Luiss University, Rome
General Secretary	Grand Mosque of Rome, Rome-Montantenne
Deputy Secretary General	Foreign Affairs Ministry, Rome
Managing Editor and Editor in Chief	*Formiche* Magazine, Rome
Embassy Staff	US Embassy, Rome
Director, International Affairs Department	ENI (Ente Nationale Idrocarburi), Rome
Head of Religious Affairs	Office of the Prime Minister, Rome
Director, Deputy Head of the Minister's Cabinet	Ministry of the Interior, Religious Affairs Office, Rome
Founder and Director	Community of Sant'Egidio, Rome

Morocco

Interviewee	*Employer, Place of Interview*
Secretary General	Consultative Council of Moroccans Residing Abroad, Rabat
Member	Consultative Council of Moroccans Residing Abroad, Rabat
Adviser to the King	Royal Palace
Professor and Ministerial Adviser	University of Mohammed VI, Rabat-Agdal
Professor and Ministerial Adviser	University of Hassan II at Casablanca
Adviser to the Minister (since 2011)	Ministry for Moroccans Residing Abroad, Rabat
Adviser to the Minister	Ministry for Moroccans Residing Abroad, Rabat
Minister	Ministry for Moroccans Residing Abroad
Adviser to the Minister*	Ministry of Islamic Affairs and Habous, Rabat
Minister and Chief of Staff	Ministry of Islamic Affairs and Habous, Rabat
Adviser to the Minister	Ministry of the Interior, Casablanca
Ambassador at Large	Ministry of Foreign Affairs, Rabat
Deputy Chairman	Hassan II Foundation, Rabat
Secretary General and Staff	Hassan II Foundation, Rabat

President	Mohammed VI Foundation for African Ulema, Rabat
President	Mohammedia Foundation for the Holy Qur'an, Rabat
Member (Justice and Development Party) and Director of International Affairs Committee	Moroccan Parliament, Rabat
First Counselor (in the Netherlands)*	Moroccan Embassy, The Hague
Ambassador to Morocco (2008–2011)	Dutch Embassy, Rabat
Ambassador to Morocco (2011–2015)	Dutch Embassy, Rabat
Ambassador to Morocco	Mission of the European Union, Rabat
Deputy Chief of Mission	French Embassy, Rabat
Ambassador to Germany	Moroccan Embassy, Berlin
Ambassador to Morocco (1990–1994)	Ministry of Foreign Affairs, Madrid
First Counselor	Spanish Embassy, Rabat
Ambassador to Morocco	Spanish Embassy, Rabat
Ambassador to Spain (1999–2001)	Hassan II Foundation, Rabat
Counselor	United States Embassy, Rabat
Professor of Law	University of Rabat
Professor of International Relations	University of Rabat
Professor of Political science	University of Casablanca
President	Strategy Consulting
Alim	High Council of Ulema, Rabat
Consul General	French Consulate General, Casablanca
Director	Moroccan Institute for Policy Analysis, Rabat
Director of Economic Promotion	Hassan II Foundation, Rabat

Netherlands

Interviewee	Employer, Place of Interview
Adviser	Ministry of the Interior, The Hague
Adviser	Ministry of the Interior, The Hague
Analyst	General Intelligence and Security Service (AIVD), The Hague

Tunisia

Interviewee	Employer, Place of Interview
President	Republic of Tunisia, Carthage
Minister	Ministry of Religious Affairs, Tunis
Chief Mufti	Republic of Tunisia, Tunis
Professor of Political Sociology	University of Carthage, Carthage
Director of Political Bureau	Nidaa Tounes Party, Carthage
President of Ennahda Faction	National Constituent Assembly, Tunis
Ambassador to Tunisia	French Embassy, Tunis
Political and Economic Public Affairs Officers	United States Embassy, Tunis
Ambassador to Tunisia	Italian Embassy, Tunis
Ambassador to Tunisia	United States Embassy, Tunis
President	High Authority of the Revolution, Tunis
Chairman	Tunisian Audiovisual Authority, Tunis
Counselor	Tunisian Embassy in Kuwait, Tunis
Diplomatic Adviser	Ministry of Foreign Affairs, Tunis
Counselor of the Minister	Moroccan Embassy in Tunisia, Tunis

Turkey

Interviewee	Employer, Place of Interview
Vice President	Presidency for Turks Abroad and Related Communities (Yurtdışı Türkler)
Staff	Presidency for Turks Abroad and Related Communities (Yürtdisi Türkler)
Director General of Foreign Affairs	Presidency of Religious Affairs (Diyanet)
Chief Adviser to Prime Minister	Office of the Prime Minister (Başbakanlık)
Deputy Secretary General	Ministry for European Union Affairs, Ankara
Director of Foreign Relations	Ministry of Education
Adviser to the President	Higher Education Council
Member of Parliament	Turkish Parliament (Nationalist Movement Party), Ankara

Member of Parliament	Turkish Parliament (Republican People's Party), Ankara
Deputy Chief of Mission	Dutch Embassy, Ankara
First and Second Counselors	French Embassy, Ankara
Referent	Turkish Embassy, Berlin
Ambassador to Turkey	European Union Mission, Ankara
Cultural Attaché	United States Embassy, Ankara
Adviser to the Secretary General	Republican People's Party (CHP), Ankara
Director of Human Rights	Foundation for Political, Economic, and Social Research (SETA), Ankara
Chair of International Relations	Middle East Technological University, Ankara
Professor of Theology	Bilgi University, Istanbul
Deputy Executive Director	Journalists and Writers Foundation, Ankara
Director	Capital Women's Association, Ankara
Columnist	*Zaman*, Istanbul
Head Librarian	Diyanet Archive, 29 May University, Istanbul
General Secretary, The Abant Platform	Journalists and Writers Foundation, Istanbul
Vice President	Journalists and Writers Foundation, Istanbul
Professor of Law	Dogus University, Istanbul
Forty-Fourth Head	House of Osman, New York
Ambassador	Turkish Embassy, Vienna
Ambassador	Turkish Embassy, Berlin

United Kingdom

Interviewee	*Employer, Place of Interview*
Member	House of Lords, London
President	Al-Khoei Foundation, London
Chairman and Former Minister	King Faisal Center for Research and Islamic Studies, London

United States

Interviewee	*Employer, Place of Interview*
Deputy Chief of Mission	United States Embassy, Algiers
Director	Gaza for Political and Strategic Studies, Washington, DC
Deputy Consul General	German Ministry of Foreign Affairs, Boston
Deputy Director	Foundation for Political, Economic, and Social Research (SETA), Washington, DC

NOTES

Archives Consulted

Turkiye Diyanet Vakfi Islam Arastirmalari Merkezi (ISAM), Istanbul

Digitized Ottoman Archives, University of Marmara, Istanbul

Ottoman Archives, Yıldız Collection, Yıldız Palace Archives, Istanbul

Roman Jesuit Archives (Archivum Romanum Societatis Jesu, ARSI), Rome

Archivio Storico della Pontificia Università Gregoriana, Rome

Archivio Storico della Congregazione de' Propaganda Fide, Rome

US Department of State (online)

Documents on British Foreign Policy and *British Documents on the Origins of War* (online)

Digital National Security Archive (online)

Chapter 1. Sunni Islam, Roman Catholicism, and the Modern State

1. "État islamique: Abou Bakr al-Baghdadi appelle les musulmans à rejoindre 'le califat,'" *France Soir*, May 15, 2014.

2. "Pope Calls on Europe to Reflect on Founders' Hopes to Create a Better Future," *Deutsche Welle*, November 25, 2014.

3. "The Sultan and the Pope," *New York Times*, October 29, 1859, p. 4.

4. Barkey, "Political Legitimacy and Islam in the Ottoman Empire: Lessons Learned."

5. "Remarks by President Obama to the Turkish Parliament," The White House, Office of the Press Secretary, April 6, 2009.

6. Haddad, *Le Reformisme musulman*.

7. Norton, *On the Muslim Question*.

8. Shaye I. D. Cohen, "The Path to Victory," from "Legitimation under Constantine," scholarly commentary accompanying *Jesus to Christ*, broadcast by PBS *Frontline*, April 6, 1998.

9. Driessen, "Religious Democracy and Civilizational Politics," p. 11.

10. Bill and Williams, *Roman Catholics and Shi'i Muslims*, pp. 97, 142.

11. Huntington, "Religion and the Third Wave," p. 42.

12. Helmy, "The Contrasting Fates of Middle Eastern Politicized Islam and European Politicized Christianity," p. 6.

13. Durkheim, *The Elementary Forms of Religious Life*.

14. Casanova, *Public Religions in the Modern World*.

15. Driessen, "Regime Type, Religion-State Arrangements, and Religious Markets in the Muslim World."

16. Thomson, "Delegitimating State-Authorized Non-State Violence."

17. Martin, *The Statesman's Year-Book* (1878). See figure 4.1 ("Longest-Lasting Caliphates and Sultanates").

18. Monastiri, "L'Isam de M. El-Qaddhafi."

19. Brown, "Is Islam Easy to Understand or Not?," p. 199; Esposito and Voll, *Islam and Democracy*.

20. An-Na'im, "Shari`a and the Secular State in the Middle East and Europe," p. 110.

21. Asad, "Secularism, Nation-State, Religion."

22. Bruce, *God Is Dead*.

23. Macedo, *Liberal Virtues*.

24. Grzymala-Busse, *Nations under God*.

25. Brake, *Shaping History*.

26. Tarrow, "The Strategy of Paired Comparison," p. 245.

27. Ibid., p. 233.

28. McAdam, Tarrow, and Tilly, *Dynamics of Contention*.

29. Ibid., p. 252.

30. Tarrow, "The Strategy of Paired Comparison," p. 245.

31. Anderson, "Religion and Politics in Libya."

32. Fabbe, *Disciples of the State? Religion and State-Building in the Former Ottoman World*, p. 64.

33. Mahoney and Rueschemeyer, *Comparative Historical Analysis in the Social Sciences*; Mahoney, "Path Dependence in Historical Sociology."

34. Hall and Taylor, "Political Science and the Three New Institutionalisms," p. 939.

35. Martin, *The Statesman's Year-Book* (1878), p. 472.

36. Froude, *Lectures on the Council of Trent*, p. 109.

37. Turner, *The Statesman's Yearbook 1876*.

38. Luizard, *Le Choc colonial et l'islam*, p. 24.

39. Kieser et al., *End of the Ottomans*, p. 326.

40. Spitz, *The Protestant Reformation, 1517–1559*, p. 3.

41. Clayer, "L'Autorité religieuse dans l'islam ottoman sous le contrôle de l'état?," p. 53.

42. Pastor, *The History of the Popes, from the Close of the Middle Ages*, p. 356.

43. Mardin, *Religion and Social Change in Modern Turkey*.

44. Itzkowitz and Shinder, "The Office of Seyh Ul-Islam and the Tanzimat."

45. Philpott, "The Religious Roots of Modern International Relations," p. 223.

46. Haddad, "The Metamorphosis of Religion."

47. Kramer, *Islam Assembled*.

48. O'Malley, *Trent: What Happened at the Council*.

49. Birt, "Preachers, Patriots, and Islamists," in *An Enquiry into the Status of the Sheikh-ul-Islam of the British Isles*, February 5, 2008, published online: https://yahyabirt1.wordpress.com /2008/02/05/an-enqurity-into-the-status-of-the-sheikh-ul-islam-of-the-british-isles/.

50. L. Carl Brown, "The Middle East: Patterns of Change 1947–1987," *Middle East Journal* 41 (1, 1987): 26–39, p. 31, http://www.jstor.org/stable/4327481 (accessed November 22, 2020).

51. Lapidus, "State and Religion in Islamic Societies," p. 17.

52. Rogan, *Frontiers of the State in the Late Ottoman Empire*, pp. 152–57.

53. Lapidus, "State and Religion in Islamic Societies," p. 17.

54. Fabbe, *Disciples of the State? Religion and State-Building in the Former Ottoman World.*

55. Mango, *Atatürk*, p. 275.

56. The solution is given theoretical elucidation by the scholar Mark Lilla in *The Stillborn God.*

57. Walzer, *The Paradox of Liberation*, p. 1.

58. Reasoner, *Church and State*, pp. 106–7.

59. Shusterman, "The French Revolution and the Civil Constitution for the Clergy," p. 67.

60. Martin, *The Statesman's Year-Book* (1878), p. 328.

61. Shusterman, "The French Revolution and the Civil Constitution for the Clergy," pp. 64–65.

62. Sarkissian, *The Varieties of Religious Repression*, p. 3.

63. Fawkes, "Prospects of the Roman Catholic Church," p. 441.

64. "The Overflow of Europe: Report of the Commission Sent to Investigate It," *New York Times*, February 8, 1892.

65. Laurence, *The Emancipation of Europe's Muslims*, pp. 30–69.

66. Maier, *Recasting Bourgeois Europe.*

67. Liegeard, "Immigration into the United States."

68. D'Agostino, *Rome in America*, p. 138.

69. Shaughnessy, *Has the Immigrant Kept the Faith?*, p. 223.

70. International Institute for Middle East and Balkan Studies, "Turkey in a Quandary between the Secular System and Its Islamic Roots," https://www.ifimes.org/en/7982-turkey-in-a-quandary-between-the-secular-system-and-its-islamic-roots.

71. Zimmer, *Immigrants against the State*, p. 122.

72. "Palmer Raids," A&E, *History*, broadcast February 1, 2018, web page updated August 21, 2018, https://www.history.com/topics/red-scare/palmer-raids.

73. Julie Bryne, "Roman Catholics and Immigration in Nineteenth-Century America," National Humanities Center, https://nationalhumanitiescenter.org/tserve/nineteen/nkeyinfo/nromcath.htm.

74. Douniol, *Le Correspondant*, p. 698.

75. Ibid., p. 700.

76. Burkle-Young, *Papal Elections in the Age of Transition.*

77. Massa, *The American Catholic Revolution*, p. xv.

78. Huntington, *The Soldier and the State*, preface, p. v.

79. Huntington, "The Change to Change," p. 317.

80. Ibid., p. 319.

81. Downing, preface to *The Military Revolution and Political Change.*

82. Huntington, *The Soldier and the State*, p. 16.

83. Hobbes, *Leviathan, or, The Matter, Forme, and Power of a Common-Wealth Ecclesiasticall and Civil.*

84. Jung, "War and State in the Middle East," p. 226.

85. Huntington, "The Change to Change," pp. 15, 20.

86. Huntington, *The Soldier and the State*, preface, p. 1.

87. Ibid., p. 34.

88. Jung, "War and State in the Middle East," p. 226.

89. Thomson, *Mercenaries, Pirates, and Sovereigns*, p. 143.

90. Ibid., p. 3.

91. Huntington, "The Change to Change," p. 93.

92. Huntington, *The Soldier and the State*, p. 84.

93. Ritzer, "Professionalization, Bureaucratization, and Rationalization," p. 632.

94. Weber, *Economy and Society*, p. 425.

95. Ibid., p. 475.

96. Mitchell, "Limits of the State," p. 93.

97. Wilensky, "The Professionalization of Everyone?"

98. Freidson, *Professional Dominance*; Haug, "1975 NCSA Presidential Address," p. 198.

99. Meyer and Rowan, "Institutionalized Organizations," p. 353.

100. Haug, "1975 NCSA Presidential Address," p. 199.

101. Abbott, *The System of Professions*, p. 76.

102. Ibid.

103. Van Maanen and Schein, "Toward a Theory of Organizational Socialization."

104. Morgan, "The Natural History of Professionalization and Its Effects on Valuation Theory and Practice in the UK and Germany," p. 189.

105. Césari, *The Awakening of Muslim Democracy*, p. 129.

106. Fox, *An Introduction to Religion and Politics: Theory and Practice*.

107. Brown, "Official Islam in the Arab World."

108. Lewis, *What Went Wrong?*; Filali-Ansary, "Islam and Liberal Democracy."

109. Hatina, *Guardians of Faith in Modern Times*, p. 250.

110. Kuru, *Islam, Authoritarianism, and Underdevelopment*.

111. Driessen, "Regime Type, Religion-State Arrangements, and Religious Markets in the Muslim."

112. Feuer, *Regulating Islam*.

Chapter 2. The Fall and Rise of Roman Catholicism

1. Froude, *Lectures on the Council of Trent*, p. 132.

2. Spitz, *The Protestant Reformation, 1517–1559*, p. 128.

3. Hertling, *Geschichte Der Katholischen Kirche*, p. 249.

4. Ibid., p. 287.

5. Ibid., p. 286.

6. Spitz, *The Protestant Reformation, 1517–1559*, p. 128.

7. MacCulloch, *The Reformation*, p. 186.

8. Hertling, *Geschichte Der Katholischen Kirche*, p. 249.

9. Ekelund, Hébert, and Tollison, "An Economic Analysis of the Protestant Reformation."

10. Troeltsch, *The Social Teaching of Christian Churches*, p. 709.

11. O'Malley, "Jesuit Survival and Restoration."

12. Owen, *The Clash of Ideas in World Politics*, p. 85.

13. Machiavelli, *The Essential Writings of Machiavelli*, p. 44.

14. Guilday, "The Sacred Congregation de Propaganda Fide (1622–1922)."

15. Brown, *The Fall of Western Christendom*, chap. 10.

16. Pastor, *The History of the Popes, from the Close of the Middle Ages*, p. 117.

17. Shea, "Great Articles of the Catholic Faith," p. 6.

18. Freston, "Christianity: Protestantism," p. 274.

19. Guilday, "The Sacred Congregation de Propaganda Fide (1622–1922)," p. 480.

20. Ekelund and Hébert, "Interest Groups, Public Choice, and the Economics of Religion," p. 432.

21. Ibid.

22. Brown, *The Fall of Western Christendom*, chap. 10; Spitz, *The Protestant Reformation, 1517–1559*, p. 109.

23. Philpott, "The Religious Roots of Modern International Relations."

24. Spitz, *The Protestant Reformation, 1517–1559*, p. 49.

25. Ibid.

26. Ekelund and Hébert, "Interest Groups, Public Choice, and the Economics of Religion," p. 434.

27. Hertling, *Geschichte Der Katholischen Kirche*, p. 550.

28. Maloney, Civan, and Maloney, "Model of Religious Schism with Application to Islam."

29. Martin Luther, *To the Christian Nobility of the German Nation* (1520).

30. Hertling, *Geschichte Der Katholischen Kirche*, p. 391.

31. Spitz, *The Protestant Reformation, 1517–1559*, p. 49.

32. Brake, *Shaping History*, p. 61.

33. Hertling, *Geschichte Der Katholischen Kirche*, p. 393.

34. Froude, *Lectures on the Council of Trent*.

35. Pastor, *The History of the Popes, from the Close of the Middle Ages*, pp. 141–42.

36. Spitz, *The Protestant Reformation, 1517–1559*, p. 89.

37. Hertling, *Geschichte Der Katholischen Kirche*, p. 240.

38. Spijker, "Early Reformation and Scholasticism," p. 290.

39. Philpott, "The Religious Roots of Modern International Relations," p. 230.

40. Ibid., p. 232.

41. Ibid., p. 230.

42. Schwiebert, "The Reformation from a New Perspective," p. 11.

43. Spitz, *The Protestant Reformation, 1517–1559*, p. 94.

44. Vincent, "When Did the Pope Rule England?"

45. A title that English monarchs have kept to this day.

46. Hertling, *Geschichte Der Katholischen Kirche*, p. 245.

47. Bailey, *The Lives and Deaths of the Illustrious Sir Thomas More and of John Fisher, Bishop of Rochester*, p. 181.

48. House of Commons, *Index to the Report from the Select Committee on Ecclesiastical Titles and Roman Catholic Relief Acts*.

49. MacCulloch, *The Reformation*, p. 194.

50. Bergin, "The Counter-Reformation Church and Its Bishops," p. 31.

51. MacCulloch, *The Reformation*, p. 196.

52. Hertling, *Geschichte Der Katholischen Kirche*, pp. 526–27.

53. Brake, *Shaping History*, p. 54.

54. Bellessort, "III. La Suède religieuse"; Battandier, *Annuaire pontifical catholique*, pp. 344–45.

55. Moller and Ostergard, "Lutheran Orthodoxy and Anti-Catholicism in Denmark, 1536–2011."

56. Ibid., p. 168.

57. Brake, *Shaping History*, p. 75.

58. Spitz, *The Protestant Reformation, 1517–1559*, p. 107.

59. Geoffrey Parker, *The Dutch Revolt, 1977* (Ithaca, NY: Cornell University Press, 1977), pp. 126–28, quoted in Philpott, "The Religious Roots of Modern International Relations," p. 232.

60. That is, Calvinism became the official state religion.

61. MacCulloch, *The Reformation*, p. 188.

62. Ibid., p. 190.

63. Froude, *Lectures on the Council of Trent*.

64. MacCulloch, *The Reformation*, p. 188.

65. Chadwick, *The Reformation*, p. 82.

66. Owen, *The Clash of Ideas in World Politics*, p. 85.

67. Spitz, *The Protestant Reformation, 1517–1559*, p. 128.

68. MacCulloch, *The Reformation*, p. 192.

69. Ibid.

70. Ibid.

71. Ibid., p. 297.

72. Ibid., p. 190.

73. Brake, *Shaping History*, p. 75.

74. Hertling, *Geschichte Der Katholischen Kirche*, pp. 521–22.

75. Hertling, *Geschichte Der Katholischen Kirche*, p. 523.

76. Brake, *Religious War and Religious Peace in Early Modern Europe*, p. 94.

77. Kamen, *The Spanish Inquisition*.

78. Brake, *Shaping History*, p. 70.

79. O'Malley, "Jesuit Survival and Restoration," p. 239.

80. Hertling, *Geschichte Der Katholischen Kirche*, p. 517.

81. Pastor, *The History of the Popes, from the Close of the Middle Ages*, p. 229.

82. Ibid., p. 316.

83. Ibid., p. 310.

84. Aron-Beller and Black, *The Roman Inquisition*.

85. Haigh, "The Continuity of Catholicism in the English Reformation," p. 57.

86. Pastor, *The History of the Popes, from the Close of the Middle Ages*, p. 381.

87. Ibid., p. 315.

88. Parigi, *The Rationalization of Miracles*.

89. Pelican, *Obedient Rebels*.

90. Gillibert, *Promenades dans le Paris Ignatien*.

91. O'Malley, *The First Jesuits*, p. 93.

92. Martin, "The Jesuit Mystique," p. 32.

93. Pastor, *The History of the Popes, from the Close of the Middle Ages*, p. 193.

94. O'Malley, *The First Jesuits*, p. 118.

95. Markham, "The Sacred Congregation of Seminaries and Universities of Studies" (PhD diss.), Canon Law Studies 384 (Washington, DC: Catholic University of America Press, 1957), https://canonlaw.catholic.edu/info-for-current-students/jcd-dissertation/index.html.

96. O'Malley, *The First Jesuits*, p. 201.

97. MacCulloch, *The Reformation*, p. 219.

98. O'Malley, *The First Jesuits*, pp. 251–52.

99. Spitz, *The Protestant Reformation, 1517–1559*, p. 307.

100. O'Malley, *The First Jesuits*, p. 201.

101. Chadwick, *The Reformation*.

102. MacCulloch, *The Reformation*, p. 300.

103. Moller and Ostergard, "Lutheran Orthodoxy and Anti-Catholicism in Denmark, 1536–2011," p. 175.

104. Grendler, *Jesuit Schools and Universities in Europe, 1548–1773*, p. 36.

105. Hertling, *Geschichte Der Katholischen Kirche*, p. 515.

106. Shea, "Great Articles of the Catholic Faith," p. 6.

107. Hertling, *Geschichte Der Katholischen Kirche*, p. 537.

108. Owen, *The Clash of Ideas in World Politics*, p. 122.

109. O'Malley, *The First Jesuits*.

110. Larkin, *The Pastoral Role of the Roman Catholic Church in Pre-Famine Ireland, 1750–1850*, p. 10.

111. Guilday, "The Sacred Congregation de Propaganda Fide (1622–1922)."

112. O'Malley, *The First Jesuits*, p. 118.

113. Hertling, *Geschichte Der Katholischen Kirche*, p. 158.

114. Schorn-Schütte, "Priest, Preacher, Pastor," p. 9.

115. Berlin, "The Counter-Reformation Church and Its Bishops."

116. Feine, *Die Besetzung der Reichsbistümer vom Westfälischen Frieden bis zur Säkularisation 1648–1803*, p. 258.

117. Ibid., p. 363.

118. Pirenne, *Mahomet et Charlemagne*, p. 156.

119. Author's archival research, Archivio Storico, Pontificia Università Urbaniana.

120. Ibid.

121. Ibid.

122. Ibid.

123. Ibid.

124. Berlin, "The Counter-Reformation Church and its Bishops," p. 32.

125. Hertling, *Geschichte Der Katholischen Kirche*, p. 286.

126. Schorn-Schütte, "Priest, Preacher, Pastor," pp. 1–39.

127. Hertling, *Geschichte Der Katholischen Kirche*.

128. Ferry, "Confessionalization and Popular Preaching," p. 1143.

129. Schorn-Schütte, "Priest, Preacher, Pastor," p. 17.

130. Kim and Pfaff, "Structure and Dynamics of Religious Insurgency."

131. Spitz, *The Protestant Reformation, 1517–1559*, p. 54.

132. Swinges, "Prestige und gemeiner Nutzen Universitätsgründungen im deutschen Spätmittelalter."

133. Ganzer, *Bischof Wilhelm Emmanuel Freiherr von Ketteler.*

134. Markham, "The Sacred Congregation of Seminaries and Universities of Studies," p. 13.

135. Fréri, "Work and Scope of the Propaganda," p. 3.

136. Markham, "The Sacred Congregation of Seminaries and Universities of Studies," p. 9.

137. Fréri, "Work and Scope of the Propaganda," p. 3.

138. Ignatius de Loyola, "Lettera al Card. De Carpi per l'erezione del Coll. Germanico—29 Luglio 1552," APUG 212rec, f. 57, Archivio Storico della Pontificia Università Gregoriana.

139. O'Malley, *The First Jesuits*, p. 238.

140. Bergin, "The Counter-Reformation Church and Its Bishops," p. 31.

141. O'Malley, *The First Jesuits*, pp. 234–45.

142. Markham, "The Sacred Congregation of Seminaries and Universities of Studies."

143. Haigh, "The Continuity of Catholicism in the English Reformation," p. 54.

144. O'Malley, *The First Jesuits*, p. 234.

145. "État des missions dans le monde à la fin du XV[i.e.] siècle," from Ecclesia Catholica, *Compendio di storia della Sacra Congregazione per l'Evangelizzazione dei Popoli o "de Propaganda Fide," 1622–1972* (1973).

146. Bergin, "The Counter-Reformation Church and Its Bishops," p. 35.

147. Ibid.

148. Ibid.

149. Ibid.

150. Ecclesia Catholica, *Compendio di storia della Sacra Congregazione per l'Evangelizzazione dei Popoli o "de Propaganda Fide," 1622–1972.*

151. Guggenberger, *A General History of the Christian Era*, p. 442.

152. Ecclesia Catholica, *Compendio di storia della Sacra Congregazione per l'Evangelizzazione dei popoli o "de Propaganda Fide," 1622–1972*, p. 116.

153. Fréri, "Work and Scope of the Propaganda."

154. Guilday, *The Life and Times of John England*, pp. 174–75.

155. Fréri, "Work and Scope of the Propaganda," p. 13.

156. Markham, "The Sacred Congregation of Seminaries and Universities of Studies," p. 13.

157. *La propagazione della fede nel mondo*, year 1, no. 1 (Rome, 1923), p. 7.

158. Owen, *Clash of Ideas in World Politics*, p. 122.

159. Fréri, "Work and Scope of the Propaganda," p. 4.

160. Pontificia Università Urbaniana, *VI. Cooperatori e Problemi in Germania e Scandinavia*, pp. 118–19.

161. O'Donnell, *The Catholic Hierarchy of the United States, 1790–1922*, p. 4.

162. Kennedy, "Catholic Missions."

163. "Istruzzione per un Cattolico necessitato a dimorare per qualche tempo in un paese ove solamente si permette la professione pubblica del Calvinismo," APUG 250, pp. 134–44, Archivio Storico della Pontificia Università Gregoriana.

164. "Intorno all'obbligazione di evitare gli scomunicati," APUG 250, pp. 157–70, Archivio Storico della Pontificia Università Gregoriana.

165. "Note dei cardinali Ferrari e Fabrizi alla Istruzione intorno alle comunicazione con gli eretici," APUG 250, pp. 146–54, Archivio Storico della Pontificia Università Gregoriana.

166. Ecclesia Catholica, *Congregato pro Pentium Evangelizzazione sei de Propaganda Fide.*

167. William, and Innocent, *A Letter from His Holiness, the Pope in Rome, to His Highness the Prince of Orange" [microform]: Containing Several Proposals and Overtures of Agreement Betwixt the Church of England, and the Church of Rome, translated out of Latin, for the benefit of all true Protestants* (Edinburgh, 1689), p. 3.

168. Moller and Ostergard, "Lutheran Orthodoxy and Anti-Catholicism in Denmark, 1536–2011," pp. 342–43.

169. DeSilva, "Senators or Courtiers."

170. *Gerarchia e Rispettiva Popolazione, 1843; Annuario Pontificio, 1912–2015.*

171. Hoffman, *Why Did Europe Conquer the World?*, p. 132.

172. Ibid., p. 22.

173. Owen, *Clash of Ideas in World Politics*, p. 86.

174. Ibid., p. 86.

175. Benincasa and Rosetti, "Chiara Borroni."

176. Beltramme, *La Storia di Roma in 100 Monumenti e Opera di Arte.*

177. Viaene, "Nineteenth-Century Catholic Internationalism and Its Predecessors," pp. 8, 84, 91, 166.

178. Wagner, "Die Reformation bis zum Ende des Bauernkriegs."

Chapter 3. The Plot against the Caliphate

1. Ardiç, *Islam and the Politics of Secularism*, pp. 188–95.

2. Birt, "Preachers, Patriots, and Islamists."

3. Motadel, "Islam and the European Empires," p. 831.

4. British and French authorities ensured that Islam would not be integrated into their own state-church relations. The British left the Shari᾽ah Department of the Justice Ministry and al Azhar in Egyptian hands; the French excluded Algerian Islam from application of the 1905 law with a 1907 decree.

5. Popovic, *L'Islam balkanique.*

6. Crews, "Allies in God's Command," vol. 1, p. 70.

7. Merad, *L'Empire ottoman et "Europe"*, p. 76.

8. Haddad, *Muslim Reformism.*

9. Motadel, "Islam and the European Empires," p. 835.

10. Clancy-Smith, "Islam and the French Empire in North Africa," p. 90.

11. Laurens, "La Projection chrétienne de l'Europe industrielle sur les provinces arabes de l'Empire ottoman," p. 266.

12. Louis, "End of the Caliphate."

13. Macfie, "The British Decision Regarding the Future of Constantinople, November 1918–January 1920."

14. Ardiç, *Islam and the Politics of Secularism*, pp. 188–95.

15. Motadel, "Islam and the European Empires: Historiographical Essay," p. 840.

16. Selim Deringil, in *The Well-Protected Domains*, draws attention to the additional parallels between Pan-Islamic tendencies and the era of Pan-Slavism under the czars. In Russia, official Orthodox Christianity played an important role in statehood and was instrumental in education reform. Czar Alexander III claimed Byzantine descent and proclaimed himself protector of all Greek Orthodox subjects in the Ottoman realm. Ottoman indignation was also a bit rich: they did their best to nationalize Christianity as much as they could, for example, with regard to the Bulgarian church.

17. Alkan, "Modernization from Empire to Republic," p. 75.

18. Deringil, *The Well-Protected Domains*, p. 17.

19. Laurens, "La Projection chrétienne de l'Europe industrielle sur les provinces arabes de l'Empire ottoman," p. 291.

20. Popovic, *L'Islam balkanique*, p. 275.

21. Yahya Birt, "An Enquiry into the Status of the Sheikh-ul-Islam of the British Isles."

22. Curic, *Situation scolaire des musulmans en Bosnie-Herzegovine (1800–1878)*.

23. Ibid.

24. Yahya Birt, "An Enquiry into the Status of the Sheikh-ul-Islam of the British Isles."

25. Reports from Basra, "Traité de Stamboul: Entre l'empire Ottoman et La Serbie; Position and Duties of Ottoman Imperial Family."

26. Ibid.

27. Laurens, "La projection chrétienne de l'Europe industrielle sur les provinces arabes de l'Empire ottoman," p. 301.

28. Ibid., p. 302.

29. A. Cabaton and M.M.L. Bouvat, "Mission scientifique du Maroc," *Revue du monde musulman* (1907) 2: 592.

30. Laurens, "La Projection chrétienne de l'Europe industrielle sur les provinces arabes de l'Empire ottoman," p. 296.

31. Ibid., p. 297.

32. Albania (71 percent Muslim) formally separated from both the Sunni Caliphate and (Bektachi) Grande Dede and instituted an elected grand mufti.

33. Motadel, *Islam and the European Empires*, p. 7.

34. Burton, review of *Insurgent Sepoys: Europe Views the Revolt of 1857* by Shaswati Mazumdar.

35. Excerpt from *The Nineteenth Century, England and Her Mussulman Subjects*, in *New York Times*, November 27, 1887.

36. Pitzipios, *The Eastern Question Solved*, p. 21.

37. Ibid.

38. Zaman, "Religious Education and the Rhetoric of Reform," pp. 303–4.

39. Büzpinar, "Abolition of the Caliphate."

40. Robinson, "The Islamic World," p. 128.

41. Wilson, *Modern Movements among Moslems*, p. 168.

42. Karpat, *The Politicization of Islam*, pp. 208–22.

43. Simsir, *British Documents on Atatürk, 1919–1938*, p. 304.

44. Ş. Tufan Buzpinar, "Opposition to the Ottoman Caliphate in the Early Years of Abdülhamid II: 1877–1882," *Die Welt Des Islams* 36 (1, 1996): 59–89, p. 82, http://www.jstor.org/stable/3693438 (accessed November 23, 2020).

45. Oliver-Dee, "The British Government Files and the Approach to Pan-Islamic Government," p. 44 .

46. Büzpinar, "Opposition to the Ottoman Caliphate in the Early Years of Abdülhamid II: 1877–1882," pp. 66–68.

47. Fabbe, "Disciples of the State: Secularization and State Building in the Former Ottoman World," p. 166.

48. O'Connor, *History of Turkey*, p. 11.

49. Walter F. Bullock, "The Fight for the Caliphate," *North American Review* 181 (585, 1905): 229–36.

50. Green, *Three Empires on the Nile*, p. 73.

51. Ibid., p. 141.

52. Lahouazi, "Mohamed Aissa: 'Al Ahmadiyya Sect's Activities Are Geared to Foreign Intelligence Purposes.'"

53. Bullock, "The Fight for the Caliphate," p. 234.

54. Büzpinar, "Opposition to the Ottoman Caliphate in the Early Years of Abdülhamid II: 1877–1882," p. 86.

55. Qureshi, *Pan-Islam in British Indian Politics*, p. 40.

56. Dynamis, "The Mohammedan Caliphate," p. 332.

57. Oliver-Dee, "The British Government Files and the Approach to Pan-Islamic Government," p. 44.

58. Farah, "Great Britain, Germany and the Ottoman Caliphate," p. 266.

59. "England Bent on Ousting Turkey from Mecca," *New York Times*, March 5, 1911.

60. Young, "Memorandum on the Future Control of the Middle East."

61. Kayali, *Arabs and Young Turks*.

62. Sweiss, "Hashemite Discourse on Wahhabi Islam as Anti-Saudi Propaganda during the Arab Revolt."

63. Young, "Memorandum on the Future Control of the Middle East."

64. MacMillan, *Paris 1919*.

65. Protheroe, *Searching for Security in Europe*, p. 18.

66. Jenkins, *Political Islam in Turkey*, p. 77; Anderson, *Lawrence in Arabia*.

67. Massignon, "Introduction à l'étude des revendications islamiques," p. 15.

68. "Telephone message by Emir Abdulla, 7 p.m., November 1, 1916," *British Documents on Foreign Policy*, vol. 2, 1902–1916, p. 693.

69. Karsh, "Turks and Arabs Welcomed the Balfour Declaration."

70. Masters, *The Arabs of the Ottoman Empire*, p. 207.

71. Feisal also needed them as an ally against the French, who were eyeing Damascus in their sphere of influence and who threatened the Hashemite Damascus-Amman-Mecca axis.

72. Emir Feisal, statement to the Chief of the General Staff, Egyptian Expeditionary Force, and the Political Officer, Damascus, August 31, 1919, in Foreign Office, *British Documents on Foreign Policy, Great Britain, 1919–1939*, p. 388.

73. Teitelbaum, "'Taking Back' the Caliphate," p. 417.

74. Hankey, "Summary of the Proceedings in Paris in Regard to the Military Occupation in Syria, Cilicia, Palestine, and Mesopotamia, 17th September 1919," CAB/21/153, Cabinet papers 1915–1978, UK National Archives.

75. Roberts, "Rethinking the Status Quo," p. 209.

76. Ibid., p. 180.

77. Ibid., p. 218.

78. Ibid., pp. 179–80.

79. Karsh, "Turks and Arabs Welcomed the Balfour Declaration."

80. Krämer, A History of Palestine, chap. 10.

81. Laurens, "La projection chrétienne de l'Europe industrielle sur les provinces arabes de l'Empire ottoman," p. 42.

82. Clancy-Smith, "Islam and the French Empire in North Africa," p. 90.

83. D'Andurain, "Le Poids du comité du Maroc et du 'parti colonial' dans la Société de l'histoire des colonies françaises," p. 314.

84. Charles-André Julien, "France and Islam," Foreign Affairs (July 1940).

85. Trumbull, An Empire of Facts, p. 94.

86. Bérard, Le Sultan, l'islam, et les puissances, p. 49.

87. Hidayette, Abdul Hamid révolutionnaire ou ce qu'on ne peut pas dire en Turquie, p. 114.

88. Farah, "Reassessing Sultan Abdülhamid II's Policy," 203.

89. D'Andurain, "Le Poids du comité du Maroc et du 'parti colonial' dans la Société de l'histoire des colonies françaises," pp. 311–23.

90. Luizard, Le Choc colonial et l'islam, p. 14.

91. This contradicted the promise in the Bourmont Convention (1830) to respect the religion of those defeated.

92. Luizard, Le Choc colonial et l'islam, pp. 207–8.

93. Gilding, "Separation of 'Church and State' in Algeria."

94. Luizard, Le Choc colonial et l'islam, p. 220.

95. Clancy-Smith, "Islam and the French Empire in North Africa," p. 94.

96. Ibid., p. 96.

97. Rid, "The Nineteenth Century Origins of Counterinsurgency Doctrine"; Clancy-Smith, "Islam and the French Empire in North Africa," p. 92.

98. Kiser, Commander of the Faithful.

99. Clancy-Smith, "Islam and the French Empire in North Africa," p. 99.

100. Luizard, Le Choc colonial et l'islam, p. 14.

101. Brown, The Tunisia of Ahmad Bey, 1837–1855.

102. Bérard, Le Sultan, l'islam, et les puissances, p. 49.

103. Clancy-Smith, "Islam and the French Empire in North Africa," p. 103.

104. Brewster, "Recent Reforms at the Zeitouna," pp. 120–22.

105. Christopher Harrison, France and Islam in West Africa, 1860–1960 (Cambridge: Cambridge University Press, 2003), p. 124.

106. Clancy-Smith, "Islam and the French Empire in North Africa," p. 94.

107. André Maurois, Lyautey (Paris: Ploton, 1931), p. 222.

108. Clancy-Smith, Rebel and Saint, p. 96.

109. They also wanted "to make it an independent kingdom with Abdul Kader as its chief," according to Pitzipios, *The Eastern Question Solved*, p. 21.

110. Ardiç, *Islam and the Politics of Secularism*, pp.188–95.

111. Istfan, "Kemal as He Looks to the Mohammedan World."

112. Roberts, "Rethinking the Status Quo," pp. 261–62.

113. Ibid., p. 263.

114. Massignon, "Introduction à l'étude des revendications islamiques," p. 15.

115. Karpat, *The Politicization of Islam*, p. 221.

116. Laurens, "La projection chrétienne de l'Europe industrielle sur les provinces arabes de l'Empire ottoman," p. 42.

117. Luizard, *Le Choc colonial et l'islam*, p. 208.

118. Jean-Louis Triaud, "Islam in Africa under French Colonial Rule," in *The History of Islam in Africa*, edited by Nehemia Levtzion and Randall Pouwels (Athens: Ohio University Press, 2000), p. 177.

119. Stepan, "Religion, Democracy, and the 'Twin Tolerations.'"

120. Wilson, *Modern Movements among Moslems*, p. 105.

121. Clancy-Smith, *Rebel and Saint*, p. 93.

122. Allan, "Nederland en 'Zijne eigene Islâmquaestie.'"

123. Tagliacozzo, "The Dutch Empire and the Hajj," p. 84.

124. Laffan, *Islamic Nationhood and Colonial Indonesia*, p. 124.

125. Around 25,000 annually in the early 1900s (up from 12 percent in the 1880s).

126. Motadel, "Islam and the European Empires: Historiographical Essay."

127. Allan, "Nederland en 'Zijne eigene Islâmquaestie.'"

128. Kaptein, "The Voice of the Ulema."

129. Sluglett and Currie, *Atlas of Islamic History*.

130. Merad, *L'Empire ottoman et l'Europe*.

131. Baldinetti, "Italian Colonial Rule and Muslim Elites in Libya," pp. 93–96.

132. Wilson, *Modern Movements among Moslems*, p. 175.

133. Woodward, *Documents on British Foreign Policy 1919–1939*.

134. Gilmour, *Curzon: Imperial Statesman*, p. 513.

135. Curzon, "Memorandum by Earl Curzon on the Future of Constantinople," pp. 992–1000.

136. Rumbold, "Sir H. Rumbold (Constantinople) to Earl Curzon (Received February 15, 1921)," in *Documents on British Foreign Policy 1919–1939*.

137. Simsir, *British Documents on Atatürk, 1919–1938*, p. 305.

138. Woodward, *Documents on British Foreign Policy, 1919–1939*, p. 730.

139. Macfie, "The British Decision Regarding the Future of Constantinople, November 1918–January 1920," p. 390.

140. Ibid.

141. Simsir, *British Documents on Atatürk, 1919–1938*, p. 186.

142. Curzon, "Memorandum by Earl Curzon on the Future of Constantinople," p. 994.

143. Farah, "Reassessing Sultan Abdülhamid II's Islamic Policy," p. 268.

144. Curzon, "Memorandum by Earl Curzon on the Future of Constantinople," p. 513.

145. Littlefield, "Why the Turks Got Rid of the Caliphate."

146. Allenby, "Field-Marshal Viscount Allenby (Cairo) to Earl Curzon (Received March 30 [1920], 12:20 p.m.)," in *Documents on British Foreign Policy 1919–1939*.

147. Ibid.

148. George Nathaniel Curzon, "Memorandum on the Future of Constantinople," January 2, 1918, British Library, IOR/L/PS/10/623 https://www.bl.uk/collection-items/memorandum-on-future-of-constantinople-lord-curzon.

149. Hansen, "Die Vatikanisierung des Sultans."

150. Oliver-Dee, "The Cairo High Command and the Caliphate Question, 1914–1919," p. 45.

151. "Notes of a Conversation at 10, Downing Street, London, S.W., on Thursday, December 11, 1919, at 3 P.M.," in *Documents on British Foreign Policy 1919–1939* (1919).

152. "General Staff Memorandum on the Situation in Turkey," [E 2207/3/44], in *Documents on British Foreign Policy 1919–1939* (1920).

153. Massignon, "Introduction à l'étude des revendications islamiques," p. 15.

154. "General Staff Memorandum on the Situation in Turkey," in *Documents on British Foreign Policy 1919–1939* (1920).

155. Massignon, "Introduction à l'étude des revendications islamiques," p. 15.

156. Robinson, "The Islamic World," p. 129.

157. Slight, "British Imperial Rule and the Hajj," p. 65.

158. Oliver-Dee, "The Cairo High Command and the Caliphate Question, 1914–1919," p. 45.

159. Willis, "Debating the Caliphate," p. 715.

160. Slight, "British Imperial Rule and the Hajj," p. 65.

161. Webb, "Admiral Webb (Constantinople) to Earl Curzon (Received February 10, 1920)," in *Documents on British Foreign Policy 1919–1939*, p. 660.

162. Ibid.

163. Kramer, *Islam Assembled*, chaps. 5 and 6.

164. "Memorandum Respecting Co-operation of Moslem Countries and Russia," in *Documents on British Foreign Policy 1919–1939* (1923).

165. Kramer, *Islam Assembled*, chaps. 5 and 6.

166. *Documents on British Foreign Policy, 1919–1939*, vol. 25, p. 14.

167. *British Documents on Foreign Affairs—Reports and Papers from the Foreign Office: Confidential Print: From the First to the Second World War*, series B, *Turkey, Iran, and the Middle East, 1918–1939* (London: Foreign Office), vol. 2, p. 181.

168. Rumbold, "Sir H. Rumbold (Constantinople) to Earl Curzon (Received February 15, 1921)," in *Documents on British Foreign Policy 1919–1939*.

169. Teitelbaum, "'Taking Back' the Caliphate," pp. 412–24.

170. Ibid., p. 417.

171. Mango, *Atatürk*, p. 363.

172. Khan, "Religion and State in Turkey (Continued)."

173. "Turkish Facts and Fantasies," *Foreign Affairs* (July 1925).

174. Mango, *Atatürk*, p. 363.

175. Teitelbaum, "'Taking Back' the Caliphate," p. 419.

176. Ibid., p. 420.

177. Ibid.

178. James, "Dropping of Sultan Worries the French," p. 14.

179. Webb, "Admiral Webb (Constantinople) to Earl Curzon (Received February 10, 1920)," in *Documents on British Foreign Policy 1919–1939*, p. 660.

180. Guida, "Seyyid Bey and the Abolition of the Caliphate," p. 279.

181. Cunliffe-Owen, "Aga Khan, Fashionable Londoner, Holds Enormous Power in Islam."

182. Ibid.

183. Teitelbaum, "'Taking Back' the Caliphate," p. 422.

184. Associated Press, "Hussein Is Descendant of Mohammed," *New York Times*, March 8, 1924, p. 3.

185. Kelley, "American Vice Consul in Charge to Secretary of State; Expulsion from Turkey of the Caliph" (1924).

186. Ibid.

187. Buhrman, "American Consul to the Secretary of State: Expulsion of the Caliph, Abdul Medjid, by the Turkish Government; Political Effect, Aleppo District" (1924).

188. Kelley, "American Vice Consul in Charge to Secretary of State; Expulsion from Turkey of the Caliph" (1924).

189. Roberts, "Rethinking the Status Quo," p. 13.

190. Buhrman, "American Consul to the Secretary of State: Expulsion of the Caliph, Abdul Medjid, by the Turkish Government; Political Effect, Aleppo District" (1924).

191. Slight, "British Imperial Rule and the Hajj," p. 10.

192. Ibid., p. 67.

193. "A Moslem Raid on Mecca," *New York Times*, October 1, 1924.

194. Allenby, "Field-Marshal Viscount Allenby (Cairo) to Earl Curzon (Received March 30 [1920], 12:20 P.M.)," in *Documents on British Foreign Policy 1919–1939*.

195. Anderson, *Lawrence in Arabia*, p. 165.

196. Mahatma Gandhi, *Young India*, July 21, 1929.

197. "General Staff Memorandum on the Situation in Turkey [E 2207/3/44]."

198. Anderson, *Lawrence in Arabia*, p. 165.

199. Parker W. Buhrman, "Selection of a New Caliph" (1924).

200. Kedourie, "Egypt and the Caliphate, 1915–1946," pp. 213–14.

201. Kramer, *Islam Assembled*.

202. Knabenahue, "To the Secretary of State; Subject: Pan-Islamic Congress."

203. Krämer, *A History of Palestine*, p. 86.

204. Louis Massignon, "Introduction à l'étude des revendications islamiques," p. 17.

205. Knabenahue, "To the Secretary of State; Subject: Pan-Islamic Congress."

206. "Indian Group Seeks to Restore Caliph" (special cable), *New York Times*, October 30 1931.

207. "Hussein Is Descendant of Mohammed," *New York Times*, March 7, 1924.

208. Kramer, *Islam Assembled*, chap. 8; Kupferschmidt, *The Supreme Muslim Council*, p. 197.

209. Littlefield, "Why the Turks Got Rid of the Caliphate."

210. Masters, *The Arabs of the Ottoman Empire, 1516–1918*, p. 227.

211. Massignon, "Introduction à l'étude des revendications islamiques," p. 21.

212. Wilson, *Modern Movements among Moslems*, p. 90.

213. Allenby, "Field-Marshal Viscount Allenby (Cairo) to Earl Curzon (Received March 30 [1920], 12:20 P.M.)," in *Documents on British Foreign Policy 1919–1939*.

214. Ibid.

215. Slight, "British Imperial Rule and the Hajj," p. 10.

216. Çetinsaya, *The Ottoman Administration of Iraq, 1890–1908*.

217. Elfenbein, "Establishing Religion in Iraq"; cf. Skovgaard-Nielson, *Defining Islam for the Egyptian State*, p. 60.

218. An-Na'im, "Shari'a and the Secular State in the Middle East and Europe," p. 106.

219. Pankhurst, *The Inevitable Caliphate?*

220. Willis, "Debating the Caliphate," pp. 711–32.

221. Vidino, *The New Muslim Brotherhood in the West*.

Chapter 4. The Rise and Fall of Pan-Islam

1. Bérard, *Le sultan, l'islam, et les puissances*, p. 49.

2. Joshi, Srinivas, and Bajaj, *Religious Demography of India*.

3. Karpat, "The Transformation of the Ottoman State, 1789–1908," p. 274.

4. Landau, *The Politics of Pan-Islam*, p. 10.

5. Tobich, "La Construction du projet."

6. White, *The Emergence of Minorities in the Middle East*, p. 31.

7. Bérard, *Le Sultan, l'islam, et les puissances*, p. 49.

8. Reed, "The Faculty of Divinity at Ankara."

9. Vikor, *Between God and the Sultan*.

10. Elfenbein, "Establishing Religion in Iraq"; cf. Skovgaard-Nielson, *Defining Islam for the Egyptian State*, pp. 37–38.

11. Khalid, "Ottoman Islamism between the Ümmet and the Nation," p. 198.

12. Merad, *L'Empire ottoman et "Europe"*, p. 75.

13. Clayer, "L'Autorité religieuse dans l'islam ottoman sous le contrôle de l'état?"

14. Güran, *Osmanlı Mali İstatistikleri ve Bütçeler (1841–1918)*; Ministry of Finance, *Osmanlı Bütçeleri (1909–1918)*; Ministry of Finance, *1917 (1333) yılı Osmanlı Bütçesi*.

15. Başkan, "Mobilizing Sheikhs and Ulama."

16. Karpat, "The Transformation of the Ottoman State, 1789–1908," p. 274.

17. Masters, *The Arabs of the Ottoman Empire, 1516–1918*, p. 236.

18. Greene, "The Ottoman Experience"; see also Deringil, *The Well-Protected Domains*, pp. 20–29.

19. Dumont, "L'Instrumentalisation de la religion dans l'Empire ottoman à l'époque de l'expansion européenne (1800–1914)," *European Journal of Turkish Studies* 27, published online January 10, 2019, http://journals.openedition.org/ejts/5933.

20. Eric Hobsbawm and Terence Ranger, *The Invention of Tradition* (Cambridge: Cambridge University Press, 1983).

21. Deringil, *The Well-Protected Domains*, p. 26.

22. Bastürk, "Understanding Turkish Motives in the Ukraine-Crimea Crisis."

23. Karpat, "The Transformation of the Ottoman State, 1789–1908," p. 271.

24. "Extract from Annual Report for Turkey 1906," in *British Documents on the Origins of War 1898–1914*, vol. 5, *The Near East: The Macedonian Problem and the Annexation of Bosnia 1903–9*.

25. Deringil, *The Well-Protected Domains*, p. 31.

26. Alkan, "Modernization from Empire to Republic," p. 53.

27. Antonius, *The Arab Awakening*, p. 70.

28. Murphy, *Exploring Ottoman Sovereignty*, p. 12.

29. Greene, "The Ottoman Experience."

30. Deringil, *The Well-Protected Domains*, p. 24.

31. Ibid., p. 17.

32. Ibid., p. 23.

33. Abu-Manneh, *Studies on Islam and the Ottoman Empire in the 19th Century*, pp. 179–80.

34. Karateke, "Legitimizing the Ottoman Sultanate."

35. Deringil, *The Well-Protected Domains*, p. 27.

36. Chirol, "Islam and the Future of Constantinople," p. 42.

37. Farah, "Reassessing Sultan Abdülhamid II's Policy," p. 208.

38. Karčić, "Supporting the Caliph's Project," p. 1.

39. Büzpinar, "Opposition to the Ottoman Caliphate in the Early Years of Abdülhamid II: 1877–1882."

40. Abu-Manneh, *Studies on Islam and the Ottoman Empire in the 19th Century (1826–1876)*, pp. 179–80.

41. Zwemer, *Arabia*, p. 208.

42. Deri, "II. Adulhamd'in Islam Birligi Siyaseti ve bu Hususta Hilafetin Rolu."

43. Farah, "Reassessing Sultan Abdülhamid II's Policy," p. 195.

44. Extract from "Annual Report for Turkey 1906," in *British Documents on the Origins of War 1898–1914*, vol. 5, *The Near East: The Macedonian Problem and the Annexation of Bosnia 1903–9*.

45. Wilson, *Modern Movements among Moslems*, pp. 63–64.

46. Deringil, *The Well-Protected Domains*, p. 57.

47. "Telephone Message from Abdullah," November 1, 1916, in ALP FO 882/5.

48. Karateke, "Legitimizing the Ottoman Sultanate."

49. Ochsenwald, "Ottoman Subsidies to the Hijaz, 1877–1886," p. 301.

50. Dwight, *Constantinople and Its Problems*.

51. Blunt, *The Future of Islam*.

52. Deringil, "Legitimacy Structures in the Ottoman State," p. 346.

53. Karpat, *The Politicization of Islam*, p. 229.

54. Abu-Manneh, "Sultan Abdülhamid II and Shaikh Abulhuda al-Sayyadi."

55. Merad, *L'Empire ottoman et "Europe"*.

56. Ibid., p. 87.

57. Brown, "The Islamic Reformist Movement in North Africa."

58. Ochsenwald, "Ottoman Subsidies to the Hijaz, 1877–1886," p. 270.

59. Farah, "Reassessing Sultan Abdülhamid II's Policy," p. 200.

60. Diamantopulo, *Le Réveil de la Turquie*, p. 198.

61. Burak, *The Second Formation of Islamic Law*, pp. 155–56.

62. Gilbert, "Institutionalization of Muslim Scholarship and Professionalization of the Ulama in Medieval Damascus."

63. Tezcan, *The Second Ottoman Empire*, p. 167.

64. Terzioglu, "Where Ilmihal Meets Catechism," p. 241.

65. Yilmaz, *The Caliphate Redefined*.

66. Inalcik, "Islam in the Ottoman Empire," pp. 21–22.

67. Tobich, *Les Statuts personnels dans les pays arabes.*

68. Landau, *The Politics of Pan-Islam*, p. 38.

69. Clayer, "L'Autorité religieuse dans l'islam ottoman sous le contrôle de l'état?," p. 52.

70. Roberts, "Rethinking the Status Quo."

71. Bayart, *L'Islam républicain*, p. 91.

72. Inalcik, "Islam in the Ottoman Empire," p. 20.

73. Turner, *The Statesman's Yearbook 1876.*

74. Karpat, "The Transformation of the Ottoman State, 1789–1908," p. 269.

75. Lapidus, "State and Religion in Islamic Societies."

76. Barnes, *An Introduction to Religious Foundations in the Ottoman Empire*, pp. 141, 155.

77. Ibid.

78. Professor Tahsin Özcan, interview with the author, Istanbul, May 2015.

79. MacFarlane, *Turkey and Its Destiny*, p. 396; Barnes, *An Introduction to Religious Foundations in the Ottoman Empire*, p. 141.

80. Turner, *The Statesman's Yearbook 1876.*

81. Kuran, "The Provision of Public Goods under Islamic Law."

82. Ochsenwald, "Islam and the Ottoman Legacy in the Modern Middle East," p. 266.

83. Başkan, *From Religious Empires to Secular States*, p. 105.

84. Akgünduz, *Osmanlı Medreseleri XIX: Asir*, p. 47.

85. Kuran, "The Provision of Public Goods under Islamic Law," 889.

86. Mardin, *Religion and Social Change in Modern Turkey*, p. 112.

87. Terzioglu, "Sunna-Minded Sufi Preachers in Service of the Ottoman State."

88. Mayaram, *Against History, Against State*, p. 113.

89. Barkey, *Empire of Difference*, p. 21.

90. Hussain, "The Tanzimat: Secular Reforms in the Ottoman Empire," p. 10.

91. Brown, "The Religious Establishment."

92. Vikor, *Between God and the Sultan*, p. 218.

93. Beydilli, *Osmanlı Döneminde Imamlar ve Bir Imamin Günlügu.*

94. Deringil, *The Well-Protected Domains*, p. 31.

95. Clayer, "L'Autorité religieuse dans l'islam ottoman sous le contrôle de l'état?," p. 50.

96. Akgünduz, *Osmanlı Medreseleri XIX: Asir*, pp. 23–28, 44–49.

97. Hathaway, *Arab Lands under Ottoman Rule, 1516–1800*, p. 119.

98. Dwight, *Constantinople and Its Problems*, p. 203.

99. Professor Tahsin Özcan, interview with the author, May 2013.

100. Dwight, *Constantinople and Its Problems*, p. 203.

101. Hathaway, *Arab Lands under Ottoman Rule, 1516–1800*, p. 119.

102. Shaw and Shaw. *History of the Ottoman Empire and Modern Turkey*, p. 115.

103. Ochsenwald, "Ottoman Subsidies to the Hejaz, 1877–1886," p. 271.

104. White, *The Emergence of Minorities in the Middle East*, pp. 22–23.

105. Fratantuono, "Religious Duties and Educational Needs."

106. Wilson, *Modern Movements among Moslems*, p. 173.

107. Ochsenwald, "Ottoman Subsidies to the Hejaz, 1877–1886," p. 270.

108. Rogan, *Frontiers of the State in the Late Ottoman Empire*, p. 157.

109. Karpat, *The Politicization of Islam*, p. 206.

110. Inalcik, Göyünç, and Lowry, "Osmanlı Arastimalari IV."

111. Yazbak, "Nabulsi Ulama in the Late Ottoman Period, 1864–1914."

112. Rogan, *Frontiers of the State in the Late Ottoman Empire*, p. 152.

113. Güran, *Osmanlı Mali Istatistikleri ve Bütçeler (1841–1918)*; Güran, "Osmanlı Kamu Maliyesi, 1839–1918."

114. Farah, "Reassessing Sultan Abdülhamid II's Policy," p. 6.

115. Barnes, *An Introduction to Religious Foundations in the Ottoman Empire*, p. 156.

116. Akarli, "Economic Policy and Budgets in Ottoman Turkey, 1876–1909."

117. Yediyildiz, "Place of the Waqf in Turkish Cultural System."

118. Kayali, *Arabs and Young Turks*, pp. 106–7.

119. Fabbe, "Disciples of the State: Secularization and State Building in the Former Ottoman World," p. 113.

120. Alkan, "Modernization from Empire to Republic," p. 69.

121. Özdalga, "Education in the Name of 'Order and Progress,'" p. 417.

122. Alkan, "Modernization from Empire to Republic."

123. Cihan, *Reform Çaginda*, pp. 243–51.

124. Inalcik, "Islam in the Ottoman Empire," p. 20.

125. Karpat, *Ottoman Past and Today's Turkey*, p. 75.

126. Fortna, "Emphasizing the Islamic."

127. Başkan, "Mobilizing Sheikhs and Ulama."

128. Rogan, *Frontiers of the State in the Late Ottoman Empire*, p. 151.

129. Rogan, *Frontiers of the State in the Late Ottoman Empire*, p. 152.

130. Açigöz, "The Civics Textbooks in the Late Ottoman Empire," p.121.

131. Alkan, "Modernization from Empire to Republic," p. 75.

132. Wilson, *Modern Movements among Moslems*, p. 182.

133. Deringil, *The Well-Protected Domains*, p. 29.

134. Ibid., p. 107.

135. Fabbe, "Disciples of the State: Secularization and State Building in the Former Ottoman World," p. 18.

136. "Chapter 30, The Turkish Empire on the Eve of Its Fall," from "Annual Report for Turkey 1906," in *British Documents on the Origins of War, 1898–1914*, vol. 5, *The Near East: The Macedonian Problem and the Annexation of Bosnia 1903–9*, pp. 24–29.

137. Amit Bein, *Ottoman Ulema, Turkish Republic: Agents of Change and Guardians of Tradition* (Stanford, CA: Stanford University Press, 2011), p. 13.

138. Hathaway, *Arab Lands under Ottoman Rule, 1516–1800*, p. 125.

139. Chirol, "Islam and the Future of Constantinople," p. 42.

140. Feener and Sevea, *Islamic Connections*.

141. Jilani, "Was the System Adopted by the Ottomans Islamic? (The Ottoman Caliphate 2/4)."

142. Ahmet Rasim, cited in Alkan, "Modernization from Empire to Republic," p. 77.

143. Kayali, *Arabs and Young Turks*, p. 16.

144. Dwight, *Constantinople and Its Problems*, pp. 207–18.

145. Antonius, *The Arab Awakening*, p. 70.

146. Wilson, *Modern Movements among Moslems*, p. 31.

147. Ibid., p. 183.

148. *The Orient*, October 7, 1914.

149. Farah, "Reassessing Sultan Abdülhamid II's Policy," p. 202.

150. Dwight, *Constantinople and Its Problems*, pp. 203, 94–177.

151. Kayali, *Arabs and Young Turks*, p. 15.

152. Dumont, "L'Instrumentalisation de la religion dans l'Empire ottoman à l'époque de l'expansion européenne (1800–1914)."

153. Deringil, *The Well-Protected Domains*, p. 24.

154. Bennison, "Muslim Internationalism between Empire and Nation-State," p. 166.

155. Farah, "Reassessing Sultan Abdülhamid II's Policy," p. 498.

156. Bennison, "Muslim Internationalism between Empire and Nation-State," p. 167.

157. Albayrak, *Last Period Ottoman Ulema Scholars*.

158. Farah, "Reassessing Sultan Abdülhamid II's Policy," p. 195.

159. Landau, *The Politics of Pan-Islam*, p. 53.

160. Ardiç, "Islam and the Politics of Secularism," pp. 188–95.

161. Oliver-Dee, "The Cairo High Command and the Caliphate Question, 1914–1919," p. 45.

162. Karpat, *The Politicization of Islam*, p. 234.

163. Ibid.

164. Landau, *The Politics of Pan-Islam*, p. 67.

165. Büzpinar, "Abdülhamid II, Islam, and the Arabs," p. 103.

166. Farah. "Reassessing Sultan Abdülhamid II's Policy," p. 196.

167. Allan, "Nederland En 'zijne Eigene Islâmquaestie.'"

168. Merad, *L'Empire ottoman et "Europe"*.

169. Minawi, *The Ottoman Scramble for Africa*, p. 2.

170. Kayali, *Arabs and Young Turks*.

171. Landau, *The Politics of Pan-Islam*, p. 71.

172. Moreau, "Politics of Religion during the First World War."

173. Colquhoun, "Pan-Islam."

174. Dwight, *Constantinople and Its Problems*, pp. 216–18.

175. Antonius, *The Arab Awakening*, p. 71.

176. Masters, *The Arabs of the Ottoman Empire, 1516–1918*, p. 208.

177. Farah, "Reassessing Sultan Abdülhamid II's Policy," p. 199.

178. Abu-Manneh, "Sultan Abdülhamid II and Shaikh Abulhuda al-Sayyadi," pp. 131–53.

179. Jenkins, *Political Islam in Turkey*, p. 60.

180. Farah, "Reassessing Sultan Abdülhamid II's Policy," p. 201.

181. Wilson, *Modern Movements among Moslems*, p. 77.

182. Mardin, *Religion and Social Change in Modern Turkey*, p. 128.

183. Hidayette, *Abdul Hamid révolutionnaire ou ce qu'on ne peut pas dire en Turquie*, p. 68.

184. Anscombe, *State, Faith, and Nation in Ottoman and Post-Ottoman Lands*, p. 115.

185. Karpat, "The Transformation of the Ottoman State, 1789–1908," p. 269.

186. Bennison, "Muslim Internationalism between Empire and Nation-State," p. 17.

187. Ibid., p. 176.

188. Ibid., p. 168.

189. Birt, "Preachers, Patriots, and Islamists."

190. Hansen, "Istanbul Blues."

191. Aydin, "The Impact of WWI on Chinese and Ottoman-Turkish Intellectuals."

192. Stoddard, "The Ottoman Government and the Arabs, 1911–1918."

193. Cleveland, *Islam against the West*.

194. Clancy-Smith, *Mediterraneans*, p. 92.

195. Baldinetti, "Italian Colonial Rule and Muslim Elites in Libya," pp. 93–96.

196. Merad, "La Turcophilie dans le débat national en Algérie au début du siècle (1911–1918)."

197. Séréni, "Algérie: l'Islam sous administration coloniale."

198. Aydin, *The Politics of Anti-Westernism in Asia*, p. 94.

199. M. Etienne to M. Jonnart, "Memorandum on the Strengthening of the German Army," March 19, 1913, dispatches and letters, 1913, in *Documents on British Foreign Policy*.

200. Sulzberger, "German Preparations in the Middle East."

201. "Our state is today at war with the governments of Russia, England and France and their allies, who are the mortal enemies of Islam. . . . The Commander of the Faithful, the Caliph of the muslims, Summons You to Jihad."

202. Howell, *Gertrude Bell*, p. 337.

203. Littlefield, "Why the Turks Got Rid of the Caliphate."

204. Louis, "End of the Caliphate."

205. Joshua Teitelbaum, "'Taking Back' the Caliphate."

206. Slight, "British Imperial Rule and the Hajj," p. 65.

207. Oliver-Dee, "The Cairo High Command and the Caliphate Question, 1914–1919," p. 45.

208. Willis, "Debating the Caliphate," p. 711.

209. Ibid.

210. Bennison, "Muslim Internationalism between Empire and Nation-State," p. 166.

211. Willis, "Debating the Caliphate," p. 714.

212. Crews, "The Russian Worlds of Islam," pp. 35–36.

213. Wilson, *Modern Movements among Moslems*, p. 177.

214. Zwemer, *Arabia*, pp. 211–15.

215. Aydin, *The Politics of Anti-Westernism in Asia*, p. 94.

216. Webb, "Admiral Webb (Constantinople) to Earl Curzon (Received February 10, 1920)," in *Documents on British Foreign Policy 1919–1939*, p. 660.

217. Turkey lost Mosul and parts of Kurdistan in a treaty that "effectively dismantled the Ottoman Empire." Sèvres "internationalized Istanbul and the Bosphorus, while giving pieces of Anatolian territory to the Greeks, Kurds, Armenians, French, British, and Italians."

218. Mango, *Atatürk*, p. 275.

219. The caliph replied that "fetvas issued at the behest of enemy states lacked validity." The antinationalist fatwas inspired armed uprisings among Circassians and Abkhazians in northwest Anatolia, where nationalist officials in a handful of towns were chased out of office. (The grandparents of the Circassians and Abkhazians had settled in Anatolia in the mid-nineteenth century, thanks to Ottoman hospitality.) The Istanbul government issued a decree establishing new "disciplinary Forces" and named them the "Army of the Caliphate" to counter the pro-Ottoman rebels.

220. Mango, *Atatürk*, p. 259.

221. Mango, *Atatürk*, p. 278.

222. Ardiç, "Islam and the Politics of Secularism," p. 488.

223. Khalidi, "The Caliph's Daughter."

224. Landau, *The Politics of Pan-Islam*, p. 56.

225. Fabbe, *Disciples of the State? Religion and State-Building in the Former Ottoman World*, p. 64.

226. Bayart, *L'Islam républicain*, p. 88.

227. Clayer, "L'Autorité religieuse dans l'islam ottoman sous le contrôle de l'état?," p. 46.

228. Owen, *The Clash of Ideas in World Politics*, p. 205.

229. Aidi, *Rebel Music*, p. 239.

Chapter 5. Nation-State Catholicism

1. D'Agostino, *Rome in America*, p. 70.

2. "Cose italiane," *Civiltà Cattolica*, March 10, 1888.

3. Hitchcock, "Church and State in Modern Europe," p. 10.

4. Manning, "The Catholic Church and Modern Society."

5. Ibid.

6. Casanova, "Globalizing Catholicism and the Return to a Universal Church," p. 13.

7. Kertzer, *The Pope Who Would Be King*, p. 254.

8. "The Pope and His Patrons," *New York Times*, February 8, 1863.

9. Manning, "The Catholic Church and Modern Society," p. 110.

10. Viaene, "Nineteenth-Century Catholic Internationalism and Its Predecessors," p. 104.

11. Hertling, *Geschichte Der Katholischen Kirche*, pp. 330–50.

12. Riedel, "Models of Church-State Relations in European Democracies," p. 255.

13. Viaene, "Nineteenth-Century Catholic Internationalism and Its Predecessors," p. 91.

14. Ibid.

15. Scott, "The Treaty between Italy and Vatican," p. 22.

16. Morris, *American Catholic*, p. 134.

17. Hitchcock, "Church and State in Modern Europe," p. 10.

18. Debidour, *Histoire des rapports de l'église et l'état en France*, p. 42.

19. Shusterman, "The French Revolution and the Civil Constitution for the Clergy," pp. 65–66.

20. Chadwick, *A History of the Popes, 1830–1914*, p. 575.

21. Shusterman, "The French Revolution and the Civil Constitution for the Clergy," pp. 64–65.

22. Chadwick, *A History of the Popes, 1830–1914*, p. 575.

23. Shusterman, "The French Revolution and the Civil Constitution for the Clergy," pp. 68–69.

24. Casanova, "Global Catholicism and the Politics of Civil Society."

25. James, "French and British Fleets," p. 304.

26. Guerlac, "The Separation of Church and State in France," p. 261.

27. Coffey, "Of Catechisms and Sermons," p. 57.

28. Baubérot, *Les Sept laïcités françaises*, pp. 40–46.

29. Gastaldi, "La Vie des paroisses," p. 5.

30. Pastor, *The History of the Popes, from the Close of the Middle Ages.*

31. Gastaldi, "Le Concordat de 1801," pp. 12–14.

32. Ibid., p. 43.

33. Chadwick, *The Popes and European Revolution,* p. 508.

34. Ibid.

35. Ibid., p. 513.

36. Gastaldi, "Le Concordat de 1801," p. 51.

37. *La Croix,* "Vocations en France"; cf. "Prêtres-Religieux, combine de 'partis,'" *Gollas* (July/August 2012); "Prêtres français dans le monde et les prêtres étrangers dans les diocèses," *Statistiques de l'Église Catholique de France,* La conférence des Évêques de France, https://eglise .catholique.fr/guide-eglise-catholique-france/statistiques-de-leglise-catholique-france-monde /statistiques-de-leglise-catholique-france/pretres-francais-monde-pretres-etrangers-france/.

38. Gastaldi, "Le Concordat de 1801," p. 31.

39. Ibid.

40. LaCapra, *Madame Bovary on Trial,* p. 7.

41. Hertling, *Geschichte Der Katholischen Kirche.*

42. Guerlac, "The Separation of Church and State in France," p. 263.

43. Ibid., p. 262.

44. Chadwick, *A History of the Popes, 1830–1914,* p. 293.

45. Coffey, "Of Catechisms and Sermons," p. 55.

46. Ibid., p. 56.

47. "Rapport au conseil d'état présenté au nom de la section de l'intérieur, des cultes . . . ," *Journal officiel de la République française* (May 1892): 2285–88.

48. Viaene, "Nineteenth-Century Catholic Internationalism and Its Predecessors," p. 97.

49. "Rapport au conseil d'état présenté au nom de la section de l'intérieur, des cultes . . . ," pp. 2285–88.

50. Guerlac, "The Separation of Church and State in France."

51. Hertling, *Geschichte Der Katholischen Kirche,* p. 266.

52. McGabe, *A History of the Popes,* p. 489.

53. Chadwick, *A History of the Popes, 1830–1914,* p. 530.

54. Hertling, *Geschichte Der Katholischen Kirche,* p. 335.

55. Ibid., p. 335.

56. Chadwick and Chadwick, *Oxford History of the Christian Church,* p. 460.

57. Ibid., p. 451.

58. Ibid., p. 452.

59. Hertling, *Geschichte Der Katholischen Kirche,* p. 335.

60. Chadwick and Chadwick, *Oxford History of the Christian Church,* p. 451.

61. Hertling, *Geschichte Der Katholischen Kirche.*

62. Holtz, "Ministerialabteilung auf Zeit," p. 142.

63. Chadwick, *A History of the Popes, 1830–1914,* p. 261.

64. Tapp, *Kardinäle und Kardinalität,* p. 149.

65. Hertling, *Geschichte Der Katholischen Kirche.*

66. Chadwick, *A History of the Popes, 1830–1914,* p. 264.

67. "Culturkampf," *Atlantic Monthly* 82 (490, August 1898) (emphasis added).

68. "French Foreign Policy: Wisdom Shown in Gambetta's New Appointments" (editorial), *New York Times*, January 18, 1882.

69. Vethake, "Prussia," *Encyclopaedia Americana: A Popular Dictionary of Arts, Sciences*, p. 501.

70. Hertling, *Geschichte Der Katholischen Kirche*, pp. 343, 347.

71. Pellicciari, *Risorgimento Anticattolico*, p. 125.

72. Chadwick, *A History of the Popes, 1830–1914*, p. 242.

73. Martina, "S.I., Il clero nell'Italia centrale dalla restaurazione all'unità."

74. Martin, *The Statesman's Year-Book* (1869).

75. "Cavour and the Pope," *New York Times*, April 12, 1861.

76. Monachino, S.I., *Problemi di storia della chiesa*, p. 259.

77. Hertling, *Geschichte Der Katholischen Kirche*, p. 335.

78. Chadwick, *A History of the Popes, 1830–1914*, p. 232.

79. O'Reilly, "Territorial Sovereignty and the Papacy."

80. Chadwick, *A History of the Popes, 1830–1914*, p. 237.

81. Lindsay and Rowe, *Constitution of the Kingdom of Italy*, p. 26.

82. *Vatican City: Business Law Handbook: Strategic Information and Basic Laws*, vol. 1 (Washington, DC: International Business Publications USA, 2015), pp. 80–81.

83. "Civil and Church Power: The Quirinal and the Vatican," *New York Times*, March 7, 1878.

84. Hertling, *Geschichte Der Katholischen Kirche*, p. 343.

85. "The Italian Government and the Papacy" (editorial), *New York Times*, March 31, 1877.

86. "Vatican Stirring Italy: Advisers to the London Times Say Church Influences Are Trying to Overthrow Monarchy," *New York Times*, May 12, 1898.

87. John Paul II, *Centesimus Annus*, in Hertzke, "The Catholic Church and Catholicism in Global Politics."

88. Manning, "The Catholic Church and Modern Society," p. 102.

89. John Paul II, *Centesimus Annus*, in Hertzke, "The Catholic Church and Catholicism in Global Politics."

90. Martina, *Pio IX (1867–1878)*, p. 275.

91. Coëtlosquet. *Theodore Wibaux, Pontifical Zouave and Jesuit*, p. 145.

92. Powell, *Two Years in the Pontifical Zouaves*, p. 297.

93. Coëtlosquet, *Theodore Wibaux, Pontifical Zouave and Jesuit*, p. 147.

94. "Pius IX and the Ecumenical Council," *New York Times*, March 11, 1869.

95. Hugo, *The Poems of Victor Marie Hugo*, p. 274.

96. O'Malley, *Vatican One*, p. 2.

97. Ibid., p. 28.

98. Viaene, "Nineteenth-Century Catholic Internationalism and Its Predecessors," p. 91.

99. Ibid., p. 83.

100. Chadwick, *A History of the Popes, 1830–1914*, pp. 553, 571.

101. The Concordat of 1827 was never applied, and after Belgium left the union in 1830, Catholics were again in the minority.

102. Chadwick, *A History of the Popes, 1830–1914*, p. 571.

103. Fabbe, "Disciples of the State: Secularization and State Building in the Former Ottoman World."

104. Viaene, "Nineteenth-Century Catholic Internationalism and Its Predecessors," p. 90.

105. Hertling, *Geschichte Der Katholischen Kirche.*

106. Chadwick, *A History of the Popes, 1830–1914,* p. 237.

107. Guasco, *Storia del clero in Italia dall'Ottocento a oggi,* p. 55.

108. Hitchcock, "Church and State in Modern Europe," p. 10.

109. Hertling, *Geschichte Der Katholischen Kirche.*

110. The United States was the most significant entrant of the period into the Congregation de *Propaganda Fide* and would remain there until 1908.

111. "Will the Pope Leave Rome?" *New York Times*, March 3, 1872.

112. Chadwick, *A History of the Popes, 1830–1914,* pp. 180, 219.

113. Burkle-Young, *Papal Elections in the Age of Transition, 1878–1972,* p. 132.

114. Hertling, *Geschichte Der Katholischen Kirche,* p. 335.

115. Martina, "S.I., Il clero nell'Italia centrale dalla restaurazione all'unità," pp. 258–59.

116. Pellicciari, "Risorgimento da riscrivere," p. 154.

117. Sala, *A Journey Due South,* p. 231.

118. Carrère, *Le Pape,* p. 190.

119. Ibid., pp. 187, 190.

120. Burkle-Young, *Papal Elections in the Age of Transition, 1878–1972,* p. 132.

121. D'Agostino, *Rome in America,* p. 60.

122. T.G. Jelen, "The American Church," in *Routledge Handbook of Religion and Politics,* ed. Jeffrey Haynes. New York: Routledge, 2009. p. 74.

123. Chadwick, *A History of the Popes, 1830–1914,* p. 293.

124. Leo XIII, *Longinqua: Encyclical of Pope Leo XIII on Catholicism in the United States,* January 6, 1895, http://www.vatican.va/content/leo-xiii/en/encyclicals/documents/hf_l-xiii_enc_06011895_longinqua.html.

125. Martina, "S.I., Il clero nell'Italia centrale dalla restaurazione all'unità," pp. 258–59.

126. "Cose italiane," *Civiltà Cattolica,* March 10, 1888.

127. Ibid.

128. D'Agostino, *Rome in America,* p. 74.

129. Hertzke, "The Catholic Church and Catholicism in Global Politics," p. 56.

130. Burkle-Young, *Papal Elections in the Age of Transition, 1878–1972,* p. 137.

131. Ibid., p. 152.

132. "Says Papal Treaty Is Blow to Freedom. Another Praises Accord," *New York Times*, June 30, 1929.

133. Chadwick, *A History of the Popes, 1830–1914,* p. 493.

134. "Pope Limits Subjects in the Vatican State," *New York Times*, March 2, 1929.

135. "Pope Becomes Ruler of a State Again," *New York Times*, June 7, 1929.

136. "Vatican and Italy Sign Pact Recreating a Papal State. 60 Years of Enmity Ended," *New York Times*, February 11, 1929.

137. Cortesi, "Pius XI: 'The Pope of the Conciliation,'" p. 3.

138. "Concordat Starts Roman Press Clash," *New York Times*, May 5, 1929.

139. D'Agostino, *Rome in America,* p. 199.

140. Fawkes, "Prospects of the Roman Catholic Church," p. 441.

141. "Concordat Starts Roman Press Clash," *New York Times*, May 5, 1929.

142. Casanova, "Global Catholicism and the Politics of Civil Society," p. 358.

143. "Pope Limits Subjects in the Vatican State," *New York Times*, March 2, 1929.

144. De Cesare, "The Pope and the Temporal Power," p. 866.

145. Ibid., p. 206.

146. Kirsch and Luksch, *Illustrierte Geschichte der Katholischen Kirche*, p. 605.

147. McGreevy, *American Jesuits and the World*, p. 2.

148. John Paul II, *Centesimus Annus*, in Hertzke, "The Catholic Church and Catholicism in Global Politics."

149. McGabe, *A History of the Popes*, p. 491.

Chapter 6. Nation-State Islam

1. Guida, "Seyyid Bey and the Abolition of the Caliphate," p. 279.

2. Rondot, "L'Islam dans la politique des états du Maghreb," p. 44.

3. Ibid.

4. Henry, "Droit musulman et structure d'état moderne en Algérie," p. 20.

5. Salamé, "L'Islam en politique."

6. Berque, "Quelques problèmes de l'Islam Maghrébin."

7. Skovgaard-Petersen, *Defining Islam for the Egyptian State*, p. 22.

8. Turner, *Weber and Islam*, pp. 151–70, p. 162.

9. See, for example, Itzkowitz, *Ottoman Empire and Islamic Tradition*.

10. Deprez, "Pérennité de l'Islam dans l'Ordre Juridique au Maghreb," p. 320.

11. Khan, "Religion and State in Turkey (Continued)."

12. Fabbe, *Disciples of the State? Religion and State-Building in the Former Ottoman World*, p. 105.

13. Clark, *Islam, Charity, and Activism*, p. 13.

14. Turner, *Weber and Islam*, pp. 151–70.

15. Clark, *Islam, Charity, and Activism*, p. 13.

16. Allam, "Opinion: Saudi Women Can Drive, but Are Their Voices Being Heard?"

17. Tobich, "La Construction du projet."

18. Elischer, "Governing the Faithful."

19. Skovgaard-Petersen, *Defining Islam for the Egyptian State*, p. 22.

20. "Iranian Revolution Boosted Self-confidence of German Muslims," *AhlulBayt News Agency*, February 14, 2011.

21. Ochsenwald, "Ottoman Subsidies to the Hijaz, 1877–1886," pp. 274–75.

22. Césari, "Religion and Diasporas."

23. Wyrtzen, "Performing the Nation in Anti-Colonial Protest in Interwar Morocco."

24. Turner, *Weber and Islam*, pp. 151–70, p. 163.

25. Faïza Tobich, *Les Statuts personnels dans les pays arabes: De l'éclatement à l'harmonisation* (Aix-en-Provence: Presses universitaires d'Aix-Marseille, 2008), p. 41.

26. Shales, *Top 10: Istanbul*, p. 33.

27. Garrison, review of *Ataturk: An Intellectual Biography* by Şükrü Hanioğlu, p. 152.

28. Khan, "Religion and State in Turkey (Continued)," p. 225.

29. Hanioğlu, *Atatürk: An Intellectual Biography*, p. 154.

30. Gülalp, "Enlightenment by Fiat," p. 356.

31. Hanioğlu, *Atatürk: An Intellectual Biography*, p. 152.

32. Solgun, "Wear Hats, Read Atatürk's Speech Instead of Koran."

33. Tezcan, *Das muslimische Subjekt*, p. 70.

34. Ardiç, *Islam and the Politics of Secularism*, p. 300.

35. Rubin, "The Status of Religion in Emergent Political Regimes."

36. Khan, "Religion and State in Turkey (Continued)."

37. Wuthnow, "Understanding Religion and Politics."

38. Khan, "Religion and State in Turkey (Continued)," p. 229.

39. Solgun, "Wear Hats, Read Atatürk's Speech Instead of Koran."

40. Maritato, "Turkish Marriages between Religion and the State."

41. Khan, "Religion and State in Turkey (Continued)."

42. Allen, "The Place of Islam in the New Turkey," p. 178.

43. Ibid.

44. Hattemer, "Atatürk and the Reforms in Turkey as Reflected in the Egyptian Press."

45. Rubin, "The Status of Religion in Emergent Political Regimes," p. 12.

46. Dreissler, "Turkey," p. 66.

47. Özdalga, "Education in the Name of 'Order and Progress,'" p. 418.

48. Mango, *Atatürk*.

49. Robinson, "Mosque and School in Turkey," p. 185.

50. Reed, "The Faculty of Divinity at Ankara."

51. Özgur, *Islamic Schools in Modern Turkey*, pp. 34–63.

52. Reed, "The Faculty of Divinity at Ankara," p. 301.

53. Gözaydın, "Religion, politique, et politique de la religion en Turquie," p. 7.

54. Reed, "The Faculty of Divinity at Ankara," pp. 305–6.

55. Taheri, "Turkey's Hundred Years of Identity Crisis," https://eng-archive.aawsat.com/amir-taheri/features/turkeys-hundred-years-of-identity-crisis.

56. Lewis, "Islamic Revival in Turkey," *International Affairs*, p. 41.

57. Reed, "The Faculty of Divinity at Ankara," p. 311.

58. Taheri, "Turkey's Hundred Years of Identity Crisis."

59. Pacaci and Aktay, "75 Years of Higher Religious Education in Modern Turkey," p. 401.

60. Özgur, *Islamic Schools in Modern Turkey*, p. 194.

61. Steppt, "Nationalismus und Islam bei Muṣṭafa Kamil," p. 258.

62. "United States Relations with Turkey: Questions of Economic and Military Assistance," *Foreign Relations of the United States, 1955–1957, Soviet Union, Eastern Mediterranean*, vol. 24, US Department of State, Central Files, 782.5-MSP/7–1656.

63. Reed, "The Faculty of Divinity at Ankara," p. 22.

64. Weiker, *The Turkish Revolution 1960–1961*, p. 9.

65. Lewis, "Islam in Politics."

66. Özgur, *Islamic Schools in Modern Turkey*, p. 194.

67. Jung and Raudvere, *Religion, Politics, and Turkey's EU Accession*, p. 13.

68. Ibid., p. 92.

69. Lewis, "Islam in Politics."

70. Ibid.

71. Tezcan, *Das muslimische Subjekt*, p. 74.

72. Scott, "Qur'an Courses in Turkey."

73. Taheri, "Turkey's Hundred Years of Identity Crisis."

74. Özgur, *Islamic Schools in Modern Turkey*.

75. Carretto, "Elezioni e Governi in Turchia nel 1977."

76. Özgur, *Islamic Schools in Modern Turkey*.

77. Taheri, "Turkey's Hundred Years of Identity Crisis," https://eng-archive.aawsat.com /amir-taheri/features/turkeys-hundred-years-of-identity-crisis.

78. Karakas, "Turkei: Islam und Laizismus zwischen Staats-, Politik- und Gesellschaft sinteressen."

79. Feroz, *The Making of Modern Turkey*, p. 221.

80. Özdalga, "Education in the Name of 'Order and Progress,'" p. 414.

81. Jung and Raudvere, *Religion, Politics, and Turkey's EU Accession*, p. 13.

82. Akyol, "The Turkish Model."

83. Özgur, *Islamic Schools in Modern Turkey*, pp. 34–63.

84. Saleem, "Effect of Islam's Role in State Nationalism on the Islamization of Government," pp. 429–34.

85. Özgur, *Islamic Schools in Modern Turkey*, pp. 34–63.

86. Tepe, "Contesting Political Theologies of Islam and Democracy in Turkey."

87. Özdalga, "Education in the Name of 'Order and Progress,'" p. 414.

88. Yavuz, *Islamic Political Identity in Turkey*, p. 216.

89. "Testing Time for Turkey," *Jerusalem Post Online*, April 27, 1997.

90. "Turkey: The Battle over Control of GOT's [Government Of Turkey's] Religious Affairs," July 28, 2003, 03ANKARA4767_a, https://wikileaks.org/plusd/cables/03ANKARA4767 _a.html.

91. Pacaci and Aktay, "75 Years of Higher Religious Education in Modern Turkey," p. 406.

92. Özgur, *Islamic Schools in Modern Turkey*, pp. 34–63.

93. "Testing Time for Turkey," *Jerusalem Post Online*.

94. Hale and Özbudun, *Islamism, Democracy, and Liberalism in Turkey*.

95. Özgur, *Islamic Schools in Modern Turkey*, pp. 34–63.

96. Scott, "Qur'an Courses in Turkey."

97. Pacaci and Aktay, "75 Years of Higher Religious Education in Modern Turkey," p. 411.

98. J. Wyrtzen, "The Commander of the Faithful and Moroccan Secularity," in *A Secular Age beyond the West: Religion, Law, and the State in Asia, the Middle East, and North Africa*, ed. M. Künkler, J. Madeley, and S. Shankar Cambridge: Cambridge University Press, 2018), p. 221.

99. Shahin, *The Restitution of Islam*, p. 56.

100. Wyrtzen, "The Commander of the Faithful and Moroccan Secularity," p. 223.

101. William N. Stokes, US Vice Consul, "Elimination of Nationalists from Karaouyine University Proposed," October 28, 1953.

102. William N. Stokes, US Vice Consul, "Religious Figures of Morocco and Their Influence" (informal department memorandum), May 19, 1953, American Consulate, Rabat, Foreign Service dispatch to the Department of State, Washington.

103. Ibid.

104. Warren, "Morocco's Sultan Loses Islamic Post."

105. Darif, "État, monarchie, et religion," p. 46.

106. Clifford Geertz, *Islam Observed: Religious Developments in Morocco* (Chicago: University of Chicago Press, 1971), p. 81.

107. Wyrtzen, "Performing the Nation in Anti-Colonial Protest in Interwar Morocco."

108. Frégosi and Zéghal, "Religion et politique au Maghreb," p. 38.

109. Gaffney, "Popular Islam," p. 43.

110. Duclos, "Rémy Leveau, le sabre et le turban, François Bourin, 1993," p. 76.

111. Frégosi and Zéghal, "Religion et politique au Maghreb," p. 40.

112. Ibid.

113. Ibid., p. 41.

114. Ibid., p. 48.

115. Bruce, "Governing Islam Abroad."

116. "Recensement des mosquées (en Arabe et Français)," Ref.: Stat 317.1.02, Premier Ministre, Secretariat chargé du plan, Division des statistiques, Service des statistiques et études démographiques, Rabat (1971).

117. Duclos, "Rémy Leveau, le sabre et le turban, François Bourin, 1993," p. 80.

118. Ibid., p. 81.

119. Frégosi and Zéghal, *Religion et politique au Maghreb*, p. 43.

120. Ibid., pp. 44–45.

121. Souriau, "Quelques données comparatives sur les institutions islamiques actuelles du Maghreb," p. 101.

122. Tozy, "L'Islam entre le contrôle de l'état et les débordements de la société civile," p. 11.

123. Frégosi and Zéghal, *Religion et politique au Maghreb*, p. 47.

124. Shahin, *The Restitution of Islam*, p. 79.

125. Tozy, "L'Islam entre le contrôle de l'état et les débordements de la société civile," p. 26.

126. Ibid., p. 19.

127. Al Ayadi, "Commentaire: État, monarchie, et religion," p. 29.

128. Souriau, "Quelques données comparatives sur les institutions islamiques actuelles du Maghreb."

129. Ibid.

130. Duclos, "Rémy Leveau, le sabre et le turban, François Bourin, 1993," p. 82.

131. Souriau, "Quelques données comparatives sur les institutions islamiques actuelles du Maghreb," p. 100.

132. Porter, "At the Base of the Pillar," p. 285.

133. Ibid., p. 249.

134. Ibid., p. 249.

135. Shahin, *The Restitution of Islam*, p. 87.

136. Souriau, "Quelques données comparatives sur les institutions islamiques actuelles du Maghreb," p. 341.

137. Ibid., pp. 353–54.

138. Ibid., pp. 352–53.

139. Eickelman, "Religion and Polity in Society," p. 91.

140. Shahin, *The Restitution of Islam*, p. 88.

141. Etienne and Tozy, "Le Glissement des obligations islamiques vers le phénomène associatif à Casablanca," p. 238.

142. Frégosi and Zeghal, "Religion et politique au Maghreb," p. 46.

143. Porter, "At the Base of the Pillar," p. 253.

144. Tamadonfar, "Islamism in Contemporary Arab Politics," p. 152.

145. Raberh, "L'islam authentique appartient à Dieu, '"l'islam algérien" à César,'" p. 64.

146. Ibid., pp. 50–51.

147. Ibid., p. 57.

148. Ibid.

149. Séréni, "Algérie: L'islam sous administration coloniale."

150. Boumghar, "Algeria."

151. Frégosi, "Les Rapports entre l'islam et l'état en Algérie et en Tunisie."

152. Deeb, "Islam and the State in Algeria and Morocco," p. 283.

153. Frégosi, "Les Rapports entre l'islam et l'état en Algérie et en Tunisie," pp. 104–8, p. 106.

154. Editor in chief of *Algeria News*, interview with the author, Algiers, February 2014.

155. Hardman, *Islam and the Métropole*.

156. Frégosi, "Les rapports entre l'islam et l'état en Algérie et en Tunisie," p. 106.

157. Rondot, L'Islam dans la politique des états du Maghreb," p. 50.

158. Frégosi, "Les Rapports entre l'islam et l'état en Algérie et en Tunisie," p. 106.

159. Ibid., p. 105.

160. Ibid., pp. 111–23, p. 120.

161. Ibid., pp. 106–8.

162. Ibid., p. 89.

163. Ibid., p. 106.

164. Walzer, *The Paradox of Liberation*, p. 14.

165. Souriau, "Quelques données comparatives sur les institutions islamiques actuelles du Maghreb," p. 372.

166. Ibid.

167. Ibid., p. 354.

168. Ibid., p. 371.

169. Frégosi, "Les Rapports entre l'islam et l'état en Algérie et en Tunisie," p. 108.

170. Tozy, "L'Islam entre le contrôle de l'état et les débordements de la société civile," p. 30.

171. Frégosi, "Les Rapports entre l'islam et l'état en Algérie et en Tunisie," p. 107.

172. Ibid., p. 108.

173. Aït-Aoudia, "La Naissance du Front Islamique Du Salut."

174. Sado Mezigh, "L'enseignement et l'islam: Une nécessité civilisationnelle," *Revolution Africaine*, October 4, 1985, pp. 18–19.

175. Frégosi, "Les Rapports entre l'islam et l'état en Algérie et en Tunisie," p. 107.

176. Séréni, "Algérie: L'islam sous administration coloniale."

177. Aït-Aoudia, "La Naissance du Front Islamique du Salut," p. 136.

178. Ministères des affaires religieuses, Direction de la planification et de la formation, République algérienne démocratique et populaire, "Situation des mosquées, écoles coraniques, et formation continue," 1989, p. 50.

179. Ministères des affaires religieuses, "Situation des mosquées, écoles coraniques, et formation continue," p. 50.

180. Moussa Sarri, interview with the author, Algiers, February 2014.

181. Driessen, "Public Religion, Democracy, and Islam," p. 24.

182. Mahiou and Henry, "Ou va l'Algérie."

183. "Algeria—Constitutional Legal Foundations," *Education Encyclopedia*, StateUniversity .com, https://education.stateuniversity.com/pages/20/Algeria-CONSTITUTIONAL -LEGAL-FOUNDATIONS.html.

184. Parteger, "Algeria's Religious Affairs Official Shot Dead."

185. Moussa Sarri, interview with the author, Algiers, February 2014.

186. Ibid.

187. Federation of American Scientists, "Patterns of Global Terrorism, 1998: Middle East Overview," https://fas.org/irp/threat/terror_98/mideast.htm.

188. Frégosi and Zéghal, *Religion et politique au Maghreb*, p. 5.

189. Brewster, "Recent Reforms at the Zeitouna," p. 122.

190. Ibid., p. 123.

191. Zeghal, "État et marché des biens religieux," p. 84.

192. Brewster, "Recent Reforms at the Zeitouna," p. 125.

193. Frégosi and Zéghal, *Religion et politique au Maghreb*, pp. 14–15.

194. Speight, "Islam in Politics," p. 282.

195. Zeghal, "État et marché des biens religieux," p. 85.

196. Ministry of Religious Affairs, "A Historical Overview of the Administrative Management of Religious Affairs in Tunisia," August 31, 2012.

197. Speight, "Islam in Politics," p. 282.

198. Frégosi, "Les Rapports entre l'islam et l'état en Algérie et en Tunisie," p. 17.

199. Zeghal, "État et marché des biens religieux," p. 85.

200. Ibid.

201. Noyon, "Tunisia's 'Managed Democracy,'" p. 96.

202. Moore, *Tunisia since Independence*, p. 57.

203. Bouhdiba, "Islam in Tunisia," p. 142.

204. Speight, "Islam in Politics," p. 283.

205. Hanna, "Changing Trends in Tunisian Socialism."

206. Speight, "Islam in Politics," p. 283.

207. Ministry of Religious Affairs, "A Historical Overview of the Administrative Management of Religious Affairs in Tunisia."

208. Shahin, *The Restitution of Islam*, p. 59.

209. Zeghal, "État et marché des biens religieux," p. 92.

210. Ibid., p. 47.

211. Moore, *Tunisia since Independence*, p. 41.

212. Zeghal, "État et marché des biens religieux," p. 85.

213. Bouhdiba, "Islam in Tunisia," p. 140.

214. Ibid.

215. Souriau, "Quelques données comparatives sur les institutions islamiques actuelles du Maghreb," p. 378.

216. Frégosi and Zeghal, "Religion et politique au Maghreb," p. 34.

217. Zeghal, "État et marché des biens religieux," p. 91.

218. Ibid.

219. Frégosi and Zéghal, "Religion et politique au Maghreb," p. 15.

220. Ibid., p. 17.

221. Ibid.

222. Ministry of Religious Affairs, "A Historical Overview of the Administrative Management of Religious Affairs in Tunisia."

223. Hanna, "Changing Trends in Tunisian Socialism," p. 232.

224. Speight, "Islam in Politics," p. 282.

225. Wolf, "An Islamist 'Renaissance'? Religion and Politics in Post-revolutionary Tunisia."

226. Frégosi, "Habib Bourguiba et la regulation institutionnelle de l'Islam."

227. Noyon, "Tunisia's 'Managed Democracy,'" p. 103.

228. Frégosi and Zéghal, Religion et politique au Maghreb, p. 20.

229. Ibid., p. 23.

230. Ibid., pp. 11–14.

231. Ibid., pp. 20, 34.

232. Ibid., p. 24.

233. Noyon, "Tunisia's 'Managed Democracy,'" p. 106.

234. Ibid., p. 104.

235. Frégosi and Zéghal, Religion et politique au Maghreb, p. 20.

236. Ibid.

237. Etzioni, Security First, p. 149.

238. Youssef ben Ismail, "Good 'Ulama' and Bad 'Ulama': History (Re-) Writing as Identity Making in Post-Colonial Tunisia," paper delivered at Middle East Studies Association annual meeting, Denver, CO, November 23, 2015.

239. Frégosi, "Les rapports entre l'islam et l'état en Algérie et en Tunisie," p. 110.

240. Zeghal, "État et marché des biens religieux," p. 80.

241. Césari, The Awakening of Muslim Democracy, p. 13.

242. Césari, "State Society Relations and Their Influence on Pakistan Stability."

243. Césari, The Awakening of Muslim Democracy, p. 30.

244. Fabbe, "Disciples of the State: Religion and State-Building in the Former Ottoman World," p. 141.

245. Nasr, Islamic Leviathan, p. 4.

246. Hefner, "Public Islam and the Problem of Democratization."

247. Zeghal, "État et marché des biens religieux," p. 91.

248. Skovgaard-Petersen, Defining Islam for the Egyptian State, p. 22.

249. Elischer, "Governing the Faithful," p. 26.

Chapter 7. Catholicism in the United States

1. McGreevy, American Jesuits and the World, p. 52.

2. Douniol, Le Correspondant 63 (1864): p. 698.

3. Shaughnessy, Has the Immigrant Kept the Faith?

4. Kirsch and Luksch, *Illustrierte Geschichte der Katholischen Kirche*, p. 603.

5. Pew Research Center, "Global Christianity."

6. Caplow, Hicks, and Wattenberg, "Religion," pp. 195–97; Saunders, *The Myth of the Muslim Tide*, p. 118.

7. Palmieri, "Il protestantesimo e gli emigranti italiani," p. 120.

8. Molteni, "La Fase odierna del problema dell'emigrazione italiana negli Stati Uniti," p. 376.

9. "Would Curb Italian Crime: Vatican Will Intensify Religious Work among Emigrants," *New York Times*, November 25, 1928.

10. Malatesta, *Life and Ideas: The Anarchist Writings of Errico Malatesta*.

11. Roy, "France's Oedipal Islamist Complex."

12. Weir, *Beyond Labor's Veil*, p. 94.

13. Abell, "Origins of Catholic Social Reform in the United States," pp. 300–301.

14. "Would Curb Italian Crime: Vatican Will Intensify Religious Work among Emigrants," *New York Times*, November 25, 1928.

15. White, *The Diocesan Seminary in the United States*, p. 87.

16. "America Not Represented," *New York Times*, December 1, 1907, p. 19.

17. "Cardinal Satolli's Successor," *New York Times*, August 19, 1896, p. 1.

18. "America Not Represented," *New York Times*, December 1, 1907, p. 19.

19. Finke and Stark, *The Churching of America, 1776–2005*, p. 125.

20. "Protestant Propaganda in the Philippines," *Catholic Fortnightly Review* 15 (18, 1908): 563.

21. "Catholics in America: Immigrants to Be Bound Together in National Bodies," *New York Times*, June 30, 1891.

22. "Care of Catholic Emigrants: A Talk with Herr Cahensly," *New York Times*, June 13, 1891.

23. Abell, "Origins of Catholic Social Reform in the United States," p. 301.

24. "Care of Catholic Emigrants: A Talk with Herr Cahensly," *New York Times*, June 13, 1891.

25. Holmes, "The American Heresy," p. 7; McGreevy, *American Jesuits and the World*, p. 41.

26. Holmes, "The American Heresy," p. 7.

27. Walburg, "The Threat of Americanization of the Immigrant,", p. 38.

28. Ibid.

29. Choate, "Sending States' Transnational Interventions in Politics, Culture, and Economics," p. 748.

30. McGreevy, *American Jesuits and the World*, p. 70.

31. Picarello, "History of Blaine Amendments."

32. Picarello et al., "School Choice: The Blaine Amendments and Anti-Catholicism."

33. "The Faribault System," *New York Times*, May 16, 1892, p. 3.

34. Curran, "Assimilation and Nativism," p. 18.

35. "Pope Praises Zeal of Catholics Here," *New York Times*, June 8, 1906.

36. *The Catholic Primer's Reference Series: Baltimore Catechism of 1891*, https://www.pcpbooks.net/docs/baltimore_catechism.pdf.

37. Finke and Stark, *The Churching of America, 1776–2005*, p. 145.

38. Marraro, "Canadian and American Zouaves in the Papal Army, 1868–1870."

39. Ibid.

40. Ibid.

41. "Celebration of High Mass at St. Peter's Church—An Address by Archbishop McCloskey—Departures of the Zouaves for Europe." *New York Times*, February 23, 1868.

42. Marraro, "Canadian and American Zouaves in the Papal Army, 1868–1870."

43. Ibid.

44. Ibid.

45. Walburg, "The Threat of Americanization of the Immigrant," pp. 37–38.

46. Abell, "Origins of Catholic Social Reform in the United States," p. 295; McGreevy, *American Jesuits and the World*, p. 43.

47. McGreevy, *American Jesuits and the World*, p. 18.

48. Andes, *The Vatican and Catholic Activism in Mexico and Chile*.

49. O'Reilly, "Territorial Sovereignty and the Papacy," p. 218.

50. Langdon, "Italy and the Papacy."

51. Ireland, "The Pope's Civil Princedom."

52. O'Reilly, "Territorial Sovereignty and the Papacy," p. 212.

53. Cioppi, "Il convegno di parigi per un istituto internazionale cristiano."

54. Ibid., p. 488.

55. Casanova, "The Politics of Nativism."

56. Morse, *Foreign Conspiracy against the Liberties of the United States*, p. 16; Moore, *Will America Become Catholic?*, p. 18.

57. McGreevy, *American Jesuits and the World*, p. 23.

58. Ibid., p. 72.

59. Morse, *Foreign Conspiracy against the Liberties of the United States*, p. 90.

60. Thomas Nast, "Religious Liberty Is Guaranteed: But Can We Allow Foreign Reptiles to Crawl All over Us?," seen June 14, 2017, at the Library of Congress, Prints and Photographs Division, https://www.loc.gov/pictures/item/2010717281/.

61. James Anthony Froude, "Romanism and the Irish Race in the United States: Part I," *North American Review* 129 (277, 1879): 519–36, p. 529. http://www.jstor.org/stable/25100813 (accessed November 24, 2020).

62. Holmes, "The American Heresy," pp. 7–8.

63. De Cesare, "The Pope and the Temporal Power," p. 864.

64. Fenton, *Religious Liberties*, p. 145.

65. Choate, "Sending States' Transnational Interventions in Politics, Culture, and Economics," p. 748.

66. Jensen, *The Battle against Anarchist Terrorism*, p. 6.

67. Ettore Zoccoli, *L'Anarchia* (Rome: Fratelli Bocca, 1907), p. vii, cited in Cilibrizzi, *Storia parlamentare politica e diplomatica d'Italia da Novara a Vittorio Veneto*, vol. 3, p. 131.

68. Turcato, "The Other Nation."

69. Petacco, *L'Anarchico che venne dall'America*, p. 23.

70. Zimmer, *Immigrants against the State*, p. 75.

71. Shea, *The Hierarchy of the Catholic Church in the United States*, p. 186.

72. Truccato, "The Other Nation."

73. "Anarchists Met Bresci," *New York Times*, August 4, 1900, p. 7.

74. Turcato, "The Other Nation."

75. Mattox, *Chronology of World Terrorism, 1901–2001*.

76. De Maria, "Anarchici italiani negli Stati Uniti."

77. Bevilacqua et al., *Storia dell'emigrazione italiana*, p. 298.

78. Petacco, *L'Anarchico che venne dall'America*, p. 42.

79. Ibid., p. 29.

80. Avrich, *Sacco and Vanzetti*, p. 95.

81. Davide Turcato, "The Other Nation," p. 47.

82. Avrich, *Sacco and Vanzetti*, p. 95.

83. Turcato, "The Other Nation," p. 45.

84. Petacco, *L'Anarchico che venne dall'America*, p. 20.

85. Zimmer, *Immigrants against the State*, p. 60.

86. Silvestri, "Le Cannonate di Beccaris sui milanesi armano la mano di Bresci."

87. Goldman, "Vaillant!," p. 110.

88. Zimmer, *Immigrants against the State*.

89. De Maria, "Anarchici italiani negli Stati Uniti"; "King Humbert Assassinated," *Sacred Heart Review* 24 (5, August 4, 1900).

90. Petacco, *L'Anarchico che venne dall'America*, p. 127.

91. "Assassin's Lot Fell upon Anarchist Here," *New York Times*, July 31, 1900, p. 1.

92. "Anarchists Met Bresci," *New York Times*, August 4, 1900, p. 7.

93. "Assassin's Comrade Nicola Quintavelli," *New York Times*, August 2, 1900, p. 3.

94. Zimmer, *Immigrants against the State*, p. 56.

95. "Searching among Paterson Anarchists," *New York Times*, August 1, 1900, p. 1.

96. "Worldwide Anarchistic Plot to Murder Monarchs," *New York Herald*, August 3, 1900.

97. "Immigration Bill Passed," *New York Times*, March 1, 1903, p. 2.

98. Czolgosz's parents were born in western Prussia (possibly Berlin). McKinley was the third US president assassinated within a thirty-six-year period (Abraham Lincoln in 1865; James Garfield in 1881; McKinley in 1901).

99. Vizetelly, *The Anarchists*.

100. "Czolgosz Says He Had No Aid," *Chicago Sunday Tribune*, September 8, 1901, pp. 1, 4.

101. Fred C. Nieman [Czolgosz alias], "Letter to John Grinder in Cleveland, Ohio," West Seneca, NY, July 30, 1901.

102. "New York Churches Pray for Mr. M'Kinley," *New York Times*, September 9, 1901, p. 3.

103. *The American Israelite*, September 15, 1901, p. 10.

104. "Czolgosz Says He Had No Aid," *Chicago Sunday Tribune*, September 8, 1901.

105. N. Currier, "The Propagation Society: More Free than Welcome," seen June 14, 2017, at the Library of Congress, Prints and Photographs Division, https://www.loc.gov/item/2003656589/; "Cardinal Hayes Tells of Visit to the Pope; Recites Pontiff's Blessing to America at Catholic School Dinner Here," *New York Times*, February 2, 1930, p. 12.

106. Birnbaum and Meehan, *The Heights*.

107. Hindus, "The Revolt of the New Immigrant," p. 848.

108. "Sorrowing Jews Pray for the Dead," *New York Times*, September 15, 1901.

109. Jensen, *The Battle against Anarchist Terrorism*, p. 234.

110. "Tracing the Bomb Throwers of New York," *New York Times*, April 12, 1908, p. 41.

111. "The Shooting of the President and the Questions It Raises," *Sacred Heart Review* 26 (11, September 14, 1901).

112. "To Drive Anarchists Out of the Country," *New York Times*, March 4, 1908, pp. 1–2.

113. "No Anarchist Immigrants," *New York Times*, May 10, 1908, p. 45.

114. "Notes of 'The Observer' in Rome," *New York Times*, December 14, 1902, p. 5.

115. "President Roosevelt's First Message," *New York Times*, December 4, 1901, pp. 6–7.

116. Gienapp, "Nebraska, Nativism, and Rum."

117. Abell, "Origins of Catholic Social Reform in the United States," p. 300.

118. McGirr, *The War on Alcohol*, p. 330.

119. Premoli, *Storia ecclesiastica contemporanea (1900–1925)*, p. 417.

120. "President Roosevelt's First Message," *New York Times*, December 4, 1901, pp. 6–7.

121. "The Shooting of the President and the Questions It Raises," *Sacred Heart Review*, September 14, 1901.

122. "Origins of Young Criminals Are Studied," *New York Times*, August 15, 1926.

123. "La Parola dei Vescovi nel Presente Movimento Sociale," *Rivista internazionale di scienze sociali e discipline ausiliari* 4 (15, March 1894): 424–35, p. 434.

124. "Care of Catholic Emigrants: A Talk with Herr Cahensly," *New York Times*, June 13, 1891.

125. Jouffroy, "Warnings and Teachings of the Church on Anarchism," p. 202.

126. Reuter, *Catholic Influence on American Colonial Policies, 1898–1904*, p. 116.

127. Vizetelly, *The Anarchists*, p. 415.

128. Shea, *The Lion and the Lamb*, p. 196.

129. Shelley, "Biography and Autobiography: James Cardinal Gibbons and John Tracy Ellis," p. 43.

130. Shea, *The Lion and the Lamb*, pp. 110–12.

131. Morris, *American Catholic*, p. 114.

132. Palmieri, "Il protestantesimo e gli emigranti italiani," p. 92.

133. Finke and Stark, *The Churching of America, 1776–2005*, p. 132.

134. Opera della propagazione della fede, *Notizia sull'opera pia della Propagazione della Fede.*

135. "Third Plenary Council," *New York Times*, November 7, 1884, p. 3.

136. White, *The Diocesan Seminary in the United States*, p. 25.

137. Brownson, *Life of Demetrius Augustine Gallatin, Prince and Priest.*

138. Curran, "Assimilation and Nativism," p. 18.

139. White, *The Diocesan Seminary in the United States*, p. 89.

140. Atwood, *Handbook of Denominations in the United States.*

141. Rev. John T. McNicholas, "The Need of American Priests for the Italian Missions," *American Ecclesiastical Review* (Philadelphia: Dolphin Press) 9 (1908): 677–87, p. 684.

142. Palmieri, "Il protestantesimo e gli emigranti italiani," p. 210.

143. Charles Douniol, *Le Correspondant* 63 (1864): p. 700.

144. Shaughnessy, *Has the Immigrant Kept the Faith?*, p. 259.

145. Finke and Stark, *The Churching of America, 1776–2005*, p. 134.

146. Catholic Church, *Priestly Vocations in the World of Today*, p. 277.

147. Curran, "Vocations Keep Climbing."

148. Bryk, Lee, and Holland, *Catholic Schools and the Common Good*, p. 25.

149. Palmieri, "L'Aspetto economico del problema religioso italiano," p. 206.

150. "The Faribault System." *New York Times*, May 16, 1892, p. 3.

151. Ibid.

152. Ibid.

153. Morris, *American Catholic*, p. 114.

154. Finke and Stark, *The Churching of America, 1776–2005*, p. 147.

155. Handy, *A History of the Churches in the United States and Canada*, p. 402.

156. Goebel, *A Study of Catholic Secondary Education during the Colonial Period up to the First Plenary Council of Baltimore*.

157. White, "Perspectives on the Nineteenth-Century Diocesan Seminary in the United States."

158. Ibid., p. 26.

159. Ibid., p. 88.

160. Ibid.

161. Ibid.

162. Ibid.

163. D'Agostino, *Rome in America*, pp. 283–85.

164. Morris, *American Catholic*, p. 117.

165. White, "Perspectives on the Nineteenth-Century Diocesan Seminary in the United States."

166. John T. McGreevy, "Jesuit Colleges in the United States in 1893," in McGreevy, *American Jesuits and the World*, p. 151.

167. Gleason, *Contending with Modernity*, p. 27.

168. McGreevy, "Jesuit Colleges in the United States in 1893," p. 100.

169. Gleason, *Contending with Modernity*, p. 12.

170. "The Faribault System." *New York Times*, May 16, 1892, p. 3.

171. Gleason, *Contending with Modernity*, pp. 84–85.

172. Ibid., p. 168.

173. National Catholic Educational Association, *Catholic Seminaries in the United States*, "Statistical Summary."

174. Kirsch and Luksch, *Illustrierte Geschichte der Katholischen Kirche*, p. 603.

175. "Sièges résidentiels par pays et par provinces," *Annuaire pontifical catholique* (Paris) (1895): 308–9.

176. "America Not Represented," *New York Times*, December 1, 1907, p. 3.

177. Shea, *Life and Times of the Most Rev. John Carroll, Bishop and First Archbishop of Baltimore*, p. 256.

178. "Pope Tests Works of Father Hanna," *New York Times*, January 5, 1908, p. 1.

179. Wilhelm, "General Councils."

180. Abell, "Origins of Catholic Social Reform in the United States," p. 295.

181. "How Cardinal Gibbons Fought Pan Germans," *New York Times*, June 3, 1917.

182. "Ireland Balked by Cardinals," *New York Times*, December 1, 1907, p. 1.

183. Holmes, "The American Heresy," p. 7.

184. Ellis, *American Catholicism*, p. 127.

185. Cassidy, *Catholic College Foundations and Development in the United States (1677–1850)*.

186. "About Us." https://www.jesuits.org/about-us/history/.

187. Stark, *One True God*, p. 239.

188. *The Pontifical North American College: Celebrating 150 Years of Priestly Formation in the Eternal City* (Washington, DC: PNAC, 2009).

Chapter 8. Islam in Europe

1. Krasner, *Sovereignty: Organized Hypocrisy.*

2. Delvecchio, "Djihadistes français: Les faux-semblants du rapport de Dounia Bouzar."

3. Orsini, "Poverty, Ideology, and Terrorism: The STAM Bond."

4. "Brother's Keeper? Toulouse Killings Still Haunt France as Trial Begins," *France 24*, October 3, 2017.

5. "Brussels Jewish Museum Murders: Mehdi Nemmouche Guilty," *BBC News*, March 7, 2019.

6. "France Remembers Victims of Kosher Supermarket Attack," *France 24*, January 10, 2016.

7. "Les Imams algériens engagés à défendre la vraie image de l'islam en Europe," *HuffPost Algérie*, Janurary 18, 2015.

8. Quatremer, "La Belgique ne s'est pas préoccupée d'aider à développer un islam européen."

9. Norris and Inglehart, "Islam and the West: Testing the Clash of Civilizations Thesis."

10. Press, "Turkish Prime Minister Says 'Assimilation Is a Crime against Humanity.'"

11. Unal Gundogan, interview with the author, Ankara, July 2011.

12. Andre Azoulay, interview with the author, Rabat, January 2011.

13. Anonymous official, interview with the author, Rabat, October 2012.

14. "Les Imams algériens engagés à défendre la vraie image de l'islam en Europe," *HuffPost Algérie*, Janurary 18, 2015.

15. Vincent, "Ecquevilly, histoire d'un satanisme français."

16. Lhomme and Davet, "Qui sont les djihadistes français tués par des 'frappes ciblées?'"

17. "Why Italy Has Not Yet Suffered Islamist Terrorism," *The Economist*, September 30, 2017.

18. Vincent, "Le Conseil d'état rejette le recours déposé par la mosquée salutiste d'Ecquevilly."

19. "One in Five Dutch People for Closing Mosques," *Euro-Islam.info*, October 17, 2016.

20. As did the 1995, 2001, and 2005 attacks before them.

21. Dr. Assia Bensalah Alaoui, interview with the author, Rabat, October 2012.

22. Jouanneau, *Les Imams en France.*

23. LeBars, "Des imams à l'école pour se former à l''islam de France.'"

24. Senay, *Beyond Turkey's Borders.*

25. Bruce, *Governing Islam Abroad*; Bruce, "Not Quite In, Not Quite Out."

26. Jouanneau, *Les Imams en France*, pp. 309–10.

27. Ibid., p. 282; Barou, "Integration of Immigrants in France."

28. US Department of State, "France 2018 Report on International Religious Freedom."

29. Talip Küçükcan, "Turkish Migrants, Social Capital, and Culturalist Discourse in Turkey-EU Relations," in *Religion, Politics, and Turkey's EU Accession*, ed. Dietrich Jung and Catharina Raudvere (New York: Palgrave Macmillan, 2008), "Figure 10.1: Turks in Selected European Countries," p. 203; Gözaydın, "Religion as Soft Power in the International Relations of Turkey."

30. Citak, "D'acteur national à transnational."

31. Bruce, "Les imams 'exportés' de la Diyanet en France."

32. Ali Kizilkaya (president of Islamrat), interview with the author, Berlin, March 2013.

33. Bruce, "Les Imams 'exportés' de la Diyanet," p. 15.

34. Özgur, *Islamic Schools in Modern Turkey*, pp. 34–63.

35. Laurence, *The Emancipation of Europe's Muslims*, p. 60.

36. "Bestandserhebung zur Ausbildung religiösen Personals islamischer Gemeinden," Deutsche Islam Konferenz, Bundesamt für Migration und Flüchtlinge, November 2020, p. 11.

37. "Türkei: Religionsbehörde Entsandte 970 Imame Nach Deutschland," *Zeit Online*, April 23, 2016.

38. Mehmet Pacaci, interview with the author, Ankara, July 2011.

39. Akgönül, "Islam turc, Islams de Turquie," p. 38.

40. Mehmet Pacaci, interview with the author, Ankara, July 2011.

41. Islamische Zeitung, interview with the author, Berlin, October 2012.

42. Akgönül, "Islam turc, Islams de Turquie," pp. 40–43.

43. Sauvaget, "Ahmet Ogras, Tête de pont d'Ankara dans l'islam français."

44. Mehmet Köse, interview with the author, Ankara, July 2011.

45. DiB, Strategic Planning Department, interview with the author, Ankara, July 2011.

46. Jouanneau, *Les Imams en France*; Mehmet Pacaci, interview with the author, Ankara, July 2011.

47. Unal Gondugan and Hasan Kaplan, interview with the author, Ankara, July 2011.

48. Arkilic, "The Limits of European Islam."

49. Spielhaus and Herzog, "Die rechtliche Anerkennung des Islams in Deutschland."

50. "Turkish Religious Official Views Situation of Muslims in Austria," *BBC Monitoring*, July 22, 2012.

51. Bruce, "Les imams 'exportés' de la Diyanet en France," p. 16.

52. Korkut, "The Diyanet of Turkey and Its Activities in Eurasia after the Cold War," p. 135.

53. Bruce, "Not Quite In, Not Quite Out."

54. Gorzewski, "DİTİB-Imame im Spagat."

55. Şenol Bal (MHP), interview with the author, Ankara, July 2011.

56. Talip Küçükçan (AKP), interview with the author, Ankara, July 2011.

57. "AVRUPA," *Hürriyet Haber*, June 23, 2017.

58. "Imame müssen die deutsche Gesellschaft verstehen," *De Zeit*, September 25, 2013.

59. J. Bouchard, Thomas Guibert, and Stéphane Palier, interview with the author, Ankara, July 2011.

60. "Zeitgeschehen," *Die Zeit*, October 2015.

61. Jean-Pierre Stroobants, "Ankara dénonce la réforme du culte islamique en Belgique," *Le Monde*, May 4, 2016.

62. Ali Dere (president of Diyanet İşleri Türk İslam Birliği), interview with the author, Berlin, December 2012.

63. Laurence, *The Emancipation of Europe's Muslims*, p. 237.

64. Ali Dere (DİTİB chairman), interview with the author, Berlin, December 2012.

65. Hüseyin Avni Karslioglu (Turkish ambassador to Germany), interview with the author, Berlin, January 2013.

66. Ali Dere, interview with the author, December 2012.

67. Ibrahim Kalin (adviser to the prime minister), interview with the author, Ankara, July 2011.

68. Sauvaget, "Turkey Invests in 'Made in France' Islam in Strasbourg."

69. Ali Kizilkaya, interview with the author, Berlin, March 2013.

70. Fondation Hassan II pour les marocains résidant à l'étranger (MRE), *Marocains de l'Extérieur 2007*, p. 15.

71. Ibid., p. 47.

72. Bruce, "Not Quite In, Not Quite Out."

73. Omar Azziman (deputy president, Foundation Hassan II pour MRE), interview with the author, Rabat, January 2011.

74. Mohamed Amine Chouaybi (president of the Mohammed VI Foundation for the Holy Qur'an in Rabat), interview with the author, Rabat, January 2011.

75. Lamfalussy, "Rabat inquiet de l'Islam belge."

76. Mohamed Amine Chouaybi, interview with the author, Rabat, January 2011.

77. Lamfalussy, "Rabat inquiet de l'Islam belge."

78. Omar Zniber (Moroccan ambassador to Germany), interview with the author, Berlin, November 2012.

79. Ibid.

80. "Rabat Toma el control del," *ABC*, November 7, 2007.

81. "Deux nouvelles mosquées à Strasbourg," *Fdesouche*, January 17, 2011, and June 24, 2017; "Le Roi du Maroc donne 787,000 euros pour achever une mosquée en France," *Le Monde*, May 31, 2012; "Maroc—Mohammed VI, un roi généreux en France," *Slate Afrique*, June 24, 2017.

82. Omar Azziman, interview with the author, Rabat, January 2011.

83. Omar Zniber, interview with the author, Berlin, November 2012.

84. Omar Azziman, interview with the author, Rabat, January 2011.

85. Bruce, "Not Quite In, Not Quite Out."

86. Omar Azziman, interview with the author, Rabat, January 2011.

87. Hakim el Ghissassi (adviser to the minister for Islamic affairs), interview with the author, Rabat, January 2011.

88. Embassy of the Kingdom of Morocco in Madrid, "Onda Cero: Más de 200 imanes evitarán que los marroquíes emigrados al extranjero se alejen del Islam moderado," June 14, 2016.

89. Mohamed Amine Chouaybi, interview with the author, Rabat, January 2011.

90. Samadi, "L'édification du moi marocain," p. 263.

91. Laurence, *The Emancipation of Europe's Muslims*, p. 66.

92. Omar Azziman, interview with the author, Rabat, January 2011.

93. Khalid Samadi, ""l'édification du Moi Marocain."" p. 281.

94. Ahmad Abbadi, interview with the author, Rabat, October 2012.

95. Omar Azziman, interview with the author, Rabat, January 2011.

96. Badía, "Marruecos formará a los imanes de la Región para evitar el radicalismo."

97. Samadi, "L'Édification du Moi Marocain," p. 282.

98. Jalal, "Le Maroc investit sur la formation des imams."

99. Ravix, "Premiers jours de cours à l'Institut Mohammed VI De Formation Des Imams"; Efe, "Marruecos formará a imanes de Nigeria, quinto país Africano que lo solicita."

100. Brown, "Is Islam Easy to Understand or Not?," pp. 117–44.

101. "Le Maroc est le mieux placé pour promouvoir un Islam de modération et du juste milieu (président UMF)." MAP Express. 25 June 2017.

102. Abdellah Boussouf, remarks in Strasbourg, January 2011.

103. Ahmed Toufiq, interview with the author, Rabat, October 2012.

104. Ahmad Abbadi, interview with the author, Rabat, October 2012.

105. Executif Musulman de Belgique, interview with the author, Brussels, September 2013.

106. "Marruecos anima a sus imanes a adaptarse a la Europa del siglo XXI," *La Vanguardia*, May 31, 2015.

107. "Islam: A Roma Primo Meeting Imam Marocchini in Italia," *Adnkronos*, February 21, 2011.

108. Abdallah Boussouf, interview with the author, Rabat, January 10, 2011.

109. Ibid.

110. Omar Azzimi and Abderrahmane Zahi, interviews with the author, Rabat, January 2011.

111. Abdellatif Maazouz, interview with the author, Rabat, October 2012.

112. Omar Azziman, interview with the author, Rabat, January 2011.

113. Yasmine Ryan, "Uncovering Algeria's Civil War," *Al Jazeera*, November 18, 2010.

114. Bouabdellah Ghlamallah (minister of religious affairs), interview with the author, Algiers, February 2014.

115. Saudi expansionism after Soviet withdrawal from Afghanistan in 1989 extended to North Africa (see chapter 7). Algeria's pragmatic embrace of anti-Islamist policies aimed to "depoliticize" religion, that is, to protect it from extraneous influences.

116. André Parant (French ambassador to Algeria), interview with the author, Algiers, February 2014.

117. President Abdelaziz Bouteflika improved national share to 90 percent in 2009, up from 85 percent in 2004.

118. Amine, "Un Algérien chargé d'installer le califat en Europe, recherché par la France et l'Espagne."

119. This amounted to one-third of the Moroccan budget for Islamic associations in Europe, but the Algerian and Moroccan transfers to their European communities separately also included other private gifts and waqf revenues.

120. The religious affairs ministry devoted nearly 2 million euros to the construction of mosques in Toulouse, Tours, and Marseille; it also added a new annual subsidy of 250,000 euros for the Grande Mosquée de Paris and, in 2012, granted final approval (together with several other countries) to build a *grande mosquée* in Marseille.

121. Bouabdellah Ghlamallah, interview with the author, Algiers, February 2014.

122. Houcine Maghar (director general of the Department for the Algerian Community Abroad, Ministry of Foreign Affairs; former Algerian ambassador to Germany; ambassador to Canada, 2014–), interview with the author, Algiers, February 2014.

123. Bouabdellah Ghlamallah, interview with the author, Algiers, February 2014.

124. Anonymous Algerian religious affairs official, interview with the author, Algiers, February 2014.

125. Bouabdellah Ghlamallah, interview with the author, Algiers, February 2014.

126. Ibid.

127. These eighteen consulates, in one country, represent more than 10 percent of its 115 consular posts worldwide.

128. Mourad, "Mohamed Aïssa aux imams délégués en France."

129. "Affaires religieuses: Rencontre nationale du conseil scientifique national (fetwa)," *El Moudjahid*, February 9, 2015.

130. Ibid.

131. Laurence and Vaisse, *Integrating Islam*.

132. Jouanneau, *Les Imams en France*, p. 348.

133. Bouabdellah Ghlamallah, interview with the author, Algiers, February 2014. Starting in 1981, according to Ghlamallah, the Algerian ministry of religious affairs required all imams to obtain a state diploma. From 1989 until 1998, an additional quota of Algerian imams on linguistic exchange were mixed into the contingent of teachers being sent.

134. Mohammed Aïssa (inspector general at the Ministry of Religious Affairs), interview with the author, Ministry of Religious Affairs, February 2014.

135. An additional 120 imams were sent temporarily to France, Germany, Spain, and Canada in 2016 to guide the *Tarouih* prayers during the month of Ramadan.

136. Laurence, *The Emancipation of Europe's Muslims*, p. 228.

137. In the same breath, Inspector General Aïssa relayed the "news that we now have two imams working full-time in Belgium."

138. Bouabdellah Ghlamallah, interview with the author, Algiers, February 2014.

139. André Parant, interview with the author, Algiers, February 2014.

140. Tlili, "L'Europe a besoin des imams algériens."

141. Houcine Maghar, interview with the author, Algiers, February 2014.

142. Mourad, "Mohamed Aïssa aux imams délégués en France."

143. Anonymous interview with French Foreign Ministry official, February 2014. The French, he noted, "know that the MARE identifies the candidates with sufficient advance time to begin on-the-job training. For several years we have been cooperating intensively before their departure."

144. Xavier Thirode and Bernard Godard (director of the Central Bureau of Religious Affairs, BCC), interview with the author, Paris, June 2013.

145. Bouabdellah Ghlamallah, interview with the author, Algiers, February 2014. He added: "There are, however, significant *losses*—a significant proportion of them simply stay in France." He knew of "at least twenty of our imams who obtained permanent residence in France."

146. Ministère des affaires religieuses et des Wakfs, "Charte de l'imam à l'étranger: Instructions et principes généraux" (Algiers: République algérienne démocratique et populaire, July 2012).

147. Some German Muslims have already made their way to the Université Abdel-Kader.

148. Mounir Tlili (minister of religious affairs), interview with the author, Tunis, May 2014.

149. The discussion with the French has been largely limited to imam training and not so much on Islam in public schools or theology faculties.

150. Guénois, "La France et l'Algérie s'accordent pour former les imams à la laïcité."

151. "Affaires religieuses: Rencontre nationale du conseil scientifique national (fetwa)," *Le Moudjahid*, February 9, 2015.

152. Mourad, "Mohamed Aïssa aux imams délégués en France."

153. Plasse, "Chems-Eddine Hafiz (CFCM): Une voix religieuse est nécessaire dans le plan anti-jihad."

154. Mourad, "Mohamed Aïssa aux imams délégués en France."

155. Chems-eddine Hafiz, "Communiqué sur les formation de l'institut Al-Ghazali de la Grande Mosquée de Paris," Institut Musulman de la Mosquée de Paris, September 15, 2020.

156. Mondher Belhadj Ali (director of the political bureau of the Nidaa Tounes Party), interview with the author, Tunis, May 2014.

157. Frégosi and Zéghal, *Religion et politique au Maghreb*, p. 24.

158. "Boosting of Religious Guidance of Tunisian Expatriates," *Agence Tunis Afrique Presse*, September 1, 2010.

159. Etzioni, *Security First*, p. 149.

160. Giannoni, "I musulmani italiani ospitano la prima visita del leader tunisino di al Nahdà."

161. "Ennahda en France: L'islamisme tranquille des Tunisiens de France/Une campagne française très efficace," *Le Monde*, December 22, 2011.

162. Moncef Marzouki (president of the republic), interview with the author, Carthage, May 20, 2014.

163. Munir Tlili (minister of religious affairs), interview with the author, Tunis, May 2014.

164. "Le Ministre des affaires religieuses propose la création du poste d'attaché religieux," May 9, 2017, in American Foreign Policy Council, *World Almanac of Islamism* (Lanham, MD: Rowman & Littlefield Publishers, 2019).

165. Ibid.

166. Hüseyin Avni Karsliogu, interview with the author, Berlin, January 2013.

167. Darmanin, "A l'Islam, nous devons imposer une concorde, afin de l'assimiler totalement à la République."

168. Ahmed Toufiq (Moroccan minister of Islamic affairs), interview with the author, Rabat, October 2012.

169. Bouabdellah Ghlamallah, interview with the author, Algiers, February 2014.

170. Ali Kizilkaya, interview with the author, Berlin, March 2013.

171. "AVRUPA," *Hürriyet Haber*, June 23, 2017.

172. Abdellatif Maazouz, interview with the author, Rabat, October 2012.

173. Lewis, *Islam and the West*, p. 42.

174. Ahmed Toufiq, interview with the author, Rabat, October 2012.

175. Unal Gundogan, interview with the author, Ankara, July 2011.

176. Guénois and Tremolet de Villers, "Jean-Pierre Chevènement, l'Islam de France."

177. "Al-Azhar Meets Marine Le Pen to 'Show True Islam,'" *Middle East Online*, May 29, 2015.

178. Julia Pascual, "Les organisations musulmanes de France proclament un 'manifeste citoyen,'" *Le Monde*, November 30, 2015.

179. Körting, "Djihadistische Radikalisierung und staatliche Gegenstrategien."

180. Sahinöz, "Vorbeter zwischen deutschen und türkischen Interessen."

181. American Foreign Policy Council, *The World Almanac of Islamism 2019*, p. 12.

182. Ibid.

183. Abdelilah, "Comment sont formés les imams de France."

184. Ibid.

185. Wilson, "Foreign Funded Islamic Extremism in the UK," p. 7.

186. Semiha Sözeri, Hulya Altinyelken, and Monique Volman, "Training Imams in the Netherlands: The Failure of a Post-Secular Endeavour," *British Journal of Religious Education* 41 (2018): 1–11, p. 7.

187. Guénois and Tremolet de Villers, "Jean-Pierre Chevènement, l'Islam de France."

188. Turkish officials, interview with the author, Ankara, July 2011.

189. Klausen, *The Islamic Challenge*.

190. In 2013, there were nearly 9,000 confessional schools—mostly Catholic but also Protestant and Jewish—and 98 percent of them received funding. The schools represented 14 percent of the educational system, and 20 percent of French secondary school students were enrolled in them. An unintended consequence of the headscarf ban was an increase, to 10 percent, in the percentage of students at Catholic schools who were young Muslim women who wore a veil.

191. Executif Musulman de Belgique, interview with the author, Brussels, September 2013.

192. Arkilic, "The Limits of European Islam."

193. Bundesministerium des Innern (BMI), "Islam an Schulen, Stand der Länder, Einrichtung islamische Religion als Regelfach, Stand Ausbau des islamischen Religionsunterrichts an deutschen Schulen," April 2015.

194. Wagtendonk, "Islamic Schools and Islamic Religious Education," p. 154; Arkilic, "The Limits of European Islam."

.19. "Bestandserhebung zur Ausbildung religiösen Personals islamischer Gemeinden," Deutsche Islam Konferenz, Bundesamt für Migration und Flüchtlinge, November 2020, p. 10.

196. Turkish embassy in western Europe, confidential interview with the author, November 2012.

197. Tim Röhn, "Wie Der Türkische Staat in Köln Weltpolitik Betreibt," TR (*timroehn.com*), June 21, 2017.

198. European ambassador to Morocco, interview with the author, Rabat, January 2011.

199. Omar Azziman, interview with the author, Rabat, January 2011.

200. Schult, "Spionage-Verdacht: Grünen-Politiker Beck Zeigt Imame an"; Schröder, "DİTİB Unter Spionage-Verdacht."

201. Vidino et al., *Fear Thy Neighbor*.

202. Omar Azziman, interview with the author, Rabat, January 2011.

203. European embassy official in Rabat, interview with the author, Rabat, October 2012.

204. Hakim el Ghissassi, interview with the author, Rabat, January 2011.

Chapter 9. Nation-State Islam versus the Islamic State

1. Ibrahim al-Badri (Abu Bakr al Baghdadi), "This Is What Allah and His Messenger Promised Us," *Rumiya* (Islamic State), Raqqa, November 11, 2016.

2. "Open Letter to Baghdadi," September 19, 2014, http://www.lettertobaghdadi.com/.

3. Ibid.

4. Inspector General of Religious Affairs, interview with the author, February 2014.

5. Northwestern University in Qatar, "Religious TV MENA Media Industry," http://www.mideastmedia.org/industry/2016/religious/.

6. Barro and McCleary, "Which Countries Have State Religions?"

7. Brown, "Official Islam in the Arab World."

8. Wiktorowicz, *The Management of Islamic Activism*; Stathis N. Kalyvas, "The 'Turkish Model' in the Matrix of Political Catholicism," in *Democracy, Islam, and Secularism in Turkey*,

ed. Ahmet T. Kuru and Alfred Stepan (New York: Columbia University Press, 2012); Jocelyne Césari, *What Is Political Islam?* (Boulder, CO: Lynne Riener Publishers, 2018); Bernard Lewis, *The Crisis of Islam: Holy War and Unholy Terror* (New York: Random House, 2003); Elie Kedourie, *Islam in the Modern World, and Other Studies* (London: Holt, Rinehart and Winston, 1980); Kuran, "The Provision of Public Goods under Islamic Law"; Feldman, *The Fall and Rise of the Islamic State.*

9. Hatina, "The Clerics' Betrayal?," pp. 250–51.

10. Kohn, "An Essay on Civilian Control of the Military," *American Diplomacy* (March 1997), http://americandiplomacy.web.unc.edu/1997/03/an-essay-on-civilian-control-of-the-military/.

11. Driessen, *Religion and Democratization*; Wainscott, *Bureaucratizing Islam.*

12. Eickelman and Piscatori, *Muslim Politics*, p. 5.

13. Hatina, "The Clerics' Betrayal?," p. 253.

14. Tepe, "Contesting Political Theologies of Islam and Democracy in Turkey," p. 175.

15. Berman, "Subsidized Sacrifice: State Support of Religion in Israel," p. 169.

16. Abootalebi, *Islam and Democracy.*

17. US Embassy and Consulates in Turkey, Public Library of US Diplomacy, "How Moderate Is Turkish Islam," Wikileaks, https://wikileaks.org/plusd/cables/05ANKARA6106_a.html.

18. "Turkey's Erdoğan Hails Push for İmam Hatip High Schools," *Hürriyet Daily News*, September 30, 2015.

19. Duran, "Understanding the AK Party's Identity Politics," p. 97.

20. Ankara, "Müftülere Nikâh Yetkisinin Fikir Babası Necmettin Erbakan."

21. Robinson, "Turkey's New Era of Restoration May Turn into Reparation."

22. Cagaptay and Jeffrey, "Turkey's 2014 Political Transition: From Erdoğan to Erdoğan?," p. 3.

23. Hamid, *Islamic Exceptionalism*, p. 159.

24. "Objections to the Islas Group Campaign against Dyane Chief Görmez," *Karar*, June 7, 2017.

25. Pacaci and Aktay, "75 Years of Religious Education in Modern Turkey," p. 406.

26. Arinc, "Devlet Protokolunde Sivillesme Donemi."

27. Mehmet Pacaci, interview with the author, Ankara, July 2011.

28. Korkmaz, "What Do People Want from Turkey's Top Religious Body?"

29. Tepe, "The Elusive Structure of State Secularism and Its Disguised Critics," p. 16.

30. "In Turkey, Erdoğan Fans an Islamic Nationalism to Build Ottoman-Style Influence," *Christian Science Monitor*, February 22, 2017.

31. Sunier, "The Turkish Directorate for Religious Affairs in a Changing Environment," p. 52.

32. "Turkey: 17,000 New Mosques Built under Erdogan," *ANSAMed*, February 19, 2013, http://www.ansamed.info/ansamed/en/news/sections/generalnews/2013/02/19/Turkey-17 -000-new-mosques-built-Erdogan_8274135.html.

33. In the early seventeenth century, the construction of six minarets on Sultanahmet in Istanbul provoked the Imam of Mecca to demand a seventh minaret at the Mosque of the Prophet in Mecca. Budge [pseud.], *The Eastern Question Solved: A Vision of the Future* (W. H. Allen, 1881), p. 8.

34. "Let There Remain No University without a Mosque," *OdaTV*, July 6, 2012 ; "Millî Eğitim Bakanliği Kurum Açma, Kapatma Ve Ad Verme Yönetmeliği," *Resmi Gazete*, June 24, 2017.

35. Turkone, "In the Education Arena the AK Party Flounders."

36. Edelman et al., *Turkey Transformed.*

37. Butler, "With More Islamic Schooling, Erdogan Aims to Reshape Turkey."

38. Ibid.

39. Solgun, "Wear Hats, Read Atatürk's Speech Instead of Koran."

40. Öztürk, "Turkey's Diyanet under AKP Rule?," p. 620.

41. "Yasaklanan Ayet Tekrar Hutbelerde," *Gazete Vatan*, December 17, 2011.

42. Öztürk, *AK Parti Döneminde AB Süreci*, p. 12.

43. "Turkey's Official Islamic Body Extends Influence Abroad," *Al-Monitor*, June 15, 2016.

44. DIB, "Hadis Arsivi," http://www.diyanet.gov.tr/turkish/hadis/; "'Reform of Religion' Claims Outright Lies, Bardakoglu Says," *Today's Zaman*, June 25, 2008.

45. Akyol, *Islam without Extremes*, p. 235.

46. Eteraz, "Not Quite the Reformation."

47. Tremblay, "Turkey's 'American Idol' of Qur'an Recitation Backfires."

48. Akyol, *Islam without Extremes*, p. 235.

49. "Mehmet Şevket Eygi Yazıları," *Milli Gazete*, April 22, 2012.

50. Mehmed Şevket Eygi, "Fazlur Rahman Toplantısı," *Milli Gazete*, June 20, 2017.

51. "Turkey's Declining Christian Population," *BBC News*, November 28, 2014.

52. Pinar, "Religion-State Relations in Turkey since the AKP."

53. Ibid., p. 514.

54. Ibid., p. 512.

55. "Diyanet: Bu Ilk Değil, Daha Önce De 14 Bin 'Mele' Aldık," *Gazete Vatan*, December 18, 2011.

56. "Government to Send 65 Alevi Dedes to Europe for Muharram," *Today's Zaman*, October 21, 2013; Kuru, *Secularism and State Policies toward Religion*, p. 36.

57. Lule, "Cemevis, ECtHR."

58. "Turkey's Erdoğan Hails Push for İmam Hatip High Schools," *Hürriyet Daily News*, September 30, 2015; "Christmas, New Year Is Pagan and Capitalist, Says Turkey's Top Cleric—Religion," *Hürriyet Daily News*, December 26, 2012.

59. "Erdoğan to Muslims: Don't Lock Women Up," *Hürriyet Daily News*, November 2, 2016.

60. Aykol, *Islam without Extremes*, p. 233.

61. "Turkish President Erdoğan Urges Women, Children to Go to Mosques—Ankara," *Hürriyet Daily News*, October 4, 2018.

62. Tepe, "The Elusive Structure of State Secularism and Its Disguised Critics," p. 16.

63. Aykol, *Islam without Extremes*, p. 203.

64. Almeida, "In Conversation with Fethullah Gülen."

65. Cemal Usak, interview with the author, Istanbul, January 2013 .

66. Prime Minister Erdoğan's post-election address, Ankara, March 30–31, 2014.

67. Carlotta Gall, "Turkey Jails Hundreds for Life over 2016 Coup," *New York Times*, November 26, 2020.

68. Keller, Mykhyalyshyn, and Timur, "The Scale of Turkey's Purge Is Nearly Unprecedented."

69. Albayrak, "The Directorate's Job Just Got a Lot Harder."

70. Ozturk, "Commentary: Two Important Developments in the Fight against FETO."

71. "FETÖ örgütlü bir din istismarı hareketidir," *Telgraf*, June 26, 2017, https://www.telgraf.net/haber/feto-orgutlu-bir-din-istismari-hareketidir-haberi-65332.html.

72. "Gülen Movement Is Fake Mahdi, Says Turkey's Religious Directorate Head," *Hürriyet Daily News*, August 24, 2016.

73. Diyanet official, interview with the author, Ankara, May 2013.

74. Maritato, "Turkish Marriages between Religion and the State."

75. Korkmaz, "What Do People Want from Turkey's Top Religious Body?"

76. Alpay, "Turkey's Big Business Opts for Consolidation of Democracy."

77. Kuru, "Policy Briefing: Muslim Politics without an 'Islamic State,'" p. 6.

78. Ibrahim Kalin, interview with the author, Ankara, July 2011.

79. Fabbe, "Historical Legacies, Modern Conflicts."

80. Uluc, "Does Habermas Shed Light on Islam in Turkey?," p. 49.

81. "Religious Affairs Director Addresses Turkish Union of Religious Affairs' Meeting," *Anatolia News Agency*, November 27, 2004.

82. "Görmez Says Diyanet Should Be Independent," *Bugun*, July 24, 2013.

83. Ibrahim Kalin, interview with the author, Ankara, March 2013.

84. Sarkissian, *The Varieties of Religious Repression*, p. 122.

85. "Diyanet Özerk Olmalı Mı, Olmamalı Mı?" *Habertürk*, December 8, 2011.

86. Sönmez, "Radicalisation, Violent Extremism, and Turkey's Fight," p. 27.

87. "Objections to Ihlas Group Campaign against Diyanet Chief Görmez," *Karar*, June 7, 2017. "No one could predict where things will stop once the reordering of the republic starts from the Diyanet," said one commentator. "We are Islamists, and our history is of opposition to regimes," said another.

88. Tepe, "The Elusive Structure of State Secularism and Its Disguised Critics," p. 8.

89. Akyol, *Islam without Extremes*, p. 225.

90. Fatih Altayli, "You Might Sow Barley but Get Sunflower Instead" [in Turkish], *Haberturk*, March 6, 2012.

91. Ahmed Toufiq, interview with the author, Rabat, January 2011.

92. *Le Matin du Sahara et du Maghreb* (Casablanca), August 11, 2002.

93. Slimani, "La Bataille du livre."

94. Radu, *Dilemmas of Democracy and Dictatorship*, p. 15.

95. Hakim el Ghissassi, interview with the author, Rabat, January 2011.

96. Omar Zniber (Moroccan ambassador to Germany), interview with the author, Berlin, November 2012.

97. *ABC News*, September 6, 2012.

98. El Ghissassi, *Regard sur le Maroc de Mohammed VI*, p. 61.

99. Ibid., p. 72.

100. Kacem, *L'Esprit du Nihilisme*, p. 118.

101. "Entretien avec Ahmed Toufiq, Ministre des Habous et des Affaires Islamiques," *Le Matin*, August 27, 2013.

102. Ahmed Toufiq, "Une Forte participation marocaine," *Le Matin*, July 6, 2011, https://lematin.ma/journal/Conference-internationale--des-oulemas-a-Dakar_Une-forte-participation-marocaine/152112.html.

103. "Government Resolves to Foil Any Attempt against 'Unity of Rite,'" *Maroc Agence Presse*, August 27, 2002.

104. Hakim el Ghissassi, "Une interview de S. M. le Roi à La Médina," *La Médina*, July 11, 2002.

105. Zerouky, "Moroccan Offensive against the 'Islamist' Book and Cassette Business Continues."

106. Ambassador Bensalah Alaoui Assia, interview with the author, Rabat, October 2012.

107. Hakim el Ghissassi, interview with the author, Rabat, 11 January 2011.

108. Ibid.

109. "Marruecos Aprueba un plan para preservar el Islam de 'Malas Interpretaciones,'" *Lainformacion*, February 16, 2016.

110. Minister Ahmed Toufiq, interview with the author, October 2012.

111. "Projet du budget sectoriel du Ministère des Habous et des Affaires Islamiques," Ministry of Endowments and Islamic Affairs website, December 2015, p. 2.

112. "Mr. Ahmed Toufiq présente le budget sectoriel 2018 du Ministère des Habous et des Affaires Islamiques à la Chambre Des Représentants," Ministry of Endowments and Islamic Affairs website, November 17, 2017.

113. Spiegel, *Young Islam*, pp. 136–37.

114. Hakim el Ghissassi, interview with the author, Rabat, July 11, 2019.

115. Youness Meskine, editorial, *Akhbar al-Youm al-Maghrebiya* [in Arabic], December 21, 2017.

116. Hakim el Ghissassi, interview with the author, January 11, 2011.

117. Ministère des Habous et des Affaires Islamiques, "L'État dépense en moyenne 500MDH pour rémunérer les imams," November 4, 2011.

118. Adviser to the minister of Habous and Islamic Affairs, interview with the author, Rabat, July 2018.

119. "Mr. Ahmed Toufiq présente le budget sectoriel 2018 du Ministère des Habous et des Affaires Islamiques à la Chambre des Représentants." Ministry of Endowments and Islamic Affairs website, November 17, 2017.

120. Wainscott, "Defending Islamic Education."

121. *Le Guide du ministère des habous et des affaires religieuses* (2013), p. 17.

122. Tozy, "L'Islam entre le contrôle de l'état et les débordeents de la société civile," pp. 17, 19.

123. "La Formation des imams étrangers au Maroc jugée 'inadaptée' par des sénateurs français," *Telquel*, July 8, 2016.

124. Spiegel, *Young Islam*, pp. 136–37.

125. "M. Toufiq appelle les Imams-encadrants à promouvoir l'attachement aux constantes religieuses et nationales," January 13, 2010, http://www.habous.net/fr/component/content/article/20-M.le%20ministre/691-13-janvier-2010-m-toufiq-appelle-les-imams-encadrants-a-promouvoir-l-attachement-aux-constantes-religieuses-et-nationales.html.

126. Ruiz Sevilla, "Marruecos entrega 27 motocicletas a imanes para predicar en El Sur."

127. Suzor, "Entretien avec Ahmed Taoufiq."

128. Sevilla, "Marruecos entrega 27 motocicletas a imanes para predicar en El Sur."

129. Ministère Des Habous Et Des Affaires Islamiques, "Dar El Hadith El Hassania," December 9, 2015.

130. "Marruecos Aprueba Un Plan para preservar el Islam de 'Malas Interpretaciones,'" *Lainformacion*, February 16, 2016.

131. "Discours de SM le Roi à l'occasion de la Fête Du Trône," *Maroc*, July 30, 2013.

132. Abdellatif and Jouhari, "Interview with Islamic Scholar Dr. Driss Kettan."

133. "Islamic Affairs Ministry Says No One Entitled to Issue Fatwas at Will," *Maroc Agence Presse*, October 10, 2001.

134. Tozy, "L'Islam entre le contrôle de l'état et les débordements de la société civile," p. 7.

135. "Le Maroc a ses mourchidates," *L'Economiste*, May 5, 2006.

136. Ahmed Toufiq, interview with the author, Rabat, October 2012.

137. "Tension between Islamists, Morocco over Ban on Extended Worship," *Al- 'Arabi al-Jadid*, May 28, 2019.

138. Ahmed Toufiq, interview with the author, Rabat, October 2012.

139. Zerouky, "Moroccan Offensive against the 'Islamist' Book and Cassette Business Continues."

140. "Minister Says Moroccan Government to Eradicate Inappropriate Prayer Spaces," *Maroc Agence Presse*, June 13, 2006.

141. "Alger Veut Encadrer l'Islam, Tout Comme Rabat," *RFI*, September 2008.

142. Belhaj, *La Dimension islamique dans la politique étrangère du Maroc Déterminants, acteurs, orientations*, p. 103.

143. "Maroc: Les délicates relations entre le ministère des habous et les imams (partie 2)," *Yabiladi*, April 19, 2015, https://www.yabiladi.com/articles/details/34909/maroc-delicates-relations-entre-ministere.html.

144. "Centri islamici fai-da-te a rischio," *Il Giornale* (January 2011).

145. Spiegel, *Young Islam*, p. 139.

146. "Les Habous et affaires islamiques: Grand retard dans la réouverture des mosquées fermées," *La Nouvelle Tribune*, May 10, 2012.

147. Youness Meskine, editorial, *Akhbar al-Youm al-Maghrebiya* [in Arabic], December 21, 2017.

148. Ahmed Toufiq, interview with the author, Rabat, October 2012.

149. Malka, "The Struggle for Religious Identity in Tunisia and the Maghreb," p. 7.

150. Ibid.

151. Bouaziz, "Marruecos mantiene a raya a los salafistas cuando atacan a los laicos."

152. "Un Imam interdit de prêche à cause de Mawazine," *Forum Marocain—Bladi.net*, June 17, 2013.

153. El Ghissassi, *Regard sur le Maroc de Mohammed VI*, p. 151.

154. Ibid., p. 180.

155. Spiegel, *Young Islam*, p. 139.

156. Louassini, "Alta tensione in Marocco."

157. "Reconstitution de la prière du vendredi à al Hoceima," *Discovery Morocco*, May 29, 2017.

158. Cembrero, "How Rabat Sought to Decapitate Rif Rebellion."

159. Ibid.

160. Iraqi, "The Controversy, for Lack of Debate."

161. "Pourquoi le PAM en veut à Ahmed Taoufik," *Maghreb Intelligence*, November 1, 2012.

162. Ahmed Toufiq, interview with the author, Rabat, October 2012.

163. Tozy, "L'Islam entre le contrôle de l'état et les débordements de la société civile."

164. Masbah, "Salafi Movements and the Political Process in Morocco," p. 88.

165. Malka, "The Struggle for Religious Identity in Tunisia and the Maghreb," p. 7.

166. Masbah, "Salafi Movements and the Political Process in Morocco," p. 86.

167. Ibid., p. 89.

168. Ibid., p. 93.

169. Adviser to the interior minister, confidential interview with the author, Casablanca, January 2011.

170. Spiegel, *Young Islam*, p. 117.

171. "Maroc: Un an de prison fermé pour une caricature portant atteinte 'à la Sacralité du Roi,'" *Oumma*, February 7, 2017.

172. Benchemsi, "Invisible Atheists."

173. Achehbar, "Médias publics: Propagande religieuse?"

174. Spiegel, *Young Islam*, p. 120.

175. Ibid., p. 119.

176. Masbah, "Moroccan Fighters in Syria."

177. Hamouda, "Entretien avec Ahmed Toufiq, ministre des habous et des affaires islamiques," Ministry of Endowments and Islamic Affairs website, August 27, 2013.

178. "Mohammed VI prohíbe a religiosos musulmanes actividades o posturas políticas," *Wanafrica*, July 4, 2014.

179. Ahmed Toufiq, interview with the author, Rabat, October 2012.

180. Anonymous, interview with the author, Algiers, February 2014.

181. Driessen, "Public Religion, Democracy, and Islam," p. 180.

182. Ibid., p. 196.

183. Press release, Ministry of Religious Affairs website, January 5, 2014.

184. "Religion: Mohamed Aissa met en garde contre les "pseudo-cheikhs," *Radio Algérienne*, December 5, 2014.

185. "Alger veut encadrer l'islam, tout comme Rabat," *RFI*, September 29, 2008.

186. Mohammed Aïssa (MARE inspector general), interview with the author, Algiers, February 2014.

187. Driessen, "Public Religion, Democracy, and Islam," p. 196.

188. Mellal, "Ce qui va changer dans les mosquées algériennes."

189. MARE official, interview with the author, Algiers, February 2014.

190. Midouni and Bounab, "Les Affaires Religieuses mettent en garde contre les avis théologiques importés."

191. Rahmani, "Les Imams étrangers 'pourraient ne pas servir le citoyen algérien.'"

192. "Algérie: Le Ministre des Affaires Religieuses interdit la prière dans les endroits publics," *Terredisrael*, December 16, 2010.

193. Benhamed, "Ministère des Affaires Religieuses et du Wakf: Bientôt un nouveau siège."

194. Driessen, "Public Religion, Democracy, and Islam," p. 187.

195. "Mohamed Aissa: 'Les Mosquées Sont Immunisées Contre Les Idéologies Extrémistes,'" *El Moudjahid*, September 15, 2014; MARE official, interview with the author, Algiers, February 2014.

196. M.C.L., "Les Sectes salafistes infiltrent les campus," *Liberté* (Algiers), May 13, 2013, https://www.liberte-algerie.com/actualite/les-sectes-salafistes-infiltrent-les-campus-189728.

197. Bouabdellah Ghlamallah (MARE minister), interview with the author, Algiers, February 2014.

198. Mohammed Aïssa, interview with the author, Algiers, February 2014.

199. Senior mosque inspector, interview with the author, Algiers, February 2014.

200. "Les Deux révolutions de Mohamed Aissa," *L'Expression*, February 12, 2015.

201. The project has given rise to a small Chinese village of 17,000 employees building the complex.

202. "Mascara: Une grande mosquée en chantier," *El Watan*, February 2, 2013.

203. "L'Année Wakf 2013 lancée à Annaba par le Ministre des Affaires Religieuses," *Djazairess*, April 25, 2013.

204. Regional director of religious affairs, interview with the author, Oran, February 2014.

205. Regional director of religious affairs, interview with the author, Oran, February 2014.

206. "Algerian Religious Affairs Minister Says Preachers under Constant Scrutiny," *BBC Monitoring*, September 23, 2007.

207. Bouabdellah Ghlamallah, interview with the author, Algiers, February 2014.

208. MARE official, interview with the author, Algiers, February 2014.

209. "La Carte nationale des mosquées réalisée à 80% (ministre)," *Algérie 360°*, January 16, 2014.

210. Bouabdellah Ghlamallah, interview with the author, Algiers, February 2014.

211. Mohamed Aïssa, interview with the author, Algiers, February 2014.

212. Chekar, "Nationale—Bouabdallah Ghlamallah se dérobe."

213. "Foreign Clerics Said Infiltrating Algerian Mosques," *BBC Monitoring*, October 25, 2006.

214. "Plus de 2,000 personnes seront recrutées en 2013," *Le Temps D'Algérie*, February 5, 2013.

215. "Mohamed Aissa: "Les Mosquées sont immunisées contre les idéologies extrémistes,"" *El Moudjahid*, September 15, 2014.

216. Ministry of Education, "Loi d'orientation sur l'éducation nationale" (official bulletin), January 23, 2008.

217. Mohammed Aïssa, interview with the author, Algiers, February 2014.

218. Mohammed Aïssa, interview with the author, Algiers, February 2014.

219. "Le jeune athlète Islam Khoualed regagnera Aujourd'hui l'Algérie," *Liberté*, January 8, 2014.

220. Bouabdellah Ghlamallah, interview with the author, Algiers, February 2014.

221. "Une Grande évolution dans l'enseignement Coranique en Algérie," *Agence Internationale de Presse Coranique. Algérie Presse Service*, February 11, 2013.

222. Ibid.

223. Regional director of religious affairs, interview with the author, Oran, February 2014.

224. Ministry of Religious affairs official, interview with the author, Algiers, February 2014.

225. "Algeria to Redefine Role of Mosques." *Africa News*, January 11 2013.

226. Taoufiq Teboun (director of Dar al Imam since 2004), interview with the author, Mohammedia, Algiers, February 2014.

227. Ministry of Religious affairs official, interview with the author, Algiers, February 2014.

228. "Les Portes du recrutement et de la promotion 'grand ouvertes' à l'élément féminin," *Le Temps D'Algérie*, March 10, 2013.

229. "Les Mourchidate appelées à oeuvrer à la préservation de la cohésion de la société (ministre)," *Djazairess*, March 25, 2013.

230. Ministry of Religious affairs official, interview with the author, Algiers, February 2014.

231. Ibid.

232. US Department of State, Office of International Religious Freedom, "Algeria," in *2010 Report on Religious Freedom*, November 17, 2010, p. 7.

233. MARE official, interview with the author, Algiers, February 2014.

234. US Department of State, Office of International Religious Freedom, "Algeria," in *2010 Report on Religious Freedom*, November 17, 2010, p. 7.

235. Ministry of Religious affairs official, interview with the author, Algiers, February 2014.

236. "Alger veut encadrer l'islam, tout comme Rabat," *RFI*, September 29, 2008.

237. "Algerian Religious Affairs Minister Says Preachers under Constant Scrutiny," *BBC Monitoring*, September 23, 2007.

238. Driessen, "Public Religion, Democracy, and Islam," p. 24.

239. Mohamed Aïssa, interview with the author, Algier, February 2014.

240. Mohamed Aïssa, interview with the author, Algier, February 2014.

241. Michael D. Driessen, correspondence with the author, January 2014.

242. Mohamed Aïssa, interview with the author, Algier, February 2014.

243. "Mes Vérités . . . ," *L'Expression*, July 22, 2014.

244. "Algerian Minister Says Mosques 'Liberated from Salafi Current," *BBC Monitoring*, May 22, 2013.

245. "Alger veut encadrer l'islam, Tout comme Rabat," *RFI*, September 29, 2008.

246. Makedhi, "Conflit de Ghardaïa et référence religieuse nationale."

247. Article 4, M-culture.gov.dz, August 23, 2003: law no. 12–05, January 2012; executive decree no. 03–278, August 23, 2003; and executive decree no. 17–08, January 4, 2017.

248. "Wave of New State Bills: Religious Freedom or License to Discriminate?" *al Jazeera America*, March 7, 2007.

249. Leila Kaddour-Boudadi, "Algérie: Les fatwas expliquées aux musulmans," *Afrik*, August 24, 2010.

250. Amir Hani, "Liberté de culte en Algérie: Mohamed Aissa réagit au rapport américain," *DIA Journal*, August 13, 2016.

251. Ibid.

252. Madjid Makedhi,"Mohamed Aïssa alerte sur les dangers du salafisme: Conflit de ghardaïa et référence religieuse nationale," *El Watan*, July 16, 2015.

253. Ramzi, "Algeria: Public Breakfast Sparks Controversy in Algeria."

254. Bouabdellah Ghlamallah, interview with the author, Algiers, February 2014.

255. Ibid.

256. Ibid.

257. "Les Mosquées 'réquisitionnées' par le régime," *AnalyseDZ*, March 25, 2012.

258. "Le Ministre des Affaires Religieuses hier à Alger," *El Watan*, February 12, 2015.

259. "All Regions Have a Bond of Solidarity with Zawiyas," *El Moujahid*, January 16, 2014.

260. "Ghoulemallah refuse la 'polémique,'" *Le Soir D'Algérie*, April 23, 2013.

261. Boukhalfa, "Les Réponses de Mohamed Aïssa."

262. [The former minister], "M. Ghlamallah: La mission de la fatwa incombe aux conseils scientifiques de wilaya," *Lemag* March 4, 2009, http://www.lemag.ma/algerie-le-ministre-des-affaires-religieuses-interdit-la-priere-dans-les-endroits-publics_a50757.html.

263. Bouabdellah Ghlamallah, interview with the author, Algiers, February 2014.

264. "Tunisia Coalition Agrees Top Government Posts," *BBC News*, November 21, 2011.

265. Hajjaj, "Hardline Currents Are Part of an All-out Crisis in the Arab World," p. 9.

266. Hafiz, "Ennahda's Religious Policies Split Tunisia's Ruling Party."

267. Faridah al'Abidi (member of the National Constituent Assembly), interview with the author, Istanbul, May 16, 2014.

268. Sahbi Atig (president of the Ennahda faction), interview with the author, Tunis, May 2014.

269. Malka, "The Struggle for Religious Identity in Tunisia and the Maghreb," p. 8.

270. "Top Tunisia Imam Calls Eid Strike," *Africa News Hub*, October 1, 2013.

271. Mondher Belhadj Ali (director of Political Bureau), interview with the author, Tunis, May 2014.

272. Moncef Marzouki (president of Tunisia), interview with the author, Tunis, May 2014.

273. Sahbi Atig, interview with the author, Tunis, May 2014.

274. Slama, "Government Seeks to Regain Control of Conservative Mosques as Ramadan Nears."

275. Yadh Ben Achour, interview with the author, Tunis, January 2015.

276. Munir Tlili (minister of religious affairs), interview with the author, Tunis, May 2014.

277. Sana Sbouai, "Grève des imams: La neutralité et l'indépendance des mosquées comme véritable enjeu," *Nawaat*, June 17, 2013, https://nawaat.org/2013/06/17/greve-des-imams-la-neutralite-et-lindependance-des-mosquees-comme-veritable-enjeu/.

278. "Tunisian Ministry Reasserts Control over 1,000 Mosques," *al Jazirah Satellite Channel Television*, May 21, 2013.

279. Hajjaj, "Hardline Currents Are Part of an All-out Crisis in the Arab World," p. 9.

280. "Tunisian Ministry Reasserts Control over 1,000 Mosques."

281. Hafiz, "Ennahda's Religious Policies Split Tunisia's Ruling Party."

282. Munir Tlili, interview with the author, Tunis, May 2014.

283. "Ministère des Affaires Religieuses Tunisie," *Huffington Post Maghreb*, May 9, 2017.

284. A. Chennoufi, "Laroussi Mizouri: Les Enseignantes religieuses passent de 3 en 1999 à 400 actuellement," *L'Expression*, March 16, 2011.

285. "ARP: Adoption du budget," *Directinfo*, November 30, 2016.

286. "ARP: Approbation du budget du MIN des Affaires Religieuses," *Mosaïque FM*, November 28, 2017.

287. "62 Recovered and 90 Mosques Still Out of Control," *Express FM*, May 3, 2014.

288. Munir Tlili, interview with the author, Tunis, May 2014; Hamdi Tlili, "187 Mosquées hors de contrôle," *France 24*, June 13, 2015.

289. Munir Tlili, interview with the author, Tunis, May 2014.

290. Chikhaoui, "Sidi Bouzid Governor Announces the Closure of Seven Local Mosques."

291. "Ministre des Affaires Religieuses Tunisie," *Huffington Post Maghreb*, May 9, 2017.

292. Ibid.

293. A. Chennoufi, "Laroussi Mizouri: Les enseignantes religieuses passent de 3 en 1999 à 400 actuellement," *L'Expression*, March 16, 2011.

294. Munir Tlili, interview with the author, Tunis, May 2014.

295. "Radwan Masmoudi à la conquête de la formation des imams," *Africa Intelligence*, June 21, 2018; "Formation des imams par le CSID," *Kapitalis*, July 1, 2020.

296. Ibid.

297. "Tunisian Exception," *al-Araby al Jadeed*, July 13, 2016.

298. Muf Hamda Saied (Mufti of the Republic), interview with the author, Tunis, May 2014.

299. Fatima, "Rabat, 04 Juin 2012: Travaux de la 2ème réunion de la Commission Mixte Maroco-Tunisienne des affaires religieuses," p. 2.

300. "Mounir Tlili: Promouvoir un discours religieux modéré et rationnel," *Directinfo*, May 4, 2014.

301. International Crisis Group, "Tunisia: Violence and the Salafi Challenge," February 13, 2013.

302. George Packer, "Exporting Jihad," *New Yorker*, March 28, 2016, p. 43.

303. Moncef Marzouki, interview with the author, Carthage, May 2014.

304. "Ennahda's Religious Policies Split Tunisia's Ruling Party," *Huffington Post*, September 4, 2013.

305. "Tunisian Government Allegedly Fires Preacher for Publicly Criticizing Ennahdha Movement," *Tunisia LIVE*, August 2, 2013.

306. Moncef Marzouki, interview with the author, Carthage, May 2014.

307. Munir Tlili, interview with the author, Tunis, May 2014.

308. Packer, "Exporting Jihad."

309. "Affaire de la Mosquée Zitouna: Ennahda 'emmêle les pinceaux," *African Manager*, July 21, 2013.

310. "Tunisie: Les prières dans la rue interdites," *Le Figaro*, April 7, 2011.

311. "Mounir Tlili: La régulation des discours des prédicateurs avant les prochaines élections," *Mosaique*, May 3, 2014.

312. La Rédaction, "Tunisie: Fermeture de mosquées et de médias suspectés de radicalisme," *SaphirNews*, July 22, 2014.

313. "Tunisia Security Forces Warn of Returning Jihadis," *Daily Mail*, December 25, 2016.

314. Vivienne Walt, "After Protests, Tunisia's Salafists Plot a More Radical Revolution," *Time*, September 21, 2012.

315. Ibid.

316. Boukhayatia, "C'est la société tunisienne qui a enfanté Daech."

317. Hafiz, "Ennahda's Religious Policies Split Tunisia's Ruling Party."

318. Dettmer, "Tunisia Moves to Rein in Islamic Hardliners."

319. "Al Qaeda Threatens Tunisia Government," *Africa News Hub*, May 23, 2013.

320. Nasri, "Mosques without Imams in Tunisia."

321. "Relations with Saudi Arabia Are Based on Harmony and Co-operation" (press release), *TAP*, November 3, 2016.

322. Adhoum, "I Support the School of Kairouan and Independent Reasoning in Religious Thinking."

323. "Tunisia: Maghreb Mouled Conference Opens in Kairouan," *Africa News Hub*, March 4, 2009.

324. Moncef Marzouki, interview with the author, Carthage, May 2014.

325. "Tunisie: Accord de la coalition au pouvoir sur le futur régime politique," *Le Monde*, October 13, 2012.

326. Stepan and Linz, "Democratization Theory and the Arab Spring," p. 18.

327. Munir Tlili, interview with the author, Tunis, May 2014.

328. Boukhayatia, "Entretien avec Hédi Yahmed."

329. Tlili, "187 Mosquées hors de contrôle."

330. "Imams Arrested on Suspicion of Aiding Terrorism," *Tunisia Live*, September 7, 2016.

331. "20 mosquées hors contrôle de l'état ont été fermées," *Business News Tunisia*, July 22, 2014.

332. Michael Brenner, "Government Accused of Firing Sheikh for Criticizing Ennahda," *Tunisialive*, August 2, 2013, http://www.tunisia-live.net/2013/08/02/government-accused-of -firing-sheikh-for-political-reasons/.

333. Nasri, "Mosques without Imams in Tunisia."

334. Mufti Hamda Saied, interview with the author, Tunis, May 2014.

335. Center for Insights in Survey Research, "Public Opinion Survey of Tunisia: April 19–April 26, 2017," pp. 27, 40, 53, 63.

336. "Tunisian Ministry Reasserts Control over 1,000 Mosques," *al Jazirah Satellite Channel Television*, May 21, 2013.

337. Essid, "Tunisia under the Yoke of Sinister Saudi Arabia."

338. "Growing Debate Centers on Tunisia's Islamist Party," *Voice of America*, March 2, 2011.

339. "Top Tunisia Imam Calls Eid Strike," *Africa News Hub*, October 1, 2013.

340. Malka, "The Struggle for Religious Identity in Tunisia and the Maghreb," p. 8.

341. Mufti Hamda Saied, interview with the author, Tunis, May 2014.

342. "Le Mufti de la république tunisienne accuse Bourguiba," *Businessnews.com*, October 2013.

343. "Two Imams Arrested on Suspicion of Aiding Terrorism," *Tunisia Live*, September 7, 2016.

344. Bax and Cohen, "Interview with Rachid Ghannouchi: 'If You Sow Dictatorship, You Harvest Terrorism.'"

345. "Khadmi promet le contrôle total de l'ensemble des mosquées avant fin 2013," *Tunisie14. tn*, May 23, 2013.

346. Marzouk, "Government Seeks Niqab Ban and Central Control of Mosques."

347. Boukhayatia, "C'est la société tunisienne qui a enfanté Daech."

348. Moncef Marzouki, interview with the author, Carthage, May 2014.

349. Ibid.

350. "Tunisia Attacks: Militants Jailed over 2015 Terror," *BBC News*, February 9, 2019.

351. "Berlin Lorry Attack: What We Know," *BBC News*, December 24, 2016.

352. Mansoor Moaddel, *Clash of Values in the Middle East and North Africa: Islamic Fundamentalism versus Liberal Nationalism: A Study of People and Their Issues* (New York: Columbia University Press, 2020), p. 199.

353. International Republican Institute, "Survey of Tunisian Public Opinion: June 22–July 1, 2014," p. 31.

354. Driessen, "Sources of Muslim Democracy."

355. Mark Tessler, Amaney Jamal, et al., "Arab Barometer: Public Opinion Survey Conducted in Algeria, Egypt, Iraq, Jordan, Kuwait, Lebanon, Libya, Morocco, Palestine, Sudan, Tunisia, and Yemen, 2012–2014" (Ann Arbor, MI: Inter-university Consortium for Political and Social Research [distributor], November 13, 2015), https://doi.org/10.3886/ICPSR36273.v1.

356. Ibid.

357. Konda Institute, "Turks Losing Trust in Religion under AKP."

358. Elischer, "How Jihadism Ends," p. 26.

359. Ibid.

Chapter 10. Out of Office: Rejoining Civil Society

1. Rizvi, "Agency of History."

2. Destremau and Moncelon, *Louis Massignon*, p. 219.

3. Khoury, "Robert de Paix et Louis Massignon."

4. Rizvi, "Agency of History."

5. Trofimov, *The Siege of Mecca*, p. 22.

6. Césari, *The Awakening of Muslim Democracy*.

7. General Secretariat of the Custodian of the Two Holy Mosques, "King Fahd Glorious Quran Printing Complex Develops Technical Services for Muslims Worldwide" (program for Hajj and Umrah).

8. "Saudi Grand Mufti Says Suicide Bombers Will Go to Hell," *Alalam News Network*, December 13, 2013.

9. Smith, "US Deployment Expected to Exceed 500,000."

10. Gerges, *ISIS: A History*, p. 271.

11. Ibid., p. 281.

12. Roy, *Jihad and Death*, p. 85.

13. Gerges, *ISIS: A History*.

14. Riedel, "The Man Who Would Be Caliph Makes a Subversive Video Debut."

15. Roy, *Jihad and Death*, p. 81.

16. Bin Laden, "The Sovereignty of the Best Ummah Lays in the Uprising of the People of the Two Holy Mosques, Episode Two."

17. Shadi Hamid and William McCants, *Rethinking Political Islam* (Oxford: Oxford University Press, 2017), p. 15.

18. Malise Ruthven, "The Map ISIS Hates," *New York Review of Books*, June 25, 2014, https://www.nybooks.com/daily/2014/06/25/map-isis-hates/.

19. Wood, "What ISIS Really Wants."

20. McCants, "The Believer: How Abu Bakr Al-Baghdadi Became Leader of the Islamic State."

21. Roy, *Jihad and Death*, p. 82.

22. Riedel, "The Man Who Would Be Caliph Makes a Subversive Video Debut"; Weidner, "History of the Caliphate: We Are All Caliphs!"

23. "Islamic State Leader Abu Bakr al-Baghdadi Encourages Emigration, Worldwide Action," SITE Intelligence Group, July 1, 2014.

24. Byman, "What Comes after ISIS?"

25. *Al-Taqrir*, July 4, 2014 (Arabic-language website now inaccessible).

26. Trofimov, *The Siege of Mecca*, p. 33.

27. Machari Al-Dhaidi, "They Are Fighting Saudi Arabia," *Middle East* [in Arabic], July 9, 2014.

28. MuslimStatistics, "92% Agree That Islamic State (ISIS) Conforms to the Values of Islam and Islamic Law," August 2014.

29. "Saudi Arabia Deploys 30,000 Soldiers to Border with Iraq: Al-Arabiya TV," *Reuters*, July 3, 2014.

30. Hamid and Mandaville, *The Geopolitics of Soft Power*.

31. Yildirim, "Religious Authority and US Foreign Policy in the Middle East."

32. "Erdoğan Islamizes Education System to Raise 'Devout Youth,'" *Al-Monitor*, December 26, 2014.

33. "Prof. Dr. Mehmet Görmez: Çarpıtılmış Fetvalarla Diyanet'e Saldırıyorlar," *Star: Milli Iradenin Sesi*, February 3, 2016.

34. Bozkurt, "Turkey's Maarif Exports Erdoğan's Ideology to Balkans."

35. Ozkan, "Turkey, Davutoğlu, and the Idea of Pan-Islamism," p. 126.

36. Ibid.

37. Öktem, "Projecting Power: Non-Conventional Policy Actors in Turkey's International System," p. 78.

38. Reynolds, "The Key to the Future Lies in the Past."

39. Öktem, "Projecting Power," p. 87.

40. Ünal, "Yunus Emre Institute Head Ateş: As an Element of Soft Power, Our Aim Is to Introduce Turkey, Its Culture to the World."

41. Öktem, "New Islamic Actors after the Wahhabi Intermezzo."

42. Recep Tayyip Erdoğan, foreword to "Yurtdisindaki Tükler: 50. Yilinda Göç ve Uyum," Ankara, May 21–23, 2009, pp. 15, 16.

43. Bahar, "Turkey's Diaspora Engagement Policy under the Justice and Development Party"; Kemal, *Turkey's New Horizon: Turks Abroad and Related Communities*.

44. Gursel, "Erdoğan Islamizes Education System to Raise 'Devout Youth.'"

45. "Religious Affairs President Bardakoglu: 'In My Opinion, Article 24 of the Constitution Is Still Valid and Will Continue to be Valid,'" *Anatolia*, October 2, 2007.

46. "Turkish Foreign Minister Pledges Strong Support for Macedonia," *Anadolu Agency*, December 21, 2012.

47. Ibrayev, "Turkish Gambit in Kyrgyzstan."

48. "Turkey: Director of Religious Affairs Visit to Cameroon," *BBC*, December 12, 2012.

49. "Erdoğan's Ottoman Dream Causes Storm in Red Sea," *Al-Monitor*, January 5, 2018.

50. Yan, "China Blasts Nomination of Rabiya Kadir as Nobel Peace Prize Candidate."

51. Duran, "Understanding the AK Party's Identity Politics," p. 94.

52. Celebi, "Turkish President Says Tunisia Second Model to Region."

53. Akgün and Gündogan, *Ortadogu'da Turkiye Algisi 2011*.

54. "Mali'de Eyüp Sultan Camii Açıldı," *Anadolu Ajansı*, December 6, 2013.

55. "Beblawy Slams Erdoğan's Remarks on Al-Azhar Sheikh," *Egypt Independent*, August 27, 2013.

56. Duran, "Understanding the AK Party's Identity Politics," p. 94.

57. Dilek, "Muslim Brotherhood Fully Supports Erdoğan, Al-Qaradawi Says."

58. "Qaradawi: Thanks to Turkey and to President Erdogan," International Union for Muslim Scholars, April 23, 2016.

59. Adnan Zeki Bıyık, "Ey Suud Yönetimi! Peygamberimiz görse size . . . ," *Radikal*, May 19, 2014, http://www.radikal.com.tr/turkiye/ey_suud_yonetimi_peygamberimiz_gorse_sizi _arabistandan_surerdi-1192889.

60. "Diyanet'ten Suudi Müftüye Kilise Cevabı" (Answer to the Saudi Cleric from the Religious Affairs Directorate), *Religious News* (Turkish), April 7, 2012.

61. Robinson, "The Caliph Has No Clothes."

62. Çakır and Görmez, "Reis Ve Raconu—Ruşen Çakır.".

63. "Colère de Recep Tayyip Erdoğan à Davos," *Le Monde*, January 30, 2009.

64. Ibid.

65. "Turkey Declares Protecting Al-Aqsa Its Mission," *Hürriyet Daily News*, November 8, 2014.

66. "Turkey's Official Islamic Body Extends Influence Abroad," *Al-Monitor*, June 15, 2016.

67. Shragay, "A New Ottoman Empire?"

68. Ibid.

69. Duran, "Understanding the AK Party's Identity Politics," p. 93.

70. Martin-Chauffier, "Erdoğan en première ligne," pp. 52–53.

71. "Full Text: Turkish PM Erdoğan's Post-election 'Balcony Speech,'" *Hürriyet Daily News*, March 31, 2014.

72. "Paper Says Turkish Religious Official, Pope Meeting Stone-walled Due to Protocol," *BBC News*, January 11, 2013.

73. "Turkey to Build Balkans' Largest Mosque in Tirana," *Hürriyet Daily News*, October 27, 2014.

74. "Turkey Rebuilds Mosques, Sends Clerics to Syria," *Daily Sabah*, June 5, 2017.

75. Takan, "Looking at the Religious Values of Turkish Society."

76. "Turkish Politician Calls for Vatican-like Administration of Mecca," *Al-Monitor*, November 2, 2014.

77. "Mankind 'Failing' Multiculturalism: Turkey's Top Cleric," *Hürriyet Daily News*, April 12, 2015.

78. "Interview with the Director of Religious Affairs Mehmet Görmez on Salafism, ISIS, and Turkey," *Rusencakir.com*, August 29, 2015.

79. Duran, "Understanding the AK Party's Identity Politics," p. 105.

80. Çakır and Görmez, "Reis Ve Raconu—Ruşen Çakır."

81. Lowther, "Sir G. Lowther to Sir Edward Grey, Letter on the Signature of Italo-Turkish Peace Protocol; Commenting on Terms," Constantinople, 1912, pp. 431–33.

82. Bekir Bozdag, speaking on the organization of the Islamic Conference, *Kanal 24 Television*, August 17, 2013.

83. Burak Akçapar, interview with the author, Boston, MA, April 2018.

84. Saoudi, "Tournée africaine du roi du Maroc."

85. Alaoui, "Formation des imams."

86. "Marruecos formará a imanes de Nigeria, quinto país africano que lo solicita," *El Confidencial*, May 26, 2014.

87. "Les 7 nouveaux accords de coopération Maroc-Sénégal," *Agence Ecofin*, July 30, 2013.

88. El Ghissassi, *Regard sur le Maroc de Mohammed VI*, p. 150.

89. Haddad, "Le Maroc, fer de lance d'un Islam éclairé."

90. Hayda, "Taoufik Denies 'Religious Diplomacy.'"

91. Director of the Mohammed VI Institute, interview with the author, Rabat, July 2018.

92. "Fundación de ulemas africanos," *El Dia*, July 14, 2015.

93. "Reprise du programme de formation des imams," *Le Matin du Sahara et du Maghreb* (Casablanca), July 19–20, 2019, p. 3.

94. "La Fondation Mohammed VI des ouléma africains se réunit en session ordinaire à Fès du 08 au 10 décembre 2017," Ministère des habous et des affaires islamiques (Morocco), http:// www.habous.gov.ma/fr/fondation-mohammed-vi-des-ouléma-africains.

95. Bouabdellah Ghlamallah, interview with the author, Algiers, February 2014.

96. Ibid.

97. Lucie Sarr, "La Ligue des Oulémas, Prêcheurs, et Imams des Pays du Sahel promeut l'enseignement d'un islam modéré," *La Croix Africa*, September 16, 2019.

98. "Afrique de l'Ouest: Ligue des Oulémas du Sahel—une expérience prisée aux niveaux régional et international," *Algérie Presse Service*, May 8, 2018.

99. Mohamed Aïssa, interview with the author, Algiers, February 2014.

100. Bouabdellah Ghlamallah, interview with the author, Algiers, February 2014.

101. *Middle East Observer* and *Saudi Arabia News*, "Eight Agreements and MoU between Tunisia and Saudi Arabia Inked," *Middle East Observer*, July 28, 2017.

102. O'Malley, "Vatican II Revisited," p. 9.

103. Morris, *American Catholic*, p. 134.

104. Morris, *American Catholic*, p.135.

105. Konrad Eubel, *Hierarchia catholica medii aevi*, vols. 1–9 (Münster, Germany: Sumptibus et Typis Librariae Regensbergianae, 1898–).

106. Graziano, *In Rome We Trust*, p. 167.

107. O'Malley, "Opening the Church to the World."

108. Mazewski, "Will the Geographic Profile of the College of Cardinals Really Change under Francis?"

109. Liu, "The Global Catholic Population."

110. Acta Benedicti XVI, "Dum Benedictus PP," p. 295.

111. "The 'Model' Has Changed as New Cardinals Are Named," *Catholic Insight* 23 (February 2, 2015): 29.

112. Hervieu-Léger, *Religion as a Chain of Memory*.

113. "1996 College Seminary Enrollment by Race," Center for Applied Research in the Apostolate (CARA), Georgetown University; "An Alphabetical List of Diocesan and Religious Priests of the United States," *Official Catholic Directory*, https://www.officialcatholicdirectory .com/assets/OCD17_PriestsIndex.pdf.

114. Faggioli et al., "Vatican II and US Catholic Communities," p. 154.

115. Murray, *The Problem of Religious Freedom*, p. 3.

116. O'Malley, "Vatican II Revisited," p. 12.

117. Massa, *The American Catholic Revolution*, p. 161.

118. Graziano, *In Rome We Trust*, p. 2.

119. Hollenbach, "Religious Freedom in Global Context Today."

120. Ibid., p. 290.

121. Ibid., p. 22.

122. Graziano, *In Rome We Trust*, p. 163.

123. R. R. Reno, "Whiter Catholicism?" *First Things* 242 (April 2014): 7.

124. "Status Here Not an Issue," *New York Times*, June 8, 1929.

125. "Says Papal Treaty Is Blow to Freedom," *New York Times*, June 30, 1929.

126. Murray, "The Problem of Religious Freedom."

127. Long, *The Development of the Roman Missal*, p. 14.

128. O'Malley, "Vatican II Revisited," p. 11.

129. Massa, *The American Catholic Revolution*, p. 5.

130. Catholic Church, *Missale Romanum*.

131. Graziano, *In Rome We Trust*, p. 152.

132. Faggioli et al., "Vatican II and US Catholic Communities," p. 153.

133. Arnold and Hahn, *Confessions of a Traditional Catholic*, p. 103.

134. Fiocchi and Welsh, "Vatican Takes on American Heresy at Rome Meeting."

135. Graziano, *In Rome We Trust*, p. 20.

136. Durantaye, "The Omen."

137. O'Malley, "Vatican II Revisited as Reconciliation," p. 3.

138. "Francis: God's Way of Writing Straight with Crooked Lines," *The Daily Nation*, November 22, 2015.

139. "Papst Franziskus Im Zeit-Interview: 'Ich Bin Sünder Und Bin Fehlbar,'" *Zeit*, March 8, 2017.

140. "Civiltà Cattolica di Spadaro bacchetta Trump, Bush, Reagan, e i 'Cattolici integralisti' degli Stati Uniti," *Formiche*, July 14, 2017; Spadaro and Figueroa, "Fondamentalismo Evangelicale e integralismo Cattolico."

141. Paul VI, "Gaudium et spes."

142. [Unsigned], "Il soffragio universale," *La Civilta Cattolica* 1 (2, 1850): 33–51.

143. "Christianity's Role in Europe Is Service, Not Colonialism, Pope Says," *Catholic Culture*, December 26, 2016.

144. Preuss, "Religion and Politics and the Constitutional Patterns of Their Mutual Accommodations."

145. Spadaro and Figueroa, "Fondamentalismo Evangelicale e Integralismo Cattolico." p. 111.

146. "Pope's Speech: Francis Tells Bishops That a Church That Excessively Explains Its Teachings Is Dangerously Unbalanced," *The Morning Call*, September 27, 2015.

147. "The Global Catholic Church by Region, 2010" (Washington, DC: Church for Applied Research in the Apostolate, 2011).

148. Boorstein, "Rare, Leaked Report Reveals Cardinal O'Malley Was a Top Vote-Getter in Last Papal Election."

149. "Global Catholic Population Tops 1.28 Billion; Half Are in 10 Countries," *National Catholic Reporter*, April 8, 2017.

150. Allen, "Africans Are No Longer Junior Partners in Catholicism Inc."

151. Allen, "Synod Is More and More Like a Soap Opera."

152. Mazewski, "Will the Geographic Profile of the College of Cardinals Really Change Under Francis?"

153. Jeff Diamant, "Under Pope Francis, the College of Cardinals Has Become Less European," Pew Research Center, November 23, 2020.

154. Ausubel and Marchetti, "Quantitative Dynamics of Human Empires."

155. Ridley, *The Rise of the Prophet Muhammad*, p. 45.

156. Weigel, "World Religion by the Numbers."

157. Casanova, *Public Religions in the Modern World*, p. 220.

158. McCants, "The Believer: How Abu Bakr Al-Baghdadi Became Leader of the Islamic State."

159. Akyol, *Islam without Extremes*, p. 216.

160. Stepan and Linz, "Democratization Theory and the 'Arab Spring,'" p. 19.

161. Ibid., pp. 16–17.

162. Locke, *A Letter Concerning Toleration*.

163. Laycock, "Church Autonomy Revisited," p. 254.

164. Carrère, *Le Pape*, p. 260.

165. Jan Grossarth-Maticek et al., "Privatschulen in Deutschland-Fakten und Hintergründe," *Destatis Kontext*, Statistisches Bundesamt (Destatis), August 10, 2020.

166. Lupu and Tuttle, "Sexual Misconduct and Ecclesiastical Immunity," p. 1795.

167. Casanova, *Public Religions in the Modern World*, p. 187.

168. Ibid., p. 205.

169. Casanova, *Public Religions in the Modern World*, p. 205.

170. Hervieu-Léger, "Une messe est possible: Les doubles funérailles du Président."

171. Graziano, *In Rome We Trust*.

172. "Number of Catholics in the World Continues Upward Trend, Thanks to Africa," *The Tablet*, April 6, 2017.

173. Kramarek and Gautier, "The Class of 2017: Survey of Ordinands to the Priesthood."

174. Fiocchi and Welsh, "Vatican Takes on American Heresy at Rome Meeting," pp. 26–28.

175. Turner, "A Complex Picture of Religion in America"; Putnam and Campbell, *American Grace*.

176. Graziano, *In Rome We Trust*, p. 159.

177. Masci and Smith, "7 Facts about US Catholics."

178. Graziano, *In Rome We Trust*, p. 10.

179. Gleason cited in Graziano, *In Rome We Trust*, p. 20.

180. Sacred Congregation of Seminaries and Universities, *Priestly Vocations in the World Today*, p. 94.

181. Catholic Church, *Priestly Vocations in the World of Today*, p. 289.

182. Sacred Congregation of Seminaries and Universities, *Priestly Vocations in the World Today*, p. 95.

183. Hollenbach, "Religious Freedom, Morality, and Law," p. 88.

184. Nairn, "Ethics—Celebrating Human Dignity."

185. Casanova, *Public Religions in the Modern World*, p. 168.

186. Ibid., pp. 70–71.

187. Graziano, *In Rome We Trust*, p. 18.

188. Ibid., p. 21.

189. Ibid., p. 20.

190. Gibson, "Cardinal Timothy Dolan: Islamic State Is Muslim Like Irish Republican Army Was Catholic."

191. Cocquet, "L'islam de France doit-il taxer le halal?"

192. Wolfgang Schwanitz, "Ridwan al-Sayyidi: The Struggle for Islam," *Qantara*, June 22, 2005, https://en.qantara.de/node/3985.

193. Haddad, "The Metamorphosis of Religion," p. 12.

194. Esposito, Rahim, and Ghobadzadeh, *The Politics of Islamism*, p. 8 .

195. Peter, Dornhof, and Arigita, *Islam and the Politics of Culture in Europe.*

196. Hefner, "Public Islam and the Problem of Democratization," p. 495.

197. Driessen, "Public Religion, Democracy, and Islam," p. 185.

198. "La Mosquée est remise aux musulmans de Suisse," *Le Matin*, January 19, 2020.

199. Bellamine, "Pour Rached Ghannouchi, 'Les Djihadistes sont l'héritage de Ben Ali.'"

200. The video can be viewed on Facebook: https://www.facebook.com/Medi1TV/videos/317581022444655/.

BIBLIOGRAPHY

Abbott, Andrew. 1988. *The System of Professions: An Essay on the Division of Expert Labor*. Chicago: University of Chicago Press.

Abdelilah, Alexander. 2017. "Comment sont formés les imams de France." *Rue 89*, January 24.

Abdellatif, El Azizi, and Noureddine Jouhari. 2001. "Interview with Islamic Scholar Dr. Driss Kettan." *Maroc Hebdo International*, October 28.

Abell, Aaron L. 1949. "Origins of Catholic Social Reform in the United States: Ideological Aspects." *Review of Politics* 11 (3, July): 294–309.

Abootalebi, Ali Reza. 2000. *Islam and Democracy: State-Society Relations in Developing Countries, 1980–1994*. New York and London: Garland Publishing.

Abu-Manneh, Butrus. 1979. "Sultan Abdülhamid II and Shaikh Abulhuda al-Sayyadi." *Middle Eastern Studies* 15 (2): 131–53.

———. 2001. *Studies on Islam and the Ottoman Empire in the 19th Century (1826–1876)*. Istanbul: ISIS Press.

Achehbar, Samir. 2012. "Médias publics: Propagande religieuse?" *Talquel*, October 31.

Açikgöz, Betül. 2013. "The Civics Textbooks in the Late Ottoman Empire: Children of Islam and the Homeland." *History of Education and Children's Literature* 8 (2): 113–57.

Acta Benedicti XVI. 2013. "Dum Benedictus PP: XVI valedicit eminentissimis dominis Cardinalibus, qui Romae adsunt." *Acta Apostolicae Sedis* 4 (March 1).

Adhoum, Ahmend. 2017. "I Support the School of Kairouan and Independent Reasoning in Religious Thinking" (interview). *Assabah News*, March 1.

Aidi, Hisham. 2014. *Rebel Music: Race, Empire, and the New Muslim Youth Culture*. New York: Pantheon.

Aït-Aoudia, Myriam. 2006. "La Naissance du Front Islamique du Salut: Une politisation conflictuelle (1988–1989)." *Critique internationale* 30 (1): 129–44.

Akarli, Engin D. 1992. "Economic Policy and Budgets in Ottoman Turkey, 1876–1909." *Middle Eastern Studies* 28 (3): 443–76.

Akgönül, Sanim. 2005. "Islam turc, Islams de Turquie: Acteurs et réseaux en Europe." *Politique étrangère* (January): 35–47.

Akgün, Mensur, and Sabiha Senyücel Gündogan. 2012. *Ortadogu'da Turkiye Algisi 2011*. Istanbul: TESEV.

Akyol, Mustafa. 2011. *Islam without Extremes: A Muslim Case for Liberty*. New York: W. W. Norton.

———. 2012. "The Turkish Model." *Cairo Review of Global Affairs* (Winter).

Alaoui, Mérième. 2015. "Formation des imams: Le Maroc décidé à être une référence internationale." *Saphir News*, April 10. http://www.saphirnews.com/Formation-des-imams-le
-Maroc-decide-a-etre-une-reference-internationale_a20633.html.

Al Ayadi, Mohamed. 2005. "Commentaire: État, monarchie, et religion." *Les cahiers bleus* 3
(February).

Albayrak, Nuh. 2017. "The Directorate's Job Just Got a Lot Harder." *Star Online* [in Turkish],
July 29.

Albayrak, Sadik. 1996. *Son devir Osmanlı uleması* (*Late Period Ottoman Ulema Scholars*), vol. 1.
Istanbul: Istanbul Metropolitan Municipality, Department of Cultural Affairs.

Al-Faruqi, Isma'il R., David Edward Sopher, and Peter Hebblethwaite. 1974. *Historical Atlas of
the Religions of the World*. New York: Macmillan.

Alkan, Mehmet Ö. 2000. "Modernization from Empire to Republic." In *Ottoman Past and
Today's Turkey*, edited by Kemal H. Karpat. Cologne: Brill.

Allam, Nermin. 2018. "Opinion: Saudi Women Can Drive, but Are Their Voices Being Heard?"
Wion, August 13.

Allan, Machteld. 2010. "Nederland en 'Zijne eigene Islâmquaestie.'" *Nde groene amsterdammer*,
November 17.

Allen, Henry Elisha. 1935. "The Place of Islam in the New Turkey." Chap. 10 in Henry Elisha
Allen, *The Turkey Transformation: A Study in Social and Religious Development*. Chicago:
University of Chicago Press.

Allen, John L., Jr. 2014. "Synod Is More and More Like a Soap Opera." *The Crux*, October 16.

———. 2014. "Africans Are No Longer Junior Partners in Catholicism Inc." *The Crux*,
October 17.

Allenby, Viscount. 1920. "Field-Marshal Viscount Allenby (Cairo) to Earl Curzon (Received
March 30 [1920], 12:20 p.m.)." In *Documents on British Foreign Policy 1919–1939*.

Almeida, Manuel. 2014. "In Conversation with Fethullah Gülen." *Asharq Al-Awsat-I*
(March).

Alpay, Sahin. 2011. "Turkey's Big Business Opts for Consolidation of Democracy." *Transcend
Media Service*, April 4.

Al-Sayyid, Ridwan. 2004. *The Struggle for Islam, Fundamentalism, Reform, and International Politics*. Beirut: Dar al Kitab al-'Arabi

American Foreign Policy Council. 2019. *The World Almanac of Islamism 2019*. Lanham, MD:
Rowman & Littlefield.

Amine, Larbi. 2014. "Un Algérien chargé d'installer le califat en Europe, recherché par la France
et l'Espagne." *Lemag*, July 11.

Anderson, Lisa S. 1981. "Religion and Politics in Libya." *Journal of Arab Affairs* 1 (1): 53–77.

Anderson, Scott. 2014. *Lawrence in Arabia: War, Deceit, Imperial Folly, and the Making of the
Modern Middle East*. New York: Anchor.

Andes, Stephen J. C. 2014. *The Vatican and Catholic Activism in Mexico and Chile: The Politics of
Transnational Catholicism, 1920–1940*. New York: Oxford University Press.

Ankara, Turan Yilmaz. 2016. "Müftülere Nikâh Yetkisinin Fikir Babası Necmettin Erbakan."
Hürriyet, June 30.

An-Na'im, Abdullahi Ahmed. 2009. "Shari'a and the Secular State in the Middle East and Europe." Carl Heinrich Becker Lecture, May 19, 2009. Cologne: Fritz Thyssen Foundation.

Anscombe, Frederick. 2014. *State, Faith, and Nation in Ottoman and Post-Ottoman Lands*. New York: Cambridge University Press.

Antonius, George. 2015. *The Arab Awakening: The Story of the Arab National Movement*. London: Allegro Publishers.

Ardiç, Nurullah. 2009. "Islam and the Politics of Secularism: The Abolition of the Caliphate (1908–1924)." PhD diss., UCLA, Sociology Department.

———. 2013. *Islam and the Politics of Secularism: The Caliphate and Middle Eastern Modernization in the Early 20th Century*. SOAS/Routledge Studies on the Middle East. London: Rutledge.

Arinc, Bulent. 2012. "Devlet Protokolunde Sivillesme Donemi." *Sabah*, May 14.

Arkilic, Z. Ayca. "The Limits of European Islam: Turkish Islamic Umbrella Organizations and Their Relations with Host Countries—France and Germany." *Journal of Muslim Minority Affairs* 35 (1): 17–42.

Arnold, Matthew, and Scott Hahn. 2017. *Confessions of a Traditional Catholic*. San Francisco: Ignatius Press.

Aron-Beller, Katherine, and Christopher F. Black. 2018. *The Roman Inquisition: Centre versus Peripheries*. Leiden: Brill.

Asad, Talal. 2018. "Secularism, Nation-State, Religion." In Talal Asad, *Formations of the Secular: Christianity, Islam, Modernity*. Stanford, CA: Stanford University Press.

Atwood, Craig D. 2010. *Handbook of Denominations in the United States*, 13th ed. Nashville: Abingdon Press.

Ausubel, Jesse, and Cesare Marchetti. 2012. "Quantitative Dynamics of Human Empires." *International Journal of Anthropology* 27 (1/2): 1–62.

Avrich, Paul. 1990. *Sacco and Vanzetti: The Anarchist Background*. Princeton, NJ: Princeton University Press.

Aydin, Cemil. 2007. "The Impact of WWI on Chinese and Ottoman-Turkish Intellectuals." International Conference on World War I and the Transformation of the Imperialist World Order, Duke University, March 2007.

———. 2007. *The Politics of Anti-Westernism in Asia*. New York: Columbia University Press.

Badía, Jorge García. 2016. "Marruecos formará a los imanes de la Región para evitar el radicalismo." *La Verdad*, April 7, 2016. http://www.laverdad.es/murcia/201604/07/marruecos -formara-imanes-region-20160407005656-v.html.

Bahar, Baser. 2017. "Turkey's Diaspora Engagement Policy under the Justice and Development Party." Oxford: International Migration Institute, Amsterdam Institute for Social Science Research (April 24).

Bailey, Thomas. 1835. *The Lives and Deaths of the Illustrious Sir Thomas More and of John Fisher, Bishop of Rochester*. Dublin: C. M. Warren.

Baldinetti, Anna. 2009. "Italian Colonial Rule and Muslim Elites in Libya: A Relationship of Antagonism and Collaboration." In *Guardians of Faith in Modern Times: "Ulema" in the Middle East*, edited by Meir Hatina. Boston: Brill.

Barkey, Karen. 2009. *Empire of Difference: The Ottomans in Comparative Perspective*. Cambridge: Cambridge University Press.

———. 2014. "Political Legitimacy and Islam in the Ottoman Empire: Lessons Learned." *Philosophy and Social Criticism* 40 (4/5): 469–78.

Barnes, John Robert. 1986. *An Introduction to Religious Foundations in the Ottoman Empire.* Leiden: E. J. Brill.

Barou, Jacques. 2014. "Integration of Immigrants in France: A Historical Perspective." *Identities* 21 (6): 642–57. doi:10.1080/1070289x.2014.882840.

Barro, Robert J., and Rachel McCleary. 2005. "Which Countries Have State Religions?" *Quarterly Journal of Economics* 120 (4): 1331–70.

Başkan, Birol, ed. 2014. *From Religious Empires to Secular States: State Secularization in Turkey, Iran, and Russia.* London: Routledge .

———. 2014. "Mobilizing Sheikhs and Ulama: Religion and the Ottoman Empire." In *From Religious Empires to Secular States: State Secularization in Turkey, Iran, and Russia,* edited by Birol Başkan. London: Routledge.

Bastürk, Levent. 2014. "Understanding Turkish Motives in the Ukraine-Crimea Crisis." *Daily Sabah,* March 16.

Battandier, Mgr. Albert. 1903. *Annuaire pontifical catholique,* vol. VI. Paris: Maison de la Bonne Presse.

Baubérot, Jean. 2015. *Les Sept laïcités françaises: Le modèle français de laïcité n'existe pas.* Paris: Éditions de la Maison des sciences de l'homme.

Bayart, Jean-François. 2010. *L'Islam républicain: Ankara, Téhéran, Dakar.* Paris: Albin Michel.

Bax, Daniel, and Tsafrir Cohen. 2014. "Interview with Rachid Ghannouchi: 'If You Sow Dictatorship, You Harvest Terrorism.'" *Qantara,* December 31.

Behar, Cem. 1996. *The Population of the Ottoman Empire and Turkey: Historical Statistics Series,* vol. 2. Ankara: Prime Ministry of the Republic of Turkey, State Institute of Statistics (May).

Belhaj, Abdessamad. 2009. *La Dimension islamique dans la politique étrangère du Maroc Déterminants, acteurs, orientations.* Louvian-le-Neuve, Belgium: Presses Universitaires de Louvain.

Bellamine, Yasmine. 2016. "Pour Rached Ghannouchi, 'Les Djihadistes sont l'héritage de Ben Ali.'" *HuffPost Tunisie,* June 27.

Bellessort, André. 1910. "III. La Suède religieuse." *Revue des deux mondes* (July).

Beltramme, Ilaria. 2016. *La Storia di Roma in 100 monumenti e opere d'arte.* Rome: Newton Compton.

Benchemsi, Ahmed. 2015. "Invisible Atheists." *The New Republic,* April 23.

Benhamed, Wassila. 2011. "Ministère des Affaires Religieuses et du Wakf: Bientôt un nouveau siege." *El Moudjahid,* September 14.

Benincasa, Fabio, and Francesco Rosetti. 2012. "Chiara Borroni." In *Forme, volti, e linguaggi della violenza nella cultura italiana,* edited by Edibom Edizioni Letterarie. Brescia: Lonato del Garda.

Bennison, Amira K. 2012. "Muslim Internationalism between Empire and Nation-State." In *Religious Internationals in the Modern World,* edited by Abigail Green and Vincent Viaene. London: Palgrave.

Bérard, Victor. 1907. *Le Sultan, l'islam, et les puissances.* Paris: Armand Colin.

Bergin, Joseph. 1999. "The Counter-Reformation Church and Its Bishops." *Past and Present* 165 (November): 30–73.

Berman, Eli. 1999. "Subsidized Sacrifice: State Support of Religion in Israel." *Contemporary Jewry* 20 (1): 167–200.

Berque, Jacques. 1957. "Quelques problèmes de l'Islam Maghrebin." *Archives des sciences sociales des religions* 3: 3–20.

Bevilacqua, Piero, et al. 2002. *Storia dell'emigrazione italiana*, vol. 2. Rome: Donzelli Editore.

Beydilli, Kemal. 2011. *Osmanlı Döneminde Imamlar ve Bir Imamin Günlügu*. Istanbul: Egitim ve Kültür Amaçli Çogaltilmistir.

Bill, James A., and John Alden Williams. 2002. *Roman Catholics and Shi'i Muslims: Prayer, Passion, and Politics*. Chapel Hill: University of North Carolina Press.

Bin-Bajjad al-Utaybi, Abdallah. 2014. *Al-Sharq al-Awsat*, July 6.

Bin Laden, Hamzah. 2017. "The Sovereignty of the Best Ummah Lays in the Uprising of the People of the Two Holy Mosques, Episode Two." *Al-Sahab Media Establishment*, May 20.

Birnbaum, Ben, and Seth Meehan. 2014. *The Heights: An Illustrated History of Boston College, 1863–2013*. Boston: Linden Lane Press at Boston College.

Birt, Yahya. 2017. "Preachers, Patriots, and Islamists: Contemporary British Muslims and the Afterlives of Abdullah Quilliam." In *Victorian Muslim: Abdullah Quilliam and Islam in the West*, edited by Jamie Gilham and Ron Geaves. London: Hurst & Co.

Blunt, Wilfred Scawen. 1882. *The Future of Islam*. Alexandria: Library of Alexandria.

Boorstein, Michelle. 2019. "Rare, Leaked Report Reveals Cardinal O'Malley Was a Top Vote-Getter in Last Papal Election." *Boston Globe*, March 23.

Bouaziz, Fatima Zohra. 2014. "Marruecos mantiene a raya a los salafistas cuando atacan a los laicos." *El Confidencial*, February 20.

Bouhdiba, Abdelwahab. 1964. "Islam in Tunisia." In *The Proceedings of the First International Congress of Africanists, Accra, 11th–18th December 1962*, edited by Lalage Brown and Michael Crowder. London: Longman.

Boukhalfa, Kheireddine. 2014. "Les Réponses de Mohamed Aïssa." *Djazairess*, August 21.

Boukhayatia, Rihab. 2015. "Entretien avec Hédi Yahmed." *Huffington Post*, April 29.

———. 2015. "C'est la société tunisienne qui a enfanté Daech." *Huffington Post*, May 1.

Boumghar, Mouloud. 2016. "Algeria." In *Encyclopedia of Law and Religion*, edited by Gerhard Robbers, W. Cole Durham, and Donlu Thayer. Leiden: Brill/Nijhoff.

Bowen, Innes. 2014. *Medina in Birmingham, Najaf in Brent: Inside British Islam*. London: Hurst.

Bozkurt, Abdullah. 2018. "Turkey's Maarif Exports Erdoğan's Ideology to Balkans." *Turkish Minute*, October 28.

Bradley, Matt, and Leila Elmergawi. 2013. "Egypt Cracks Down on Radical Muslim Clerics." *Wall Street Journal*, September 11.

Brake, Wayne te. 1998. *Shaping History: Ordinary People in European Politics: 1500–1700*. Berkeley: University of California Press.

———. 2017. *Religious War and Religious Peace in Early Modern Europe*. Cambridge: Cambridge University Press.

Brewster, D. 1968. "Recent Reforms at the Zeitouna." *The Muslim World* 58 (2, April): 120–27.

Brown, Jonathan A. C. 2015. "Is Islam Easy to Understand or Not? Salafis, the Democratization of Interpretation, and the Need for Ulema." *Journal of Islamic Studies* 26 (2, May): 117–44.

Brown, Leon Carl. 1964. "The Islamic Reformist Movement in North Africa." *Journal of Modern African Studies* 2 (1, March): 55–63.

———. 1974. *The Tunisia of Ahmad Bey, 1837–1855*. Princeton, NJ: Princeton University Press.

———. 1974. "The Religious Establishment." In Leon Carl Brown, *The Tunisia of Ahmad Bey, 1837–1855*. Princeton, NJ: Princeton University Press.

Brown, Nathan J. 2017. "Official Islam in the Arab World: The Contest for Religious Authority." Washington, DC: Carnegie Endowment for International Peace (May 11). https://carnegieendowment.org/2017/05/11/official-islam-in-arab-world-contest-for-religious-authority-pub-69929.

Brown, Peter. 2013. *The Fall of Western Christendom: Triumph and Diversity, AD 200–1000*. Malden, MA: Wiley-Blackwell Publishing.

Brownson, Sarah M. 1873. *Life of Demetrius Augustine Gallatin, Prince and Priest*. New York: Fr. Plustet & Co.

Bruce, Benjamin. 2012. "Les Imams 'exportés' de la Diyanet en France: Enjeu de politique étrangère, enjeu de politique intérieure." *Cahiers de l'obtic* (2, December): 16.

———. 2013. "Not Quite In, Not Quite Out: Islamic Organizations in France and Germany and Their Ties to Their States of Origin." In *Islamic Organizations in Europe and the USA: A Multidisciplinary Perspective*, edited by Matthias and Kerstin Rosenow-Williams Kortmann. London: Palgrave Macmillan.

———. 2015. "Governing Islam Abroad: The Turkish and Moroccan Muslim Fields in France and Germany." PhD diss., Institut d'études politiques de Paris, Political Science Department.

———. 2019. *Governing Islam Abroad: Turkish and Moroccan Muslims in Western Europe*. Cham, Switzerland: Palgrave Macmillan.

Bruce, Steve. 2011. *God Is Dead: Secularization in the West*. Oxford: Blackwell.

Bryk, Anthony S., Valerie E. Lee, and Peter B. Holland. 1993. *Catholic Schools and the Common Good*. Cambridge, MA: Harvard University Press.

Buhrman, Parker W. 1924. "American Consul to the Secretary of State: Expulsion of the Caliph, Abdul Medjid, by the Turkish Government; Political Effect, Aleppo District." Edited by the Department of State. Aleppo, Syria: American Consulate in Syria.

———. 1924. "Selection of a New Caliph," edited by the Department of State. No. 169. Aleppo, Syria: American Consulate in Syria.

Burak, Guy. 2015. *The Second Formation of Islamic Law: The Hanafi School in the Early Modern Ottoman Empire*. Cambridge: Cambridge University Press.

Burkle-Young, Francis A. 2000. *Papal Elections in the Age of Transition, 1878–1922*. Lanham, MD: Lexington Books.

Burton, Antoinette. 2012. Review of *Insurgent Sepoys: Europe Views the Revolt of 1857* by Shaswati Mazumdar. *Victorian Studies* 54 (4, Summer): 729–31.

Butler, Daren. 2018. "With More Islamic Schooling, Erdogan Aims to Reshape Turkey." *Reuters*, January 25.

Büzpinar, Ş. Tufan. 1991. "Abdülhamid II, Islam, and the Arabs: The Cases of Syria and the Hijaz (1878–1882)." University of Manchester.

———. 1991. "Abolition of the Caliphate." PhD diss., University of Manchester.

———. 1996. "Opposition to the Ottoman Caliphate in the Early Years of Abdülhamid II: 1877–1882." *Die Welt des Islams* 36 (1, March): 59–89.

Byman, Daniel. 2019. "What Comes after ISIS?" *Foreign Policy*, February 22.

Cagaptay, Soner, and James F. Jeffrey. 2014. "Turkey's 2014 Political Transition: From Erdoğan to Erdoğan?" Policy Note 17. Washington, DC: Washington Institute (January).

Çakır, Ruşen, and Mehmet Görmez. 2015. "Reis Ve Raconu—Ruşen Çakır." Ruşen Çakır Medyascope, August 2. https://www.youtube.com/watch?v=TH9BcA3NScI.

Caplow, Theodore, Louis Hicks, and Ben J. Wattenberg. 2001. "Religion." Chap. 6 in *The First Measured Century: An Illustrated Guide to Trends in America, 1900–2000*, edited by PBS. Washington, DC: American Enterprise Institute.

Carrère, Jean. 1923. *Le Pape: Rome éternelle, Pierre et César, Canossa Dante, Charles-Quint, Napoléon, la Question Romaine*. Paris: Plon Nourit et Cie.

Carretto, Giacomo E. 1977. ""Elezioni e Governi in Turchia nel 1977." *Oriente Moderno* 57 (11/12, November/December): 489–518.

Casanova, José. 1994. "Globalizing Catholicism and the Return to a Universal Church." In *Transnational Religion and Fading States*, edited by Susanne Rudolph and James Piscatori. New York: Routledge.

———. 1996. "Global Catholicism and the Politics of Civil Society." *Sociological Inquiry* 66 (3): 367–73.

———. 2011. *Public Religions in the Modern World*. Chicago: University of Chicago Press.

———. 2012. "The Politics of Nativism: Islam in Europe, Catholicism in the United States." *Philosophy and Social Criticism* 38 (4/5): 485–96.

Cassidy, Francis Patrick. 1924. *Catholic College Foundations and Development in the United States (1677–1850)*. Washington, DC: Catholic University Press.

Catholic Church. 1880. *Missale Romanum*. Mechliniae: H. Dessain.

Catholic Church. 1963. *Priestly Vocations in the World of Today: Acts of the First International Congress for Priestly Vocations, Rome, 22–26 May 1962*. Vatican City: Congregatio de Seminariis et Studiorum Universitatibus.

Cavatorta, Francesco, and Fabio Merone, eds. 2016. *Salafism after the Arab Awakening: Contending with People's Power*. Oxford: Oxford University Press.

Celebi, Yusuf. 2012. "Turkish President Says Tunisia Second Model to Region." *Anatolia*, March 9.

Cembrero, Ignacio. 2017. "How Rabat Sought to Decapitate Rif Rebellion." *Le Desk*, May 28.

Center for Insights in Survey Research. 2017. "Public Opinion Survey of Tunisia: April 19–April 26, 2017." Washington, DC: International Republican Institute.

Césari, Jocelyne. 2012. "State Society Relations and Their Influence on Pakistan Stability." In South Asia Stability Assessment Academic Consortium, *Strategic Multilayer Assessment (SMA) and Minerva Research Initiative*. October 31.

———. 2013. "Religion and Diasporas: Challenges of Emigration Countries." Research Report 2013/01. Fiesole, Italy: Robert Schuman Centre for Advanced Studies, San Domenico di Fiesole, European University Institute (November 1).

———. 2014. *The Awakening of Muslim Democracy: Religion, Modernity, and the State*. New York: Cambridge University Press.

———. 2018. *What is Political Islam?* Boulder, CO: Lynne Riener Publishers.

Çetinsaya, Gökhan. 2006. *The Ottoman Administration of Iraq, 1890–1908*. New York: Routledge.

Chadwick, Henry, and Owen Chadwick. 1981. *Oxford History of the Christian Church*. Oxford: Oxford University Press.

Chadwick, Owen. 1964. *The Reformation*, vol. 3, *The Pelican History of the Church*. Harmondsworth: Penguin Books.

———. 1980. *The Popes and European Revolution*. Oxford: Oxford University Press.

———. 2003. *A History of the Popes, 1830–1914*. Oxford: Oxford University Press.

Chekar, Amar. 2013. "Nationale—Bouabdallah Ghlamallah se dérobe." *L'Expression*, April 23.

Chikhaoui, Yosra. 2016. "Sidi Bouzid Governor Announces the Closure of Seven Local Mosques." *Hakaek*, November 9.

Chirol, Valentine. 1919. "Islam and the Future of Constantinople." In *The Fortnightly Review*, edited by W. L. Courtney. London: Chapman and Hall, Ltd.

Choate, Mark I. 2007. "Sending States' Transnational Interventions in Politics, Culture, and Economics: The Historical Example of Italy." *International Migration Review* 41 (3, Fall): 728–78.

Cihan, Ahmet. 2004. *Reform Çaginda: Osmanlı Ilmiyye Sinifi*. Istanbul: Birey Yayincilik/Sosyal Tarih Dizisi.

Cilibrizzi, Saverio. 1929. *Storia parlamentare politica e diplomatica d'Italia da Novara a Vittorio Veneto*, vol. 3, *1896–1909*. Milan: Societa editrice Dante Alighieri.

Cioppi, Guido. 1912. "Il convegno di parigi per un istituto internazionale cristiano." *Rivista Internazionale di Scienze Sociali e Discipline Ausiliarie* 59 (235): 338–53.

Citak, Zana. 2012. "D'acteur national à transnational: La Diyanet en Europe." *Cahiers de l'obtic* (2, December): 11.

Clancy-Smith, Julia Ann. 1997. *Rebel and Saint: Muslim Notables, Populist Protest, Colonial Encounters (Algeria and Tunisia, 1800–1904)*. Berkeley: University of California Press.

———. 2010. *Mediterraneans: North Africa and Europe in an Age of Migration, c. 1800–1900*. Berkeley: University of California Press.

———. 2014. "Islam and the French Empire in North Africa." In *Islam and the European Empires*, edited by David Motadel. Oxford: Oxford University Press.

Clark, Janine A. 2010. *Islam, Charity, and Activism: Middle-Class Networks and Social Welfare in Egypt, Jordan, and Yemen*. Bloomington: Indiana University Press.

Clayer, Nathalie. 2004. "L'Autorité religieuse dans l'islam ottoman sous le contrôle de l'état?" *Archives de sciences sociales religions* 49 (125): 45–62.

Cleveland, William L. 1985. *Islam against the West*. Austin: University of Texas Press.

Cocquet, Marion. 2015. "L'islam de France doit-il taxer le halal?" *Le Point*, August 3.

Coëtlosquet, Marie Emmanuel du. 1887. *Theodore Wibaux, Pontifical Zouave and Jesuit*. London: Catholic Truth Society.

Coffey, Joan L. 1997. "Of Catechisms and Sermons: Church-State Relations in France, 1890–1905." *Church History* 66 (1): 54–66.

Colquhoun, A. R. 1906. "Pan-Islam." *North American Review*.

Cortesi, Arnaldo. 1929. "Pius XI: 'The Pope of the Conciliation.'" *New York Times*, April 7.

Cox, Kathryn Lilla. 2015. *Water Shaping Stone: Faith, Relationships, and Conscience Formation*. Collegeville, MN: Liturgical Press.

Crews, Robert. 1999. "Allies in God's Command: Muslim Communities and the State in Imperial Russia." 2 vols. PhD diss., Princeton University, Department of History.

———. 2014. "The Russian Worlds of Islam." In *Islam and the European Empires*, edited by David Motadel. The Past and Present Book Series. Oxford: Oxford University Press.

La Croix. 2013. "Les Vocations en France." Dossier du No.2444, *La Croix*, April 9. https://www .la-croix.com/Urbi-et-Orbi/Archives/Documentation-catholique-n-2444/Les-vocations -en-France-elements-statistiques-2013-04-09-932105.

Cunliffe-Owen, F. 1923. "Aga Khan, Fashionable Londoner, Holds Enormous Power in Islam." *New York Times*, July 8.

Curic, Hajrudin. 1965. *Situation scolaire des musulmans en Bosnie-Herzegovine (1800–1878)*. Belgrade: Scientific Work Publishing House/Izdavačka Ustanova Naučno Delo.

Curran, Francis X. 1957. "Vocations Keep Climbing." *America* 96 (19, February).

Curran, Thomas J. 1966. "Assimilation and Nativism." *International Migration Digest* 3 (1, Spring): 15–25.

Curzon, Earl. 1920. "Memorandum by Earl Curzon on the Future of Constantinople." [168210/151671/44]. In *Adriatic and the Near East 1919–February 1920: Documents on British Foreign Policy 1919–1939*, series 1, vol. 4.

D'Agostino, Peter. 2004. *Rome in America: Transitional Catholic Ideology from the Risorgimento to Fascism*. Chapel Hill: University of North Carolina Press.

D'Andurain, Julie. 2012. "Le Poids du comité du Maroc et du 'parti colonial' dans la Société de l'histoire des colonies françaises (1902–1912)." *Outremers* 9: 311–23.

Darif, Mohammed. 2005. "État, monarchie, et religion." *Les Cahiers bleus* 3 (February).

Darmanin, Gérald. 2016. "A l'Islam, nous devons imposer une concorde, afin de l'assimiler totalement à la République." *L'Opinion*, June 6.

Debidour, Antonin. 1898. *Histoire des rapports de l'église et l'état en France*. Geneva: Slatkine-Megariotis.

De Cesare, R. 1901. "The Pope and the Temporal Power." *North American Review* 172 (535): 863–66.

Deeb, Mary-Jane. 1996. "Islam and the State in Algeria and Morocco: A Dialectical Model." In *Islamism and Secularism in North Africa*, edited by John Ruedy. Basingstoke: Macmillan.

Delvecchio, Alexandre. 2014. "Djihadistes français: Les faux-semblants du rapport de Dounia Bouzar." *Le Figaro*, November 20.

De Maria, Carlo. 2011. "Anarchici italiani negli Stati Uniti." *Diacronie: Studi di Storia Contemporanea* (January 29).

Deprez, Jean. 1981. "Pérennité de l'Islam dans l'Ordre Juridique au Maghreb." *Ordre religieux et norme juridique* (3): 315–53.

Deri, Mehmet. 2008. "II. Adulhamd'in Islam Birligi Siyaseti ve bu Hususta Hilafetin Rolu." *Sosyal BilgilerGen.tr*, September 28. https://www.sosyalbilgiler.org/ii-abdulhamidin-islam -birligi-siyaseti-ve-bu-hususta-hilafetin-rolu/.

Deringil, Selim. 1991. "Legitimacy Structures in the Ottoman State: The Reign of Abdülhamid II (1876–1909)." *International Journal of Middle East Studies* 23 (3, August): 345–59.

———. 1999. *The Well-Protected Domains: Ideology and the Legitimation of Power in the Ottoman Empire, 1876–1909*. Cambridge: Cambridge University Press.

DeSilva, Jennifer M. 2008. "Senators or Courtiers: Negotiating Models for the College of Cardinals under Julius II and Leo X." *Renaissance Studies* 22.

Dessouki, Ali E. Hillal. 1987. "Official Islam and Political Legitimation in the Arab Countries." In *The Islamic Impulse*, edited by Barbara Freyer Stowasser. Washington, DC: Georgetown University Press.

Destremau, Christian, and Jean Moncelon. 2005. *Louis Massignon: Le cheikh admirable*. Paris: Capucin.

Dettmer, Jamie. 2013. "Tunisia Moves to Rein in Islamic Hardliners." *Voice of America*, May 16.

Diamantopulo, Hercule. 1909. *Le Réveil de la Turquie: Études et croquis historiques*. Alexandria: Typo-Lithographie Centrale Della Rocca.

Dilek, Emine. 2013. "Muslim Brotherhood Fully Supports Erdoğan, Al-Qaradawi Says." *Progressive Press*, June 13.

Douniol, Charles. 1864. [No title]. *Le Correspondant* 63: 693–702.

Dowley, Tim, and Nick Rowland. 2018. *Atlas of World Religions*. Minneapolis: Fortress Press.

Downing, Brian M. 1992. Preface to *The Military Revolution and Political Change: Origins of Democracy and Autocracy in Early Modern Europe*. Princeton, NJ: Princeton University Press.

Dreissler, Markus. 2008. "Turkey." In *The Islamic World*, edited by Andrew Rippin. New York: Routledge.

Driessen, Michael. 2012. "Public Religion, Democracy, and Islam: Examining the Moderation Thesis in Algeria." *Comparative Politics* 44 (2, January): 171–89.

———. 2013. "Religious Democracy and Civilizational Politics: Comparing Political Islam and Political Catholicism." Occasional Paper 12. Washington, DC: Georgetown Qatar School of Foreign Service in Qatar, Center for International and Regional Studies.

———. 2014. "Regime Type, Religion-State Arrangements, and Religious Markets in the Muslim World." *Sociology of Religion* 75 (3, September): 367–94.

———. 2014. *Religion and Democratization: Framing Religious and Political Identities in Muslim and Catholic Societies*. Oxford: Oxford University Press.

———. 2017. "Sources of Muslim Democracy: The Supply and Demand of Religious Policies in the Muslim World." *Democratization* 25 (1): 115–35.

Duclos, Louis-Jean. 1993. "Rémy Leveau, le sabre et le turban, François Bourin, 1993." *Cultures et Conflits* (11).

Dumont, Paul. 2019. "L'Instrumentalisation de la religion dans l'Empire ottoman à l'époque de l'expansion européenne (1800–1914)." *European Journal of Turkish Studies* 27. Published online January 10, 2019. http://journals.openedition.org/ejts/5933.

Duran, Burhanettin. 2013. "Understanding the AK Party's Identity Politic: A Civilizational Discourse and Its Limitations." *Insight Turkey* 15 (1, Winter): 91–109.

Durantaye, Leland de la. 2005, "The Omen." *Village Voice*, August 2.

Durkheim, Émile. 1995 [1912]. *The Elementary Forms of Religious Life*, translated by Karen E. Fields. New York: Free Press.

Dwight, Henry Otis. 1901. *Constantinople and Its Problems: Its Peoples, Customs, Religions, and Progress*. New York: Fleming H. Revell.

Dyer, Jeffrey. 2016. "The Ottomans in the Age of Empire." PhD. diss., Boston College, Department of History.

Dynamis. 1916. "The Mohammedan Caliphate." *Studies: An Irish Quarterly Review* 5 (19): 325–38.

Ecclesia Catholica. 1973. *Compendio di storia della Sacra Congregazione per l'Evangelizzazione dei Popoli o "de Propaganda Fide," 1622–1972: 350 anni al servizio delle missioni,* edited by Congregatio pro Gentium Evangelizatione seu de Propaganda Fide. Rome: Pontificia Università Urbaniana.

Edelman, Eric, et al., principal investigators. 2015. *Turkey Transformed: The Origins and Evolution of Authoritarianism and Islamization under the AKP.* Washington, DC: Bipartisan Policy Center (October).

Edelund, Robert B., Hébert, Robert F., Tollison, Robert D. 2002. "An Economic Analysis of the Protestant Reformation." *Journal of Political Economy* 110 (3):646–671.

Efe. 2014. "Marruecos formará a imanes de Nigeria, quinto país Africano que lo solicita." *El Confidencial,* May 26.

Eickelman, Dale. 1987. "Religion and Polity in Society." In *The Political Economy of Morocco,* edited by I. William Zartman. New York: Praeger.

Eickelman, Dale F., and James P. Piscatori. 2004. *Muslim Politics.* Princeton, NJ: Princeton University Press.

Ekelund, Robert B., and Robert F. Hébert. 2010. "Interest Groups, Public Choice, and the Economics of Religion." *Public Choice* 142: 429–36.

Ekelund, Robert B., Robert F. Hébert, and Robert D. Tollison. 2002. "An Economic Analysis of the Protestant Reformation." *Journal of Political Economy* 110 (3): 646–71.

Elfenbein, Caleb. 2007. "Establishing Religion in Iraq: Islam and the Modern State." *Comparative Islamic Studies* 3 (1): 57–71.

El Ghissassi, Hakim. 2006. *Regard sur le Maroc de Mohammed VI.* Neuilly-sur-Seine: Michel Lafon.

Elischer, Sebastian. 2017. "How Jihadism Ends: The State, Critical Antecedents, and the Demobilization of Violent Salafism in East Africa." Unpublished manuscript.

———. 2017. "Governing the Faithful: State Management of Salafi Activity in the Francophone Sahel." Unpublished manuscript.

Ellis, John Tracy. 1956. *American Catholicism.* Chicago: University of Chicago Press.

———. 1971. "The Catholic Priest in the US." In *The Catholic Priest in the United States: Historical Investigations.* Collegeville, MN: Liturgical Press.

Erdoğan, Recep Tayyip. 2013. *Al Masri al Youmi.* August 27.

Erikson, Edward J. 2003. *Defeat in Detail: The Ottoman Army in the Balkans, 1912–1913.* Santa Barbara, CA: Praeger Publishers.

Esposito, John L., Lily Zubaidah Rahim, and Naser Ghobadzadeh. 2018. *The Politics of Islamism: Diverging Visions and Trajectories.* London: Palgrave Macmillan.

Esposito, John L., and John O. Voll. 1996. *Islam and Democracy.* Oxford: Oxford University Press.

Essid, Yassine. 2016. "Tunisia under the Yoke of Sinister Saudi Arabia." *Kapitalis,* November 10.

Eteraz, Ali. 2008. "Not Quite the Reformation." *Guardian,* February 29.

Etienne, Bruno, and Mohamed Tozy. 1979. "Le Glissement des obligations islamiques vers le phénomène associatif à Casablanca." *Annuaire de l'Afrique du Nord, Aix-en-Provence.*

Etzioni, Amitai. 2007. *Security First: For a Muscular, Moral Foreign Policy.* New Haven, CT: Yale University Press.

Eubel, Konrad. 1898–. *Hierarchia catholica medii aevi*, vols. 1–9. Münster, Germany: Sumptibus et Typis Librariae Regensbergianae.

Fabbe, Kristin Elisabeth. 2012. "Disciples of the State: Secularization and State Building in the Former Ottoman World." PhD. diss., Massachusetts Institute of Technology. Department of Political Science.

———. 2013. "Historical Legacies, Modern Conflicts: State Consolidation and Religious Pluralism in Greece and Turkey." *Southeast European and Black Sea Studies* 13 (3): 435–53.

———. 2019. *Disciples of the State? Religion and State-Building in the Former Ottoman World.* Cambridge: Cambridge University Press.

Faggioli, Massimo, et al. 2015. "Vatican II and US Catholic Communities." in *The Legacy of Vatican II*, edited by Massimo Faggioli and Andrea Vicini, SJ. Mahwah, NJ: Paulist Press.

Fatima, Stiki. 2012. "Rabat, 04 Juin 2012: Travaux de la 2ème réunion de la Commission Mixte Maroco-Tunisienne des affaires religieuses." وزارة الأوقاف والشؤون الإسلامية—الرئيسية (Ministry of Endowments and Islamic Affairs) (June).

Farah, Caesar E. 1995. "Reassessing Sultan Abdülhamid II's Islamic Policy." *Archivum Ottomanicum*, 191–212.

———. 1998. "Great Britain, Germany, and the Ottoman Caliphate." *Der Islam (Zeitschrift für Geschichte und Kultur des Islamischen Orients)* 66 (2): 264–88.

Fawkes, Alfred. 1915. "Prospects of the Roman Catholic Church." *Harvard Theological Review* 8 (4): 439–58.

Feener, R. Michael , and Terenjit Sevea, eds. 2009. *Islamic Connections: Muslim Societies in South and Southeast Asia.* Singapore: Institute of South Asian Studies.

Feine, H. E. 1964 [1921]. Die *Besetzung der Reichsbistümer vom Westfälischen Frieden bis zur Säkularisation, 1648–1803.* Stuttgart: Schippers.

Feldman, Noah. 2011. *The Fall and Rise of the Islamic State.* Princeton, NJ: Princeton University Press.

Fenton, Elizabeth. 2011. *Religious Liberties: Anti-Catholicism and Liberal Democracy in Nineteenth-Century Literature and Culture.* Oxford: Oxford University Press.

Feroz, Ahmad. 2015. *The Making of Modern Turkey.* London: Routledge.

Ferry, Patrick T. 1997. "Confessionalization and Popular Preaching: Sermons against Synergism in Reformation Saxony." *Sixteenth Century Journal* 28 (4): 1143.

Feuer, Sarah J. 2018. *Regulating Islam: Religion and the State in Contemporary Morocco and Tunisia.* Cambridge: Cambridge University Press.

Filali-Ansary, Abdou. 1996. "Islam and Liberal Democracy: The Challenge of Secularization." *Journal of Democracy* 7 (2): 76–80.

Finke, Roger, and Rodney Stark. 2005. *The Churching of America, 1776–2005: Winners and Losers in Our Religious Economy.* New Brunswick, NJ: Rutgers University Press.

Fiocchi, Maria Cristina, and Susan Welsh. 1989. "Vatican Takes on American Heresy at Rome Meeting." *Executive Intelligence Review* 16 (15, 7 April): 26–28.

Flanagan, Kathleen. 1999. "The Changing Character of the American Catholic Church 1810–1850." *Vincentian Heritage Journal* 20 (1, Spring).

Fortna, Benjamin. 2007. "Emphasizing the Islamic: Modifying the Curriculum of Late Ottoman State Schools." In *Enfance et jeunesse dans le monde musulman*, edited by Klaus Kreiser and Francois Georgeon. Paris: Maissonneuve et Larose.

Fox, Jonathan. 2018. *An Introduction to Religion and Politics: Theory and Practice*, 2nd ed. London: Routledge.

Fratantuono, Ella. 2015. "Religious Duties and Educational Needs." Paper delivered at Middle East Studies Association annual meeting, Denver, CO, November 23.

Frégosi, Franck. 1997. "Les Rapports entre l'islam et l'état en Algérie et en Tunisie: De leur revalorisation à leur contestation." In *L'État de droit dans le monde arabe (sous la direction de): Extrait de l'Annuaire de l'Afrique du Nord 1995*, edited by Ahmed Mahiou. Paris: CNRS Éditions.

Frégosi, Franck. 2004. "Habib Bourguiba et la régulation institutionnelle de l'Islam." In *Habib Bourguiba: La trace et l'héritage*, edited by Vincent Geisser and Michel Camau. Paris: Karthala.

Frégosi, Franck, and Malika Zéghal. 2005. "Religion et politique au Maghreb: Les exemples tunisien et marocain." Policy Paper 11. Paris: Institut français des relations internationales (March).

Freidson, Eliot. 1970. *Professional Dominance: The Social Structure of Medical Care*. New Brunswick, NJ: Aldine Transaction.

Fréri, J. 1903. "Work and Scope of the Propaganda." *American Ecclesiastical Review* 28 (10): 162–81.

Freston, Paul. 2016. "Christianity: Protestantism." In *Routledge Handbook of Religion and Politics*, edited by Jeffrey Haynes. New York: Routledge.

Froude, James Anthony. 1879. "An American Problem: Romanism and the Irish Race in the United States." *Chicago Daily Tribune*, November 19. Also published as "Romanism and the Irish Race in the US," *North American Review* 129 (277, 1879): 519–36.

———. 1896. *Lectures on the Council of Trent, Delivered at Oxford 1892–3*. New York: Scribner.

———. 1901. *Selections from the Writings of James Anthony Froude*. London: Longmans, Green.

Gaffney, Patrick D. 1992. "Popular Islam." *Annals of the American Academy of Political and Social Science* 524 (November): 44–46.

Ganzer, Klaus. 2002. *Bischof Wilhelm Emmanuel Freiherr von Ketteler*. Stuttgart: Franz Steiner Verlag.

Garrison, Douglas H. 2012. Review of *Ataturk: An Intellectual Biography* by Şükrü Hanioğlu. *Digest of Middle East Studies (DOMES)* 21 (1, Spring 2012): 205–7.

Gastaldi, Nadine. 2002. "La Vie des paroisses." In *De la concorde à la rupture, un siècle de vie religieuse en France (1801–1905)* (exhibit catalog). Paris: Musée de l'histoire de France, Centre historique des archives nationales.

———. 2004. "Le Concordat de 1801." *Histoire par l'image* (November 2004): 12–14.

Geertz, Clifford. 1988. *Religiöse Entwicklungen im Islam: Beoachtet in Marokko und Indonesien*. Frankfurt: Suhrkamp Verlag.

Genç, Mehmet, and Özvar, Erol. 2006. *Osmanlı maliyesi: Kurumlar ve bütçeler, 1. baskı*. Istanbul: Osmanlı Bankası Arşiv ve Araştırma Merkezi, Karaköy.

Gerges, Fawaz A. 2016. *ISIS: A History*. Princeton, NJ: Princeton University Press.

Giannoni, Alberto. 2011. "I musulmani italiani ospitano la prima visita del leader tunisino di al Nahdà." *Il Giornale*, December 20.

Gibson, David. 2015. "Cardinal Timothy Dolan: Islamic State Is Muslim Like Irish Republican Army Was Catholic." *Religion News Service*, March 4.

Gienapp, William E. 1985. "Nebraska, Nativism, and Rum: The Failure of Fusion in Pennsylvania, 1854." *Pennsylvania Magazine of History and Biography* 109 (4, October): 425–71.

Gilbert, Joan E. 1980. "Institutionalization of Muslim Scholarship and Professionalization of the Ulama in Medieval Damascus." *Studia Islamica* 52: 105–34/

Gilding, Ben. 2011. "Separation of 'Church and State' in Algeria: The Origins and Legacies of the Régime." University of Cambridge.

Gilham, Jaime. 2013. "Britain's First Muslim Peer of the Realm—Henry, Lord Stanley of Alderley and Islam in Victorian Britain." *Journal of Muslim Minority Affairs*.

Gillibert, Bernard. 2010. *Promenades dans le Paris Ignatien*. Paris: Guide Médiasèvres.

Gilmour, David. 1994. *Curzon: Imperial Statesman*. London: John Murray Ltd.

Gleason, Philip. 1995. *Contending with Modernity: Catholic Higher Education in the Twentieth Century*. New York: Oxford University Press.

Goebel, Edmund J. 1852. *A Study of Catholic Secondary Education during the Colonial Period up to the First Plenary Council of Baltimore*. New York: Benziger.

Goldman, Emma. 1910. "Vaillant!" In *Anarchism and Other Essays*. New York: Mother Earth Publishing Association.

Gorzewski, Andreas. 2016. "DİTİB-Imame Im Spagat." *MiGAZIN*, May 4.

Gözaydın, Iştar B. 2012. "Religion, politique, et politique de la religion en Turquie." *Cahier de l'obtic* 2: 4–8.

Gözaydın, İştar. 2011. "Religion as Soft Power in the International Relations of Turkey." Istanbul: Istanbul Technical University, Department of Humanities and Social Sciences.

Graziano, Manlio. 2017. *In Rome We Trust: The Rise of Catholics in American Political Life*. Stanford, CA: Stanford University Press.

Green, Abigail, and Vincent Viaene, eds. 2012. *Religious Internationals in the Modern World*. London: Palgrave Macmillan.

Green, Dominic. 2007. *Three Empires on the Nile: The Victorian Jihad, 1869–1899*. New York: Free Press.

Greene, Molly. 2005. "The Ottoman Experience." *Daedalus* 134 (2, Spring): 88–99.

Grendler, Paul F. 2019. *Jesuit Schools and Universities in Europe, 1548–1773*. Leiden: Brill.

Grzymala-Busse, Anna. 2015. *Nations under God: How Churches Use Moral Authority to Influence Policy*. Princeton, NJ: Princeton University Press.

Guasco, Maurilio. 1997. *Storia del clero in Italia dall'Ottocento a oggi*. Roma-Bari: Editori Laterza.

Guénois, Jean-Marie. 2014. "La France et l'Algérie s'accordent pour former les imams à la laïcité." *Le Figaro*, December 19.

Guénois, Jean-Marie, and Vincent Tremolet de Villers. 2016. "Jean-Pierre Chevènement, l'Islam de France." *Le Figaro*, August 31.

Guerlac, Othon. 1908. "The Separation of Church and State in France." *Political Science Quarterly* 23.

Guggenberger, Anthony. 1931. *A General History of the Christian Era: For Catholic Colleges and Reading Circles, and for Self-instruction*. St. Louis: B. Herder.

Guida, Michelangelo. 2008. "Seyyid Bey and the Abolition of the Caliphate." *Middle Eastern Studies* 44 (2): 275–89.

Guilday, Peter. 1921. "The Sacred Congregation de Propaganda Fide (1622–1922)." *Catholic Historical Review* 6 (4): 478–94.

———. 1927. *The Life and Times of John England.* New York: America Press.

Gülalp, Haldun. 2005. "Enlightenment by Fiat: Secularization and Democracy in Turkey." *Middle Eastern Studies* 41 (3): 351–72.

Güran, Tevfik. 1997. *Osmanlı Devleti'nin ilk istatistik yilligi, 1897.* Ankara: T.C. Başbakanlık Devlet İstatistik Enstitüsü (State Institute of Statistics).

———. 2003. *Osmanlı malî istatistikleri bütçeler, 1841–1918* (Ottoman financial statistics budgets). Publication 2878. Ankara: T.C. Başbakanlık Devlet İstatistik Enstitüsü (State Institute of Statistics).

———. 2006. "Osmanlı Kamu Maliyesi, 1839–1918." In *Osmanlı Maliyesi: Kurumlar ve Bütçeler,* vol. 1, edited by Mehmet Genç and Erol Özvar. Istanbul: Ottoman Bank Archive and Research Center, pp. 65–95.

Gursel, Kadri. 2014. "Erdoğan Islamizes Education System to Raise 'Devout Youth,'" translated by Sibel Utku Bila. *Al-Monitor,* December 9.

Haddad, Lahcen. 2016. "Le Maroc, fer de lance d'un Islam éclairé." *Huffington Post,* October 5.

Haddad, Mohammad. 2015. "The Metamorphosis of Religion: North Africa in the Modern Era." Working Paper 15. Rome: Istituto Affari Internazionali (September).

———. 2016. *Le Réformisme musulman,* translated by Sarya Baladi. Cham, Switzerland: Springer Publications.

Hafiz, Yasmine. 2013. "Ennahda's Religious Policies Split Tunisia's Ruling Party." *Huffington Post,* September 4.

Haigh, Christopher. 1981. "The Continuity of Catholicism in the English Reformation." *Past and Present* 93: 37–69. Published by Oxford University Press on behalf of the Past and Present Society. http://www.jstor.org/stable/650527.

Hajjaj, Hanan. 2016. "Hardline Currents Are Part of an All-out Crisis in the Arab World" (interview with Abdeljellil Ben Salem). *Al Ahram,* October 13.

Hale, William, and Ergun Özbudun. 2010. *Islamism, Democracy, and Liberalism in Turkey: The Case of the AKP.* New York: Routledge.

Hall, Peter A., and Rosemary C. R. Taylor. 1996. "Political Science and the Three New Institutionalisms." *Political Studies* 44 (5): 936–57.

Hamid, Shadi. 2016. *Islamic Exceptionalism: How the Struggle over Islam Is Reshaping the World.* New York: St. Martin's Press.

Hamid, Shadi, and Peter Mandaville, eds. 2018. *The Geopolitics of Soft Power.* Washington, DC: Brookings Institution Press.

Handy, Robert T. 1976. *A History of the Churches in the United States and Canada.* Oxford: Clarendon Press.

Hanioğlu, M. Sükrü. 2011. *Atatürk: An Intellectual Biography.* Princeton, NJ: Princeton University Press.

Hankey, M.P.A. 1919. "Summary of the Proceedings in Paris in Regard to the Military Occupation in Syria, Cilicia, Palestine, and Mesopotamia, September 1919." No. 18/Q/252 [130943/2117/44A]. In *Documents on British Foreign Policy 1919–1939.*

Hanna, Sami A. 1972. "Changing Trends in Tunisian Socialism." *The Muslim World* 62 (3, July): 230–40.

Hansen, Suzy. 2018. "Istanbul Blues." *New York Review of Books,* February 22.

Hansen, N. 1920. "Die Vatikanisierung des Sultans." *Nord und Süd* (Berlin) (July).

Hardman, Ben. 2009. *Islam and the Métropole: A Case Study of Religion and Rhetoric in Algeria.* New York: Peter Lang.

Hathaway, Jane. 2008. *Arab Lands under Ottoman Rule, 1516–1800.* Harlow: Pearson Longman.

Hatina, Meir, ed. 2009. *Guardians of Faith in Modern Times: "Ulama" in the Middle East.* Boston: Brill.

———. 2009. "The Clerics' Betrayal? Islamists, 'Ulema,' and the Polity." In *Guardians of Faith in Modern Times: "Ulama" in the Middle East,* edited by Meir Hatina. Boston: Brill.

Hattemer, Richard. 2000. "Atatürk and the Reforms in Turkey as Reflected in the Egyptian Press." *Journal of Islamic Studies* 11 (1): 21–42.

Haug, Marie R. 1975. "1975 NCSA Presidential Address: The De-professionalization of Everyone?" *Sociological Focus* 8 (3, August): 197–213.

Hayda, Abdelatif. 2017. "Taoufik Denies 'Religious Diplomacy.'" *Al-Yaoum24* [in Arabic], November 15.

Hefner, Robert W. 2001. "Public Islam and the Problem of Democratization." *Sociology of Religion* 62 (4): 491–514.

Helmy, Khaled. 2006. "The Contrasting Fates of Middle Eastern Politicized Islam and European Politicized Christianity." Religion and Democracy Seminar, Columbia University.

Hennesey, James J. 1981. *American Catholics: A History of the Roman Catholic Community in the United States.* Oxford: Oxford University Press.

Henry, Jean-Robert. 1981. "Droit musulman et structure d'état moderne en Algérie: L'héritage colonial." In *Ordre Religieux et Norme Juridique,* edited by Ernest Gellner, Jean-Claude Vatin, and Abdallah Hammoudi. Paris: Éditions du Centre national de la recherche scientifique (CNRS).

Hertling, Ludwig. 1949. *Geschichte der katholischen Kirche.* Berlin: Morus-Verl.

Hertzke, Allen D. 2009. "The Catholic Church and Catholicism in Global Politics." In *Routledge Handbook of Religion and Politics,* edited by Jeffrey Haynes. New York: Routledge.

Hervieu-Léger, Danièle. 1996. "Une messe est possible: Les doubles funérailles du Président." *Le Débat* 91 (4): 23–30.

———. 2006. *Religion as a Chain of Memory.* Oxford: Polity Press.

Hidayette [pseud.]. 1986. *Abdul Hamid révolutionnaire ou ce qu'on ne peut pas dire en Turquie.* Zurich: O. Füssli.

Hindus, Maurice G. 1922. "The Revolt of the New Immigrant." *The Century* 105 (November): 847–54.

Hitchcock, James. 2012. "Church and State in Modern Europe." Chap. 1 in *Religion and the State: Europe and North America in the Seventeenth and Eighteenth Centuries,* edited by Joshua B. Stein and Sargon G. Donabed. Plymouth: Lexington Books.

Hobbes, Thomas. 1651. *Leviathan, or, The Matter, Forme, and Power of a Common-Wealth Ecclesiasticall and Civil.* London.

Hoffman, Philip T. 2015. *Why Did Europe Conquer the World?* Princeton, NJ: Princeton University Press.

Hollenbach, David. 2012. "Religious Freedom, Morality, and Law: John Courtney Murray Today." *Journal of Moral Theology* 1 (1): 69–91.

———. 2013. "Religious Freedom in Global Context Today: Some Contributions by Vatican II and John Courtney Murray." Washington, DC: Georgetown University, Berkeley Center for Religion, Peace, and World Affairs (September 24).

Holmes, J. Derek. 1979. "The American Heresy." *The Tablet* (January 13): 7–8.

Holtz, Barbel. 2012. "Ministerialabteilung auf Zeit—Die Katholische Abteilung zwischen "Kölner Wirren" und Kulturkampf." Chap. IV in *Das preussische Kultusministerium als Staatsbehörde und gesellschaftliche Agentur (1817–1934)*, edited by Barbel Holtz, Christina Rathgeber, Hartwin Spenkuch, and Reinhold Zilch. Berlin: Akad-Verl.

House of Commons, Parliament of Great Britain. 1867. *Index to the Report from the Select Committee on Ecclesiastical Titles and Roman Catholic Relief Acts*. London: House of Commons.

Howell, Georgina. 2008. *Gertrude Bell: Queen of the Desert, Shaper of Nations*. New York: Sarah Crichton Books.

Hugo, Victor. 1888. *The Poems of Victor Marie Hugo*. New York: Fred DeFau & Co.

Huntington, Samuel P. 1957. *The Soldier and the State: The Theory and Politics of Civil-Military Relations*. Cambridge, MA: Harvard University Press.

———. 1971. "The Change to Change: Modernization, Development, and Politics." *Comparative Politics* 3 (3, April): 283–322.

———. 1991. "Religion and the Third Wave." *The National Interest* 24 (Summer): 29–42.

Hussain, Ishtiaq. 2011. "The Tanzimat: Secular Reforms in the Ottoman Empire." *Faith Matters*, February 15.

Ibrayev, Baytemir. 2012. "Turkish Gambit in Kyrgyzstan." *Belvy Parus (Bishkek)*, August 28.

Inalcik, Halil. 1968–1970. "Islam in the Ottoman Empire." *Cultura Turcica* 5–7: 19–29.

Inalcik, Halil, Nejat Göyünç, and Heath W. Lowry. 1984. "Osmanlı Arastimalari IV," *Journal of Ottoman Studies* 4: 166–67.

Inalcik, Halil, and Donald Quataert, eds. 1994. *An Economic and Social History of the Ottoman Empire, 1600–1914*, vol. 2. Cambridge: Cambridge University Press.

International Republican Institute (IRI). 2014. "Survey of Tunisian Public Opinion: June 22–July 1, 2014." Washington, DC: IRI.

International Union for Muslims Scholars. 2016. "Qaradawi: Thanks to Turkey and to the President Erdogan." April 23.

Iraqi, Fahid. 2013. "The Controversy, for Lack of Debate." *Telquel*, May 8.

Ireland, John C. 1901. "The Pope's Civil Princedom." *North American Review* 172 (532): 337–51.

Istfan, Habeeb G. 1922. "Kemal as He Looks to the Mohammedan World." *New York Times*, December 17.

Itzkowitz, Norman. 1972. *Ottoman Empire and Islamic Tradition*. Chicago: University of Chicago Press.

Itzkowitz, Norman, and Joel Shinder. 1972. "The Office of Seyh ul-Islam and the Tanzimat: A Prospographic Enquiry." *Middle Eastern Studies* 8 (1): 93–101.

Jalal. 2015. "Le Maroc investit sur la formation des imams." *Katibin*, March 29.

James, Edwin L. 1922. "Dropping of Sultan Worries the French; They Fear the Effect of Angora's Action on Their Moslem Empire—Distrust Kemal." *New York Times*, November 5.

James, William. 2002 [1837]. "French and British Fleets." In *The Naval History of Great Britain: From the Declaration of War by France in 1793 to the Accession of George IV*, vol. 2, 1797–1799. Mechanicsburg, PA: Stackpole Books.

Jelen, T. G. 2009. "The American Church." In *Routledge Handbook of Religion and Politics*, edited by Jeffrey Haynes. New York: Routledge.

Jenkins, Gareth. 2008. *Political Islam in Turkey: Running West, Heading East?* London: Palgrave Macmillan.

Jensen, Richard Bach. 2014. *The Battle against Anarchist Terrorism.* New York: Cambridge University Press.

Jilani, Muhammad. 2013. "Was the System Adopted by the Ottomans Islamic? (The Ottoman Caliphate 2/4)." *New Civilisation,* November 14. http://www.newcivilisation.com/home /islamic-civilisation/was-the-system-adopted-by-the-ottomans-islamic-the-ottoman -caliphate-24/.

John Paul II. 2009. "Centesimus Annus (1991)." In *Routledge Handbook of Religion and Politics,* edited by Jeffrey Haynes. New York: Routledge.

Joshi, A. P., M. D. Srinivas, and J. K. Bajaj. 2005. *Religious Demography of India.* New Delhi: Dr. J. K. Bajaj for the Centre for Policy Studies.

Jouanneau, Solène. 2013. *Les Imams en France: Une autorité religieuse sous contrôle.* Paris: Agone.

Jouffroy, Theodore L. 1901. "Warnings and Teachings of the Church on Anarchism." *The Catholic World* (December).

Jung, Dietrich. 2017. "War and State in the Middle East: Reassessing Charles Tilly in a Regional Context." In *Does War Make States? Investigations of Charles Tilly's Historical Sociology,* edited by Lars Bo Kaspersen and Jeppe Strandsbjerg. Cambridge: Cambridge University Press.

Jung, Dietrich, and Catharina Raudvere. 2008. *Religion, Politics, and Turkey's EU Accession.* New York: Palgrave Macmillan.

Kacem, Mehdi Belhaj. 2009. *L'Esprit du Nihilisme: Une ontologique de l'histoire.* Paris: Fayard.

Kalyvas, Stathis N. 2012. "The 'Turkish Model' in the Matrix of Political Catholicism." In *Democracy, Islam, and Secularism in Turkey,* edited by Ahmet T. Kuru and Alfred Stepan. New York: Columbia University Press.

Kamen, Henry. 1998. *The Spanish Inquisition: A Historical Revision.* New Haven, CT: Yale University Press.

Kant, Neil. 2000. *The Soul of the North: A Social, Architectural and Cultural History of the Nordic Countries: 1700–1940.* London: Reaktion Books.

Kaptein, Nico J. G. 2004. "The Voice of the Ulema: Fatwas and Religious Authority in Indonesia." *Archives de sciences sociales des religions* (January/March): 115–30.

Karakas, Cemal. 2007. "Turkei: Islam und Laizismus zwischen Staats-, Politik-, und Gesellschaftsinteressen." Report 1/2007. Frankfurt am Main: Hessische Stiftung Friedens- und Konfliktforschung (HSFK).

Karateke, Hakan T. 2005. "Legitimizing the Ottoman Sultanate: A Framework for Historical Analysis." In *Legitimizing the Order: The Ottoman Rhetoric of State Power,* edited by Hakan Karateke and Maurus Reinkowski. Leiden: Brill.

Karčić, Hamza. 2014. "Supporting the Caliph's Project: Bosnian Muslims and the Hejaz Railway." *Journal of Muslim Minority Affairs* 34 (3): 282–92. doi:10.1080/13602004.2014.939555.

Karpat, Kemal H. 1972. "The Transformation of the Ottoman State, 1789–1908." *International Journal of Middle East Studies* 3: 243–81.

———, ed. 2000. *Ottoman Past and Today's Turkey.* Cologne: Brill.

———. 2001. *The Politicization of Islam: Reconstructing Identity, State, Faith, and Community in the Late Ottoman State.* Oxford: Oxford University Press.

Karsh, Efraim. 2018. "Turks and Arabs Welcomed the Balfour Declaration." *Middle East Forum* 25 (1, Winter): 1–13.

Kayali, Hasan. 1997. *Arabs and Young Turks: Ottomanism, Arabism, and Islamism in the Ottoman Empire, 1908–1918.* Berkeley: University of California Press.

Kedourie, Elie. 1963. "Egypt and the Caliphate, 1915–1946." *Journal of the Royal Asiatic Society of Great Britain and Ireland* 95 (3/4, October): 208–48.

———. 1980. *Islam in the Modern World, and Other Studies.* London: Holt, Rinehart and Winston.

Keller, Josh, Iaryna Mykhyalyshyn, and Safak Timur. 2016. "The Scale of Turkey's Purge Is Nearly Unprecedented." *New York Times,* August 2.

Kelley, J. H., Jr. 1924. "American Vice Consul in Charge to Secretary of State; Expulsion from Turkey of the Caliph." Edited by the Department of State. Damascus, Syria: American Consulate in Syria.

Kemal, Yurtnaç. 2012. *Turkey's New Horizon: Turks Abroad and Related Communities.* Ankara: Center for Strategic Research.

Kennedy, Thomas. 1911. "Catholic Missions." In *The Catholic Encyclopedia,* vol. 10, edited by Charles G. Herbermann et al. New York: Robert Appleton Co.

Kertzer, David I. 2018. *The Pope Who Would Be King: The Exile of Pius IX and the Emergence of Modern Europe.* New York: Random House.

Khalid, Adeeb. 2001. "Ottoman Islamism between the Ümmet and the Nation." *Archivum Ottomanicum* 19: 197–211.

Khalidi, Omar. 2004. "The Caliph's Daughter." *Cornucopia Magazine* 31.

Khan, Mohamed Samin. 1958. "Religion and State in Turkey (Continued)." *Pakistan Horizon* 11 (4, December): 221–37.

Khoury, Gérard D. 2004. "Robert de Caix et Louis Massignon: Deux visions de la politique française au Levant en 1920." In *The British and French Mandates in Comparative Perspectives,* edited by Nadine Méouchy and Peter Sluglett. Leiden: Brill.

Kieser, Hans-Lukas, Margaret Lavinia Anderson, Seyhan Bayraktar, and Thomas Schmutz, eds. 2019. *End of the Ottomans: The Genocide of 1915 and the Politics of Turkish Nationalism.* London: I. B. Tauris.

Kim, Hyojoung, and Steven Pfaff. 2012. "Structure and Dynamics of Religious Insurgency: Students and the Spread of the Reformation." *American Sociological Review* 77 (2): 188–215.

Kirsch, Johann P., and Vincent Luksch. 1905. *Illustrierte Geschichte der Katholischen Kirche.* Munich: Allgemeine Verlags-Gesellschaft.

Kiser, John W. 2008. *Commander of the Faithful: The Life and Times of Emir And el-Kader: A Story of True Jihad.* Rhinebeck, NY: Monkfish Book Publishing.

Klausen, Jytte. 2005. *The Islamic Challenge: Politics and Religion in Western Europe.* New York: Oxford University Press.

Knabenahue, P. 1931. "To the Secretary of State; Subject: Pan-Islamic Congress." Jerusalem: American Consulate (November 17).

Kohn, Richard H. 1997. "How Democracies Control the Military." *Journal of Democracy* 8 (4).

Konda Institute. 2019. "Turks Losing Trust in Religion under AKP." *Al-Monitor,* January 9.

Korkmaz, Özgür. 2015. "What Do People Want from Turkey's Top Religious Body?" *Hürriyet Daily News,* April 30.

Korkut, Şenol. 2010. "The Diyanet of Turkey and Its Activities in Eurasia after the Cold War." *Acta Slavica Iaponica*.

Körting, Erhart. 2015. "Djihadistische Radikalisierung und staatliche Gegenstrategien." *Arbeitspapier Religion und Politik* 2.

Kramarek, Michal J., and Mary L. Gautier. 2017. "The Class of 2017: Survey of Ordinands to the Priesthood: A Report to the Secretariat of Clergy, Consecrated Life and Vocations, United States Conference of Catholic Bishops." Washington, DC: Center for Applied Research in the Apostolate (CARA), Georgetown University (April).

Krämer, Gudrun. 2008. *A History of Palestine: From the Ottoman Conquest to the Founding of the State of Israel*, trans. Graham Harman and Gudrun Kramer. Princeton, NJ: Princeton University Press.

Kramer, Martin. 1986. *Islam Assembled: The Advent of the Muslim Congresses*. New York: Columbia University Press.

Krasner, Stephen D. 1999. *Sovereignty: Organized Hypocrisy*. Princeton, NJ: Princeton University Press.

Kupferschmidt, Uri M. 1987. *The Supreme Muslim Council: Islam under the British Mandate for Palestine*. Boston: Brill.

Kuran, Timur. 2001. "The Provision of Public Goods under Islamic Law: Origins, Impact, and Limitations of the Waqf System." *Law and Society Review* 35 (4): 841–98.

Kuru, Ahmet T. 2009. *Secularism and State Policies toward Religion: The United States, France, and Turkey*. Cambridge: Cambridge University Press.

———. 2013. "Policy Briefing: Muslim Politics without an 'Islamic State.'" Washington, DC: Brookings Doha Center (February).

———. 2019. *Islam, Authoritarianism, and Underdevelopment: A Global and Historical Comparison*. Cambridge: Cambridge University Press.

LaCapra, Dominick. 1982. *Madame Bovary on Trial*. Ithaca, NY: Cornell University Press.

Laffan, Michael Francis. 2003. *Islamic Nationhood and Colonial Indonesia: The Umma below the Winds*. London: Routledge, 2003.

Lahouazi, Mohamed. 2017. "Mohamed Aissa: 'Al Ahmadiyya Sect's Activities Are Geared to Foreign Intelligence Purposes.'" *Echourouk El-Youmi*, March 27. https://www.echoroukonline.com/mohamed-aissa-al-ahmadiyya-sects-activities-are-geared-to-foreign-intelligence-purposes/.

Lamfalussy, Christophe. 2010. "Rabat inquiet de l'Islam belge." *Le Soir*, June 28.

Landau, Jacob. 1990. *The Politics of Pan-Islam: Ideology and Organization*. Oxford: Clarendon Press.

Langdon, William Chauncy. 1894. "Italy and the Papacy." *International Journal of Ethics* 5 (1, October): 103–6.

Lapidus, Ira M. 1996. "State and Religion in Islamic Societies," *Past and Present* 151 (1): 3–27.

Larkin, Emmet. 2006. *The Pastoral Role of the Roman Catholic Church in Pre-Famine Ireland, 1750–1850*. Washington, DC: Catholic University of America Press.

Laurence, Jonathan. 2012. *The Emancipation of Europe's Muslims: The State's Role in Immigration Integration*. Princeton, NJ: Princeton University Press.

Laurence, Jonathan, and Justin Vaisse. 2006. *Integrating Islam: Political and Religious Challenges in Contemporary France*. Washington, DC: Brookings Institution.

Laurens, Henri. 2006. "La Projection chrétienne de l'Europe industrielle sur les provinces arabes de l'Empire ottoman." In *Le Choc colonial et l'Islam: Les politiques religieuses des puissances coloniales en terres d'Islam*, edited by Pierre-Jean Luizard. Paris: Découverte.

Laycock, Douglas. 2009. "Church Autonomy Revisited." *Georgetown Journal of Law and Public Policy* 7 (1): 253–78.

LeBars, Stéphanie. 2014. Des imams à l'école pour se former à "L'islam de France." *Le Monde*, April 23.

Lepeska, David. 2015. "Turkey Casts the Diyanet." *Foreign Affairs* (May).

Lewis, Bernard. 1952. "Islamic Revival in Turkey." *International Affairs* 28 (1, January).

Lewis, Bernard. 1994. *Islam and the West*. New York: Oxford University Press.

———. 2001. *The Emergence of Modern Turkey*. Oxford: Oxford University Press.

———. 2002. *What Went Wrong? Western Impact and Middle Eastern Response*. Oxford: Oxford University Press.

———. 2003. *The Crisis of Islam: Holy War and Unholy Terror*. New York: Random House.

Lewis, Geoffrey. 1966. "Islam in Politics." *The Muslim World* 56 (4, October): 235–311.

Leyshon, Gareth. 2004. *Catholic Statistics: Priests and Population in England and Wales, 1841–2001*. Wonersh, Guildford: St. John's Seminary (August).

Lhomme, Frabrice, and Gérard Davet. 2017. "Qui sont les djihadistes français tués par des 'frappes ciblées?'" *Le Monde*, January 4.

Liegeard, Armand. 1884. "Immigration into the United States." *Journal of the Statistical Society of London* 47 (3, September): 496–515.

Lilla, Mark. 2007. *The Stillborn God: Religion, Politics, and the Modern West*. New York: Alfred A. Knopf.

Lindsay, S. M., and Leo S. Rowe, trans. 2017. *Constitution of the Kingdom of Italy*, with a historical introduction and notes. Philadelphia: American Academy of Political and Social Science.

Littlefield, Walter. 1924. "Why the Turks Got Rid of the Caliphate." *New York Times*, March 9.

Liu, Joseph. 2013. "The Global Catholic Population." Washington, DC: Pew Research Center/ Religion & Public Life Project (February 12).

Locke, John. 1680. *A Letter Concerning Toleration*, edited by William Popple.

Long, Alexander Dennis. 2016. *The Development of the Roman Missal: Fostering the Growth of the Ordinary and Extraordinary Forms of the Roman Rite*. Dayton, OH: University of Dayton.

Louassini, Zouhair. 2017. "Alta tensione in Marocco." *Rainews*, June 30.

Louis, William Roger. 2015. "End of the Caliphate." *Wall Street Journal*, September 4.

Lowther, Sir G. 1912. "Sir G. Lowther to Sir Edward Grey, Letter on the Signature of Italo-Turkish Peace Protocol; Commenting on Terms," Constantinople, 1912. In chap. 74, "The Tripoli War, V. The Treaty of Peace," in *British Documents on the Origins of the War 1898–1914* (no. 459).

Luizard, Pierre-Jean. 2006. *Le Choc colonial et l'Islam: Les politiques religieuses des puissances coloniales en terres d'islam*. Paris: Decouverte.

Lule, Zeynel. 2018. "Cemevis, ECtHR." *T24* [in Turkish], November 29.

Lupu, Ira C., and Robert W. Tuttle. 2004. "Sexual Misconduct and Ecclesiastical Immunity." *Brigham Young University Law Review* 2004 (5): 1789–1896.

MacCulloch, Diarmaid. 2003. *The Reformation: A History*. New York: Viking.

Macedo, Stephen. 2010. *Liberal Virtues: Citizenship, Virtue, and Community in Liberal Constitu-tionalism*. Oxford: Clarendon Press.

MacFarlane, Charles. 1850. *Turkey and Its Destiny: The Result of Journeys Made in 1847 and 1848 to Examine into the State of That Country*. London: John Murray.

Macfie, A. L. 1975. "The British Decision Regarding the Future of Constantinople, November 1918–January 1920." *The Historical Journal* 18 (2, June): 391–400.

Machiavelli, Niccolò. 2007. *The Essential Writings of Machiavelli*, selected and translated by Peter Constantine. New York: Random House.

MacMillan, Margaret. 2001. *Paris 1919: Six Months That Changed the World*. New York: Random House.

Mahiou, Ahmed, and Jean-Robert Henry, eds. 2001. *Où va l'Algérie*. Paris: l'Institut de recherches et d'études sur les mondes arabes et musulmans (IREMAM).

Mahoney, James. 2000. "Path Dependence in Historical Sociology." *Theory and Society* 29 (4): 507–48.

Mahoney, James, and Dietrich Rueschemeyer, eds. 2003.*Comparative Historical Analysis in the Social Sciences*. Cambridge: Cambridge University Press.

Maier, Charles S. 2015. *Recasting Bourgeois Europe: Stabilization in France, Germany, and Italy in the Decade after World War I*, with a new preface. Princeton, NJ: Princeton University Press.

Makedhi, Madjid. 2015. "Conflit de Ghardaïa et référence religieuse nationale: Mohamed Aïssa alerte sur les dangers du Salafisme." *El Watan*, July 16.

Malanima, Paolo. 2010. "Energy and Population in Europe: The Medieval Growth (10th–14th Centuries." Institute of Studies on Mediterranean Societies (ISSM) and National Research Council (CNR). http://www.paolomalanima.it/default_file/Papers/MEDIEVAL _GROWTH.pdf.

Malatesta, Errico. 2015. *Life and Ideas: The Anarchist Writings of Errico Malatesta*. Oakland, CA: PM Press.

Malka, Haim. 2017. "The Struggle for Religious Identity in Tunisia and the Maghreb." Washington, DC: Center for Strategic and International Studies (June 14).

Maloney, M. T., Abdulkadir Civan, and Mary Frances Maloney. 2010. "Model of Religious Schism with Application to Islam." *Public Choice* 142 (3/4): 441–60. doi:10.1007/ s11127-009-9533-9.

Mango, Andrew. 2002. *Atatürk: The Biography of the Founder of Modern Turkey*. Woodstock, NY: Overlook Press.

Manning, Henry Edward. 1880. "The Catholic Church and Modern Society." *North American Review* 130 (279, February): 101–15.

Mardin, Serif. 1989. *Religion and Social Change in Modern Turkey: The Case of Bediuzzaman Said Nursi*. Albany: State University of New York Press.

Maritato, Chiara. 2017. "Turkish Marriages between Religion and the State." *Reset DOC*, November 6.

Markham, James J. 2013. *The Sacred Congregation of Seminaries and Universities of Studies*. Washington, DC: Catholic University of America Press.

Marraro, Howard R. 1944–1945. "Canadian and American Zouaves in the Papal Army, 1868–1870." *Canadian Catholic Historical Association Report* 12: 83–102. https://www.umanitoba.ca /colleges/st_pauls/ccha/Back%20Issues/CCHA1944-45/Marraro.html.

Martin, Frederick. 1869. *The Statesman's Year-Book: A Statistical, Mercantile, and Historical Account of the States and Sovereigns of Civilised World.* London: MacMillan and Co.

———. 1878. *The Statesman's Year-Book: Statistical and Historical Annual of the States of the Civilised World for the Year 1878.* London: Macmillan and Co.

Martin, A. Lynn. 1973. "The Jesuit Mystique." *Sixteenth Century Journal* 4 (1): 31–40.

Martina, Giacomo. *Pio IX (1867–1878).* Roma: Editrice Pontificia Universitá Gregoriana.

———. 1985. "S.I., Il clero nell'Italia centrale dalla restaurazione all'unità." In *S.I., Problemi di storia della chiesa,* edited by Vincenzo Monachino. Napoli: Edizioni Devoniane.

Martin-Chauffier, Gilles. 2014. "Erdoğan en première ligne." *Paris Match,* June 19.

Marzouk, Zeineb. 2016. "Government Seeks Niqab Ban and Central Control of Mosques." *Tunisia Live,* April 2.

Masbah, Mohammed. 2014. "Moroccan Fighters in Syria." Washington, DC: Carnegie Endowment for International Peace (April 10).

Masbah, Mohammed. 2016. "Salafi Movements and the Political Process in Morocco." In *Salafism after the Arab Awakening: Contending with People's Power,* edited by Francesco Cavatorta and Fabio Merone. Oxford: Oxford University Press.

Masci, David, and Gregory A. Smith. 2018. "7 Facts about US Catholics." Washington, DC: Pew Research Center (October 10).

Massa, Mark Stephen, SJ. 2010. *The American Catholic Revolution: How the '60s Changed the Church Forever.* Oxford: Oxford University Press.

Massignon, Louis. 1920. "Introduction à l'étude des revendications islamiques." *Revue du monde musulman* 39.

Masters, Bruce. 2013. *The Arabs of the Ottoman Empire, 1516–1918: A Social and Cultural History.* New York: Cambridge University Press.

Mattox, Henry E. 2004. *Chronology of World Terrorism, 1901–2001.* Jefferson, NC: McFarland.

Mayaram, Shail. 2006. *Against History, Against State.* New Delhi: Permanent Black.

Mazewski, Matt. 2014. "Will the Geographic Profile of the College of Cardinals Really Change under Francis?" *Reasonably Moderate,* February 23.

McAdam, Doug, Sidney Tarrow, and Charles Tilly. 2008. *Dynamics of Contentio.* Cambridge: Cambridge University Press.

McAvoy, Thomas Timothy. 1909. "The Immigrants Dominate the American Church, 1850–1866." *North American Review* 190 (647, October). Reprinted in Thomas Timothy McAvoy, *A History of the Catholic Church in the United States.* Notre Dame, IN: University of Notre Dame Press.

———. 1969. *A History of the Catholic Church in the United States.* Notre Dame, IN: University of Notre Dame Press.

McCants, William. 2015. "The Believer: How Abu Bakr Al-Baghdadi Became Leader of the Islamic State." *The Brookings Essay,* September 1, 2015. http://csweb.brookings.edu/content/research/essays/2015/thebeliever.html.

McGabe, Joseph. 1939. *A History of the Popes.* London: Watts & Ox.

McGirr, Lisa. 2016. *The War on Alcohol: Prohibition and the Rise of the American State.* New York: W. W. Norton & Co.

McGreevy, John T. 2016. *American Jesuits and the World: How an Embattled Religious Order Made Modern Catholicism Global.* Princeton, NJ: Princeton University Press.

Mecham, R. Quinn. 2004. "From the Ashes of Virtue, a Promise of Light: The Transformation of Political Islam in Turkey." *Third World Quarterly* 25 (2): 339–58.

Mellal, Nadia. 2007. "Ce qui va changer dans les mosquées algériennes." *Algeria-Watch: Informations sur la situation des droits humaines en Algérie*, July 4.

Merad, Ali. 2007 [1914]. *L'Empire ottoman et "l'Europe": D'après les pensées et souvenirs du sultan Abdul-Hamid II (1876–1909)*, reprint ed. Paris: Publisud.

———. 1983. "La Turcophilie dans le débat national en Algérie au début du siècle (1911–1918)." in *Les Provinces arabes et leurs sources documentaires à l'époque ottomane: (partie française et anglaise)*, edited by Abdeljelil Tamimi. Tunis: La Fondation Temini.

Meyer, John W., and Brian Rowan. 1977. "Institutionalized Organizations: Formal Structure as Myth and Ceremony." *American Journal of Sociology* 83 (2, September): 340–63.

Midouni, H., and H. Bounab. 2013. "Les Affaires Religieuses mettent en garde contre les avis théologiques importés." *Algérie Actualités*, July 26.

Miller, Paula Jean, and Richard Fossey. 2004. *Mapping the Catholic Cultural Landscape*, Lanham, MD: Rowman & Littlefield.

Minawi, Mostafa. 2016. *The Ottoman Scramble for Africa: Empire and Diplomacy in the Sahara and the Hijaz*. Stanford, CA: Stanford University Press.

Ministry of Finance. 2003. *Osmanlı Bütçeleri (1909–1918)*. Publication 358. Ankara: Ministry of Finance.

———. 2003. *1917 (1333) Yılı Osmanlı Bütçesi*. Publication 363. Ankara: Ministry of Finance, Research, Planning and Coordination Board.

Mitchell, Timothy. 1991. "Limits of the State." *American Political Science Review* 85 (1, March): 77–96.

Moller, Jes Farbicius, and Uffe Ostergard. 2013. "Lutheran Orthodoxy and Anti-Catholicism in Denmark, 1536–2011." *European Studies* 31: 165–89.

Molteni, Giuseppe. 1924. "La Fase odierna del problema dell'emigrazione italiana negli Stati Uniti." *Rivista Internazionale di Scienze Sociali e Discipline Ausillarie* 98 (376): 375–422.

Monachino, Vincenzo. 1985. *S.I., Problemi di storia della chiesa*. Napoli: Edizioni Devoniane.

Monastiri, Taoufik. 1979. "L'Isam de M. El-Qaddhafi." *Middle East Studies Association Bulletin* 13 (2, December).

Moore, Clement Henry. 1965. *Tunisia since Independence: The Dynamics of One-Party Government*. Berkeley: University of California Press.

Moore, John F. 1931. *Will America Become Catholic?* New York: Harper and Brothers.

Moreau, Odile. 2017. "Politics of Religion during the First World War: Ottoman Islamic Rhetoric in Morocco." Session P4913, annual meeting of the Middle East Studies Association, Washington, DC, November 18–21.

Morgan, John F. W. 1983. "The Natural History of Professionalization and Its Effects on Valuation Theory and Practice in the UK and Germany." *Journal of Property Valuation and Investment* 16 (2): 185–206.

Morris, Charles R. 1997. *American Catholic: The Saints and Sinners Who Built America's Most Powerful Church*. New York: Random House.

Morse, Samuel F. B. 1855. *Foreign Conspiracy against the Liberties of the United States: The Numbers under the Signature of Brutus, Originally Published in the New York Observer*. Cambridge, MA: Harvard University Press.

Motadel, David, 2012. "Islam and the European Empires: Historiographical Essay." *The Historical Journal* 55 (3): 831–56.

———, ed. 2014. *Islam and the European Empires*. The Past and Present Book Series. Oxford: Oxford University Press.

Mourad, A. 2015. "Mohamed Aïssa aux imams délégués en France: 'Il faut préserver la référence religieuse Algérienne.'" *El Moudjahid*, January 5.

Murphy, Rhoads. 2008. *Exploring Ottoman Sovereignty: Tradition, Image, and Practice in the Ottoman Imperial Household*. London: Continuum.

Murray, John Courtney. 1964. "The Problem of Religious Freedom." *Theological Studies* 25 (4): 130–37.

———. 1965. *The Problem of Religious Freedom*. Gastonia, NC: Neumann Press.

Mutlu, Servet. 2003. "Late Ottoman Population and Its Ethnic Distribution." *Nüfusbilim Dergisi/ Turkish Journal of Population Studies* 25.

Nairn, Thomas. 2015. "Ethics—Celebrating Human Dignity: Two Documents of Vatican II." *Catholic Health Association of the United States* (November/December).

Nasr, Seyyed Vali Reza. 2001. *Islamic Leviathan: Islam and the Making of State Power*. New York: Oxford University Press.

Nasri, Mariam. 2017. "Mosques without Imams in Tunisia." *al ʾArabi al Jadid*, January 17.

National Catholic Educational Association. 1966. *Catholic Seminaries in the United States*. Washington, DC: National Catholic Educational Association.

Norris, Pippa, and Ronald Inglehart. 2002. "Islam and the West: Testing the Clash of Civilizations Thesis." *SSRN Electronic Journal* (April).

Norton, Anne. 2013. *On the Muslim Question*. Princeton, NJ: Princeton University Press.

Noyon, Jennifer. 2003. "Tunisia's 'Managed Democracy.'" In Jennifer Noyon, *Islam, Politics, and Pluralism: Theory and Practice in Turkey, Jordan, Tunisia, and Algeria*. Washington, DC: Royal Institute of International Affairs.

Ochsenwald, William L. 1975. "Ottoman Subsidies to the Hijaz, 1877–1886." *International Journal of Middle East Studies* 6 (3, July): 300–307.

———. 2010. "Islam and the Ottoman Legacy in the Modern Middle East." In *Religion, Economy, and State in Ottoman-Arab History*. Piscataway, NJ: Gorgias Press/Isis Press.

O'Connor, J. D. 1877. *History of Turkey: Comprising the Geography, Chronology, and Statistics of the Empire; the Ethnology, Primitive Traditions, and Sociology of the Turks; the Genealogy of the Existing Osmanli Dynasty; and the Causes of the War of 1877*. Chicago: Moses Warren.

O'Donnell, John Hugh. 1922. *The Catholic Hierarchy of the United States, 1790–1922*. Washington, DC: Catholic University of America.

Öktem, Kerem. 2010. "New Islamic Actors after the Wahhabi Intermezzo: Turkey's Return to the Muslim Balkans." Oxford: European Studies Centre, University of Oxford (December).

Öktem, Kerem, Ayşe Kadioğlu, and Mehmet Karlı. 2009. *Another Empire? A Decade of Turkey's Foreign Policy under the Justice and Development Party*. South East European Studies at Oxford. Istanbul: Bilgi University Press.

Oliver-Dee, Sean. 2009. *The Caliphate Question: The British Government and Islamic Governance*. Lexington: Lexington Books.

———. 2009. "The Cairo High Command and the Caliphate Question, 1914–1919." In Sean Oliver-Dee, *The Caliphate Question: The British Government and Islamic Governance*. Lexington: Lexington Books.

———. 2009. "The British Government Files and the Approach to Pan-Islamic Government." In Sean Oliver-Dee, *The Caliphate Question: The British Government and Islamic Governance*. Lexington: Lexington Books.

O'Malley, John W. 1995. *The First Jesuits*. Cambridge, MA: Harvard University Press.

———. 2012. "Vatican II Revisited: The Apostolic Visitation Revives Some Unresolved Conflicts." *America Magazine*, December 8.

———. 2012. "Opening the Church to the World." *New York Times*, October 10.

———. 2013. *Trent: What Happened at the Council*. Cambridge, MA: Harvard University Press.

———. 2015. "Vatican II Revisited as Reconciliation: The Francis Factor." In *The Legacy of Vatican II*, edited by Massimo Faggioli and Andrea Vicini, SJ. Mahwah, NJ: Paulist Press.

———. 2018. *Vatican One: The Council and the Making of the Ultramontane Church*. Cambridge, MA: Harvard University Press.

O'Malley, Sean. 2014. "Jesuit Survival and Restoration." Jesuit Survival and Restoration Conference, Boston College, June 11.

Opera della propagazione della Fede. 1841. *Notizia sull'opera pia della propagazione della fede a prò delle missioni straniere ne' due mondi*. Napoli: Dei Tipi dei Fratelli de Bonis nel Palazzo Arcivescovile.

O'Reilly, Bernard. 1894. "Territorial Sovereignty and the Papacy." *North American Review* 158 (447, February): 211–21.

Orsini, Alessandro. 2012. "Poverty, Ideology, and Terrorism: The STAM Bond." *Studies in Conflict and Terrorism* 35 (10): 665–92.

Owen, John M. 2010. *The Clash of Ideas in World Politics: Transnational Networks, States, and Regime Change, 1510–2010*. Princeton, NJ: Princeton University Press.

Özdalga, Elizabeth. 1999. "Education in the Name of 'Order and Progress': Reflections on the Recent Eight Year Obligatory School Reform in Turkey." *The Muslim World* 79 (3/4, July/October).

Özgur, Iren. 2015. *Islamic Schools in Modern Turkey: Faith, Politics, and Education*. Cambridge: Cambridge University Press.

Ozkan, Behlül. 2014. "Turkey, Davutoğlu, and the Idea of Pan-Islamism." *Survival: Global Politics and Strategy* (July 23): 119–40.

Öztürk, Ahmet Erdi. 2016. "Turkey's Diyanet under AKP Rule: From Protector to Imposer of State Ideology?" *Southeast European and Black Sea Studies* 16 (4): 619–35.

———. 2016. *AK Parti Döneminde AB Süreci: Çok Boyutlu İnşacılığın Pragmatizm Ile Sentezi*. https://www.academia.edu/25983715/AK_PART%C4%B0_D%C3%96NEM%C4%B0NDE_AB_S%C3%9CREC%C4%B0_%C3%87OK_BOYUTLU_%C4%B0N%C5%9EACILI%C4%9EIN_PRAGMAT%C4%B0ZM_%C4%B0LE_SENTEZ%C4%B0.

Ozturk, Kemal. 2017. "Commentary: Two Important Developments in the Fight against FETO." *Yeni Safak*, July 27.

Pacaci, Mehmet, and Yasin Aktay. 1999. "75 Years of Higher Religious Education in Modern Turkey." *The Muslim World*, October 1.

Palmieri, P. Aurelio. 1918. "Il protestantesimo e gli emigranti italiani." *Rivista Internazionale* 76 (302, February): 85–98.

———. 1918. "L'Aspetto economico del problema religioso italiano." *Rivista internazationale* 77 (307, July): 184–210.

Pamuk, Şevket. 2009. "The Ottoman Economy in World War I." In *The Economics of World War I*, edited by Stephen Broadberry and Mark Harrison. Cambridge: Cambridge University Press.

Pankhurst, Reza. 2013. *The Inevitable Caliphate? A History of the Struggle for Global Islamic Union, 1924 to the Present*. London: Hurst & Co.

Parigi, Paolo. 2012. *The Rationalization of Miracles*. Cambridge: Cambridge University Press.

Parteger, Alison. 1995. "Algeria's Religious Affairs Official Shot Dead." *Financial Times*, July 26.

Pastor, Ludwig von. 1908. *The History of the Popes, from the Close of the Middle Ages, Drawn from the Secret Archives of the Vatican and Other Original Sources*, vol. 6 of *The History of the Popes*, edited by Frederick Ignatius Antrobus. London: Kegan Paul, Trench, Trübner & Co.

Paul VI. 1965. "Gaudium et spes." In Vatican Council II, *Pastoral Constitution on the Church in the Modern World*, December 7.

Pelican, Jaroslav. 1964. *Obedient Rebels: Catholic Substance and Protestant Principle in Luther's Reformation*. London: SCM Press.

Pellicciari, Angela. 2000. "Risorgimento da riscrivere." Unpublished manuscript.

———. 2011. *Risorgimento Anticattolico*. Verona: Fede & Cultura.

Petacco, Arrigo. 1969. *L'Anarchico che venne dall'America*. Milano: Mondadori.

Peter, Frank, Sarah Dornhof, and Elena Arigita, eds. 2013. *Islam and the Politics of Culture in Europe: Memory, Aesthetics, Art*. Bielefeld: Transcript Verlag.

Pew Research Center. 2011. "Global Christianity: A Report on the Size and Distribution of the World's Christian Population." December 19. https://www.pewforum.org/2011/12/19/global-christianity-exec/.

Philpott, Daniel. 2000. "The Religious Roots of Modern International Relations." *World Politics* 52 (2): 206–45.

Picarello, Anthony R., Jr. 2007. *School Choice: The Blaine Amendments and Anti-Catholicism*. Washington, DC: US Commission on Civil Rights. https://www.usccr.gov/pubs/docs/BlaineReport.pdf.

Picarello, Anthony R., K. Hollyn Hollman, Ellen Johnson, and Richard D. Komer. 2007. *School Choice: The Blaine Amendments and Anti-Catholicism*. Testimony before the US Commission on Civil Rights, June 1, 2007, Washington, DC.

Pinar, Candas. 2013. "Religion-State Relations in Turkey since the AKP: A Changing Landscape? Evidence from Parliamentary Debates on the Alevi Matter." *Journal of Muslim Minority Affairs* 33 (4): 507–20.

Pirenne, Henri. 1961 [1937]. *Mahomet et Charlemagne*. Paris: Club de Libraries de France.

Pitzipios, Jakobos Georgios. 1881. *The Eastern Question Solved*. London: W. H. Allen.

Plasse, Stéphanie. 2014. "Chems-Eddine Hafiz (CFCM): Une voix religieuse est nécessaire dans le plan anti-jihad." *Jeune Afrique*, April 29.

Popovic, Alexandre. 1986. *L'Islam balkanique: Les musulmans du sud-est européen dans la période post-ottomane*. Berlin: Berlin University Press.

Porter, Geoffrey David. 2002. "At the Pillar's Base: Islam, Morocco and Education in the Qarawiyin Mosque, 1912–2000." PhD diss., New York University.

Powell, Joseph. 1871. *Two Years in the Pontifical Zouaves*. London: Washbourne.

Premoli, Orazio. 1925. *Storia ecclesiastica contemporanea (1900–1925)*. Torino: Marietti.

Press, Elizabeth. 2008. "Turkish Prime Minister Says 'Assimilation Is a Crime against Humanity.'" *The Local De*, February 11.

Preuss, Ulrich K. 2004. "Religion and Politics and the Constitutional Patterns of Their Mutual Accommodations." University of Chicago Law School (January).

Protheroe, Gerald J. 2006. *Searching for Security in Europe: The Diplomatic Career of Sir George Russell Clerk*. Abingdon: Routledge.

Putnam, Robert D., and David E. Campbell. 2012. *American Grace: How Religion Divides and Unites Us*. New York: Simon & Schuster.

Quatremer, Jean. 2016. "La Belgique ne s'est pas préoccupée d'aider à développer un islam européen." *Libération*, last modified April 20.

Qureshi, M. Naeem. 1999. *Pan-Islam in British Indian Politics*. Leiden: Brill.

Raberh, Achi. 2007. "L'islam authentique appartient à Dieu, '"l'islam algérien" à César': La mobilisation de l'association des oulémas d'Algérie pour la séparation du culte musulman et de l'état (1931–1956)." *Genèses* 4 (69): 49–69.

Radu, Michael. 2006. *Dilemmas of Democracy and Dictatorship: Place, Time, and Ideology in Global Perspective*. New Brunswick, NJ: Transaction Publications.

Rahmani, Ejedjiga. 2013. "Les Imams étrangers 'pourraient ne pas servir le citoyen algérien.'" *Slate Afrique*, August 3.

Ramzi, Walid. 2013. "Algeria: Public Breakfast Sparks Controversy in Algeria." *All Africa*, August 12.

Ravix, Anna. 2015. "Premiers jours de cours à l'Institut Mohammed VI De Formation Des Imams." *Huffington Post*, April 3.

Reasoner, Calvin. 2013 [1896]. *Church and State*. London: Forgotten Books.

Reed, Howard A. 1956. "The Faculty of Divinity at Ankara." *The Muslim World* 46 (4, October): 295–312.

Reports from Basra. "'Traité de Stamboul: Entre l'empire Ottoman et La Serbie'; Position and Duties of Ottoman Imperial Family" (copy). Selected files from series AIR, CAB, CO, FCO, FO, PREM, T, WO, National Archives, Kew, UK.

Reuter, Frank. 1967. *Catholic Influence on American Colonial Policies, 1898–1904*. Austin: University of Texas Press.

Reynolds, Michael A. 2015. "The Key to the Future Lies in the Past: The Worldview of Erdoğan and Davutoğlu." Hudson Institute, September 3.

Rid, Thomas. 2010. "The Nineteenth Century Origins of Counterinsurgency Doctrine." *Journal of Strategic Studies* 33 (5): 727–58.

Ridley, Yvonne. 201. *The Rise of the Prophet Muhammad: Don't Shoot the Messenger*. Newcastle upon Tyne, UK: Cambridge Scholars Publishing.

Riedel, Bruce. 2014. "The Man Who Would Be Caliph Makes a Subversive Video Debut." *Brookings*, July 6. https://www.brookings.edu/blog/markaz/2014/07/06/the-man-who-would-be-caliph-makes-a-subversive-video-debut/.

Riedel, Sabine. 2008. "Models of Church-State Relations in European Democracies." *Journal of Religion in Europe* 1(3): 251–72.

Ritzer, George. 1975. "Professionalization, Bureaucratization, and Rationalization: The Views of Max Weber." *Social Forces* 53 (4, June): 627–34.

Rizvi, Kishwar. 2015. "Agency of History: The Symbolic Potential of the Transnational Mosque." In Kishwar Rizvi, *The Transnational Mosque: Architecture and Historical Memory in the Contemporary Middle East*. Chapel Hill: University of North Carolina Press.

Roberts, Nicholas E. 2010. "Rethinking the Status Quo: The British and Islam in Palestine, 1917–1929." PhD. diss., New York University, History and Middle Eastern and Islamic Studies Department.

Robinson, Chase. 2014. "The Caliph Has No Clothes." *New York Times*, July 16.

Robinson, Firdevs. 2014. "Turkey's New Era of Restoration May Turn into Reparation." *Firdevs Talk Turkey*, August 28.

Robinson, Francis. 2012. "The Islamic World: World System to 'Religious International.'" In *Religious Internationals in the Modern World*, edited by Abigail Green and Vincent Viaene. Palgrave Macmillan Transnational History Series. London: Palgrave Macmillan.

Robinson, Richard D. 1961. "Mosque and School in Turkey." *The Muslim World* 51 (April).

Rogan, Eugene L. 2002. *Frontiers of the State in the Late Ottoman Empire: Transjordan, 1850–1921*. Cambridge Middle East Studies. Cambridge: Cambridge University Press.

Rondot, Pierre. 1973. "L'Islam dans la politique des états du Maghreb." *Politique Etrangère* 1: 41–50.

Roy, Oliver, 2016. "France's Oedipal Islamist Complex." *Foreign Policy*, March 23.

———. 2017. *Jihad and Death: The Global Appeal of Islamic State*. New York: Oxford University Press.

Rubin, Aviad. 2013. "The Status of Religion in Emergent Political Regimes: Lessons from Turkey and Israel." *Nations and Nationalism* 19 (3): 493–512.

Ruiz Sevilla, Adolfo S. 2016. "Marruecos entrega 27 motocicletas a imanes para predicar en El Sur." *La Vanguardia*, February 27.

Rumbold, H. 1921. "Sir H. Rumbold (Constantinople) to Earl Curzon (Received February 15, 1921)." [E 2021/1/144]. In *Documents on British Foreign Policy 1919–1939*.

———. 1921. "Sir H. Rumbold (Constantinople) to Earl Curzon (Received March 30, 1921)." No. 300 [E 3765/1/44]. In *Documents on British Foreign Policy 1919–1939*.

Ruthven, Malise. 2014. "The Map ISIS Hates." *New York Review of Books*, June 25.

———. 2015. "Lure of the Caliphate." *New York Review of Books*, February 28.

Sacred Congregation of Seminaries and Universities. 1963. *Priestly Vocations in the World Today: Acts of the First International Congress for Priestly Vocations, Rome, 22–26 May 1962*. Vatican City: Sacred Congregation of Seminaries and Universities.

Sahinöz, Cemil. 2016. "Vorbeter zwishen deutschen und türkischen Interessen." *MiGAZIN*, May 4.

Sala, George Augustus. 1885. *A Journey Due South: Travels in Search of Sunshine*. London: Vizetelly & Co.

Salamé, Ghassane. 1982. "L'Islam en politique: Les Expériences arabes d'aujourd'hui." *Politique Etrangère* 47 (2): 365–84.

Saleem, Raja. 2015. "Effect of Islam's Role in State Nationalism on the Islamization of Government: Case Studies of Turkey and Pakistan." PhD diss., George Mason University, Department of Policy, Government, and International Affairs.

Samadi, Khalid. 2010. "L'Édification du moi marocain." In *La Formation des cadres religieux musulmans: Perspectives de l'expérience marocaine*. Rabat: Consultative Council for Moroccans Residing Abroad.

Saoudi, Hasna. 2014. "Tournée africaine du roi du Maroc: 'Les liens entre le Maroc et l'Afrique sont quasiment constitutifs de la nation marocaine' (expert Afrique)." *Atlasinfo*, March 2.

Sarkissian, Ani. 2015. *The Varieties of Religious Repression: Why Governments Restrict Religion.* Oxford: Oxford University Press.

Saunders, Doug. 2012. *The Myth of the Muslim Tide: Do Immigrants Threaten the West?* New York: Vintage.

Sauvaget, Bernadette. 2013. "Turkey Invests in 'Made in France' Islam in Strasbourg." *Libération*, October 7.

———. 2016. "Ahmet Ogras, Tête de pont D'Ankara dans l'islam français." *Libération*, August 2.

Schorn-Schütte, Luise. 2000. "Priest, Preacher, Pastor: Research on Clerical Office in Early Modern Europe." *Central European History* 33 (1): 1–39.

Schröder, Alwin. 2017. "DİTİB Unter Spionage-Verdacht." *Der Spiegel*, January 18.

Schult, Christoph. 2016. "Spionage-Verdacht: Grünen-Politiker Beck Zeigt Imame an." *Der Spiegel*, December 17.

Schwiebert, Ernest G. 1948. "The Reformation from a New Perspective." *Church History* 17 (1): 3–31.

Scott, James Brown. 1929. "The Treaty between Italy and Vatican." *Proceedings of the American Society of International Law at Its Annual Meeting (1921–1969)*, vol. 23. Cambridge: Cambridge University Press.

Scott, Richard B. 1971. "Qur'an Courses in Turkey." *The Muslim World* 61 (4): 239–55.

Senay, Banu. 2013. *Beyond Turkey's Borders: Long-Distance Kemalism, State Politics, and the Turkish Diaspora.* London: I. B. Tauris.

Séréni, Jean-Pierre. 2013. "Algérie: L'islam sous administration coloniale." *Orient* 21: November 27. https://orientxxi.info/lu-vu-entendu/algerie-l-islam-sous-administration-coloniale,0432.

Shahin, Emad Eldin Ali. 1989. "The Restitution of Islam: A Comparative Study of the Islamic Movements in Contemporary Tunisia and Morocco." Diss., Johns Hopkins University.

Shales, Melissa. 2013. *Top 10: Istanbul.* London: DK Publishing.

Shaughnessy, Gerald. 1025. *Has the Immigrant Kept the Faith? A Study of Immigration and Catholic Growth in the United States, 1790–1920.* New York: Macmillan.

Shaw, Stanford J., and Ezel Kural Shaw. 1977. *History of the Ottoman Empire and Modern Turkey*, vol. 2, *Reform, Revolution, and Republic: The Rise of Modern Turkey 1808–1975.* Cambridge: Cambridge University Press.

Shaw, Stanford J. 1978. "Ottoman Expenditures and Budgets in the Late Nineteenth and Early Twentieth Centuries." *International Journal of Middle East Studies* 9 (3, August): 373–78.

———. 1978. "The Ottoman Census System and Population, 1831–1914." *International Journal of Middle East Studies* 9 (3, August): 325–38.

Shea, John G. 1886. *The Hierarchy of the Catholic Church in the United States*. New York: Office of Catholic Publications.

———. 1886. "Great Articles of the Catholic Faith." In *The Hierarchy of the Catholic Church in the United States*. New York: Office of Catholic Publications.

———. 1888. *Life and Times of the Most Rev. John Carroll, Embracing the History of the Catholic Church in the United States, 1763–1810*. New York: John G. Shea.

Shea, William M. 2004. *The Lion and the Lamb: Evangelicals and Catholics in America*. Oxford: Oxford University Press.

Shelley, Thomas J. 2003. "Biography and Autobiography: James Cardinal Gibbons and John Tracy Ellis." *US Catholic Historian* 21 (2).

Shragay, Nadav. 2017. "A New Ottoman Empire?" *Israel Hayom*, June 23.

Shusterman, Noah. 2012. "The French Revolution and the Civil Constitution for the Clergy: The Unintentional Turning Point." In *Religion and the State: Europe and North America in the Seventeenth and Eighteenth Centuries*, edited by Joshua B. Stein and Sargon G. Donabed. Plymouth, UK: Lexington Books.

Silvestri, Enrico. 2013. "Le Cannonate di Beccaris sui milanesi armano la mano di Bresci." *Il Giornale*, May 5.

Skovgaard-Petersen, Jakob. 1997. *Defining Islam for the Egyptian State: Muftis and Fatwas of the Dar al-Ifta*. Leiden: Brill.

Slama, Nissaf. 2014. "Government Seeks to Regain Control of Conservative Mosques as Ramadan Nears." *Tunisia Live*, September 29.

Slight, John. 2014. "British Imperial Rule and the Hajj." In *Islam and the European Empires*, edited by David Motadel. Oxford: Oxford University Press.

Slimani, Leila. 2010. "La Bataille du livre." *Jeune Afrique*, August 10.

Sluglett, Peter, and Andrew Currie. 2015. *Atlas of Islamic History*. Oxford: Routledge.

Smith, R. Jeffrey. 1991. "US Deployment Expected to Exceed 500,000." *Washington Post*, January 25.

Smith, Ryan K. 2006. *Gothic Arches, Latin Crosses: Anti-Catholicism and American Church Designs in the Nineteenth Century*. Chapel Hill: University of North Carolina Press.

Snyder, Thomas D. 1993. "120 Years of American Education: A Statistical Portrait." Washington, DC: U.S. Department for Education, Center for Education Statistics, Office of Educational Research and Improvement (January).

Solgun, Cafer. 2013. "Wear Hats, Read Atatürk's Speech Instead of Koran." *HaberDiyarbakir*, July 10.

Sönmez, Göktuğ. 2017. "Radicalisation, Violent Extremism, and Turkey's Fight." Report 209. Ankara: ORSAM (May).

Souriau, Christiane, ed. 1981. *Le Maghreb musulman en 1979*. Paris: Éditions du Centre national de la recherche scientifique.

———. 1981. "Quelques données comparatives sur les institutions islamiques actuelles du Maghreb." In *Le Maghreb musulman en 1979*, edited by Christiane Souriau. Paris: Éditions du Centre national de la recherche scientifique.

Spadaro, Antonio, and Marcelo Figueroa. 2017. "Fondamentalismo Evangelicale e integralismo Cattolico." *La Civiltà Cattolica* (July 13): 105–13.

Speight, R. Marston. 1966. "Islam in Politics." *The Muslim World* 56 (4, October).

Spiegel, Avi Max. 2015. *Young Islam: The New Politics of Religion in Morocco and the Arab World.* Princeton, NJ: Princeton University Press.

Spielhaus, Riem, und Martin Herzog. 2015. "Die rechtliche Anerkennung des Islams in Deutschland." *Friedrich-Ebert-Stiftung.*

Spijker, Willem van 't. 2001. "Early Reformation and Scholasticism." *Dutch Review of Church History/Nederlands archief voor kerkgeschiedenis* 81 (3): 290–305.

Spitz, Lewis W. 2003. *The Protestant Reformation, 1517–1559.* St. Louis: Concordia Publishing House.

Stark, Rodney. 2001. *One True God: Historical Consequences of Monotheism.* Princeton, NJ: Princeton University Press.

The Statesman's Year-Book. N.d. London and New York: Macmillan/St. Martin's Press.

Stepan, Alfred C. 2000. "Religion, Democracy, and the 'Twin Tolerations.'" *Journal of Democracy* 11 (4, October): 37–57.

Stepan, Alfred, and Juan J. Linz. 2013. "Democratization Theory and the Arab Spring." *Journal of Democracy* 24 (2, April).

Steppt, Fritz. 1956. "Nationalismus und Islam bei Muṣṭafa Kamil: Ein Beitrag zur Ideengeschichte der ägyptischen Nationalbewegung." *Die Welt des Islams* 4 (4): 241–341.

Stoddard, Philip Hendrick. 1963. "The Ottoman Government and the Arabs, 1911–1918: A Preliminary Study of the Teşkilat-ı Mahsusa." PhD. diss., Princeton University.

Sulzberger, C. L. 1942. "German Preparations in the Middle East." *Foreign Affairs* (July).

Sunier, Thijl. 2011. "The Turkish Directorate for Religious Affairs in a Changing Environment." *Diyanet Report* (January).

Suzor, Cecilia Fernández. 2006–2007. "Entretien avec Ahmed Taoufiq." *Afkar/Idées* (Winter): 11–14.

Sweiss, Sami. 2017. "Hashemite Discourse on Wahhabi Islam as Anti-Saudi Propaganda during the Arab Revolt." Session P4913, annual meeting of the Middle East Studies Association, Washington, DC, November 18–21.

Swinges, Rainer Christoph. 1998. "Prestige und gemeiner Nutzen Universitätsgründungen im deutschen Spätmittelalter." *Berichte zur Wissenschaftsgeschichte* 21.

Tagliacozzo, Eric. 2014. "The Dutch Empire and the Hajj." In *Islam and the European Empires,* edited by David Motadel. Oxford: Oxford University Press.

Taheri, Amir. 2014. "Turkey's Hundred Years of Identity Crisis." *Asharq Al-Awsat,* February 19.

Takan, Ahmet. 2017. "Looking at the Religious Values of Turkish Society." *Gazete Yenicag: Türkiye Turkleindir,* June 20.

Tamadonfar, Mehran. 2002. "Islamism in Contemporary Arab Politics: Lessons in Authoritarianism and Democratization." In *Religion and Politics in Comparative Perspective: The One, the Few, and the Many,* edited by Ted G. Jelen and Clyde Wilcox. New York: Cambridge University Press.

Tapp. Christian. 2005. *Kardinäle und Kardinalität. Stuttgart:* Franz Steiner Verlag.

Tarrow, Sidney. 2010. "The Strategy of Paired Comparison: Toward a Theory of Practice." *Comparative Political Studies* 43 (2): 230–59.

Teitelbaum, Joshua. 2000. "'Taking Back' the Caliphate: Sharīf Ḥusayn Ibn ʿAlī, Mustafa Kemal, and the Ottoman Caliphate." *Die Welt des Islams* (new series) 40 (3, November): 412–24.

Tepe, Sultan. 2015. "The Elusive Structure of State Secularism and Its Disguised Critics." Paper presented at the annual meeting of the American Political Science Association.

———. 2016. "Contesting Political Theologies of Islam and Democracy in Turkey." *Journal of Religious and Political Practice* 2 (2, July 1): 175–92.

Terzioglu, Derin. 2010. "Sunna-Minded Sufi Preachers in Service of the Ottoman State: The Nasihatname of Hassan Addressed to Murad IV." *Archivum Ottomanicum* 27: 241–312.

———. 2013. "Where Ilmihal Meets Catechism: Islamic Manuals of Religious Instruction in the Ottoman Empire in the Age of Confessionalization." *Past and Present* 220 (1): 79–114.

Tezcan, Baki. 2010. *The Second Ottoman Empire: Political and Social Transformation in the Early Modern World*. Cambridge: Cambridge University Press.

Tezcan, Levent. 2012. *Das muslimische Subjekt: Verfangen im Dialog der Deutschen Islam Konferenz*. Konstanz: Konstanz University Press.

Thomson, Janice E. 1996. "Delegitimating State-Authorized Non-State Violence." In Janice E. Thomson, *Mercenaries, Pirates, and Sovereigns: State-Building and Extraterritorial Violence in Early Modern Europe*. Princeton, NJ: Princeton University Press.

Tlili, Hamdi. 2015. "187 Mosquées hors de contrôle." *France 24*, June 13.

Tlili, Madjid. 2014. "L'Europe a besoin des imams algériens." *Liberté-Algérie*, September 22.

Tobich, Faïza. 2008. *Les Statuts personnels dans les pays arabes*. Marseille: Presses universitaires d'Aix-Marseille.

———. 2008. "La Construction du projet." Chap. 1 in Faïza Tobich, *Les Statuts personnels dans les pays arabes*. Marseille: Presses universitaires d'Aix-Marseille.

Tozy, Mohamed. 1992. "L'Islam entre le contrôle de l'état et les débordements de la société civile: Des nouveaux clercs aux nouveaux lieux de l'expression religieuse." In *Le Maroc actuel: Une modernisation au miroir de la tradition*, edited by Jean-Claude Santucci. Aix-en-Provence: Institut de recherches et d'études sur le monde arabe et musulman.

Tremblay, Pinar. 2017. "Turkey's 'American Idol' of Qur'an Recitation Backfires." *Al-Monitor*, June 8.

Triaud, Jean-Louis. 2000. "Islam in Africa under French Colonial Rule." In *The History of Islam in Africa*, edited by Nehemia Levtzion and Randall Pouwels. Athens: Ohio University Press.

Troeltsch, Ernst. 1931. *The Social Teaching of Christian Churches*, vol. 2. New York: Macmillan,

Trofimov, Yaroslav. 2007. *The Siege of Mecca: The Forgotten Uprising in Islam's Holiest Shrine and the Birth of Al Qaeda*. New York: Doubleday.

Trumbull, George R., IV. 2009. *An Empire of Facts: Colonial Power, Cultural Knowledge, and Islam in Algeria 1870–1914*. Cambridge: Cambridge University Press.

Turcato, Davide. 2018. "The Other Nation: The Places of the Italian Anarchist Press in the US." In *Historical Geographies of Anarchism*, edited by Federico Ferretti, Gerónimo Barrera de la Torre, Anthony Ince, and Francisco Toro. New York: Routledge.

Turkone, Mumtazer. 2013. "In the Education Arena the AK Party Flounders." *Today's Zaman*, November 26.

Turner, Barry. 2014. *The Statesman's Yearbook 1876: The Politics, Cultures, and Economies of the World*. London: Palgrave Macmillan.

Turner, Darrell. 2011. "A Complex Picture of Religion in America." *National Catholic Reporter*, March 16.

Turner, Bryan S. 1974. *Weber and Islam: A Critical Study*. Abingdon, UK: Routledge & Kegan Paul.

Uluc, Ozlem. 2015. "Does Habermas Shed Light on Islam in Turkey?" In *The Role of Religions in the Public-Sphere: The Post-Secular Model of Jürgen Habermas and Beyond*, edited by Plamen Makariev. Washington, DC: Council for Research in Values and Philosophy.

Ünal, Ali. 2017. "Yunus Emre Institute Head Ateş: As an Element of Soft Power, Our Aim Is to Introduce Turkey, Its Culture to the World." *Daily Sabah*, July 23.

US Department of State. 2019. "France 2018 Report on International Religious Freedom." https://www.state.gov/wp-content/uploads/2019/05/FRANCE-2018 -INTERNATIONAL-RELIGIOUS-FREEDOM-REPORT.pdf.

Van Maanen, John, and Edgar H. Schein. 1977. "Toward a Theory of Organizational Socialization," Massachusetts Institute of Technology. https://dspace.mit.edu/bitstream/handle /1721.1/1934/SWP-0960-03581864.pdf.

Vethake, Henry, ed. 1847. "Prussia." In *Encyclopaedia Americana: A Popular Dictionary of Arts, Sciences*, vol. 14. Philadelphia: Lea and Blanchard.

Viaene, Vincent. 2012. "Nineteenth-Century Catholic Internationalism and Its Predecessors." In *Religious Internationals in the Modern World*, edited by Abigail Green and Vincent Viaene. London: Palgrave Macmillan.

Vidino, Lorenzo. 2010. *The New Muslim Brotherhood in the West*. New York: Columbia University Press.

Vidino, Lorenzo, et al. 2017. *Fear Thy Neighbor: Radicalization and Jihadist Attacks in the West*. Milan: Ledizioni Publishing.

Vikor, Knut S. 2005. *Between God and the Sultan: A History of Islamic Law*. London: Hurst & Co.

Vincent, Elise. 2016. "Ecquevilly, histoire d'un satanisme français." *Le Monde*, March 12.

———. 2016. "Le Conseil d'état rejette le recours déposé par la mosquée salutiste d'Ecquevilly." *Le Monde*, December 6.

Vincent, Nicholas, 2010. "When Did the Pope Rule England?" *BBC History Magazine* (October).

Vizetelly, Ernest Alfred. 1911. *The Anarchists: Their Faith and Their Record Including Sidelights on the Royal and Other Personages Who Have Been Assassinated*. London: John Lane.

Wagner, Andreas. "Die Reformation bis zum Ende des Bauernkriegs (1517–1529)." PhD diss., Freie University Berlin.

Wagtendonk, K. 1991. "Islamic Schools and Islamic Religious Education: A Comparison between Holland and Other West European Countries." In *The Integration of Islam and Hinduism in Western Europe*, edited by W.A.R. Shadid and P. S. Koningsveld. Kampen: Kok Pharos.

Wainscott, Ann Marie. 2015. "Defending Islamic Education: War on Terror Discourse and Religious Education in Twenty-First-Century Morocco." *North African Studies* 20 (4).

———. 2018. *Bureaucratizing Islam: Morocco and the War on Terror*. Cambridge: Cambridge University Press.

Walburg, Anton H. 1968. "The Threat of Americanization of the Immigrant." In *American Catholic Thought on Social Questions*, edited by Aaron L. Abell and Bobbs-Merrill. New York: Bobbs-Merrill.

Walt, Vivienne. 2012. "After Protests, Tunisia's Salafists Plot a More Radical Revolution." *Time*, September 21.

Walzer, Michael. 2015. *The Paradox of Liberation: Secular Revolutions and Religious Counterrevolutions*. New Haven, CT: Yale University Press.

Warren, Lansing. 1953. "Morocco's Sultan Loses Islamic Post." *New York Times*, August 16.

Webb. 1920. "Admiral Webb (Constantinople) to Earl Curzon (Received February 10, 1920)." No. 122 [177629/521/44]. In *Documents on British Foreign Policy 1919–1939*.

Weber, Max. 1968. *Economy and Society*, edited by Guenther Roth and Claus Wittich. Berkeley: University of California Press.

Weidner, Stefan. 2014. "History of the Caliphate: We Are All Caliphs!" *Qantara—Dialogue with the Islamic World*, July 18.

Weigel, George. 2006. "World Religion by the Numbers." *The Catholic Difference*, March 6.

Weiker, Walter F. 1963. *The Turkish Revolution 1960–1961: Aspects of Military Politics*. Washington, DC: Brookings Institution.

Weir, Robert E. 1996. *Beyond Labor's Veil: The Culture of the Knights of Labor*. University Park: Penn State University Press.

White, Benjamin Thomas. 2012. *The Emergence of Minorities in the Middle East: The Politics of Community in French Mandate Syria*. Edinburgh: University of Edinburgh Press.

White, Joseph Michael. 1989. *The Diocesan Seminary in the United States: A History from the 1780s to the Present*. Notre Dame, IN: University of Notre Dame Press.

———. 2001. "Perspectives on the Nineteenth-Century Diocesan Seminary in the United States." Special issue of *US Catholic Historian* ("The American Catholic Experience: Essays in Honor of Jay P. Dolan") 19 (1, Winter): 21–35.

Wiktorowicz, Quintan. 2001. *The Management of Islamic Activism: Salafis, the Muslim Brotherhood, and State Power in Jordan*. Albany: State University of New York Press.

Wilensky, Harold L. 1964. "The Professionalization of Everyone?" *American Journal of Sociology* 70 (2): 137–58.

Wilhelm, Joseph. 2019. "General Councils." *Catholic Encyclopedia*, July 5.

Willis, John. 2010. "Debating the Caliphate: Islam and Nation in the Work of Rashid Rida and Abul Kalam Azad." *International History Review* 32 (4): 711–32.

Wilson, Samuel Graham. 1916. *Modern Movements among Moslems*. New York: Fleming H. Revell Co.

Wilson, Tom. 2017. "Foreign Funded Islamic Extremism in the UK." Research Paper 9. London: Centre for the Response to Radicalisation and Terrorism, Henry Jackson Society.

Wirtschafter, Jacob, and Amr El Tohamy. 2018. "Fearing Extremist Violence, Egypt Silences 20,000 Storefront Mosques." *Religion News Service*, May 28.

Wolf, Anne. 2013. "An Islamist 'Renaissance'? Religion and Politics in Post-revolutionary Tunisia." *Journal of North African Studies* 18 (4): 560–73.

Wood, Graeme. 2016. "What ISIS Really Wants." *Atlantic*, April 14.

Woodward, Ernest L. 1939. *Documents on British Foreign Policy 1919–1939*, 3rd series, vol. VII. Internet Archive.

Wuthnow, Robert. 1991. "Understanding Religion and Politics." *Daedalus* 120 (3, Summer): 1–20.

Wyrtzen, Jonathan. 2011. "Colonial State-Building and the Negotiation of Arab and Berber Identity in Protectorate Morocco." *International Journal of Middle East Studies* 43: 227–49.

———. 2013. "Performing the Nation in Anti-Colonial Protest in Interwar Morocco." *Nations and Nationalism* 19 (4, August 23).

Yakut, Esra. 2005. *Seyhulislamlik. yenileşme döneminde devlet ve din*. Istanbul: Kitap Yayinevi.

Yan, Yangtze. 2006. "China Blasts Nomination of Rabiya Kadir as Nobel Peace Prize Candidate." *Gov.cn*, September 12.

Yavuz, M. Hakan. 2003. *Islamic Political Identity in Turkey*. Oxford: Oxford University Press.

Yazbak, Mahmoud. 1997. "Nabulsi Ulama in the Late Ottoman Period, 1864–1914." *International Journal of Middle East Studies* 29 (1, February): 71–91.

Yediyildiz, Bahaeddin. 1996. "Place of the Waqf in Turkish Cultural System." in *Habitat II*, edited by Ankara Hacettepe University, Istanbul.

Yikdirim, A. Kadir. 2019. "Religious Authority and US Foreign Policy in the Middle East." Baker Institute, Rice University.

Yilmaz, Hussein. 2018. *The Caliphate Redefined: The Mystical Turn in Ottoman Islamic Thought*. Princeton, NJ: Princeton University Press.

Young, Major H.W. 1920. "Memorandum on the Future Control of the Middle East." [E 4870/4870/44]. In *Documents on British Foreign Policy 1919–1939*, series 1, vol. 13: *Turkey, February–December 1920; Arabia, Syria, and Palestine, February 1920–January 1921; Persia, January 1920–March 1921*. London: Foreign Office.

Zaman, Muhammad Qasim. 1999. "Religious Education and the Rhetoric of Reform: The Madrasa in British India and Pakistan." *Comparative Studies in Society and History* 41 (2).

Zeghal, Malika. 1999. "État et marché des biens religieux: Les voies égyptienne et tunisienne." *Critique internationale* (5).

Zerouky, Hassane. 2002. "Moroccan Offensive against the 'Islamist' Book and Cassette Business Continues." *Le Matin*, September 8.

Zimmer, Kenyon. 2015. *Immigrants against the State: Yiddish and Italian Anarchism in America*. Urbana: University of Illinois Press.

Zwemer, Samuel Marinus. 2013 [1900]. *Arabia: The Cradle of Islam*. Piscataway, NJ: Gorgias Press.

ILLUSTRATION CREDITS

1.1.1. © Claude Truong-Ngoc/Wikimedia Commons

1.1.2. Bridgeman Images/US Department of Defense

1.2.1. Bibliothèque nationale de France/Collection De Vinck (histoire de France, 1770–1871)

1.2.2 Wikimedia Commons

1.3. Data compiled from Malanima, "Energy and Population in Europe"; Al-Faruqi, Sopher, and Hebblethwaite, *Historical Atlas of the Religions of the World*; Dowley and Rowland, *Atlas of World Religions*; Erickson, *Defeat in Detail*; Kirsch and Luksch, p. 603

1.4. Data compiled from Ministry of Finance, *Osmanlı Bütçeleri (1909–1918): Maliye Bakanlığı Yayınları*; Yakut, *Seyhulislamlik*; Güran, *Osmanlı Mali Istatistikleri ve Bütçeler (1841–1918)*; Pamuk, p. 112; Inalcik and Quataert, *An Economic and Social History of the Ottoman Empire*, 2:779; Yakut, *Seyhulislamlik*, p. 160; Ochsenwald, "Ottoman Subsidies to the Hijaz, 1877–1886"; Barnes, *An Introduction to Religious Foundations in the Ottoman Empire*, p. 149; Martin, *The Statesman's Year-Book*, p. 1463.

1.5. Data compiled from Flanagan, "The Changing Character of the American Catholic Church 1810–1850"; Shea, *The Hierarchy of the Catholic Church in the United States*, p. 58; Hennesey, *American Catholics*; McAvoy, "The Immigrants Dominate the American Church, 1850–1866"; Kirsch and Luksch, *Illustrierte Geschichte der Katholischen Kirche*; Smith, *Gothic Arches, Latin Crosses*; Miller and Fossey, *Mapping the Catholic Cultural Landscape*, p. 92; Eurostat, "Population on January 1, 2013"; Jørgen S. Nielsen et al., *Muslims in Western Europe* (Edinburgh: Edinburgh University Press, 2004); Brian Arly Jacobsen, "Muslim Population Trends in Western Europe," Oxford Islamic Studies Online, http://www.oxfordislamicstudies.com/article/opr/t343/e0136?_hi=0&_pos=1#match; Turkinfo.nl, "Hollanda'da 395 bin Türk yaşiyor," April 23, 2014, https://www.turkinfo.nl/hollandada-395-bin-turk-yasiyor/8694/; "Belcika'da 218.832 Türk Kökenli Vatandaş Yaşiyor," *Gündem*, http://www.gundem.be/tr/belcika/belcika-da-218-832-turk-kokenli-vatandas-yasiyor; "Turks in Selected European Countries: Figure 10.1, 'Turkish Migrants,'" p. 203; Statistiques de la Direction des Affaires Consulaires et Sociales du Ministère marocain des Affaires Etrangères et de la Coopération, March 2002

1.6. Data compiled from *Annuario Ecclesiastico*, 1900; Salvador Miranda, "The Cardinals of the Holy Roman Church, 1998–2018," Florida International University Libraries,

http://cardinals.fiu.edu/cardinals.htm; Go Catholic, "Living Cardinals (by Country)"
http://www.gcatholic.org/hierarchy/cardinals-alive-country.htm; Chow, "Living
Cardinals (by Country)"; John F. Broderick, "The Sacred College of Cardinals: Size
and Geographical Composition (1099–1986)," *Archivum Historiae Pontificiae* 25 (1987):
7–71

1.7. Data compiled from Institut national de la statistique, *La Tunisie en chiffres,
2008–2010* (2011); Ministère tunisien des finances, *Le Budget de l'état 2014 en chiffres;*
Ministère des Habous et des Affaires Religieuses, *Le Guide,* 2013; *Projet de loi de
finances 2004–2014* (Morocco); Diyanet İşleri Başkanlığı, *2000 yılı istatistikleri*
(Ankara: Diyanet İşleri Başkanlığı, Araştırma Planlama ve Koordinasyon Dairesi,
2001); *Algeria:* Bouabdellah Ghlamallah (minister of religious affairs), interview
with the author, Algiers, February 2014; *Journal Officiel de la république algérienne
démocratique et populaire* 39 (76, December 13, 2000), http://www.vitaminedz.com
/articlesfiche/1233/1233092.pdf; *Journal officiel de la république algérienne
démocratique et populaire,* 1963–2016 (reference numbers by year available from
author on request); Loi 327, October 23, 2001 (6 Chaabane 1422); "Administration
centrale—Conférences et séminaires," Budget de fonctionnement du ministère, Loi
des finances, article 3, http://www.andi.dz/PDF/loifinance/2006-04.pdf; Décret
présidentiel no. 10–174 du 24 Rajab 1431correspondant au 7 juillet 2010 portant
transfert de crédits au budget de fonctionnement du ministère des affaires
religieuses et des wakfs; Décret présidentiel no. 10–241 du 5 Dhou El Kaada 1431
correspondant au 13 octobre 2010 portant transfert de crédits au budget de
fonctionnement du ministère des affaires religieuses et des wakfs, http://univ
-ouargla.dz/docs/tlr/decret_executif_10-250_instituant_le_regime_indemnitaire
_du_chercheur_permanent_fr.pdf; Décret présidentiel no. 12–330 du 19 Chaoual
1433 correspondant au 6 septembre 2012 portant transfert de crédits au budget de
fonctionnement du ministère des affaires religieuses et des wakfs; Décret
présidentiel no. 13–365 du 29 Dhou El Hidja 1434 correspondant au 3 novembre 2013
portant transfert de crédits au budget de fonctionnement du ministère des affaires
religieuses et des wakfs. *Morocco:* Ahmed Toufiq, interview with the author, Rabat,
October 2012; Mohsine Elmahdi, *Une décennie de réformes au Maroc (1999–2009)*
(Rabat: Karthala, 2009), p. 126; "Rapport sur les comptes spéciaux du Trésor: Projet
de loi de finances pour l'année budgétaire" (2009); Royaume du Maroc: Ministère
des habous et des affaires islamiques, "Toufiq: 740 millions de dirhams alloués à
l'amélioration de la situation des imams des mosquées," June 1, 2012, http://habous
.gov.ma/fr/m-le-ministre-3/712-toufiq-740-millions-de-dirhams-alloues-a-l
-amelioration-de-la-situation-des-imams-des-mosquees.html; Royaume du Maroc:
Ministère des habous et des affaires islamiques, "Projet du budget sectoriel du
ministère des Habous et des Affaires Islamiques pour l'annèe 2012," April 4, 2012,
http://habous.gov.ma/fr/component/content/article/20-M.le%20ministre/562
-projet-du-budget-sectoriel-du-ministere-des-habous-et-des-affaires-islamiques
-pour-l-annee-2012.html; Royaume du Maroc: Ministère des habous et des affaires
islamiques, "Présentation au Souverain du Programme de Qualification des imams,"
January 7, 2011, http://habous.gov.ma/fr/component/content/article/20-M.le%20
ministre/564-presentation-au-souverain-du-programme-de-qualification-des

-imams.html; Royaume du Maroc: Ministère des habous et des affaires islamiques, "Ahmed Toufiq présente le budget sectoriel 2014 du ministère devant la commission de l'éducation et des affaires culturelles et sociales à la chambre des conseillers," December 9, 2013, http://habous.gov.ma/fr/component/content/article/36 -Annonces-et-activités-ministère/1649-ahmed-toufiq-présente-le-budget-sectoriel -2014-du-ministère-devant-la-commission-de-l'éducation-et-des-affaires-culturelles -et-sociales-à-la-chambre-des-conseillers.html; *Bulletin officiel du royaume du Maroc* (2000–2016); *Tunisia*: Munir Tlili, interview with the author, Tunis, May 2014; Loi no. 2012–1 du 16 mai 2012, portant loi de finances complémentaire pour l'année 2012 (1); Loi no. 2010–58 du 17 décembre 2010, portant loi de finances pour l'année 2011 (1); Budget du ministère des Affaires religieuses (Ministère tunisien des finances) (archive), http://v2.portail.finances.gov.tn/index.php?option=com _jdownloads&Itemid=613&view=finish&cid=52&catid=1&lang=fr; Budget du ministère des Affaires religieuses (Ministère tunisien des finances) (archive): http://v2.portail.finances.gov.tn/index.php?option=com_jdownloads&Itemid =613&view=finish&cid=52&catid=1&lang=fr; Frégosi and Zéghal, "Religion et politique au Maghreb," p. 20; *Journal officiel de la république tunisienne* (1993–2016); *Turkey*: 30 İstatistiksel Tablolar: 2008–2009 Yılları Bütçe Ödenekleri (Statistical Tables: Budget Appropriation of 2008–2009), Diyanet website, http://www.diyanet .gov.tr/turkish/tanitim/istatistiksel_tablolar/6_butce/2009_yili_butce_odenegi .xls; İştar Gözaydın, *Diyanet: Türkiye Cumhuriyeti'nde Dinin Tanzimi* (Diyanet: Arranging Religion in the Turkish Republic) (Istanbul: İletişim Yayınları, 2009), p. 224; Statistical Figures on Turkish Islam and Diyanet personnel from: http:// www.diyanet.gov.tr/english/default.asp; "Ministers Get in Line to Sing Diyanet Praises," *Hurriyet Daily News*, January 4, 2013, http://www.hurriyetdailynews.com /ministers-get-in-line-to-sing-diyanet-praises.aspx?pageID=238&nID =38325&NewsCatID=338; Yavuz Baydar, "Diyanet Tops the Budget League," *Today's Zaman Online* October 21, 2013; Turkish Grand National Assembly, *Journal of the Minutes* 36 (December 14, 1989): 105, http://www.tbmm.gov.tr/tutanaklar /TUTANAK/TBMM/d18/c036/tbmm18036046.pdf

2.1. Data compiled from Malanima, "Energy and Population in Europe"; Al-Faruqi, Sopher, and Hebblethwaite, *Historical Atlas of the Religions of the World*; Dowley and Rowland, *Atlas of World Religions*

2.2. Jean Pol Grandmont, "Gallery of Maps," Wikimedia Commons

2.3. Wikimedia Commons

2.4. Wikimedia Commons

2.5. Photograph by the author

2.6. De Agostini Picture Library/G. Dagli Orti/Bridgeman Images

2.7. *Catechismus ex decreto Concilii Tridentini, ad parochos, Pij 5. pont. max. iussu editus*, National Central Library of Rome, 1574, http://books.google.com/books?id =eARtkRKYoeAC&hl=&source=gbs_api

2.8. Data compiled from Eubel, *Hierarchia catholica medii aevi*; Pius Bonifacius Gams, *Series episcoporum Ecclesiae Catholicae* (Graz, Austria: Akademische Druck, 1957)

2.9. Wikimedia Commons

2.10. Data compiled from P. Pasquale D'Elia SJ, "Le Missioni Cattoliche nel mondo: A proposita della 'Guida delle Missioni,' 'La Civiltà cattolica,'" notebook 2037, May 4, 1935; *Notizia statistica delle missioni cattoliche in tutto il mondo* (Rome: Sacra Congregazione di Propaganda Fide, 1843), year 1; Kirsch and Luksch, *Illustrierte Geschichte der Katholischen Kirche*; Hertling, *Geschichte der katholischen Kirche*, p. 287

2.11. "Lettera al Card: De Carpi per l'erezione del Coll. Germanico, 29 Luglio 1552," Archivio Storico di Propaganda Fide

2.12. Bridgeman Images/Achenbach Foundation for Graphic Arts

2.13. Copyright Archivio Storico di Propaganda Fide (S.C. Tipografia 1, f. 122)

2.14. De Agostini, "Galleria Garisenda," Bridgeman Images

2.15. Data compiled from *Annuario Pontificio*, 1912–2015; Eubel, *Hierarchia catholica medii aevi*

3.1. Wikimedia Commons

3.2. Bérard, *Le Sultan, l'Islam, et les puissances*

3.3. *New York Times* archives, March 5, 1911

3.4. *Iznogoud*, comic series by René Goscinny and Jean Tabary (Imav Editions, 1995–)

3.5. Henry Guttmann/Getty Images/Hulton Archive, 1925

3.6. *Bilder-Atlas zu Mekka von Dr. C. Snouck Hurgronje* (The Hague: Martinus Nijhoff, 1888)

3.7. H. C. King and C. R. Crane, "Disputed Lands of Near East That Hold World Attention Today" (1919), World War I Document Archive, http://wwi.lib.byu.edu /images/2/2c/King-Crane_Report_Disputed_Lands.jpg (*Literary Digest Atlas*, 1922)

3.8. Wikimedia Commons

3.9. John Stanmeyer/National Geographic Creative, Image 1961671

3.10. Zwemer, *Arabia: The Cradle of Islam*

4.1. Compiled by the author

4.2. Courtesy of Yitik Hazine Yayınları

4.3. Library of Congress, Prints and Photographs Division, LC-USZ62–81227

4.4. Library of Congress, Prints and Photographs Division

4.5. Wikimedia Commons

4.6. Library of Congress, Prints and Photographs Division

4.7. Leiden University Library

4.8. Library of Congress, Prints and Photographs Division

4.9. Library of Congress, Prints and Photographs Division

4.10. Data compiled from Mutlu, "Late Ottoman Population and Its Ethnic Distribution"; Erikson, *Defeat in Detail*; Inalcik and Quataert, *An Economic and Social History of the Ottoman Empire*, p. 779; Shaw and Kural, *History of the Ottoman Empire and Modern Turkey*, 2:117; Shaw, "The Ottoman Census System and Population, 1831–1914," p. 334;

Behar, *The Population of the Ottoman Empire and Turkey*; "Late Ottoman Population and Its Ethnic Distribution," *Turkish Journal of Population Studies* 25 (2003): 3–38, http://www.hips.hacettepe.edu.tr/nbd_cilt25/mutlu.pdf; "Osmanli butçeleri (1909–1918)," Ministry of Finance publication 2000/358 (Ankara: Ministry of Finance, 2003)

4.11. Shaw, "The Ottoman Census System and Population, 1831–1914," p. 334; O'Connor, *History of Turkey*, p. 111

4.12. Photograph by the author, Oran

4.13. Data compiled from Güran, "Osmanlı Kamu Maliyesi, 1839–1918"; Ochsenwald, "Ottoman Subsidies to the Hijaz, 1877–1886"; Hicaz Demirolyu Müdüriyet (Secretariat of the Hijaz Railway), *Osmanli Imparatorlugu'na ve Türkiye Cumhuriyeti'ne gelen Balkan göcmenleri*, p. 62; Behar, *The Population of the Ottoman Empire and Turkey*; Pamuk, "The Ottoman Economy in World War I," p. 11; Güran, *Osmanlı Mali Istatistikleri ve Bütçeler (1841–1918)*; Ministry of Finance, *Osmanlı Bütçeleri (1909–1918): Maliye Bakanlığı Yayınları*; Ministry of Finance, *1917 (1333) yılı Osmanlı Bütçesi*; Shaw, "Ottoman Expenditures and Budgets in the Late Nineteenth and Early Twentieth Centuries"; Güran, "Hicaz ve Yemen ve surre-i hümayûn muhassâti" in *Osmanlı Mali Istatistikleri ve Bütçeler (1841–1918)*; "Hicaz ve Yemen ve surre-i hümayûn muhassâti," in Güran, *Osmanlı Mali Istatistikleri ve Bütçeler (1841–1918)*, State Institute of Statistics No. 2878, Historical Statistics Series, vol. 7); Yakut, *Seyhulislamlik*, p. 165; Martin, *The Statesman's Year-Book*, p. 1463

5.1. T. Fabbri, "Inauguration of the Statue of Giordano Bruno," Parker Collection in the City Photo Archive, Museum of Rome

5.2. Data compiled from Hertling, *Geschichte der katholischen Kirche*; G. Simson, "L'évolution du droit moderne du divorce," *Revue internationale de droit comparé* 9 (2, 1957): 379–94; Berhard Duhr, S.J., *Geschichte der Jesuiten in den Ländern Deutscher Zunge*, vol. 1 (Freiburg im Breisgau: Herder, 1907), pp. xvi, 876; H. Dannreuther, "L'Église catholique et les confiscations," *Bulletin de la Société de l'Histoire du Protestantisme Français (1903–)* 54 (2, 1905): 121–23; R. N. Shain, "A Cross-Cultural History of Abortion," *Clinics in Obstetrics and Gynaecology* 13 (1, February 28, 1986): 1–17; A. Green, *Education and State Formation in Europe, East Asia, and the USA* (London: Palgrave Macmillan, 2013)

5.3. R. Desjardins, 1931/Wikimedia Commons

5.4. Data compiled from *Gerarchia e Rispettiva Popolazione*, 1843, p. 283; Eubel, *Hierarchia catholica medii aevi*

5.5. Wikimedia Commons

5.6. © SZ Photo/Scherl/Bridgeman Images

5.7. Wikipedia Commons

5.8. *Geschiedenis Beleven*. On April 25, 1870, Pope Pius IX blesses his troops for the last time before the defeat of the Papal States in the capture of Rome later that year (Wikimedia Commons/Burzagli Family Archives)

5.9. Compiled by the author

5.10. Data compiled from Leyshon, *Catholic Statistics, Priests and Population in England and Wales, 1841–2001*; Haigh, "The Continuity of Catholicism in the English Reformation"; Trystan Owain Hughes, "The Roman Catholic Church and Society in Wales 1916–62" (ProQuest Dissertations Publishing, 1998)

5.11. Luigi Leoni/Leoni Archive/Alinari Archives/Alinari via Getty Images

6.1. Compiled by the author

6.2. Compiled by the author; Giovanni Oman, "La Questione del digiuno di ramaḍān in tunisia," *Oriente Moderno* 40 (11/12, November/December 1960): 763–74

6.3. Data compiled from Diyanet 1927–2000, "1926 senesi muvazenei umumiye kanunu," no. 848; Grand National Assembly of Turkey, Sira Sayısı, 559; Turkish Statistical Institute database, population census; "1950 yılı Bütçe Kanunu," no. 5561; Mustafa Peköz, "Siyasal İslamın örgütlenme merkezi: Diyanet İşleri Başkanlığı (I)"; "1926 General Equity Law," Senesi Muvazenei Umumiye Kanunu (Eesmî Ceride ile neşir ve ilâm: 6/VI/1926—Sayı: 391), no. 848, https://www.tbmm.gov.tr/tutanaklar /KANUNLAR_KARARLAR/kanuntbmmc004/kanuntbmmc004/kanun tbmmc00400848.pdf; Gotthard Jaeschke, "Yeni Türkiye'de İslamcılık" (Ankara, 1972), s. 65–66, http://www.odatv.com/n.php?n=evet-inonu-bazi-camileri-depoya-cevirdi -2804121200; Lewis, "Islam in Politics"; *Millet Meclisi Tutanak Dergisi, Cumartesi* 49 (4, February 1977), https://www.tbmm.gov.tr/tutanaklar/TUTANAK/MM__/d04 /c024/mm__04024049.pdf; Karakas, "Turkei: Islam und Laizismus"; Çakır Ruşen, İrfan Bozan, and Balkan Talu, *İmam Hatip Liseleri: Efsaneler ve Gerçekler* (Ankara: TESEV, 2004)

6.4. Data compiled from Turkish Statistical Institute database, population census, "Post-Coup Hiring Spurts by the Diyanet," 1950–2000, https://biruni.tuik.gov.tr /nufusapp/idari.zul; Lewis, "Islam in Politics"; "Info-Türk," *Monthly Bulletin Brussels Collectif Info-Türk*, March 1987, http://www.odatv.com/n.php?n=evet-inonu-bazi -camileri-depoya-cevirdi-2804121200; Jaeschke, "Yeni Türkiye'de İslamcılık"; Meclisi, "Tutanak Dergisi," pp. 383, 378, 396; Özgur, *Islamic Schools in Modern Turkey*, p. 60

6.5. Data compiled by author from Inikat Ellinci, "T.B.M.M. Zabit Ceridesi," *Pazar* 11 (3, November 1960), https://www.tbmm.gov.tr/tutanaklar/TUTANAK/TBMM/d11 /c012/tbmm11012050.pdf; Damsma Meclisi, 10. 10. 1983, p. 51, https://www.tbmm.gov .tr/tutanaklar/TUTANAK/DM__/d02/c023/b174/dm__020231740051.pdf; Içindekiler, "T.B.M.M. Tutanak Dergisi," *Yasama Yili* (2, December 1988), https:// www.tbmm.gov.tr/tutanaklar/TUTANAK/TBMM/d18/c020/tbmm18020041.pdf; Tezcan, *The Second Ottoman Empire*, p. 82; *Millet Meclisi Tutanak Dergisi* (*Journal of National Assembly Minutes*), 1977–1989

6.6. Data compiled from Özgur, *Islamic Schools in Modern Turkey*; "T.B.M.M. Zabit Cerıdesi Ellinci İnikat," November 28, 1960; "1950 yılı Bütçe Kanunu," no. 5561; Lewis, "Islam in Politics"; Pacaci and Aktay, "75 Years of Higher Religious Education in Modern Turkey," p. 411; Turkish Grand National Assembly, "T.B.M.M. Zabit Cerıdesı, Ellinci İnikat," August 4, 1929, Pazartesi; Reed, "The Faculty of Divinity at Ankara," p. 310; Özgur, *Islamic Schools in Modern Turkey*, p. 36; Özdalga, Elizabeth. "Education in the Name of 'Order and Progress,'" p. 432; Richard B. Scott, "Turkish Village

Attitudes toward Religious Education," *The Muslim World* 55 (3, July 1965): 222–29; Ruşen Çakır, *Mehmet Görmez'e yönelik cüretkar saldirilar var* (video), filmed August 2017, https://www.youtube.com/watch?v=TH9BcA3NScI

6.7. Wikimedia Commons

6.8. Data compiled from Suzor, "Entretien avec Ahmed Taoufiq"; Bruce, "Les Imams 'exportés' de la Diyanet en France," pp. 166–67 Mohamed Tozy, "Champ et contrechamp politico-religieux au Maroc," PhD diss., Université de Droit, Économie, et des Sciences, Aix-Marseille, p. 164; Souriau, *Le Maghreb musulman en 1979*; Etienne and Tozy, "Le Glissement des obligations islamiques vers le phénomène associatif à Casablanca," p. 238; Malka, "The Struggle for Religious Identity in Tunisia and the Maghreb," p. 15; "Budget économique exploratoire, 1973–1978," Haut Commissariat au Plan, Royaume du Maroc; Joseph Luccioni, *Les Fondations pieuses "habous" au Maroc: Depuis les origines jusqu'à 1956* (Rabat: Imprimerie Royale, 1982); Tozy, "L'Islam entre le contrôle de l'état et les débordements de la société civile"

6.9. Bridgeman Images/PVDE

6.10. Radio Tataouine

7.1. Data compiled from McAvoy, "The Immigrants Dominate the American Church," p. 166; Shea, *The Hierarchy of the Catholic Church in the United States*; Smith, *Gothic Arches, Latin Crosses*; Flanagan, "The Changing Character of the American Catholic Church 1810–1850"

7.2. Library of Congress, Prints and Photographs Division

7.3. Miriam and Ira D. Wallach Division of Art, Prints and Photographs, Print Collection, New York Public Library Digital Collections; "Cathedral of the Holy Cross, Boston, Mass." (Detroit Publishing Co., c. 1900–1906), image retrieved from Library of Congress

7.4. *Saint Joseph Baltimore Catechism: The Truths of Our Catholic Faith Clearly Explained and Illustrated: With Bible Readings, Study Helps, and Mass Prayers* (Baltimore, MD: Catholic Book Publishing, 1964)

7.5. "The Pope's Army Comes to New York," *Patheos* [McNamara's Blog], https://www .patheos.com/blogs/mcnamarasblog/2011/03/the-popes-army-comes-to-new-york -1868.html

7.6. Eugene Zimmerman/Library of Congress, Prints and Photographs Division

7.7. *Le Petit Journal* (supplément illustré), December 23, 1893/Wikimedia Commons

7.8. "Bombing of the Liceu Theater, Barcelona," *Le Petit Journal*, November 25, 1893/ Wikipedia Commons

7.9. Bain News Service/Library of Congress, Prints and Photographs Division

7.10. Getty Images/*Le Petit Journal*

7.11. De Agostini Picture Library/A. Dagli Orti/Bridgeman Images

7.12. Bain News Service/Library of Congress, Prints and Photographs Division

7.13. Library of Congress, Prints and Photographs Division

7.14. Compiled from US State Department Archives

7.15. Data compiled from Smith, *Gothic Arches, Latin Crosses*, p. 20; McAvoy, *A History of the Catholic Church in the United States*, p. 166; Miller and Fossey, *Mapping the Catholic Cultural Landscape*, p. 92; Hennesey, *American Catholics*

7.16. Data compiled from Ellis, "The Catholic Priest in the U.S.," p. 31; Shea, *The Hierarchy of the Catholic Church in the United States*, p. 58

7.17. Data compiled from Goebel, *A Study of Catholic Secondary Education*; Morris, *American Catholic*; Bryk, Lee, and Holland, *Catholic Schools and the Common Good*, p. 33

7.18. Data compiled from McAvoy, "The Immigrants Dominate the American Church," p. 166; Handy, *A History of the Churches in the United States and Canada*, p. 402; Morris, *American Catholic*; Snyder, "120 Years of American Education: A Statistical Portrait"

7.19. Wikimedia Commons

7.20. E. H. Pickering/Library of Congress, Prints and Photographs Division

7.21. Data compiled from William Crosby and H. P. Nichols, *The Unitarian Annual Register, for the Year, 1845* (Boston: W. M. Crosby & H. P. Nichols, 1846); *Dizionario storico ecclesiastico*, vol. IX (1852)

7.22. Wikimedia Commons

7.23. Library of Congress

7.24. J. T. Vintage/Bridgeman Images

8.1. Compiled by the author

8.2. *La Voix du Nord*, defense blogs/Facebook, 2016

8.3. Mac, *Daily Mail*, January 9, 2015

8.4. © Hugues Seumo and Simon Moussi/*Afrik Actuelle*

8.5. "Belçika'da 218.832 Türk Kökenli Vatandaş Yaşıyor," *Gündem*, http://www.gundem.be /tr/belcika/belcika-da-218-832-turk-kokenli-vatandas-yasiyor; Abone Ol, "Hollanda da 395 bin Türk yasiyor," *Turkinfo*, 2014, http://www.turkinfo.nl/hollanda-da-395-bin -turk-yasiyor/8694/; Bruce, "Les Imams 'exportés' de la Diyanet en France," p. 16; "Turks in Selected European Countries," figure 10.1, "Turkish Migrants," 203; Catherine Borrel, "Être né en France d'un parent immigré," *Institut national de la statistique et Des études économiques* (1287, March 2010), https://www.insee.fr/fr /statistiques/1283065#consulter; L. Talha, ed., *The Immigrant Wage in Crisis: The Labor Maghreb in France (1921–1987)* (Marseille: CNRS, 1989); El Ghissassi, "Regard sur le Maroc de Mohammed VI"; Jochen Blaschke and Martin van Bruinessen, eds., *Islam und Politik In Der Turkei* (Berlin: Verlagsabteilung des Berliner Instituts für Vergleichende Sozialforschung e.V. [Edition Parabolis], 1989), p. 233; Etienne and Tozy. "Le Glissement des obligations islamiques vers le phénomène associatif à Casablanca," p. 239; Cemal Usak, interview with the author, Istanbul, May 2015

8.6. Turkish-Islamic Union for Religious Affairs, Germany

8.7. *Rue89 Strasbourg*, Facebook post, October 2015

8.8. Compiled by the author from "Origins and Destinations of the World's Migrants, 1990–2017," Pew Research Center, February 28, 2018, https://www.pewresearch.org /global/interactives/global-migrant-stocks-map/; Houssain Kettani, "Muslim

Population in Europe: 1950–2020," *International Journal of Environmental Science and Development* 1 (2, June 2010): 154–64; Brian Arly Jacobsen, "Muslim Population Trends in Western Europe," Oxford Islamic Studies Online, http://www .oxfordislamicstudies.com/article/opr/t343/e0136?_hi=0&_pos=1#match

8.9. © Alain Jocard/Getty Images

8.10. *Public Sénat*

8.11. Patrick Kovark/AFP/Getty Images

8.12. © D.R. / *Liberté Algérie*, 2015

8.13. Mahatatou/Wikimedia Commons

8.14. Ministry of Religious Affairs and Waqfs, Algeria

8.15. Michael Gottschalk/Photothek/Getty Images

8.16.1. Archeologo / Wikimedia Commons

8.16.2 Claude Truong-Ngoc/Wikimedia Commons

8.16.3 Raimond Spekking/Wikimedia Commons

9.1. Redrawn by the author

9.2. Compiled by the author from the sources listed for figure 1.7

9.3. Compiled by the author from the sources listed for figure1.7; additional sources include: The World Bank, "Data: Morocco," http://data.worldbank.org/country /morocco; Countrymeters, "Morocco Population," http://countrymeters.info/en /Morocco/; Countrymeters, "Tunisia Population," http://countrymeters.info/en /Tunisia; Central Intelligence Agency, "The World Factbook: Tunisia," https://www .cia.gov/library/publications/the-world-factbook/geos/ts.html; The World Bank, "Data: Algeria," http://data.worldbank.org/country/algeria

9.4. "Number of Mosques, Statistical Data on Preachers, Statistical Data on Religious Landmarks and Mosques in Tunisia (1959–2017): Statistical Data on Training Courses for Agents of the Ministry of Religious Affairs" (Tunis: Ministry of Religious Affairs), www.affaires-religieuses.tn/index.php?id=174; Bouabdellah Ghlamallah (MARE minister), interview with the author, Algiers, February 2014; Minister Ahmed Toufiq, interview with the author, Rabat, October 2012; Munir Tlili (minister of religious affairs), interview with the author, Tunis, May 2014

9.5. Compiled by the author from the sources listed at figure 1.7; "Ahmed Toufiq présente le budget sectoriel 2014 du ministère devant la commission de l'éducation et des affaires culturelles et sociales à la chambre des conseillers," Royaume du Maroc Ministere des Habous et des Affaires Islamiques, December 9, 2013, http://habous.gov .ma/fr/component/content/article/36-Annonces-et-activités-ministère/1649-%20 ahmed-toufiq-présente-le-budget-sectoriel-2014-du-ministère-devant-la-commission -de%20l'éducation-et-des-affaires-culturelles-et-sociales-à-la-chambre-des-conseillers .html; *Le Guide du Ministère des Habous et des Affaires Religieuses* (2013), p. 15

9.6. Compiled by the author from Gözaydın, *Diyanet: Türkiye Cumhuriyeti'nde Dinin Tanzimi*, p. 224; Mustafa Pekoz, *Sendika.org*, http://www.sendika.org/2006/11/siyasal -islamin-orgutlenme-merkezi diyanet-isleri-baskanligi-i-mustafa-pekoz/; Turkish

Grand National Assembly, "Turkiye Buyuk Millet Meclisi Tutanak Dergisi," 22/104/4, December 18, 2005, http://www.tbmm.gov.tr/tutanaklar/TUTANAK/TBMM/d22 /c104/tbmm22104035.pdf; Ende Werner and Udo Steinbach, *Islam in the World Today: A Handbook of Politics, Religion, Culture, and Society*, p. 234; İstatistiksel Tablolar, 2008–2009, Yılları Bütçe Ödenekleri (Statistical Tables, Budget Appropriation of 2008–2009), Diyanet, http://www.diyanet.gov.tr/turkish/tanitim/istatistiksel _tablolar/6_butce/2009_yili_butce_odenegi.xls; Bruce, "Governing Islam Abroad," p. 119; "Ministers Get in Line to Sing Diyanet Praises," *Hurriyet Daily News*, January 4, 2013, http://www.hurriyetdailynews.com/ministers-get-in-line-to-sing-diyanet-praises .aspx?pageID=238&nID=38325&NewsCatID=338; Yavuz Baydar, "Diyanet Tops the Budget League," *Hurriyet*, hurriyet.com.tr/ekonomi/24893813.asp, http://www .hurriyetdailynews.com/intelligence-religious-affairs-set-to-take-huge-share-of -turkeys-2016-budget--aspx?pageID=238&nID=89761&NewsCatID=344

9.7. Compiled by the author from "Istanbul Home to Most Mosques in Turkey," March 5, 2013, http://www.hurriyetdailynews.com/istanbul home-to-most-mosques-in-turkey. aspx?pageID=238&nid=42361; Gözaydın, *Diyanet: Türkiye Cumhuriyeti'nde Dinin Tanzimi*, p. 224; Turkish Grand National Assembly, "Turkiye Buyuk Millet Meclisi Tutanak Dergisi," vol. 49, February 19, 1977, http://www.tbmm.gov.tr/tutanaklar /TUTANAK/MM__/d04/c024/mm__04024049.pdf; "Türkiye'de hangi ilde kaç cami var?," *Haber7.com*, https://www.haber7.com/foto-galeri/65234-turkiyede hangi-ilde-kac-cami-var 10.10.2020

9.8. Compiled by the author from Ilhan Yildiz, "Turkiye'nin Avrupa Birligine," Girisinin Din Boyutu Sempzyumi, http://www.dinihaberler.com/diyanet-te-kac-imam-var -biliyor-musunuz--58187.html, 30; İstatistiksel Tablolar, 2008–2009. Yılları Bütçe Ödenekleri (Statistical Tables, Budget Appropriation of 2008–2009), Diyanet, http://www.diyanet.gov.tr/turkish/tanitim/istatistiksel_tablolar/6_butce/2009_yili _butce_odene gi.xls

9.9. Compiled by the author from T. C. Kumluca Kaymakamliği Kumluca İlçe Milli Eğitim Müdürlüğü Anadolu İmam Hatip Lises Kumluca Anadolu İmam Hatip Lisesi 2011–2014 Stratejik Plani, Kumluca 2012; İstatistiki bölge birimleri sınıflamasına göre Kur'an kursu, kursiyer ve bitiren kursiyer sayısı [Öğretim yılı sonu, 2009–2010, Diyanet; Çakır, Bozan, and Talu, *İmam Hatip Liseleri: Efsaneler ve Gerçekler*

9.10. Compiled by the author from Elmahdi, *Une décennie de réformes au Maroc (1999– 2009)*, p. 126; *Le Guide du Ministère des Habous et des Affaires Religieuses* (2013), p. 15; Minister Ahmed Toufiq, interview with the author, Rabat, October 2012; Projet de loi de finances pour l'annee 2012, 2013, and 2014; "Maroc: Un 'plan de soutien à l'encadrement religieux' dans les mosques," *Fait-Religieux.com*, June 19, 2014; Projet du budget sectoriel pour l'année 2012–2014, Ministere des Habous et des Affairs Islamiques; Stephane Papi, "L'influence juridique Islamique au Maghreb," *L'Harmattan*, 2009

9.11. Compiled by the author from Bouabdellah Ghlamallah, interview with the author, Algiers, February 2014; Mohammed Aïssa, interview with the author, Algiers, February 2014; Décret exécutif no. 09–282 du du 9 Ramadhan 1430 correspondant au

30 août 2009, http://www.pdf-repo.com/pdf_1a/6fbgc07cm951e7f91b.html; "Lois," Journal Officiel de la République Algérienne no. 86 (December 27, 2006), http://www .mf.gov.dz/article_pdf/uplb987b1ef012cabc69c44dcadb3e6ee85.pdf; "Lois," *Journal Officiel de la République Algérienne* no. 85 (December 25, 2002), http://www.mf.gov.dz /article_pdf/upl8cd0962b7c0d2ab91439e432aea64912.pdf; "Ordonnances," *Journal Officiel de la République Algérienne* no. 52 (July 26, 2005), http://www.mf.gov.dz/article _pdf/upl536efc255626397c71d8bf4104862e41.pdf; "Lois," *Journal Officiel de la République Algérienne* no. 78 (December 31, 2009), http://www.mf.gov.dz/article_pdf/ upl58f737e7a8ec7ee77d499f92dbcc09b0.pdf

9.12.1 PVDE/Bridgeman Images

9.12.2 Sandervalya/Wikimedia Commons

9.13. Photograph by the author

9.14. Photograph by the author

9.15. *Leaders* (Tunis), March 2013

9.16. Compiled by the author

9.17. *Jawhara*, 2014 (www.jawharafm.net)

10.1. Soufan Group

10.2. Balkanique/Wikimedia Commons

10.3. © Adem Altan/Reuters

10.4. Metin Pala/Anadolu Agency/Getty Images

10.5. Drawn by the author using Piktochart

10.6. *RP Médias* (Bagnolet, France)

10.7. Data compiled from Hertling, *Geschichte Der Katholischen Kirche*; "Titular Sees: The Hierarchy of the Catholic Church," *Catholic-Hierarch.org*, http://www.catholic -hierarchy.org/diocese/lt.html; Eubel, *Hierarchia catholica medii aevi*; "Frequently Requested Church Statistics," Center for Applied Research in the Apostolate, Georgetown University, http://cara.georgetown.edu/frequently-requested-church -statistics/; "Status of Global Mission," *International Bulletin on Missionary Research* 37, no. 1, January 2013, January 2000, p. 25, January 1985, p. 31

10.8. Data compiled from Battandier, *Annuaire pontifical catholique*; Eubel, *Hierarchia catholica medii aevi*; "Geography of the Conclave: Where Do the Cardinals Come From?," Pew Research Center, March 8, 2013

10.9. "Foreign Relations of the Holy See," Wikipedia, https://en.wikipedia.org/w/index .php?title=Foreign_relations_of_the_Holy_See&oldid=986978 128 (accessed November 8, 2020)

10.10. Data compiled from "The Future of World Religions: Population Growth Projections, 2010–2050," Pew Research Center, April 2, 2015, https://www.pewforum.org/2015/04 /02/religious-projections-2010-2050/; "The Changing Global Religious Landscape," Pew Research Center, April 15, 2017, https://www.pewforum.org/2017/04/05/the -changing-global-religious-landscape/#global-population-projections-2015-to-2060

10.11. Data compiled from O'Donnell, *The Catholic Hierarchy of the United States, 1790–1922*; Guilday, "The Sacred Congregation de Propaganda Fide (1622–1922)"; Eubel, *Hierarchia catholica medii aevi*; *The Religious Creeds and Statistics of every Christian Denomination in the United States and British Provinces with some account . . .* (Boston: John Hayward, 1836); Shea, *The Hierarchy of the Catholic Church in the United States*, p. 58; Hertling, *Geschichte der katholischen Kirche*, p. 162; McAvoy, "The Immigrants Dominate the American Church, 1850–1866"; Kirsch and Luksch, *Illustrierte Geschichte der Katholischen Kirche*, p. 603

10.12. Data compiled from Ausubel and Marchetti, "Quantitative Dynamics of Human Empires"

10.13. St. Peter's, Vatican City/Bridgeman Images

INDEX

Abbassid Caliphate 104, 399

Abdel Nasser, Gamal 228, 230

Abduh, Muhammed 434

Abdülhamid I 444

Abdülhamid II xii, xix, 24, 86, 91, 95, 98,
103–104, 113, 121, 123, 126, 128–130, 138–139,
141–151, 411, 437, 444, 467n46, 467n54,
468n88, 469n143, 473n37, 473n43,
473n54, 473n59, 475n114, 476n149,
476n155, 476n158, 476n165, 476n166,
476n177, 476n178, 476n180, 519, 524, 527,
530; dethronement of, 141

Abdülaziz 24, 444

Abdullah bin Hussein bin Ali 88, 110, 112

Abdülmecid I xi, 5–6, 24, 108, 129, 133,
144–145, 444

Abdülmecid II 108–115, 155, 205, 216, 409, 444

Abel, Cain and 205

Aceh War (1873–1910) 98

Act of Supremacy (1534) 53

Adolescentium Aetas 68

Afghanistan 79, 89, 110, 362

Ahmadiyya 86, 467n52, 538

Aïssa, Mohammed xv, 311, 362, 364, 367, 371–375,
467n52, 497n128, 498n134, 498n137,
498n142, 498n152, 498n154, 506n184,
506n186, 506n195, 507n198, 508n239,
508n240, 508n242. 508n252, 509n261,
515n99, 523, 538, 540, 543, 564

AK Party (Turkey). *See* Justice and
Development Party

Akyol, Mustafa 350, 427, 484n82, 502n45,
502n48, 503n89, 517n159, 519

Al Hoceima 358, 505n157

Al Istiqlāl Party (1976–1983) 218–219

Al-Adl wal lhsane 218, 360

Al-Afghani, Jamal al-Din 139, 144, 147, 149

Al-Aqsa Mosque 397, 407–408, 514n65

Alawites 93, 344. *See also* Alaouites; Alevis

Al-Azhar, 328; Sheikh of, 117, 321, 324, 514n55

Al-Azhar University 86, 90, 98, 114, 143–144,
403,

Al-Baghdadi, Abu Bakr xi, 4, 9, 328, 330, 388,
397–399, 407, 444, 457n1, 500n1, 500n2,
512n20, 513n23, 517n158, 541

Al-Din al-Afghani, Jamal 139, 144, 147, 149

Alevis, Alevism 337–338, 343–345,385,437

Alexander III, Czar 466n16,

Algeria: French Control of, 92; Civil War, 204;
Islam in 226–227, 235, 361–363, 379, 479n113

Al-Ghannouchi, Rachid 230, 318, 382, 385,
387, 401, 406, 511n344, 518n199, 522

Al-Ghazali Institute xv, 312–314, 316–317,
499n155

Al-Harameyn 129–130

Al-Madani, Hamza Zhafir 147–148

Al-Qaeda, xxi, 8, 285, 302, 322, 338, 343, 352,
361, 383–384, 396–398, 434, 510n319, 551;
attacks of 2001, 397

Al-Qaradawi, Yusuf 9, 360, 401, 406, 514n57,
514n58, 528, 535

Al-Qarawayin 215, 217, 219, 221, 328, 484fn101

Al-Quds 408, Committee for Jerusalem, 219

al-Rabita (Muslim World League) 157, 326

Al-Rahman al-Kawakibi, Abd (1849–1902) 144

Al-Saud 112, 399. *See also* Saudi

Al-Sayyadi, Abulhuda 147–148, 473n54,
476n178, 519

Al-Utaybi, Juhayman 398

Al-Zeitouna 93, 99, 228–233, 378–387; Sheikh of, 328

Amir Amanulla 110

Amizigh358. *See also* Berber

Anarchists xiv, 32–34, 186, 239, 241, 255, 258–261, 263–265, 279, 489n10, 490n66, 490n73, 491n91, 491n92, 491n95, 491n96, 491n99, 491n109, 492n112, 492n113, 492n127, 521, 536, 540, 551, 552

Ancien régime 108, 157, 169, 196, 377, 382–383

Angiolillo, Michele 242, 258

Anglo-Mohammedan College 80, 84

Anti-Saloon League 264

Arab League 220, 231, 406, 426

Arab Spring 43, 334, 336, 353, 359, 361, 365, 385, 511n326, 517n160, 550

Archangel Raphael Society 244

Archbishop 28, 61, 70, 167, 171, 179, 268, 277, 281, 308 ; of Baltimore 266, 279; of Canterbury, 53; of Chicago, 269; of Cologne 50, 175; of Gnesen-Posen, 176; of Milan, 59; of Minnesota, 252, 272; of New York, 246, 250, 269; of Wisconsin, 279; in Japan and China, 71; of San Francisco, 278; under Pope Francis, 418; excommunication of, 422

Archdiocese 63, 277, 307, 436, 445

Arinç, Bülent 338, 501n26, 521

Atatürk, Mustafa Kemal 28, 95, 105–110, 153, 154, 157, 196, 200, 205–208, 215, 228, 338, 459n55, 466n43, 469n111, 469n137, 469n141, 470n171, 470n174, 477n218, 477n220, 478n221, 482n29, 483n31, 483n32, 483n39, 483n44, 483n48, 502n39, 513n43, 531, 533–535, 540, 549–550

Attacks of September 11, 2001 290

Auto-da-fé 56

Awqaf, Ministry of 197, 229. *See also* Waqf

Aya Sofia mosque 5, 206, 349

Ayatollah Khomenei 202, 218, 220

Aziz al-Shaykh, Grand Mufti Abdul 397

Bab al-Oued riots (1988) 201, 225

Bad Kissingen 180, 242

Balfour Declaration 116, 467n69, 468n79, 537

Balkan Wars (1910–2) 103, 149, 150–151

Balkans 8, 20, 24, 26, 77, 79, 81, 97–99, 118–119, 150, 197, 394, 401–404, 406, 409, 416, 437, 513n34, 514n73, 523, 529, 543

Baltimore Catechism xiv, 246, 250, 315, 489n36, 561

Bapst, Johann 241, 253

Bedini, Archbishop Gaetano: Papal Nuncio 274, 303

Belhadj, Mondher 377, 499n156, 509n271

Bell, Gertrude L. 102, 112–113

Ben Badis, Abdelhamid 144, 151, 223

Ben Bella, Ahmed 200, 221–223

Ben Salem, Abdeljalil 384–385, 533

Benedict XV, Pope 418, 443

Benedict XVI, Pope 409, 422, 443, 515n110, 519

Benedictines 58, 65, 70, 166, 270, 422

Benincasa, Fabio xxv, 423, 465n175, 522

Benjedid, Chadly 224–225

Benkirane, Abdellah 357

Berbers 358, 437

Bergoglio, cardinal Jose Mario 418, 422–423. *See also* Francis, Pope

Bismarck, Otto von 176, 242

Blaine Amendments 489n31, 489n32

Blunt, William S. 86, 473n51, 523

Böhm, Paul: Kölner Moschee (2014) 324

Bonaparte, Napoléon 82, 86, 90, 167, 169, 173

Book of Common Prayer 53

Bosnia-Herzegovina 22, 82, 150, 322

Boston College xxiii, xxiv, 273, 277, 523, 528, 544

Boubakeur, Dalil xv, 308–309, 311–312

Boudiba, Abdelwahab 229–230, 487n203, 487n213, 523

Boumediènne, Houari 223–224

Bourguiba, Habib 28, 200, 228–233, 318, 376, 383, 387, 488n226, 511n324, 531

Bouteflika, Abdelaziz 227, 361–362, 366, 497n117

British Empire xix, 79, 85–86, 145, 147, 149

British India 81, 85, 103, 112, 117, 137, 284, 554

Bruno, Giordano xiii, 161, 162, 180, 559

Bulgaria 80–81, 83, 197, 404

Caesaropapism 27, 163

Cahensly, Peter 244, 265, 489n22, 492n124

Caliphate, abolition of (1922–1924) 7, 103, 110, 113, 116, 196, 205, 466n39, 471n180, 482n1, 521, 524, 532

Calvin, Jean 55, 60; Calvinism, 170, 185, 445, 462n60

Calvinists 56, 58, 73, 74

Canon Law 163, 198, 278, 281, 304, 418, 430, 445, 463n95

Canisius, Peter 58–59

Cardinal Ratzinger, Joseph 422

Carroll, John xv, 239, 243, 268, 273, 277–278, 280, 493n177, 549

Castel Sant'Angelo 169

Cathedral of St. Andrews xi, 53, 54

Cathedral of the Holy Cross xiv, 246–247, 561

Catholic Church xi, xix, 7, 11, 16, 19–20, 29–30, 50, 55, 71, 75, 96, 150, 161, 176, 193, 198, 241, 243, 264–266, 268, 323, 393, 427, 430, 437, 438, 445–448, 459n63, 463n110, 478n4, 478n9, 480n87, 480n88, 480n89, 481n129, 481n140, 482n148, 490n71, 492n146, 516n130, 517n181, 525, 530, 534, 538, 540–541, 549, 555, 560–562, 565, 566; Papal Zouaves: Army of, 182, 248, 251, 447; in Germany, 176; Catholic Civil War, 182

Cem Houses 344

Césari, Jocelyne 332, 501, 525

Charlemagne 23

Charles X 194

Charlie Hebdo 34, 287, 289, 317, 321

Churches xiii, xiv, 10, 15–17, 19, 21, 24, 33–35, 47, 49, 51, 53–54, 56, 74–75, 79, 161, 166, 171, 173, 179, 184–185, 188, 190, 243, 252, 262, 264, 266, 268, 269–270, 272, 281, 292, 312, 343–344, 374, 407, 419, 429, 446, 460n10, 491n102, 493n155, 532, 533, 551, 562; Anglican and Swedish, 21; in Saudi Arabia, 292, 407; schismatic, 33, 47, 49, 75, 79, 264

Cocco-Ortu Memorandum (1901) 190

Cold War 203, 330, 397, 401, 495n52, 538

College of Cardinals 51, 173, 187, 266, 277, 281, 283, 515n108, 517n152, 541, 555

Collegio Romano 23, 59, 66, 69–70, 186

Colosseum 179, 394

Comité de Coordination des Musulmans Turcs de France (CCMTF) xxi, 293

Committee on Union and Progress 105, 150

Concordat of 1801 167, 479n31, 531

Concordat of 1851 173

Concordat of 1953 173, 419, 427, 432

Confessionalization 132, 223, 463n128, 530, 551

Confucianism 11

Congregatio studiorum (1870) 186, 525

Congregation of the Doctrine of the Faith 422

Congregations Law 176

Congress of Berlin 82

Conseil français du culte musulman (CFCM) 308, 321

Conseil Supérieur des Ouléma 353, 356, 416

Constantine: ruler, 23, 424, 445; city in Algeria, 151, 162, 225, 227, 363, 457n8

Consultative Council for Moroccans Residing Abroad (CCME) xxi, 306–307, 452, 548

Council of European Moroccan Ulama (COEM) xxi, xxiv, 303, 305–306

Council of Trent xi, 19, 23, 50, 60–62, 68, 119, 183, 276, 330, 417, 423, 458n36, 460n1, 461n34, 462n63, 531; Tridentine, 62, 277, 297, 305, 312

Counter-Reformation 13, 19, 24–26, 36, 44, 49, 58–60, 62, 66, 76, 132, 152, 184, 193, 331, 431, 462n50, 463n115, 463n124464n140, 464n146, 522,

Couvent de Saint-Jacques 166

Crispi, Francesco 190, 242

Crusaders 398, 410

Cuma Selamligi. 125 See also Selamlik

Custodians of Mecca and Medina: 13, 21, 407, 426; Otttoman, 128–131, 152; Saudi, 285, 326, 395; and ISIS, 398. See also Khadimü'l-Harameyn

Czolgosz, Leon xiv, 242, 261–262, 264

Dar al-Hadith 217, 355, 358

Dar al-Harb 35, 104, 286, 327, 446

Dar al-Imam 315, 331, 363, 369–370, 415, 446, 507n226

Dar al-Islam 35, 104, 286, 300, 327, 437, 446, 449

Dar al-Ulum 80

Darul Uloom 139, 143

Davutoğlu, Ahmet 338, 401–402, 407, 513n35, 544, 546

Declaration of the Rights of Man and Citizen 166

Decolonization, European 117

Deoband 84, 139, 143

Deutsche Islam Konferenz 495n36, 500

Dioceses xi, xv, xvii, 12, 23–24, 34, 36, 49, 54, 61–63, 69, 71, 73, 120, 134, 163, 165–167, 169, 173, 176, 179–180, 192, 243–244, 246, 262, 268–270, 273–278, 283, 307, 416–417, 423, 431–432, 436, 445–446, 448, 479n37, 565; increase of, 36, 49, 120, 165, 169; reduction of, 166

Diocesization 144, 438

Diyanet Işleri Başkanliği (DIB) xiii, xxi, 206–213, 218, 294–299, 301, 319, 324, 326, 337–340, 342–350, 376, 385, 390, 401, 403–404, 407, 409–410, 446, 454, 455, 457, 494n31, 494n33, 495n45, 495n51, 495n52, 495n62, 502n40, 502n44, 502n55, 503n73, 503n82, 503n85, 503n87, 513n33, 514n60, 524, 526, 538–539, 544, 550, 556, 557, 560, 561, 562, 563, 564; president of, 295–296, 297, 299, 319, 339, 344–345, 349–350, 376, 410, 403, 407, 409, 495n62

Diyanet Işleri Türk-İslam Birliği (DITIB) xxi, 416, 446, 451, 495n54, 495n64, 500n200, 532, 548

Dolmabahçe 155, 196, 205

Dutch East Indies 81, 104, 137

Eastern Question 84, 100, 157, 329, 394, 435, 466n36, 469n109, 501n33, 545

Edison, Thomas 98, 128; new wax cylinders of, 98, 128

Education, Ministry of 139, 165, 225, 289, 298, 299, 341, 347, 367–368, 381

Edward VI 53

Egypt 9, 18, 22, 80–82, 84–86, 90, 97–98, 101, 102, 104–105, 109–110, 113–117, 122–123, 128, 137, 140, 142–145, 147–148, 150, 153–154, 197, 220, 230, 329–330, 353, 382, 403, 406, 409, 471n200, 512n355, 514n55, 523, 526, 537, 553; British occupation of, 144; egyptian, 9, 18, 80, 85, 86, 90, 113–114, 148, 228, 230, 385, 445, 465n4, 467n72, 472n217, 472n10, 482n7, 482n19, 483n44, 488n248, 534, 549; Grand Sheikh, 406; Mamluks in, 122, 440

El Ghissassi, Hakim xxv, 351, 352, 354, 357, 414, 496n87, 500n204, 503n95, 503n98504n104, 504n107, 504n114, 504n116, 505n153, 515n88, 529, 562

Emir al-Mu'minin (Commander of the Faithful) 93, 96, 109, 111, 123, 200, 217, 307, 350–352, 359–360, 389, 412, 415, 446, 468n98, 477n201, 484n98, 484n100, 537

Enlightenment 135, 161, 442

Ennahda 231–233, 318, 375–377, 380–385, 406, 454, 499n161, 509n266, 509n268, 509n281, 510n304, 510n309, 510n317, 511n332, 533

Erbakan, Necmettin 210–212, 337, 343, 501n20, 520

Erdoğan, Recep Tayyip 299, 405–406, 411, 501n18, 501n22, 501n30, 502n37, 502n58, 502n59, 502n61, 502n66, 513n32, 513n34, 513n42, 513n44, 513n49, 514n55, 514n57, 514n63, 514n70, 514n71, 523–525, 528–529, 533, 535 541, 546; government of, 403

Esau, Jacob and 65

European Institute for Human Sciences 321

European Islam 286, 298, 312, 319, 495n48, 500n192, 500n194, 521

European Turkish Democrats (EUTD) xxi, 295

Evkaf (Religious foundations) 25, 121, 133–134, 140, 448

Evkaf, Ministry of (Ottoman Empire) 98, 121, 133–134, 138–139, 144–145, 154, 205

Expatriation Law of 1890 177

Eyup Sultan Mosque 123

Faqih 204
Fatwa Council 84, 141, 145, 197, 328, 357, 372, 446
Fédération Nationale des Musulmans de France (FNMF) xxi, 293, 302
Feisal bin Hussein bin Ali 88–89, 93–95, 112, 467n71, 467n72
Fasci Siciliani 258
Fatwa (Fetva ; Fetvas) 154, 446, 477n219
Fitna 14, 43, 332, 349, 358, 363, 374–375, 446
Fiqh 35, 93, 141, 286, 329, 356, 375, 446
Fondation pour l'Islam de France (2017) 322, 496n70, 515n94, 542
Foreign fighters 26, 126, 250–1, 291, 388, 398, 400
France xiii, xv, xxi, xxii, xxv, 17, 20, 27–29, 33, 38, 47, 50, 54–58, 62–64, 69, 75–77, 80, 89, 91, 92–96, 100–101, 103, 113–114, 116, 133, 151–152, 163, 164–167, 169–170, 177, 181, 185–187, 190, 194, 215, 239, 242, 244, 255, 263, 270, 276–277, 281, 285, 287–291, 293, 295–296, 298–305, 307–319, 321–323, 326, 329, 342, 358, 373, 414, 416, 419, 427, 429, 439, 449, 450, 457n1468n84, 468n105, 477n201, 478n18, 478n26, 479n37, 479n42, 479n50, 494n4, 494n6, 494n22, 494n23, 494n26, 494n27, 494n28, 494n31, 495n46, 495n51, 495n68, 496n81, 497n118, 497n128, 498n132, 498n135, 498n142, 498n145, 498n150, 498n152, 498n154, 499n161, 499n176, 499n178, 499n183, 500n187, 509n288, 518n191, 519–522, 524, 526–527, 531–532, 535–536, 538–540, 543, 545, 548, 551–552, 561–562, 565; 28, 47, 50, 56, 64, 166, 170, 173, 187, 244, 263, 277, 429; 89; Catholicism in, xiv-xv, xix, xxi, 5, 7, 12, 13–14, 20, 22–23, 26, 29–30, 40, 55–56, 58–60, 63, 70, 73, 75, 79–82, 87, 89–96, 98–101, 105–106, 109–111, 113–117, 120–122, 125–126, 130, 142, 144, 146, 148, 151, 154, 161, 166–167, 169–171, 173–174, 182, 185, 196, 198, 200, 206, 213–217, 221, 223, 228, 239, 242, 255, 271, 283–284, 287, 289–291, 293, 296, 298, 300, 304–322, 358, 361, 373, 394, 397, 415, 417, 419, 421, 429–430, 434, 437–439, 441, 446, 449, 453, 454, 455, 459n59, 459n61, 465n4,

465n10, 467n71, 468n82, 468n95, 468n97, 468n99, 468n103, 468n106, 469n118, 470n178, 477n217, 478n19, 478n21, 478n23, 478n25, 480n68, 497n116, 498n143, 498n149, 500n190, 526, 535, 537, 549, 551, 553
Franklin, Benjamin 239
Franzelin, Cardinal Johannes 276
Friday Cumalik (Cuma selamligi) 125
Front de Libération Nationale 200
Front Islamique du Salut 486n173, 486n177, 519

Gallican Church 95–96, 169, 184, 446
Gambetta, Léon 171, 480n68
Garibaldi, Giuseppe 182, 248
Gaudium et Spes (1965) 423, 516n141, 545
Georgetown University 239, 268, 515n113, 528, 534, 538, 565
Germany xi, xv, xxii, 17, 19, 22, 29, 35, 47, 50–53, 58, 62–63, 66, 74, 76, 101, 147, 151–152, 163–166, 174, 176–177, 181, 185–187, 190, 193, 242, 264, 281, 285, 287–288, 294–300, 302, 305, 308, 316, 319, 321, 323, 388, 403, 416, 419, 429, 434, 439, 440, 446, 450, 451, 453, 460n104, 467n58, 495n65, 496n78, 497n122, 498n135, 503n96, 515n105, 521, 524, 530, 540, 542, 562; christian, 285, 296, 298–300, 319, 321, 323; Catholics in, 19, 22, 50–51, 53, 58, 63, 66, 185; German, 152; Islam in, xi, xxi, xvi, xxiii, 9, 12, 23, 51–53, 55, 58, 62, 64–65, 67, 70, 72, 74, 76, 79, 101, 103, 130, 146–147, 151, 174–177, 180, 182, 184, 187, 188, 244, 265, 269–271, 279, 291, 296–301, 305, 320, 322–324, 411, 429, 437, 439–440, 450–451, 456, 461n29, 477n199, 477n200, 482n0, 498n147, 550; Lutheran Reformation in, 52–53; southern, 74, 187, 193, 429
Ghlamallah, Boabdallah 310–311, 313, 315, 362, 363, 366, 368, 370, 372–375, 497n114, 497n121, 497n123, 497n125, 498n133, 498n138, 498n145, 499n169, 507n197, 507n207, 507n210, 507n212, 507n220, 508n254, 509n262, 509n263, 515n95, 515n100, 526, 556, 563, 564

Gladstone, William 85

Goldman, Emma 259, 491n87, 532

Görmez, Mehmet 347–348, 407–410, 501n24, 503n82, 503n87, 513n33, 514n62, 514n78, 514n80, 525, 561

Gözaydin, Istar xxiv, 483n53, 494n29, 532, 557, 563, 564

Grand Mosque of Algiers (Djamaa el Djazaïr) 364

Grand National Assembly 105, 107–109, 154, 156, 201, 206–207, 557, 560, 563–564

Grande Mosquée de Paris (GMP) xxi, 293, 308, 311, 314, 316–316

Great Mosque of al-Nuri (Al Nuri Mosque) 328

Great Schism 13

Gregory XVII, Pope 421

Groupe Islamique Combattant Marocain, GICM xxi, 302

Guantánamo Bay 350

Gülen, Fethullah 213, 218, 295, 300, 337, 346–347, 406, 446, 502n64, 503n72, 520; Gülenists, 300–301, 324, 342, 346–348, 446

Gulf Cooperation Council (GCC) xxi, 396, 406, 416

Habous Ministry xxiii, 197, 204, 218, 220, 302–303, 352–354, 452. *See also* Islamic Affairs, Ministry of

Habsburg dynasty, 439–440; administration, 82

Hadiths 128, 331, 343, 367, 399, 430, 446–448

Hajj 77, 84, 97, 129, 130–131, 229–230, 232, 301, 323, 335, 390, 408–409, 446, 469n123, 470n157, 470n160, 471n191, 472n215, 477n206, 512n7, 549, 550; Ottoman administration of, 129–131; Turkish, 408

Halki seminary 343

Hanafi Tradition 132, 134–135, 140–141, 344, 385, 404, 410, 412, 416, 446, 524

Hanbali Tradition 132, 134–135, 446

Haram al-Sharif (al Haram) (the Dome Mosque) 89, 114, 407

Hashemite 21, 88, 89, 107, 111, 113, 115–116, 126, 146, 219, 396–397, 447, 467n62, 467n71, 550

Hassan II Foundation 302–304, 327, 452, 453, 496n70, 496n73

Headscarf 292, 337

Hejaz 24–25, 88, 93, 97, 111, 113, 128–130, 137, 140, 146, 148, 152, 157, 329, 409, 440, 446–447, 474n103, 474n107; Railway, xii-xiii, 87, 130–131, 145, 149, 155, 536

Henry VIII 21, 53, 75

Higher Islamic Council (1966) 223, 227

Hijra Movement 104

Hizmet Movement. *See* Fethullah Gülen

Holy See 23, 30, 65, 76, 164, 171, 177, 189, 191, 193, 281, 283, 428, 447, 565; diplomatic relations with, 171. *See also* Roman Church; Vatican

Hudud punishments 120

Hughes, Bishop John 246, 273

Hugo, Victor 182, 480n95, 535

Humbert I, King 261, 491n89. *See also* Umberto, King

Hussein bin Ali 81, 88–89, 93–95, 101, 103–105, 109–114, 116, 146, 152, 397, 447, 471n184; British relations with, 101, 105, 111, 152

Hussayni, Kemal 88, 89, 93, 447

Hussainid (Dynasty) 447

ibn Abd al-Wahhab, Muhammad. *See also* Wahhabism 448

ibn Muhieddine, Abd el-Kader 223, 225, 315, 469n109, 498n147, 537

Ibn Saud, 'Abd-al-'Aziz 101, 448

Ibn-Arafa, Mohammed 215, 441

Ignatius of Loyola, Saint xi-xii, 57–59, 66–67, 70, 75–76, 423, 464n138. *See also* Jesuits

Ikhwan 117, 410; Ikwanism, 204, 331. *See also* Muslim Brotherhood

Ilmiye 140. *See also* Ulema

Imam Hatip Schools xiii, xvi, xxi, 139, 206–214, 294, 298, 337, 339, 341–342, 345, 347, 350, 401, 501n18, 502n58, 560, 564

Imams xx, 3, 14, 43, 77, 80–81, 83, 86, 88–89, 93, 104, 125, 135, 141, 204, 215–216, 225, 227,

229, 230–231, 293, 295, 304, 305, 312, 315–317, 321, 331–332, 337, 344, 346, 349, 353–355, 357–358, 362–363, 366–371, 376, 378, 380–381, 386, 390, 406, 414–416, 446–447, 451, 497n107, 498n149, 505n152, 507n226, 509n270, 511n339, 564; Imamat, 200, 330, 447; of the Two Holy Cities, 81, 88, 89, 93, 104

Immortale Dei (1885) 189

Indigenous Code 92

Inquisition, Roman 56–57, 119, 169, 462n84, 521

Institut des sciences islamiques 225

Institut Supérieur de théologie 381

Institut Français xxiv, 313

Iran; Revolution in 202–204, 227, 328, 349, 362, 395, 406, 444, 470n167, 522; Revolution, 202, 482n20

Islam, Maliki 34, 35, 94, 134–135, 306, 326, 351, 352, 360, 362, 374–375, 385, 386, 412, 413, 415–416, 447

Iran-Iraq War 203

Islamic Affairs and Habous, Moroccan Ministry of xvi, xxiii, 197, 204, 218, 220, 302, 303, 304, 305, 352, 353, 354, 446, 452, 503, 504, 505, 506, 515, 556, 557

Islamic Question 7

Islamic Salvation Front (FIS) xxi, 225–227

Islamic Shura Council 205

Islamic State (ISIS) ix, xvi, xxii, 8, 309, 318, 330–331, 338, 343, 361, 388, 390, 397–399, 402, 407, 410, 434, 512n10, 512n13, 512n18, 512n19, 513n24, 513n28, 514n78, 519, 524, 531, 543, 547, 553

Islamkolleg 323

Islamrat 300, 319, 451, 494n32

Israel 116, 197, 220, 373–374, 397, 407, 408, 440, 501n15

Istanbul, Inter-Allied Occupation of 81, 101, 115, 149

Istanbul-Marmara xv, xxv, 297, 403, 407–408, 457

Istituzione Leopoldina 187

i-Tabligh, Jamaat 117

Italy, xi, xiv, 8, 17, 20, 24, 27, 29, 35–37, 47, 56–59, 62–64, 69, 74, 76, 81, 98–99, 119, 133, 162–166, 173–174, 177, 179, 181–182, 186–187, 189–191, 194, 241–242, 248, 250, 252, 255, 257–258, 260–261, 263–264, 268–270, 275, 281, 291, 301–302, 416, 419–421, 427, 429, 440, 451, 478n15, 480n81, 480n86, 481n136, 490n50, 494n17, 525–526, 538–540, 548; Italian, 3, 7, 22, 26–30, 33–34, 36, 49, 57, 59, 63, 81, 98–99, 105–106, 109, 126, 144, 146, 151, 161, 169–170, 174, 177, 179–183, 186–192, 240–241, 243–244, 246, 248, 251–253, 257, 258–260, 262, 264–267, 269–271, 275–276, 279, 289, 291, 305–306, 388, 393, 398, 417–418, 420, 423, 437, 440, 447, 454, 469n131, 477n195, 480n85, 489n9, 489n14, 492n141, 521, 551, 554; northern, 58–59, 76, 257; Reformation in, 57; southern, 179; unified, 181–182

Italian Law of Guarantees (1871) 180, 186

Jacobins 166–167

Jerusalem xx, 13, 22–24, 55, 65, 81, 87–89, 95, 98, 113–115, 122, 130, 138–139, 143, 152, 154, 219, 328, 395, 397, 405–408, 440, 446–447, 484n89, 489n93, 537

Jessie J 357

Jesuits 23, 57–60, 65–66, 70, 146, 164, 173–174, 176–177, 270, 276, 281, 423, 463n91, 463n94, 463n96, 463n98, 463n100, 463n109, 463n112, 464n139, 464n141, 464n144, 482n147, 488n1, 489n25, 489n30, 490n46, 490n47, 490n57, 493n166, 493n186, 541, 544

Jesus, Society of. *See* Jesuits

Jewish 43, 88, 99, 116, 128, 169, 159, 251, 259, 287, 289, 291, 297, 323, 329, 337, 373–374, 385, 425, 438

John Paul II, Pope 418, 422, 430, 443, 480n87, 480n89, 482n148, 536

John XXIII, Pope 23, 421

Josephism 27, 163, 176

Justice and Development Party: in Turkey (AKP), xxi, 298, 337–339, 341, 343–346, 349–350, 385, 389, 401, 403–404, 406, 409–410, 495n56, 502n40, 502n52, 512n357, 529, 533, 537, 544–545; in Morocco (PJD), 357, 359

Ka'bah 112,116,129–131
Kahn, Sayid Ahmad 84
Kairouan 93–94, 154, 231–232, 380–381, 385, 387, 511n322, 511n323, 519
Kalin, Ibrahim 300, 348, 495n67, 503n78, 503n83
Kavakçe, Merve 345
Kbibeche, Anouar 321
Kennedy, John F. 432
Khadimü'l-Harameyn 129–130. See also Custodian of Mecca and Medina
Khilafa movement: 26, 103, 117, 126; Abu Bkr al Baghdadi and, 399
Khilafat, Central Committee 103–104, 112
Know-Nothing Movement 252
Küçük Kainardja,Treaty of (1774) 80, 82, 92, 411, 444
Küçükçan, Talip xxiv, 298, 494n29, 495n56
Kulturkampf 176, 180, 447, 535
Kultusministerium, Prussian 176, 535
Kurds 342, 344–345, 477n217
Kurfürst 162
Kuru, Ahmet 43, 341, 348
Kuttabs 86, 228

La Questione Sociale xiv, 258, 259, 260, 492n123
Laïcité 92, 215, 221, 319, 478n28, 498n150, 522, 532
Länder 296, 429, 500n193, 559
Lateran Accords (1929) 8, 29, 191, 194, 281, 285, 324
Law of Guarantees, Italian (1871) 180, 186
Lawrence, T. E. 21, 113
Le Pen, Marine 320, 499n177
Lefebvre, Archbishop Marcel 421–422
Leo XIII, Pope 185, 189–190, 253, 265, 279, 443, 481n124
Letter Concerning Toleration (1689) 428, 517n162, 539
Libya 9, 18, 21–22, 25, 98, 113, 137, 144, 146–147, 197, 203–204, 288, 302, 330, 353, 359, 384, 388, 397–398, 411, 414–415, 451, 458n31, 469n131, 477n195, 512n355, 520–521
Lilla, Mark xxiii, 459n56

Lloyd George, David 100–102
Louis XVI 162, 167
Louis XVIII 194
Louisiana Purchase 239
Louvain, Catholic University of 58, 65, 274, 522
Luther, Martin 21–22, 47, 51–53, 55, 60, 75–76, 205, 328–330, 461n29; Lutheran, 20–22, 48–51, 53–54, 57, 66, 73, 76, 79, 165, 184–185, 462n55, 463n103, 465n168, 542; Lutheranism, 19, 21, 23, 63, 65, 71, 170, 241

Macron, Emmanuel 319
Madaniyya 147–148
Madrassas 15, 25, 84, 92–94, 135, 138, 142, 206, 223–224, 356, 447 . See also Imam Hatip Schools; Medreses
Madrid Riots (1835) 173
Mahdi 21, 80, 86, 90, 96, 148, 330, 347, 434, 503, 556, 564
Mahmud II 123, 129, 130, 133, 135, 139, 141, 145, 444
Mainz 244, 245
Makhzen 217, 302
Malatesta, Errico 241, 258, 260, 264, 489, 540
Maliki Tradition 34, 35, 94, 134–135, 306, 326, 351, 352, 360, 362, 374–375, 385, 386, 412, 413, 415–416, 447
Mardin, Serif 26, 143, 148
Marzouki, Moncef 318, 377, 499, 509, 510, 511
Masonic Flags 161, 225
Massignon, Louis 95, 114, 115, 394, 471, 512, 528, 537
Mawlana Hasan 104
May Laws (Maigesetze, 1873) 176
McCloskey, John 15, 250, 268, 277, 280
McGirr, Lisa 264
McKinley, William 14, 242, 261, 262
McMahon, Henry: McMahon Letter 88, 116
Mecca xii, 5–22, 77–157, 202–220, 385, 326, 328, 341, 372, 397–409, 440–471, 501, 512–514, 551
Medreses (Ottoman Empire) 139, 141–143, 145, 355, 447. See also Madrassas; See also Imam Hatip Schools

Medjid Asylum 471, 524

Mehmed V, Sultan 26, 89, 99, 106, 145, 150, 156, 444

Mehmed VI (Vahdettin), Sultan 99, 106–107, 156, 444

Mejelle 134

Menderes, Adnan 201, 208

Mitterand, François 430, 485

Mohammed VI Institute for Imams 304, 305, 414, 415

Mohammed V 360

Mohammed VI 221, 302, 306, 334, 350–361, 401, 413, 438, 441

Molenbeek, Belgium 33, 289, 292, 302

Morocco; Moroccan XXV, 14–17, 29, 35, 42, 79–117, 150–151, 197–235, 284–338, 301–307, 350–416, 437–453

Moroccans Residing Abroad (MRE) XXI, XXII, 33, 290, 306, 350, 412, 414, 452

Morse, Samuel F. B. 127; and know-nothing movement, 252

Mouvahidin 153, 154

Mudawana 352

Muezzin 25, 28, 83, 137, 230, 338, 366, 372, 447

Mufti: Ottoman Grand; of Jerusalem 204, 209, 228

Mujahid; Mujahidin 200, 398, 407, 434

Mujtahid 200, 230–231

Münster 54, 76, 298

Muslim Brotherhood 8, 18, 117, 202, 203, 204, 227, 235, 362, 403, 406. See also *Ikhwan*

Mussolini 191, 440

Napoleon III 92, 170

Nasserism 27

National Order Party 210

National Security Council 213

National Shrine of the Assumption 243, 244, 268

Nida Tounes Party 377, 454

Nigerian Fatwa Council 328

Niqab 310, 376, 381

Non Expedit, Encyclical (1868) 182, 190

North Africa 7, 8, 9, 13, 17, 20, 22, 24, 26, 27, 28, 31, 32, 33, 42, 43, 77, 79, 90, 91, 92, 94, 98, 99, 103, 116, 119, 120, 126, 128, 134, 144, 146, 148, 150, 151, 195, 196, 197, 215, 228, 264, 286, 301, 314, 328, 331, 335, 336, 338, 394, 401, 403, 406, 411, 416, 435, 436, 437, 438

North Atlantic Treaty Organization (NATO) XXII, 350, 356, 430, 436

Northern Europe 19, 49, 52, 56, 66, 74, 75, 81, 149, 239, 437

nudum jus 24, 29

Nuncio 163, 253, 274, 308, 447

Nusayri 344. See also Alawis

O'Malley, John 58

Öktem, Kerem 403

Omar Mujahid, Mullah Muhammad 398

Opera della Propagazione della Fede (1922) 245

Order of the Dutch Lion 98

Order of the Mass (1969) 421

Orenburg Muhammadan Ecclesiastical Assembly (1782) 80

Organization of Islamic Cooperation (OIC) xxii, 220, 345

Osama bin Laden 9, 398, 399

Osman, House of 24, 108, 113, 154, 157, 206, 455

Ottoman Caliph 13, 27, 32, 77–101, 118, 155, 196, 217, 234, 285, 394, 446, 447. *See also* Ottoman Caliphate

Ottoman Caliphate (Osmanli Devleti, 1299–1924) 13, 126, 140

Ottoman Empire 7–30, 44, 79–104, 115–121, 134–156, 228, 322, 398, 401, 410, 440, 441, 445

Ottoman Refugee Code of 1857 136

Özal, Turgut 211

Palestine 25, 77, 85, 88, 89, 95, 104, 112, 116, 126, 134, 137, 287, 329, 409

Pan-Islam 7–24, 84, 93–121, 130–157, 225, 228, 285, 326, 410

Pan-Slavism 82, 466n16

Papacy 10–32, 47, 49, 60, 75–79, 106, 163, 180–205, 268, 285, 323, 394, 409, 418, 422, 442, 446. *See also* Holy See; Roman Church

Papal Diplomatic Corps 193

Papal States 7–29, 56–66, 153–169, 181, 191, 239–252, 277, 447

Paterson, New Jersey 33, 34, 257, 258, 259, 260, 261, 263, 264, 289

Patronage 25, 34, 62, 217, 286, 303, 330

Paul III, Pope 23, 47, 49, 57

Pentecost Sunday 161

Peres, Shimon 407

Philopoppoli 83

Pius IX, Pope 3, 6, 26, 145, 182, 183, 251, 398,

Pius X, Pope 173

Pius XI, Pope 191

Portoghesi, Paolo 324

Prefect of the Congregation for the Doctrine of the Faith 243, 422

Presidency for Turks Abroad and Related Communities 403, 454. See also *Yürtdisi Türkler*

Presidency of Religious Affairs, Turkish 206–218, 294–301, 319–350, 376, 390, 401–409, 446, 454, 455. *See also* Diyanet

Priests 12, 15, 21–35, 47–75, 161–194, 243–281, 312, 317, 421–432

Professionalization 14, 16, 18, 19, 23, 34, 38, 39, 40, 43, 49, 58, 69, 119, 121, 150, 165, 174, 193, 199, 202, 243, 266, 283, 292, 293, 330, 334, 336, 337, 350, 369, 388, 393

Propaganda Fide, Holy Congregation of 23, 35, 50, 51, 70, 71, 72, 73, 76, 119, 146, 272, 274, 279, 416, 447

Protestant Reformation 10, 13, 19, 47, 75, 157; Protestantism, 33, 62, 71, 173, 245, 319, 423

Qaddafi, Muammar 327, 397, 458n18

Qarawiyin, al-. *See* Al-Qarawiyin

Quds, al-. *See* Al-Quds

Quilliam, Abdullah 147, 149

Quirinale Palace 179, 394

Qur'an 128, 203, 218, 232, 234, 285, 302–304, 310, 319, 326, 330; Arabic, 90; Association to Preserve, 230; Recitation of, 313, 317; Schools, 25, 137, 141–142, 207–211, 213, 217, 219, 223–224, 226, 289, 298, 341–415; 447–453, 484; Swearing upon, 223

Qureyshi 88, 97, 114, 126, 328, 396, 397, 398, 399

Rabi'a Square Massacre 406

Rais ul-Islam 26, 80, 116, 145, 149, 150, 447

Rais al Ulema 22, 82

Ramadan 117, 125, 215, 220, 222, 223, 227, 229, 230, 231, 232, 303, 307, 313, 318, 328, 333, 349, 356, 363, 372, 373, 378, 379, 404, 409, 446, 447

Rassemblement des Musulmans de France (RMF) xxii, 293, 303, 304, 307

Ratzinger, Cardinal Joseph (*See* Benedict XVI, Pope) 422

Reconquista 302, 406

Red Crescent Society 156

Redouane, Abdellah 288

Reformist movements 21, 50

Refugees 25, 32, 33, 119, 136, 137, 156, 257, 258, 284, 406, 411, 450, 451

Religion Supreme Council (*Din Üst Kurulu*) 349

Religious Affairs, Ministry of xxi, xxiii, 13, 17, 37 80, 197, 204, 212, 231, 294, 295, 333, 334, 337, 339, 348, 352, 436, 446

Republican People's Party (CHP) xxi, 207, 209, 212, 334, 455

Rerum Novarum (1891) 189, 420

Revolution, Jasmine 317, 377, 379, 441

Right-wing and ethno-national terrorism 292

Risorgimento 177, 190, 246, 447, 480, 481

Roman Church 10–32, 47, 49, 60–79, 106, 163, 180–205, 268, 283, 285, 323, 394, 409, 418, 422, 442, 446. *See also* Holy See; Papacy

Roman Curia 71, 188, 279

Roman Question 8, 26, 29, 30, 99, 157, 179, 184, 187, 188, 190, 191, 240, 251, 281, 443

Russia 73, 79, 83, 136, 137, 176

Russian-Turkish War of 1877–78 83

Saddam Hussein: execution 397, 398

Sadiqi College 93

Saint Benedict (Benoît) 422